Between Asymmetry and Secession

Federico Savastano • Laura Frosina
Giulia Caravale
Editors

Between Asymmetry and Secession

Territorial Issues in Europe

Springer

Editors
Federico Savastano
Department of Political Sciences
Sapienza University of Rome
Rome, Italy

Laura Frosina
Department of Political Sciences
Sapienza University of Rome
Rome, Italy

Giulia Caravale
Department of Political Sciences
Sapienza University of Rome
Rome, Italy

ISBN 978-3-032-29602-3 ISBN 978-3-032-29603-0 (eBook)
https://doi.org/10.1007/978-3-032-29603-0

This work was supported by Sapienza Università di Roma (RM12117A88470161).

This Springer imprint is published by the registered company Springer Nature Switzerland AG
The registered company address is: Gewerbestrasse 11, 6330 Cham, Switzerland

Preface

The relationship between territories and constitutional orders has always been a central issue in the study of public law and political science. In Europe, this dynamic is particularly complex, shaped by historical legacies, diverse cultural identities, and the continuous evolution of supranational integration within the European Union. The volume *Between Asymmetry and Secession: Territorial Issues in Europe* seeks to explore these multidimensional challenges through a comparative constitutional lens, offering both theoretical reflections and detailed case studies. This work is the product of the Sapienza University Research Project "*Territorio, confini e istituzioni tra secessione e tendenze centrifughe*," initiated and inspired by Professor Beniamino Caravita, one of Italy's most distinguished scholars on federal models and territorial governance. His vision and encouragement have been instrumental in shaping the research that underpins this volume.

The themes of territorial asymmetries and secession are particularly significant within comparative constitutional law, as they challenge the foundational principles of state sovereignty, unity, and democracy. Territorial asymmetries—such as differentiated autonomy or federal structures—often serve as tools for accommodating diverse regional identities within a single constitutional framework, as seen in cases like Spain, Italy, and Belgium. Scholars like Giovanni Bognetti and John McGarry have long argued that these arrangements, while stabilizing, can also fuel perceptions of inequality and sow discontent, especially when asymmetry is seen as favoring certain regions over others. Secession, on the other hand, represents a more dramatic rupture, testing the resilience of constitutional systems to balance self-determination against territorial integrity. Prominent examples in Europe include the Scottish independence referendum, the Catalan crisis, and the ongoing debates in Flanders. These cases demonstrate how asymmetries and secessionist movements are often intertwined, reflecting both the promises and pitfalls of constitutional design in managing diversity.

By engaging with these issues from both theoretical and practical perspectives, *Between Asymmetry and Secession: Territorial Issues in Europe* offers valuable insights for scholars, policymakers, and practitioners grappling with the evolving landscape of territorial governance in Europe.

Rome, Italy Federico Savastano
Rome, Italy Laura Frosina
Rome, Italy Giulia Caravale
15 November 2025

Contents

List of Contributors

Antonia Maria Acierno Luiss Guido Carli University, Rome, Italy

Francesco Barbaro Sapienza University of Rome, Rome, Italy

Jorge Cagiao y Conde University of Nantes, Nantes, France

Giulia Caravale Department of Political Sciences, Sapienza University of Rome, Rome, Italy

Adriano Dirri LUISS Guido Carli University, Rome, Italy

Federica Fabrizzi Sapienza University of Rome, Rome, Italy

Gennaro Ferraiuolo Federico II University of Naples, Napoli, Italy

Andrea Fiorentino UnitelmaSapienza University of Rome, Rome, Italy

Laura Frosina Department of Political Sciences, Sapienza University of Rome, Rome, Italy

Emanuele Gabriele Sapienza University of Rome, Rome, Italy

Alain-G. Gagnon Université du Québec à Montréal, Montréal, Canada

Rosa Iannaccone University of Sassari, Sassari, Italy

Eleonora Iannario LUISS Guido Carli University, Rome, Italy

Giulia Aravantinou Leonidi Zayed University, Abu Dhabi, United Arab Emirates

Anna Mastromarino University of Turin, Torino, Italy

Andrea Patroni Griffi Federico II University of Naples, Napoli, Italy

Antonio Perez Miras University of Granada, Granada, Spain

Paola Piciacchia Sapienza University of Rome, Rome, Italy

Anna Maria Poggi University of Turin, Torino, Italy

Federico Savastano Department of Political Sciences, Sapienza University of Rome, Rome, Italy

Francesco Severa Sapienza University of Rome, Rome, Italy

Edin Skrebo University of Milan-Bicocca, Milan, Italy

An Introduction

Anna Maria Poggi

The conceptual inquiry into the notion of "territory" stands as one of the foundational pillars of constitutional science and of the broader discipline of public law.

Territory, as a constitutive component of the State, is not merely an element that statically delineates a given material reality; it is, at the same time, the firm foundation upon which the entire edifice of statehood has rested. As Jared Diamond reminds us, it was with the advent of the "farmers"—whose sedentary existence, marked by the stable occupation of land and the ensuing need for enduring forms of organization, transformed human societies—that the passage from bands to tribes, to chiefdoms, and finally, around 3700 B.C., to the emergence of the first States in Mesopotamia took place (Diamond 2006).

In earlier times, territory was merely the expanse within which hunter-gatherers could roam unimpeded—wandering aimlessly among bands and tribes, securing what they required, taking what proved useful, and leaving behind what did not, untroubled by any concern for establishing a stable or enduring form of organization. The cultivation of the land by the early farmers—their deliberate care for the territory and their will to render it an element of stability intertwined with the growth of communities—gradually led to the momentous enterprise, conceptual as well as institutional, that culminated in the birth of the State.

The transition was an epochal one, for it introduced the very notion of territory as a politically governed space; and through successive stages of this evolution, there gradually emerged the conceptual pairing of territory and state sovereignty.

With a secular leap forward, the notion of territory became, in the course of the nineteenth century, the very foundation of the birth of nation-states—animated by a clear intent of almost physical "protection" of specific communities.

Pierre Rosanvallon reconstructs that historical passage through what took shape in France in the early 1840s: protectionism as a social response and as an alternative

A. M. Poggi (✉)
University of Turin, Torino, Italy
e-mail: annamaria.poggi@unito.it

F. Savastano et al. (eds.), *Between Asymmetry and Secession*,
https://doi.org/10.1007/978-3-032-29603-0_1

to the mounting inequalities that accompanied the emergence of a new industrial proletariat. In that context, as Rosanvallon acutely observes, *"democratic equality began to be understood as belonging to a community of protection and of distancing"* (Rosanvallon 2016).

From that original intent, however, there unfolded a perverse trajectory that led to nationalism—to a conception of protection understood no longer as inclusion, but as the exclusion of the "other" beyond the defensive wall.

The overcoming of nationalism did not entail the overcoming of the State itself, but rather the historical, political, and intellectual transition to the redistributive State—a transformation that occurred, with similar modalities, across most of the Western world, inspired by a renewed understanding of equality and solidarity. A different *assemblage*, as Saskia Sassen would say, among Territory, Authority, and Rights (Sassen 2008).

Thus, one of the conceptual paradigms of the nation-state—whose disappearance many scholars had deemed irreversible—is now re-emerging in the unprecedented form of a renewed demand for protection by communities.

Theories of so-called functional geography, which seek to depict the dematerialization of territory as the physical locus of state sovereignty, may indeed capture a factual reality, yet they remain purely descriptive and cannot sustain a constitutional theory. Hence, when Parag Khanna asserts that Europe has become an archetype of functional geography, he accurately describes an undeniable reality: *"After the end of the Cold War, Europe has focused more on building bridges and tunnels than walls and trenches... European nations are functionally inseparable, an omelette that cannot be unscrambled into its original ingredients. Monetary systems, transport corridors, energy grids, financial networks, industrial supply chains: all are deeply integrated"* (Khanna 2016). Yet he misses the mark when he concludes that *"the age of organizing the world according to political space (the way we legally divide the globe) is giving way to its organization according to functional space (the way we use it). In this new era, the de jure world of political borders is being supplanted by the de facto world of functional connections"* (Khanna 2016).

The fallacy of such a conclusion is today self-evident: functional geography—as exemplified by the global spread of the COVID-19 virus—still requires to be governed by political geography. For, as Gino Scaccia has sharply observed, the individual *"who, from his firm terrestrial belonging to the national civitas, once derived both a collective vision of the common good and the sense of responsibility within the enterprise of coexistence, may now find himself deprived of social protections – of that web of public and intersubjective solidarity which once rendered existence less precarious. He discovers himself richer than ever in opportunities for life and in spaces of freedom, yet bereft of bonds, solitary in the void left by the delocalization of law and the deconstruction of the State form and of sovereignty as the principle of political unity"* (Scaccia 2017).

In short, the triad sovereignty-representation-territory has not been swept away by globalization; rather, it continues to embody the very conceptual nucleus of statehood itself.

Territory, as *sovereignty*—that is, as the normative political space abstracted from the mere concreteness of the Earth—appears once again as one of the defining exigencies of our time, urging renewed reflection on the meaning it assumes, or may assume, within the framework of European unity.

The pandemic period made this abundantly clear: the closure of borders by certain States—the consequence of a narrow-minded protectionism—risked undermining the entire European project, striking at its original and most vital inspiration, namely, the free movement across the territories of the Member States of the Union. That crisis revived long-dormant doubts concerning the effectiveness of the integration process and the very configuration of the Union—whether as a mere aggregation of States or as a genuine unitary polity. Beyond the domestic conflicts between majorities and oppositions, it was the majority of scholars and commentators who began to question the role of the European Union itself.

These issues cannot be regarded as fully resolved with the end of the pandemic. The geopolitical dynamics that emerged during that period compel serious reflection, for certain foundations of the European experience must find a renewed path of viability. In particular, the objective of European unity—as a form of completed integration—likely requires a revisiting of the prevailing conception of *territory*. This should not come as a surprise if one follows Sassen's teaching that the assemblage among Territory, Authority, and Rights is indeed subject to transformation, albeit infrequently.

The very dynamics surrounding the *fate* of state territory lie at the heart of the volume *Between Asymmetry and Secession: Territorial Issues in Europe*, which advances the thesis that the evolving relationship between territories and constitutional orders in Europe is particularly complex—shaped by historical legacies, divergent cultural identities, and the continuous evolution of supranational integration within the European Union.

The subject is of profound significance for scholars of constitutional systems: the European construction is not merely an object of study in itself, but, by extension, a prism through which the transformative dynamics of the individual States can also be examined.

It is a precious volume in which reflections on the geopolitics of separatism intersect and complement one another, revealing with remarkable clarity how the crisis of the foundational categories of the modern political order has given rise to *hybrid* forms of power distribution of immense theoretical interest. Likewise, the analysis of conflicts of various kinds and magnitudes leads to thought-provoking reflections on contemporary issues—from the evolution of the Western Balkans (Albania, Greece, the successor States of the former Yugoslavia) to the current state of asymmetries in other countries such as Spain, Italy, and Belgium.

What emerges is that federalism no longer possesses a strictly "formal" structure; rather, asymmetries now demand to be governed through a judicious mix of centralization and unity, oriented around *loyalty* as the central and fundamental principle of territorial governance.

To transcend the homogenizing tendencies of the nation-state—when these constrain and risk suffocating diversity—a structural form of pluralistic governance is required, one grounded in solidarity and democratic legitimacy.

In sum, this constitutes a formidable challenge—one that simultaneously engages the Member States and the very construction that, in Europe, has given birth to the European Union.

References

Diamond J (2006) Armi, acciaio e malattie. Breve storia del mondo negli ultimi tredicimila anni. Einaudi, Turin

Khanna P (2016) Connectography. Le mappe del futuro ordine mondiale. Fazi, Rome

Rosanvallon P (2016) La società dell'uguaglianza. Castelvecchi, Rome

Sassen S (2008) Territorio, autorità, diritti. Assemblaggi dal Medioevo all'età globale. Mondadori, Milan

Scaccia G (2017) Il territorio tra sovranità statale e globalizzazione dello spazio economico. Rivista AIC 3:1–58

Theoretical and Systemic Perspectives

Regionalism and Asymmetric Federalism in Europe

Anna Mastromarino

Abstract This essay examines the role of asymmetry in accommodating diversity within European constitutional systems, focusing on Italy and Spain. Challenging the nation-state model rooted in homogeneity, it argues that asymmetry should be viewed not as an exception but as a structural tool for managing pluralism. Through a comparative and interdisciplinary approach, the paper explores how asymmetrical decentralisation—when grounded in trust, solidarity, and democratic legitimacy—can enhance institutional effectiveness and social cohesion. It highlights the importance of a decentralisation culture and criticises the lack of systemic vision in current practices. Ultimately, the essay presents asymmetry as a key to revitalising democratic participation and building inclusive constitutional orders in increasingly diverse societies.

1 From Uniformity to Asymmetry: Rethinking Diversity in Constitutional Democracies

It cannot be denied that in recent years reflection on the accommodation of diversity has reached very high levels of interdisciplinary depth in the attempt to provide solutions to the challenges that social super-diversity imposes (Vertovec 2007). Legal science has tried to play its part, coming to terms with resistance that has conditioned reflection, also from structural points of view.

In fact, the contemporary constitutional project has had to deal with prospects of pluralism that go far beyond former expectations, with diversity seemingly reduced to units and therefore considered potentially capable of shaking the foundations of the State's organisation (aided by the expansion of the supranational dimension of human rights protection, which has undermined the basis of the State's monopoly on the protection of citizens).

A. Mastromarino (✉)
University of Turin, Torino, Italy
e-mail: anna.mastromarino@unito.it

F. Savastano et al. (eds.), *Between Asymmetry and Secession*,
https://doi.org/10.1007/978-3-032-29603-0_2

In this sense, the friction that manifests itself in our societies as far as diversity is concerned can be understood both as a cause and as a symptom of the system's fragile condition: on the one hand, it fuels the consensus of those political forces hostile to cultural change, and, on the other, it is nourished by those same forces that resort to the weapons of fear and uncertainty to secure legitimacy in the public space.

I am fully aware of the cultural coordinates within which I am moving, characterised by strong populist dynamics. Nevertheless, in this brief essay I would like to approach the phenomenon in a more positive way.

I therefore wonder why we do not reverse the scenario and move from the idea that diversity and its manifestation in the public space – rather than being viewed as an accident or a side effect of the system that has got out of hand – represent, on the contrary, the product of a constitutionalism that has truly been capable of unleashing the forces contained in the social body. In this sense, the super-diversity of liberal societies can be seen as proof of a goal achieved by constitutional democracy, aiming to guarantee the free development of the individual, despite differences and not by virtue of a right to equality representing expectations of uniformity.

From this point of view, the difficult management of high-intensity pluralism would not be a symptom of the failure of the system, but rather an opportunity to ask ourselves whether the tools used to deal with reality are adequate.

And this is where the constitutionalist's headaches start. At first glance, the answer appears to be negative because efforts made to consolidate a state of freedom and 'confidence' in which to express one's identity have not been accompanied by an equally successful transformation of the legal framework (Karmis & Rocher, 2012; Putnam, 2000, Fukuyama, 1995). In fact, the constitutional paradigm of the nation-state has continued to represent the framework in which the change is viewed. The tools of jurists (and not only those of jurists) have also—in most cases—continued to be insufficient. In no way can we assert that the national perspective should not be granted the merit of initially establishing the predominantly theoretical approach to the universalism of rights; it must, however, be recognised that it came about to design a uniform framework for 'uniform' citizens, which is totally unsuited to the features of the current social body. Thus, we find ourselves wanting to govern to neutralise the differentiating forces that the system itself has triggered.

If 'symmetry' means the condition of harmony and coherence in which two or more elements find themselves, then, on the contrary, 'asymmetrical' would refer to something that has no correspondence with any other element. It would therefore seem logical that asymmetry—and not its opposite—is the natural state of a human being's existence and environment.

Nonetheless, this is not the idea that the term 'asymmetry' in public law gives the observer, particularly when one considers its use in conjunction with concepts such as 'differentiation' and 'speciality'. In fact, it is evident that speaking about asymmetry in law means above all drawing attention to situations of non-conformity with standards, immediately evoking a state of derogation.

Without doubt there are several reasons for this approach, but in my opinion the first motivation can be sought in the historical roots of the nation-state. Resistance that systems apply to asymmetrical formulas also has its roots in French Revolutionary thought, which by enshrining the principle of equality seemed to envisage cultural homogeneity as a guarantee for efficient governing of the nation.

In no way do I deny the usefulness of the national context in which the liberal State was conceived.

I would like you to reflect on the structural conditions that have led to the conception of homogeneity of the social body and, consequently, institutional symmetry as the key to understanding the entire legal system. In the context that has uniformity as its goal—understood as a legal and conceptual space in which equality can be managed more easily—what is dissimilar seems to be only something that can be experienced as an exception to be tolerated within certain limits. It is in this sense that asymmetry is transformed from status quo to something that needs to be contained, circumscribed and regulated.

But is this really the only possible vision? Perhaps not. If, in fact, for a moment we abandon the traditional view of the State built around a homogeneous nation—which, moreover, has been going through a deep crisis for some time, despite the regurgitations of 'national sovereignty' in many countries of contemporary Europe—we would find ourselves in a position of setting aside the idea of homogeneity as an established standard: by taking 'diversity' as the point of observation, with perhaps a more realistic perspective, it is asymmetry that becomes standardised and differentiation that becomes a parameter of evaluation (Bush 2011).

On the basis of these considerations the following pages intend to propose new insights into the concept of asymmetry: moving from studies carried out on the theme of trust as a path of social interaction in systems characterised by strong clivages, I would like to assess the possibility of accepting asymmetry as a paradigm of the contemporary constitutional State and, therefore, of diversity as a standard representing a compulsory step in consolidating a climate of convergence and social unity in contexts of social conflict and as a fundamental step in the consolidation of citizens' trust in State institutions. These are goals that should definitely not be underestimated in a context of growing social conflict and increasing distrust in both institutions and their representative circuits.

Rather than treating asymmetry as an 'accident', I think one should begin by noting that it can represent a key to the accommodation of differences—be they geographical, economic, socio-political, cultural or ethnic-social—and therefore a path to explore, given that diversity now constitutes the way of being of contemporary societies: this is as true in the presence of evident fractures in the social body as it is in correspondence with contexts naturally characterised by a certain homogeneity (Delledonne 2017). In fact, it should not be overlooked that since decentralisation has become one of the features of contemporary constitutionalism, it is the very practice of autonomy—of any nature or degree—that generates differentiation. That is, if by autonomy we mean that normative space is delimited regarding the boundaries but never in its contents.

From this point of view, it is not so much a matter of assessing the compatibility of asymmetry per se with respect to each individual system, but it is rather a matter of verifying—also taking into account the geographical, social and economic features of the system—'how much' asymmetry can be absorbed by the system. In other words, what degree of asymmetry can be injected into the system without provoking a physiological rejection, in search of a balance between quantum and quomodo that can guarantee the achievement of the potential benefits that its implementation can bring in terms of political integration.

In fact, what has been said so far emphasises the need for asymmetry to take on a new conceptual and practical dimension in public law: a less timid, less circumscribed dimension will only gain in value if we pause to consider the advantages that asymmetrical arrangements can bring to the system as a whole.

However, it will be a matter of moving into a discourse that is no longer only legal, as it is characterised by aspects that also have to do with 'legal culture', i.e. with a sphere in which law is intertwined with concepts that are only apparently extraneous to the legal sphere: the interdisciplinary, comparative perspective once again is the only one capable of totally addressing certain challenges of contemporary constitutionalism.

2 Reframing Asymmetry: From Exception to Principle of Governance

Reasoning about asymmetry in this day and age is therefore not only useful but has become indispensable. This is clear when we pause to reflect on the role that decentralisation has acquired in democratic constitutionalism. In fact, I have no qualms about calling it the veritable hallmark of constitutional democracy.

Whether this trend still stands in the face of growing populist, illiberal dynamics—fertile soil for abusive forms of democracy—remains to be seen, but the question makes sense given that, to date, multi-level systems have been helping to build public forums in which to exercise democracy.

On the other hand, the democratic nature of the legal system presents itself as an indispensable precondition for the establishment of authentic decentralisation, flanking the more traditional horizontal separation of powers with a vertical separation of powers in order to complete the project of guaranteed citizen participation in the State.

Where the liberal paradigm of the rule of law is not ensured, in fact, it is unthinkable to consider the possible evolution of a multilevel government: without space pluralism as a prerequisite for a condition of social existence, the systemic premises which we are reasoning about are lost. This is why asymmetry is proposed here as a key to understanding decentralisation in systems that have achieved a considerable degree of internal democracy, regardless of their multinational nature.

Differentiation, in fact, is inherent in the very concept of decentralisation because allowing different entities to act implicitly means accepting a space of autonomy, i.e. a sphere in which self-determining power allows an entity to make decisions which might be conflicting with or at least different from those made by other decentralised entities or by the central government itself (Fossas Espadaler, 2009;

Burgess, 2009). From this perspective, two different types of asymmetry can be identified. The first, de facto, derives from the possibility, inherent in the very concept of autonomy, of 'getting one's act together' and doing it differently from others: it follows that even when the autonomy granted to various peripheral entities is identical in degree and content, a certain differentiation may nevertheless occur, and is likely to occur as a result of the different use made of that autonomy by individual entities.

The second type of asymmetry, the ex-lege type, derives from the granting—through a regulatory act—of prerogatives that are different for each entity in degree and content. In this case we are faced with specialisation policies aimed at recognising the existence of elements that, by their mere existence, make it possible to resort to differentiating—but not discriminating—treatment. As an example, among the factors that have legitimised differentiation policies over the years, we can recall—thinking in particular of the condition of insularity—economic ones, historical ones and, especially in recent years, those linked to the identity of indigenous communities, such as language, culture or ethnicity (Palermo 2018).

This is not without consequences since asymmetry has generally been regarded as an 'extraordinary' and therefore exceptional condition, favouring a logic of identity and neglecting other paths, which have nothing 'special' about them and are well present in other decentralised systems, especially in recent years.

The principle of differentiation can, in fact, also be invoked from an 'enabling' perspective, i.e. supporting administrative effectiveness and efficiency. And it is not strange to note that it is precisely in this idea of asymmetry that the greatest resistance has been catalysed by those who do not wish to admit that it is not differentiated decentralisation as an organisational instrument but the values by which it is inspired that represent the real watershed in the debate.

The differentiation/equality relationship actually becomes central, depending on the principles by which one is inspired, and it is evident, after all, that it is in organisational differentiation rather than in identity asymmetry that the reasons for asymmetry become more difficult to understand, and therefore to convey in order to be accepted. Thus, it becomes a more concrete danger that differences in poorly conveyed treatment will be perceived as unjustified discrimination, capable of profoundly altering the principle of equality, not conceived outside a context of uniformity, precisely because it has grown in the framework of the nation-state.

As a matter of fact, it is precisely in the differentiation/equality junction that the success of asymmetrical decentralisation is decided, i.e. in the capacity to distinguish differentiation processes, sustained by the principle of solidarity, from the ones sustained by mere competitive dynamics. It is one thing to envisage an asymmetrical organisation as a functional key to good governance; it is quite another to favour a concept of social as well as institutional relations that both imply and claim the right of those who live and operate in certain parts of the State territory to differentiate in order to differentiate, maintaining or amplifying a gap (Grosso 2020).

The intertwining of the asymmetry discourse with the principle of equality undoubtedly makes the path more slippery. But it does not make it impracticable. It is true, in fact, that, given the premises that have been proposed, it would be better to begin by considering as fixed the 'ifs', taking as inevitable the start of a path of differentiation in those systems—where Italy is no exception—which have started decentralisation. We should concentrate on the 'hows', analysing assumptions and characteristics that better than others can help to set virtuous paths of asymmetry in motion—also of an organisational nature, especially in contexts necessarily devoted to territorial solidarity by will of the constitutional text.

3 Beyond Numbers: Towards a Reasoned and Sustainable Asymmetry

The experiences of decentralisation, in particular, highlight a path of progressive emancipation of asymmetry with respect to those theories that place it in opposition to the principle of equality. It has long been emphasised that there is no contradiction between the protection of non-discrimination principles and the recognition of differentiated formulas of recognition of rights, provided that this does not imply inequality in the enjoyment of political freedom and fundamental rights.

It is, in fact, a principle that accepts the existence of differences leading to the application of distinct treatments, when argued and justified based on reasonable grounds (Luciani 2011, p. 7). It follows that not differentiation per se, but rather differentiation whose reasons seem unfounded or, worse, appear to be founded in privilege, can contribute to generating tensions and sometimes conflicts that are destined to take root endemically in the social body.

The definition of a reasonableness to differentiation is the basis for initiating a process of sustainable asymmetry, capable of enhancing rather than disrupting the system's assumptions of unity, giving the measure of distance between this concept and uniformity. It is precisely the effort of argumentation that highlights the risks involved in not knowing how to verbalise this difference in rational terms on a social and economic level, pursuing paths of dematerialisation of diversity that are gradually based on exclusionary and ambiguous elements that inhibit the construction of pathways of solidarity at State level.

This is not the place to recall the damage to the system's resilience that fomenting exclusionary identities can produce. Certainly, however, this may be an opportunity to emphasise the limits of differentiation that aims only at cultural data, but also to question the objections of those who, on the contrary, deny any relevance to the cultural profile, forgetting that for a long time equality has also been declined in community forms (for example through the constitutionalisation of collective rights) and in treating equal cases equally and different cases differently, even when it comes to social formations.

So, if it is true that the critical issues lie in the construction of asymmetry and its narration and not in asymmetry itself, then the 'what' to differentiate must be as important as the 'how', since consistency between the reasons for asymmetry and 'differentiating facts' facilitates policies of recognising diversity and consolidates processes of trust and reliance, overcoming possible objections arising from the interaction of differentiation with the principle of equality. It is easy to understand the fears that this interaction may generate, touching on one of the totems of contemporary constitutionalism, namely equality declined in a formal sense. But it is also necessary to contextualise this interaction in the reflection of contemporary constitutionalism, which, albeit with difficulty, has found a way to distinguish egalitarianism from non-discriminatory treatment, relating, as mentioned, the right to social reality (Basso 1971, p. 654).

It is no coincidence that the introduction of asymmetrical arrangements can never be reduced to a mere quantitative issue. Asymmetry should not be measured by the number and degree of differentiations introduced into the system. In fact, the qualitative aspect also matters, requiring a careful political analysis of the fields in which differentiation is to be introduced. This is a delicate operation that implies a profound knowledge of the context and requires a careful identification of the various elements on which the asymmetry is to be based: elements that, by virtue of the force of attraction and cohesion that they are capable of developing, appear in themselves fundamental in defining the identity of a place and its population, now and in the future.

This order of reflections obliges us to think about the spaces in which it is possible to differentiate without losing sight of the protection of the whole, i.e. without facilitating the creation of identity clivages, economic fractures, cultural distances and breaches in the system of solidarity-based decentralisation. I am thinking in particular of the issue of schools, of the debate about the differentiation of educational paths or the training of teaching staff, which, in the name of a claimed and entirely unproven need to rationalise the administration of the school system, can build territorial barriers based on cultural assumptions nurtured precisely at school, i.e. in that space that more than any other is called upon to form citizens around shared values.

Reasoning about what and how to differentiate then raises a time-related issue: in my opinion, it is reductive and very unprofitable to reason about asymmetry in the short term. Differentiation projects must be designed to last over time, to stabilise and thus be able to produce benefits in the system. They need a structural perspective. That is why they cannot be improvised and need an organisational system whose maintenance over time must be guaranteed. The intention here is not to reopen the age-old issue of the representation of territorial entities, i.e. whether it is necessary to provide for a second chamber to represent sub-state entities or whether this centre-periphery coordination can be better performed by intergovernmental circuits. I have said on other occasions that I strongly believe that these two paths are not mutually exclusive, but must be thought of harmoniously because they are called upon to perform different functions and operate in a synergetic manner (Mastromarino 2016). Rather, I would like to emphasise here the need for differentiated decentralisation paths to be accompanied by a rethinking of the forums for cooperation between the different levels of government so as not to lose sight of the unitary character that even the composite state, federal or non-federal, retains. Differentiation, in fact, entails changes at the level of choices concerning the country's territorial articulation, but it also inevitably determines heavy repercussions at the level of political organisation which can hardly be absorbed naturally by the system.

4 Asymmetry as Recognition: Rebuilding the State-Citizen Relationship

Asymmetry, thus conceived, can be converted into a structural element of the plural State, capable of acknowledging and shaping pluralism not only in its more traditional ideological-political aspect, but also in its territorial, institutional and cultural one.

Taking asymmetry as the key to understanding democracy means, in fact, giving legal form to diversity and structural recognition to pluralism beyond constitutional rhetoric. In a condition of chronic crisis of representation—understood as the system's ability to intercept, project and respond to the needs of the social body—asymmetry, understood in its complexity, neither trivialised nor demonised a priori, presents itself as a tool to revitalise the circuit of participation through a process of rediscovery of the institution-citizen bond that can only be two-way.

Reflection necessarily becomes interdisciplinary and must broaden its field of investigation, dwelling on elements that are extra-legal, but that can no longer be excluded from the horizon of analysis of the legal sciences.

In this sense, it must be said from the outset that a correct practice of differentiation presupposes the assimilation of a genuine culture of decentralisation. This does not mean pretending that the federal option is the privileged one in the choice of territorial organisation. Rather, it means demanding that in composite systems a knowledge and practice of the principles and values of federalism—as an ideology of shared government, of participatory democracy, of the coordination of levels and of the coexistence of diversities—should take root on the part of the institutions, as well as among citizens.

On the other hand, if it is reduced to legislative discourse, the discourse on asymmetry runs the risk of becoming a suffocating one.

We must begin by saying that, to be fully understood, differentiation requires a predisposition to knowledge of the other, of his essence and of his peculiarities; and it also calls for a legitimate subject who will act as guarantor of that path of approach, knowledge and acceptance: otherwise, the knowledge of the differentiation needs advanced by the other must be certified by a subject capable of legitimising his differentiating action without being questioned.

The idea that precisely the sense of 'confidence' is one of the glues on which social as well as institutional relations are built is not new. Understood as reliance, confidence increases bonds of affiliation and thus contributes to the construction of political integration and identity, as well as consolidating processes of social pacification (Mastromarino 2018). In the political and social sphere, in fact, it coincides with the expectation of others' propensity to abide by those same rules considered cogent for peaceful coexistence and replaces dynamics such as the threat of sanction and coercive imposition (Caminal i Badia 2013).

It may not be straightforward to establish in what terms this attitude to work on aspects such as citizens' confidence in institutions and fellow citizens can be grafted onto a reflection about the formulas of asymmetry. At first glance, in fact, it is differentiation itself—if we insist on diversities rather than similarities—that could slow down or hinder processes of trust, and thus integration, by amplifying territorial and identity claims, thereby fuelling dissociative processes capable of endangering the territorial unity of the state.

Nevertheless, the study of practices in place in systems characterised by deep social fractures leads one to accept the fact that recognising differences in the distribution of power at the territorial level denotes an attention of the central State to the characteristics and needs of local populations that can defuse centre-periphery competition, above all between peer entities (Gagnon 2013, p. 77). This is thanks to the activation of an interaction, based on the recognition of diversity, be it cultural, social, economic and geographical: as the desire for participation grows at the local and national level, the opportunities for listening to and getting to know diversity increase and thus the distrust of one group towards the other diminishes; those collective narratives on which prejudices are based are remodelled and end up favouring a common and solidarity-based identity, improving social relations; work is done on the symbolic aspects by elaborating inclusive languages that are less tied to the myth of the nation-state on which the idea of community in public law is traditionally fixed.

Confidence becomes the engine of a consociative system that, as Arend Lijphart teaches, is not exhausted in a style of government, but presupposes an institutional architecture that is strengthened in asymmetry, since experience shows that a decentralised set-up can only function if a relational attitude is established, thus becoming decisive for the overall effectiveness of the system.

It would be a matter, taking up Giorgio Lombardi's teaching (1985, p. 495), of recovering the sense of the 'internal frontier' understood «non già come lo spazio di validità della norma, il limite fisico di essa, ma come l'ambito entro il quale si esprime un'aggregazione idonea a esprimere una struttura sociale tale da riconoscersi secondo criteri dell'uguaglianza e della sovranità popolare»: asymmetry presupposes recognition, recognition presupposes knowledge and acceptance of those characteristics around which identity awareness of the other is consolidated. The differentiations made by the legal system, when they are the fruit of a political will to accommodate, end up testifying to the bond established between the State and the various parts of its territory: a bond founded on mutual respect and also concretised in the definition of common rules, beyond diversities, those same rules being the fruit of a shared formation process. One does not aspire to the homologation of interests to be pursued, but rather to the definition of a system of interests that, even when they do not appear convergent, can be said to be connected. Inevitably, the acceptance of a condition of unstable equilibrium in correspondence with decentralised systems, the result of an inexhaustible balancing act between 'containment' and 'contentment'.

5 Frozen Federalism: Spain's Incomplete Journey Towards Territorial Pluralism

For a long time, the presence or absence of a culture of decentralisation within a legal system, even if only in embryonic form, was underestimated.

It is the culture of decentralisation that gives meaning to words like loyal cooperation, coordination and loyalty to institutions and makes paths of differentiation and, in some cases, community reconciliation possible.

On the other hand, the culture of decentralisation needs seeds but also places where those seeds can germinate. It can find fertile soil in institutions, but that is not enough. It does not proliferate if it is not supported in the party system, by their dynamics, strategies, but also by their language. Nor does it take root if there is not an adequate information system to foster and nurture it.

To become a promoter of autonomy, culture must take root in a public opinion that defends decentralisation by recognising it as the essence of democracy (Putnam 1993).

The culture of decentralisation, after all, is not a congenital aspect of a particular society. It is both project and perspective. There are human organisations that for historical reasons may be more inclined than others to find their way of being in decentralised formulas. But, having said that, it must be remembered that the culture of decentralisation, like consensus, must be built, sustained, and fomented; it is no coincidence that precisely where this culture is lacking—I am thinking of Spain, but also of Italy—it is difficult to elaborate projects of differentiation, to convey them and to understand them.

The events of recent years have undoubtedly shown how, in Spain, resistance to nurturing a political culture of decentralisation has progressively frozen the potential of the territorial model of 1978 (Cámara Villar 2018).

It must be remembered that the 1978 text is, indeed, full of hypotheses of differentiation, never realised. And it is in this non-fulfilment of constitutional promises that one must seek, on the one hand, the reasons for that sense of betrayal that has progressively grown in the nationalist discourse and, on the other, the causes of that convinced opposition shown by a part of public opinion and political forces to any real project of institutionalised asymmetry.

What was at first a purely constitutional question has become first a political question, in the process of implementing the Constitution, and then a cultural question, when the constitutional and political dimension thus shaped became the horizon of meaning within which the public opinion and institutional culture of the Spanish people were formed.

For years, in Spain, there has been talk of constitutional reforms to close the inacabado territorial process; for years, the subject has been fathomed by the doctrine, which has highlighted the areas that need updating (Tudela Aranda 2016; Cubas et al. 2013).

Indeed, many of the institutional and political difficulties in which Spain finds itself are precisely the result of the unfinished space around which the practices of an institutionalised political formula have been consolidated.

At the same time, however, despite the knowledge that what is needed is an intervention of constitutional regeneration, capable of modifying certain neuralgic concepts such as those of sovereignty, culture and nationhood, such reforms have been postponed for years. An intervention for which Spain is not ready at the moment.

Although we can rely on Article 168 EC, which allows for a total revision of the Constitution without opening a constituent phase, even in this case it is difficult to escape the 'paradox of constitutional reform' (Zagrebelsky 1985, p. 927). On the other hand, the very level reached by the crisis, both socially and politically, makes it totally inadvisable, if not impossible, to initiate, for the time being, any process of amending the Constitution, since the prerequisites of planning and communion of intentions, which are the inescapable basis of any process for the definition of a constitutional pact between citizens, are lacking.

It is necessary to strengthen the foundations of the Spanish order, but to do so, we need to create the conditions to clarify what has remained understood for decades and call a spade a spade. If it is a matter of multinational federalism, let us call it that (Seymour and Laforest 2011; Saymour and Gagnon 2012) and let us do it openly by facing the consequences of this choice.

First and foremost, we have to accept an asymmetrical set-up, connatural to the processes of a disaggregative federalism (Mastromarino 2010) towards which the evolution of the Spanish state type may tend. Acknowledging the plurality of the components of the social body is the first act, to be followed by the knowledge of diversity and the acceptance of differentiated regimes that in no way presuppose discriminatory treatment, but rather constitute the first step to avoid it, adhering to a vision of justice in which human dignity is represented not only in its individual meaning, but also collectively, as belonging to a common identity project, which does not necessarily coincide with the State, but flows into it.

The change would not only be formal, as claimed by many, but also substantial, as shown by the reluctance of nationalist forces to favour reforming the constitution in a federal direction. This behaviour is only apparently incomprehensible.

Federalism, as has been said, emphasises the protagonism of all the subjects that contribute to animating the political-institutional arena of the order. At the same time, however, although it is a flexible formula for organising the centre-periphery dynamics, the federal state presupposes the definition of a constitutional pact, which is based on predetermined, albeit elastic, procedures and is founded on multilateral relations of cooperation and recognition of the other. All in all, uncomfortable conditions for the nationalists, who have so far been able to take advantage of the accommodating attitude of governments in need of support by changing their strategies from time to time, sometimes bypassing constitutional limits. But also uncomfortable for the political forces at the central level, which, finding themselves in an unstable context of party system evolution, find it hard to imagine what future political scenarios they might be confronted with in terms of electoral consensus.

As long as the federal option continues to be a cause of fear, it is difficult for Spain to really find its way out of its latent situation of tension. It is only to be hoped that between periods of institutional pax they will have the courage to continue to reason in systemic terms, widening their gaze beyond the contingent, even when that contingent takes on the gravity of a crisis like the Catalan one, a symptom and not a cause of the malaise in which the Spanish order finds itself.

A quick glance at how the current Sanchez government was formed, on the other hand, seems to tell us that the time for rethinking has not yet come.

It is not possible to reconstruct a well-known affair here. It should be recalled that rumours have been spread about the constitutional legitimacy of the amnesty law approved by Sanchez for the facts related to the so-called Procés and provided for in an agreement signed in Brussels on 9 November 2023. Its political expediency has been questioned on many sides; little or nothing has been said about the potential weakening that not so much the amnesty institute itself but the iter that led to its adoption has determined on the application of certain cardinal principles of decentralisation, such as subsidiarity, proximity, loyal collaboration and cooperation, and the harmonious development of the constitutional project. These are elements designed to ensure an organic vision of the sub-state entities and the central system that have been crushed by political contingency, aiming to enhance some positions rather than others and undermining the entire multi-level system.

I am well aware that this is not the first time that the support of territorial parties to the central government has been played out on a quid pro quo basis and that bilateralism is the feature that has always distinguished centre-periphery relations in Spain. Nevertheless, what makes the difference here is the willingness to abandon any institutional perspective in the management of political relations that have a much broader constitutional scope than other agreements on the transfer of competences may have had. Consequently, what is missing is that systemic vision capable of practising differentiation as an instrument of unity, irrespective of uniformity, as a means of recognising the plural nature of the social body without lapsing into discrimination, as an opportunity to revitalise solidarity relations, rather than an occasion for political competition between political forces.

There are certain aspects, in fact, that hint at a profound change in the modalities of centre-periphery interaction in the Spanish case. If it is true that bilateralism is a constant in the Spanish legal system, given the scarce institutional success of the multilateral concertation venues, it must be stressed that here the negotiations were carried out not on an institutional basis, albeit through informal channels, as happened in other instances, but explicitly within the party system. The latter has been the protagonist of an affair that has had and will have serious structural repercussions on the Spanish model of territorial organisation, which appears definitively and openly subject to the action and contingent aims of the political forces.

In this specific case, the agreement that Pedro Sanchez signs with the Catalan Independents represents much more than the fall-out of concessions aimed, as in the past, at securing Catalonia's differentiation from the other Communities.

Here, in fact, the territorial claims put forward by some Catalan political forces have ended up becoming the backbone of the definition of the new government's political direction and thus of the evolution of the territorial model.

6 Differentiation Without Direction: The Crisis of Asymmetrical Regionalism in Italy

If one looks at it from the point of view of comparative law, the debate on Italian regionalism appears somewhat asphyxiated. It is all bent on a diatribe that in some respects seems to be more ideological than juridical—notwithstanding the intrinsically political nature of the issue—and on reflections that often completely disregard a more general analysis.

It has been said that if the regions are one of the most important innovations of the Republican Constitution, the introduction of differentiated regionalism in the Charter is perhaps the most significant datum of the reform of Title V of the Constitution, brought about by Constitutional Law No. 3/2001 (Patroni Griffi 2021, p. 318). The bibliography on the subject is endless and cannot be recalled here.

What is of interest here, on the other hand, is trying to make considerations from the pre-legal perspective in which we have been moving so far.

In other words, the question remains as to whether, before embarking on the disputes that animate the strongest opponents of differentiated regionalism and its defenders, we have dwelled on the context, on the existence of factual and legal prerequisites that might favour the establishment of a satisfactory differentiated system.

Dwelling on the existence of potential limits to fruitful differentiated regionalism taking root in Italy is, in fact, not meant to discourage the full implementation of Article 116, but rather to spur us to act as soon as possible to prepare the field and to ask the right questions. Thus, the de facto conditions may be created so that once it is fully operational, differentiated regionalism may truly act as an agent of the country's harmonious development, as a glue between differences.

Going back to what has been said, we must recall that the absence of a deep-rooted culture of decentralisation does not allow for the serene cooperation of the different levels of government—and thus the consolidation of a solid confidence-building process—even in those matters in which no demands for differentiation have ever been made, let alone if this absence of culture does not have immediate and undesirable consequences on the debate—at times entirely focused on the question of the North-South divide—in those matters with a higher degree of differentiation.

It is the absence of this culture—not a real attitude against asymmetry – that has not allowed the seeds of differentiation already present in our Charter to germinate, beyond Article 116: starting from the constitutionalisation of horizontal subsidiarity, passing through the provisions on the form of regional government and residual legislative power. Without training in de facto differentiation, it is difficult to find the road to mature de jure differentiation (Castella Andreu-Mastromarino and Castellà Andreu 2009).

The demands for differentiation have followed one another in a confrontation lacking transparency—a circumstance never favourable to the development of relations based on trust—with little rationality and therefore appearing unsustainable. All has been reduced to the electoral here-and-now, in a centre-periphery contraposition that lends itself to party-politics logic, hardly feeling the weight of the epochal change in store for the Republic.

The regions have demanded a lot, a little of everything and perhaps too much, some after dragging the population into referenda that, beyond the judgment on their legitimacy or otherwise, highlight a series of objectives to be achieved at a political level that are difficult to trace and consider compatible with the fine-tuning of the regional system through the provisions of Article 116 (Morelli 2017).

When everything is requested, it is difficult to understand the rationale behind the request; that is, it is difficult to read—without any solution—the contents of the request for differentiation and the organisational reasons that in specific terms underpin that request. One also finds a certain discontinuity between the policy documents approved by the individual regional councils and the concrete demands and reasons put forward with respect to the increased legislative and administrative competences.

The result is that one senses in the debate, on the one hand, a resistance to change that at times takes on derisive tones, not entirely honest in reconstructing the reasons for the 'southern question'. On the other hand, a sense of economic revenge on one part of the country, made all the heavier by the feeling of wanting to create a sort of 'ethical' regionalism in which the right to differentiation represents the prize to which virtuous regions, and therefore richer in merit, can legitimately aspire (Viesti 2019).

There is a lack of knowledge, a lack of recognition. There is a lack of telling, a lack of listening. Awareness gives way to a clear sensation of a lack of awareness, which becomes certainty if we move on to the level of the institutional context that that path of differentiation should support and accommodate.

Indeed, it must be acknowledged that it is always difficult to think about the structural reform of a system when one moves in a context of delegitimisation of the subject that that reform must bring about. As in the Italian case, where the State, rather than being a protagonist subject, seems to be, in all respects, considered an actor among many, inadequate to take on the role of guarantor in the construction of the prerequisites for the success of the operation. It is well demonstrated by the legislative outcome that led to the approval of a law implementing Article 116 (no. 84 of 26 June 2024) that the Constitutional Court has emptied completely (sentence no. 192/2024), highlighting the shortcomings and dissimilarities of an intervention that failed to grasp the spirit of the constitutional norm and of the structure of the 2001 reform, to which many faults can be acknowledged, certainly, but not the total responsibility for the failure of our regional model, since that reform remained substantially on paper.

From a comparative perspective, the structural limitations of our system, in particular the total lack of a system of financial and tax autonomy and the absence of dynamics and places of the centre-periphery connection, which are now, after the difficulties experienced during the pandemic, can no longer be disguised in any way.

Everyone feels the weight of the context in which we are moving, to the point that it is worth wondering whether there is really any point in debating Article 116(3): so many knots remain to be unravelled in the regional system as a whole that any legal solution is doomed to failure.

The truth is that the differentiated regionalism of Article 116 Const. is a glimpse into the broader panorama that has remained largely outside the Parliament's lens: first, with the approval of the reform of Title V, acting as if those changes that were going to affect the organisation of the territory were not part of a broader harmonious project strongly pursued by Leopoldo Elia during the work of the D'Alema Bicameral, but lost. Then, with the implementation of the provisions of the reform that required at least the setting up of a bicameral that was able to give breathing space to the multilevel dialogue of Italian regionalism within the form of government while waiting for the modification of Parliament in a territorial key to be finally reached.

Well, then, it is inevitable to formulate doubts when one expects to implement, with a twenty-year delay, a piece of reform that has never been fully implemented. We persist in criticising the idea of differentiated regionalism, displaying a certain doctrinal provincialism with respect to a subject that has acquired wide consensus in the comparative debate, without taking the trouble to understand that any intervention is destined to yield meagre results and perhaps some problems, owing to the lack of a prior analysis of the context and assumptions. This is precisely the most important lesson that the comparative perspective can bring to legal science.

References

Basso L (1971) Giustizia e potere. La lunga via al socialismo. Quale giustizia 11–12:644–659

Burgess M (2009) The paradox of diversity – asymmetrical federalism in comparative perspective. In: Palermo F, Zwilling C, Kössler K (eds) Asymmetries in constitutional law. Recent developments in federal and regional systems. Eurac Research, Bolzano

Bush L (2011) Standards: recipes for reality. MIT Press, Cambridge

Cámara Villar C (2018) La organización territorial de España. Una reflexión sobre el Estado de la cuestión y claves para la reforma constitucional. Revista de Derecho Político 101

Caminal i Badia M (2013) El federalismo pluralista. Del federalismo nacional al federalismo plurinacional. Paidos, Barcelona

Cubas AM, Pérez JA, Romero J, Soler M, Vidal JM (2013) El federalismo plurinacional. Fin de viaje para el Estado autonómico? Diaz & Pons, Madrid

Delledonne G (2017) L'omogeneità costituzionale negli ordinamenti composti. Editoriale Scientifica, Naples
Fossas Espadaler E (2009) Estado autonómico: plurinacionalidad y asimetría. In: Mastromarino A, Castellà Andreu JM (eds) Esperienze di regionalismo differenziato. Il caso italiano e quello spagnolo a confronto. Giuffrè, Milan
Fukuyama F (1995) Trust: the social virtues and the creation of prosperity. Free Press, New York
Gagnon AG (2013) L'età delle incertezze. Saggio sul federalismo e la diversità nazionale. Cedam, Padova
Grosso E (2020) Intervento introduttivo. In: Bertolino C, Morelli A, Sobrino G (eds) Regionalismo differenziato e specialità regionale: problemi e prospettive, Università degli Studi di, Torino, Turin
Karmis D, Rocher F (2012) La dynamique Confiance/méfiance dans les démocraties multinationales. Le Canada sous l'angle comparatif. Presses de l'Université Laval, Laval
Lombardi G (1985) Spazio e frontiere tra eguaglianza e privilegio: problemi costituzionali fra storia e diritto. In: Scritti sulle fonti normative e altri temi di vario diritto in onore di Vezio Crisafulli, vol. II. Cedam, Padova
Luciani M (2011) Forma di Stato e forma di governo. Quale rapporto tra federalismo e democrazia? In: Vitale E (ed) Quale federalismo? Giappichelli, Turin
Mastromarino A (2010) Il federalismo disaggregativo. Un percorso costituzionale negli stati multinazionali, Giuffrè, Milan
Mastromarino A (2016) Audizione del 9 giugno 2016 alla Commissione parlamentare per le questioni regionali nell'ambito dell'indagine conoscitiva sulle forme di raccordo tra lo Stato e le autonomie territoriali, con particolare riguardo al "sistema delle conferenze". Osservatorio costituzionale 2:1–14
Mastromarino A (2018) Percorsi di asimmetria e relazioni di fiducia nei processi di integrazione politica. La prospettiva belga. Le Istituzioni del Federalismo 2:411–429
Mastromarino A, Castellà Andreu JM (2009) Esperienze di regionalismo differenziato. Giuffrè, Milan
Morelli A (2017) Ascese e declini del regionalismo italiano. Quali prospettive dopo i referendum di Lombardia e Veneto. Le Regioni 3:321–328
Palermo F (2018) Asimmetria come forma e formante dei sistemi composti. Istituzioni del federalismo 2:255–271
Patroni Griffi A (2021) Regionalismo differenziato. Digesto delle Discipline Pubblicistiche, Aggiornamento, Utet, Turin
Putnam RD (1993) La tradizione civica nelle regioni italiane. Mondadori, Milan
Putnam RD (2000) Bowling alone: the collapse and revival of american community. Simon and Schuster, New York
Saymour M, Gagnon AG (2012) Multinational federakusms, problems and prospects. Palgrave, London
Saymour M, Laforest G (2011) Le fédéralisme multinational Un modèle viable? Peter Lang, Bruxelles
Tudela Aranda J (2016) El fracasado éxito del Estado autonòmico. Una historia española. Marcial Pons, Madrid.
Vertovec S (2007) Super-diversity and its implications. Ethnic Racial Stud 30(6)
Viesti G (2019) Verso la secessione dei ricchi. Laterza, Roma-Bari
Zagrebelsky G (1985) Adeguamenti e cambiamenti della Costituzione. Scritti sulle fonti normative e altri temi di vario diritto in onore di Vezio Crisafulli, II, Cedam, Padova

Constitutional Asymmetries in Federal and Regional Systems

Antonio Pérez Miras

Abstract The essay examines constitutional asymmetries in federal and regional systems, arguing that the opposition between symmetrical and asymmetrical federalism is a false dilemma. Starting from the link between territorial pluralism, federalism and democracy, it shows that all composite systems display, to varying degrees, differences in status, powers, institutions and finance among territorial units. Drawing on Tarlton, Watts and Blanco Valdés, the author distinguishes de jure and de facto asymmetry, temporary and permanent models, as well as simple diversity, inhomogeneity and "true" asymmetry, and discusses their limits in light of the principles of equality and fundamental rights. A comparative analysis of several cases (USA, Germany, Austria, Belgium, Italy, Spain, Canada, India, Malaysia and the European Union) illustrates that, when "sustainable" and constitutionally framed, asymmetry can operate as an instrument of integration and cohesion, improving democratic quality and enabling a better balance between unity and diversity. Differentiation, properly designed, may thus strengthen rather than weaken state unity.

1 Introduction

The balance between unity and diversity is the great challenge of any complex legal system, that is, of any democratic State that assumes the existence of a political and territorial pluralism that conditions its institutional political life and the development of constitutional principles. There are indeed uniform States, both in terms of the size of the territory and the size of the population, which normally imply a strong cultural cohesion and a solid identity that limit pluralism to the horizontal axis of the political spectrum. Thus, it is difficult for territorial tensions to exist in this type of State that have not been resolved through dissolution, aggregation, or reconversion. Obviously, these types of states are the least common on the world

A. P. Miras (✉)
University of Granada, Granada, Spain
e-mail: perezmiras@ugr.es

F. Savastano et al. (eds.), *Between Asymmetry and Secession*,
https://doi.org/10.1007/978-3-032-29603-0_3

scene; in practically all modern States, the different constitutions must face the challenge of accommodating the differences that arise from the territories (and the population that inhabits them) due to geographical, historical, economic, and cultural facts. The response to this need has been disparate throughout history, and especially with the emergence of liberal states since the end of the eighteenth century; on the one hand we find the articulation of forms of government in common of the different parts through confederal and federal formulas; on the other hand, the denial or concealment of differences due to their incompatibility with the thriving nations that needed to reinforce the common elements that evidenced the reasons for unity, even if this meant the construction of a fictitious uniformity that, as the passage of time has shown, has not managed to hide the impulses and desires in favor of the recognition of autonomy or independence. This drift has been accompanied by the assimilation of the democratic idea as the matrix of the rule of law. Therefore, this balance between unity and diversity can be achieved in an optimal way if democratic forms and principles are followed that respect not only political pluralism but also territorial pluralism. Thus, federalism is not only a way of understanding the territorial organization of a State but also a way of understanding the plural relations that coexist within a political community. It implies a federal culture.[1]

Today, the idea of federalism has spread throughout the world as an ideal way to capture and solve the internal tensions of a State because of the various realities derived from territorial fit, as a way to neutralize centrifugal tendencies but also to strengthen central power. Thus, federalism behaves as communicating vessels that balance the autonomy of territorial entities to maintain the unity of the complex legal system. It is in this flux that the game of asymmetries is understood: the asymmetrical constitutional design responds to that superior need for the very survival of the State even at the cost of sacrificing (apparently) the basic principle of contemporary constitutionalism, such as equality.

Starting from this premise, we will wonder in this paper about the constitutional asymmetries in federal and regional countries, which leads us to make a preliminary clarification. So far we have made a generic reference to federalism as a singular idea (and in the singular) but in reality there is not a single type or an ideal of federalism but our position is based on the recognition of a plurality of federalisms,[2]

[1] Vid. Galera Victoria (2024a). When analysing the federal process in Spain, this important expert points out that "the direct relationship between federalism and democracy and how this relationship is projected in the current globalised context is a necessary prerequisite for the analysis of this formula for the organisation of power. In democratic spaces, federalism manages to cohere and integrate pluralism into a political organization through institutional and competence responses, concrete mechanisms of integration and coordination. And at the same time, in a relationship of interdependence, federal techniques and culture are valuable tools in this respect because they appeal to very clear democratic principles and far from extreme positions, such as respect for diversity and pluralism, solidarity, cooperation or loyalty." (2024a, 862) [own translation from Spanish].

[2] This plurality can be seen both in doctrinal references and in the treatment of their study and understanding. In this sense, the famous and prestigious Italian review founded by Beniamino

which means, on the one hand, that today federalism needs an adjective, a label that identifies it both on its theoretical level and in its identifying relationship of a concrete experience in some State; on the other hand, the federal idea transcends the mere formal nomination and allows an analysis of all the States that present a system composed of different territorial levels (regardless of the political scope and the level of autonomy they present), including cases of supranational grouping, as exemplified by the creation of the European Union. Thus, following the classic division between formal and material constitution, we can extrapolate a formal and material federalism, which necessarily means that attention must be paid to the states considered regional (as an intermediate stage between the federal states and the unitary states), a category that we do not really consider useful because for us what is important is the degree of autonomy and the interrelation of the different territorial entities, whose study is redirected to the federal analysis. Therefore, in this paper we will jointly address the federal and regional systems in which the doctrine coincides in dealing in a similar way with constitutional asymmetries, which will allow us to conclude on the effectiveness and possible benefits of this recognition to maintain the cohesion of the legal system and territorial unity, always with an eye on the principle of equality.

To this end, we will structure this study in two sections and conclusions. In Sect. 2, we will carry out a bibliographic review on the concept of asymmetrical federalism, where we will consider the dilemma of its real opposition to the so-called symmetrical federalism, which is presented to us as the model of federalism and, therefore, as the ideal to be accommodated. Symmetrical federalism takes on its meaning from the origin of the leading states in the field: the United States and its dual federalism and Germany and its cooperative federalism, both based on an application of constitutional equality to interterritorial relations and the pact origin of their foundation.[3] By analyzing the elements of differentiation that can lead to constitutional asymmetry, we will try to demonstrate that the so-called asymmetrical federalism is in fact the rule that governs constitutional design, although with different scopes and consequences. For this reason, in Sect. 3 we will carry out a

Caravita di Toritto in 2003, whose name declines federalism in the plural, is very eloquent: Federalismi.it. In doctrine we can highlight the monograph by Blanco Valdés (2012).

[3] I would like to refer to my work Pérez Miras (2020, 241): “two classic tensions when it comes to understanding a composite State: on the one hand, the union of separate parts that of their own free will decide to form a common entity; on the other hand, the conversion of an existing unitary State into a decentralised and, therefore, plural State in the recognition of the diversity that is integrated within it. The first case is what has traditionally been known as federation and has always had a direct relationship with sovereignty. The second case, on the other hand, based on the existence of a sovereign State, has tended to be approached from the point of view of decentralization, which has sometimes led to confusion between the mere, and necessary, administrative organization of any State, and the political organization of the territories of a State that, due to their idiosyncrasies and particularities, they form differentiated cultural communities. The political aspiration of these differentiated political communities is the common denominator to these two tensions.” [own translation from Spanish].

comparative review of the main case studies that assert this idea, choosing for this purpose the States that have commonly been addressed by the doctrine.

The importance of this election is that it will take place in the Constitution, that is, in a normative framework of a legal-political organization that brings together the common elements of the communities that make up the State with the diversities that emerge from each component for geographical, historical, social, economic, and cultural reasons. The Constitution, as a legal norm that articulates coexistence, inexorably appears as the frame of reference to be able to manage the territorial differences that coexist, although it sounds paradoxical, in the common territory. In this sense, the Constitution represents better than any other norm the foedus, that territorial pact with which different sovereign States formed a new federal sovereign that materialized in the form of a federal Constitution (cf. La Pergola 1969/2016). But the Constitution has also shown itself to be an ideal norm to guarantee a decentralization that would adapt the structures of the State to the political and social reality of the people it represents. In any case, a correct conceptual determination will be crucial that leads us to the common understanding of federalism as a multifunctional power and independent of the dynamic process of determining the centers of power (cf. La Pergola 1973).

In this constitutional framework, there is a symbiosis between federalism and democracy, the paradox of which Burgess (2013, p. 10) summarizes in these words: "it is important to consider that the peculiar context wherein the new federal models are located can produce an interesting paradox: federation is both the means and the end of democratisation just as democratisation is a necessary instrument of a self-sustaining federalism. They are, in short, mutually reinforcing influences."

As Balaguer Callejón (2019, p. 430) rightly points out, territorial pluralism incorporates a new separation of powers, which increases the possibilities of control over majorities at each level of government. And it goes on to state that the contribution of federalism to constitutional democracy is based precisely on the existence of different territorial levels of government, whose dialectical tension favors the formation of different majorities with implications in both the political and legal spheres, which leads to an increase in the quality of democracy at all levels.

2 Symmetrical Federalism vs. Asymmetrical Federalism: A False Dilemma?

The doctrinal debate on the distinction between symmetrical federalism and asymmetrical federalism starts from the famous study by Tarlton (1965) in which he asks in a speculative essay about the elements that make up federalism in order to be cautious of a high degree of recognition of asymmetry, since it would be a factor for disintegration. In contrast, a high degree of symmetry would ensure the cohesion and unity of the federation. This idea-force has accompanied the most varied doctrine by analyzing the risks in specific cases and being reluctant to recognize differences that create such statuses that they become the prelude to independence demands, as history has shown that this future is a verifiable reality and not just a hypothetical prophecy. Thus, for example, Häberle (2006) perceives differentiated federalism with skepticism if its differences are so deep that they threaten unity (which would apply, for example, to Germany); however, this differentiation seems admissible if we find regional models (such as Spain and Italy), in such a way that differentiated regionalism can be considered as a pragmatic tool to manage diversity, especially cultural, within the limits of a cohesive State. In this sense, García Roca (1997) is against the adoption of a pure asymmetrical federalism as an ideal of territorial organization, warning about its potential disintegrating effects and its negative impact on the governability and cohesion of the State; However, it does not deny the existence of asymmetries in practice, as long as it advocates a balanced institutional design that preserves unity and equality. This caution is shared by Montilla Martos (2015). In fact, as Martinico (2018) points out, asymmetry has been viewed with suspicion among comparatists, as it has traditionally been associated with fragmentation.

From the criticisms made by reluctant authors to the concept of asymmetry, a continuity with Tarlton's first suggestive idea can be observed, which is the premise that there are two opposing models of federalism, the symmetrical and the asymmetrical, and that, therefore, each of these options can be analyzed in such a way that their advantages and disadvantages are extracted when betting on the best design of a given State. This oppositional character is already seen in the first two meanings that Tarlton (1965, p. 861) offers us: the notion of symmetry shows the concerns for the federal system as a whole, while, on the contrary, the concept of asymmetry expresses the degree to which the component states do not share these common characteristics. From this opposition, the author extracts the following idea: "Whether the relationship of a state is symmetrical or asymmetrical is a question of its participation in the pattern of social, cultural, economic, and political characteristics of the federal system of which it is part. This relation, in turn, is a significant factor in shaping its relations with other component states and with the national authority."

But what if there were no such opposition? Or, asked another way: do these opposing (i.e., pure) theoretical models really exist in practice? We have already seen how authors who show their concern about the drift and consequences of asymmetry do not fail to accept a degree of asymmetry in certain circumstances, even attributing beneficial effects to it [for example, Häberle (2006) on differentiated regionalism or Montilla Martos (2015, p. 211)] who, betting on a symmetrical federalism, is in favor in the Spanish case of recognizing certain identity singularities in the constitutional framework, that is, it welcomes the possibility of an asymmetrical federalism in the sense that we will explain below.

To do this, it is necessary that we first make a series of conceptual assessments. While federalism seeks unity within diversity, the theory of asymmetrical federalism postulates that not all the units that make up a federal or composite state must necessarily have the same status, competencies, or relations with the central power. This implies that asymmetry can manifest itself in different areas—which will determine, in our opinion, the acceptability and functionality of the asymmetry in the specific case—such as differences in the competences assumed by the federated entities, with an impact even on legislative power, the recognition of their own historical features that determine the existence of different institutions in each entity; a disparate relationship between each federated entity and the federal group (or among federated entities) that affects not only intergovernmental relations (for example, bilaterality) but also the very presence and participation of the federated entities in the federation (for example, unequal distribution of seats in the Senate); or the no less important issue of financing. Note that we have not mentioned the differences to be expected to justify the asymmetry: first and foremost, geographical features (e.g., insularity) but also the plurinational or multicultural character. In fact, we could say that, as obvious, they are the first causes for a constitutional recognition of asymmetry, but by themselves they do not imply a genuine differentiation with respect to the whole: the mere existence of an island or the presence of a differentiated linguistic community does not imply that its recognition in the Federal Constitution entails an articulation of power in an asymmetrical way, that is, by recognizing a specific competence, establishing an autonomous government or imposing its own financing. All this will always be nuanced, first, by the historical processes of formation, and second, by its capacity to influence general policy. Continuing with these examples: it is not the same that the treatment of insularity affects the whole of the archipelago or islands understood in isolation; whether the linguistic community is considered a minority, whether they can achieve political representation at the federal level with the capacity to influence in their favor.

In the end, what we are talking about is the capacity of the State to respond to the different demands that intrinsic diversity can or should produce in the constitutional design. Thus, if the territorial organization must respond to geographical, historical, cultural, and economic realities and if the federal commitment seems the ideal solution, it must necessarily attend to the differences that originate its adoption and, therefore, must be sensitive to them to the point of being able to make an asymmetrical design. This can be seen very well if we look at the formation of federal states, which can emerge as a union of previous sovereign states, as a process of decentralization from a unitary state, or as a decision from the center (top-down) or following a dispositive principle (bottom-up). For all these procedures, asymmetrical federalism is more flexible, dynamic, and adaptive than a mere symmetrical design that does not respond to the diversities to which it tries to give autonomy and differentiation. These asymmetries can, in turn, be understood in a particular way, "à la carte," to solve a festering problem that destabilizes territorial unity, or they can be seen for all territories in search of a homogenization of difference, as is the case with the famous "coffee for all" of the Spanish autonomy process.

In this way, we can affirm that asymmetry is not only not an exception but is a constitutive and essential element of federalism and composite systems. Many authors have contested the positions of Tarlton, who was skeptical about the ability of federalism to ensure unity in situations of high asymmetry. In response to the criticism of ungovernability and secessionist potential, Watts (2005) considers that asymmetry is a mechanism for accommodating diversity within unity, being a response to entities that want a degree of autonomy that corrects excessive centralization, which can certainly generate tensions but can also overcome them by strengthening territorial cohesion by recognizing the particularities. This mechanism of accommodation is better understood by Watts' classification of asymmetry and the conception of symmetrical federalism as uniformity between the parts, while asymmetrical federalism makes it possible to differentiate between different degrees of power and autonomy enjoyed by the federated entities. Thus, Watts distinguishes, first, between conditions (historical, economic, social, ethnic and cultural) and outcomes (the actual relations between governments). Second, perhaps his distinction that has most influenced the doctrine is de jure and de facto asymmetry. De jure asymmetry is legally recognized inequality, a formal asymmetry recognized in constitutional and legal processes; therefore, a constitutional asymmetry that affects the status and competences of sub-state entities. De facto asymmetry is the inequality that exists in practice, driven by socioeconomic and cultural realities, which manifests itself even if entities are treated equally. The de jure asymmetry can be, in turn, transitory or permanent; respectively, we would be facing a process "at several speeds" tending to gradually achieve uniformity or symmetry, or before the creation of a system of "variable geometry."

Blanco Valdés (2018, p. 301) further refines this classification and proposes distinguishing between diversity, inhomogeneity, and asymmetry itself. Diversity is the demographic, geographical, and economic contrasts that tend to occur in all states. Inhomogeneity is the differences in competences that arise from natural elements or political decisions but that do not alter the political-constitutional position. And the asymmetry itself would be the true asymmetry that arises from political decisions, generally at the constitutional level, that establish differences in competence or of another nature that do alter the political-constitutional position of the federated entities; that is, they do affect their status.

Such is the evidence that differences of different kinds determine and condition in some way the constitutional design of the territorial organization of a State, which means that, in the first place, States are looking for federal formulas (especially those included as regional systems) that try to respond to their idiosyncrasies that avoid a disintegrating drift, and hence the solution always involves welcoming and recognizing a certain degree of asymmetry, as this would be the way to guarantee cohesion. In other words, a unity, even a federal one, that tended only to uniformity would imply a rigidity that was easy to break, while the development of contemporary federalism through the recognition of different degrees of asymmetry would help to give the system the necessary elasticity to cohere the unity (federal or regional). This represents an important change in doctrine, since an important sector already clearly shows that far from being a rupture, asymmetry manages to reinforce cohesion and can even tend to homogenization within respect for diversity (constitutionally recognized). Thus, for example, Seijas Villadangos (2013) points out that asymmetry is a constitutive and essential element of federalism and not a simple exception that is functional for the system: it links asymmetry with the workability of the federal system, which implies that differentiation can be a pragmatic solution to make a federal system viable in contexts of diversity, in which the component units of the State do not share the same and identical common characteristics. In fact, this differentiation implies positions of weakness between entities that imply divergences and differences in conditions that must be treated differently. This allows us to seek a point of balance that treats the equal as the same and the different differently. For his part, Palermo (2018) focuses on asymmetry as a fundamental pillar of territorial organization in composite states and defends a comprehensive analysis beyond competencies to understand its impact on the unity of the system. It also starts from asymmetry as an inherent and fundamental characteristic of composite systems, rather than an exception. Thus, asymmetry in status, powers, and functions among territorial entities is the rule rather than the exception, although it recognizes that the extent and nature of the asymmetry is often implicit ("criptotype"). The ambivalence and breadth of its recognition means that asymmetry is an instrument of integration (even differentiated) rather than a factor of disintegration as long as it is "sustainable,"[4] i.e., that it is developed in compliance with a series of procedural and substantive guarantees aimed at safeguarding the constitutional core of the system (Martinico 2018, p. 299).

The recognition of asymmetry and its different impact on the constitutional order will find a limit in the principle of equality and in the recognition of rights and, therefore, in the position of citizenship in the legal system as a whole. In the end, both ideas are connected because they respond to the same logic on which the contemporary rule of law is based: equality is not incompatible with difference if individual positions are safeguarded that allow people to exercise their rights under the same conditions of equality. In fact, D'Ignazio (2018, p. 253) considers that asymmetry must be harmonized with the system of protection of fundamental rights in such a way that a balance is achieved between unity, equality and autonomy without emptying them of content. Achieving this balance is crucial in federal and composite states, since diversity is by its very nature. Preserving this diversity while maintaining unity is one of the challenges of asymmetrical systems.

This leads us to ask ourselves then about the role of equality in asymmetrical states. As Seijas Villadangos (2013, p. 687) rightly points out: "There are two references for comparing, constituent units and citizens, and two conceptualizations of equality, arithmetic equality and geometric equality." Thus we find that "[on] the one hand, arithmetic equality postulates absolutely equal treatment under the law. On the other hand, geometric equality requires differentiation of treatment according to real differences. This was Plato's main theory. If we apply this theory to constituent units, under an arithmetic equality all these units would be considered absolutely equal under the law. If we differentiate the legal status between them according to real differences, such as territorial size, population, tradition, language, religion, we should apply a geometric concept of equality. The justice of this application depends on the reality of these differences and on the limits to the consequences of the assignment of that singular status."

[4] Ragone (2013) also speaks of sustainable federalism.

3 Comparative Analysis of Case Studies

In line with what was expressed in the previous section, today we can observe that the ideal or type of symmetrical federal State does not exist in a pure way since all States, whether nominally a federation or ascribed as regional systems, present some type of asymmetry, in the expressed sense of differentiation in their constitutional status. It is true that the degree of intensity of the asymmetry can lead to a greater or lesser risk of breakdown of unity or, as we have been arguing, they can simply help to maintain state cohesion by recognizing a difference that, by nature, is justified. Perhaps the most palpable evidence of this issue is found in the existence of differentiations expressly included in the constitutions of classic federal states for their capitals: this is the case with Washington and the District of Columbia in the United States, Mexico City (formerly a federal district) in Mexico, the unique position of Brasilia in Brazil as a federal district or of Buenos Aires in Argentina as an autonomous city. In Australia, we would also find a specialty in the Australian Capital Territory that had to be defined by Parliament, being different from the rest of the federated states. In Europe, we could place in this situation the special intermediate position of Brussels in the Belgian federal framework and, if approved, the brand-new proposal for constitutional reform in Italy for Rome Capital.

Beyond the capitals, territorial differences with a direct impact on the relationship between territories are also observed in the United States, which exercises sovereignty, in addition to the 50 states, over five unincorporated territories (Puerto Rico, Northern Mariana Islands, Guam, the United States Virgin Islands and American Samoa). Something similar occurs in Canada, where, in addition to the ten provinces, there are three territories (Northwest Territories, Yukon and Nunavut), incorporated into the Federation as entities with delegated powers (non-native, such as the provinces) by the federal authorities. And it was also the case in Brazil, where originally the 1988 Constitution provided in Article 18 for the existence of federal territories dependent on the Union—therefore outside the three levels of Union, States and Municipalities—but with the possibility of becoming States, as has finally happened, tending towards symmetry in this sense, with the entire territory divided into 26 states (plus the Federal Capital).[5] In Spain we also find a difference between the 17 Autonomous Communities and the two Autonomous Cities of Ceuta and Melilla, which, as Montilla Martos (1999, pp. 68–69) expresses, exemplify an "asymmetry from below," that is, "they do not reach that lowest common denominator typical of the Autonomous Communities," and have fewer powers and a more limited institutional design. In this case, structural asymmetry leads to a lower degree of autonomy.

From a geographical point of view, Portugal exemplifies, with the autonomies of the archipelagos of the Azores and Madeira, the evolution of decentralization on an asymmetrical basis, because only the insular speciality of these territories justifies a

[5] On the evolution of federalism in Brazil, see Fernandes Guimarães (2025: 55–63) and Da Silva (2005).

constitutional differentiation, which has not been extended to the peninsular territory, overcoming its strong centralist tradition (Orrù 2018).

Focusing on cases of classical federalism, we find Germany, Austria and Belgium. In the first case, the German model, whose cooperative federalism shows a strong symmetrical sense, instead presents asymmetrical features. For example, among the Länder one can differentiate city-states (Hamburg, Bremen, Berlin) and free states (Bavaria, Thuringia, Saxony) with their own particularities. In addition, although representation in the Bundesrat is proportional to the population, some guarantees give more favorable treatment to smaller territories. On the other hand, the constitutional reforms of 2006, 2009, 2017 and 2019 show the debate between competitive and cooperative federalism, which has been reinforced by regaining the prominence of joint decisions. As Kölling (2024, pp. 93–94) points out, the asymmetries have deepened: "While prosperous Länder have more fiscal resources for their own policy initiatives, economically weaker Länder are increasingly dependent on the federal level and supplementary federal subsidies."[6]

Austria has similar features and evolution to Germany. Here too, there have been intense debates that affect the distribution of competences and constitutional reform, although the political debate has not yet found an ideal formula, so the system follows the vicissitudes of each time.[7] The case of Belgium is paradigmatic because, first, it involves the transformation of a unitary State into a federal State through constitutional reform, which has opted for a complex asymmetrical system that tries to respond to the cultural complexity of the country with the firm intention of maintaining unity even at the cost of creating entities that respond to cultural and linguistic criteria, which exacerbates the lack of a sense of national cohesion (Lucas Murillo de la Cueva 1997). Thus, Belgium is divided between the Regions of Flanders, Wallonia and Brussels and at the same time recognizes three linguistic communities, which do not correspond to the territorial base of the aforementioned regions; A French, a Flemish and a German-speaking community are also envisaged. Therefore, linguistic communities overlap with territorially based regions. These communities and regions are, since the constitutional reform of 1993, the entities that make up the Belgian federal State, according to Article 1 of its Constitution. The high degree of asymmetry is therefore evident, since not all constituent entities have the same status or the same competencies. This is explained by the "consociational power-sharing agreement" on which the Belgian system is based (Popelier 2024, p. 103). In fact, Mastromarino (2018, p. 427) considers that the search for balance (albeit unstable) is the key to Belgian law, which constantly seeks compromise as a privileged dynamic to avoid the prevalence of one political force over another or the interests of one community over the other.

Focusing now on two States that have traditionally been framed as regional systems, we find Italy and Spain, which, despite this classification, today the most

[6] Own translation from Spanish.

[7] Vid. Schäffer (2005). On the constitutional reform project in an asymmetrical sense, see the study by Pernthaler (1999).

advanced doctrine has no hesitation in classifying both States as materially federal and, in fact, both with a strong asymmetrical component. In the case of Italy, the federal spirit is evident and gains special strength with the constitutional reform of 2001,[8] although the Constitution of 1948 originally made an asymmetrical regional design based on regions of special statute and ordinary statute. The former responded to geographical issues, in particular the insular element of Sicily and Sardinia, linguistic issues, and borders. Thus, the rich regions of the north were excluded from the special scope, which, over time, showed differentiating aspirations, which led to the inclusion of section 3 in Article 116, which recognized particular forms of autonomy for ordinary regions in accordance with a development law, giving rise to the so-called differentiated regionalism.[9] The controversial Law No. 86 of 2024 on differentiated autonomy has been submitted to a judgment of constitutional legitimacy. The Constitutional Court, in its ruling 192/2024, has endorsed the general principles of the law but has declared the nullity of several of its important precepts.[10]

The case of Spain has also given rise to a wide doctrinal debate and has required a great deal of attention from many scholars, which is impossible to attend to in all its variety. A common idea is shared: we are facing an asymmetrical system that still lacks determining elements to be defined as federal, but that can be totally comparable. Many of us believe that Spain needs a constitutional reform in the federal sense (Pérez Miras 2020; Montilla Martos 2015; Cámara Villar 2018; Galera Victoria 2024a, b), although it is true that many voices call for federalism as a way of solving the so-called Catalan and Basque issues. The first has come to challenge the unity of the State through an independence process, and the second has been marked by the existence in the first decades of a young democracy of the terrorist movement ETA. Beyond these specific issues, the territorial organization in Spain is "deconstitutionalized," according to the fortunate expression of Cruz Villalón (1981), which has led to the formation of an autonomous process on the basis of the dispositive principle that has decentralized the entire territory into 17 Autonomous Communities and two Autonomous Cities, whose main asymmetrical characteristic is the distribution of powers, which does not provide for a residual federal clause and allows each Autonomous Community to assume in its Statute of Autonomous Communities the powers it wishes to exercise, which has forced a marked bilateral nature and a problem around the financing for the execution of all these powers. This dispositive principle has explained the oscillations between differentiation and homogenization that have followed one another through the regional agreements of

[8] Very early on, D'Atena (2001) manifested this federal drift, ideas that he has subsequently developed in the immediate development phase (D'Atena 2005, 2007) and the work he coordinated in D'Atena (2008). Also important are the two collective works by Gambino (2003a and 2003b) that studied the changes that had taken place very early on; and with historical repose see Gambino (2013). For his part, Mezzetti (2005) qualifies it as quasi-federal.

[9] Without wishing to be exhaustive, for a first analysis, D'Ignazio (2003) and D'Ignazio and Carballo Armas (2003). For an analysis that includes the debates on its implementation, see Russo (2018).

[10] See the comments made by Poggi (2025), Torretta (2025).

the 80s and 90s and the statutory reforms initiated in 2006, which have given rise to the so-called Second-Generation Statutes, which sought to strengthen self-government and improve existing competence relations through what is known as competence shielding. This last great wave of statutory reforms has been conditioned in its development by the Constitutional Court judgments 247/2007 (Valencian Statute) and 31/2010 (Catalan Statute); the latter was a turning point for the beginning of the independence challenge in Catalonia, whose consequences we are still experiencing with a direct impact on the current governmental stability as a result of the pardons and Organic Law 1/2024 on amnesty for institutional, political and social normalization in Catalonia (endorsed in its constitutionality by the Constitutional Court in sentence 137/2025). Many proposals seek to establish the asymmetrical system, although there is a strong concern to maintain the homogeneity of the system, surely due to the existence of strong nationalist movements that tend to be disintegrating and, therefore, their federalist (asymmetrical) aspirations may be a certain risk for the unity and permanence of the Spanish State (Blanco Valdés 2018; Mastromarino 2013). However, the adoption of an asymmetrical system in Spain is the way that best responds to what the doctrine calls "differential facts," which would be authentic constitutional asymmetries in the sense set out above.[11] Undoubtedly, there are many challenges facing the Spanish autonomous model but the doctrine has them in general localized, as observed in the book coordinated by Galera Victoria "The territorial question in Spain: a necessary historical, political and constitutional debate"; thus we see how a new vision of the distribution of competences is crucial (Montilla Martos 2024; López-Basaguren 2024), coordination, cooperation and collaboration relations (Cámara Villar 2024), especially in the health field (Guillén López 2024) and, most especially, the issue of regional financing (Pérez Zúñiga 2021, 2024).

Outside Europe, we find paradigmatic cases of asymmetry such as the particular statutes of Jammu and Kashmir, Maharashtra and Gujarat in India[12] or the states of Sabah and Sarawak in Malaysia. But perhaps the most relevant is the case of Canada, which has produced a huge amount of academic literature because of the Quebec question, which oscillates between the study of constitutionally recognized asymmetries and the (orderly) process of independence of the French-speaking province.[13]

Finally, we would like to mention the special case of the European Union, since it is not a State but a process of integration, which has been debated since its origins between a federal soul and a confederal one, which ultimately responds to the

[11] Aja (1999). In the words of López Aguilar (1998, 42), "constitutionally relevant differential facts are those, in our opinion, from which a reasonable constitutional consignment can be predicated, directly or indirectly, from which a mandate of protection, a 'wager' or expression of the constitutional will to protect that fact can be deduced" [own translation from Spanish].

[12] On developments in India, see Bahttacharyya (2005) and Singh (2005).

[13] Without wishing to be exhaustive, see: Woehrling (2005), Craigie (2013), Pelletier (2013), Simeon (2013), Noël (2013).

question of its constitutional nature or as an international organization. Our position, obviously, is aligned with the constitutional understanding, despite the vicissitudes, of the construction of Europe. As Aguilar Calahorro (2024) demonstrates, the functionalist method promoted by Robert Schumann and Jean Monnet, with which progress has been made in the European Union since the beginning of the Communities, although it has a federalist intention, has created a neutral Union Law in terms of the system of territorial planning of the power of the Member States. For this reason, he classifies the Union as "a new type of quasi-federal entity" (Aguilar Calahorro 2024, p. 218). Therefore, the federal fate of the Union runs parallel to its very process of constitutionalizing, in the sense, therefore, expressed in this study. Thus, the distinction between formal and material constitution that is so opportunely applied to the Union also finds an echo in its federal process. Continuing with Aguilar Calahorro (2024, p. 242): "although the formal federalisation of the Union has stopped, the substantive and material possibilities of the Treaty of Lisbon (which not in vain incorporated practically all the novelties of the European Constitutional Treaty) allow the development of integration in materially constitutional terms. Although, in the absence of form, the substance continues to develop in a praetorian way, through dialogue and disagreements between the constitutional courts and the Court of Justice. The federal development of the Union will have to continue along this path, in a material sense, strengthening the role of the judge to the detriment of parliaments. Be that as it may, the principles that structured a future United States of Europe remain intact, in a praetorian way, and reinforced if possible thanks to the appearance of the Charter and European Values as a new legal element that aims at the integration and ordering of power in the European Union."[14] For his part, Martinico (2018) observes an asymmetrical system in the European integration process and, as we have already pointed out, this can help cohesion.

4 Conclusions

We have made a brief review of some states that present elements of constitutional asymmetry, that is, that which really modifies the status or power relations between federal and federated entities. Following the thesis that has been developed in this essay that the opposition between symmetrical and asymmetrical federalism is a false dilemma because it does not actually occur in its pure state in any state, whether federal or regional, it has been possible to verify how these elements of asymmetry occur with greater or lesser scope even in classic federal states, such as the USA or Germany. This review has included countries from several continents:

[14] Own translation from Spanish.

from India and Malaysia, Australia, Argentina, Mexico, Brazil, Canada, Austria and Belgium, as well as the cases of Italy and Spain, which, although they are not formally federal states, their constitutional orders provide for models of strong asymmetrical tendency. Likewise, the case of supranational construction of the European Union has been studied.

Starting with these last three examples, in which there is obviously no formal federalism, we can see how asymmetrical federalism is undoubtedly the reference model for achieving authentic formal and material adequacy. However, in the sense that we have been defending, the commitment to a pure asymmetrical federalism would impede, in our opinion, the value of cohesion that a large majority of authors advocate as one of the benefits of the recognition of difference with an impact on its constitutional status. In fact, even the critics of asymmetrical federalism, on the conceptual opposition initially raised by Tarlton (1965), do not deny a certain asymmetrical recognition precisely in the references to the cases mentioned here. Thus, the positive value that Häberle (2006) gives to differentiated regionalism or the nuanced positions of Montilla Martos or García Roca are a good example of this. Behind these criticisms there is a widely shared concern, such as the possible breakdown of equality, as there is a slippery slope that the asymmetry between territories could imply a breakdown of the equal rights of citizens. As Galera Victoria (2024a, 2024b) rightly insists, the adoption of a federal system for these states (nominally incomplete) would also represent a democratic advance that would allow political debates and operational problems to be faced in a calmer way and, especially, with a federal culture that places loyalty as a central and basic principle of territorial coexistence. Thus, there is no need to fear the recognition of asymmetry at the constitutional level, since it would not be a door to disintegration but a bridge to the improvement of collective life.

In fact, these debates on improving the functioning of the federal system are observed in the states that are formally so, which translate into constitutional reforms, as can be seen in Germany or Austria. This would lead us to wonder whether the formal recognition of the federal state helps to focus on problems and even seek asymmetrical solutions. This would be consistent with the idea shared by many authors that asymmetry, far from being an element of separation, would help to maintain cohesion through the recognition of differences. Let us not forget that the conception of equality is based on a recognition of what is different, and as Seijas Villadangos (2013) has observed, asymmetry can make equality effective by treating those who are different differently.

The idea of the recognition of constitutional asymmetry as an instrument to guarantee unity (Palermo 2018, p. 266) is, from our point of view, a crucial element in betting on its adoption. However, this does not avoid the debate about potential slippage depending on the degree of asymmetry. Or in other words, the mere recognition of asymmetry is not a panacea; it must be accompanied by a reflection on the quantum and the manner of this recognition. Perhaps the cases of Belgium and

Canada are paradigmatic in this regard. In the case of Belgium, the asymmetrical federal reform of 1993 served to maintain the unity of the Kingdom of Belgium, but (also perhaps) the institutional design chosen has not been the most ideal because, with such marked and differentiated sociolinguistic bases, common and unifying elements have not been sought, but have limited themselves to recognizing differences without establishing channels that promote plural coexistence. The Canadian solution, on the other hand, seems to have even served to stop the independence of Quebec. This risk, which Blanco Valdés considers possible in Spain because of the existence of strong separatist nationalist sentiments, is basically a confirmation of an asymmetrical recognition contrary to the foundation that we have been defending in these pages: the structuring of diversity derived from territorial pluralism contributes to the strengthening of democratic pluralism and better control of power. An important lesson can also be drawn from this for the constitutional construction of the European Union.

In short, the asymmetrical governance derived from the constitutional design has an impact on general political stability and better territorial integration. Differentiated autonomy responds to the particular needs of the various territorial entities and can achieve a balance between unity and diversity.

References

Aguilar Calahorro A (2024) La Unión Europea: de la internacionalización a la federalización. In: Arbós Marín X, Romano A (eds) El federalismo contemporáneo en Europa. Editorial Hacer, Barcelona, pp 213–243

Aja Fernández E (1999) El Estado Autonómico. Federalismo y hechos diferenciales. Alianza Editorial, Madrid

Bahttacharyya H (2005) Federalism and regional accommodation of identity in India. In: Valadés D, Serna de la Garza JM (eds) Federalismo y regionalismo, UNAM - Tribunal Superior de Justicia del Estado de Puebla, México, pp 471–504

Balaguer Callejón F (2019) Federalism and democratic quality: the contribution of territorial pluralism to constitutional democracy. In: López-Basaguren A, Escajedo San-Epifanio L (eds) Claims for secession and federalism. Springer, Cham, pp 423–431

Blanco Valdés RL (2012) Los rostros del federalismo. Alianza Editorial, Madrid

Blanco Valdés RL (2018) Sobre la asimetría en los Estados federales y la utilidad práctica de una buena teoría. Istituzioni del Federalismo 2:301–322

Burgess M (2013) Opening Pandora's box: process and paradox in the federalism of political identity. In: López-Basaguren A, Escajedo San-Epifanio L (eds) The ways of federalism in western countries and the horizons of territorial autonomy in Spain, Vol. 1. Springer, Cham, pp 3–14

Cámara Villar G (2018) La organización territorial de España. Una reflexión sobre el estado de la cuestión y claves para la reforma constitucional. Revista de Derecho Político 101:395–430

Cámara Villar G (2024) Reflexiones sobre las relaciones de coordinación, cooperación y colaboración en el estado autonómico en el marco de una posible reforma constitucional en sentido federal. In: Galera Victoria A (eds) La cuestión territorial en España: un debate histórico, político y constitucional necesario. Comares, Granada, pp 105–124

Craigie A (2013) Defending the federation: the federal challenge to national defence policy making in Canada. In: López-Basaguren A, Escajedo San-Epifanio L (eds) The ways of federalism in western countries and the horizons of territorial autonomy in Spain, Vol. 1. Springer, Cham, pp 155–164

Cruz Villalón P (1981) La estructura del Estado o la curiosidad del jurista persa. Revista de la Facultad de Derecho de la Universidad Complutense 4:53–63

D'Atena A (2001) L'Italia verso il "federalismo." Taccuini di Viaggio. Giuffrè, Milan

D'Atena A (2005) Le Regioni dopo il Big Bang. Giuffrè, Milan

D'Atena A (2007) La reforma constitucional del regionalismo italiano. Revista d'Estudis Autonòmics i federals 4:9–34

D'Atena A (ed) (2008) I nuovi Statuti delle Regioni ad autonomia ordinaria. Giuffrè, Milan

D'Ignazio G (2003) Asimetrie e differenziazioni regionali dopo la riforma del Titolo V della Costituzione. In: Gambino S (ed) Il "nuovo" ordinamento regionale. Competenze e diritti. Giuffrè, Milan, pp 263–274

D'Ignazio G (2018) Asimmetrie e "Costituzioni territoriali" nel quadro giuridico europeo: un'analisi comparata. Istituzioni del Federalismo 2:245–254

D'Ignazio G, Carballo Armas P (2003/2004) Asimetrías y diferenciaciones regionales tras la reforma del Título V de la Constitución italiana. Teoría y Realidad Constitucional 12–13:385–396

Da Silva JA (2005) Dos Estados federados no federalismo brasileiro. In: Valadés D, Serna de la Garza JM (eds) Federalismo y regionalismo. UNAM - Tribunal Superior de Justicia del Estado de Puebla, México, pp 155–178

Fernandes Guimarães D (2025) Os sintomas do federalismo cooperativo brasileiro. In: Pérez Miras A, Teruel Lozano GM, Romboli S, Palombino G (eds) Constitucionalismo: diálogos intergeneracionales entre España e Italia, Vol. II. BOE-CEPC, Madrid, pp 55–76

Galera Victoria A (2024a) Sobre la federalización del Estado autonómico. In: Balaguer Callejón F, López Aguilar JF, Balaguer Callejón ML (eds) Estudios sobre el Estado social y democrático de Derecho. Liber amicorum Gregorio Cámara Villar, Tomo II. CEPC, Madrid, pp 855–872

Galera Victoria A (2024b) Evolución y perspectivas de futuro del estado autonómico. In: Galera Victoria A (ed) La cuestión territorial en España: un debate histórico, político y constitucional necesario. Comares, Granada, pp 203–222

Gambino S (2003a) Regionalismo, Federalismo, Devolution. Competenze e diritti. Giuffrè, Milan

Gambino S (2003b) Il 'nuovo' ordinamento regionale. Competenze e diritti. Giuffrè, Milan

Gambino S (2013) The road towards federalism in Italy?. In: López-Basaguren A, Escajedo San-Epifanio L (eds) The ways of federalism in western countries and the horizons of territorial autonomy in Spain, Vol. 1. Springer, Cham, pp 351–374

García Roca J (1997) España asimétrica (Descentralización territorial y asimetrías autonómicas: una especulación teórica). In: Asimetría y cohesión en el estado autonómico. Jornadas sobre el Estado autonómico: integración y eficacia. Instituto Nacional de Administración Pública, Madrid

González Pascual M (2018) La asimetría consensuada y opcional como solución constitucional al conflicto catalán. La necesaria reforma constitucional, Istituzioni del Federalismo. Rivista di studi giuridici e politici 2:323–342

Guillén López E (2024) Descentralización territorial, estado de alarma y consejo interterritorial del Sistema Nacional de Salud. In: Galera Victoria A (ed) La cuestión territorial en España: un debate histórico, político y constitucional necesario. Comares, Granada, pp 125–145

Häberle P (2006) El federalismo y el regionalismo: una estructura modélica del Estado constitucional. Experiencias alemanas y proyectos. Memorándum para un proyecto español. Revista Española de Derecho Constitucional 77:9–25
Kölling M (2024) La organización territorial de Alemania: un balance de los últimos veinte años In: Arbós Marín X, Romano A (eds) El federalismo contemporáneo en Europa. Editorial Hacer, Barcelona, pp 79–99
La Pergola A (1969/2016) Vestigios «contractualistas» y estructura federal en la Constitución de los Estados Unidos. Tecnos, Madrid
La Pergola A (1973) El empirismo en el estudio de los sistemas federales: en torno a una teoría de Karl Friedrich. Revista de Estudios Políticos 188:21–79
López Aguilar JF (1998) Estado autonómico y hechos diferenciales. Centro de Estudios Políticos y Constitucionales, Madrid
López-Basaguren A (2018) L'autonomia del Paese basco tra asimmetrie interne e riconoscimento europeo. Alla ricerca di un rapporto confederale e del riconoscimento del "diritto a decidere". Istituzioni del Federalismo 2:343–364
López-Basaguren A (2024) La distribución de competencias en el sistema autonómico: la necesidad de la reforma. In: Galera Victoria A (ed) La cuestión territorial en España: un debate histórico, político y constitucional necesario. Comares, Granada, pp 75–90
Lucas Murillo de la Cueva P (1997) El federalismo asimétrico en Bélgica. Revista Vasca de Administración Pública 47(II):173–198
Martinico G (2018) Quanto è sostenibile l'integrazione (asimmetrica) sovranazionale. Note di diritto comparato. Istituzioni del Federalismo 2:287–300
Mastromarino A (2013) The Adhesion of the Spanish autonomic state to the disaggregative model of federalism: a possible way. In: López-Basaguren A, Escajedo San-Epifanio L (eds) The ways of federalism in western countries and the horizons of territorial autonomy in Spain, Vol. 2. Springer, Cham, pp 711–730
Mastromarino A (2018) Percorsi di asimmetria e relazioni di fiducia nei processi di integrazione politica. La prospettiva belga. Istituzioni del Federalismo 2:411–430
Mezzetti L (2005) Il sistema (quasi) federale italiano. In: Valadés D, Serna de la Garza JM (coords.), Federalismo y regionalismo (Valadés D, Serna de la Garza JM (eds)) UNAM - Tribunal Superior de Justicia del Estado de Puebla, México. Federalismo y regionalismo (Valadés D, Serna de la Garza JM (eds)) UNAM - Tribunal Superior de Justicia del Estado de Puebla, México, pp 525–546
Montilla Martos JA (1999) La asimetría de las Ciudades Autónomas. Revista Española de Derecho Constitucional 57:65–86
Montilla Martos JA (2015) Reforma federal y Estatutos de segunda generación. Cizur Menor, Aranzadi
Montilla Martos JA (2024) El debate competencial en el estado autonómico. In: A. Galera Victoria (eds) La cuestión territorial en España: un debate histórico, político y constitucional necesario. Comares, Grenada, pp 91–103
Noël A (2013) ¿Café para todos? Homogeneity, Difference, and Canadian Federalism. In: López-Basaguren A, Escajedo San-Epifanio L (eds) The ways of federalism in western countries and the horizons of territorial autonomy in Spain, vol 2. Springer, Cham, pp 359–374
Orrù R (2018) Asimmetrie formali e materiali nel sistema territoriale portoghese. Istituzioni del Federalismo 2:451–470
Palermo F (2018) Asimmetria come forma e formante dei sistemi composti. Istituzioni del Federalismo 2:255–272

Pelletier B (2013) Intergovernmental relations in Canada: a horizontal perspective. In: López-Basaguren A, Escajedo San-Epifanio L (eds) The ways of federalism in western countries and the horizons of territorial autonomy in Spain, Vol. 2. Springer, Cham, 13–38
Pérez Miras A (2020). La reforma federal de la Constitución española: ¿una necesidad simbólica?. In: Pérez Miras A, Teruel Lozano GM, Raffiotta EC, Iadicicco MP, Romboli S (eds) Setenta años de Constitución italiana y cuarenta años de Constitución española. Volumen I Balances y perspectivas en la Europa constitucional. BOE-CEPC, Madrid, pp 239–261
Pérez Zúñiga JM (2021) Estado Autonómico y Federal. Thomson Reuters Aranzadi, Cizur Menor
Pérez Zúñiga JM (2024) El federalismo fiscal en la Constitución Española. In: Galera Victoria A (ed) La cuestión territorial en España: un debate histórico, político y constitucional necesario. Comares, Granada, pp. 147–182
Pernthaler P (1999) El Estado federal asimétrico. Fundamentos teóricos, consecuencias prácticas y ámbitos de aplicación en la reforma del Estado federal austriaco. IVAP, Oñati
Poggi A (2025) Il referendum sul regionalismo differenziato: i principi, l'attuazione, le Corti e la sovranità popolare. Federalismi.it, 1
Popelier P (2024). Dinámicas federales en Bélgica: orígenes, path dependency y acontecimientos clave que dan forma al equilibrio federal entre cohesión y autonomía. In: Arbós Marín X, Romano A (eds) El federalismo contemporáneo en Europa. Editorial Hacer, Barcelona, pp 101–127
Ragone S (2013) "Sustainable Differentiation": the twenty-first century challenge to decentralization (a comparative study of Italy and Spain, with special attention to constitutional case law. In: López-Basaguren A, Escajedo San-Epifanio L (eds) The ways of federalism in western countries and the horizons of territorial autonomy in Spain. Springer, Cham, pp 191–200
Russo AM (2018) Il regionalismo italiano nel vortice autonomistico della differenziazione: l'asimmetria sperimentale tra integrazione e conflitti. Istituzioni del Federalismo 2:365–392
Schäffer H (2005) The Austrian Federalism: Situation and Perspectives. In: Valadés D, Serna de la Garza JM (eds) Federalismo y regionalismo. UNAM - Tribunal Superior de Justicia del Estado de Puebla, México, pp. 119–154
Seijas Villadangos E (2013) Asymmetry as an element of federalism: a theoretical speculation fifty years later - readdress the Spanish case. In: López-Basaguren A, Escajedo San-Epifanio L (eds) The Ways of Federalism in Western Countries and the Horizons of Territorial Autonomy in Spain. Springer, Cham, pp. 679–690
Simeon R (2013) Reflections on diversity in Canada: competing models. In: López-Basaguren A, Escajedo San-Epifanio L (eds) The ways of federalism in western countries and the horizons of territorial autonomy in Spain, Vol. II. Springer, Cham, pp 331–340
Singh MP (2005) Federalism, democracy and human rights: some reflections with special reference to India. In: Valadés D, Serna de la Garza JM (eds) Federalismo y regionalismo, UNAM - Tribunal Superior de Justicia del Estado de Puebla, México, pp 505–524
Tarlton CD (1965) Symmetry and asymmetry as elements of federalism: a theoretical speculation. J Polit 27(4):861–874
Torretta P (2025) La disciplina dei LEP per l'autonomia differenziata (ma non solo) al vaglio della Corte costituzionale. Note a margine della sentenza n. 192/2024. Federalismi.it, 13
Watts RL (2005) A comparative perspective on asymmetry in federations. In: Asymmetry Series, 4. IIGR, Queen's University
Woehrling J (2005). Canada: The state of federation. In: Valadés D, Serna de la Garza JM (eds) Federalismo y regionalismo. UNAM - Tribunal Superior de Justicia del Estado de Puebla, México, pp 179–218

Pluralist Democracy, Unity of the State, Secession: A Journey Through Indivisible Legal Orders

Gennaro Ferraiuolo

Abstract This essay examines how democratic constitutional systems address secessionist claims, with particular attention to the tension between unity and pluralism. Using Italy, Spain, Germany, Canada, and the United Kingdom as case studies, it contrasts legal frameworks that categorically exclude secession (Italy, Germany) with those that, at least formally, envisage a constitutional path (Spain, Canada). The analysis shows, however, that such classifications are often illusory: rigid constitutional procedures or political vetoes render secession practically unattainable. Against this background, the essay advocates a dynamic approach that integrates not only legal-constitutional rules but also the political processes in which secessionist claims emerge. Canada's "adherence to the law/legitimacy" balance and the UK's accommodation of "moral authority/legal authority" illustrate models of democratic responsiveness, whereas Spain's and Italy's rigid stances risk suppressing minority nations' political subjectivity. Ultimately, the paper argues that constitutional debate on secession remains meaningful only if legality is complemented by legitimacy, ensuring recognition of internal pluralism.

1 Premise

This chapter aims to outline, through a limited comparative lens, the different approaches adopted by democratic systems in safeguarding the principle of territorial unity. The focus on democracy is crucial: only within such a framework does the demand for secession arise as a genuinely political issue, whereas "in other contexts [...] it is merely a military matter, resolved either by coercion or by the victory of secessionist forces" (Cantaro 1996, p. 22).

The analysis begins with the cases of Italy and Spain, two constitutional orders that, at least in principle, provide distinct responses to the prospect of a rupture in the territorial integrity of the State. From this starting point, the discussion proceeds

G. Ferraiuolo (✉)
Federico II University of Naples, Napoli, Italy
e-mail: gennaro.ferraiuolo@unina.it

F. Savastano et al. (eds.), *Between Asymmetry and Secession*,
https://doi.org/10.1007/978-3-032-29603-0_4

to uncover discursive ambiguities and argumentative pitfalls that have shaped legal and political debates, ultimately paving the way for a broader and more critical reflection on the normative scope of the principle of unity.

2 A World Divided Into Two Blocks?

At first glance, an analysis of Italian and Spanish constitutional jurisprudence may suggest the existence of markedly different approaches to both the scope of the principle of unity and, correspondingly, to the phenomenon of secession.

The Italian Constitutional Court classifies secession among those "institutional upheavals radically incompatible with the fundamental principles of unity and indivisibility of the Republic enshrined in Article 5 of the Constitution. The unity of the Republic is one of those elements so essential to the constitutional order that it is even removed from the scope of constitutional amendment" (Judgment No. 118/2015). The legal impossibility of secession translates, in terms of constitutional conformity, into the legal impossibility of consulting citizens on that outcome: indeed, the Court declared unconstitutional a Veneto regional law (No. 16/2014) providing for a referendum on independence. What cannot be legally achieved cannot even be legally asked, not even through a merely consultative referendum. A comparable stance was adopted by the German Constitutional Court in 2016: secession, as such, is contrary to the constitutional order; the Länder are not the masters of the Constitution (2 BvR 349/16).

It is therefore necessary to ask on what grounds this notion of indissoluble unity rests, especially considering that Article 5 of the Italian Constitution contains no explicit entrenchment clause excluding it from constitutional amendment. In this respect, Alessandro Pace has argued that "even if Article 5 did not exist, consent to the dismemberment of the State (or even to the secession of only part of it) would nonetheless constitute a revolutionary act; and it would remain such regardless of the (even peaceful) means envisioned to bring it about." Consequently, "all legal acts adopted for that purpose (e.g., a popular consultative referendum) must be regarded as radically null and void, giving rise to civil, criminal, and administrative liability, and inapplicable by anyone" (Pace 1999, p. 1139, emphasis added). At the bottom lies the idea that States are territorially indissoluble by their very nature, since their constitutive elements—among them territory and, accordingly, the population inhabiting it—cannot be altered.

This approach appears to be rejected by the Spanish Constitutional Court (Tribunal Constitucional, TC). Spain is not a *militant democracy* in which "what is imposed is not only respect for, but also positive adherence to, the constitutional order, and in the first place to the Constitution"; accordingly, there is no "core of norms inaccessible to constitutional amendment procedures" (Judgment No. 48/2003).[1] Under this vision, even a secessionist project may be legitimately

[1] In a similar vein, see also TC Judgments Nos. 103/2008, 31/2009, and 42/2014.

pursued through the procedures of constitutional revision: "if the Legislative Assembly of an Autonomous Community, which is granted by the Constitution the power to initiate constitutional amendment […], were to submit such a proposal, the Spanish Parliament would be obliged to consider it" (STC 42/2014).

In contrast to the radical closure adopted by the Italian Court, the position of the TC has been considered very close to that of the Canadian Supreme Court (Delledonne 2017: 145), as expressed in its well-known 1998 *Reference re Secession of Quebec* ([1998] 2 SCR 217), rightly regarded as a "global benchmark, containing what is arguably the most advanced constitutional doctrine on the right of secession" (Fossas Espadaler 2014, p. 287). In fact, the Spanish Constitutional Court, in its 2014 decision, explicitly drew on this foreign precedent.

If, in light of the foregoing, one were to attempt a preliminary and provisional classification of how States approach the prospect of a rupture in territorial unity, a world of democracies would seem divided into two clearly distinct blocks: on the one hand, systems in which secession cannot be achieved by legal means (Italy and Germany); on the other, systems that envision a legal pathway to secession through constitutional amendment procedures (Spain and Canada).

Yet a closer look reveals that such a classification suffers from excessive abstraction. This becomes particularly clear in the Spanish case. The principle of unity, enshrined in Article 2 of the Constitution's Preliminary Title, could theoretically be overridden through the procedure set forth in Article 168. Yet this procedure is so complex that scholarship has often described it less as a tool for constitutional reform than as a device designed to prevent it—an implicit entrenchment clause (*cláusula de intangibilidad oculta*) (De Vega 1985, p. 148). If this procedure is already close to impossible to implement in practice, one can imagine how much more so it is for structural minorities such as peripheral nationalisms—typically the political actors advancing independence claims. However strong their majority support within their territories, they will never command, in the national Parliament, the supermajorities required by a procedure modeled on Article 168 CE.

Accordingly, even if one accepts that certain constitutional democracies formally include clauses allowing secession through constitutional amendment, the fairness of such clauses must be assessed in light of the weight they accord to the will of peripheral nations (Norman 2002, pp. 94–95; Modugno 1999, p. 1029). Without such consideration, the prospect of secession by way of constitutional amendment—however theoretically possible—may prove unattainable in practice. Thus, the presentation of such a pathway risks becoming a rhetorical device, invoked primarily to foreclose debate by denying the legitimacy of secessionist claims at their root.

3 Welcome to *Flatland*

These considerations suggest that the limited data examined thus far should be organized according to a criterion informed by greater realism. With regard to the issue at hand—the responses of democratic constitutionalism to secessionist demands—the constitutional landscape ultimately appears rather uniform. No particular irregularities emerge; the map is shaded in largely homogeneous tones: secession presents itself as a claim that cannot be legally accommodated, at least not in practice, if not already at the level of principle.

Some territories, however, ought to be erased from this map. The United Kingdom, which has not yet been addressed, would in fact belong to a different planet, one where the gravitational force of constitutional rigidity is absent, and the principle of parliamentary sovereignty reigns supreme. These features make that system hardly comparable to those considered here (Montilla Martos 2016). Alongside these legal considerations, one must also acknowledge a more recent political tendency—particularly in the aftermath of Brexit, a development that at least echoes secessionist dynamics (Savastano 2019, p. 161 ff.)—to strip the British system of its longstanding status as a constitutional model.[2]

Within this framework, the models taken into account (more precisely: the models worthy of consideration—Italy, Germany, Spain, and Canada) prove, at bottom, to be highly similar, despite certain divergent conceptual premises. The resulting map evokes the world of *Flatland*, depicted by Edwin Abbott in his 1882 tale: a country inhabited by flat geometric figures, devoid of any perception of a third dimension. There are triangles, squares, pentagons, hexagons, and circles. Yet they move only by sliding along the plane on which they rest; unable to rise above it and observe their world from above, Flatland's inhabitants perceive themselves merely as lines, distinguished only by the varying intensity of their light. Figures who, having come into contact with another world—*Spaceland*—attempt to reveal the existence of an additional dimension are silenced, imprisoned, or killed (Abbott 1882).[3]

It is worth asking, then, whether in our representation of the issue at stake some dimension has likewise been overlooked, and whether it is precisely this omission that renders, in substance, the approaches of different democratic systems to secessionist claims so indistinguishable.

[2] In Italy, for example, the British parliamentary system served for decades as a primary point of reference—explicitly acknowledged in much of the legal and political science scholarship—for electoral and constitutional reforms, whether enacted or merely envisaged, at all levels of government since at least the 1990s. For a critical analysis of these legislative interventions—and in particular of the misunderstandings underpinning references to the British parliamentary model—see Ferraiuolo 2018; Ferraiuolo and Praino 2018.

[3] I am indebted for this image to Sandro Staiano, who employs it in relation to a different field of analysis—namely, the relationship between the rules governing the organization of political power and the party system (Staiano 2019, p. 30).

4 The Forgotten Dimension

The dimension that has been neglected may well be that of the political processes within which secessionist claims arise: a dynamic (rather than static) dimension that unfolds not only on the strictly legal plane but also within the broader politico-legal sphere (Bastida 2016, p. 218 ff.; Amoroso and Ferraiuolo 2019, p. 93 ff.).

Adopting this perspective, the responses provided by state institutions may appear more nuanced than the classificatory scheme sketched thus far, and therefore more—or less—consistent with the logic of pluralist democracies. At this stage, what emerges are no longer indistinct lines, but distinct geometric figures, each bearing its own specific characteristics.

4.1 Exploring Canada: Adherence to the Law and Legitimacy

From this new vantage point, the distinctive feature of the Canadian paradigm is not secession through constitutional amendment, but rather the relationship the Supreme Court establishes between the democratic principle and the principle of legality/constitutional rigidity (Gaudreault-Desbiens 2014, pp. 768–769). This relationship is articulated in a bidirectional sense: the legal rule (in this case, the constitutional rule) is not merely an external limit to political decision-making; law must also provide the instruments that allow the rule, at least in principle, to reflect the will of the people. For the Canadian Court, a democratic system of government cannot subsist solely on *adherence to the law* but also requires *legitimacy* (§ 67 of the Reference). The tension between the static dimension (*adherence to the law*) and the dynamic dimension (*legitimacy*) is vividly captured in the vision offered by the guardian of the constitutional order.

In this perspective, a fragmented manifestation of the popular will is accepted as a democratic possibility, one implied by pluralism in general and, more specifically, by national pluralism. Two equally legitimate majorities may come into conflict, without one being entitled to silence the other: the majority of the population of Québec and the majority of Canada as a whole (§§ 93, 66). The instrument through which the national minority expresses its will regarding the relationship it wishes to maintain with the federal State is the referendum—fully embraced within the democratic logic as a method for ascertaining citizens' views on fundamental political questions (§ 87)—even though this institution is not expressly provided for in the Canadian Constitution, and thus cannot be endowed with any automatic or legally binding effect.

On this premise, constitutional amendment is not conceived as a blocking device firmly controlled by the political forces that dominate central institutions. Rather, it represents a stage in a more complex procedural sequence, designed to maintain a democratic balance between *adherence to the law* and *legitimacy*: referendum of the national minority; a "clear majority on a clear question"; and the obligation of the

Federation and the Provinces (both the secessionist province and the others) to negotiate in good faith in order to achieve, through constitutional amendment, an outcome that responds to the demands expressed by the territorial minority through referendum (§ 88).

Within this framework, both the attempt by the national minority to achieve secession unilaterally and the "unreasonable intransigence" of the Federation (and the other Provinces) in refusing to engage in the necessary negotiations fall outside the bounds of good faith (and of constitutional compliance). In the latter case, the Court appears to open the door to a form of *just cause* for secession, updated to reflect the democratic evolution of constitutional systems: refusal to negotiate may, in fact, confer legitimacy on a unilateral secession, even at the international level (§ 103). This approach is shared by a part of the specialized literature (Seymour 2010, p. 62 ff.; Buchanan 2013, pp. 19–21), which illustrates how the distance between different theoretical categories of secession (remedial, ascriptive, voluntarist)—so clear in the abstract—may narrow considerably in practice.

4.2 Returning to the United Kingdom: Making the Process Legal

Adopting the dynamic perspective suggested here allows us to reintroduce the United Kingdom into the analysis, even though it initially appeared to belong to a different world, far removed from the realm of rigid constitutions. Despite the absence of the latter, by substituting the tension between *adherence to the law* and *legitimacy* with that between *moral authority* and *legal authority*—formulas recurrent in the Scottish experience culminating in the 2014 independence referendum—one can discern a certain proximity to the Canadian paradigm. The crucial difference, however, is that here we are faced not with a judicially crafted design, but with a process constructed entirely through political negotiation between London and Edinburgh (for a detailed analysis, see Caravale 2017, p. 45 ff.). As in Canada, moreover, the legal instruments required to achieve independence are not immediately available to national minority groups, who remain dependent on decisions formally taken at the central level.

Both sides of the British territorial conflict shared the understanding that the Scottish Parliament lacked the *legal authority* to call a referendum: "without amendment, the Scotland Act 1998 confers no legislative power on the Scottish Parliament to pass an Act purporting to authorise a referendum about independence."[4] Once the Scottish National Party secured a *moral authority* to hold such a consultation,

[4] Thus, see the *Referendum on Scottish Independence*, Select Committee on the Constitution of the House of Lords (February 2012), pp. 12–13, §§ 30–31. In the same vein, see also *Scotland's Constitutional Future: A Consultation on Facilitating a Legal, Fair and Decisive Referendum on Whether Scotland Should Leave the United Kingdom*, January 2012, p. 6.

following its electoral victory in 2011,[5] the central authorities nonetheless recognized the democratic necessity of devising, through political channels, the legal framework capable of realigning the moral and the legal dimensions. No words better capture this dynamic than those of the then Conservative Prime Minister and his Liberal Democrat deputy:

> The Scottish National Party entered the May 2011 election with a manifesto pledge for a referendum on independence. They have campaigned consistently for independence, and while the UK Government does not believe this is in the interests of Scotland, or the rest of the United Kingdom, we will not stand in the way of a referendum on independence: the future of Scotland's place within the United Kingdom is for people in Scotland to vote on (Cameron and Clegg 2012, p. 5).

As in the Canadian experience, then, when confronted with a gap between the two planes (legality and legitimacy, moral and legal), the dominant nation—structurally majoritarian within central institutions—took its decision while taking into account the will of the structurally minoritarian national group within the State. The Westminster Parliament, by amending the *Scotland Act* (the materially constitutional statute governing the relationship between the levels implicated in the political conflict), delegated ad hoc to Holyrood the competence to regulate and convene the referendum, subject to the constraints established in the Edinburgh Agreement.[6] Particularly telling in this regard is the title of a dossier commissioned by the House of Commons and prepared with input from constitutional scholars to identify possible regulatory solutions for the referendum: *"The Referendum on Separation for Scotland: Making the Process Legal."*[7]

From this perspective, the United Kingdom's experience differs from that of continental democratic systems only in quantitative, not qualitative, terms (more generally, see Chessa 2017, pp. 21–22). The procedures employed in the latter will be more complex and demanding, but remain available whenever state-level actors deem it preferable to address political–territorial conflicts through means consistent with democratic pluralism. From this vantage point, the treatment afforded to Scottish claims during the 2010–2014 period has been regarded as a democratic demonstration of the State's "flexibility to adjust to such a challenge and the capacity also to recognise the multinational character of the State which underpins the political aspirations of its different peoples" (Tierney 2013, pp. 141–142); "a sign of strength, the latest example of the state's pragmatic reconsolidation in response to internal stresses" (Walker 2014, p. 745).

---

[5] In this sense, see the programmatic manifesto *Re-elect. A Scottish Government Working for Scotland (2011). Scottish National Party Manifesto 2011*, p. 28.

[6] The agreement between the United Kingdom and Scotland was reached in October 2012: *Agreement between the United Kingdom Government and the Scottish Government on a Referendum on Independence for Scotland.*

[7] *The Referendum on Separation for Scotland: Making the Process Legal*, House of Commons Scottish Affairs Committee, August 2012.

4.3 *The Journey of the Spanish Tribunal Constitucional: From Canada to Italy…*

At this stage, it becomes possible to appreciate the considerable distance separating the approach of the Spanish *TC* from the Canadian paradigm in matters of secession, and, consequently, the misleading nature of the reference made by the former to the latter in Judgment No. 42/2014: *"En el marco de la Constitución [...] una Comunidad Autónoma no puede unilateralmente convocar un referéndum de autodeterminación para decidir sobre su integración en España. Esta conclusión es del mismo tenor que la que formuló el Tribunal Supremo del Canadá en el pronunciamiento de 20 de agosto de 1998, en el que rechazó la adecuación de un proyecto unilateral de secesión por parte de una de sus provincias tanto a su Constitución como a los postulados del Derecho internacional."*

It is surprising—given the rigor expected of constitutional adjudication—that the Canadian precedent (where several independence referenda were in fact held in Québec, convened by the province itself) should be invoked to categorically deny the possibility of holding a popular consultation on the same issue in an Autonomous Community.

The surprise is compounded when one considers the subsequent case law of the *TC*. The 2014 decision, in its ambiguity, was at the time read in different ways: some saw in it an opening to the so-called *derecho a decidir* of the Catalans (Vintró 2014; Vilajosana 2014),[8] which the Court characterized as an "*aspiración política susceptible de ser defendida en el marco de la Constitución*." Yet this door was immediately shut: barely a year later, the *TC*—reverting to its earlier jurisprudence—affirmed that "*el respeto a la Constitución impone que los proyectos de revisión del orden constituido [...] se sustancien abierta y directamente por la vía que la Constitución ha previsto para esos fines*"; therefore, "*no caben actuaciones por otros cauces ni de las Comunidades Autónomas ni de cualquier órgano del Estado*" (STC 31/2015).

The holding of a referendum—even when initiated by state institutions—is categorically excluded, on the ground that it would undermine the integrity of the constitutionally defined amendment procedures: a position clearly aligned with Italian constitutional jurisprudence[9] (Viver I Pi-Sunyer 2014: 94). The indispensable starting point of the procedural sequence established in the Canadian paradigm is thus foreclosed.[10] That paradigm, though formally invoked, is in fact entirely alien to the *TC*'s approach, rightly criticized for the incoherence between accepting the juridical possibility of secession and then denying the instruments necessary to pursue it: *"sería absurdo iniciar el procedimiento de reforma constitucional para conseguir*

---

[8] See also *Institut d'Estudis Autonòmics, Informe sobre la Sentencia del Tribunal Constitucional, de 25 de marҫ de 2014, relativa a la Resolució 5/X del Parlament de Catalunya, per la qual s'aprova la Declaració de sobirania i del dret a decidir del poble de Catalunya*, 1 April 2014.

[9] See Italian Constitutional Court, Judgments Nos. 470/1992, 496/2000, and 118/2015.

[10] Sullo stretto rapporto tra separatismi e referendum, see Frosina (2024).

la independencia de Cataluña antes de comprobar que los catalanes quieren realmente separarse de España" (Ferreres Comella 2012; see also Aláez Corral 2015, pp. 160–161).

Secession by way of constitutional amendment is thereby revealed as an empty rhetorical device: separatist claims cannot even take form in their clear and concrete (Canadian-style) dimension. Tensions between rigidity and democracy, legality and legitimacy, legal authority and moral authority are removed from constitutional discourse and mechanically resolved in favor of the first terms of each pair; the same fate befalls the dialectic between unity and pluralism, between nations coexisting within the same political space, which is rejected outright in the name of an unassailable demotic monism (Tierney 2012, p. 138).

Spain, therefore, despite the *TC*'s declarations, in substance departs from Canada only to converge on the Italian position: a system that radically excludes any rupture of unity, even through constitutional amendment. This shift in perspective results in a stance—shared by both constitutional courts—of closure toward referenda intended to ascertain the will of territorial minorities seeking independence. Such a stance risks amounting to the denial of the political subjectivity of those minorities, a failure to recognize and accommodate internal national pluralism, and a rejection of a genuine "federal logic" (Cagiao y Conde 2015, p. 115; Sanjaume 2015, p. 187). More precisely, this risk becomes serious in constitutional systems built within political–social contexts marked by an internal national pluralism that is historically and empirically observable (Cagiao y Conde 2018, p. 188 ff.).

It is precisely this lack of recognition of the minority nation that the Canadian Court sought to avoid by premising its construction on the assertion that "*the social and demographic reality of Quebec*" allows the Province to be qualified as a "*political unit*" (§ 59 of the Reference); thereby making it clear that "*a people* may include only a portion of the population of an existing state. The juxtaposition of these terms is indicative that the reference to 'people' does not necessarily mean the entirety of a state's population" (§ 124).

This idea is, by contrast, clearly rejected in the approach of the constitutional judges of Italy and Spain. Faced with responses that are, in substance, identical across the two systems, one must nonetheless ask whether the secessionist claims they confronted are truly comparable—in their historical–political dimension—in terms of legitimacy, and thus genuinely deserving of responses framed solely in legal–juridical terms. One must further ask whether, after rejecting the demand for secession (and the referendum so closely intertwined with it), the central authorities in these two systems have offered alternative democratic political solutions capable of at least partially accommodating the claims of territorial minorities.

Answering these questions would require an inquiry too complex to undertake here. On the basis of a preliminary analysis, however, it may be observed that Spain's "plurinational question" appears to be marked by a historical depth absent from Italy's "Northern question," advanced in the final decades of the twentieth century by the *Lega Nord* (Dogliani 2012). The former constitutes a dominant cleavage in Rokkanian terms (Rokkan 1999), leaving a clear and enduring imprint on the multilevel party system and on the democratic Constitution itself (Trujillo 1977,

p. 258; Solé Tura 1985, p. 88; Herrero De Miñón 1993, p. 123; Rubio Llorente 2014, pp. 163–164). The latter, by contrast, burst onto the Italian democratic scene suddenly and improvisedly, overlapping with (and replacing) the Southern question, which did provide a foundational cleavage for the Italian democratic order (Barucci 1975; Staiano 2020).

Signs of incoherence soon revealed the improvisational nature of the Northern question (Mény, Surel 2000, p. 283 ff.; Segatti and Guglielmi 2012; Segatori 2010): most evident was the rapid transformation of the *Lega Nord* into a national political actor (more precisely: of the Italian nation), centering its ideological platform on a populist exaltation of national (Italian) sovereignty that it had initially sought to dismantle; and forging alliances across Europe with nationalist–centralist forces of the far right, from France's *Front (Rassemblement) National* to Hungary's *Fidesz* and Spain's *Vox*—preferring, in the latter case, complicity with neo-Francoist unionism rather than with Catalan independentism.

This divergence of situations—amply confirmed over time—was already clearly grasped by Augusto Barbera, who emphasized that while Catalan and Basque movements have "evident historical, ethnic, linguistic, and cultural reasons to claim a Catalan nation or a Basque nation as separate, the separatist movements of Padania can rely exclusively on economic malaise" (Barbera and Miglio 1997, p. 142).

4.3.1 Passing Through Germany

The 2016 decision of the German Constitutional Court (2 BvR 349/16), previously mentioned, was interpreted in public debate as reaffirming the idea that the only possible legal response by a democratic constitutional state to secessionist claims is one of radical closure. Yet considering the dimension of the political process may also, in this case, contribute to a fuller understanding of the matter, by examining how the independence claim—ultimately struck down by the German Court—was constructed. In other words, alongside the brief content of the judgment, it is also necessary to take into account the broader context in which it was delivered.

The dispute originated with an initiative launched by members of the *Bayernpartei*, who submitted at the regional level a popular legislative proposal calling for a referendum on Bavarian self-determination. Under the Land Constitution, popular initiatives are subject to preliminary review by the regional government. When the government refused to advance the proposal, the promoters brought a direct appeal to the Constitutional Court, which, in the decision under consideration, dismissed their claim. These are the essential legal steps of the controversy. Viewed dynamically, however, the political process preceding the litigation reveals that, in the relevant years, the *Bayernpartei* had obtained 1.7% of the vote in the 2018 Land elections and 2.1% in 2013, in both cases failing to secure representation due to the electoral threshold; indeed, the 2013 result was the party's best performance in Bavaria since 1970 (including national parliamentary elections).

Such data cast some doubt on the urgency, salience, and depth of the so-called Bavarian question. Comparing this with the Catalan case underscores the contrast: in Catalonia, beginning in 2012, four consecutive regional elections (2012, 2015, 2017, 2021) produced a majority in favor of holding a referendum on independence; in 2015 and 2017, an outright majority of seats supporting independence; and in 2021, pro-independence parties achieved a majority both in seats and in votes. These results emerged in a context where political parties competing for office clearly and consistently articulated their positions on both the referendum and independence, in electoral platforms and public debates. This pattern persisted despite the intense pressure deployed against Catalan independentism, particularly around the 2017 and 2021 elections, by Spanish state institutions on both the political and, above all, judicial fronts (Selmini 2020; Selmini, Salellas i Vilar 2022). On these premises, even a scholar such as Victor Ferreres—critical of Catalan separatism in his analyses—observed that an electoral victory in votes by openly pro-independence parties would inevitably usher in a "new political time," in which the Generalitat de Catalunya would acquire the legitimacy to negotiate with the State on the holding of a self-determination referendum (Ferreres Comella 2014, p. 83).

Here too, then, the question arises whether the elements recalled above align Catalonia's claims of recent years more closely with Bavaria—and perhaps Veneto—or, rather, with Quebec and Scotland; and, consequently, whether the formulas employed in the former cases or the latter appear better suited to unlocking territorial conflict through democratic means.

4.4 A Legitimacy Juridically Disarmed?

At this stage, the reader may well agree with some of the arguments developed, while nonetheless observing that, in the end, there seems to be no way to overcome the responses offered by central authorities strictly within a legal–juridical framework—however unreasonable or unbalanced they may appear. Secessionist claims, even when endowed with strong legitimacy, will always lack the instruments to assert their strength on the constitutional–legal plane: although firmly rooted in political and social dynamics, their fate will always remain subordinated to the will of the State, which, in rejecting them, will always be able to invoke legality on its side.

It is precisely here that the Canadian framework itself reveals significant weaknesses. To sanction the Federation's "unreasonable intransigence" in refusing to negotiate, the Supreme Court affirmed that in such a case unilateral secession might acquire the legitimacy it ordinarily lacks; yet the assessment of such legitimacy was placed on the international plane—an arena where the Court's jurisdiction does not apply. It is, at the very least, doubtful that the path indicated by the Canadian Court is the one embraced by international law, which remains, after all, the law of relations among sovereign States (on this point, with differing nuances, see Gagnon 2011, p. 125 ff.; Tancredi 2015, p. 473 ff.; Mancini 2014, p. 630 ff.).

The shortcomings in democratically accommodating legitimate secessionist claims nonetheless produce consequences that are themselves legally and constitutionally relevant; indeed, one might even argue that such consequences constitute, in some measure, a confirmation of the legitimacy of those claims. This requires moving beyond a restrictive conception of legal sanction understood solely in jurisdictional terms (for reconstructive accounts in this sense, see Modugno 1978, p. 346 ff.; Staiano 2019, p. 36 ff.). The point may be illustrated by the Spanish case, where the gap has been most visible between the strength of the Catalan independence movement (in terms of popular support and persistence over time) and the stance of state authorities, who have consistently confined their response to the strictly legal–juridical dimension.

The first consequence suffered by the Spanish system was the erosion of the stability that had characterized its entire democratic experience of government: Catalan nationalist parties, long a key factor in ensuring governability, withdrew from negotiations to form national executives, rendering government formation particularly problematic. It is no coincidence that between 2015 and 2019—during the most intense phase of radicalization of the Catalan question—Spaniards were called to the polls four times, testing the complex procedural solutions of Article 99 CE, until then never used. The troubled formation of Sánchez III's government after the 2023 elections likewise testifies clearly to the enduring impact of the Catalan conflict, even in its ebb phase, on national political equilibria (Ferraiuolo 2023).

The risk of territorial crisis erupting into the dynamics of state politics (Nevola 1997, pp. 824–825; Jovanović 2009, p. 77) is, moreover, inherent in the plurinational character of the system: that is, in a constitutional reality where the "*composición nacional no se encuentra definitivamente resuelta y es objeto de debate político*," and whose principal indicator is precisely "*la presencia de fuerzas políticas nacionalistas que se encuentran fuertemente implantadas en sus respectivos territorios, y además juegan un papel decisivo en el conjunto del sistema político estatal*" (Fossas Espadaler 2009, p. 94; see also Bossacoma i Busquets 2015, p. 27 ff.). It should not be surprising, then, that in such contexts failures to accommodate plurinationalism may translate into dysfunctions of the democratic system of government as a whole.

These considerations may also be extended to a broader dimension, one that encompasses not only political–institutional relations but also the protection of rights, where the system may suffer democratic backsliding of even greater magnitude. Numerous observers have pointed to serious shortcomings in the State's handling of Catalan claims. The 2017 report of *The Economist Intelligence Unit*, for example, noted the deterioration of Spain's democratic credentials due to the violence employed by police forces to prevent the holding of the 1 October 2017 referendum and the repressive measures adopted against pro-independence politicians and activists. Indeed, the entire "highlight" of the report's Western Europe section focused on the Catalan events, with Spain registering—on the study's indicators—a democratic regression greater than that of Turkey in the same year.[11]

Spain thus presents the paradox of a system which, in the words of the TC, proclaims itself a *"democracia no militante"* that does not impose *"adhesión positiva al ordenamiento y a la Constitución,"* but in which leaders of associations without public office were sentenced to lengthy prison terms for sedition merely for exercising constitutionally protected rights—above all, the right of peaceful assembly—while the Speaker of the Catalan Parliament was likewise convicted for having allowed parliamentary debate.[12] Hannah Arendt forcefully reminded us of the "substantial difference between the criminal who tries to conceal his acts from public view and the civil disobedient who openly challenges the law." This distinction between a clandestine violation and an overt, public violation of the law, she argued, "is so evident that it can be ignored only out of prejudice or bad faith." Notably, in making this point, Arendt invoked John C. Calhoun and his notion of "concurrent majorities," warning that "to treat disobedient minorities as rebels or traitors is contrary to the letter and the spirit of the Constitution [the reference being to the American experience], whose framers were particularly sensitive to the dangers of unqualified majority rule" (Arendt 1970, pp. 30–32).

The principle of unity, if asserted in unyielding absoluteness, risks becoming tyrannical, crushing all other constitutional principles—including, ultimately, democracy itself: an outcome the Supreme Court of Canada explicitly rejected by seeking a reasonable balance among the Constitution's underlying principles.[13] By contrast, *tyrannical unity* rests upon a perspective that can only be described as nationalist: that of the dominant nationalism of the State, which operates in the banal dimension so effectively described by Michael Billig (Billig 1995) and which,

[11] *The Economist Intelligence Unit, Democracy Index 2017. Free Speech Under Attack*, London, 2018, p. 10. These are not isolated observations: among the many documents on the subject, see also *Amnesty International, Amnesty International Report 2017/18. The State of the World's Human Rights*, London, 2018, pp. 339–341; *Amnistía Internacional España, 1-O en Cataluña: obstáculos para la investigación del uso excesivo de la fuerza*, Madrid, 2018; *Human Rights Watch, World Report 2019. Events of 2018*, USA, 2019, p. 237; *United Nations Human Rights Office of the High Commissioner—Working Group on Arbitrary Detention, Opinions* No. 6, 13 June 2019, and No. 12, 10 July 2019; *Amnistía Internacional España, España: libertad de reunión y de expresión, y principio de legalidad, a la luz de la sentencia del Tribunal Supremo en la causa especial 3/20907/2017*, Madrid, 2020; *Council of Europe—Parliamentary Assembly, Should Politicians Be Prosecuted for Statements Made in the Exercise of Their Mandate?*, Resolution No. 2381, 21 June 2021.

[12] This was the outcome produced by the well-known judgment of the *Tribunal Supremo* (Criminal Chamber) No. 459/2019, delivered in *causa especial* No. 20907/2017. On this matter, and for numerous bibliographic references, see (Marcelli 2020; Queralt Jiménez 2020); and, for the more specific aspects discussed in the text, Luís Martí (2019).

[13] These are, specifically, the federal principle, democracy, constitutional rigidity (*constitutionalism and the rule of law*), and respect for minority rights: the very principles that "inform and sustain the constitutional text," that constitute "the vital unstated assumptions," and that function "in symbiosis: no single principle can be defined in isolation from the others, nor does any one principle trump or exclude the operation of any other" (§ 49 of the *Reference re Secession of Quebec*).

when challenged, does not hesitate to assert its supremacy in radical—and at times outright authoritarian—forms.

5 Concluding Remarks: For the Constitutional Debate on Secession to Continue—And to Serve a Purpose

This essay has sought to demonstrate that it makes sense to discuss secession in legal terms only if the analysis is open—dynamically—to the perspective of *legitimacy* (in the Canadian sense) or *moral authority* (in the British sense). Otherwise, without also engaging with these dimensions, legal scholarship will have very little to contribute: secession will appear as a mere "matter of fact, and not of law," belonging not to the legal world but to that "of the infinite possibilities of human beings" (Barbera 1997, pp. 153–155). To borrow the critical words of Javier Pérez Royo: *"no hay nada que discutir, porque todo está resuelto por la Constitución"* (Pérez Royo 2013). Along this path, the thousands of pages devoted by public law scholarship to the subject would appear of little interest, serving merely to reiterate this simple and, at the same time, insurmountable postulate.

By contrast, if the study is extended to the dynamic dimension, the principal task of social scientists becomes the identification of the indicators that, in democratic contexts, signal the need to complement the legal–juridical approach with a politico–legal one. In this way, scholarship may contribute to identifying pathways for resolving territorial conflicts that are democratically satisfactory: on the one hand, without overlooking the profound impact that the rupture of unity has on a state order—thus requiring procedures of considerable complexity; on the other, by attributing decisive weight to the democratically expressed decisions of national–territorial minorities, to prevent central institutional closures from degenerating into a failure of recognition (or its exacerbation), which is often the deepest cause of legitimate separatist claims (Gagnon 2011, p. 5).

References

Abbott EA (1882) Flatland. A Romance of Many Dimensions. Trad. italiana (1966). Flatlandia. Racconto fantastico a più dimensioni, Adelphi, Milan

Aláez Corral B (2015) Constitucionalizar la secesión para armonizar la legalidad constitucional y el principio democrático en estados territorialmente descentralizados como España. Revista d'Estudis Autonòmics i Federals 22:136–183

Amoroso D, Ferraiuolo G (2019) Breaking a 'Taboo': the case for a dynamic approach to secessionist claims. Rivista di diritti comparati 3:93–123

Arendt A (1970) "Civil Disobedience." The New Yorker, 12 settembre. Trad. italiana (2020). Disobbedienza civile, Chiarelettere, Milan

Barbera A, Miglio G (1997) Federalismo e secessione. Un dialogo. Libero, Milan

Barucci P (ed) (1975) Il Mezzogiorno alla Costituente. Giuffrè, Milan

Bastida X (2016) El derecho a la autodeterminación como derecho moral: una apología de la libertad y del deber político. In: Cagiao J, Ferraiuolo G (eds) El encaje constitucional del derecho a decidir. Un enfoque polémico. Catarata, Madrid, pp 218–268

Billig M (1995). Banal Nationalism. Sage, London. Trad. italiana (2018). Nazionalismo banale, Rubettino, Soveria Mannelli

Bossacoma i Busquets P (2015) Justícia i legalitat de la secessió. Una teoria de l'autodeterminació nacional des de Catalunya. IEA, Barcelona

Buchanan A (2013) Prólogo a la edición española. ¿Tiene Cataluña derecho a la secesión? In: Buchanan A (ed) Secesión. Causas y consecuencias del divorcio politico. Ariel, Barcelona, pp 11–21

Cagiao y Conde J (2015) El federalismo ante la consulta catalana. Una lectura federal del derecho a decidir. In: Cagiao y Conde J, Martin V (eds) Federalismo, autonomía y secesión en el debate territorial español. El caso catalán. Le Manuscrit, Paris, pp 77–128

Cagiao y Conde J (2018) Un sassolino nella scarpa. La Catalogna come chiave della crisi del modello territoriale spagnolo. In: Cagiao y Conde J, Ferraiuolo G, Rigobon P (eds) La nazione catalana. Storia, lingua, politica, Costituzione nella prospettiva plurinazionale. Editoriale scientifica, Napoli, pp 143–192

Cameron D, Clegg N (2012) Preface. Scotland's constitutional future. A consultation on facilitating a legal, fair and decisive referendum on whether Scotland should leave the United Kingdom, www.official-documents.gov.uk

Cantaro A (1996) Introduzione. In: De Fiores C, Petrosino D (eds) Secessione. Ediesse, Rome, pp 7–24

Caravale G (2017) A family of nations Asimmetrie territoriali nel Regno unito tra devolution e Brexit. Jovene, Naples

Chessa O (2017) Sovranità: temi e problemi di un dibattito giuspubblicistico ancor attuale. Rivista AIC 3:1–28

De Vega P (1985) La reforma constitucional y la problemática del poder constituyente. Tecnos, Madrid

Delledonne G (2017) I Länder non sono i padroni della Costituzione: il Bundesverfassungsgericht di fronte a un tentativo secessionista bavarese. Quaderni costituzionali 1:145–147

Dogliani M (2012) Questione settentrionale e Costituzione. In: Alle frontiere del diritto costituzionale. Scritti in onore di Valerio Onida. Giuffrè, Milan, pp 741–757

Ferraiuolo G (2018) La transizione maggioritaria in Italia: equivoci, paradossi, distorsioni della realtà. Astrid Rassegna 10:1–17

Ferraiuolo G (2023) Accordi e disaccordi. Il patto di investitura PSOE-Junts per Catalunya nella crisi costituzionale spagnola. Federalismiit 29:23–37

Ferraiuolo G, Praino D (2018) The role of political parties in the Italian electoral reforms. Revista Catalana de Dret Públic 57:154–165

Ferreres Comella V (2012) The Secessionist Challenge in Spain: An independent Catalonia?. I-Connect. Blog of International Journal of Constitutional Law, 22 novembre

Ferreres Comella V (2014) Intervento. Federalismi.it 22:80–86

Fossas Espadaler E (2009) Estado autonómico: plurinacionalidad y asimetría. In: Mastromarino A, Castellá Andreu JM (eds) Esperienze di regionalismo differenziato. Il caso italiano e quello spagnolo a confronto. Giuffrè, Milan, pp 89–120

Fossas Espadaler E (2014) Interpretar la política. Comentario a la STC 42/2014, de 25 de marzo, sobre la Declaración de soberanía y el derecho a decidir del pueblo de Cataluña. Revista Española de Derecho constitucional 101:273–300

Frosina L (2024) Separatismi e referendum. Teoria e prassi in prospettiva comparata. Jovene, Naples

Gagnon AG (2011) L'Âge des incertitudes: essais sur le fédéralisme et la diversité nationale, Université Laval. Trad. italiana (2013). L'età delle incertezze. Saggio sul federalismo e la diversità nazionale, Cedam, Padua

Gaudreault-Desbiens JF (2014) Secession blues: some legal and political challenges facing the Independence movement in Quebec. Percorsi costituzionali 3:765–786

Herrero De Miñón M (1993) Memorias de estío. Temas de Hoy, Madrid
Jovanović MA (2009) Can constitutions be of use in the resolution of secessionist conflicts? Journal of International Law and International Relations 5(2):59–87
Luís Martí J (2019) An Exotic right: protest and sedition in the Spanish Supreme Court's ruling on Catalan secessionism. VerfBlog, 18 ottobre [https://verfassungsblog.de/an-exotic-right/]
Mancini S (2014) Ai confini del diritto: una teoria democratica della secessione. Percorsi costituzionali 3:623–638
Marcelli F (2020) Catalogna, una questione di democrazia. In: Marcelli F (ed) Il problema catalano tra diritto a decidere ed autodeterminazione. Editoriale scientifica, Naples, pp 9–104
Mény Y, Surel Y (2000) Par le peuple, pour le peuple. Fayard, Paris. Trad. italiana (2004). Populismo e democrazia, Il Mulino, Bononia
Modugno F. (1978) "Norma (teoria generale)" Enciclopedia del Diritto, vol. XXVIII, Giuffrè, Milan, 328–393
Modugno F (1999) Unità-indivisibilità della Repubblica e principio di autodeterminazione dei popoli (riflessioni sull'ammissibilità-ricevibilità di un disegno di legge costituzionale comportante revisione degli artt. 5 e 132 Cost.). Studi in onore di Leopoldo Elia, II, Giuffrè, Milan, 1011–1044
Montilla Martos JA (2016) El referéndum de secesión en Europa. Revista de Derecho Constitucional Europeo 26
Nevola G (1997) Capire la secessione. Il Mulino 5:814–827
Norman W (2002) Secesión y democracia (constitucional). In: Requejo F (ed) Democracia y pluralismo nacional. Ariel, Barcelona, pp 89–105
Pace A (1999) Processi costituenti italiani 1996–1997. Studi in onore di Leopoldo Elia, II, Giuffrè, Milan, 1127–1149
Pérez Royo J (2013) El tiempo se agota. El País, 13 dicembre
Queralt Jiménez J (ed) (2020) La sentencia del procés. Una aproximación académica. Atelier, Barcelona
Rokkan S (1999) State formation, nation-building, and mass politics in Europe. The theory of Stein Rokkan. Clarendon Press, Oxford. Trad. italiana (2012). Stato, nazione e democrazia in Europa, Il Mulino, Bononia
Rubio Llorente F (2014) Defectos de forma. Revista Española de Derecho Constitucional, 100, 133–165
Sanjaume M (2015) Federalismo, pluralismo nacional y autodeterminación: la acomodación de Cataluña y Quebec. In: Cagiao y Conde J, Martin V (eds) Federalismo, autonomía y secesión en el debate territorial español. El caso catalán. Le Manuscrit, Paris, pp 151–189
Savastano F (2019) Uscire dall'Unione europea. Brexit e il diritto di recedere dai Trattati. Giappichelli, Turin
Segatori R (2010) Le debolezze identitarie del regionalismo italiano. Le istituzioni del federalismo 5(6):435–467
Segatti P, Guglielmi S (2012) Padani o italiani? I sentimenti nazionali degli elettori leghisti. Il Mulino 3:431–438
Selmini R (2020) Criminalizzazione e repressione del dissenso politico. Il caso della mobilitazione indipendentista catalana. Criminalia:431–459
Selmini R, Salellas i Vilar B (2022) Da Barcellona a Leningrado: riflessioni sulla criminalizzazione del movimento indipendentista catalano. Studi sulla questione criminale 2:7–28
Seymour M (2010) Els pobles i el dret a l'autodeterminació. In: Gagnon AG, Requejo F (eds) Nacions a la recerca de reconeixement: Catalunya i el Quebec davant el seu future. IEA, Barcelona, pp 55–73
Solé Tura J (1985) Nacionalidades y nacionalismos en España. Autonomías, federalismo, autodeterminación. Alianza, Madrid. Trad. italiana (2016). Nazionalità e nazionalismo in Spagna. Autonomie, federalismo e autodeterminazione. Editoriale scientifica, Naples

Staiano S (2019) La forma di governo nella Costituzione come norma e come processo. In: Musella F (ed) Il governo in Italia. Profili costituzionali e dinamiche politiche. Il Mulino, Bononia, pp 29–70
Staiano S (2020) La frattura Nord-Sud. L'asimmetria territoriale come questione democratica. Il Politico 251(2):268–307
Tancredi A (2015) Secessione e diritto internazionale: un'analisi del dibattito. Diritto pubblico comparato ed europeo 2:449–478
Tierney S (2012) Constitutional Referendums. The theory and practice of Republican deliberation. Oxford University Press, Oxford
Tierney S (2013) «The Three Hundred and Seven Year Itch»: Scotland and the 2014 Independence Referendum. In: Qvortrup M (ed) The British constitution: continuity and change. A Festschrift for Vernon Bogdanor. Hart Publishing, Oxford, pp 141–152
Trujillo G (1977) Relaciones interpartidistas en un marco político descentralizado. In: De Vega P (ed) Teoría y práctica de los partidos politicos. Cuadernos para el Diálogo, Madrid, pp 257–267
Vilajosana JM (2014) La interpretación del derecho a decidir. El País, 5 aprile
Vintró J (2014) El Tribunal Constitucional y el derecho a decidir de Cataluña: una reflexión sobre la STC de 25 de marzo de 2014. Blog de la Revista catalana de dret public, 2 aprile
Viver I Pi-Sunyer C (2014) Intervento. Federalismi.it 22:94–100
Walker W (2014) International reactions to the Scottish referendum. Int Aff 90(4):743–759

Nation Trouble: What Is Wrong with the Most Influential Theory of Secession?

Jorge Cagiao y Conde

Abstract The most influential understanding of secession and secessionist conflicts is provided by remedial theories. Normatively, both lawyers and philosophers view secession as a highly negative phenomenon and advocate for solutions to avoid it. Interestingly, this perspective is also dominant among social scientists. This chapter will explain what is wrong with this dominant path and why we can see something like nation trouble at its very core.

1 Premise

In this chapter, the main argument is that the prevailing theory of just secession faces a significant methodological challenge that must be addressed. This issue arises from the theorists who have neglected the insights from the literature on nationalism. Consequently, the most influential theory of secession presents an uninformed and oversimplified perspective on the relationship between nationalism and secession.

The question of whether this failure is deliberate or unconscious, as can be gleaned from Michael Billig's (1995) seminal study, is not the primary concern here. Instead, the focus is on elucidating the ramifications of this unexpected oversight. It is challenging to comprehend how one can aspire to construct a just reflection on secession, or the equivalent, on national self-determination, without acknowledging the contributions of social scientists on the human collectives that

I would like to warmly thank Carine Berbéri for his considerable help with the English version of this chapter.

J. Cagiao y Conde (✉)
University of Nantes, Nantes, France
e-mail: jorge.cagiaoyconde@univ-nantes.fr

F. Savastano et al. (eds.), *Between Asymmetry and Secession*,
https://doi.org/10.1007/978-3-032-29603-0_5

provide full meaning to the normative reflection on secession or self-determination[1]—that is, nations.

In the first section, a concise exposition will be provided on the foundational elements of the remedial theory, which currently dominates the discourse on just secession. It is noteworthy to observe the significant impact this theory has exerted on the field, prompting even its detractors to adopt its central tenets. In my opinion, this phenomenon poses a significant challenge, as it suggests the possibility of a correct understanding of just secession only within the confines of the remedial theory.

In the second section, the shortcomings of remedial theory in addressing the justice of secession within democratic frameworks will be elucidated. A thorough examination will reveal that the remedial theory suffers from methodological nationalism, a problem that should be eschewed in any academic reflection on just secession. This obviously requires a position of neutrality with respect to the claims and positions of the two opposing national groups in a secessionist conflict. This requires an impartial point of view that can only be reached in our deeply nationalized societies through a good knowledge of the intricacies of nationalism and nationalist conflicts (Cagiao y Conde 2018).

2 Remedial Theory of Secession

The prevailing theory in the field is the Remedial Right Only theory. Allen Buchanan is the author of the main and most commented reference (1991). Buchanan's work can be characterized as an academic articulation of pragmatic solutions that are already present in the corpus of international law. It is important to note that the latter codifies a right to external self-determination in very specific circumstances. According to the prevailing perspective in international law, secession is recognized as a legitimate option when a population is subjected to external domination, has experienced pervasive violations of fundamental rights, or is in a colonial context (UN 1960a, 1960b, 1970). In addition to the aforementioned cases, the sole remaining avenue (as a right) available to people for exploration would be that of internal self-determination within the state in which they find themselves—that is to say, the attainment of some form of territorial autonomy, whether larger or smaller in scope.

The logic of remedial theory is consistent with this perspective, as it posits that secession is only deemed justifiable when the proponents of secession find themselves in a dire situation. The right to secession is predicated on the condition that

[1] In this analysis, the term "self-determination" is employed as a synonym for "secession." The concept of self-determination is more extensive than that of secession, as it encompasses options beyond independence, such as territorial autonomy and federalism. Nevertheless, the notion of self-determination, conceptualized as a process entailing a decision, invariably encompasses the option of independence. That is to say, the possibility is presented to the human collective asserting this right to disassociate from the State within which it is incorporated, to establish a sovereign State, should that be its aspiration.

the group in question has been subjected to grave and pervasive injustices. Moreover, secession is regarded as a means of redressing and ultimately resolving the injustices endured by the group. This consequentialist logic—very important in the remedial theory—opposes secessions that could generate new situations of injustice or violations of human rights. As asserted by Buchanan (1998, p. 230), "Remedial Right Only theories assert that a group has a general right to secede if, and only if, it has suffered certain injustices, for which secession is the appropriate remedy of last resort."

Buchanan's theory of secession, while acknowledging the legitimacy of secession agreed by a state and one of its territorial parts (as each state retains the right to relinquish a part of its territory), is thus predicated on a logic of victimhood and reparation. Consequently, as previously expounded in my existing publications (Cagiao y Conde 2021, 2022a, b, 2024a, b), it is also reasonable to conclude that his theory has no application in the framework of Western democracies,[2] except for certain colonial cases that are still pending, such as that of the United Kingdom or France with Gibraltar and New Caledonia, respectively.

In recent years, however, the remedial theory has undergone a small and interesting evolution. Indeed, it may be argued that the theory is now far removed from its original logic. Buchanan has argued that the systematic violation of existing autonomy agreements by a state could be included in the list of just causes for secession. The following statement can be found in the preface to the Spanish version of Buchanan's 1991 book:

> Intrastate autonomous agreements that can be unilaterally annulled by one party, in this case Spain, are not a plausible means to avoid non-consensual secession. If Spain is unwilling to actually engage in a renegotiation of Catalonia's self-governing powers within the state, this will increase the case for a right to non-consensual secession (Buchanan 2013: 21).

As previously mentioned, it appears that Buchanan is shifting his focus away from the cases and dramatic situations (such as colonialism and violations of human rights) that were previously the focal point of the remedial theory. In the case referenced in Buchanan's quote, there does not seem to be any significant issue that would suggest the existence of a Catalan people that is a victim of the Spanish state. It is crucial to acknowledge the substantial political autonomy enjoyed by the Catalans, who have their own government and significant powers. Moreover, Catalan is officially recognized as one of the languages of the Catalan administration, alongside Spanish, and is spoken by a substantial proportion of the Catalan population. Consequently, there appears to be an absence of any form of oppression against the Catalan people. Their fundamental rights are enshrined in both the Spanish Constitution and the Statute of Autonomy of Catalonia. In light of these considerations, it makes sense to inquire what forms of oppression or injustices, if any, should be addressed according to Buchanan's perspective.

Even though this issue is not the primary focus of this chapter, it is crucial to emphasize that Buchanan, in arriving at a conclusion regarding a case akin to that of

[2] See, for instance, Supreme Court of Canada (1998).

Catalonia, appears to relinquish the victimizing and reparative logic of his own theory of secession. However, as explained in some previous publications, there is an absence of compelling evidence that would permit the application of the logic of the remedial theory of secession in cases like Catalonia, Quebec, or Scotland.

In any event, it is important to note that the latest evolution of Buchanan's theory of secession has been positively received by a sector of the doctrine that, unlike him, had been defending in some way a primary right to self-determination—that is to say, a right that would not be justified by the conditions or the particular context in which a people's demand for secession would arise. This is the case, for example, of authors who have recently written several important works in the field, such as Michel Seymour (2017, 2024) or Pau Bossacoma (2020).

The former, attentive to the debate and context in which the demands for self-determination in Canada arise—in the case of Quebec and the First Nations specifically—has argued in a sense analogous to Buchanan's. Seymour posits that, while there is no primary or unconditional right to external self-determination (as opposed to internal self-determination, which would be unconditional, in Seymour's view), repeated abuses and breaches by the Canadian government with respect to power-sharing and provincial autonomy could be considered as a serious fault or injustice that would make the remedial theory operative in the Canadian case.

Bossacoma's work has as its background and main concern the situation generated in Spain around the demands for improved self-government and the subsequent secessionist conflict in Catalonia during the last decade. This author also defends the need to recognize a right of secession in cases of persistent disagreement over the distribution of power and autonomy between the state and a part of its territory. However, as acknowledged by Bossacoma, such a right would need to be so strictly regulated that secession would likely become an unfeasible option in practice.

In this chapter, I will not delve into the theoretical coherence issues that may arise from the attempts to harmonize the theory of secession as a primary right and the theory of secession as a remedy. I will not address the contradictions in Buchanan's own efforts to introduce a non-victimizing logic into his theory either. However, these deviations from the original remedial theory can be regarded as its inherent limitations in addressing the salient issues under consideration. Specifically, if the remedial theory, as initially conceived, is only applicable to contexts as extreme and grave as those previously mentioned, it would suggest that the theory is entirely devoid of any propositions for cases such as Quebec, Catalonia, or Scotland. Consequently, in such scenarios, the theory would provide the state (in this case, Canada, the United Kingdom, or Spain) with a systematic justification to deny the secessionist party any form of legitimacy for its claims. Nevertheless, the evolution previously referenced in the remedial theory of secession appears to suggest an antithetical conclusion. Specifically, it can be interpreted as a sign of an inherent flaw when applied to democratic contexts. This observation might imply an implicit acknowledgment that the remedial logic is ineffective in such settings and that its implementation could potentially serve to reinforce or exacerbate the existing conflict between the state and the people claiming the right to self-determination.

3 What Is Wrong with "National" Self-Determination?

The concept of secession or self-determination is generally associated with a collective entity, frequently termed the "people" or the "nation." This is an indisputable fact. The contemporary world is comprised of nations, or states, and, as a result, the human collectives that attain independence and establish a new state are regarded as nations. It is also customary for new states to present themselves as sovereign nations. Consequently, it is imperative to possess a comprehensive and informed understanding of the nation, as it serves as the primary subject of interest for the theory of secession. And it is clear that the most reliable guidance on this subject is provided by the literature on the nation and nationalism. As previously mentioned, this is the primary issue with the theory of secession as a remedy. As will be demonstrated subsequently, the argumentation of the aforementioned theory appears to disregard the findings of the literature in that field.

In this section, two arguments posited by Buchanan will be examined. The first argument pertains to the potential dangers associated with the acceptance of a theory of secession, such as that advanced by primary right theorists (in its two versions, the plebiscitary theorists and the nationalist ones), which may be considered overly permissive. The second argument cautions against the moral challenges associated with secession from a nationalist perspective.

3.1 The Domino Effect Argument

The domino effect (or slippery slope) argument argues that overly generous conditions to allow secession would generate an escalation of the demands for independence, leading to a major and undesirable destabilization of the national and international order. This argument has been used not only against the nationalist secession theory, "recipe for limitless political fragmentation," in Buchanan's view (1991, p. 49), but also, more surprisingly, against the plebiscitary theory of secession.

The latter conceptualizes secession as an individual right that enables individuals to associate with whomever they choose (Beran 1984, 1998; Wellman 2005). The principle of voluntariness, which governs social relations, is a fundamental tenet of liberalism. This theoretical framework posits that this principle should also govern the formation of state borders. The exercise of this right would thus allow a territorially concentrated collective of individuals—a priori, regardless of their cultural, ethnic, religious, etc. characteristics—to legitimately claim secession in order to constitute a new political association—that is, a new state.

The distinguishing feature of this theory is its emphasis on a fundamental right to secession. However, the plebiscitary theory typically makes the possibility of secession conditional upon a series of factors, such as the viability of the new state or the relative insignificance of the loss of economic or military resources for the state experiencing secession. These conditions, when actualized, can effectively render secession as challenging as remedial theory.

However, one can leave aside this nuance, which nevertheless drastically reduces the number of potential and serious candidates for secession according to the plebiscitary theory. Consequently, the relevance of the slippery slope argument is called into question. I am especially interested in showing how empirically unfounded is the fear that the number of secessionist projects would greatly increase if the plebiscitary approach were to prevail in our debate. Indeed, the theorists who criticize the plebiscitary theory are effectively lending credibility to the possibility that any group of territorialized individuals (a wealthy town, a neighborhood of a city, a group of caravan travelers settling in the desert, etc.) may wish to create a new state and initiate a process of secession. But this is not realistic. Statehood does not constitute a demand among these and other groups. In suggesting otherwise, both the plebiscitary theory and its critics are equating implausible hypotheses with the well-known secessionist experiences, which are invariably processes of self-determination by a people or nation. These secessions are therefore provoked by nationalist movements that aspire to establish their own states for their own nations. As Mancini puts it (2012, p. 486), secession is a matter that pertains to national groups, and not to the other groups that individuals can freely constitute according to diverse interests and affinities: "In practice, in the overwhelming majority of cases, the right to secede ends up by being granted mainly on the basis of nationality."

A variant of this remedial argument against secession can be found in the "ethnic" thesis defended by Buchanan following Gellner's reflection (1991, p. 49). As is known, the renowned scholar of nationalism pointed to the existence of a very high number of stateless nations in the world, much higher than the relatively low number of existing nation-states. This observation led Gellner to conclude that the demand for statehood by nationalists (the principle of nationalities, which asserts that each nation should have its own State) is, in effect, unattainable. It is not feasible for every nation to possess its own state (Gellner 1983, p. 2). In this instance, the argument is not used against the plebiscitary theory; rather, it is directed against nationalist theory. According to the nationalist theory, the fundamental subject of self-determination or secession is not some group of geographically concentrated individuals motivated by some elective affinity, but rather the nation as a whole (Margalit & Raz 1990; Tamir 1993; Miller 1995). Buchanan's argument in this instance functions similarly to his previous argument: he uses it to demonstrate that if all nations, a countless number of which could claim a legitimate right to secession, were to do so, the resultant increase in demands would significantly impact global stability. It is imperative to reevaluate the empirical foundation of this objection.

It is a well-established fact that the number of nation-states around the world has increased significantly over the last two centuries. Of the nearly two hundred nation-states currently recognized by the United Nations, more than half have been established during the latter half of the twentieth century. This phenomenon appears to lend credence to the slippery slope argument. However, the relatively limited number of nation-states in existence today, particularly when juxtaposed against the significantly larger number of stateless nations, enables a reevaluation of the perceived threat of secessionist movements. The crux of the issue, as articulated by Gellner and Buchanan, pertains to the conceptualization of the term "nation" (or "people": Buchanan, 1991, p. 49). This term encompasses a wide spectrum of realities, some of which may be starkly divergent. If one examines the case of Spain, one finds that territories such as Galicia, the Canary Islands, Andalusia, and Aragon can be regarded as "nations" (or "nationalities," according to the Spanish Constitution). These territories are considered alongside other human groups that also self-identify as nations, such as the Catalans, the Basques, and the Spaniards themselves. A similar phenomenon can be observed in other states, where the term "nation" can acquire an ethnic connotation (as seen with the First Nations in North America, the indigenous nations in Central or South America, or even the term "Black Nation" in the United States, which is a more distant example from the subject under discussion). The term "nation" can even be used to refer to a group of supporters of a particular sports team (for example, "Lakers Nation"). Notwithstanding the polysemy of the term "nation," it should not distract us when one reflects normatively on secession to the point of equating groups of individuals who have no interest in secession or even self-government with those who do.[3]

This is the primary rationale behind the failure of the ethnic argument employed by Buchanan against secession. The number of stateless nations, as understood in ethnic terms, may be substantial. Nevertheless, the number of nations, in the political sense, that are potential candidates for secession is comparatively modest, and even relatively low when considered against the high figures frequently quoted in discussions about potential nations worldwide. In this regard, it is noteworthy that Sorens' seminal study on secessionism concludes that the number of ethno-national minority groups with a strong territorial focus is approximately 200, a figure that is significantly lower than the thousands often cited. Furthermore, the study notes that in the majority of these groups, the presence of secessionist organizations is minimal, with such organizations being present in 107 out of 283 groups (Sorens 2012, p. 56). It would be important to know the proportion among these 107 groups that constitutes a pro-independence majority or at least an influential social movement. But this information would likely result in a further reduction in the number of serious secession candidates. In any case, these data would serve to mitigate the fear expressed by Buchanan, thereby substantiating Gellner's contention regarding the number of nations. Assuming that the option of independence is appealing only to

[3] This is undoubtedly a widespread problem, also present in the remedial theory: the nation claimed by nationalists tends to be understood excessively in an ethnic or cultural key, as if it were not fundamentally a political phenomenon, in which both emotions and reason are appealed to, influenced as much by affections as by interests (Delanty and O'Mahony 2002, p. 35). This "only cultural" and "depoliticized" reading of nationalism and of the idea of nation ("he [Buchanan] conceives it apolitically"—Verges 2021, p. 30), contrary to what the literature explains, would justify this amalgam that is made between what one can call "political nations" and "cultural nations," between nations with interest and capacity to initiate a political process of secession and the rest of the nations (ethnic or cultural groups), with different and in any case less ambitious claims.

territorially concentrated human groups with a distinct perception of themselves as a political entity distinct from the state in which they reside, the concern of a secessionist domino effect appears to lack empirical support.[4] As Bossacoma notes, this fear seems to be at least exaggerated (2020, p. 64). It is noteworthy that Buchanan, after initially adopting Gellner's thesis (thus lending credibility to the prospect of an escalation of nationalist secessions), ultimately concedes that in reality, "there have been relatively few serious secessionist movements" (1991, p. 103).

The slippery slope argument posited in the remedial theory is therefore without foundation. In Spain, for instance, it is nowadays difficult to imagine more than two potential candidates for secession (Catalonia and the Basque Country). Likewise, the notion that secession could be a viable prospect for Canada, outside the context of Quebec, appears to be a rather implausible proposition. A similar argument can be made for the United Kingdom, where the possibility of secession is unrealistic outside of Scotland or Northern Ireland. A similar analysis can be extrapolated to the rest of the states. Within the European Union, the number of secession projects that could reasonably emerge in the next 10 to 20 years is extremely limited. The slippery slope argument lacks, therefore, empiricism, using an overly expansive conception of the term "nation" that makes it ill-suited for today's normative debate on secession.

3.2 *Nationalism as an Immoral Basis for Secession*

The remedial theory argues that nationalism would be an immoral basis for secession. Buchanan puts it by saying that "the moral *costs* of even attempting to implement it [the normative nationalist principle] are prohibitive" (1991, p. 49), "one of the least plausible justifications" (1991, p. 48). The question that immediately comes to mind is: Why?

To comprehend Buchanan's point of view, one should contextualize it within the prevailing public opinion on nationalism. Nationalism is a concept that usually has pejorative connotations. People tend to associate it with far-right, illiberal, or antidemocratic political projects. As Billig explained, this is how nationalism is often seen in our societies, with very threatening profiles for Western democracies. These are profiles that people tend to identify with extreme right-wing movements and, where they exist, with sub-state nationalist movements (Billig 1995).

If nationalism were characterized by the aforementioned attributes, Buchanan's skepticism towards nationalist secessions would be justified. However, it would be relevant to inquire whether this conception of nationalism accurately or reasonably encapsulates its essence. To address this inquiry, one must refer again to the existing

[4] Obviously, the context is always a pertinent factor to consider. Indeed, a state may act in such a way that a national minority is sufficiently comfortable and recognized in its constitutional system without wishing to have a state of its own, as has been the case in Spain, Canada, and the United Kingdom for several decades.

literature on the subject. What insights does this literature provide? As shall be demonstrated, the literature predominantly reveals that the fear expressed by Buchanan is not rooted in absolutes. Indeed, it may lack a solid foundation in the democratic contexts that are of particular concern in this study.

The existing literature on nationalism has been able to sound a note of warning against its destructive and anti-democratic potential. Indeed, a review of history and contemporary events reveals numerous instances of nationalist movements pursuing political agendas that are in direct opposition to the principles and values of liberal democracies. However, this observation does not provide sufficient evidence to conclude that nationalism is inherently anti-democratic. Indeed, scholars have identified a diverse array of nationalist expressions throughout history, including instances that align with democratic values and principles (Calhoun 1997; Tamir 1993).

If the main argument of nationalism studies is accepted—namely, that the nation is a product or construction of nationalism in our modern world—and if, simultaneously, it is acknowledged that societies such as the United States, Germany, France, and numerous others constitute what is conventionally understood as a nation, then one should recognize that nationalism has necessarily created, promoted, and sustained these nations over the years. Otherwise, as Wayne Norman points out, "nation-building is a natural consequence of perfectly legitimate government programs and political discourse. And mobilizing support for just policies by appealing to aspects of citizens' national identities is also, within limits, a normal part of democratic politics" (2006, p. 216). Therefore, the globally recognized existence of a significant number of democratic nations on the global stage must also imply the existence of democratic state nationalisms. Contrary to the implications suggested by Buchanan's argument, there is no inherent relationship between nationalism and political immorality (nationalism perceived as an anti-democratic political project, obsessed with ethnic or cultural purity, etc.). Buchanan's methodological error is characterized by the presentation of nationalism as a phenomenon that is exclusively defined by its most unfortunate experiences.

Once established that there have been both nationalist and somewhat democratic independence processes, and that all current nations (states) have been and continue to be promoted and sustained by nationalism, one can ask the following question: What moral dilemmas might arise from a secessionist process driven by a democratic nationalism, as exemplified by the cases of Scotland, Quebec, Catalonia, and the Basque Country?

In Western democracies, this question is generally answered by adopting two distinct strategies. They are both working to prevent nationalist secession. However, both approaches seem incompatible with the findings of nationalism studies. The first option seeks to repudiate any process of national self-determination founded upon the nationalist principle. Nevertheless, the critics of "nationalist secessionism" would have to explain to expert social scientists how nations, even democratic ones, can exist without nationalism. It appears that this approach is clearly wrong. The second option would be to acknowledge the existence of a nationalist (i.e., patriotic) project in every independent nation-state. Typically, this is the approach often preferred in Western democracies. Its purpose is to emphasize the democratic or civic aspects of state nationalism. This approach enables a distinction between the nationalist project of nation-states and secessionist nationalist projects, which are often characterized as illiberal and antidemocratic. However, this attempt at differentiation is arguably futile, as the distinction between civic and ethnic nationalisms has been largely eclipsed in recent studies on nationalism. In fact, the prevailing academic consensus suggests that there is no such thing as a purely civic and democratic nationalism, nor a purely ethnic or cultural (anti-democratic) nationalism. In modern times, nationalism has always encompassed a civic (or political) and an ethnic (or cultural) dimension (Kymlicka 2001; Maiz 2004, 2005; Archiles 2018). In summary, the prevailing consensus among scholars on nationalism suggests that the criticism over the moral foundations of nationalist secessionism is unfounded in the democratic systems I have referred to in this chapter.

In today's modern politics, if all national projects (all nation-states) are considered as the products of nationalism, then the assertion made by Buchanan that a secessionist national project would inherently entail "prohibitive moral costs" due to its nationalist character seems unjustified. If, in accordance with the principle of nationalities, all national entities seek the formation of a state, what issues can arise? Buchanan's argument is both unsustainable and unjust, as it does not see the nationalism of existing nation-states while opposing the nationalism of emerging state-building projects in Western democracies.

4 Concluding Remarks

Buchanan's argument on nationalism, in general, and nationalist secession, in particular, is not an exceptional case. Many renowned intellectuals and academics have been identified by experts on nationalism as prone to interpreting the concept in a simplistic way. In his book entitled *Banal Nationalism*, Billig offers a noteworthy commentary on Richard Rorty, a perspective that can be applied to numerous other intellectuals, such as Rawls, Habermas, and others (see Requejo 2009).

In any case, it is interesting to note that our most renowned philosophers and intellectuals often display a rather simplistic and conservative stance when it comes to nationalism. This is even more obvious when faced with the emergence of a political movement that challenges the national integrity of one of the established nation-states. This phenomenon has been thoroughly examined by experts in the field of nationalism. The assertion posits that individuals are born, raised, and socialized in societies that are perpetually exposed to a process of nationalization (Billig 1995; Edensor 2005; Throssell 2015). This suggests that the transition from childhood to adulthood is accompanied by a process of socialization in national values, principles, and representations. These values, principles, and representations are internalized unconsciously, and as a general rule, they are rarely questioned by adults. In fact, adults have no reason to question their own nation and nationalism. They are indeed incapable of seeing themselves as part of a collective process that is broadly and transversally marked by nationalism. This well-known sociological phenomenon (present at other levels in social hierarchies: class, race, gender, religion, etc.) is what Billig has called "banal nationalism."

This issue has a significant impact even on our leading intellectuals. It is important to recognize that long before they became accomplished academics, writers, or philosophers (normally not before the age of 30), these individuals were already patriotic young adults who had developed a profound and unconditional love for their nation (Viroli 1995). Nevertheless, they are nationalists who cannot see or recognize themselves in this light. This phenomenon results from the remarkable influence of nationalism on today's political climate. Its influence is pervasive. As Benedict Anderson notes, "since World War II every successful revolution has defined itself in *national* terms" (2016, p. 2). Yes, every revolutionary process has defined itself in national terms, but it has rarely identified itself as "nationalist."

Therefore, the influence of nationalism, as well as the literature explaining this phenomenon, should seriously be taken into account if secession and other related issues are to be addressed in a rigorous and fair manner. Otherwise, the methodological mistake discussed in this chapter is unavoidable.

References

Anderson B (1983 [2016]) Imagined communities. Reflections on the origin and spread of nationalism. Verso, London

Archiles F (ed) (2018) No sólo cívica. Nación y nacionalismo cultural español. Tirant humanidades, Valencia

Beran H (1984) A Liberal theory of secession. Political Studies 32(2):21–31

Beran H (1998) A democratic theory of political self-determination for a new world order. In: Lehning PB (ed) Theories of secession. Routledge, London, pp 32–59

Billig M (1995) Banal nationalism. Sage, London

Bossacoma P (2020) Morality and legality of secession. A theory of national self-determination. Palgrave MacMillan, London

Buchanan A (1991) Secession: the morality of political divorce from Fort Sumter to Lithuania and Quebec. Westview Press, Boulder

Buchanan A (1998) The international institutional dimension of secession. In: Lehning PB (ed) Theories of secession. Routledge, London and New York, pp 225–253

Buchanan A (2013) Secesión. Causas y consecuencias del divorcio político. Planeta, Barcelona

Cagiao y Conde J (2018) Micronacionalismos. ¿No seremos todos nacionalistas? Catarata, Madrid

Cagiao y Conde J (2021) La soberanía discutida. Una aproximación analítica y normativa a los conflictos territoriales de soberanía. In: Almeda P (ed) Cataluña-España. ¿Del conflicto al diálogo político? Catarata, Madrid, pp 522–553

Cagiao y Conde J (2022a) Miseria de la causa justa. Una lectura critica de las teorías de la secesión-remedio en contextos democráticos. In: Cagiao y Conde J, Ferraiuolo G (eds) La legitimidad de la secesión a debate. Catarata, Madrid, pp 118–156

Cagiao y Conde J (2022b) Democracia y nación. España en el laberinto plurinacional. Catarata, Madrid

Cagiao y Conde J (2024a) Nada que remediar: sobre la incompatibilidad teórica entre la secesión como remedio y la secesión como derecho primario en contextos democráticos. In: Compte Nunes G, Bossacoma Busquets P (eds) La autodeterminación de los pueblos: con-

troversias en Europa y las Américas. Universidad Nacional Autónoma de México, Instituto de Investigaciones Sociales, Mexico City, pp 173–194
Cagiao y Conde J (2024b) Autodétermination, démocratie et nation. A la recherche d'une cohérence théorique. In: Cagiao y Conde J, Ferraiuolo G (eds) Les frontières de la démocratie. De l'autodétermination nationale au XXIe siècle. Kimé, Paris, pp 107–150
Calhoun C (1997) Nationalism. Open University Press, Buckingham
Delanty G, O'Mahony P (2002) Nationalism and social theory. Sage, London
Edensor T (2005) National identity, popular culture and everyday life. Berg Publishers, Oxford-New York
Gellner E (1983) Nations and nationalism. Blackwell, Oxford
Kymlicka W (2001) Politics in the vernacular. Nationalism, multiculturalism, and citizenship. Oxford University Press, Oxford
Maiz R (2004) *Per Modium Unius*: más allá de la dicotomía nacionalismo cívico vs. nacionalismo étnico. In: Gurrutxaga Abad A (ed) El presente del estado-nación. UPV, Bilbao, pp 107–130
Maiz R (2005) Republicanismo e inmigración en Francia. *La République une et indivisible* y el *affaire du foulard*. Revista de Estudios Políticos (nueva época) 129:5–37
Mancini S (2012) Secession and Self-Determination. In: Rosenfeld M, Sajó A (eds) The Oxford handbook of comparative constitutional law. Oxford University Press, Oxford, pp 481–500
Margalit A, Raz J (1990) National Self-determination. J Philos 87(9):439–446
Miller D (1995) On nationality. Oxford University Press, Oxford
Norman W (2006) Negotiating nationalism. Nation-building, federalism, and secession in the multinational state. Oxford University Press, Oxford
Requejo F (2009) Fédéralisme multinational et pluralisme de valeurs. Le cas espagnol. Peter Lang, Bruxelles
Seymour M (2017) Demain, Québec: autodétermination interne ou autodétermination externe? In: Noreau P, Gagnon AG (eds) Constitutionnalisme, droit et diversité. Mélanges en l'honneur de José Woehrling. Thémis, Montréal, pp 547–581
Seymour M (2024) Nation et autodétermination au XXIe siècle. Les Presses de l'Université de Montréal, Montréal
Sorens J (2012) Secessionism: identity, interest, and strategy. McGill-Queen's University Press, Montreal-Kingston
Supreme Court of Canada (1998) Reference re Secession of Quebec [1998] 2 SCR 217
Tamir Y (1993) Liberal nationalism. Princeton University Press, Princeton
Throssell K (2015) Child and nation: a study of political socialisation and banal nationalism in France and England. Peter Lang, Bruxelles-New York
UN (1960a) 14 December, General Assembly resolution 1514 (XV)
UN (1960b) 15 December, General Assembly Resolution 1541 (XV)
UN (1970) 24 October, General Assembly Resolution 2625 (XXV)
Verges J (2021) In a democracy, what makes an external self-determination claim reasonable? Some reflections on the moral aspect of the question. Las Torres de Lucca 10(18):19–42
Viroli M (1995) For love of country: an essay on patriotism and nationalism. Oxford University Press, Oxford
Wellman C (2005) A theory of secession. The case for political self-determination. Cambridge University Press, Cambridge

Failures of the Nation-States and Promises of Liberal Nationalism and Multinational Federalism

Alain-G. Gagnon

Abstract This chapter challenges conventional portrayals of nationalism by distinguishing between majority nationalism—which often pursues homogenization—and the nationalism of minority nations, which can foster diversity and democratic renewal. Gagnon argues that nationalism is not inherently destructive; under certain conditions, it can empower culturally distinct communities, enhance political accountability, and strengthen democratic practices. After examining the "dark side" of nationalism described by critics such as Kedourie and Hechter, the chapter highlights the failures of traditional liberal democracies to accommodate deep diversity, noting their tendencies toward cultural homogenization, monistic understandings of the demos, and myths of state neutrality. Gagnon then outlines two promising pathways: liberal nationalism, which reconciles cultural membership with universal rights, and democratic multinational federalism, which offers institutional mechanisms for shared rule and self-rule within diverse polities. Together, these approaches redefine nationalism as a potentially "diversity-developing" force capable of revitalizing democracy and addressing the aspirations of minority nations.

Preface

Let me first provide you with a brief overview of a few key points I wish to make in this chapter. First, I should point out that it is important to demarcate two modalities of nationalism: nationalism writ large and nationalism advocated by minority nations. The former corresponds to the imposition of a set of hegemonic practices on political communities with a view to fusing them with an all-encompassing nation; the latter—that is, nationalism advocated by minority nations—focuses on the pursuit of national belonging from minorities, which could take place inside or outside existing nation-states.

A.-G. Gagnon (✉)
Université du Québec à Montréal, Montréal, Canada
e-mail: gagnon.alain@uqam.ca

F. Savastano et al. (eds.), *Between Asymmetry and Secession*,
https://doi.org/10.1007/978-3-032-29603-0_6

Tensions between these two modalities—and this is a central point I wish to make—reveal intentions in the case of majority nationalism to undermine and, at times, even repress diversity, or, to formulate it differently, it corresponds to a "diversity-eliminating" process, whereas the second trend consists in empowering small nations and in opening the way to a "diversity-developing" process.

So, to put it bluntly, I challenge the view—so dominant in the social sciences—that all expressions of nationalism lead to the elimination of diversity. Rather, I suggest that nationalism can also lead to its growth.

If one accepts this revised premise, one will then be open to questioning approaches disseminated by standard textbooks. I am of the view that it could do a lot of good if we undertake to make this case, especially considering the plight of many ethnic, cultural, and national minorities evolving in deeply diverse democracies.

As I see it, my *problématique* is that there could be a dark side to nationalism—as many have argued—but we should not be too quick to quarrel with it. Instead, we ought to view nationalism—under certain conditions—as an avenue (first) to redress current failings of liberal democracies, and (second) as a way to enhance democracy per se.

1 Introduction: Defining Nationalism[1]

Nationalism has become the most frequent expression of claims for political autonomy and self-realization in the modern world. It is significant to note that in territories as diverse as Canada and Spain, for example, nationalism has constituted simultaneously the struggle against a domineering view of the state imposed by central institutions and the attempt to refine democratic practices.

Any study of the phenomenon of nationalism should point out its impressive capacity to renew itself through transformative myths, narratives, normative arguments, and, more concretely, through a variety of political actions.

Several of the main authors who study the national phenomenon converge on a famous dictum made by Ernest Gellner in the opening statement of his book on *Nations and Nationalism* to the effect that "Nationalism is primarily a political principle, which holds that the political and national unit should be congruent." This point raises immediately a series of questions pertaining to state sovereignty and territorial integrity as two central pillars of the continuing existence of the nation-state.

At the very outset, let me formulate a working definition of what I mean when I use the concept of nationalism. Nationalism is to be depicted as a political process

[1] This chapter builds on and synthesizes two earlier conferences. The first conference was delivered on May 15, 2017 at Sciences Po Paris as part of a conference series on "The Future of Nations" that I had co-organised with Alain Dieckhoff, and the second conference was delivered on January 11, 2024 as the 34th Annual McDonald Lecture under the auspices of the Centre for Constitutional Studies of the University of Alberta, Canada.

on the part of culturally differentiated groups, characterized by a sense of togetherness on a specific territory, that pursue the objective of transforming themselves from cultural subjects into political subjects with a view to potentially reap the benefits of full statehood.

Students of nationalism, including Eric Hobsbawm, are often of the view that the new century would see the decline of nationalism thanks to progress made by forces of liberalism and cosmopolitanism. In the conclusion to his major book, *Nations and Nationalism since 1760: programme, myth, reality*, Hobsbawm declared, however, that: "The owl of Minerva which brings wisdom, said Hegel, flies out at dusk. It is a good sign that it is now circling round nations and nationalism" (1989, p. 183).

It seems though that Hobsbawm confused the decline of communism in Central and Eastern Europe with the disappearance of nationalism (Laforest 1995, p. 225). Some colleagues have taken an additional step and even stated that we have ushered into a post-sovereign era (Keating 2001).

Nationalism remains a central component of modern societies that we need to be able to cope with, and that comes in various shapes and shades—at times destructive and, at other moments, constructive.

It could be both backward-leaning and forward-leaning (Nairn 1975, 1997). In short, nationalism is a polysemic concept that cannot be reduced to a single thing.

Here, it is worthwhile to pay closer attention to the work of Hans Kohn—especially *The Idea of Nationalism*—Kohn was probably the first one to distinguish between ethnic and civic forms of nationalism as he differentiated the development of distinct state traditions occurring in Central and Eastern Europe (illiberal) with the ones taking hold in Western Europe (liberal)—similar to the work produced by Istvan Bibo (1911–1979).

Many motives have been identified by theorists of nationalism to account for its emergence and spread. These include the desire to obtain one's own state for a national group in quest of historical repairs, or else for political recognition or for the will to retain or acquire accrued powers to be in a position to enter the international fray with a potent voice.

Part 1 is composed of two segments.

I will first be exploring what the main authors have depicted as the dark side of nationalism, so that we have a better idea of what is being conveyed and discussed.

Second, I will be turning my attention to the challenges and shortcomings of traditional liberal democracies, which have produced the conditions that have led to the emergence of nationalist attitudes.

In part 2, after having shown that traditional liberal democracies have failed to cope in a fair manner with nationalism as a "diversity-developing" project, I will be advancing two distinctive roads that can offer concrete promises for the future of nation-states as well as for the maintenance of the world order, namely through the advancement of liberal nationalism and the development of multinational federalism.

2 Nationalism: Its Dark Side

Critics of nationalism abound both in the field of social sciences and in the political arena. Michael Hechter goes as far as arguing that nationalism has become the most prevalent source of political conflicts and violence in the world today.

Hechter gives examples of parochialism, systemic abuses, outmoded and backward attitudes, aggressions, crimes, racism, xenophobia of various types, ethnic cleansing, genocide, and other forms of violent behavior to make his point. Such a position echoes statements made by Elie Kedourie (1960) and Pierre Trudeau (1962–1968) in which they denounce nationalism for its inherent destructive and reactionary nature.

Kedourie is particularly critical of nationalist claims. He concludes his book *Nationalism* by arguing that "Nationalism, then, does not make easy the relations of different groups in mixed areas. Since it advocates a recasting of frontiers and a redistribution of political power to conform with the demands of a particular nationality, it tends to disrupt whatever equilibrium had been reached between different groups, to reopen settled questions and to renew strife. Because these claims are uncompromising nationalists must always cast about/ for opportunities to reopen an issue which/, for the time being, they might consent to consider closed. Far from increasing political stability and political liberty, nationalism in mixed areas makes for tension and mutual hatred" (1960, p. 115).

Pierre Elliott Trudeau spoke of "tribalism" to depict French-Canadian (Quebec) nationalism, suggesting that the values being heralded were based on affective and ascriptive group ties. Values heralded by nationalists were said to be premodern and to be in sharp opposition with the rich legacy of the Enlightenment and the virtuous goals pursued by liberalism.

Influential philosopher Karl Popper [1902–1992] was never a fan of nationalist inclinations. Indeed, he condemned vehemently any expressions of nationalism / that he considered/ to correspond to "tribal instincts, to passion and to prejudice, and to our most nostalgic desire to be relieved from the strain of individual responsibility /which it attempts to replace/ by a collective or group responsibility."[2]

One can find many illustrations of this suggested trend in an expanding literature which oppose particularist and universalist viewpoints or else nationalist and cosmopolitan standpoints. The best illustration is offered by Michael Ignatieff in *Blood and Belonging*.

Writing at the time of the collapse of the Soviet Empire, Michael Ignatieff wrote in *Blood and Belonging* that "For what has succeeded the last age of empire is a new age of violence. The key narrative of the new world order is the disintegration of nation-states into civil war; the key architect of that order are warlords; and the key language for our age is ethnic nationalism (…) we assumed that the world was moving irrevocably beyond nationalism, beyond tribalism, beyond provincial confines of the identities inscribed in our passports, toward a global market culture that was

[2] *The Open Society and its Enemies*, 1962: 49 (quoted in Tamir 1993: 80).

to be our new home. In retrospect, we were whistling in the dark. The repressed has returned, and its name is nationalism."

Authors such as Eric Hobsbawm and Terence Ranger, in *The Invention of Tradition*, made the argument that nationalism is simply an invention created by politicians and political entrepreneurs keen to serve their own interests.

These authors often are of the view that nationalism constitutes an historical error. During his first presidential campaign, Emmanuel Macron spoke of the forces of progress (republican patriotism) that he contrasted with reactionary elements (nationalism). "Nationalism is war" ("Le nationalisme, c'est la guerre") or, when Macron got to the final presidential ballot and declared that he wanted to be "the president of all the people of France, the president of all patriots to respond to all nationalist threats" ... ("le président de tout le peuple de France, le président des patriotes face à la menace des nationalistes").

Such positions leave no room for any genuine reflections on the means to be taken and measures to be adopted to cope with nationalism as a challenge for a world that ought to be more accommodating of deep diversity, and especially so in cases of advanced democratic polities.

Commenting on the work of Michael Keating in *Nations against the State* as well as the work I have done with James Tully in *Multinational Democracies*, Stephen Tierney notes that nationalist movements, such as the ones manifested in Catalonia, Quebec and Scotland "are, contrary to many negative stereotypes, not atavistic or romantic but in fact are well in tune with contemporary democratic attitudes to social policy, civic conceptions of citizenship and universal human rights standards" (Tierney 2015, p. 62).

His colleague Michael Keating develops the point in *Plurinational Democracy* that "nationality conflicts [ought to be understood] as a form of politics to be negotiated continually, rather than as a problem to be resolved once and for all, after which 'normal politics' can resume" (2001, p. 3).

In short, nationalism, contrary to what has been argued without much nuance by Kedourie, Trudeau, and many others, who refused to give nationalism any credit for its achievements, has contributed in at least four ways to make our world a better one:

1. its capacity to mobilize people and advance popular sovereignty;
2. its ability to organize political communities and create ties of solidarity that bind its members;
3. its power to force decision-makers to be more accountable to the population; and
4. its strength in advancing both individual and community rights within liberal democratic settings (Gagnon & Keating 2012).

This takes me to my discussion of traditional liberal democracies.

3 Traditional Liberal Democracies: An Exploration

Traditional liberal democracies have occupied the center stage ever since the advent of the nation-state. They contributed (1) to imagine political life based on notions of individualism and universalism and (2) to give meaning to the state as a potent instrument to mobilize various interests in an effort to construct the nation-state. This led to some important developments.

However, several authors coming from Canada, Spain, and the United Kingdom have been at the forefront in identifying and debating a series of shortcomings on the part of liberal democracies. These shortcomings have taken many forms, among which four have greater importance in explaining what I consider to be their central weaknesses.

First, through their natural inclination and persistent push in favor of cultural and national homogenization, liberal democracies have often forced minority nations and ethnic groups to take strange forms and to adopt new cultural and social practices, short of which they would be further isolated and alienated in the emerging nation-state. Ferran Requejo reminds us, for example, that "All states impose particular national, linguistic and cultural features on their citizens. [To be fair so do] Minority nations (…) when they have their own institutions of self-government. Some of the nation-building processes used by democracies in the past are unacceptable nowadays in normative terms (assimilation, deportation, repression, stigmatisation of minorities, etc.)" (Requejo 2010, p. 152).

Second, traditional democracies have assumed that the demos cannot be fragmented (state monism *obliges*) or that it cannot be shared. Or, formulated differently, that the polity can only be single, therefore making it impossible for minority nations to be properly heard or to have their views seriously taken into account, both in the policy process and in constitution-making.

Third, traditional democracies also take for granted that the state is neutral—in fact, this standpoint constitutes one of the most enduring myths since the establishment of the liberal states. Both as we are reminded by various authors, the normative foundations of the liberal democratic rights and freedoms "have never been 'neutral' as far as individual identities are concerned, because those rights and rules include a whole range of implicit *particularist* cultural values (such as language, reconstruction of history, 'common' traditions etc.) which go beyond mere procedural and universal values" (Requejo 1999, pp. 260–61).[3]

And, fourth, traditional liberal democracies are said to stand up for universal and individualistic values, and anything short of those would be considered to be reactionary and retrograde. This position is particularly well-argued by Pierre Trudeau, Canada's former prime minister from 1968 to 1984 (with a brief period out of power

[3] A similar argument has been made by Yael Tamir in *Liberal Nationalism* when she discussed the "illusion of neutrality" (1993: 145–147)—or else by Cass Sunstein in his famous book *The Partial Constitution* (1993).

in 1979). Trudeau's moral theory is said to be first and foremost individualistic, which means that his position is not influenced by collective values or projects.

More to the point, Trudeau "rejects the collectivist [and, he would have said, reactionary] idea that values, traditions, and languages deserve respect and protection as a matter of right and justice. Too much cultural protectionism, he defended, inevitably shades into intolerance and finally a totalitarian denial of personal freedom in the name of group identity" (Bickerton et al. 2006, p. 139).

In such a setting, states play a crucial role in advancing the values of individuals who are said to be free to choose their cultural, ethnic, linguistic, national, and religious identities. But, as Requejo has illustrated in his work, such "identities are usually not chosen. In reality, they are the foundations on which one's choices are based (political, social, and cultural contexts in which individuals socialize, and are usually the result of processes that include historical events of both a peaceful and violent nature—wars of annexation, territorial conquests, etc.). The struggles are often the root of present-day struggles for the recognition and accommodation of minority nations" (Requejo 2010, p. 153), as I will illustrate in the following section.

What is most problematic for liberal democrats is to see their national projects being challenged from within, at different territorial scales, by concurrent national projects that often pursue similar objectives, namely the advancement of a civic project and the construction of a political community. In the cases of Catalonia, Québec, and Scotland, such projects are founded less, I would argue, on ethnic fragmentation and values differentiation than on the importance of social cohesion, increased accountability, and the search for self-rule.

In the next segment of this chapter, I am advancing what I consider to be two optimal ways to accommodate fragmented polities, namely, institutional arrangements based on liberal nationalism, or else, institutional arrangements that will contribute to the blossoming of democratic multinational federalism.

4 Road 1: Liberal Nationalism

Twenty-five years ago, Yael Tamir published a path-breaking book, *Liberal Nationalism*, in which she brought together the literature on liberalism and nationalism. For most authors before her, the two concepts were in sharp opposition.

In *Liberal Nationalism*, Tamir produced one of the most advanced theoretical analyses to debunk shortsighted accounts of the national phenomenon. She did so by underscoring the idea that "Liberal nationalism requires a state of mind characterized by tolerance and respect for diversity for members of one's own group and for outsiders" (1993, p. 90).

Tamir also insisted on a key idea that at the center of both nationalist and liberal claims lies "the right to culture" (Tamir 1993, p. 34). In other words, "Liberal nationalism thus celebrates the particularity of culture together with the universality of human rights, the social and cultural embeddedness of individuals together with their personal autonomy" (Tamir 1993, p. 79).

This idea is also well formulated by Peter Alter, who, writing at about the same time as Tamir, made the point that liberal nationalism represented nothing less than "a protest movement against an existing system of political domination, against a state which destroys the nation's traditions and prevents its flourishing. Its adherents stress the right of every nation, and with it the right of *each* and *every* member of a nation, to autonomous development, for in their minds, individual freedom and national independence are closely connected" (1994, p. 29).

Among the best known pioneers of liberal nationalism are the German, Johann Herder, the Italian Giuseppe Mazzini, and the Frenchman, Ernest Renan, for whom nationalism is aimed at constructing a world based on human values of equality, fraternity, and liberty. The concept of nation as defined by Ernest Renan receives favorable echoes among Catalans, Quebecers, and Scots:

> A nation is a soul, a spiritual principle. Only two things, actually, constitute this soul... One is the possession in common of a rich legacy of remembrances the other is the actual consent, the desire to live together, the will to continue to value the heritage of which all hold in common ... The existence of a nation ... is an everyday plebiscite (Renan 1994 [1882], p. 26).

Tamir's seminal contribution builds on the legacy of Herder, Mazzini, and Renan as she goes on to develop the view that 'personal autonomy' and 'communal belonging' are natural allies. Such "concepts are viewed here as complementary rather than conflicting, suggesting that no individual can be context-free, but that all can be free within a context" (Tamir 1993, p. 14).

This allows us to make the point that nationalism, especially liberal nationalism, constitutes a modern phenomenon and represents a tool that can assist political communities to seek the establishment of just relations and to pursue mutual recognition.

The main challenge here, for both liberals and liberal nationalists, is to guarantee that the pursuit of cultural membership, historical continuity, and their future is shared with, and is inclusive of all others, so that its liberal character is maintained and fully sustained. This is what I applied myself to discuss at length in my book *Minority Nations in the Age of Uncertainty: New Paths to National Emancipation and Empowerment.*

In the same vein, David Miller, in his book, *On Nationality*, points out that nationality [that he distinguishes from nationalism] is a source of ample goods since it contributes to building personal identity and to mobilizing individuals as members of a given collectivity for which they engage in activities of solidarity. Nationality, does he stress, can also be an operative principle for political communities that feel treated unfairly and, as a result, could justify claims leading to regional or political autonomy and, in the most extreme cases, leading to secession.

Will Kymlicka (1995) and Joseph Carens are probably the two scholars who have most convincingly invited philosophers and policymakers to take seriously claims made by liberal nationalists, considering that—like liberals—they stand up for liberty, equality, fairness, and justice. The only difference is that proponents of liberal nationalism aspire to implement them on another scale.

I wish to emphasize the point that liberal nationalism constitutes nothing less than a more rooted expression of cosmopolitanism, but that it simply takes place at the level of the political community, exactly where it is possible for political agents to act and to intervene to guarantee the advancement of democratic practices.

Liberal nationalism then entails a commitment to universal ideals and values. In other words, in its liberal form, nationalism is the embodiment of an anchored cosmopolitanism.

All in all, I would argue that cosmopolitanism and liberal nationalism take their source from the same intellectual traditions. Both seek to instill human rights and human dignity. However, they use different strategies and operate at a different scale.

Such a change in focus could bring new life into the concept of nationalism, which can be interpreted as an expression of political will through the advent of loyalty, community, solidarity, justice, and, to use Will Kymlicka's terminology, can constitute an added context of choice for smaller political communities. It is through this process that we can really enter into a phase of "diversity-enabling" and avoid the current process of "diversity-eliminating" that has been so pervasive at the international level ever since the beginning of the Westphalian age.

What becomes clear is that nationalism, such as depicted by Kedourie and Trudeau, does not have to be conceived from a dark side—that is to say, conservative, reactionary, chauvinist, or racist. The work of Craig Calhoun—whom we heard a few weeks ago—is particularly relevant as he invites us to avoid discussing nationalism as simply being instances of passionate excesses or successful manipulations by demagogues and identity entrepreneurs.

For Calhoun, "nationalism is equally a discursive formation that facilitates mutual recognition among polities that mediate different histories, institutional arrangements, material conditions, cultures, and political projects in the context of intensifying globalization. Nationalism offers both a mode of access to global affairs [as we see in the cases of Catalonia, Québec, and Scotland] and a mode of resistance to aspects of globalization. To wish it away is more likely to invite the dominance of neoliberal capitalism than to usher in an era of world citizenship" (Calhoun 2007, p. 166).

5 Road 2: Democratic Multinational Federalism

As we engage in the exploration of democratic multinational federalism as a potential way out of current impasses in several political settings, we need first to note that nationalist movements prevailing in several regions confirm that nation-states have often failed on two important aspects. First, nation-states have, time and again, been unable to accommodate national diversity, and second, they have proven incapable of meeting the needs of individuals, coming from different cultural backgrounds, in their quest for personal autonomy.

In *The Rights Revolution*, Michael Ignatieff, revisiting and correcting his earlier sweeping criticisms of nationalist movements such as the ones he expressed in

Blood and Belonging, concludes that, in the Canadian case, "At the moment, might lies with the majority and right with the minority. Mutual recognition must rebalance the relationship, with power and legitimacy finding new equilibrium. Then, and only then, will we be able to live together in peace in two countries at once, a community of rights-bearing equals and a community of self-governing nations" (Ignatieff 2000, p. 84).

I fully endorse Ignatieff's new take on the Canadian situation. But let us face it, there exists a major current in liberalism that tends to undermine the necessity to recognize cultural diversity—a current that is deeply "diversity-eliminating." We need to take this trend very seriously and consider new options.

For authentic liberals, though, assimilation and cultural homogenization cannot be considered to be acceptable answers to present-day challenges.

My colleague James Tully, a well-known political philosopher, advances that this condition constitutes one of the most destructive forces of modernity, which needs to be rapidly identified and contained, reminding us that it was in the name of modernity that campaigns of colonization in North America, with the corresponding genocide of Aboriginal peoples, were justified. The concept of modernity has too often served to rationalize the quest to eradicate cultural differences and to impose a uniform model of governance on all citizens residing in a given territory.

A few decades ago, Yael Tamir alerted us that: "The popularity of [the concept of nation-state] rests on several widely held fallacies, namely free institutions can only operate within a homogeneous nation-state, that a state can mobilize its citizens only by invoking the power of national ideas, and that economic development and modernization require cultural homogeneity" (Tamir 1993, p. 163).

This is in good part why we need to embark on a higher road. To do so, I have advanced democratic multinational federalism as a second-best option. Considering that most countries today are, in fact, multinational polities (India, China, the United Kingdom, Spain, Canada, etc.), we shall do more than pay lip service to this crucial fact.

Why, then, propose multinational federalism as one of my two optimal ways to accommodate divided polities? The best response has probably been offered by Michael Burgess, who argues that "Multinational federalism, then, conveyed a sense of 'separateness' within the state rather than a separation from the state. It presumed the protection, preservation, and promotion of distinct substate nations that would be able to determine themselves as nations within the larger federal state" (Burgess 2012, p. 24).

In connection with this, Lord Acton has, much earlier on, made a major contribution to the advancement of a modern theory of multinationalism. One of his most often quoted essays on "nationality" comes to mind. After juxtaposing the values inherent to a theory of unity and a theory of liberty, Acton concluded that the theory of unity leads to despotism and revolution, while the theory of liberty leads to self-government. He then goes on to affirm that:

> "The presence of different nations under the same sovereignty (…) provides against the servility which flourishes under the shadow of a single authority, by balancing interests, multiplying associations, and giving to the subject the restraint and support of a combined

> opinion. (…) Liberty provokes diversity, and diversity preserves liberty by supplying the means of organization" (Acton 1949, p. 185).

Although he was the first one to denounce narrow nationalism and national homogeneity, Acton supported the view of multinational states as the best guarantee for freedom. In Acton's view: "a State which labours to neutralize, to absorb, or to expel them [different peoples and nationalities], destroys its own vitality; a State which does not include them is destitute of the chief basis of self-government" (Acton 1949, p. 193).

In the Canadian context, Pierre Trudeau could never have been more perceptive and attuned to Lord Acton's philosophical stand, than when he wrote in 1962 his text on "The Multi-National State in Canada" when he argued that "it is necessary to divorce the concept of the state and of the nation and to make Canada a society truly pluralist and multinational" (1962, p. 53). I should point out though that his policy positions as Canada's Prime minister were often out of synch with this position.

Come to mind his forceful opposition to minority nationalist claims made by Indigenous communities and the Quebec National Assembly. In fact, Trudeau stood in favor of the all-encompassing nation-state against all other expressions of nationalism. We could even say that Trudeau was a forceful nationalist. His main battle was first and foremost his fight against separatism, as is clearly illustrated by this statement:

> One way of offsetting the appeal of separatism is by investing a tremendous amount of time, energy, and money in nationalism *at the federal level*. (…) Resources must be diverted into such things as national flags, anthems, education, arts councils, broadcasting corporations, film boards (Trudeau 1968, p. 193).

Trudeau did understand the workings of nationalism both as an engaging political process and, similarly to Michael Billing, as the expression of a variety of banal expressions.

As a student of both nationalism and federalism, I am of the view that these two concepts, rather than being antithetical, can inform and emulate each other. This is the main reason why I have invested much energy during the last two decades in advocating for Belgium, Canada, Spain, and, among other political regimes, the United Kingdom, in multinational federalism. I should also point out that Alain Dieckhoff has, with much drive and determination, embarked on this journey with his book, *Nationalism and the Multinational State*.

Nationalism does not have to be primordialist, exclusionary, or ethnically driven. Federalism does not have to be imperialistic, hierarchical, or authoritarian.

The idea is to find a proper balance so that all voices are heard and respected. This is why I believe that, in complex political settings, multinational federalism constitutes the best available option.

Federalism can also institutionalize equal, respectful power relationships among national communities and enable stakeholders to focus on relations of non-domination among different orders of government. Federalism also makes it possible to think about sovereignty as being shared between political subjects.

The central objective to be pursued by political actors ought to be clear: it should be to find a healthy balance between different political communities, such that members of the minority nations can realize possibilities that are comparable to those enjoyed by members of the majority nations. In other words, my proposal stands in sharp opposition with the phenomenon of "diversity-eliminating," rather, it consists in feeding conditions that would lead to a fairer deal for all partners in the federal compact.

Democratic multinational federalism provides new possibilities for a world in need of added contexts of choice, both for political communities and for citizens. It is also capable of producing a context that would allow a culture of constitutional pluralism to take hold.

6 Concluding Remarks

So far, the majority of nations have overwhelmingly been hesitant, when not simply opposed to advanced shared rule and self-rule strategies. Instead, states have been investing lots of energy to discredit nationalist movements, like in the case of Catalonia. Meanwhile, international organizations (the European Union, for example) have also been keen to oppose sub-national claims and, generally, to defend the status quo (Tierney 2004).

Such attitudes seem to give no other options to minority nations than to continue their quest for internal or even external self-determination due to the presence of a set of overlapping and reinforcing trends that undermine their position in the changing international order.

One can readily identify four challenges that are confronting minority nations and that they need to be able to respond to: (1) the consolidation of a global market accompanied by the continued wave of cultural Americanization; (2) the decline of civic engagement; (3) the growing uniformity between formerly distinct societies and cultures; and (4) the continuing atomization of the individual.

Advocates of democratic forms of nationalism have been capable of advancing strong narratives to the effect that nations evolving within multinational states can develop successful economic strategies on the world stage and contribute to democratizing the hegemonic nation-state as they make it more accountable at the sub-state as well as at the state levels.

Nationalism is here to stay and cannot simply be wished away. In other words, we need to cope with it. The nation-state remains a powerful instrument for nations in search of recognition and empowerment, as we have been reminded in various contexts such as East Timor, Kosovo, and South Sudan, all of which have been in a position to acquire the status of nation-states under very challenging circumstances.

Situations prevailing respectively in Canada, Spain, and the United Kingdom, with Quebec, Catalonia, and Scotland, are also reminders that liberal nationalism has not lost its capacity to mobilize and that its political salience and purchase remain very high, although, paradoxically, it will be much harder for these political communities to acquire the status of a nation-state.

The fact that concurrent national projects have a lot in common makes it harder for political elites to identify workable solutions—especially in cases such as the Catalan, Scottish, and Quebecois, where cultural differences are not that wide. Michael Keating reminded us that "History remains the battleground for rival nationalist projects" (2012, p. 115).

In brief, the pursuit of liberal nationalism is important for at least four main reasons. (1) It constitutes a buffer against cultural homogenization (Craig Calhoun). (2) It feeds the affirmation of political identities (Craig Calhoun, Liah Greenfeld, Michael Keating). (3) It contributes to the advancement of additional contexts of choice (Will Kymlicka). And (4) it helps in refining the demos and in giving a constitutional voice to minority nations (Ferran Requejo, Stephen Tierney, James Tully).

As a result, and to provide a caveat to Popper's one-sided account, nationalism does not have to "freeze" the idea of belonging and to pursue the institutional means to ensure the permanence of a particular mode of belonging through exclusion, ethnic cleansing, and similar despicable measures.

Liberal nationalism has all the ingredients to lead the way to an "open society" as it reveals its compatibility with democracy and adheres to a diversity-developing system of meaning. As a student of federalism and nationalism, I feel comforted that we are capable today of discussing foundational values of liberal nationalism.

References

Acton JE (1949) Nationality. In: Himmelfarb G (ed) Essays on freedom and power, vol III. The Free Press, Glencoe

Alter P (1994) Nationalism. E. Arnold, London

Bickerton J, Brooks S, Gagnon AG (2006) Freedom, equality, community: the political philosophy of six influential Canadians. McGill-Queen's University Press, Montreal and Kingston

Burgess M (2012) Multinational federalism and multinational federation. In: Seymour M, Gagnon AG (eds) Multinational federalism: problems and prospects. Palgrave Macmillan, Basingstoke, pp 23–44

Calhoun C (2007) Nations matter: culture, history, and the cosmopolitan dream. Routledge, London

Gagnon AG, Keating M (eds) (2012) Political autonomy and divided societies. Imagining democratic alternatives in complex settings. Palgrave Macmillan, Basingstoke

Hobsbawm E (1989) Nations and nationalism since 1780: programme, myth, reality. Cambridge University Press, Cambridge

Ignatieff M (2000) The rights revolution. Anansi, Toronto

Keating M (2001) Plurinational democracy: stateless nations in a post-sovereignty era. Oxford University Press, Oxford

Keating M (2012) Reforging the nation: Britain, Scotland and the crisis of unionism. In: Seymour M, Gagnon AG (eds) Multinational federalism: problems and prospects. Palgrave Macmillan, Basingstoke, pp 107–128

Kedourie E (1960) Nationalism. Hutchinson University Library, London

Kymlicka W (1995) Multicultural citizenship: a Liberal theory of minority rights. Oxford University Press, Oxford

Laforest G (1995) Le Québec et l'éthique libérale de la secession. In: Seymour M (ed) Une nation peut-elle se donner la constitution de son choix? Bellarmin, Montréal, pp 215–227
Nairn T (1975) The modern Janus. *New Left Review*, November–December
Nairn T (1997) Faces of nationalism: Janus revisited. Verso, London
Renan E. (1994). [1882]. Qu'est-ce qu'une nation? Calmann-Levy, Paris
Requejo F (1999) Cultural pluralism nationalism and federalism: a revision of democratic citizenship in plurinational states. European Journal of Political Research 35(2), pp. 255–286
Requejo F (2010) Revealing the dark side of traditional democracies in plurinational societies. Nations and nationalism, vol. 16, no 1, 148–168.
Sunstein C (1993) The partial constitution. Harvard University Press, Cambridge
Tamir Y (1993) Liberal nationalism. Princeton University Press, Princeton
Tierney S (2004) Constitutional law and nationalism pluralism. Oxford University Press, Oxford
Tierney S (2015) Sub-state nations and strong sstates: the accommodation impasse. In: Nationalism and globalization : new settings, new challenges. Hart Publishing, Oxford, 55–71.
Trudeau PE (1968) Federalism and the French Canadians. Macmillan, Toronto
Trudeau PE (1962) The multi-National State in Canada. The Interaction of Nationalism in Canada. Canadian Forum, June

Territories, Partitions, and Rights: Brief Reflections Starting from the Idea of Borders and Differentiation

Federica Fabrizzi

Abstract The contribution examines the theme of borders and territorial differentiation from a constitutional and legal perspective, emphasizing how borders—whether physical, economic, social, or cultural—are mutable and artificial, yet indispensable for administrative organization and the delivery of public services. Globalization, flows of capital and people, and technological innovation have increasingly blurred boundaries, requiring a critical rethinking of governance models. Particular attention is devoted to the Italian case, marked by a rigid and inefficient territorial grid that fails to reflect actual socio-economic and spatial dynamics. The lack of a coherent reform strategy has produced significant misalignments between institutional frameworks and functional realities. In light of these challenges, the analysis highlights the need to value differentiation as a tool for administrative efficiency, social inclusion, and the protection of rights, in line with the constitutional principles of subsidiarity, solidarity, and cohesion.

1 Brief Introduction to the Concept of "Border" and its Randomness

In a written work significantly entitled *Frontiers, boundaries, limits: and geography?*, the geographer Marcello Tanca, questioning the meaning of the border in geography, recalls that for Richard Hartshorne, geography is precisely defined as the *science of spatial differentiation* because the geographer's task consists, precisely, in identifying regions that are homogeneous within themselves and different from what surrounds them. He also recalls that in *La Terre et l'évolution humaine*, the historian Lucien Febvre states that "Point de problème plus important, en géographie, que celui des divisions" (Febvre 1949).

To summarize—at the risk of oversimplifying—any act of subdivision is essentially the drawing of a boundary, the tracing of a line that separates *different* things.

F. Fabrizzi (✉)
Sapienza University of Rome, Rome, Italy
e-mail: federica.fabrizzi@uniroma1.it

F. Savastano et al. (eds.), *Between Asymmetry and Secession*,
https://doi.org/10.1007/978-3-032-29603-0_7

If geographers question the role of geography in this "marking of differences," so too should legal scholars who specialize in public law, particularly local government law. So, the title of these brief reflections could be something like: Frontiers, boundaries, limits: and public law?

The purpose, in fact, is to attempt to frame the issue of borders within the concept of difference and the resulting differentiation from a legal point of view.

Now, differences can be of various types: for instance, geography teaches us that the delimitation of a physical unit with geomorphological and geological characteristics different from those of the surrounding area marks what is known as a physical boundary. The difference in *landforms*, therefore, represents a possible criterion for distinction. But the physical boundary is not the only possible territorial subdivision; there are also divisions based on different types of criteria, such as economic, social, cultural, or historical.

From a legal perspective, the crucial element is that all these potential subdivisions, different in origins, must eventually be summarized, reconciled, and translated into the identification of a political and administrative boundary that will separate *what lies on this side* from *what lies on that side*. It is an operation as complex as necessary: not by chance, in the very first lessons of public law, we are taught that territory is a constitutive element of the State; and territorial public entities are such precisely because they are autonomous entities that distinguish themselves from other public entities specifically due to the element of territory. Thus, the Italian state is distinguished from the French state by a political boundary, just as the Italian municipality of Todi is separated from neighboring Collazzone by an administrative line—as happens with the French municipalities of Saint-Genis-Pouilly and Sergy.

The subdivision into different levels of territorial governance takes on fundamental importance in administrative geography—which has rightly been called "the most political of the geographies" (Dini and Zilli 2021).

The line that distinguishes, both vertically and horizontally, the different entities is nothing more than an "institutional fact," a superstructure that attempts to make fixed what, in reality, is not fixed. In fact, the administrative boundary, understood as what defines the difference between entity A and entity B, does not exist in nature, or at least is highly porous and susceptible to change based on countless stimuli and to settle in different ways over time.

Suffice it to say that in March 2009, it was reported that, due to the melting of glaciers, some parts of the boundary between Switzerland and Italy, originally drawn in 1861, had shifted by several dozen meters, rendering previous reference points obsolete; this phenomenon forced geographers to update measurements, topography, and maps, and at the same time pushed authorities to consider the idea of a "mobile boundary."

Now, if even physical, "natural" boundaries shift and change, it is easy to imagine how mutable boundaries based on economic or social phenomena might be.

As is well known, the new dynamics arising from global flows of capital and people, from the production and management of goods and services, as well as from technological development and new forms of communication, all contribute to a rapid and ever-changing redefinition of economic-social boundaries—boundaries that are undeniably different even compared to just a few decades ago. To this, we must add the global scale of certain phenomena: the environment and digital technologies—to name the two most obvious cases—do not conform well to boundaries and subdivisions, as by definition they cannot be confined within politically and administratively finite territories.

Essentially, borrowing the words of Marcello Tanca, "the very idea of the border as we understand it is increasingly in crisis, because the rationality of political space—and of forms of belonging—is itself in crisis, due both to autonomist pressures emerging at the local level and to the dynamics generated by global flows of capital and people, of production, management, technology, and communication" (Tanca 2011).

Nevertheless, partitions—boundaries—are not only necessary between States, but also within them, as they provide the basis for the delivery of essential administrative services: despite variations in legal systems and in the distribution of powers, a key element in the planning and implementation of regional policies lies in identifying the geographic units to which those policies will be applied.

Thus, the exercise of governing authority has always taken place within a territorial framework that, by separating what might not otherwise be separate, inevitably produces differences—differences which, in some cases, may have significant consequences in terms of the enjoyment of rights and access to services. Otherwise, we would not be able to explain why, between 2005 and 2015, residents of as many as 25 municipalities in Veneto (a region with ordinary statute) requested to be incorporated into the territorial jurisdiction of Trentino-Alto Adige (a region with special statute).

Administrative boundaries are not only necessary; they also tend to remain relatively stable. States usually maintain them unchanged for long periods, since frequently altering the administrative framework would be difficult to manage and might lead to inefficiencies.

Thus, even though the principle of maximum alignment between the territorial area in which daily activities occur and the area of governance over those activities is considered good practice to apply, this principle is sometimes sacrificed. With the result of a misalignment between the *de jure* and de facto situation.

Although this gap between real boundaries of so-called "life basins" and the administrative boundaries is recognized as a problem, it remains evident that territorial reforms only occur when the territory—which naturally tends to adapt—can no longer compensate for the inefficiencies caused by that misalignment.

2 What Is Urban? What Is Metropolitan? What Are Inner Areas?

From the brief overview provided, two key aspects clearly emerge: on the one hand, the necessity for States to define administrative units, essentially territorial sections that designate a geographical area for which an administrative authority is empowered to take administrative or strategic decisions, in accordance with the judicial and institutional framework of the State; on the other hand, the significant difficulty in identifying delimitation criteria that are sufficiently validated and shared, due to the broad discretionary power involved in determining indicators, thresholds, and weightings.

Even the European Union—which, as is well known, lacks competence in the territorial organization of its Member States—has felt the need to establish a common statistical nomenclature for territorial units, known as NUTS (*Nomenclature of Territorial Units for Statistics*), to facilitate the collection, development, and publication of harmonized regional statistics in the EU and to conduct socio-economic analyses of the regions and the framing of interventions in the context of EU cohesion policy.

The resulting framework is highly heterogeneous: based on demographic thresholds, three NUTS levels are identified across the 27 EU Member States, comprising 92 NUTS 1 regions (such as Germany's federal Länder or entire countries like Denmark and Sweden), 268 NUTS 2 regions (such as Italian regions or Spain's Autonomous Communities), and 1214 NUTS 3 regions, which include Italian provinces, Greece's Nomoi, Finland's Maakunnat, Sweden's Län, Germany's Kreise, France's Départements, and Spain's provinces.

This classification is complemented by the LAU (Local Administrative Units), which are the building blocks of NUTS and correspond to municipalities across the EU. Each Member State subdivides its NUTS 3 level into one or two additional tiers of territorial units under the LAU system.

If the NUTS structure is already quite varied, the LAU level is even more fragmented. As noted in the literature: "The average size of the English local government is almost 100 times larger than that of a typical French commune. There is nothing like a typical or even dominant European 'model' of territorial organisation at the municipal level. There is huge diversity in this respect and reforms relating to the size of municipal authorities are still topics of very hot debate and conflict in several countries" (Swianiewicz et al. 2017).

However, the issue is not merely one of size. Reducing the complexity of administrative zoning to demographic or territorial extension alone is clearly reductive, as the functional dimension holds equally significant weight.

One illustrative case of the difficulty in reducing territorial complexity into clear-cut and reproducible "models" is the challenge of defining urban areas, particularly cities with metropolitan features.

First, it is important to highlight that the concept of "city" encompasses at least three meanings: physical, referring to the built environment; political-administrative, linked to the area defined by administrative boundaries; functional, related to the flows and activities that occur within it.

A vast part of academic literature on urban systems and metropolitan areas confirms the significant challenges in identifying universally accepted and empirically validated delimitation criteria.Geographic studies, for example, increasingly describe the city as an ever-expanding territory with blurred boundaries: some refer to the concept of "diffused city" (Indovina 2009); others conceptualize it as a "mosaic" of heterogeneous fragments, using metaphors such as archipelago, islands, urban villages, or patchwork (Lanzani and Pasqui 2011).

In these studies, the city is no longer understood as a homogeneous entity, but rather as characterized by discontinuities, disruptions, and fragmentation of the metropolitan fabric.

This discontinuity has also been acknowledged by ISTAT (Italy's national statistics institute), which notes: "in the contemporary city, the intensification of flows, the spread of settlement patterns scattered heterogeneously across the territory, and the blending of urban uses into agricultural space make the urban boundary increasingly blurred and weaken its conceptual link with the traditional ways of constructing the city" (Istat 2017).

Several studies have highlighted new relational principles underlying settlement forms and urban morphology, which stand in open contrast to the conventional conception of urban space as distinct from non-urban space.

As settlement patterns evolve, so too does urban morphology, the very concept of "city" itself, and, consequently, the notion of what is "non-city." It has become increasingly complex to define urban cores, just as the concepts of "peripheral areas" or "inner areas" have lost some of their traditional meanings.

In a digitally connected society, how is the criterion of "proximity to the citizen" defined?Does it still coincide with physical spatiality, or does it instead align with digital accessibility to services?

If the transition toward smart infrastructures is viewed as essential in urban environments, it becomes even more critical in sparsely populated and less interconnected areas, where digitalization and innovation can help bridge access gaps.

The €ten million grant awarded in May 2025 by Italy's Agency for Digitalization (AgID) is a strategic initiative aimed at digitizing rural villages, to enhance cultural heritage and revitalizing tourism in peripheral areas. This initiative aligns with a broader European strategy increasingly focused on expanding the scope of smartness beyond urban contexts.

As Teresa Graziano notes: "Despite differences in policies and practices across national contexts (from reciprocity contracts in France to Finland's 'smart countryside', and the platforms of German digital villages), the initiatives launched so far interpret *smartness* not only in terms of technological infrastructure and digitalization, but also as social innovation and inclusion" (Graziano 2022).

In Italy, municipalities classified as "inner areas" are those with spatial peripherality relative to service hubs. This classification is time-based: 20–40 min, intermediate; 40–75 min, peripheral; over 75 min, ultra-peripheral. Clearly, this time-distance criterion is becoming outdated. Indeed, recent critical-geographic analyses increasingly consider how digital technologies have not only modified and mediated existing social processes but also transformed the very forms and operations of physical space.

What, then, are the legal and administrative implications?

A first observation is that spatial planning experts have long shown a growing interest in variable-geometry governance systems. In this approach, the metropolitan area loses its character as a fixed physical agglomeration, and its boundaries gradually dissolve into the surrounding territory.

A network-based governance model, where functions are distributed according to non-hierarchical, reticular structures, appears, at least in theory, to be the most suitable for managing the increasing complexity of contemporary territories. In fact, a comparative look at European experiences reveals an evident trend: internal differentiation within the same level of government is growing across all states.

From this perspective, the French example is particularly significant, as France is traditionally seen as the "homeland of uniformity." Yet today, its legal framework allows for substantial institutional differentiation among metropolitan areas, which are now distinguished not only from the rest of the country but also from each other. For example, the *Métropole* of Lyon adopts governance solutions that differ significantly from those of Paris, Marseille, and other cities as they are progressively established (Vandelli 2019).

3 An Example of Dysfunctionality: The Italian Case

In the context of this general European trend toward, on the one hand, rationalizing administrative subdivisions and, on the other, fostering differentiation, Italy stands out—unfortunately—as an exception. Despite clear evidence emerging from statistical, economic, and geographic studies, Italy has not only failed to update its territorial grid, but when it did so—by intervening on the provinces and establishing metropolitan cities through Law 56/2014—it did so without any coherent plan or functional criteria.

The misalignment between administrative areas and the actual forms of residence, production, and circulation is undeniably a longstanding issue in Italy. However, the absence of a territorial reorganization strategy—at the municipal, provincial, and even regional levels—has become especially evident in recent years. Reforms have been driven solely by cost-cutting objectives (as seen in the drastic budget reductions imposed on provinces between 2008 and 2014), with questionable results. The spending review targeted the intermediate level of the so-called "area vasta," essentially reducing provinces to second-tier elected bodies. Yet, no structural reform has been undertaken at the municipal level, despite an equally pressing need for rethinking.

These inconsistencies are well known. In particular, the territorial configuration of municipalities no longer reflects the spatial distribution of residential and productive activities. As previously discussed, the territorial basins where daily activities—living, working, consuming—take place have expanded significantly. As a result, Italy now lacks any correspondence between the framework of territorial entities and the actual "area-population relations" of its citizens.

This disconnect is clearly illustrated in ISTAT's analysis of the distribution of Local Labor Systems (Sistemi Locali del Lavoro, SLL). The report notes: "There are 611 local labour systems (LLS) identified by Istat in 2011 during the 15th

Population Census, using daily home–work commuting patterns. Compared to 2001, this represents a reduction of 72 units. Local labour systems are independent of administrative boundaries: 56 of them (9.2%) straddle more than one region, and 185 (30.3%) involve two or more provinces. The systems of Voghera (Pavia) and Melfi (Potenza) are the only ones that include municipalities belonging to three different regions. The local system of Milan, in addition to being the largest in terms of resident population (almost 3.7 million inhabitants), encompasses 174 municipalities spanning seven of Lombardy's twelve provinces" (Istat 2014).

This functional zoning thus reveals numerous organizational patterns that cut across provincial and regional boundaries.

The report also highlights how socio-economic developments have altered population distribution over time: "The size of the 2011 systems is larger than in 2001, both in terms of the number of municipalities composing them (13.2 versus 11.9) and in terms of resident population (97,000 inhabitants versus 83,000). Overall, 221 local systems (36.2%) recorded a decline in resident population between 2001 and 2011, located predominantly in the Mezzogiorno."

This range of data and insights should serve as a foundation for policymakers to legally formalize concepts such as "metropolitan area," "metropolitan city," "inner area," or "peripheral area." Moreover, anyone reading these numbers critically must recognize that a one-size-fits-all legal framework—applied uniformly across the entire national territory, as Italy has done to date—no longer corresponds to the actual dynamics on the ground.

For instance, the document notes: "In general, the Mezzogiorno, unlike the Centre-North, is characterized to a greater extent by small-sized local systems, as a result of the overall weakness of its labour market, where interactions between labour supply and demand are limited. On the other hand, however, the regions of the Mezzogiorno tend to have local systems that are, on average, more self-contained, both on the demand side and on the supply side."

This raises important questions about the legal and territorial implications of such findings: yet, to date, no regulatory adjustments have been made to reflect these realities.

The data on Local Labor Systems also highlight inconsistencies in the organization of the "area vasta" level, which in Italy encompasses both provinces and metropolitan cities.

Some numbers help illustrate the existing asymmetries: ten provinces have more than one million inhabitants, while six of Italy's twenty regions have fewer; twenty-two provinces have more than 800,000 inhabitants; only three metropolitan cities (which are also provinces) include more than 100 municipalities, whereas 22 provinces have over 100 municipalities; out of nearly 8000 municipalities, 69% have fewer than 5000 inhabitants, and their distribution is highly uneven (e.g., Piemonte has 1046 such municipalities, while Puglia has only 84).

The 2014 legislative choice to equate provincial boundaries with metropolitan cities is universally recognized in academic literature as illogical and, consequently, inefficient.

Provincial boundaries—except for a few exceptions such as the systems of Milan, Rome, and Naples with populations of 3.7, 3.5, and 2.5 million, respectively—cannot be considered metropolitan areas because they do not correspond to the functional spatial and relational densities that characterize today's Italian territory.

Indeed, none of the 84 Functional Urban Regions identified in Italy by Eurostat and the OECD through a common methodology corresponds to a provincial territory.

As various studies have emphasized: "in a territory marked by hierarchical polycentrism such as Italy—though the German case, for example, is by no means different—the metropolitan question takes shape as the consolidation of an asymmetric interdependence among neighbouring municipalities, where the asymmetry stems from the presence of one municipality far larger than the others, whose 'pulling power' structures the surrounding area. This asymmetry—and the form of interdependence that follows from it—calls into question the (social, political, and economic) rationality of the decision-making autonomy of individual municipal administrations and, more generally, of the current political–administrative organization of the territory in question" (Calafati 2014).

If Italy were to seriously reflect on the "metropolitan question" based on empirical territorial evidence—which clearly has not occurred and does not seem to be on the institutional agenda—it would become obvious, for example, that Monza (today not part of Milano's metropolitan city) could never truly be considered separate from Milano, just as Sesto San Giovanni (which is today part of Milano's metropolitan city) cannot be considered separate. The same applies to Prato (today excluded from Firenze's metropolitan city) and Scandicci (today included within it).

Elsewhere in Europe, large cities have gradually extended their boundaries to incorporate neighboring municipalities with which they have developed spatial and relational integration: examples include Manchester and Munich. In Italy, however, municipal boundaries have remained unchanged, even in major urban areas: metropolitan cities continue to suffer from pronounced asymmetry between the core city and the surrounding municipalities.

As Antonio Calafati wrote: "The problem of governing metropolitan territory can be solved only by acknowledging the differences in the degree and type of territorial interdependencies. There are many cases in which municipal boundaries must first be redrawn to transform *de facto* cities into *de jure* cities: among neighbouring municipalities within a metropolitan area, the level of spatial integration is often so high as to suggest their outright merger" (Calafati 2013).

At the very end, the crucial problem is that the map of Italy's administrative organization offers a blurred—if not wholly misleading—image of the national territory. As the Italian Geographical Society noted in its 2014 report: "the grid separates places that would be better off together, and holds together others whose union is simply inefficient" (Società Geografica Italiana 2015).

4 Differentiation as a Tool for Effective Governance

If it was not already clear, it is evidently time for Italy to engage in a serious interdisciplinary reflection on zoning, thereby reconsidering administrative boundaries, while considering their artificial nature and the difficulty of applying uniform and rigid criteria. Despite the complexity of such an undertaking, economic, statistical, and geographical studies demonstrate that a breaking point has been reached between the administrative structure and the real structure of the country. Consequently, rather than being a driver of economic efficiency, the territorial grid has become a source of inefficiencies, making intervention unavoidable.

This is not only a matter of improving system efficiency; it also concerns citizens' enjoyment of rights and the attainment of essential levels of performance for the entire population. One need only consider that in the case of small and medium-sized cities and metropolitan areas, the demand for public services is consistently underestimated, as it is calculated on the basis of the administrative city rather than the actual city. Furthermore, public policies that are excessively localized—particularly in matters of spatial planning—often lack long-term vision.

It would therefore be highly desirable for such territorial reorganization to stem from a serious reflection on functions, following a logic that starts from the functions themselves and moves toward determining the optimal territorial division, not the other way around. As already noted, such a reflection would likely lead to the conclusion that a differentiated regime is necessary, marking a significant departure from the logic that has until now characterized Italian legislation, an approach described as "blind to differentiation" (BIN), if not actually resistant to it.

The only path taken toward differentiation has been that outlined in Article 116, paragraph 3, of the Constitution, with all the issues and debates it has entailed.

It is not the purpose of these brief reflections to dwell on the complex theoretical issue of asymmetries and their relationship with federal systems, although this issue undoubtedly underlies the arguments presented here.

In comparative legal frameworks—and particularly in the Italian context—scholarly positions are, as is well known, highly divergent. Some argue, for instance, that one must "distinguish between differences or differentiations and asymmetries: differentiations are those that necessarily exist among the constituent units of any composite entity, such as a federal state, and they may be of various kinds (geographical, economic, demographic, and so on); asymmetries, on the other hand, are something else entirely and may or may not be present within the same federal state." According to this view, "If it is true that differentiations are present in every composite unitary state, it is equally true that differences do not necessarily give rise to asymmetries" (Bifulco 2020).

Others argue that "autonomy can only mean differentiation, or at least the possibility of differentiation — that is, the ability of different territories to adopt different rules. Indeed, it is evident, even from the etymology, that where the same rules apply uniformly, one cannot speak of autonomy" (Palermo 2018).

The core question then becomes: how far can differentiation (and asymmetry) be tolerated in a unitary state?

A response was offered by the Constitutional Court in Judgment No. 192/2024, which examined the constitutionality of the so-called Calderoli Law (Law 86/2024) and stated:

"Certainly, any regional system contains elements of competition among regions, since it allows each of them, within the scope of their constitutional powers, to pursue different policies in the search for better outcomes. However, the *inevitable competition and differences among regions and territories* — which can indeed help improve the quality of public services — cannot go so far as to undermine solidarity between the State and the regions and among the regions themselves, the legal and economic unity of the Republic (Art. 120 Const.), the equality of citizens in the enjoyment of rights (Art. 3 Const.), or the effective guarantee of the essential levels of services relating to civil and social rights (Art. 117, second paragraph, letter m, Const.). Nor may it jeopardize social cohesion and national unity — defining features of the form of the State — whose weakening may lead to a crisis of democracy itself" (emphasis added).

In that decision, the Court made extensive and detailed reference to the principle of subsidiarity, which it identified as the foundation of the entire reasoning behind the possibility/necessity of differentiation. It is, in fact, subsidiarity that renders Article 116, paragraph 3, consistent with the constitutional framework. It is also subsidiarity that "rules out an abstract model for allocating functions and instead requires that, for each specific function, the most appropriate territorial level be selected, *in relation to the nature of the function, the local context, and the broader context* in which it is assigned" (emphasis added).

The differentiation provided for in Article 116, paragraph 3, is not, according to the Court, a factor of national disintegration or social fragmentation, but rather "a tool serving the common good of society and the protection of the rights of individuals and social groups."

It represents a factor of intrinsic flexibility, clearly stated in Article 118, which governs administrative functions and where, not coincidentally, the principle of subsidiarity is framed through the lenses of differentiation and appropriateness.

As the Court writes: "From a constitutional perspective grounded in the principle of subsidiarity, the allocation of legislative and administrative functions between the State and the regions — or a specific region, in the case of differentiation under Article 116(3) of the Constitution — cannot be reduced to a logic of power aimed at resolving conflicts among political actors, nor can it depend on merely political considerations. The principle of subsidiarity requires that the distribution of functions, and therefore differentiation, be viewed not *ex parte principis* but *ex parte populi.*"

Describing the mechanism as an elevator that must stop at the right floor, the principle of subsidiarity "rules out an abstract model of functional allocation and instead requires that, for each specific function, the most appropriate territorial level be chosen, in relation to *the nature of the function, the local context, and the broader context in which it is allocated*" (emphasis added). In other words, a flexible model.

Flexibility must not be confused with arbitrariness: the allocation must follow principles of effectiveness and efficiency in the distribution of functions and related resources, equity in their distribution, and public accountability to the populations affected by those functions.

As long as oversight and accountability are ensured *ex parte populi*, there are no obstacles to envisioning flexible models.

What seems indisputable, however, is the existence of a "right of territories" based on their differences, and, as has been effectively noted, the existence of "a physiological need for differentiation" (D'Orlando 2025).

This is demonstrated by the fact that when we talk about regions, we inevitably refer to the profound differences—in terms of demographic, territorial, altimetric, productive, social, and administrative tradition (BIN 2016)—that distinguish them. Similarly, for provinces and metropolitan cities, scholars have rightly noted that "to reduce Provinces and Metropolitan Cities to uniformity in terms of administrative functions and even their form of government […] would be "not only short-sighted but also contrary to the constitutional framework"" (De Donno 2025). Even for urban municipality cities, it has been noted that there exists a local administrative reality with characteristics that warrant specific legal recognition. There is, therefore, a need for a differentiated structure of public powers that better considers "those centres that are situated, so to speak, in the middle — that is, they are neither small enough to fall under the specific legislation currently in force, nor are they incorporated into the Metropolitan Cities" (Giglioni 2025).

Thus, when it is stated that "autonomy and differentiation are not curious claims that need to be justified, but precise constitutional requirements — features of our legal system that cannot be removed" (Bin 2016), what is being articulated is the constitutional translation of the empirical evidence discussed above.

The principles of differentiation and appropriateness, present in the constitutional text, provide the foundation for the differentiated exercise of power, an exercise that must not become a weapon (differentiation is not "a free space" used to "arm" regions seeking more political leverage against national uniformity (Carloni 2025)), but should instead serve to deliver differentiated, specific responses to specific problems.

If, as widely recognized in academic discourse, the classical model of rigid and uniform distribution has long proven inadequate, then the solution can only lie in differentiation.

This differentiation, moreover, is required, as argued in Judgment 240/2021, by Article 114 of the Constitution, which opens the entire Title V and describes the "identity card" of the Italian Republic. In that ruling, the Constitutional Court, addressing the coherence of the solution for area vasta governance under Law 56/2014, criticized the process by which "the territory of the Metropolitan Cities was made to coincide with that of the Provinces, thus failing *to differentiate the respective communities* according to appropriate criteria of efficiency and functionality — something that, under Article 114 of the Constitution, would instead be necessary in order for Metropolitan Cities and Provinces to be able *to best serve the interests arising from their territories*" (emphasis added).

Constitutional case law thus supports the interpretation of Article 114 as a principle of differentiation, rightly linking it both to the territorial delineation of entities and to the enjoyment of rights by citizens within those entities.

Meeting the specific needs of each community and socio-economic reality may well require abandoning the paradigm of uniformity and adopting flexible systems, without this implying the dissolution of national unity.

Ultimately, the same principle that applies to individuals also applies to territories: equal treatment for equal situations, and different treatment for different situations. Not to deepen divisions, but rather to ensure equality among citizens.

References

Bifulco R (2020) Differenziazioni e asimmetrie nella teoria federale. *Diritti regionali*. Rivista di diritto delle autonomie territoriali, 1/2020

Bin R (2016) Chi ha paura delle autonomie? In: AA.VV. Scritti in ricordo di Paolo Cavaleri, Napoli

Calafati A (2013). Città e aree metropolitane in Italia (cities and metropolitan areas in Italy). GSSI Urban Studies Working Paper, No. 1

Carloni E (2025) Dove va il regionalismo italiano. Considerazioni su differenziazione, amministrativizzazione, sussidiarietà. Le Istituzioni del Federalismo, 1/2025

D'Orlando E (2025) Lo Stato (regionale) come integrazione. Asimmetrie e contrappesi. Le Istituzioni del Federalismo, 1/2025

De Donno M (2025) Gli insegnamenti della Corte costituzionale nella sentenza n. 192/2024. Quale lezione per le riforme locali? Le Istituzioni del Federalismo, 1/2025

Dini F, Zilli S (2021) Sul cambiamento interno della geografia politica italiana. In: Dini F, Martellozzo F, Randelli F, Romei P (eds) Oltre la globalizzazione–Feedback, Società di Studi Geografici, Memorie geografiche NS 19, 817–824

Febvre L (1949) La Terre et l'évolution humaine. A. Michel édit

Giglioni F (2025) Differenziare i Comuni: le città come nuovo soggetto di diritto? Diritto pubblico, fasc. 1, gennaio–aprile 2025

Graziano T (2022) Gli smart villages per lo sviluppo delle comunità rurali: politiche, pratiche e modelli di innovazione in Europa. Geotema, Supplemento 2022

Indovina F (2009) Dalla città diffusa all'arcipelago metropolitano. Milano

ISTAT (2014). I Sistemi locali del lavoro. Report

ISTAT (2017) Forme, livelli e dinamiche dell'urbanizzazione in Italia

Lanzani AS, Pasqui G (2011) L'Italia al futuro. Città e paesaggi, economie e società. Franco Angeli, Milano

Palermo F (2018) Asimmetria come forma e formante dei sistemi composti. Le Istituzioni del Federalismo, 2/2018

Società Geografica Italiana (2015) Il riordino territoriale dello Stato. Rapporto annuale della Società Geografica Italiana

Swianiewicz P, Gendźwill A, Zardi A (2017) Territorial reforms in Europe: does size matter? Territorial amalgamation toolkit. Centre of Expertise for Local Government Reform, Council of Europe

Tanca M (2011) Frontiere, confini, limiti: e la geografia? Between vol. I(1) (Maggio/May 2011)

Vandelli L (2019) Il regionalismo differenziato. Rivista AIC, 3/2019

The Territorial Dimension and the Process of European Integration

Andrea Patroni Griffi

Abstract This essay examines the role of the territorial dimension in the European integration process, highlighting its potential to strengthen democracy and pluralism by complementing traditional channels of legitimacy. Subnational entities—regions, autonomous communities, and local authorities—emerge as basic democratic institutions capable of mitigating the Union's so-called democratic deficit. Instruments such as decentralization, autonomy, and subsidiarity, already entrenched within Member States, acquire further significance when projected onto the supranational level. The essay analyzes institutional mechanisms enhancing territorial participation, including the European Charter of Local Self-Government, the presence of regional representatives in the Council, and, above all, the Committee of the Regions, whose consultative but evolving role reflects both progress and persistent limitations. The discussion then addresses the impact of recent crises—pandemic, economic, and geopolitical—on territorial governance, with particular reference to Italy's National Recovery and Resilience Plan. These dynamics reveal a paradoxical tension between recentralization and the indispensability of regional implementation, underscoring loyal cooperation as the constitutional keystone. Ultimately, territorial autonomy is framed as a driver of democratic legitimacy in a multilevel Europe.

1 Europe and Regions

The territorial dimension acquires the potential to serve as an instrument, linked to the principle of autonomy, capable—if duly acknowledged—of reinforcing democracy and pluralism in Europe within a process attentive not only to economic but also to political integration.

Subnational levels of government, particularly where endowed with representative bodies and regulatory competences, emerge as *"basic democratic institutions"*

A. Patroni Griffi (✉)
Federico II University of Naples, Napoli, Italy
e-mail: andrea.patronigriffi@unina.it

F. Savastano et al. (eds.), *Between Asymmetry and Secession*,
https://doi.org/10.1007/978-3-032-29603-0_8

that may help offset the so-called democratic deficit within European institutions (Antonelli 2012; Habermas 2012). Regional and local actors can thus complement European democracy, which remains, to a significant extent, "mediated" by the Member States (Mancini 2007). Principles such as decentralization, territorial autonomy, and subsidiarity, where recognized, already serve within national systems to strengthen active citizenship and citizens' participation in public power, thereby consolidating decision-making mechanisms that give expression to the democratic *volonté générale*. By the same token, these very principles may acquire significance if adequately recognized at the supranational European level.

As the European Charter of Local Self-Government affirms, *"local authorities are one of the main foundations of any democratic regime,"* and their empowerment represents *"an important contribution to the construction of a Europe founded on the principles of democracy and the decentralization of power."*

A stronger recognition of the territorial dimension within the EU would therefore make decision-making circuits more proximate to citizens and expand European political pluralism, without disrupting the existing institutional framework either at the state level or at the supranational European level. In this respect, territorial autonomies become relevant to the very debate on the alleged democratic deficit of the European Union. This debate is not merely theoretical, but one that would require, as a preliminary step, clarification of what is meant by "democracy" within a legal order whose contours—summarized in the formula of a supranational organization—remain in constant evolution and adjustment.[1]

The European Union is not yet a federal state, but it already constitutes a territorial, multipolar, and multilevel system of governance (Pernice 2015). In this context, the traditional channels of democratic legitimation (the European Parliament and national parliaments) risk proving insufficient.

The principle of subsidiarity, enshrined in Article 5 TEU as the foundation of the exercise of Union competences, requires that decisions be taken as closely as possible to the citizen. More recently, however, it has been reconceptualized: from a subjective criterion focused on identifying the holder of competence, to an objective standard for assessing the *"best"* exercise of functions. Concrete experience nonetheless shows that where subsidiarity and local participation are effectively applied, forms of more participatory democracy multiply. Indeed, the Preamble of the TEU already demands that *"decisions be taken as closely as possible to the citizen, in accordance with the principle of subsidiarity"* (TEU Preamble).

Beyond the undeniably emphatic tone of certain expressions, the emergence of the territorial and local dimension at the European level can nevertheless serve as an "auxiliary" element of democratic legitimation and as a factor in the possible

[1] In his writings as early as the 1960s, Benedetto Conforti distinguished between classical intergovernmental international organizations and those exhibiting supranational features—namely, endowed with powers capable of directly affecting the legal orders of the Member States. This distinction finds its fullest expression in the *unicum* of the former European Communities, which did not merely bind states at the contractual level but produced direct and overriding effects within domestic legal systems (Conforti 1968, 1975, 2015).

improvement of integration processes and related decision-making mechanisms. Indeed, where territorial autonomies actively participate in the formulation of European environmental, social, and economic policies, the integration process is increasingly perceived not as a heteronomous phenomenon imposed "from above," but as the outcome of a shared pathway. Such a dynamic helps root the idea of a European Union that is not detached from the concrete needs of local communities, but rather capable of receiving and translating their demands into regulatory and programmatic measures whose legitimacy derives precisely from their participatory origins. In this perspective, the involvement of territorial autonomies not only enhances the democratic quality of decision-making but also strengthens its effectiveness, as policies prove more attuned to the socio-territorial contexts for which they are intended.

In this sense, territorial autonomies are not merely an internal factor irrelevant to the Union; they become natural interlocutors of European institutions, both in the definition of national positions and in the implementation of directives and the management of European funds. It is worth noting that no Member State of the Union still follows a fully centralized model of statehood in the Napoleonic tradition—not even France. The principle of autonomy, in its territorial articulation, permeates the legal orders of Member States, albeit in diverse forms of composite statehood.[2]

The Union has long abandoned its former *"Länder-Blindheit"* (blindness to federal structures); it is no longer indifferent to the composite nature of statehood, particularly where this is expressed in the existence of representative assemblies with legislative functions. The *Länder*, autonomous communities, regions, and territorial entities of composite states, however denominated, assume an important role in the integration process, not least because of the recognition accorded to them in the constitutions of Member States. This multiple phenomenon of federal and regional interconnections implies that the European dimension of autonomies must increasingly be interwoven with the internal forms of statehood (D'Atena 2018).

2 The Enhancement of the Territorial Dimension within the Union's Legal Order

In recent decades, significant institutional instruments have been introduced to enhance the territorial dimension within the Union. Primarily, the already mentioned European Charter of Local Self-Government, adopted by the Council of Europe in 1985, explicitly affirms that citizen participation in local governance is a shared democratic principle in Europe and that strengthening local autonomy constitutes an essential contribution to the construction of a democratic and

[2] Subnational levels, by bringing citizens' demands to the attention of EU institutions, help to "distribute" democracy more effectively and to "contribute to mitigating the 'democratic deficit' of the European institutions," providing a "surplus of legitimacy" that complements the Union's dual channel (Antonelli 2012; Caciagli 2011).

decentralized Europe (see Preamble), also by guaranteeing effective forms of judicial protection (Art. 11).

Although the Charter is not binding on the EU, as it is a Council of Europe treaty, it has nonetheless acquired relevance and is often cited, at times, in the case law of the Italian Constitutional Court.[3] Despite its formal exclusion from the EU Treaties, the convergence between the principles enshrined in the Charter and the *"common constitutional traditions"*—among which the principle of autonomy must be included (Pizzorusso 2002)—could lead the Court of Justice itself to treat them as general principles of European law. This would pave the way for their direct application, at least in cases where Member States fail to fully guarantee local self-government rights, thereby further consolidating the legal status of territorial autonomy within the corpus of supranational European integration.

Among the instruments aimed at increasing territorial visibility within the Union, the admission of representatives of regional governments from the Member States to Council sessions represents an important step.[4] The direct participation of regional representatives, particularly in federal states or in those with composite forms of statehood, constitutes an implicit recognition of the role of sub-state entities in shaping state positions at the European level, especially in policy areas subject to regional implementation.[5] Nonetheless, the arrangement remains heterogeneous, essentially dependent on the discretion of Member States, resulting in limited autonomous influence of the regions on the substance of European decisions and clear asymmetries in territorial representation.

---

[3]The Constitutional Court, in Judgment No. 50 of 2015, referred to it as a *"policy document"* which nonetheless *"leaves intact the basic competences of local communities [...] as established by the Constitution or by statute,"* as had already been recognized in Judgment No. 325 of 2010. It has been observed that the Delrio Act raises questions concerning its conformity with the provisions of the European Charter of Local Self-Government (Lucarelli 2015). On the relevance of the Charter of the Council of Europe before the Constitutional Court, see also Judgment No. 33 of 2019.

[4]Article 16(2) of the Treaty on European Union (TEU) provides that *"The Council shall consist of a representative of each Member State at ministerial level, who may commit the government of the Member State in question and cast its vote ..."* The clause *"at ministerial level"* makes it possible, in federal or regional systems, for the representative in the Council to be a member of a subnational government, as is the case with the German *Länder*, the Spanish Autonomous Communities, or the regions themselves, in matters falling within their competences. In Italy, Article 5 of Law No. 131 of 5 June 2003 stipulates that *"The Regions and the Autonomous Provinces of Trento and Bolzano shall participate directly, in matters falling within their legislative competences, in the formulation of Community acts, by taking part, within the Government's delegations, in the activities of the Council and of the working groups and committees of the Council and of the European Commission, according to modalities to be agreed within the State–Regions Conference, taking into account the specificities of the special autonomies and, in any case, guaranteeing the unity of Italy's representation through the Head of Delegation designated by the Government."*

[5]With the Maastricht Treaty, one can observe the transition from the so-called *"functionalist regionalism"* of the European Community—where the involvement of regional and local authorities was limited to the pursuit of certain objectives of economic and social cohesion policy, in the formulation of which those very local governments did not participate—to the so-called *"institutionalist regionalism"* (Tarli Barbieri 2024).

While the admission of regional representatives to Council sessions is a step toward the Europeanization of multilevel governance, in the absence of a binding and uniform supranational framework, there is a risk that such openness remains of limited effectiveness, heavily conditioned by political will and national institutional architectures. A stronger institutionalization of the role of regions and sub-state territories in the European decision-making process should instead be pursued by reinforcing the role of the Committee of the Regions.

Within the EU, it is indeed the European Committee of the Regions—established by the Maastricht Treaty of 1992—that embodies an institutional body composed of representatives of regions and municipalities. The Committee is consulted by the Parliament, the Council, and the Commission on crucial matters such as economic and social cohesion, trans-European infrastructure, regional policies, environment, energy, and other areas of local concern.

The Committee is certainly not a third "chamber of territorial representation" (assuming one were to construe, albeit somewhat artificially, the Council as a de facto second chamber of state representation). Nonetheless, it serves as an institutional channel through which territorial autonomies receive formal recognition within the European legal order. It thus constitutes a privileged forum of interaction between sub-state levels and Union institutions, ensuring that the claims of local communities are not confined within the boundaries of national orders but find legitimate expression and consideration in the supranational decision-making space. One must also recall, at the national level, the ongoing—at least doctrinal—debate on the reform of the Italian system of strict bicameralism, aimed at differentiating the two chambers through the creation of a "Senate of Autonomies" (Patroni Griffi 2018), partly to grant regional entities greater weight in the European integration process.

Despite initial expectations, however, the Committee does not possess autonomous decision-making powers and remains an advisory body. The first protocol, which entered into force in 1993, entrusted national parliaments alone with monitoring compliance with the principle of subsidiarity, with no explicit reference to the role of local and regional authorities. The second protocol, by contrast, provides in Article 2 that the European Commission, prior to formulating a legislative proposal, must initiate a broad consultation process, taking into account, where appropriate, the regional and local implications of the proposed measures. Similarly, Article 5 requires legislative drafts to consider the need to limit, proportionately to the objectives pursued, the economic and administrative burdens placed on sub-state entities. Additional progress includes the possibility for national parliaments to consult regional territorial bodies (Art. 6(2) of the Protocol), and the explicit recognition of the Committee's standing before the Court of Justice of the European Union.

This latter prerogative enables the Committee to challenge a Union act to *"safeguard its own prerogatives"* (Art. 263(3) TFEU). It follows, however, that the Committee must demonstrate a concrete and direct legal interest in protecting such prerogatives against Union legislative acts perceived as invasive. Yet Article 8 of Protocol No. 2 on the principle of subsidiarity recognizes the Committee's standing before the CJEU not only to defend its own prerogatives but also, more broadly, to seek annulment of Union acts which, in breach of the principle of subsidiarity, encroach upon the competences of regional and local authorities. Nonetheless, the Committee's right of action remains subject to the conditions laid down in Article 263 TFEU.[6] In practice, therefore, this instrument has not succeeded in realizing its full potential.

As regards composition, depending on the choices made by individual Member States, guaranteed individual representation for regional entities within the Committee is found in the Union's three federal states in the strict sense,[7] as well as in Spain and Portugal, both characterized by territorial communities vested with legislative powers. Italy, however, constitutes an exception: despite being a state with twenty regions vested with legislative competences, it does not secure individual representation for the regions within the Committee. The Italian delegation, in fact, comprises 24 members, of whom only 14 represent the regional level, while the remaining members represent the local level (D'Atena 2022), perhaps reflecting the peculiarities of Italy's system of territorial autonomies.

As to its functioning, although traditional scholarship has often emphasized the Committee's limited impact on the European decision-making process due to its purely consultative role (Hönnige et al. 2015), empirical studies have shown that a significant percentage of Commission proposals in the field of regional policy effectively incorporate the Committee's opinions (Neshkova 2010). At the same time, relations with the European Parliament—initially marked by distrust—have evolved positively thanks to the reforms introduced by the Treaties of Amsterdam and Lisbon, culminating in the conclusion of an interinstitutional cooperation agreement between the two bodies (Decoster et al. 2019). The overall assessment of the Committee and its role is therefore mixed, reflecting both progress achieved and persisting limitations.

3 The Territorial Dimension in the Face of Recent Crises

The avenues for strengthening—albeit, as noted, still in need of further improvement—the territorial dimension within the Union's institutional architecture come into potential tension in the face of recent crises: first the pandemic, then the economic, military, and migratory emergencies, and more generally the global geopolitical instability that has frequently given rise to tendencies toward the reassertion of national sovereignty, both within Member States and in their relations with the Union.

[6] In particular, the impugned measure must possess a legislative character, meaning that it must have been adopted through either the ordinary or a special legislative procedure; furthermore, the Treaty on the Functioning of the European Union must expressly provide for consultation of the Committee in relation to such measure; and, finally, the action must be lodged within the peremptory time limit of two months following the publication of the measure.

[7] Germany, Austria, and Belgium.

Against this backdrop, the signals concerning the territorial dimension in the integration process appear contradictory and, to some extent, troubling: if not entirely sidelined, it has certainly not experienced the further development that might have been envisaged or deemed desirable.

The pandemic crisis undoubtedly delivered a significant signal of *"European federalism"* through the Union's resort, for the first time in its history, to common debt via the Next Generation EU mechanism and the issuance of Eurobonds to finance loans and grants to Member States. Yet the message conveyed by this instrument to the system of territorial autonomies is at best ambivalent.

While territorial entities have historically played a central role in the management of structural funds—thus constituting a fundamental instrument of territorial development and economic cohesion—the National Recovery and Resilience Plan (NRRP), defined at the state level, though recognizing in principle the importance of regional involvement,[8] has largely operated according to recentralizing logics designed to ensure the effectiveness of the measures adopted. Such centralization was fostered by the *"governance method"* (Lupo 2024) inaugurated by the NGEU, which presupposes ongoing—and often informal—interaction between the European Commission and national governments.

Moreover, the NRRP, triggered by the Recovery and Resilience Facility,[9] conditions the disbursement of resources on the achievement of milestones and targets, ultimately verified at the supranational level by the Commission. This introduces a logic of *ex post* conditionality that reverses the traditional paradigm of public expenditure. Within this framework, a constant tension emerges: on the one hand, the need to valorize the role of regions and local authorities as actors closest to the territories in implementing measures; on the other, the need to centralize functions of coordination, monitoring, and, if necessary, substitution, to ensure compliance with deadlines and commitments undertaken at the European level.

The establishment of the *Cabina di regia* (steering committee), the monitoring system, and the substitution mechanisms in the event of non-compliance by regional or local implementing bodies,[10] as well as the further centralization represented by the *Struttura di missione PNRR* at the Presidency of the Council of Ministers, all point to a clear recentralization.[11]

---

[8] One may consider, for instance, the establishment—aimed at ensuring the coordination of relations between state administrations responsible for implementing measures under the NRRP and territorial entities—of the *NRRP State–Regions Unit* (*Nucleo PNRR Stato-Regioni*), set up within the Department for Regional Affairs and Autonomies of the Presidency of the Council of Ministers, to which a range of essentially technical support functions has been entrusted.

[9] Regulation (EU) 2020/241 (the so-called RRF Regulation).

[10] Decree-Law No. 77 of 31 May 2021, *Governance of the National Recovery and Resilience Plan and Initial Measures for Strengthening Administrative Structures and for the Acceleration and Streamlining of Procedures*, converted into Law No. 108 of 29 July 2021.

[11] Decree-Law No. 152 of 6 November 2021, *Urgent Provisions for the Implementation of the National Recovery and Resilience Plan (PNRR) and for the Prevention of Mafia Infiltrations*, and Decree-Law No. 1 of 24 February 2023, *Urgent Provisions for the Implementation of the National*

The *Cabina di regia* is also entrusted with ensuring cooperation with the economic, social, and territorial partnership, a function previously carried out by the permanent forum abolished by Decree-Law No. 13/2023. In the meetings dedicated to this activity, the President of the Conference of Regions, the President of the National Association of Italian Municipalities (ANCI), the President of the Union of Provinces of Italy (UPI), the Mayor of Rome, and representatives of social partners, the productive and financial system, academia, civil society, and organizations of active citizenship participate, as identified by decree of the Prime Minister on the basis of representativeness.

The result is a performance-based plan that restructures the relationship between the center and the autonomies toward forms of coordination and accountability for outcomes that transcend the ordinary dialectic of concurrent legislation and even of shared administration.

Thus, the logic underlying the NRRP reflects a coexistence—indeed, a tension—between the drive to centralize the core of governance and the functional need to empower regions and local authorities as implementing actors. This tension may be inevitable, given the *"ambivalence"* of the NRRP: autonomies are indispensable for implementation, yet recentralization is ultimately necessary to secure the certainty of results. On a pragmatic level, beyond theoretical considerations, this has produced a new overall arrangement: regions should be protagonists in identifying regional projects, while the state must ensure the plan's effectiveness, efficiency, and strategic coherence throughout the national territory. The involvement of regional levels in the preparation of recovery plans is beyond dispute; equally undisputed is the need to guarantee achievement of the objectives, which underpins the very logic of recentralization.

From this unresolved tension arises a paradox within the structure of the NRRP: regions are weak in political decision-making, yet heavily burdened with executive and managerial responsibilities.

Indeed, periodic reports of the Court of Auditors have highlighted difficulties linked to the territorial disparities in administrative capacity, and the consequent risk that local delays may compromise the attainment of European targets.[12] Hence, the genuine necessity of strengthening personnel, technical expertise, and support instruments for territorial entities, without which there is a danger of creating mere alibis for local inefficiency and reducing the principle of autonomy to a purely formal proclamation.

The Constitutional Court has also had occasion to pronounce on the substitution powers linked to the NRRP. Notably, in Judgment No. 31 of 2024, the Court

---

Recovery and Resilience Plan (PNRR). The Mission Structure was established by Decree-Law No. 13/2023, as subsequently amended by Decree-Law No. 19/2024.

[12] Cf. *Report on the State of Implementation of the National Recovery and Resilience Plan (PNRR)*, Italian Court of Auditors, Joint Sections in the Supervisory Capacity, May 2024, 9, which also emphasizes that *"the implementation difficulties connected with relations with territorial entities acquire significance, as they affect in various ways both the programming phase and the executive phase of the interventions."*

reiterated that the exercise of such powers must be subject to procedural guarantees in compliance with the principle of loyal cooperation, and can legitimately operate only as an *extrema ratio*, after activating appropriate venues of negotiation. In so doing, the Court, through an additive decision, declared unconstitutional Decree-Law No. 13/2013 *"insofar as it did not require the acquisition of the agreement of the Region of Apulia for the adoption of the interministerial decrees approving the infrastructure program."*

The essential point in the Court's reasoning is the distinction between mere procedural forms of involvement and cases in which genuine agreement (*intesa*) is required as an expression of substantive accord (Guerrieri 2024). The Court stressed that simple consultation or information of the region cannot be deemed sufficient to respect the principle of loyal cooperation in cases where state intervention has a structural and permanent impact on the regional territory. In such contexts, especially in matters falling within the concurrent or residual legislative competences of the region, agreement constitutes *"the only adequate instrument,"* standing as an indispensable constitutional guarantee of balance between levels of government—though still surmountable in cases of persistent divergence *"despite repeated negotiations"* between state and region. The mere invocation of urgency cannot suffice to override this requirement.[13]

Without genuine attention to the principle of loyal cooperation, properly understood, there is a risk of what might be termed a form of *"suspended autonomy"* (Bergo and Cecchetti 2024). The NRRP centralizes the role of territorial entities in the implementation phase while simultaneously reducing their decision-making space and subjecting them to stringent state oversight that goes well beyond formal control. This alters the very configuration of Italian regionalism in the name of ensuring results—results whose failure would trigger serious supranational consequences for the entire system of autonomies (Cecchetti 2022; Pajno 2022), including the risk of undermining the *"reduction of territorial disparities as a non-negotiable constraint"* (Sciortino 2022).

The disruptive impact of the NRRP on autonomies is undeniable, and the concerns it raises are well-founded (Ferraiuolo 2022; Parisi 2022). For this reason, the principle of loyal cooperation remains the keystone, particularly if extended not only to the planning phase—through agreements or, where appropriate, forms of concertation that genuinely ensure participatory involvement—but also to implementation and monitoring. The task is, in some sense, to move beyond a narrow logic of competence allocation, and instead to establish—without excuses and with adequate instruments—a collaborative chain of responsibility aimed at outcomes (Dirri 2024).

The dialectic inherent in the NRRP between recentralization and the role of autonomies should not be read as a clash of competing competences and responsibilities, but as a functional integration. Genuine loyal cooperation, not emptied of substance, once again emerges as decisive: both *ex ante*, in programming, and *ex*

[13] See Italian Constitutional Court, Judgment No. 31 of 2024, para 6.2.

post, in monitoring and substitution. In this light, recentralization can be transformed from a limitation of autonomy into a means of ensuring its effective realization within the framework of republican unity.

Despite the manifold tensions brought to light by today's crisis scenarios, the principle of territorial autonomy ultimately remains a potential driver of democracy, even at the European level. It compels us to conceive of the state (and the Union) not as a monolith, but as a *"community of communities,"* embodying *"unity in diversity"* (Patroni Griffi 2024), in line with the long-noted phenomenon of *"double federal intertwining"* (D'Atena 2022). The horizon that emerges is that of a Europe that includes subnational levels as integral components of its own democratic, circular, and multilevel process—enriching both European and national sovereignty with territorial plurality. If managed properly, this double federal intertwining between the internal and the European dimensions may enhance governmental legitimacy and allow for more effective representation of local interests in Union decision-making.

References

Antonelli V (2012). Le autonomie locali: una questione europea. Amministrazioneincammino.it, 16

Bergo M, Cecchetti M (2024) Il PNRR e l'autonomia regionale "sospesa": tra urgenze del presente e Costituzione del futuro. Istituzioni del Federalismo 1:17 ff

Caciagli M (2011) L'Europa delle Regioni? Regionalismi e regionalizzazioni nell'Unione Europea. In: Mangiameli R (ed) Autonomia. Micronazionalismi e regionalismi in Europa. Editpress, Florence-Catania

Cecchetti M (2022) L'incidenza del PNRR sui livelli territoriali di governo e le conseguenze nei sistemi amministrativi. Rivista AIC, 3

Conforti B (1968) La funzione dell'accordo nel sistema delle Nazioni Unite. Cedam, Padua

Conforti B (1975) Le Nazioni Unite. Lezioni di Organizzazione Internazionale Vol. I - Introduzione, l'appartenenza all'organizzazione, gli organi. Cedam, Padua.

Conforti B (2015) Diritto internazionale. Editoriale scientifica, Naples, 170 ff

D'Atena A (2018) Il doppio intreccio federale: le Regioni nell'Unione europea. Le Regioni, 6

D'Atena A (2022) Diritto regionale. Giappichelli, Turin

Decoster F, Delhomme V, Rousselle J (2019) The committee of the regions and the European Parliament: an evolving relationship? In: Costa O (ed) The European Parliament in times of EU crisis. Dynamics and transformations. Palgrave Macmillan

Dirri A (2024). La leale cooperazione nell'assestamento del PNRR: un regionalismo "esecutivo" per il superamento dei divari territoriali. Osservatorio AIC, 1

Ferraiuolo G (2022) PNRR e correzione delle asimmetrie territoriali. Rivista AIC, 3

Guerrieri E (2024) La chiamata in sussidiarietà e il "mutevole" principio di leale collaborazione. Nota alla sentenza Corte cost. n. 31 del 2024. Osservatorio costituzionale, 4

Habermas JH (2012) The crisis of the European Union: a response. Polity Press, Malden

Hönnige C et al (2015) Consultative committees in the European Union. No vote-no influence? ECPR Press, Colchester

Lucarelli A (2015) La sentenza della Corte costituzionale n. 50 del 2015. Considerazioni in merito all'istituzione delle città metropolitane. federalismi.it, 8

Lupo N (2024) Il nuovo "metodo di governo" delineato dal PNRR e i suoi incoraggianti primi passi. In: Bilancia P (ed) L'impatto del PNRR sul sistema di governo multilivello. Opportunità e criticità, Bononia

Mancini M (2007) Regioni e Unione europea: il mancato "aggiramento" dello Stato. Le Regioni
Neshkova MI (2010) The impact of subnational interests on supranational regulation. J Eur Public Policy 17:8
Pajno S (2022) Il crepuscolo dell'autonomia regionale di fronte al PNRR. In: Antonetti N, Pajno A (eds) Stato e sistema delle autonomie dopo la pandemia. Problemi e prospettive, Bononia, 241 ff
Parisi S (2022) PNRR e meccanismi di raccordo: c'è vita oltre gli esecutivi? In: Antonetti N, Pajno A (eds) Stato e sistema delle autonomie dopo la pandemia. Problemi e prospettive. Bononia, pp 257–268
Patroni Griffi A (2018) Per il superamento del bicameralismo paritario e il Senato delle autonomie: lineamenti di una proposta. federalismi.it, 17
Patroni Griffi A (2024). E pluribus unum: le identità in Europa. Diritto pubblico europeo-Rassegna online, 1
Pernice I (2015) Multilevel constitutionalism and the crisis of democracy in Europe. Eur Const Law Rev 11(3), December
Pizzorusso A (2002) Il patrimonio costituzionale europeo. Il Mulino, Bologna
Sciortino A (2022) L'impatto del PNRR sulle diseguaglianze territoriali: note introduttive. Rivista AIC, 3

Case Studies

The Path of Devolution Between Centripetal and Centrifugal Forces

Giulia Caravale

Abstract The UK is described as a 'voluntary union of four nations… coming together to share resources and risks'. It is more than 25 years since the creation of the devolved institutions, which marked an indelible transformation in what has been called the 'new British Constitution'. Although the four nations have taken different and specific paths, formalised through legislation pertaining exclusively to their territories, it is undeniable the mutual influence among them and their shared drive to obtain a greater number of powers. This work proposes a classification of the devolutionary process into three phases, each characterised by distinctive features, and contends that, in the aftermath of Brexit, devolution must further develop through a reconfiguration of the legislative consent convention and a strengthening of intergovernmental relations, to promote a coordinated and shared evolution of the territorial constitution.

1 Introduction

The devolution introduced in 1998 in Scotland, Wales, and Northern Ireland significantly impacted the territorial constitution of the United Kingdom, establishing an original institutional framework that is particularly distinctive, also due to the absence of a written constitution, which would otherwise allow for a coordinated allocation of competences and a clear definition of specific powers (Schwartz 2022). Prior to 1998, the United Kingdom was regarded as one of the most centralised unitary states in Europe, with a governance structure heavily oriented around England. Since the late nineteenth century, a system of 'administrative devolution' began to apply, and even before 1998, some scholars had preferred to describe the UK not as a *unitary state* but as a *union state*, to point out that its political entity was formed through the historical union of four distinct nations: England, Scotland, Wales, and Ireland (Rokkan and Urwin 1982; Mitchell 2000; Jeffrey 2013). These

G. Caravale (✉)
Department of Political Sciences, Sapienza University of Rome, Rome, Italy
e-mail: giulia.caravale@uniroma1.it

F. Savastano et al. (eds.), *Between Asymmetry and Secession*,
https://doi.org/10.1007/978-3-032-29603-0_9

nations were brought together over time through a series of political acts and treaties (England's union with Wales in the 1530s, the Acts of Union in 1707 between England and Scotland, and in 1801 with Ireland, though only Northern Ireland remains part of the UK today) (Tierney 2004; Tierney 2012; Walker 2000). This origin is evident in the name *United Kingdom of Great Britain and Northern Ireland.* Unlike a unitary state, where power is centralised and uniform across the territory, or a federal state, where sovereignty is constitutionally divided between central and local governments, the UK represents a unique form of union even before 1998, while characterised by a centralised government and a single sovereign Parliament, it nonetheless preserved the integrity of its constituent parts, enabling them to retain their unique cultural, linguistic, and legal traditions (Bogdanor 1999a).

This paper aims to explore several key aspects characterising the United Kingdom's devolution process, beginning with its asymmetrical nature. Given the different political realities, distinct identities, legal traditions and cultures in each territory, Westminster has conferred varying degrees of power upon the devolved governments and assemblies.

This asymmetry has persisted over time, as each of the constituent nations of the UK has followed its own path, resulting in diverse and not always coordinated developments. The introduction of legal frameworks tailored to individual nations in a piecemeal manner, often lacking a coherent or shared vision, has prompted reflections on the need to approach constitutional reform in a more systemic and integrated way, placing greater emphasis on the constitutional implications of each reform.

The following pages will reconstruct the main features of the devolution processes, with particular emphasis on some of the most significant issues that define devolution in the UK. The main one is the preservation of Westminster as the sole sovereign Parliament of the United Kingdom. In accordance with the foundational principle of the British constitution—the sovereignty of the King in Parliament—the devolved systems have been structured as derivative entities, lacking original sovereign powers. Westminster has retained the authority to legislate even in devolved matters, and whenever it legislates in areas within its competence, the Scottish, Welsh, and Northern Ireland Assemblies must pass a legislative consent motion (Hazell & Rawlings 2005; Bromley 2006). However, this motion does not have the legal capacity to constrain Westminster's authority. Moreover, all the acts passed by the devolved legislatures are subject to various and complex forms of review, both *ex ante* and *ex post*, particularly when considered *ultra vires*, and may ultimately be declared 'not law' by the Supreme Court. The British government may also lay before Westminster a negative statutory instrument preventing the bill passed by the devolved Parliament from being submitted for royal assent.

Second, the UK's decision to leave the European Union significantly impacted the devolution framework, thereby affecting the cohesion of the Union. The repatriation of powers from Brussels to London had consequences on a wide range of devolved matters, necessitating a reassessment of centre-periphery dynamics and the frameworks of intergovernmental cooperation. The impact of Brexit was particularly significant in Scotland and Northern Ireland, the nations that had voted to remain in the European Union. In this evolving context, the Supreme Court was repeatedly called upon to rule on matters related to devolution (e.g. the Miller case, the Continuity Bill case, the reference on Scottish independence referendum, the Northern Ireland Protocol case), making a substantial contribution to the definition of the territorial settlement (Tirapu-Sanuy 2025). Devolution has therefore not only transformed the territorial constitution but has also affected the nature of the UK's constitutional order and the country's politico-constitutional architecture.

2 The Evolution of Devolution

Tony Blair's victory in the 1997 general election marked the beginning of what has been described as the 'modern era of constitutional reform' (Gordon 2015), culminating in the introduction of devolution in 1998. The development of devolution can be divided into three distinct phases: the first one, which we can define as the Labour Era, spanned from 1997 to 2010 and was characterised by the establishment, the consolidation, and the institutionalisation of devolved governance structures. The second phase, which extended from 2010 to early 2017, witnessed an intensification of the devolutionary process so profound that it posed a challenge to the integrity of the United Kingdom itself. This period included the 2014 Scottish independence referendum, the outcome of which had far-reaching implications not only for Scotland but for the other constituent nations as well. During this period, Scotland was granted expanded legislative powers, and Wales similarly gained enhanced authority. Concurrently, alternative approaches to addressing the so-called 'English Question' began to emerge, diverging from the original proposals envisioned in the early stages of devolution. Finally, Northern Ireland experienced an uninterrupted phase of devolved governance, albeit not without significant challenges. This period may be seen as concluding in the early months of 2017 (Caravale 2017). In January, the Miller judgment clarified the meaning of the legislative consent convention and reaffirmed the principle of Westminster sovereignty. In March, the formal procedure for the United Kingdom's withdrawal from the European Union was initiated, culminating in 2020. This marked the beginning of a third phase, which extends to the present day and is defined by the constitutional and territorial consequences of Brexit. This phase is also characterised by the emergence of new challenges and the ongoing search for institutional and political equilibrium.

3 The First Phase 1997–2010: The Labour Era

Following the publication of two white papers outlining the devolution proposals for Scotland and Wales, and the subsequent pre-legislative referendums held to consult Scottish and Welsh citizens on the establishment of their respective Parliaments—and, in the case of Scotland, also on the conferral of limited fiscal autonomy—the

Blair government introduced the Scotland Act 1998 and the Government of Wales Act 1998. At the same time, following the Good Friday Agreement of 1998, the Northern Ireland Act 1998 was passed, and the Northern Ireland Assembly was resumed. The three laws of devolution established the competences of the institutions, highlighted that the three nations remained an integral part of the United Kingdom, and that the devolved Assemblies were constitutionally subordinate bodies, whose powers are assigned by London (Bogdanor 1999b). In May 1999, the first elections for the three Assemblies were held. Therefore, under the UK constitutional tradition of 'parliamentary sovereignty', devolution is reversible, and the devolved institutions are products of UK statutes.

The Westminster Parliament has remained sovereign throughout the United Kingdom and has retained implicit powers enabling it to extend its legislative competence in pursuit of predetermined objectives, including in areas of devolved responsibility. A constitutional convention, known as the 'legislative consent convention' (or Sewel convention), has been established to govern inter-parliamentary legislative cooperation. This convention provides that the devolved legislatures may pass a legislative consent motion agreeing to Westminster legislation in areas within their legislative competence, or when an Act of the UK Parliament would modify the legislative powers of a devolved legislature or the executive functions of devolved ministers or departments. In such instances, the UK government is required to engage in consultation with the devolved administrations, which, in accordance with the Standing Orders of the devolved legislatures, issue a legislative consent memorandum outlining the terms and scope of the proposed consent (Dalyell 2000; Keating 2001; Keating 2009; Mitchell 2009; Cairney 2011). As a constitutional convention, the legislative consent convention is not legally binding. In a large majority of cases, the convention has operated without controversy: the convention's application with Brexit highlighted the difficulties in interaction between levels of government, as we will see later.

From the outset, the three devolved legislatures were granted different levels of competence and were composed of varying numbers of members, reflecting both the population size and the constitutional responsibilities of each institution. In Scotland, a Parliament of 129 members was established, elected through a mixed electoral system. A parliamentary form of government was introduced, whereby the First Minister is elected by the Parliament and must retain its confidence. The Scotland Act 1998 conferred primary legislative powers upon the Scottish Parliament, and a reserved powers model was adopted in the allocation of competences.

Following two parliamentary terms (1999–2003 and 2003–2007) under Labour-led coalition governments with the Liberal Democrats, the 2007 Holyrood elections were won by the Scottish National Party (SNP), which has maintained either an absolute or relative majority in every subsequent election since then. The 2007 elections marked a significant turning point not only because, for the first time since 1999, an administration politically distinct from the UK central government was formed, but also because the newly appointed First Minister, Alex Salmond, immediately declared his intention to hold a referendum on Scottish independence.

In an effort to curb the spread of autonomist sentiment and to respond to growing demands for the devolution of greater powers, the British government established the Commission on Scottish Devolution in 2008. Chaired by Sir Kenneth Calman, this independent body was tasked with reviewing the provisions of the Scotland Act 1998 and proposing reforms in light of the first 10 years of devolved governance. The reports published in 2008 and 2009 offered a generally positive assessment of the functioning of Scottish institutions, firmly rejected any move towards independence, and advocated for a strengthening of devolution, particularly through the expansion of fiscal powers. In 2010, the recommendations of the Calman Commission led to the introduction of a bill, which was enacted two years later (Scotland Act 2012). The Act significantly enhanced the Scottish Parliament's taxation powers and expanded certain devolved competences.

The asymmetric nature of the UK's devolution framework becomes particularly evident when comparing Scotland to Wales, whose process was markedly slower. This volume examines the evolution of Welsh devolution through a paper by Giulia Aravantinou Leonidi. This divergence can be attributed to the differing historical contexts of the two nations and the weaker sentiment of autonomy or independence in Wales. The Government of Wales Act 1998 introduced a form of 'executive devolution' that left considerable authority in the hands of the Secretary of State for Wales of the British government and conferred only secondary legislative powers on the Assembly. The legislative powers could be exercised only with the prior approval of a legislative competence order passed by Westminster. The Act did not grant any fiscal powers and did not adopt the reserved powers model.

The Cardiff Assembly, which comprises 60 AMs elected by a mixed system, was conceived as a corporate body responsible for legislative and executive functions. The government and Assembly were intended to operate as a unified entity within this body. Following the 1999 election, a Labour-Liberal Democrat coalition government was formed. The complex structure of the government and its associated difficulties prompted Blair to introduce a clearer distinction between the institutions shortly afterwards. Thanks to the Richard Commission report, Westminster passed the Government of Wales Act 2006, providing for a clearer separation of powers between the Welsh legislature (the National Assembly for Wales) and the executive (the Welsh Assembly Government) (Trench 2008; McEldowney 2013). The Government of Wales Act 2006 did not immediately grant primary legislative powers upon the Assembly; instead, it defined a complex system of 'step-by-step' empowerment to raise awareness of the topic among the population, culminating in the approval referendum on 3 March 2011. The Assembly gained legislative powers only after the referendum (Gibson-Morgan 2014). The first phase of devolution thus served as a kind of 'apprenticeship', enabling the Assembly to establish its identity and begin exercising its legislative powers effectively (Melding 2012). However, the Government of Wales Act 2006 did not change the distribution of powers, which remained based on the conferred powers model until 2017.

The situation in Northern Ireland is more complex and is explored in depth in this volume, in the paper by Emanuele Gabriele. A particular model of devolution based on the content of the Good Friday Agreement was envisaged for Northern

Ireland, including the possibility of holding a referendum to decide whether to remain part of the United Kingdom. Institutions inspired by the consociational democracy model were required, providing for the election of a diarchy consisting of a First Minister and Deputy First Minister with similar powers, as well as a complex Assembly voting system to ensure consensus among the two communities. The Assembly originally consisted of 108 deputies elected by Single Transferable Vote, who were reduced to 90 in 2016. Compared to Scotland, the Stormont Assembly was endowed with limited powers. Moreover, the most controversial matters were not devolved immediately, but only from 2010 onwards, following the Hillsborough Agreement between the DUP and Sinn Féin. After the 1999 elections, the Northern Ireland institutions only functioned for a few years due to ongoing conflicts between the two communities, which resulted in their suspension by Westminster in October 2002. This suspension lasted until 2007, when the Northern Ireland institutions resumed functioning following the St Andrew's Agreement of 2006.

To highlight the asymmetrical nature of the territorial distribution of powers, the reconstruction of the essential features of the first phase of devolution must include England. The territorial heterogeneity, the absence of a tradition of regional governance and the lack of a distinct English nationalist identity led the Blair government to exclude solutions for England comparable to those implemented in the devolved nations. Instead, the government envisaged a strengthening of the local government system and a gradual introduction of regional-level structures, which had never been part of England's long-standing tradition of self-government. Consequently, Parliament passed the Regional Development Agencies Act 1998 and made provisions for the establishment of elected regional Assemblies in those English regions that explicitly requested them and approved them through a referendum (Smith and Wistrich 2010; Ayres et al. 2018). However, the proposal was never implemented: the first and only region to hold such a referendum, the North East, overwhelmingly rejected it in November 2004, with 78% voting against. As a result, the other planned referendums were cancelled. Subsequent attempts by Labour governments to reform English regionalism and address territorial asymmetry were ultimately reversed in 2011 by the newly formed coalition government (Pearce and Ayres 2009).

4 The Second Phase 2010–2017: Between Two Referendums

The second phase of devolution was characterised by two referendums: the Scottish independence referendum in 2014 and the Brexit referendum in 2016. Rosa Iannaccone's paper in this volume covers the independence referendum. Two key aspects warrant emphasis: first, the independence referendum, considered as a 'once-in-a-generation opportunity', allowed the territorial nature of the United Kingdom to be definitively considered as a 'voluntary union', in which the devolved administrations are fundamental and permanent components. Second, following the granting of greater powers to Scotland after the 'No' vote, an original—even if temporary—solution was found to the English Question. Furthermore, Wales saw the recognition of greater powers, including in fiscal matters, thanks to the recommendations of the Holtham Commission and the Silk Commission. These recommendations were incorporated into the Wales Act 2014 and the Wales Act 2017, which introduced the reserved powers model, among other things.

It should be noted that the recommendations of the Smith Commission, set up in the aftermath of the referendum, led the Westminster Parliament to pass the Scotland Act 2016, which, together with the Wales Act 2017, introduced particular constitutional novelties. The Acts have granted enhanced powers to the devolved institutions, and have recognised the existence of the legislative consent convention, while designating the devolved institutions as 'permanent'. This designation entails that their abolition by Westminster would require a preceding referendum. These provisions are primarily symbolic in nature and must be interpreted in the light of the principle of parliamentary sovereignty. The formal entrenchment of the permanence of the institutions represents a political undertaking that cannot be regarded as legally binding upon Westminster in perpetuity, nor as imposing any limitation on its sovereign authority. The permanence of the Scottish and the Welsh Parliaments can only have 'a political claim rather than a legal one' (Himsworth 2016). The devolved institutions were recognised as permanent, only in the sense that they are regarded as such by Westminster. This recognition did not take away Westminster's power to abolish them, although such a decision is politically unlikely (Tierney 2019). The permanence of the institutions established in the Scotland Act 2016 and in the Wales Act 2017 is eminently political in nature, and the British Parliament could still repeal the Acts, removing the requirement for a referendum. However, through the approval of these Acts, Westminster assumed a form of moral obligation to respect the will of the people, as expressed in a referendum (White 2020).

Questions were raised about the consequences of translating the legislative consent convention into law, and whether parliamentary recognition of the existence of a convention could change the nature of that convention. The Supreme Court clarified these doubts with the Miller case of 24 January 2017 and specified how the courts should interpret the introduction of the legislative consent convention into the 2016 and 2017 Acts (Keating 2021). The Court ruled that the convention is merely a 'statement of political intent [that does] not create legal obligations. So the only purpose of recognising the convention in statutory form was to give it greater political weight, as a convention' (Murkens 2017). According to the ruling, therefore, the Acts merely introduced 'legislative recognition' of a 'political convention': a recognition of purely political and symbolic value by which Westminster also wished to highlight the 'co-operative relationships between the UK Parliament and the devolved institutions, where there were overlapping legislative competences' (Tierney 2019). The inclusion of the legislative consent convention in the devolution Acts did not give the Courts the right to intervene in the event of a hypothetical breach of the convention, because the latter's application and operation 'does not lie within the constitutional remit of the judiciary'.

During this phase, it became evident that devolution constitutes an essential component of the United Kingdom's territorial and constitutional structure. It also emerged that the core principle of the British constitution—the sovereignty of the

King in Parliament—may admit certain forms of self-limitation, such as the requirement of a referendum for the abolition of devolved institutions. Nonetheless, the legislative supremacy of Westminster remains unaffected by the will of the devolved legislatures. Potential conflicts between the different levels of government must be resolved both through political channels, by means of intergovernmental cooperation mechanisms, and through judicial adjudication by the UK Supreme Court.

To complete the analysis of this second phase, it is important to note that Northern Ireland experienced a relative period of institutional stability, with fewer interruptions compared to the other two phases. However, tensions between the two main communities persisted, particularly on symbolic and identity-related issues, many of which are rooted in the complex legacy of the Troubles. A significant setback occurred in January 2017, in the aftermath of the Brexit referendum, with the collapse of the Foster government following the resignation of Deputy First Minister Martin McGuinness. The subsequent elections in March 2017 marked the beginning of a new and protracted period of deadlock in Northern Ireland's devolution process.

Finally, the referendum for Scottish independence also had effects for England, since in the aftermath of the consultation, David Cameron tied the granting of more powers to Scotland to the resolution of the long-standing 'English Question' and the anomaly under which the MPs elected to Westminster from Scottish, Welsh, and Northern Irish constituencies still had the right to vote on matters relating exclusively to England. In October 2015, the House of Commons passed an amendment to its standing orders introducing a significant change to the way government bills that affected only England were passed in the Commons. According to the 'English Votes for English Laws' (EVEL) procedure, during the second reading of a bill in the House of Commons, if the text concerned England alone (or England and Wales), a committee comprising only MPs elected in English (or Welsh) constituencies was involved. The final decision about the bill, however, was made by the entire Chamber. The reform has not altered the internal balance of the Commons in any way, since the majority in the House has always coincided with the majority in English constituencies, and it was repealed in 2021.

5 The Third Phase 2017: Brexit and the New Challenges for Devolution

The third phase of devolution is defined by the repercussions of the Brexit referendum. The repatriation of competences from Brussels to London affected numerous devolved matters and inevitably prompted a redefinition of centre-periphery relations, particularly due to the absence of the European Union's harmonising role in the implementation of EU policies. Successive Conservative governments adopted a neo-unionist stance and sought to strengthen the powers of the central government. Consequently, the devolved administrations perceived the post-Brexit measures introduced by the government as a power grab undermining the democratic authority of devolved institutions and as an assault on devolution.

These dynamics unfolded in parallel with Supreme Court rulings reaffirming the principle of Westminster sovereignty and its authority to override devolved legislation, especially in cases of legislative conflict. The Supreme Court further clarified that the powers of the devolved legislatures are both limited and conditional, and that the legislative consent convention constitutes a political understanding rather than a legally enforceable obligation.[1] It is worth noting that, in November 2022, the UK Supreme Court delivered a unanimous judgment on a Reference by the Lord Advocate on devolution issues under paragraph 34 of Schedule 6 to the Scotland Act 1998 concerning whether a referendum on Scottish independence is within the legislative competence of the Scottish Parliament. The Court concluded that the Scottish Parliament could not legislate for a referendum on the question of whether Scotland should become an independent country. Even though the referendum would have been advisory, without any legal effect on the Union, it would have had important political consequences. The reference judgment confirmed that the 2014 procedure was the only legitimate way to hold the referendum.

It is worth emphasising that while the repatriation of competences strengthened the central government and Brexit fuelled pro-independence sentiments, particularly in Scotland and Northern Ireland, the withdrawal from the European Union coincided with the management of the pandemic, whose handling, by contrast, enhanced territorial autonomy. Health is one of the devolved policy areas, which allowed the devolved executives to operate alongside the UK national government four. The 'four nations approach' to managing the emergency constituted an unprecedented opportunity to experiment with a 'quasi-federal' model of state action, facilitating internal comparison of both the effectiveness of the measures adopted by individual governments and the varying degrees of parliamentary involvement in decisions with direct and substantial effects on citizens' lives (Higgins 2023; Torrance 2024a; Torrance 2024b).

As we previously stated, in Scotland, the referendum on leaving the European Union rekindled independence sentiments and plans for a new referendum. However, the British government always rejected the idea of a new referendum, and the Supreme Court's reference judgment ruled out the possibility of an autonomous initiative by Scotland. It is worth noting that independence feelings have mutated significantly in recent years: signs of a deep crisis in the Scottish National Party include financial scandals within the party, Sturgeon's resignation in February 2023, the resignation of her successor Humza Yousaf in 2024, his replacement by John Swinney, and the heavy loss of seats in the 2024 Westminster elections. However, at the May 2026 Scottish Parliament election, the SNP remained the largest party despite a loss of six seats, and formed a new government.

The effects of Brexit have been particularly severe in Northern Ireland, where the fragile equilibrium between communities established by the Good Friday Agreement rested in part on the fact that both the United Kingdom and the Republic of Ireland

[1] Miller & Anor, R (on the application of) v Secretary of State for Exiting the European Union (Rev 3) [2017] UKSC 5; Reference by the Attorney General and the Advocate General for Scotland - UK Supreme Court, [2018] UKSC 64.

were member states of the European Union, thereby removing the need for a physical border (Saputelli 2020; Doyle et al. 2021). In this third phase, Northern Ireland institutions remained suspended from 2017 to 2020 and again from 2022 to 2024, in part due to tensions stemming from the United Kingdom's decision to leave both the Single Market and the Customs Union, the unionist opposition to the customs border in the Irish Sea, and the nationalist resistance to the reintroduction of a border within the island. The Northern Ireland Protocol, agreed by Boris Johnson in October 2019 as part of the Withdrawal Agreement, enabled the removal of the backstop included in Theresa May's deal and granted Northern Ireland a unique status: it remained part of the UK's customs territory while simultaneously being subject to the EU Customs Code and Single Market regulations for goods. In accordance with the Good Friday Agreement, which prohibits the establishment of a hard border within the island of Ireland, the Protocol stipulated that goods arriving from Great Britain into Northern Ireland ports would be subject to complex customs procedures. The Northern Ireland Protocol has been strongly opposed by unionist communities and has been challenged by unionist politicians who say it breaches the Act of Union, which guarantees parity between the citizens of Northern Ireland and those of Great Britain, and the Northern Ireland Act, which stipulates that any change to the constitutional status of Northern Ireland must be subject to a referendum. The Supreme Court unanimously rejected their appeal on all grounds in February 2023.[2] In February 2023, the Windsor Framework eased trade between Great Britain and Northern Ireland, safeguarding Northern Ireland's place in the UK and addressing democratic concerns related to EU law application in the region. Furthermore, the Windsor Framework introduced the Stormont Brake mechanism, which allows for a request to disapply specific pieces of EU legislation in cases where it can be demonstrated that such rules would have a significantly negative and lasting impact (Douglas-Scott 2023). Following the May 2022 elections, Sinn Féin emerged as the largest party for the first time, and a new executive was formed only in February 2024.

In Wales, even in the absence of independence aspirations comparable to those in Scotland, the devolution process appears to have been consolidated during this third phase, due to the acquisition of enhanced powers and competences, as well as a strengthened sense of identity and institutional awareness. This awareness was expressed in 2020 through the renaming of the National Assembly as the Welsh Parliament/Senedd Cymru, a change that reflected its expanded powers and its status as a national legislature. The decision followed a public consultation intended to improve citizens' understanding of the Welsh Parliament's role and its newly conferred powers. In 2024, the Senedd increased its membership from 60 to 96, pursuant to the Co-operation Agreement between Welsh Labour and Plaid Cymru. This expansion was deemed essential in light of the Chamber's broadened legislative responsibilities. In the 2026 Senedd Cymru election the Plaid Cymru emerged as

[2] In the matter of an application by James Hugh Allister and others for Judicial Review (Appellants) (Northern Ireland) In the matter of an application by Clifford Peeples for Judicial Review (Appellant) (Northern Ireland).

the largest party, followed by Reform UK Wales. This was the first election since Welsh devolution in which the Labour Party failed to win the largest number of seats

Finally, in England, the abolition of the EVEL procedure in July 2021 was due not only to the substantial ineffectiveness of such a complex mechanism for the legislative process, but also to the fact that, in Johnson's neo-centrist vision, Brexit had strengthened the Union, whereas EVEL could have undermined the role of Parliament as the Union Parliament. Following the failure of the EVEL mechanism, both successive Conservative governments and the current Labour government have shifted their focus towards strengthening local governance. In December 2024, the Starmer government presented a white paper on English devolution, proposing what has been described as 'the biggest transfer of power out of Westminster this century'. This ambitious reform aims to extend devolution across the entirety of England, thereby addressing the current gaps represented by 'devolution deserts', the areas in which devolution is entirely absent, and tackling the deeply rooted issue of regional economic inequality by fostering growth in the most disadvantaged areas. In April 2026, Westminster enacted the English Devolution and Community Empowerment Act 2026, introducing a major reform of English local government.

6 Conclusions: The Legislative Consent Convention as a Mechanism for Structuring the Evolving Balance of Devolution

During the third phase of devolution, the operation of the legislative consent convention has exposed both internal tensions within the United Kingdom and structural weaknesses inherent in the devolution framework. It has likewise prompted consideration of whether reforming this mechanism might strengthen the effectiveness and coherence of the devolved settlement. Since 1999, legislative consent motions have been sought in relation to more than 220 Acts passed by the Westminster Parliament. In approximately 30 cases, consent was withheld by one or more of the devolved legislatures.

This figure must be understood within the broader historical and political context we described above. In the first phase of devolution, no significant frictions emerged, primarily because, until 2007, the governing majority in Scotland aligned with the party in power at Westminster. In Wales, the Assembly lacked primary legislative powers, while in Northern Ireland, devolved institutions operated intermittently and exercised limited authority. Even during the second phase, the devolved legislatures generally granted consent to Westminster legislation affecting devolved matters without substantial conflict.

The UK Supreme Court's decision in Miller marked a transition to the third phase of devolution, clarifying that the legislative consent convention, even when included in statutory form, remains a political convention and is not legally enforceable. It is primarily in this third phase that the limitations of the convention have become apparent, particularly in response to the introduction of highly contentious Brexit-related legislation during the 2017–2019 parliamentary session. The convention has come under sustained criticism due to Westminster's repeated unilateral interventions in devolved areas. While in a limited number of cases the UK government accommodated the concerns raised by devolved administrations, in most instances it proceeded notwithstanding explicit and vigorous opposition from the devolved legislatures. This pattern of behaviour has underscored the merely conventional—rather than legally binding—nature of the legislative consent convention and has reaffirmed the doctrine of parliamentary sovereignty centred in Westminster.

It is worth noting that the most relevant Acts relating to Brexit were passed without the support of the devolved nations. For example, the EU Withdrawal Act 2018 was initially opposed by Scotland and Wales (at that time, the Northern Ireland Assembly was suspended); Wales subsequently gave its consent. The European Union Withdrawal Agreement Act 2020 was passed without the consent of any of the three devolved legislatures. The battle over the passage of the Internal Market Act 2020[3] was particularly heated, with the three devolved Assemblies opposing it. The Subsidy Control Act 2022 received opposition from the devolved institutions during the legislative consent process. Thus, during this third period, it was confirmed that the opposing votes of the Scottish, Welsh and Northern Ireland Assemblies could not limit the exercise of sovereignty by Westminster, whose formal power has remained unchanged.[4]

In a constitutional context where the boundary between law and politics is often blurred, it is noteworthy that the codification of the legislative consent convention has, at the very least, amplified the political salience of conflict when divergences arise between Westminster and the devolved legislatures (Ewing 2017; Perry and Tucker 2018). The constitutional tensions witnessed in recent years, along with the

---

[3] The complexity of intergovernmental relations is exemplified by the contentious UK Internal Market Act 2020. In order to prevent the emergence of barriers between the nations of the United Kingdom and the resulting distortions to the market, the Act regulates the internal market on the basis of two Market Access Principles. The devolved nations criticised the legislation, expressing concern that it would impose uniform standards on food products, goods, and services, thereby constraining their decision-making autonomy and limiting the ability of devolved legislatures to establish their own regulatory frameworks. Indeed, the Act precludes devolved institutions from applying devolved policies to incoming goods and services. In practice, the legislation has, for example, prevented Scotland from implementing a glass recycling scheme and Scotland and Wales from legislating to restrict single-use plastics ahead of the UK Government's timetable for England, due to discrepancies with UK-wide standards. While the position of the central government remains predominant, it must nonetheless be acknowledged that the 2020 Act has incentivised administrations to cooperate in identifying and adopting common standards for the entire United Kingdom. In early 2025, the Starmer government launched a public consultation aimed at informing reflection on the management of intergovernmental relations and the prospective revision of the 2020 Act (Dougan et al. 2022; Horsley et al. 2024; Horsley 2025).

[4] Furthermore, in December 2022, the British government invoked for the first time Section 35 of the Scotland Act 1998 to prevent the Gender Recognition Reform (Scotland) Bill from receiving royal assent. The government believed that the bill would create contradictions between the nations of the Kingdom.

increasing need for renewed mechanisms of collaboration and contestation within the United Kingdom, suggest that the future of the territorial union depends significantly on reforming the principle of legislative consent, a cornerstone of the devolution settlement. Passing legislation at Westminster without the consent of Scotland, Wales, or Northern Ireland risks destabilising the devolution framework and, more broadly, undermining the integrity of the Union itself. Thus, it has become necessary to enhance the status of the legislative consent convention by placing greater constraints on Westminster's ability to legislate unilaterally in devolved areas. Several proposals have emerged in both political and academic discourse. Some have advocated that it should be deemed procedurally improper to introduce legislation requiring devolved consent unless the responsible Whitehall department has first engaged in meaningful consultation with the relevant devolved government on the draft bill. Others have proposed the establishment of an internal mechanism within Westminster whereby, in cases of contested consent, the matter would be referred to a dedicated parliamentary committee tasked with scrutinising the government's approach and reporting its findings prior to full parliamentary debate. Further suggestions include making consultation with devolved administrations a mandatory requirement, subject to a standardised minimum period, rather than merely an advisory practice. It is worth noting that these are all interesting proposals, albeit of a purely political or conventional nature, which could be reconciled with the principle of parliamentary sovereignty only insofar as they retain their conventional status.

In order to strengthen political forms of interaction between levels of government, the centre-periphery dynamics and intergovernmental relations have been reconsidered in the post-Brexit context: the Joint Ministerial Committee—a consultative body of limited effectiveness—was replaced in 2022 by a new intergovernmental framework. This is structured as a three-tier model, headed by the Prime Minister and the Heads of Devolved Governments Council, and based on Interministerial Standing Committees, which meet bi-monthly to oversee cross-cutting issues across governments. These committees provide a forum for regular engagement between ministers from the four administrations and facilitate dialogue on bills under consideration at Westminster that are of relevance to the devolved nations. In addition, Interministerial Groups (IMGs) focused on specific policy areas have been established, with chairing responsibilities rotated among the governments (Select Committee on the Constitution 2024).

More than 25 years after the first elections to the devolved legislatures—and following the three phases of devolution outlined above—it now appears necessary to embark upon a fourth phase, marked by coordinated reforms, a revision of the legislative consent convention, and a strengthening of intergovernmental relations. The consolidation and enhancement of the devolution framework will require sustained commitment to constructive engagement and the cultivation of 'goodwill' as a guiding principle in intergovernmental relations, fostering early dialogue and the development of shared understandings.

References

Ayres S, Flinders M, Sandford M (2018) Territory, power and statecraft: understanding English devolution. Region Stud, 853–864
Bogdanor V (1999a) Devolution in the United Kingdom. Oxford University Press, Oxford
Bogdanor V (1999b) Devolution: decentralisation or disintegration? Polit Quart, 185–194
Bromley C (2006) Has devolution delivered? Edinburgh University Press, Edinburgh
Cairney P (2011) The Scottish political system since devolution: from new politics to the New Scottish Government. Imprint Academic, Exeter
Caravale G (2017) Family of Nations. Asimmetrie territoriali nel Regno Unito tra devolution e Brexit. Jovene, Napoli
Dalyell T (2000) Devolution: the end of Britain. In: Sutherland K, Beloff M (eds) The rape of the constitution? Imprint Academic, Thorventon
Dougan M, Hunt J, McEwen N, McHarg A (2022) Sleeping with an elephant: devolution and the United Kingdom Internal Market Act 2020. Law Quart Rev, 650–676
Douglas-Scott S (2023) Brexit, Union, and disunion. Cambridge University Press, Cambridge
Doyle O, McHarg A, Murkens JE (eds) (2021) The Brexit challenge for Ireland and the United Kingdom: constitutions under pressure. Cambridge University Press, Cambridge
Ewing K (2017) Brexit and parliamentary sovereignty. Mod Law Rev, 711–726
Gibson-Morgan E (2014) The United Kingdom Supreme Court and devolution issues: towards constitutional review? Miroirs: Revue des civilisations anglophone, ibérique et ibéro-américaine, 84–111
Gordon M (2015) Parliamentary sovereignty in the UK constitution. Hart, Oxford
Hazell R, Rawlings R (2005) Devolution, law making and the constitution. Imprint Academic, Exeter
Higgins J (2023) Scottish devolution, deconstruction, and change. J Intersect, 45–48
Himsworth C (2016) Legislating for permanence and a statutory footing. Edinburgh Law Rev, 361–367
Horsley T (2025) Reforming the UK internal market: the UK Government's response to the review of the United Kingdom Internal Market Act 2020. U.K. Const Law Blog
Horsley T, Swan CB, McEwen N, Whitten LC (2024) Westminster rules: the United Kingdom internal market act and devolution. U.K. Const Law Blog
Jeffrey C (2013) Devolution in the United Kingdom. In: Loughlin J, Kincaid J, Swenden W (eds) Routledge handbook of regionalism & federalism. Routledge, New York, pp 317–330
Keating M (2001) So many nations so few states: territory and nationalism in the global era. In: Gagnon AG, Tully J (eds) Multinational democracies. Cambridge University Press, Cambridge, pp 39–64
Keating M (2009) The independence of Scotland: self-government and the shifting politics of Union. Oxford University Press, Oxford
Keating M (2021) State and nation in the United Kingdom. The fractured Union. Oxford University Press, Oxford
McEldowney J (2013) The impact of devolution on the UK parliament. In: Horne A, Drewry G, Oliver D (eds) Parliament and the law, Hart, pp 197–220
Melding D (2012) Issues on Welsh devolution. Statute Law Rev, 97–102
Mitchell J (2000) Territorial politics and change in Britain. In: Catterall P, Kaiser W, Walton-Jordan U (eds) Reforming the constitution: debates in twentieth-century Britain. Frank Cass, London, pp 225–249
Mitchell J (2009) Devolution in the UK. Manchester University Press, Manchester
Murkens J (2017) Mixed messages in bottles: the European Union, devolution, and the future of the constitution. Mod Law Rev, 685–696
Pearce G, Ayres S (2009) Governance in the English regions: the role of the regional development agencies. Urban Studies, 535–557
Perry A, Tucker A (2018) Top-down constitutional conventions. Mod Law Rev, 765–789

Rokkan S, Urwin DW (1982) Introduction: centres and peripheries in Western Europe. In: Rokkan S, Urwin DW (eds) The politics of territorial identity: studies in European regionalism. Sage, London, pp 1–17
Saputelli G (2020) Brexit e devolution nel Regno Unito: quando è lo Stato (e non l'UE) a mostrare i suoi limiti. DPCE online, 4, 4707–4734
Schwartz A (2022) The changing concepts of the constitution. Oxford J Legal Stud 758–786
Select Committee on the Constitution (2024) The Governance of the Union: Consultation, Co-operation and Legislative Consent. 1st Report of Session 2024-25, HL Paper 13
Smith DM, Wistrich E (2010) Regional Government in England: democratic governance and Central Government Direction. Regional Studies Association, Annual International Conference, 4
Tierney S (2004) Constitutional law and national pluralism. Oxford University Press, Oxford
Tierney S (2012) Quiet devolution: sub-state autonomy and the gradual reconstitution of the United Kingdom. In: Burgess M, Tarr GA (eds) Constitutional dynamics in federal systems. Sub-national perspectives, Forum of Federations & McGill-Queen's University Press, Montreal, p 197
Tierney S (2019) The territorial constitution and the Brexit process. Curr Leg Probl, 59–83
Tirapu-Sanuy JM (2025) Devolution, national pluralism and the role of the UK Supreme Court. Oxford J Legal Stud, 1–29
Torrance D (2024a) Devolution in Scotland: "The settled will"?. House of Commons Library, Research Briefing
Torrance D (2024b) Introduction to devolution in the United Kingdom. House of Commons Library. Research Briefing
Trench A (2008) Scotland and Wales: the evolution of devolution. In: Hazell R (ed) Constitutional futures revised. Britain's Constitution to 2020. Palgrave Macmillan, London, pp 29–55
Walker N (2000) Beyond the unitary conception of the United Kingdom constitution? Public Law, 384–404
White SG (2020) The referendum in the UK's constitution: from parliamentary to popular sovereignty? Parliam Aff, 263–280

The Parable of Scottish Independence

Rosa Iannaccone

Abstract The purpose of this contribution is to analyse, within the framework of a peculiar British regionalism and also a peculiar Scottish constitutionalism, the most recent evolution of the independence issue and of the party that has made it its main cause, the Scottish National Party, whose fortunes are closely linked to it. The apex of this parabola was the 2014 independence referendum, to which this chapter devotes particular attention, given the considerable interest, in the comparative landscape, in some of the connotations that allow it to be considered, from a technical point of view, the 'most successful' independence referendum.

1 Some Notes on the Independence Issue: From Its Origins to the Scottish National Party (SNP)

The referendum on the independence of Scotland from the United Kingdom is part of a recent wave of new independence movements in states with a well-established democratic states (Frosina 2017a, pp. 1–2), as – in addition to the case mentioned – has also occurred in Canada and Spain. These movements have led to the holding of secessionist referendums (Auer 2007; De Caria 2014; Volpi 2016; Montilla Martos 2016; Frosina 2024), held sometimes in accordance with the existing legal framework, sometimes in defiance of it. This is not a new phenomenon; in fact, secession referendums have been conducted in a variety of legal and geopolitical contexts. The referendum, which at the European level represents one of the most institutionalised and widely used mechanisms of participatory democracy, has assumed a central role precisely in independence dynamics, particularly in the United Kingdom and Spain. This relevance has also extended at the level of relations with the European Union, as demonstrated by the British referendum on Brexit.

In a study on asymmetry and secession in Scotland, possible lines of inquiry include the study of the issue of devolution and the question of independence. These

R. Iannaccone (✉)
University of Sassari, Sassari, Italy
e-mail: riannaccone1@uniss.it

F. Savastano et al. (eds.), *Between Asymmetry and Secession*,
https://doi.org/10.1007/978-3-032-29603-0_10

two aspects are closely interconnected, two sides of the same coin: in fact, a progressive expansion of the competences devolved to the Scottish bodies—in particular on the occasion of the legislative interventions of 2012 and 2016—has been followed by a strengthening of independence sentiment, in a stringent cause-and-effect relationship, which, however, seems to have recently weakened. The subject of this contribution will be the second of these profiles, since, from a technical and legal perspective, the consultation on Scottish independence can be considered the most structured and 'successful' example of an independence referendum in Europe. The present work, however, does not seek to examine, directly, the theme of secession, nor its interaction with internal or international law, but will concentrate on the analysis of the Scottish case, also formulating, in the concluding considerations, some comparative reflections in consideration of the peculiar 'parabola' of the so-called 'Scottish Question', the historical roots of which are intertwined, in the most recent phase, with the political and institutional events of a political party: the Scottish National Party (SNP).

The origin of the 'Scottish Question' can be traced back to the Act of Union of 1707, which was the result of long negotiations and determined by a number of competing factors. Among these, of particular importance was the failure of the Scottish project to settle in Panama, which had serious economic repercussions, leading to a deep financial crisis (Flamini 2013). Frome the English perspective, on the other hand, the Union mainly responded to strategic and military considerations, related to the need for defence against invasion by Louis XIV's French troops. The Anglo-Scottish Joint Commission, appointed by the Crown and charged with drafting the articles of the Act of Union to be submitted to their respective Parliaments for ratification, abandoned the initial hypothesis of concluding a treaty, believing that this solution would not resolve the incompatibility arising from the coexistence of two distinct legislative bodies, and therefore proceeded to draft a unification formula, which was approved by an absolute majority of both Parliaments.

It is worth noting that no popular consultation by referendum was envisaged, and that the two legislatures were not an expression of democratic representation, being predominantly composed of large landowners. The Union was therefore established in a context characterised by widespread feelings of suspicion and resentment: during the drafting phase of the Act, there were numerous protests, particularly in Edinburgh and Glasgow, linked to the fear of an increase in the taxation on essential goods in an already economically fragile area. There were numerous proposals for its abolition from the outset, including the motion tabled as early as 1713 in the House of Lords and rejected by only 4 votes against (Martino 2015, pp. 409–510). Added to this were the insurrectionary attempts promoted by the Jacobites, supporters of the 'Young Pretender', the Catholic son of James II, who had been forced to abdicate following the Glorious Revolution of 1688, which had led to the establishment of a Protestant monarchy under the Hanover dynasty. The Jacobites attempted to subvert the Union through two armed revolts in 1715 and 1745, both of which failed.

The abolition of the Scottish Parliament was accompanied by a severely limited representation in Westminster, with only 45 seats in the House of Commons and fourteen Scottish lords admitted to the Upper House.[1] Following the Union, the Scots were subject to the English tax regime, while retaining their own legal system, ecclesiastical institutions and university system (Flamini 2013, p. 61).

Indeed, Scotland has retained a legal system characterised by continuity between the pre-unification Scottish institutions and the post-1707 institutional set-up. This continuity has, on the one hand, fuelled a persistent sense of national identity (Martino 2015, p. 407), resulting in the definition of a 'nationalist' sentiment, and on the other, motivated the prominent role played by Scotland among the sub-state areas of the United Kingdom, making it the focus of devolution. Within the complex framework of the devolutionary settlement of the United Kingdom, the peculiar institutional configuration of Scotland – which some scholars closest to nationalist positions has defined as an entirely *sui generis* political system, endowed with a coherent and separate system of government from what is commonly known about the 'English' constitutional form of the United Kingdom – has given this area a privileged role in the origin of the devolution process. This was in stark contrast to the Welsh context, historically marked by full political-institutional and legal integration with England, where the distinctive features of national identity was expressed mainly through folklore and language, and to the Northern Irish context, compromised by a conflict that produced a permanent constitutional crisis (Torre 2013, pp. 139–40).

The Scottish devolution (Bogdanor 1999; Torre 2007, 2010; Del Conte 2011; Poggeschi 2016; Guastaferro 2019, 2020), among its various peculiarities, is characterised by a close ideological and political interrelationship between autonomist and secessionist demands. These two options are not considered antithetical but rather seen as complementary expressions of the same identity tension, ready to prevail one over the other depending on the political context, the overall social context, and the different historical phases experienced by the Scottish people. Although devolution has been formally incorporated into the constitutional order of the United Kingdom, and Scotland represents the main testing ground of this model, with a Parliament invested with legislative powers also in fiscal matters, as expected, aspirations for full national independence have not diminished. This is also because, since the 1930s, these claims have been politically channelled by the Scottish National Party, a political party characterised by notable distinctive traits compared to other European nationalist movements, among which are inclusiveness and a marked pro-European orientation (Martinelli 2022, p. 210 ff.).

[1]According to Dicey, the Scottish Parliament had been subsumed and incorporated into the Westminster Parliament, which remained sovereign, as attested by the subsequent reform of some of the guarantees contained in the Union Acts (Dicey 1915, pp. 21–22).

2 The SNP and the Construction of Scottish Independence

The Scottish National Party, founded in 1934, has over time supported Scottish 'Home Rule', the recognition of Scotland as a dominion within the British Empire, as well as independence. The latter, since the 1980s, has declined in the formula 'independence in Europe', with the assumption that Scotland would retain its membership of the British Commonwealth and recognise the Queen as an unelected head of state. Traditionally, the SNP pursued the goal of gaining the most seats in the UK general election in order to legitimise, through this parliamentary mandate, the path to independence. However, this strategy underwent a significant evolution with the start of the devolution process and, starting in 1999, the party included in its election programmes a pledge to hold a referendum on independence through the Holyrood Parliament, formally established that same year (Lynch 2005, p. 504).

Two fundamental characteristics of the political dynamics of the twentieth century are relevant to understanding the ways in which the Scottish base has been activated to support autonomist demands. The first is represented by the evolution of an interventionist welfare state and the fact that important areas of public policy, with a direct impact on the daily lives of citizens resident in Scotland, were managed through Scottish local institutions, helping to consolidate the perception of Scotland as an entity with its own institutional specificity. The second major development can be traced back to the process of democratisation. Politics ceased to be a sphere reserved exclusively for the elite, gradually opening up to the participation of ever wider sections of the population. The interplay between the widening of democratic participation and the consolidation of the welfare state, within an institutional framework that recognised a marked Scottish dimension, constituted the prerequisite for the mobilisation of demands centred both on an increase in resources for Scotland, mainly through an expansion of public expenditure, and on greater autonomy in internal affairs.

Scottish nationalism did not emerge in the second half of the twentieth century, but rather evolved towards an unprecedented configuration, based on the demand for autonomy and greater control over resources, in parallel with the consolidation of the Scottish National Party. After remaining in a marginal position in the Scottish political landscape for some three decades, the SNP won its first seat in the House of Commons in a by-election in 1967 and has since gained a continuous presence in the Westminster Parliament, albeit with limited numerical representation.

The turning point for the SNP came in 1974, when it won 11 seats in Westminster with 30% of the Scottish vote, which led the then Labour government to propose the establishment of a devolved assembly (Dardanelli and Mitchell 2014, pp. 89–90). This was followed by a failed referendum on 2 March 1979, which rejected the Scotland Bill for failure to reach a structural quorum, despite the fact that 51.6% of voters had voted in favour. The Scottish nationalists supported a motion of no confidence in the Labour government and radicalised their demands for independence.

The beginning in 1979 of a Conservative government, led by Margaret Thatcher, traditionally opposed to the demands for self-government, did not stop the debate on Scottish autonomy, fuelled by the Labour Party, the majority political force in a context favourable to the establishment of a devolutionary order, flanked as a second political force by the SNP, advocating radical independence positions.

In this context, the Scottish Constitutional Convention, established in 1989 and composed of representatives of the political forces (except for the Scottish Conservative Party, which refused to participate, and the SNP, which later withdrew from the work), localities and civil society, successfully mediated between the two positions, the moderate and the radical, by proposing a devolved arrangement that would not be limited to formal recognition of Scottish autonomist demands, but which would ensure a more representative parliamentary system, encourage greater political participation and favour the expression of a specific identity. This proposal consisted of a departure from the Westminster model of parliamentary government through the introduction of a mixed electoral system and a devolution accompanied by instruments of direct democracy.

When the Labour Party won the 1997 general election, the devolution project was high on the new executive's political agenda: following the publication of two white papers in July of that year and the favourable outcome of the referendum on 11 September 1997, the Scotland Act 1998 was passed, establishing a unicameral Executive and Parliament for Scotland, elected on a proportional basis (the Additional Member System) and with residual primary legislative competence over the subjects listed as the exclusive competence of the London Parliament, without prejudice to Westminster's power to intervene in the devolved legislative competences by voting on a legislative 'sharing' motion, the so-called 'Sewel motion' (Martino 2015, p. 413 ff.).

The referendum of 11 September 1997 included a twofold question: the establishment of a Scottish Parliament and the legislative devolution of a number of matters. With a turnout of 60.3%, in which 74.3% were in favour of the establishment of the parliament and 63.5% in favour of devolution, the legal and institutional foundations were laid for the configuration of an asymmetrical regional state. On this referendum occasion, the Scottish National Party proposed the inclusion of a third question with secessionist content, but the proposal was not accepted by the then British Prime Minister, Tony Blair (Ruggiu 2016, p. 85).

The turning point in the evolution of the autonomy process can be traced back to the SNP's conquest of a parliamentary majority, with the consequent formation—against a Labour national government—of a minority executive, led by Alex Salmond, who in August 2007 launched a public consultation known as the National Conversation, on Scotland's constitutional future and formally identified the independence issue as a priority on the government agenda (Martino 2015, p. 415).

With only 47 seats out of 129, the SNP took over the leadership of the Scottish government for the first time and managed to complete the entire legislature, subsequently being rewarded by its electorate in the 2011 elections, in which it won an absolute majority of seats. This result, however, was not due to the independence issue but to the electorate's confidence in the party's record in government, which was considered more effective than its political opponents. The SNP's absolute majority did not, therefore, coincide with an equally large majority in favour of independence. Indeed, polls indicated that popular support for independence had remained almost stable: Scottish voters valued the independence party more than independence itself (Dardanelli and Mitchell 2014, p. 92). Nevertheless, the SNP began a lengthy negotiation with the government in London aimed at holding a referendum on independence.

3 The 2014 Independence Referendum

The referendum held in Scotland on 18 September 2014 (Milani 2013; Leyland 2014; Tomkins 2014; Frosini 2014; Mainardi 2014; Mullen 2014; Keating 2015; Tierney 2015; Marzulli 2016; McHarg et al. 2016), as anticipated, must be understood in the context of the devolution process that began in the United Kingdom at the end of the twentieth century, which has constitued one of the most significant innovations in British political-institutional life in recent decades (Caravale 2024a, p. 4). On account of its potential constitutional repercussions, this referendum—the culmination of a chain of popular consultations held in the territories affected by devolution—cannot be regarded as a marginal expression of the secessionist wave that has swept through numerous European democratic systems, or as a localist manifestation circumscribed to a peripheral area of a post-imperial United Kingdom, or, finally, as an isolated or accidental episode in the broader process of constitutional transformation initiated during the New Labour experience of government (Torre 2017, pp. 1–2).

The request to hold the referendum was formally made on 25 January 2012 by the Scottish First Minister, Alex Salmond, and was endorsed by the government led by David Cameron, who, while expressing his opposition to independence, recognised from the outset the right of the Scottish people to choose their own constitutional future. This openness on the part of London led to the signing of the Edinburgh Agreement in October 2012, under which all the preparatory and procedural stages leading to the holding of the referendum were articulated. The two executives, in fact, undertook to collaborate on the organisation of the referendum, reaching an agreement on some essential aspects related to its holding, as formalised by the Memorandum of Agreement. In addition, through an order in council, the Scottish Parliament was granted the power to call the referendum and to regulate some specific issues, including the date of the vote and the rules concerning the electorate (Frosina 2017b, pp. 15–16).

London could, therefore, have refused to authorise the transfer of one of its own competences, but it consented mainly for two reasons: it recognised, on the one hand, Scotland's right to self-determination and, on the other hand, the mandate given to the Scottish National Party following its electoral victory in the election in which it had presented the referendum as an integral part of its programme of government.

In the Edinburgh Agreement, it was stipulated that the referendum would concern a single question on independence: 'Should Scotland be independent?', thus resulting following recommendations made by the National Electoral Commission for Referendums, which had found that the previous proposal, containing the phrase 'Do you agree', could have steered the electorate towards an affirmative answer. In addition to changing the original wording, Alex Salmond also waived a second referendum question, concerning access to the highest degree of devolution ('devolution-max') through the extension of powers under the Scotland Act 1998. This option, originally conceived by the Scottish government in order to offer a broader range of solutions concerning Scotland's future constitutional arrangements, was subsequently re-proposed by unionist forces during the referendum campaign (Torre 2017, p. 4 ff). It was also decided that the referendum would be held according to the procedural rules of the Political Parties, Elections and Referendums Act 2000 (PPERA), the national legislation governing referendums in the United Kingdom, which ensures a number of procedural guarantees, including control by an independent Electoral Commission. In relation to this general regulatory framework, Scotland was nevertheless able to enact some detailed laws to define the procedure; to imit the electorate to Scottish residents aged 16 or over; and to set the date by which the consultation was to be held (Ruggiu 2016, pp. 83–84).

It should also be noted that, prior to the holding of the referendum and during the months of debate on the matter, the Westminster parliament had passed the Scotland Act 2012, tabled on 30 November 2010. This Act, implementing what had been suggested by the Calman Commission in 2009, extended the taxation powers granted to the Scottish Parliament from 2015, extended certain areas of devolution and redefined the competences of the UK Supreme Court with regard to devolution issues (Caravale 2017, p. 52).

The referendum took place on 18 September 2014. There was a particularly high turnout of 84.6% of eligible voters, of whom 55.3% voted No and 44.7% Yes. The majority of voters, therefore, voted to remain in the UK (Frosina 2017b, pp. 19–20). An in-depth analysis of the outcome of the referendum, which recorded a turnout of 85%, reveals a secessionist propensity among the economically better-off, particularly among men, and a greater unionist inclination among the older electorate; 80% of SNP supporters, 40% of Lib Dems, 31% of Labour supporters and only 2% of Conservatives declared that they supported independence. Out of 32 electoral constituencies, corresponding to Scottish local authorities, only 4 voted in favour of independence (Dundee, Glasgow, West Dunbartonshire, North Lanarkshire), while the highest percentages of votes against were registered in the areas closest and furthest from England (Martino 2015, p. 422).

4 The Call for a Second Chance

The referendum result led to the resignation of Alex Salmond, who was succeeded on 19 November 2014 by Nicola Sturgeon, simultaneously assuming the leadership of the party and the post of First Minister of Scotland. Despite the result, the 'Scottish Question' did not actually end there, and already in the aftermath of the vote, Prime Minister Cameron, as announced in the closing stages of the referendum campaign (Clegg 2014), had initiated a process of reform through the establishment of the Smith Commission, charged with drawing up a proposal on the further devolution of powers to the Assembly of Holyrood. This process was concluded with the final approval, in February 2016, of the Scotland Act 2016. The latter enshrined the permanent and irrevocable nature of the Scottish Parliament and Government and gave the legislature greater powers across a wide range of areas, including taxation, electoral and natural resource management, and also gave it the power to repeal the electoral provisions of the Scotland Act 1998. In addition, the measure formalised on a legislative level the recognition of the legislative consent motion[2] and the Barnett formula, which provides Scotland with particularly favourable fiscal and financial treatment (Frosina 2017b, pp. 19–20).

Further accelerating the independence issue was First Minister Sturgeon, when, during her second term in office, at the end of August 2022, she announced in a speech to the Parliament at Holyrood that a new referendum on independence, to be held in October 2023, would be called 'IndyRef.2'. Moreover, to overcome the opposition expressed by the British Executive, it instructed, on the same occasion, the Lord Advocate to refer the matter to the Supreme Court of the United Kingdom for a ruling on whether the referendum was a matter falling within the exclusive jurisdiction of the UK authorities, or whether it could fall within the unilateral prerogatives of the devolved bodies, in accordance with the constitutional provisions (Martinelli 2022, p. 209). In fact, although it was generally agreed that the question of independence could only be dealt with in a referendum 'once in a generation', the political scenario had radically changed—at least for the Scottish National Party—following the outcome of the Brexit referendum, in wich the 'Leave' campaign prevailed and, in particular, in the light of the fact that a large majority of the Scottish electorate (62%) had voted 'Remain', in stark contrast to the rest of the United Kingdom. It is worth pointing out that, at this juncture, the position taken by the Scottish government was not shared by the UK Government, which has always considered the request to hold a new referendum a few years after the previous one to be inadmissible.

According to the Scottish Government's argument before the Supreme Court, although the Scotland Act of 1998 exclusively reserved to the Westminster Parliament the power to regulate matters relating to 'the Union of the Kingdoms of Scotland and England', this reservation did not exclude the possibility for the Holyrood Parliament to hold a referendum whose character, as specified in the first article of the bill and in accordance with the constitutional practice of the United Kingdom, would be merely advisory. In this sense, the purpose of the draft legislation to hold the referendum would not have been independence as such but to ascertain the orientation of the Scottish people on this issue. However, the President of

[2] In the event that the Westminster Parliament decides to legislate on devolved matters, on matters of Scottish legislative competence and on matters of executive competence, it is necessary for the Scottish Government to table a 'motion for legislative approval' to be passed by the Holyrood Parliament.

the Court, Lord Reed, ruling on behalf of a unanimous Court, stated that the subject matter of the bill – which had not yet been introduced by the Scottish Government – fell within the scope of matters reserved for the exclusive competence of the British Parliament. Consequently, the Scottish Parliament could not have independently passed a bill in that area unless it had been expressly authorised by Westminster. The only legitimate procedure for calling any future popular consultation, therefore, remained the one followed in the 2014 referendum.

The Supreme Court also fully rejected the arguments presented by the Scottish National Party, both with regard to the restrictive interpretation of matters reserved to Westminster and, above all, with regard to the concept of self-determination of the Scottish people. In this regard, the reference to the leading judgment of the Canadian Supreme Court of 1988, cited by the SNP, was used by the British counterpart to affirm that, similarly to the situation in Quebec, the prerequisites of international law for a right to self-determination of the peoples do not exist for Scotland (Caravale 2022, p. ix ff. see Conti 2017; Martino 2023a; Martino 2023b). The judgment represented a significant setback in Scotland's pursuit of self-determination and, initially, triggered a wide-ranging internal debate within the Scottish National Party regarding the strategies, both political and legal, to be adopted in order to continue the path towards independence.

Furthermore, shortly after the Supreme Court's ruling in February 2023, Scotland's First Minister, Nicola Sturgeon, resigned for personal reasons, stating that she was doing so out of a sense of duty and because of the great love she felt for her party and her country. She was succeeded on 29 March 2023 by Humza Yousaf, whose term of office ended after just over a year. Yousaf had inherited from the previous First Minister the cooperation agreement with the Green Party that had provided for their participation in the government, but relations between the two parties had deteriorated in April 2024, following the SNP's renunciation of its commitment to reduce pollutant emissions by 75% by 2030, as well as the decision to stop administering puberty-suspension drugs to transgender children. In this context, two no-confidence motions were tabled, prompting the First Minister to resign before they could be voted on. Yousaf remained in office until 7 May, when he was succeeded by John Swinney, who was elected as the new party leader.

The SNP has been going through a particularly complex phase in recent years, determined as much by the objective obstacles to holding a new independence referendum as by the investigations into the party's financial management. The crisis of the nationalist party became evident during the general elections of 4 July 2024, even though Prime Minister John Swinney had opted to relegate the issue of independence to the margins of the electoral debate, aware of the fact that this issue was less popular than in the past and of the repercussions that the internal difficulties within the party could have had on the outcome of the vote. Previously, both Nicola Sturgeon and Humza Yousaf had argued that, in the absence of the possibility of holding a referendum on independence, the Westminster general election should be regarded as a *de facto* referendum, but the outcome of the consultation in the Scottish constituencies differed significantly from that of previous legislatures, causing the SNP to lose the position of third party in Westminster, which it had occupied since 2015. At the 2024 general election, the Labour Party gained 35% of the vote and 37 seats, compared to only 1 seat gained at the 2019 election, while the Scottish National Party fell from 48 to 9 seats, picking up 30% of the vote. The Liberal Democrats, with 9.7% of the vote, gained 6 seats, an increase of 4 compared to 2019; the Conservatives, with 12.5% of the vote, gained 5 seats, one less than in the previous election. Already in May, the Scottish First Minister had eliminated the post of Minister for Independence, established by his predecessor, thereby signalling his government's intention to focus on the immediate priorities of the Scottish people. The election result has, in this sense, provided the party with a further opportunity to reflect on the independence issue and, in view of the Scottish Parliament elections scheduled for 2026, an in-depth reflection on the party's identity and priorities, which has already been initiated by the SNP, has become necessary (Caravale 2024b, pp. 18–19).

5 A 'Successful' Referendum Beyond the Outcome: Comparative Reflections

Referendum practice in the United Kingdom[3] is rooted in a well-established tradition and represents one of the main innovations within the traditional Westminster model, as well as one of the most effective instruments of governance available to policymakers (Martinelli 2021, p. 762). For 25 years, the legislation governing the 1975 referendum on British membership of the EEC served as the general regulatory framework, to which the provisions contained in the specific laws instituting the numerous referendums were conformed. This role was subsequently assumed by the Political Parties, Elections and Referendums Act 2000 (PPERA). However, both laws limited themselves to regulating only certain procedural aspects of referendums, such as the powers attributed to the Electoral Commission, in particular the power to reformulate the referendum question to ensure its clarity and comprehensibility for the electorate, as well as the supervision of the incoming and outgoing financial flows relating to referendum campaigns. They do not affect Westminster's power to determinate whether, when and how a referendum is to be held, leaving the UK Parliament, acting in agreement with the Government, full discretion in determining the political and legal framework of each referendum (Martinelli 2019, pp. 14–15).

With regard to the issues that can be submitted to referendums, guidance on this issues was provided by a report of the Select Committee on the Constitution of the House of Lords ('Referendums in the United Kingdom', HL Paper 99, 12th Report of Session 2009–10, 17 March 2010, para 210) in which—although the report nevertheless expresses reservations about the routine use of referendums, because

[3] See *ex pluribus*, Dicey (1890); Qvortrup (2006); Torre and Frosini (2012); Leyland (2013); Parolari and Woelk (2015); Atkinson and Blick (2017); De Grazia (2019); Gordon (2020).

'there are significant drawbacks'—the Lords point out that 'if referendums are to be used, they are most appropriately used in relation to fundamental constitutional issues', listing among these the possible abolition of the Monarchy, the withdrawal from the European Union, the secession of one of the Nations, the abolition of the House of Lords, the reform of the electoral system for the House of Commons, the question of the pound sterling, as well as the possible adoption of a written constitution (Giannello 2022, p. 53).

In the Scottish context, this participatory instrument form part of a broader framework aimed at enhancing citizen participation. Indeed, as in other devolved systems, there are two closely related conceptual link: on the one hand, that between devolution and direct democracy, and on the other, that between devolution and mixed electoral systems. The wide range of devolution reforms has been accompanied by numerous referendums conceived as opportunities for public participation through which the electorates of individual areas have been called upon to express their views on the legal effectiveness of transfers of competences. In Scotland, furthermore, there are further mechanisms, non-electoral parliamentary mechanisms, aimed at strengthening the participatory component of parliamentary democracy. These include, for example, the widespread availability, since 1999, of television and online coverage of the activities of the Edinburgh Parliament, as well as the adoption of Standing Orders of the Scottish Parliament that have led to an organisational and functional structure of the assembly that is significantly different from the Westminster model, although without disowning its inspiring principles. In particular, a system of standing committees of a multi-functional role was established, with powers of both legislative initiative and scrutiny (although rarely exercised), control over the work of the executive and parliamentary inquiries. In addition, within the same parliament, there is the institution of popular petitioning, whose petitions are compulsorily referred to the Public Petitions Committee, whose meetings are entirely public and broadcast through the usual television and telematic channels. Lastly, the Scottish Executive, politically accountable to the legislature, makes extensive use of pre-legislative consultation, involving associations and other representatives of civil society (Torre 2013, p. 164 ff.).

The centrality played by the participatory element in the Scottish context is therefore evident. In this regard, it should be borne in mind that, following the negative outcome of the 1979 referendum, which did not lead to the establishment of a devolved Scottish Assembly, the Scottish Constitutional Convention was set up in 1989 to develop more detailed constitutional reform proposals. This body brought together Labour and Liberal Democrat MPs elected in Scottish constituencies, additional left-wing and environmentalist political formations, various trade union organisations, the Presbyterian Church, and various local government authorities. The publication of a series of documents and reports—among which the Towards Scotland's Parliament (1990) and Scotland's Parliament, Scotland's Right (1995) are worth mentioning—enabled the Convention to establish itself as a leading actor in constitutional reform. In this context, it elaborated a conception of devolution that would not merely imitate the Westminster parliamentary model but would promote a form of parliamentary government that was more accessible, more fairly representative and more responsive to the participatory demands of Scottish civil society (Torre 2013, p. 12).

In addition to these peculiarities of the Scottish system, it must be considered that the Scottish referendum experience is unlikely to be trasposed in the same form within constitutional systems founded on structural and cultural assumptions radically different from the British one (Martinelli 2022, p. 236). Despite this, the Scottish independence referendum and the legal framework that governed its conduct, guaranteeing a fully democratic consultation, may provide an example of good practice (Frosina 2017b, p. 20) that could also be drawn upon in different contexts.

The first relevant element in this perspective is the agreement between the parties involved and their shared commitment. The analysis of the political-institutional and legal process that led to the holding of the referendum clearly shows how the will of both actors involved was to give rise to a genuine democratic process, in which the people would make a decisive decision, through a highly structured and transparent procedure. The law adopted by the Parliament of Holyrood thus represented the culmination of a path of negotiation and a formal agreement between the governments of London and Edinburgh (Martinelli 2022, pp. 225–226).

The relevance of this element is also evident when comparing it with the 2016 referendum on Brexit,[4] with which the Scottish one shares the constitutional and cultural context, and with the Catalan independence consultations, with which it shares the secessionist purpose instead. With regard to the former, the laws instituting the referendum merely formalised the unilateral will of the Westminster Parliament to refer a decision of particular constitutional importance (Martinelli 2022, pp. 225–226) to the electoral body of the United Kingdom, in the absence of any prior agreement with the devolved governments. This distance was particularly evident in the fragmented interpretation of the outcome. The 'Leave' victory came with a majority of 51.89%, against a turnout of 72.21% (Savastano 2016), higher than that recorded in the 2015 general election (66.4%). However, the vote revealed deep territorial, generational and cultural rifts. Indeed, the referendum not only showed a polarisation between those in favour and against Europe, but also highlighted a clear divide between different geographical areas and social segments: London and the rest of England, Scotland and Northern Ireland on the one hand and England and Wales on the other, older generations and younger voters, affluent and less affluent groups (Martinelli 2019, p. 17).

With reference to the Catalan case, it is well known how the institutional conflict between the central and territorial levels has constituted a permanent, dramatic feature with no prospects for reconciliation. This dynamic emerges particularly clearly from a brief reconstruction of the salient phases of the affair. Following the failure of the negotiations on the adoption of the *Fiscal Pact*, the Catalan Parliament

---

[4] For a reconstruction of the assumptions of the referendum, the vote and its legal and political implications both domestically and in the EU framework, *ex multis*, see Gordon and Moffatt (2016); Caravita (2016); Curti Gialdino (2016); Palici di Suni (2016); Carboni (2016); Armstrong (2017); Mariani (2018); Martinico (2019); Savastano (2019); Martinelli (2017); Caravale (2019); Gordon (2020); Saputelli (2020); Fabbrini (2020); Baldini et al. (2021).

approved Resolution 5/X on the *Declaración de soberanía y del derecho a decidir del pueblo de Cataluña* (Declaration of sovereignty and the right to decide of the people of Catalonia), which affirmed the Catalan people's *derecho a decidir* ('right to decide')[5] on their political future, invoking the principles of democratic legitimacy, transparency, dialogue, social cohesion, Europeanism, legality and participation (Bindi 2019, pp. 6–7). This act marked the start of a unilateral process of independence and secession, conducted autonomously by the Catalan Community.[6] Faced with initiatives that could be regarded as acts of constitutional disobedience on the part of Catalan institutions, the Spanish government reacted with extreme firmness and intransigence. In a first phase, until the 2015 autonomous elections were held, the Catalan institutions acted formally within the constitutional framework, pursuing the objective of holding a referendum on independence. In this context, there was an evolving interpretation of the constitutional provisions and the adoption of Regional Law 10/2014 on non-referendum consultations.[7] Subsequently, the Constitutional Tribunal declared the unconstitutionality of both the regional regulations on popular consultations (STC 31/2015) and the specific convocation of the independence consultation (STC 32/2015). Following these pronouncements, the President of the *Generalitat* launched a 'participatory process', known as *procés*, consisting of a vote that was not formally convened, with the same questions as the original consultation, but organised with the support of volunteers and outside the formal institutional framework. At the *procés de participació ciutadana sobre el futur polític de Catalunya*, 80.72% of the participants were in favour of full independence. However, the turnout was only 35.9% of those eligible.

Despite the lack of legal effect of the consultation, it was considered by secessionist forces as sufficient to confer political legitimacy to the continuation of the process leading towards independence. This was followed by a gradual judicialisation of the independence movement, as the State Attorney General's Office brought criminal charges against various members of the Catalan government for organising the consultation. However, this did not stop the secessionist dynamic: indeed, the Catalan Parliament passed Resolution 1/XI, declaring the start of a constituent process, which was later declared unconstitutional in very harsh terms by the Constitutional Tribunal (STC 259/2015). In the following 2 years (2016–2017), the Catalan legislative assembly adopted several parliamentary resolutions that openly defied the authority of the Constitutional Court and were systematically annulled by

---

[5] In doctrine, it is considered that this right derives from the democratic principle and the right of political participation recognised by the Spanish Constitution in Articles 1.1 and 23.1. It is defined as an individual right to be exercised collectively by the members of a given community, territorially localised and democratically organised, which allows them to express, through a democratic process, their will to redefine their political-institutional status, including the possibility of constituting an independent state. In this sense, Frosina (2017b, pp. 21–22). On the subject, see Cappuccio and Corretja Torrens (2014); Castellà i Andreu (2014); Jiménez Sánchez (2014); Vilajosana (2014); González Bondia et al. (2015); Tudela Aranda (2016).

[6] See Generalitat De Catalunya (2014).

[7] See *ex multis*, Frosina (2012, 2013, 2014); Iacometti (2013).

the latter. The culminating point of this path of challenging the existing legal order and the pronouncements of the courts, both ordinary and constitutional, was the approval, in September 2017, of two regional laws: one aimed at regulating the holding of a self-determination referendum, the other aimed at the proclamation of an independent Catalan Republic. Both, after being challenged by the Madrid government, were immediately suspended and subsequently declared unconstitutional by the highest national court in Judgments114/2017 and 124/2107. Despite this and the intervention of the security forces, the referendum was nevertheless carried out, and the *procés* ended with the unilateral declaration of independence by the Catalan institutions. Official figures show a turnout of less than half the eligible voters (43.03%) and an overwhelming majority of votes in favour of independence (90.18%). Following these events, the Spanish Government triggered the procedure to apply the so-called 'coacción federal',[8] provided for in Article 155 of the Constitution, to be adopted in case of violation of constitutional obligations or actions contrary to the general interest. Following the Senate's approval of the measure, the President of the *Generalitat* and the entire Regional Executive were removed, as well as numerous organs and administrative structures of the Autonomous Community. At the same time, new elections were called for the Catalan Parliament.[9]

There are, then, further distinctive features that distinguished the Scottish case, in addition to the agreement on the holding of the referendum, which assume particular relevance in the context of an overall assessment of its strengths. Among these, it is worth mentioning the definition of the procedural framework, which took place in accordance with the recommendations expressed by the committees of the House of Commons and the House of Lords, as well as those of the Electoral Commission (Caravale 2024b, p. 16), thereby guaranteeing enhancing the legitimacy of the referendum process.

With specific reference to referendums on independence, one of the immediate questions and, at the same time, among the most complex from both a theoretical and a practical perspective, concerns the identification of the electorate entitled to participate in the decision, whether it should include only residents of the territory concerned, the only ones formally entitled to the relevant nationality even if they are non-residents, or the entire citizenship of the State to which they belong. The Scottish case represented an important innovation in this regard, including among those entitled to vote persons other than Scottish nationals in the strict sense. In fact, the Parliament of Holyrood, exercising the power conferred on it by the draft Order in Council, approved, on the proposal of the Government of Edinburgh, the Scottish Independence Referendum (Franchise) Act 2013, by which the personal scope of

[8] See Vírgala Foruria (2005); Frosina (2017); Lafuente Balle (2018); Ferraro (2018).

[9] Montilla Martos (2018, p. 261 ff.). For a reconstruction of the events and the positions of the actors involved, as well as the doctrine, Spanish and Italian, see Bar Cendón (2016); Caravita (2017); Gambino (2017); Plutino (2017): Mastromarino (2017); Ceccanti (2017); Poggeschi (2018); Ferraiuolo (2018); Cagiao Y Conde (2018); Aragón Reyes (2018); Azpitarte Sánchez (2018); Alberti Rovira (2019); Frosina (2019); Nicotra (2019); Jordana (2019).

voting rights was defined, including citizens resident in Scotland aged 16 years or over; citizens of the United Kingdom, a Member State of the European Union or a Commonwealth country, provided that they are resident in Scotland and duly registered on the local electoral registers or, in the case of those under 18 years of age, on the registers specifically established for 'young voters'.

On the other hand, Scots residing in other regions of the United Kingdom were excluded from the electoral body, thus marking a territorially based approach in accordance with the principle of actual residence (Frosina 2017b, pp. 16–17). As highlighted in this contribution, the referendum on Scottish independence was characterised by a number of qualifying elements, which helped to disprove the widespread scepticism in the literature of the referendum, often considered, in doctrine, to be easily manipulated by political elites and inadequate to guarantee fully informed and conscious deliberative processes on the part of the electorate (Tierney 2015, p. 633).

In short, the referendum was the outcome of a lengthy and carefully negotiated institutional process underpinned by a bilateral political agreement, the so-called Edinburgh Agreement. The Edinburgh Agreement, which ensured that both parties involved—at the central and regional level—were committed to respecting the outcome, thereby conferring a high degree of democratic legitimacy on the referendum. Of particular note is also the fact that the consultation took place within a fully structured legal framework, the result of the integration of UK state legislation, represented by the Political Parties, Elections and Referendums Act 2000 (PPERA), and two laws adopted *ad hoc* by the Scottish Parliament, namely the Scottish Independence Referendum (Franchise) Act 2013 and the Scottish Independence Referendum Act 2013. Finally, to guarantee the impartiality and transparency of the process, the action of an independent electoral authority, the Electoral Commission, which had already been in operation for some time and which has specific responsabilities in the area of the control of referendum questions and the conduct of referendum campaigns, played a central role (Ruggiu 2016, pp. 85–86).

A comparative analysis of the referendum experiences in Scotland, Catalonia and the United Kingdom in the Brexit case, on the one hand, clearly shows the profoundly heterogeneous nature that referendums can assume in the different legal contexts, and on the other, highlights how they represent instruments whose democratic effectiveness depends to a large extent on how they are conceived, regulated and managed.

References

Alberti Rovira E (2019) El conflicto de Cataluña como crisis constitucional. Cuadernos Monográficos de Teoría del Estado, Derecho Público y Historia Constitucional, 10/2019

Aragón Reyes M (2018) El desafío en Cataluña: Comentario constitucional. Revista Electrónica de Estudios Internacionales, 35/2018

Armstrong K (2017) Brexit time: leaving the EU – why, how and when? Cambridge University Press, Cambridge

Atkinson L, Blick A (2017) Referendums and constitution. The Constitution Society, London

Auer A (2007) National referendum in the process of European Integration: time for change. In: Albi A, Ziller J (eds) The European Constitution and National Constitutions. Ratification and beyond. Kluwer Law International, Netherlands
Azpitarte Sánchez M (2018) La defensa de la Constitución frente al secesionismo. Crónica política y legislativa del año 2017. Revista Española de Derecho Constitucional, 112/2018
Baldini G, Bressanelli E, Massetti E (2021) Il Regno Unito alla prova della Brexit. Il Mulino, Bologna
Bar Cendón A (2016) El proceso independentista de Cataluña y la doctrina jurisprudencial: una visión sistemática. Teoría y Realidad Constitucional, 37/2016
Bindi E (2019) Oltre i confini dell'autonomia. Osservatoriosullefonti.it, 3/2019
Bogdanor V (1999) Devolution: decentralisation or disintegration. Polit Quart 2/1999
Cagiao y Conde J (2018) Un sassolino nella scarpa. La Catalogna come chiave della crisi del modello territoriale spagnolo. federalismi.it, 17/2018
Cappuccio L, Corretja Torrens M (eds) (2014) El derecho a decidir: un diálogo italo-catalán. Barcellona.
Caravale G (2017) A family of nations. Asimmetrie territoriali nel Regno Unito tra devolution e Brexit. Jovene, Napoli
Caravale G (2019) Brexit e Costituzione britannica. Jovene, Napoli
Caravale G (2022) Il giudizio di reference della Corte suprema sul referendum scozzese: una political question. federalismi.it, 31/2022
Caravale G (2024a) Britain chooses its future: le elezioni della Camera dei Comuni del 4 luglio 2024 e il ritorno al potere del Partito Laburista. Nomos – Le attualità nel diritto, 2/2024
Caravale G (2024b) Il referendum del 18 settembre 2014: Scotland chooses the best of both worlds. federalismi.it, 18/2024
Caravita B (2016) Brexit: keep calm and apply the European Constitution. fe eralismi.it, 13/2016
Caravita B (2017) La Catalogna di fronte all'Europa. federalismi.it, 19/2017
Carboni GG (2016) A proposito della Brexit: gli effetti del referendum sul Regno Unito e l'Unione europea. DPCE Online, 2/2016
Castellà i Andreu JM (2014) Secesión y referéndum sobre el "derecho a decidir" en Cataluña: una aproximación desde el Derecho Constitucional. In: AA.VV., El futuro territorial del Estado español. Tirant lo Blanch, Valencia
Ceccanti S (2017) Catalogna e Spagna al momento senza uscita. DPCE Online, 4/2017
Clegg D (2014) David Cameron, Ed Miliband and Nick Clegg sign joint historic promise which guarantees more devolved powers for Scotland and protection of NHS if we vote No. Daily Record, 15/09/2014
Conti G (2017). Un secondo referendum scozzese tra parliamentary sovereignty e popular sovereignty. Rivista AIC, 3/2017
Curti Gialdino C (2016) Oltre la Brexit: brevi note sulle implicazioni giuridiche e politiche per il futuro prossimo dell'Unione europea. federalismi.it, 13/2016
Dardanelli P, Mitchell J (2014) An independent Scotland? The Scottish National Party's bid for independence and its prospects. The International Spectator, 3/2014
De Caria VR (2014) I referendum indipendentisti. Diritto pubblico comparato ed europeo, 4/2014
De Grazia L (2019) Oltre la democrazia rappresentativa? Sovranità popolare e referendum nell'esperienza britannica, spagnola e francese. Nuove Autonomie, 3/2019
Del Conte F (2011) La Devolution nel Regno Unito. Percorsi di analisi sul decentramento politico-costituzionale d'oltremanica. Giappichelli, Torino
Dicey AV (1890) Ought the Referendum to be Introduced into England? Contemp Rev 57/1890
Dicey AV (1915) Introduction to the Study of the Law of the Constitution (1885). Macmillan, London
Fabbrini F (2020) Brexit and the future of the European Union: the case for constitutional reforms. Oxford University Press, Oxford
Ferraiuolo G (2018) Non far niente. È democratico? federalismi.it, 17/2018
Ferraro L (2018) Un nuovo governo autonomico e la fine della coercizione statale in Cataluña: un consuntivo sull'art.155 della Costituzione spagnola. federalismi.it, 17/2018
Flamini R (2013) Scotland's Independence bid: history, prospects, challenges. World Affairs 176:57

Frosina L (2012). La sfida dell'indipendentismo catalano nella perdurante emergenza economica. Nomos – Le attualità nel diritto, 3/2012
Frosina L (2013) Dall'austerità al c.d. austericidio. Aggravamento e nuovi rimedi della crisi spagnola. Nomos – Le attualità nel diritto, 1/2013
Frosina L (2014) Il c.d. derecho a decidir nella sentenza n.42/2014 del Tribunale costituzionale spagnolo sulla dichiarazione di sovranità della Catalogna. federalismi.it, 2014
Frosina L (2017a) La deriva della Catalogna verso la secessione unilaterale e l'applicazione dell'articolo 155 Cost. Nomos – Le attualità nel diritto, 3/2017
Frosina L (2017b) Profili giuridici e aspetti problematici dei referendum di secessione. Un'analisi comparata. Nomos – Le attualità nel diritto, 3/2017
Frosina L (2019) Conflitto catalano tra giustizia e politica. Prime osservazioni sulla sentenza del Tribunale Supremo sul cd. Procés. federalismi.it, 20/2019
Frosina L (2024) Separatismi e referendum. Teoria e prassi in prospettiva comparata. Jovene, Napoli
Frosini JO (2014) C'è chi dice no: la Scozia non abbandona l'Unione. Quaderni Costituzionali, 4/2014
Gambino S (2017) Pretese sovranistiche della Catalogna e unità indissolubile della Nazione spagnola. DPCE Online, 3/2017
Generalitat de Catalunya (2014) Libro Blanco de la Transición Nacional de Cataluña. Síntesis, Departamento de la Presidencia, Entidad Autónoma del Diario Oficial y de Publicaciones, Barcelona
Giannello S (2022) Il referendum nel Regno Unito prima e dopo la Brexit. In: Fasone C, Martinelli C (eds) Le conseguenze costituzionali della Brexit. federalismi.it, 10/2022
González Bondia A, López Hernández J, Vilajosana Rubio JM, Barceló M, Serramalera I, Corretja Torrens M (2015) El derecho a decidir. Teoría y práctica de un nuevo derecho. Atelier, Barcelona
Gordon M (2020) Referendums in the UK constitution: authority, sovereignty and democracy after Brexit. Eur Const Law Rev, 16/2020
Gordon R, Moffatt R (2016) Brexit: the immediate legal consequences. The Constitution Society
Guastaferro B (2019) Parlamenti, Corti e struttura territoriale dello Stato: il Regno Unito tra Brexit e devolution. DPCE Online, 4/2019
Guastaferro B (2020) Autonomia Sovranità Rappresentanza. L'evoluzione della forma di Stato in Italia e Regno Unito. CEDAM, Padova
Iacometti M (2013) L'accidentato cammino dello Stato autonómico spagnolo tra crisi economica e deriva soberanista: primi passi verso l'indipendenza della Catalogna? Diritto pubblico comparato ed europeo, 3/2013
Jiménez Sánchez J (2014) Principio democrático y derecho a decidir. *Revista d'Estudis Autonòmics i Federals*, 19/2014
Jordana J (2019) Barcelona, Madrid y el Estado. Ciudades globales y el pulso por la independencia en Cataluña. Los Libros de la Catarata, Madrid
Keating M (2015) The Scottish independence referendum and after. Revista d'Estudis Autonòmics i Federals, 21/2015
Lafuente Balle JM (2018) El artículo 155 de la Constitución española: examen doctrinal y comparado. Revista de Derecho Político, 102/2018
Leyland P (2013) Referendums, popular sovereignty, and the territorial constitution. In: Rawlings R, Leyland P, Young A (eds) Sovereignty and the Law. Oxford University Press, Oxford
Leyland P (2014) The Scottish Referendum and the funding of territorial governance in the United Kingdom and the legislative role of the Westminster Parliament. Istituzioni del Federalismo, 4/2014
Lynch P (2005) Scottish independence, the Quebec model of secession and the political future of the Scottish National Party. Nationalism and Ethnic Politics, 4/2005
Mainardi E (2014) Il referendum in Scozia: tra devolution e indipendenza. federalismi.it, 17/2014
Mariani P (2018). Lasciare l'Unione Europea. Riflessioni giuridiche sul recesso nei giorni di Brexit, Igea, Milano
Martinelli C (2017) Il referendum Brexit e le sue ricadute costituzionali. Sant'Arcangelo di Romagna

Martinelli C (2019) Il ruolo del referendum nella British Constitution. Federalismi.it, Interventi al Seminario "Brexit e il diritto di recedere dai trattati," 23/11/2019
Martinelli C (2021) Bilanci costituzionali e prospettive referendarie alla luce della Brexit. Diritto pubblico comparato ed europeo, 3/2021
Martinelli C (2022) La Scozia tra autonomia e secessione: riflessioni sul referendum indipendentista nel processo devolutivo. federalismi.it, 23/2022
Martinico G (2019) Il diritto costituzionale come speranza. Giappichelli, Torino
Martino P (2015) La questione indipendentista scozzese: le nuove frontiere della Britishness. Diritto pubblico comparato, 2/2015
Martino P (2023a) La comfort zone della Corte suprema del Regno Unito nel giudizio di reference sul secondo referendum indipendentista scozzese, Diritti comparati, 2/2023
Martino P (2023b) La Corte suprema del Regno Unito sul secondo referendum indipendentista scozzese: una partita chiusa? Diritti comparati – Blog, 9/01/2023
Marzulli G (2016) Il nomos della Scozia: il referendum sull'indipendenza nella rete ingarbugliata della sovranità. In: Martinelli C (ed) La Scozia nella Costituzione britannica. Giappichelli, Torino
Mastromarino A (2017) La dichiarazione di indipendenza della Catalogna. Rivista AIC, 3/2017
McHarg A, Mullen T, Page A, Walker N (2016) The Scottish independence referendum. Constitutional and political implications. Oxford University Press, Oxford
Milani G (2013) Regno Unito – Firmato l'accordo sul referendum per l'indipendenza della Scozia. DPCE Online, 2/2013
Montilla Martos JA (2016) El referéndum de secesión en Europa. ReDCE, 26/2016
Montilla Martos JA (2018) Evolución y retos de la organización territorial en España. Revista Valenciana d'Estudis Autonòmics, 63/2018
Mullen T (2014) The Scottish Independence referendum 2014. J Law Soc 4/2014
Nicotra IA (2019) La "sfida" secessionista e il valore "unificante" della solidarietà territoriale. federalismi.it, 16/2019
Palici di Suni E (2016) I britannici hanno detto sì alla Brexit: uno choc per l'Europa. DPCE Online, 2/2016
Parolari S, Woelk J (2015) The referendum in the United Kingdom: instrument for greater constitutional legitimacy, tool of political convenience, or first step to revitalize democracy? In: Fraenkel C, et al. (eds) Citizen participation in multi-level democracies. Boston
Plutino M (2017) La vicenda catalana tra istanze politiche malposte e la dura logica dello Stato di diritto. Dirittifondamentali.it, 2/2017
Poggeschi G (2016) Il processo di devolution: una storia che parte da lontano. In: Martinelli C (ed) La Scozia nella Costituzione britannica. Giappichelli, Torino
Poggeschi G (2018) La Catalogna: dalla Nazione storica alla Repubblica immaginaria. Napoli
Qvortrup M (2006) Democracy by Delegation: The Decision to Hold Referendums in the United Kingdom. Representation, 1/2006
Ruggiu I (2016) Referendum e secessione l'appello al popolo per l'indipendenza in Scozia e in Catalogna. Costituzionalismo.it, 2/2016
Saputelli G (2020) Brexit e devolution nel Regno Unito: quando è lo Stato (e non l'UE) a mostrare i suoi limiti. DPCE Online, 4/2020
Savastano F (2016) Brexit. Un'analisi del voto. federalismi.it, 13/2016
Savastano F (2019) Uscire dall'Unione europea. Brexit e il diritto di recederedai Trattati. Giappichelli, Torino
Tierney S (2015). Direct democracy in the United Kingdom: reflections from the Scottish independence referendum. Public Law 4/2015
Tomkins A (2014) Scotland's choice, Britain's future. Law Quart Rev 130/2014
Torre A (2007) Le metamorfosi del governo territoriale (lo Stato devoluto è una nuova forma di Stato?). In: Torre A (ed) Processi di devolution transizioni costituzionali negli Stati unitari (dal Regno Unito all'Europa). Giappichelli, Torino

Torre A (2010) Pluralismo e asimmetrie in uno stato unitario: istituzioni, caratteri e politiche della devolution nel Regno Unito. In: Benazzo A (ed) Federalismi a confronto. Dalle esperienze straniere al caso veneto. Cedam, Padova

Torre A (2013) Scozia: devolution, quasi-federalismo, indipendenza? Istituzioni del Federalismo, 1/2013

Torre A (2017) Una Costituzione sotto stress. Riflessioni sul referendum scozzese del 18 settembre 2014. Rivista AIC, 2/2017

Torre A, Frosini JO (eds) (2012) Democrazia rappresentativa e referendum nel Regno Unito. Sant'Arcangelo di Romagna

Tudela Aranda J (2016) El derecho a decidir y el principio democrático. Teoría y Realidad Constitucional, 37/2016

Vilajosana JM (2014) Principio democrático y justificación constitucional de derecho a decidir. Revista d'Estudis Autonòmics i Federals, 19/2014

Vírgala Foruria E (2005) La coacción estatal del artículo 155 de la Constitución. Revista Española de Derecho Constitucional, 73/2005

Volpi M (2016) L'organizzazione costituzionale. In: Morbidelli G et al. (eds) Diritto pubblico comparato. Giappichelli, Torino

Secession by Design: Northern Ireland's Consociational Model in Comparative Perspective

Emanuele Gabriele

Abstract This chapter examines the constitutional architecture of Northern Ireland as a paradigmatic case of post-conflict consociationalism within a plurinational State. Anchored in the 1998 Good Friday Agreement and implemented through the Northern Ireland Act 1998, the model institutionalises ethno-national power-sharing, procedural vetoes, and proportional representation, while uniquely codifying a conditional right to secession. Through a comparative constitutional lens, the study analyses how Northern Ireland's 'rigid-flexible' framework reconciles democratic self-determination with systemic intercommunal guarantees. Situated between federacy and asymmetrical devolution, this model exemplifies a resilient yet fragile constitutional design that transforms conflict management into legally mediated coexistence.

1 Introduction

From the perspective of the territorial relations that characterise decentralised legal systems, Northern Ireland provides an interesting and peculiar case study. Differing from the other devolutive processes in the United Kingdom—those of Scotland and Wales—which are mainly based on a logic of functional decentralisation or national recognition, Northern Ireland's devolution is shaped as a post-conflict and consociational, institutionalised model, rooted in a context of long-standing political-religious conflict, and established explicitly to guarantee a coexistence between two historically antagonistic communities: the Unionist/Protestant (in favour of remaining in the United Kingdom) and the Nationalist/Catholic one (in support of unification with the Republic of Ireland) (O'Leary 2019c, pp. 216–219).

At the domestic level, the juridical foundation of the system resides in the Northern Ireland Act 1998 (c. 47), adopted to implement the Belfast Agreement (or Good Friday Agreement) of the same year, an international treaty and multilevel

E. Gabriele (✉)
Sapienza University of Rome, Rome, Italy
e-mail: emanuele.gabriele@uniroma1.it

F. Savastano et al. (eds.), *Between Asymmetry and Secession*,
https://doi.org/10.1007/978-3-032-29603-0_11

political agreement, signed by the United Kingdom, the Republic of Ireland and the main Northern Irish parties to effectively end the turbulent Troubles period. Not only did this agreement establish a system of asymmetrical devolution, but it also introduced an innovative 'mandatory power-sharing' model, in which executive offices are allocated proportionally, and major decisions require the cross-party consent of the two national communities. In this sense, Northern Irish devolution can be described as one of the most complex and atypical institutional architectures in comparative constitutional law (Whitten 2023, p. 2).

This study investigates the constitutional configuration of Northern Ireland through a comparative public law lens, focusing on how post-conflict consociational design interfaces with codified, though contingent, pathways to secession. It analyses the normative architecture of Northern Irish devolution, paying particular attention to three interrelated dimensions: the structural balance between territorial autonomy and central oversight; the legal mechanisms ensuring intercommunal parity and identity protection; and the formalisation of self-determination through the border poll provision.

Methodologically, the study adopts an integrated approach, combining doctrinal analysis of normative sources (both statutory and international) with consideration of effective institutional experiences (Örücü 2006; Jackson 2012, pp. 66–67; Hirschl 2014). Special emphasis is placed on the tension between the stabilising logic of consociational power-sharing and the latent volatility introduced by a constitutionalised, but politically discretionary, right to secede. In light of Brexit and the shifting demographic and electoral equilibrium, Northern Ireland emerges as a paradigmatic – albeit fragile – laboratory for examining the interplay between devolution, identity-based pluralism, and negotiated secession within plurinational constitutional systems (McGarry and O'Leary 2008).

2 A Brief History of Devolution in Northern Ireland

The development of devolution in Northern Ireland is inextricably linked to the historical and constitutional genesis of the ethno-national conflict that has shaped the region, reaching its peak during the second half of the twentieth century. As already noted, the Northern Irish case, unlike other devolved processes within the United Kingdom, stands apart as the direct result of a constitutional attempt to transform antagonism into a stable institutional settlement, in what can be described as a post-conflict consociational model (Wolff 2011, pp. 1785–1786).

English rule in Ireland was formally established in 1171, when Henry II declared himself Lord of the *Dominium Hiberniae* (Veach 2018, pp. 160–166). This lordship was transformed into the Kingdom of Ireland in 1542 via the Crown of Ireland Act (33 Hen. 8 c. 1), creating a viceroyal dependency (Brady 2018, p. 31) governed through a bicameral parliament modelled on Westminster, with a House of Lords appointed by the King and a House of Commons elected by a significantly limited franchise. This arrangement effectively facilitated the political control maintained by the Protestant minority, commonly referred to as the 'Protestant Ascendancy' (Edwards 2018, p. 67). Despite this institutional framework, real English authority prior to the sixteenth century was largely confined to the Pale – a colonial enclave around Dublin, inhabited by the *Saxain* (those of English origin)—while regions like Ulster—characterised by a complex social landscape in which *Gaill* (individuals of English descent who had long resided in Ireland) and *Gáedhil* (native Irish) coexisted – remained beyond effective control (O'Leary 2019a, p. 154).

In the northern part of the island, the situation began to change in the early seventeenth century, when the English Crown intensified colonisation by dispossessing Gaelic lords and settling Protestant populations, notably Presbyterian Scots and Anglican English. This plantation policy entrenched a tripartite social order: Gaelic Catholic natives, Scottish Presbyterian settlers, and English Anglican elites—divided by language, religion, and legal status (O'Leary 2019a, p. 170). These divisions, initially imposed to neutralise the Irish Catholic threat and to culturally reorient the region, to the extent that Ulster eventually came to represent a prototype of the British colonial model (Canny 1998, p. 12), later solidified into deep ethno-religious cleavages that became enduring impediments to Irish national unification.

Following the Acts of Union enacted in 1800,[1] the Irish Parliament was dissolved, and from 1 January 1801, Ireland was represented in the Imperial Parliament at Westminster. Throughout the nineteenth century, calls for Irish Home Rule—seeking devolution within the UK—gained traction, notably with Liberal support in 1886. Early legislative efforts to establish a devolved Irish parliament in 1886 and 1893 failed (O'Leary 2019a, pp. 290–294), but debates around the Third Home Rule Bill (1912–1914) marked a turning point (O'Leary 2019a, pp. 299–302). These discussions highlighted growing demands for differentiated governance and encountered strong resistance from the increasingly influential Ulster Unionist Party, which had initially mobilised as a political force against the First Home Rule Bill in 1886 (O'Leary 2019a, p. 355).

Amid the failure of prior Home Rule efforts and the outbreak of armed resistance, the fourth Government of Ireland Bill was introduced during the Irish War of Independence (1919–1921), a protracted guerrilla conflict waged between the Irish Republican Army (IRA) and British Crown forces. The subsequent Government of Ireland Act 1920 (10 & 11 Geo. 5 c. 67) established separate parliaments for Southern and Northern Ireland (O'Leary 2019a, pp. 338–339), but while the Southern assembly collapsed under the Sinn Féin nationalist rejection (Ward 1994, pp. 153–156), the Northern Parliament functioned as intended, dominated by Unionists as a result of the adoption of the first past the post electoral formula (Caravale 2017, p. 118).

A pivotal development occurred on 6 December 1921, when representatives of the British Government and Sinn Féin signed the Anglo-Irish Treaty. This

[1] The Acts are the British Parliament Union with Ireland Act 1800 (39 & 40 Geo. 3 c. 67) and the Irish Parliament Act of Union (Ireland) 1800 (40 Geo. 3 c. 38 (I).

agreement established the Irish Free State as a self-governing Dominion within the British Empire—effectively granting it a status analogous to that of Canada or Australia—, offering Northern Ireland the choice to join or remain in the UK. It opted for the latter, formalising partition. By 1923, a customs border separated the two jurisdictions, and in 1937, the Free State adopted a republican constitution as Éire, consolidating Ireland's political bifurcation.

In the 1960s and early 1970s, Ulster witnessed a surge in paramilitary activity, with the emergence of the Provisional Irish Republican Army (IRA) and the growth of loyalist groups like the Ulster Defence Association (UDA) and the Ulster Volunteer Force (UVF). The ensuing period, known as 'The Troubles' (1968–1998), was marked by sustained sectarian violence, including assassinations and bombings (O'Leary 2019b, pp. 176–195). Amid escalating instability, the Northern Ireland Parliament was suspended in 1972 and abolished in 1973.[2] Attempts to reintroduce devolved power-sharing governance in 1973–74 and 1982–86 failed (O'Leary 2019c, pp. 33–85), leading to prolonged Direct Rule from London.

Efforts to foster peaceful coexistence between unionists and nationalists gained traction in the 1990s. A key milestone was the 1993 British and Irish Joint Declaration on Peace, which affirmed mutual recognition, endorsed self-determination, and required cross-jurisdictional consent for reunification (Caravale 2017, pp. 120–121). The 1995 Framework for the Future—informed by consociational theory articulated by Arend Lijphart and other theorists (Lijphart 1977; Bogaards 1998; McGarry and O'Leary 2004; Wolff 2011)—further shaped the conceptual basis for power-sharing.

In May 1997, the electoral victory of Tony Blair's Labour Party marked a pivotal moment in British politics, bringing with it renewed emphasis on devolution and institutional innovation across the United Kingdom (Bogdanor 2009, pp. 89–119). This domestic shift aligned the British Government's stance more closely with that of the Irish authorities. Contributing to this convergence was the broader European context, particularly the process of European Union integration, which since the 1980s had increasingly promoted cross-border cooperation among member states. Moreover, the evolving global emphasis on peacebuilding—visible in efforts to resolve ethno-national conflicts in regions such as South Africa, Palestine, Lebanon, and Bosnia—fostered an international environment conducive to negotiated settlements (Caravale 2017, p. 122).

In this context, and with United States mediation, the Good Friday Agreement was signed at Stormont on 10 April 1998, establishing the foundation for Northern Ireland's post-conflict constitutional order.

[2] Direct Rule was introduced through the Northern Ireland (Temporary Provisions) Act 1972 (c. 22).

3 The Good Friday Agreement

The Belfast/Good Friday Agreement consists of two different components: the Multi-Party Agreement, involving the United Kingdom and Irish governments along with the eight Northern Irish political parties, and the British-Irish Agreement, a formal treaty concluded between the UK and Irish governments.

The Multi-Party Agreement[3] opened with a joint declaration of support by all signatories, followed by a substantive section titled 'Constitutional Issues'. In this section, both the British and Irish governments affirmed their commitment to uphold the democratic will of the people of Northern Ireland concerning the region's constitutional future. This included explicit recognition of the right to self-determination and the freedom of individuals to identify as Irish, British, or both, and to hold the corresponding citizenship. The section was accompanied by two annexes aimed at revising each State's constitutional and legislative frameworks. The United Kingdom acknowledged Northern Ireland's status as part of its sovereign territory, conditional upon the majority preference of its population and, accordingly, repealed the Government of Ireland Act 1920. Simultaneously, the Republic of Ireland undertook significant constitutional reform, particularly amending Articles 2 and 3 of the 1937 Constitution. These amendments marked a departure from earlier nationalist and irredentist rhetoric, instead articulating a peaceful aspiration for Irish unity grounded in mutual respect for diverse national identities.

The Agreement was subsequently structured into three distinct Strands. Strand One addressed the devolution of certain powers from the United Kingdom to Northern Ireland and provided for the establishment of new political institutions designed to reflect the region's diverse shared composition. Central to this was the creation of the Northern Ireland Assembly and a new power-sharing Executive accountable to it. This component represented a cornerstone of the Agreement and laid the foundation for the passage of the Northern Ireland Act 1998 by the Westminster Parliament. The newly established institutional framework in Northern Ireland, departing significantly from the arrangements set out in 1920, embraced a model that can be described as a '*sui generis* form of consociationalism'. This model was regarded as the most effective means of ensuring the protection of communal rights and fostering peaceful coexistence. Its principal features will be examined in the subsequent sections.

Strand Two of the Agreement established the North-South Ministerial Council (NSMC), a formal mechanism for cooperation between the Irish Government and the Northern Ireland Executive. Its purpose was to enable joint decision-making, dialogue, and coordinated policy initiatives on issues of shared concern across the island of Ireland. This cooperation was to extend to both all-island and cross-border dimensions, within the areas of competence held by each administration.

The NSMC was designed to function on the basis of mutual consent, with all decisions requiring the agreement of both the Government of Ireland and the

[3] The Multi-Party Agreement text is available at assets.publishing.service.gov.uk.

Northern Ireland Executive. Representation from Northern Ireland included the First Minister, the Deputy First Minister, and any Ministers relevant to the specific policy area under discussion. On the Irish side, the Taoiseach and corresponding Ministers would participate. The Council was expected to meet in plenary format twice annually, and to hold frequent sectoral meetings focused on specific areas of cooperation. Additionally, it would convene as needed in suitable configurations to address institutional or cross-cutting matters—including those related to European Union affairs—or to manage disputes between the parties.

Strand Three of the Agreement introduced the British-Irish Council (BIC), envisioned as a forum to foster constructive and mutually advantageous relations among all the peoples of the British Isles. Its core objective was to encourage cooperation and dialogue across the various jurisdictions through the exchange of information, consultation, and efforts to achieve consensus on issues of shared concern falling within the remit of each administration. The Council's membership was to include representatives from the UK and Irish governments, as well as the devolved administrations of Northern Ireland, Scotland, and Wales (once established). It also extended to representatives from the Isle of Man and the Channel Islands, and potentially other parts of the United Kingdom, where appropriate. The BIC was structured to convene semi-annual summit meetings, alongside regular gatherings in sector-specific formats.

Strand Three also established the British-Irish Intergovernmental Conference (BIIGC), a permanent mechanism designed to enhance bilateral cooperation between the United Kingdom and Ireland. Its purpose was to provide a forum for engagement on matters of mutual interest that fall within the jurisdiction of both governments. The Conference was intended to convene at summit level when necessary—bringing together the UK Prime Minister and the Irish Taoiseach—but it was also structured to meet regularly and frequently at ministerial level. The BIIGC was tasked with addressing non-devolved Northern Ireland issues. Its sessions would also cover matters of all-island or cross-border relevance that lie outside the scope of devolved powers. Within this framework, cooperation would extend to sensitive areas such as security, justice, policing, and the prison system, unless and until these responsibilities were transferred to the Northern Ireland Assembly under devolution arrangements.

The Multi-Party Agreement was followed by the British-Irish Agreement, an international treaty between the United Kingdom and Ireland. This legally binding accord obligated both governments to implement the terms outlined in the Multi-Party Agreement.

Public endorsement was sought through referendums held simultaneously on 22 May 1998. In Northern Ireland, a majority of political parties—including the Ulster Unionist Party, the Social Democratic and Labour Party (SDLP), and Sinn Féin—supported a 'Yes' campaign, while opposition came primarily from the Democratic Unionist Party (DUP) and certain dissident republican groups. The result was a decisive endorsement: 71.1% voted in favour, 28.9% against, with a high turnout of 81%. In the Republic of Ireland, the referendum asked voters to approve the Government's authority to sign the Agreement and amend the Constitution accordingly, through the Nineteenth Amendment. Turnout stood at 56%, with 94% voting in favour of the proposed constitutional changes, demonstrating overwhelming support.[4]

Following these dual referendums, the British Government introduced the Northern Ireland Bill to Parliament to provide a legislative basis for implementing aspects of the Agreement. This culminated in the enactment of the Northern Ireland Act 1998, which received Royal Assent on 19 November 1998. Notably, Lord Bingham, then serving as a Lord of Appeal in Ordinary, later described the Act as 'in effect a constitution'[5] for Northern Ireland, underscoring its foundational significance in the region's governance.

4 The Northern Irish Constitutional Laboratory in Comparison

The constitutional framework established by the Multi-Party Agreement—endorsed through referendums in both the monarchical and republican jurisdictions on the island of Ireland and subsequently enshrined in domestic law by the Northern Ireland Act 1998—integrated key features of Lijphart's consociational model. It fulfilled all four core principles that define a full consociational democracy: power-sharing within a cross-community executive, proportional representation across governmental structures, electoral systems, and policymaking processes; guaranteed autonomy and cultural parity; and institutionalised minority veto rights (Lijphart 1977, p. 25). Within this framework, political actors in the newly created Northern Ireland Assembly were formally categorised into three designations: unionists, nationalists, and 'others', thereby codifying the partnership structure at the heart of the consociational arrangement.

While the Agreement incorporated the key elements of a consociational model, it also deviated from Lijphart's classical formulation in several significant ways. Firstly, its architecture extended beyond internal power-sharing to include external, intergovernmental dimensions, most notably the North–South Ministerial Council (NSMC), the British–Irish Council (BIC), and the British–Irish Intergovernmental Conference (BIIGC). Moreover, what further distinguished the Northern Irish arrangement was its dual endorsement through concurrent referendums in two separate jurisdictions—Northern Ireland and the Republic of Ireland—marking the first instance of a consociational framework ratified by cross-border popular consent (O'Leary 2019c, p. 178). The Agreement itself emerged from an interstate pact, rather than solely from intra-state negotiation. Additionally, the oversight role assumed by the British and Irish governments introduced elements of co-sovereignty.

[4] Referendum data are available at https://www.ark.ac.uk/elections/fref98.htm.

[5] *Robinson v Secretary of State for Northern Ireland* [2002] UKHL 32, para 11.

Typical of the Northern Irish experience is, then, the explicit legal provision for a referendum aimed at the secession of Ulster from the United Kingdom in order to complete the unification of the island of Ireland. This formalisation—or 'objectification'—of secession within a legal instrument, while providing considerable discretion to political actors and a lack of automaticity for its activation, stands out as a significant development. It warrants particular attention in the broader context of referendums as a primary mechanism for addressing territorial disputes, which seems to be a typical feature of modern constitutional practice in the area of secessionism and separatism (Palermo 2019, p. 267).

The Northern Irish constitutional laboratory thus assumes characteristics that are both peculiar and thus unique to the specific case, and common to other consociational models. This combination provides a foundation for comparative analysis, which will be undertaken in the next sections of this chapter.

4.1 Proportional Representation, Veto Mechanisms and Community Safeguards in Stormont Assembly

Strand One of the Multi-Party Agreement, given legal force through the *Northern Ireland Act 1998*, established a devolved legislative assembly at Stormont.

Devolved matters under the Northern Ireland constitutional framework are organised into three distinct categories: (a) excepted matters remain under the exclusive jurisdiction of the UK Parliament at Westminster and are not subject to devolution; (b) reserved matters also fall within Westminster's competence, but they retain a flexible character, allowing for potential involvement by the Northern Ireland Assembly; (c) transferred matters are those areas over which the Assembly holds full legislative authority.[6]

The Assembly was initially composed of 108 members, elected through a system of proportional representation using the single transferable vote (STV) in 18 six-member constituencies. However, ahead of the 2016 Assembly elections, the number of seats was reduced to 90, achieved by lowering the number of representatives per constituency from six to five.[7]

The electoral system employed for the Northern Ireland Assembly mirrors that used in all elections to collegiate bodies within the Republic of Ireland, including elections to the *Dáil Éireann*, the elective component of the *Seanad*, the Irish seats in the European Parliament, and local government councils. The adoption of a proportional representation system for electing members to the Stormont Assembly thus represents a significant departure from historical electoral practices in Northern Ireland. It aligns closely with the principles of democratic consociationalism by

[6] See Schedules 2 and 3 of the Northern Ireland Act 1998.

[7] The reduction was introduced through the Assembly Members (Reduction of Numbers) Act (Northern Ireland) 2016 (c. 29).

promoting inclusivity and balanced representation. Furthermore, the Multi-Party Agreement reinforces this consociational orientation through the use of the d'Hondt formula for the allocation of executive positions—a mechanism that will be examined in the following section.

Under the terms of the Agreement, all 108 (now 90) elected Members of the Legislative Assembly (MLAs) were required to self-identify as either 'nationalist', 'unionist', or 'other'. This provision stands in contrast to normative principles advocating for self-determination over predetermined classification—an approach critiqued by Lijphart (Lijphart 1995). Unlike their counterparts in the UK Parliament at Westminster or in the devolved legislatures of Scotland and Wales, Northern Ireland MLAs are not required to swear an oath of allegiance to the Crown. However, they must formally commit to a pledge renouncing paramilitary activity.[8]

A defining feature of consociational systems—particularly evident in the Northern Ireland model—is the incorporation of inter-community veto mechanisms within the legislative process. While most legislation can be enacted by a simple majority of members present and voting, so-called 'key decisions'—which include contentious measures such as the budget, the election of the Speaker and Deputy Speaker, and amendments to standing orders—are subject to enhanced cross-community consent procedures (O'Leary 2019c, p. 180).

These special procedures are implemented through two distinct rules. The first is *parallel consent*, which requires a majority of votes among all MLAs present and voting, in addition to separate concurrent majorities among those designated as nationalists and those designated as unionists. The second mechanism is the *weighted majority* rule, whereby a proposal must receive the support of at least 60% of voting MLAs, and simultaneously, no less than 40% of both designated nationalist and unionist representatives. These safeguards are designed to ensure that critical legislative outcomes enjoy broad support across the community divide, reinforcing the consociational foundation of the Assembly's operations.

An additional significant feature of the Assembly's voting procedures is the *Petition of Concern*.[9] Under this provision, if 30 MLAs formally submit a petition expressing concern over a particular matter scheduled for a vote, the issue in question must then be decided through cross-community voting procedures. However, due to criticisms that this mechanism had been used to obstruct legislation, the process was reformed under the Northern Ireland (Ministers, Elections and Petitions of Concern) Act 2022. While the threshold of 30 MLAs remains unchanged, several new safeguards have been introduced. A mandatory 14-day consideration period must now elapse before a petition can be validated. Furthermore, petitioners must represent more than one political party, and neither the Speaker of the Assembly nor their deputies are permitted to sign a petition. Additionally, the mechanism cannot be invoked during the second stage of a bill.

[8] See Section 40A of the Northern Ireland Act 1998.

[9] See Section 42(1) of the Northern Ireland Act 1998.

The Assembly's procedural mechanisms—*parallel consent*, the *weighted majority* rule, and the *Petition of Concern*—are designed to safeguard communal interests by establishing veto points that prevent unilateral imposition of legislation. However, they have also been strategically employed in ways that diverge from their original intent. Notably, the Democratic Unionist Party (DUP) has utilised mechanisms originally intended to protect the nationalist minority to obstruct the functioning of the institutions themselves and to block progressive social legislation unrelated to constitutional questions. In later years, the DUP invoked these procedural tools to resist reforms concerning abortion, same-sex marriage, and LGBT rights (McCulloch 2018).

By contrast, members of the Assembly designated as 'others' receive comparatively weaker institutional protections. They may be overridden by a simple majority or by a cross-community supermajority, and their current numbers typically fall short of the threshold required to trigger a Petition of Concern. Nonetheless, given that 'others' were not central actors in the ethno-national conflict that the Agreement sought to resolve, their limited influence in the design of its institutional safeguards is perhaps unsurprising (O'Leary 2019c, p. 201).

While proportional representation within government institutions and intercommunal veto powers are widely recognised as defining features of consociational models, their significance is particularly pronounced in post-conflict constitutional arrangements. In such contexts, the coexistence of these mechanisms becomes a critical condition for the viability and stability of power-sharing frameworks. A prominent example is found in Bosnia and Herzegovina, where the constitutional order established by the 1995 Dayton Accords institutionalises a model of rigid ethnic federalism. Under this system, all principal State organs—most notably the upper chamber of the Sarajevo Parliament, the House of Peoples—are structured to maintain ethnic parity among the three constituent groups: Croats, Serbs, and Bosniaks. Article IV(e) and (f) of the Bosnian Constitution enshrines the right of each of these communities to block legislative or administrative measures deemed to infringe upon their 'vital national interests'. This right is operationalised through a formal veto mechanism, which may be invoked when a majority of representatives from any one of the three ethnic groups in the House of Peoples supports such a motion (Bieber 2006, p. 55).

The Lebanese political system, originally established under the 1943 National Pact and later restructured through the Ta'if Accords of 1989, is based on a consociational confessional framework. This model allocates the highest offices of State—namely, the Presidency, the Premiership, and the Speakership of Parliament—to members of specific religious communities: Maronite Christians, Sunni Muslims, and Shia Muslims, respectively. Following the constitutional reforms introduced by the Ta'if Accords, the Lebanese Constitution also introduced provisions for executive-level veto power. Specifically, Article 65 of the Constitution stipulates that the Cabinet shall strive to make decisions by consensus. In cases where consensus cannot be reached, decisions concerning so-called 'basic issues'—which are explicitly listed, including constitutional amendments, declarations of emergency, the national budget, dissolution of the Chamber of Deputies, and electoral legislation—must secure the approval of two-thirds of the Cabinet members. This effectively grants an implicit veto power to a minority comprising one-third of the

Cabinet ministers—a threshold that, in the Lebanese context, typically corresponds to representatives of a specific religious community through their affiliated political parties (Salamey 2013, p. 74; Bogaards 2019, pp. 32–33).

In the aftermath of the 2001 Ohrid Agreement, which sought to resolve the conflict between ethnic Macedonians and Albanians, the North Macedonian Constitution was amended to incorporate provisions for proportional representation within public institutions. Additionally, it introduced the principle of 'double majority', requiring that legislation in key areas such as culture, language, and education obtain the approval of representatives from both major ethnic communities.[10]

The comparative analysis shows how post-conflict consociational orders resort, with varying degrees of formalisation, to normative instruments that combine ethnic/confessional proportionality and veto rights. Within this landscape, the Northern Ireland model, compared to contexts such as Bosnia or Lebanon, stands out for achieving a more sophisticated equilibrium between legal rigidity and procedural adaptability. Moreover, it is distinguished by its foundation in dual legitimacy—both internal, through domestic political consensus, and external, through international endorsement.

4.2 The Power-Sharing Model of Government

The Multi-Party Agreement introduced a wholly restructured Executive Committee, led by a diarchic arrangement featuring two quasi-presidential figures. This structure is grounded in a mandatory power-sharing framework designed to ensure equal representation and participation of the two principal ethno-political communities in executive governance and decision-making. The First Minister (FM) and the Deputy First Minister (DFM), although formally distinct, jointly exercise the leadership of the executive and act on a basis of functional and decision-making parity, by virtue of the principle of joint office (Wilford 2009, p. 187).

Once appointed, the First Minister and Deputy First Minister exhibit several presidential features, primarily due to the significant difficulty in removing them from office before the next general election, provided they maintain their joint position. The defining characteristic of presidentialism thus lies not in the title, but in the executive's resilience against dismissal by the legislature (O'Leary 2019c, p. 182).

Initially, under the provisions of the Agreement, the FM and DFM were elected jointly through the parallel consent procedure and could only be removed through mutual resignation or a triggering of joint loss of office by either office-holder. However, following the St Andrews Agreement (2006) and subsequent legislative amendments, the method of appointment changed. The First Minister is now nominated by the largest party within the largest political designation in the Assembly, while the Deputy First Minister is nominated by the largest party within the second largest designation.[11]

---

[10] See Constitution of the Republic of North Macedonia, amendment X.

[11] See Section 8 of the Northern Ireland (St Andrews Agreement) Act 2006.

Ministerial posts within the Executive are allocated using the d'Hondt formula, which distributes portfolios proportionally based on party strength in the Assembly. Parties select their respective ministers accordingly. An exception applies to the post of Minister of Justice, which—following the devolution of policing and justice functions in 2010—is appointed through a cross-community vote in the Assembly, based on a joint nomination from the First Minister and Deputy First Minister.[12]

In the Northern Irish context, therefore, the concept of 'grand coalition' is realised through the formation of the devolved executive based on legally mandated proportionality (McEvoy 2006), the codification of co-decision-making between identity-based communities, and the institutionalisation of functional parity in executive coordination. While this framework has at times fostered constitutional stability, it also reflects characteristics of a sort of 'hyper-consociational model', rendering it vulnerable to decision-making gridlock and operational paralysis when inter-community cooperation breaks down.

The requirement for dual legitimacy means that withdrawal or obstruction by either of the two main communities can paralyse governance, preventing the formation of an executive or the passage of a budget—as happened on several occasions, and especially between 2002 and 2007, 2017 and 2020, 2022 and 2024. In comparison with other devolved systems in the United Kingdom, the Northern Irish model is distinguished by the absence of a majority/opposition dynamic, replaced by a compulsory co-governing pluralism.

The institutional design of Northern Ireland thus constitutes a notable deviation from the traditional majoritarian parliamentary model, and finds close parallels only in other consociational systems, such as Bosnia and Herzegovina's tripartite collegial presidency or Lebanon's confessional allocation of senior political offices.

The Northern Irish dual-leadership executive encapsulates the core principles of a 'rigid consociational constitutionalism': a structure that privileges communal equality over majoritarian decision-making and transforms ethno-political conflict into a framework of institutionalised co-governance. Nevertheless, the system's reliance on reciprocal dependence—without adequate compensatory safeguards—represents a significant structural weakness. This raises concerns about the long-term resilience of the Northern Irish model, particularly in the face of repeated political crises and evolving intercommunal power dynamics.

4.3 The Constitutional Objectification of Secession

The 1998 settlement extends beyond its consociational framework and also engages directly with the underlying issue of national self-determination. A central feature of the Multi-Party and the British-Irish Agreements was the establishment of reciprocal forms of recognition between the two States and communities. Through a

[12] See Section 2 of the Department of Justice Act (Northern Ireland) 2010.

constitutional amendment, the people of Ireland acknowledged the current status of Northern Ireland as part of the United Kingdom, while simultaneously affirming their aspiration for Irish unification, contingent upon the future majority consent of both jurisdictions on the island. Conversely, the United Kingdom, through an international treaty, formally recognised the right of the people of Ireland—understood collectively as encompassing both North and South—to exercise self-determination.

The Good Friday Agreement, along with its domestic implementation through the Northern Ireland Act 1998, thus codifies the possibility of altering the region's constitutional status via referendum. Article 1(1) of the Agreement affirms:

> It is for the people of the island of Ireland alone [...] to bring about a united Ireland, if that is their wish, freely exercised and without external impediment.

This provision was transposed into UK law through Schedule 1 of the Northern Ireland Act 1998, which grants the Secretary of State for Northern Ireland the authority to call, by order, a referendum—commonly referred to as a 'border poll'—if a majority of voters in Northern Ireland are likely to support unification with the Republic of Ireland.

However, this recognition of a right to internal self-determination is subject to a series of limitations, since (a) it rests on the discretionary judgment of the UK Government, without an objective or mandatory threshold for action; (b) there is no automatic or legally triggered mechanism to initiate the referendum; (c) the arrangement presumes the constitutional integrity of the United Kingdom remains intact until any vote is held. Furthermore, if a referendum results in a vote against unification, no subsequent poll may be held within a minimum of seven years.

The Secretary of State's determination regarding the 'likelihood' of majority support is entirely political in nature and is not subject to judicial review. Additionally, there is no requirement for a formal quorum—either in terms of voter turnout or supermajority threshold. As a result, this provision does not establish a legally enforceable right for citizens or devolved institutions, but instead offers a conditional political mechanism, fully controlled by the central Government. The absence of clearly defined, objective criteria—such as opinion polls, electoral trends, or demographic shifts—for assessing the 'likelihood' of a referendum outcome has drawn criticism for introducing a significant degree of ambiguity and discretion into the decision-making process (Whysall 2019; Frosina 2024, p. 243).

The right to self-determination in Northern Ireland is thus an expression of a negotiated constitutionalism, based on equality between communities and the proceduralisation of secession. It does not amount to an immediately exercisable subjective right, but represents a conditional constitutional option, the exercise of which depends on political assessments and community balances. This distinctive arrangement renders Northern Ireland a constitutional *unicum*, in which elements of international law, domestic constitutional frameworks, and democratic legitimacy are interwoven. The result is a multilevel constitutionality that seeks to reconcile the integrity of the State with the recognition of self-determination claims.

Despite the distinctive multilevel framework through which the right to self-determination is recognised, the Northern Irish case aligns with the broader trend of the 'objectification' of secession. This refers to the capacity of contemporary legal systems to translate separatist claims from the realm of political discourse into the legal-constitutional domain, thereby formalising and regulating the conditions under which secession may occur (Haljan 2014; Frosina 2024, p. 33).

In this context, constitutional systems seek to address the crisis of the unitary State by distinguishing between two distinct models of secession: unilateral separation, which occurs through an *extra ordinem* rupture from the constitutional framework, and consensual secession, which unfolds through negotiated—bilateral or multilateral—processes guided by institutionalised procedures between central and peripheral authorities. Within this interpretive framework, legal scholarship increasingly explores the development of a theory of 'democratic secession', grounded in predetermined rules and procedures that confer legitimacy on the secessionist process when specific criteria are met (Closa et al. 2020).

A notable trend in comparative constitutional scholarship is the growing support for addressing secessionist conflicts through the constitutionalisation of secession—that is, the formal incorporation of specific clauses into the constitutional framework that not only regulate the process but also function, primarily, as disincentives (Weinstock 2001; Norman 2006). In systems such as the United Kingdom, which lacks a single written constitution, this form of constitutionalisation is achieved through primary legislation that carries constitutional weight—commonly referred to as 'constitutional statutes' (Ahmed and Perry 2017)—with the Northern Ireland Act 1998 serving as a paradigmatic example. On the other hand, in systems with a formal constitution, although the objectification of the phenomenon is still scarcely practised, the text directly outlines the rules governing secession.

A noteworthy historical instance of a constitutional provision regulating the right to secession is found in the Constitution of the Czechoslovak Republic. Constitutional Law No. 327 stipulated that any proposal for secession by either the Czech or Slovak Republics must be decided through a referendum. Furthermore, it provided that if such a proposal had been approved in at least one of the republics, the Czech and Slovak Federal Republic would have been dissolved one year after the official announcement of the referendum result (Hofmann 2009).[13] Modern legal systems offer several examples of the constitutionalisation of the secession process, notably in the constitutional charters of the Principality of Liechtenstein (1921),[14] Saint

[13] See Constitutional Law on Referendum [done 18 July 1991] č. 327/1991 Sb.

[14] See Article 4(2) of the Liechtenstein Constitution, according to which: 'Individual communes have the right to secede from the State. A decision to initiate the secession procedure shall be taken by a majority of the citizens residing there who are entitled to vote. Secession shall be regulated by a law or, as the case may be, a treaty. In the latter event, a second ballot shall be held in the commune after the negotations have been completed'.

Kitts and Nevis (1983),[15] Uzbekistan (1992),[16] and the Federal Democratic Republic of Ethiopia (1995).[17] In other jurisdictions, while secession may not be explicitly enshrined in constitutional texts, it has been acknowledged through judicial interpretation—often contingent upon the requirement of a referendum. A paradigmatic example is the Canadian Supreme Court's landmark 1998 Reference on the secession of Quebec.[18]

In such cases, popular consultation assumes the character of a direct expression of sovereignty, manifesting in what are termed 'sovereignty referendums' (Şen 2015). These referendums address constitutionally significant issues, particularly those involving territorial reconfiguration and questions of State sovereignty.

Within the comparative spectrum, Northern Ireland occupies an intermediate position between permissive and prohibitionist constitutional models. Unlike rigid models that categorically forbid secession and uphold the inviolability of State unity, the Northern Irish arrangement includes an explicit statutory mechanism allowing for a change in constitutional status. However, this provision is distinct from more permissive systems in that it is contingent upon the discretionary political judgment of the British executive and is deeply influenced by a delicate intercommunal equilibrium.

Ultimately, the Northern Irish model represents a conditional and pact-based form of self-determination—grounded in principles of negotiated transition and mutual accommodation, rather than in an absolute or unilateral right to secede.

[15] See Article 113(1) and (2) of Saint Kitts and Nevis Constitution, according to which: 'The Nevis Island Legislature may provide that the island of Nevis shall cease to be federated with the island of Saint Christopher and accordingly that this Constitution shall no longer have effect in the island of Nevis. A bill for the purposes of subsection (1) shall not be regarded as being passed by the Assembly unless on its final reading the bill is supported by the votes of not less than two-thirds of all the elected members of the Assembly and such a bill shall not be submitted to the Governor-General for his assent unless [...] after it has been passed by the Assembly, the bill has been approved in a referendum held in the island of Nevis by not less than two-thirds of all the votes validly cast on that referendum [...]'.

[16] See Article 74 of the Uzbekistan Constitution, which states that: 'The Republic of Karakalpakstan shall have the right to secede from the Republic of Uzbekistan on the basis of a nation-wide referendum held by the people of Karakalpakstan'.

[17] See Article 39(4) of the Ethiopian Constitution, according to which: 'The right to self-determination, including secession, of every Nation, Nationality and People shall come into effect: (a) When a demand for secession has been approved by a two-thirds majority of the members of the Legislative Council of the Nation, Nationality or People concerned; (b) When the Federal Government has organized a referendum which must take place within three years from the time it received the concerned council's decision for secession; (c) When the demand for secession is supported by a majority vote in the referendum [...]'.

[18] *Reference Re Secession of Quebec* [1998] 2 SCR 217.

5 Northern Irish Constitutional Resilience between Consociational Logic and Secessionist Strains

British devolution, which has evolved since the late 1990s, is characterised by a flexible and asymmetrical approach to decentralisation, lacking a rigid constitutional framework. The most pronounced normative and functional divergence is found in the comparison between Scottish and Northern Irish devolution, which represent the two poles of the United Kingdom's constitutional pluralism.

The Scottish model mirrors Westminster's majoritarian logic, albeit within a devolved context. In contrast, the Northern Irish framework diverges fundamentally, since: (a) it does not permit the formation of a majority government, (b) mandates a compulsory cross-community coalition between Unionist and Nationalist parties, (c) structures the Executive on a dual-leadership model with equal powers, and (d) requires cross-community support for many key decisions. These institutional differences reflect distinct underlying purposes: in Scotland, devolution responds to a demand for national self-government, whereas in Northern Ireland, it functions primarily as a mechanism for conflict resolution and intercommunal power-sharing.

Furthermore, unlike Scotland—where the 2014 independence referendum was a one-off political concession with no codified right to self-determination—Northern Ireland possesses a formal, though conditional, legal pathway to secession. This is grounded in a bilateral, treaty-based framework, offering a recognised mechanism for constitutional change.

In fact, unlike Scottish and Welsh devolution, the Multi-Party Agreement was embedded in an international treaty between the UK and Ireland, grounded in mutual recognition of Irish self-determination. Its institutions were endorsed through concurrent referendums in both Northern Ireland and the Republic, underscoring its all-island legitimacy. The operation of the Northern Ireland Assembly was made interdependent with that of the North–South Ministerial Council (NSMC), a cross-border body established by treaty, reflecting a shared jurisdiction with the Irish Government.

This arrangement gives the UK–Northern Ireland relationship a partially federal character, aligning with Daniel Elazar's concept of a *federacy*—an autonomous entity in a predominantly unitary State (O'Leary 2019c, pp. 312–313). Externally, the Agreement introduced both confederal and federal features. The NSMC operates similarly to the EU Council of Ministers, facilitating cross-border cooperation while preserving ministerial accountability. A broader, though weaker, confederal structure was also created through the British–Irish Council (BIC), allowing sovereign and devolved governments, along with Crown dependencies, to coordinate policy and delegate functions across these islands (Elazar 1987, p. 7).

Northern Ireland's constitutional future remains marked by significant legal and political fluidity, shaped by both domestic and international dynamics. While politically part of the UK, Northern Ireland's geographic proximity to the Republic of Ireland—and thus the EU—has created tensions, especially following Brexit. The UK's withdrawal from the EU introduced a legal rupture between British parliamentary sovereignty and the consociational framework established by the Northern Ireland Act 1998.

The Northern Ireland Protocol, part of the 2019 Withdrawal Agreement, kept the region aligned with the EU single market for goods and imposed customs checks between Great Britain and Northern Ireland. This arrangement drew strong opposition from unionist parties, particularly the DUP, which triggered a governance crisis by refusing to appoint a Deputy First Minister, leading to executive paralysis from 2022 to early 2024. The Windsor Framework (2023) sought to ease tensions by introducing the 'Stormont brake', allowing the Assembly to block new EU rules deemed harmful to local interests. However, this safeguard relies on the functioning of devolved institutions—making it vulnerable to the very instability it aims to address.

Northern Ireland thus presents a constitutional paradox: it stands as a region where institutional rigidity coexists with political fluidity, and where legal mechanisms of inclusion are persistently tested by underlying aspirations for exclusion or departure. At the core of this paradox lies a deeply consociational arrangement that is both the product and the guarantor of peace, yet remains structurally susceptible to the centrifugal forces of secessionist nationalism and unionist retrenchment. This unique equilibrium offers a revealing case study in the constitutional resilience of plurinational States navigating the turbulent waters between unity and fragmentation.

Despite these limitations, the Northern Irish constitutional framework has demonstrated a remarkable capacity for endurance. Its survival through multiple crises—most notably the suspension of devolved government from 2002–2007, 2017–2020, and again from 2022 to early 2024—speaks not only to the tenacity of its legal scaffolding, but to the international, cross-community, and procedural legitimacy it continues to command. The hybridisation of internal power-sharing with external guarantees—particularly through the involvement of the Republic of Ireland and codification in treaty form—renders the Northern Irish model an institutional innovation, one that is both sub-state and transnational in scope.

In this context, the constitutional resilience of the Northern Irish model is contingent not merely on legal robustness, but on its adaptive capacity to moderate demographic, electoral, and geopolitical change. Nowhere is this more evident than in the post-Brexit landscape, where the Northern Ireland Protocol and subsequent Windsor Framework have introduced new regulatory borders and heightened the symbolic salience of identity politics. These post-Brexit developments have intensified perceptions of dislocation among unionist communities, while simultaneously strengthening the arguments of nationalist and reunification advocates.

Yet despite these structural limitations and recurring episodes of deadlock, the Northern Irish constitutional model has not collapsed. On the contrary, its resilience lies precisely in its ability to absorb shocks, adjust procedures (as seen with recent reforms to the Petition of Concern), and preserve a framework of mutual recognition in the face of deep-rooted antagonisms. This enduring adaptability affirms its value as a post-conflict constitutional paradigm. It shows that in deeply divided societies, sustainable peace may come not through erasing difference, but by embedding it into the heart of constitutional design, allowing space for both power-sharing and the managed possibility of secession.

References

Ahmed F, Perry A (2017) Constitutional statutes. Oxford J Legal Stud 37(2):461–481
Bieber F (2006) Post-War Bosnia. Ethnicity, inequality and public sector governance. Palgrave Macmillan, Cham
Bogaards M (1998) The favourable factors for consociational democracy: a review. Eur J Polit Res 33(4):475–496
Bogaards M (2019) Formal and informal consociational institutions: a comparison of the national pact and the Taif Agreement in Lebanon. Natl Ethnic Polit 25(1):27–42
Bogdanor V (2009) The New British Constitution. Hart, Oxford-Portland
Brady C (2018) Politics, policy and power, 1550–1603. In: J. Ohlmeyer (ed) The Cambridge history of Ireland. Volume II. 1550-1730. CUP, Cambridge, pp 23–47
Canny NP (1998) The origins of empire. In: Canny NP (ed) The Oxford history of the British Empire. Volume I. The Origins of Empire: British Overseas enterprise to the close of the 17th century. OUP, Oxford, pp 1–33
Caravale G (2017) A family of nations. Asimmetrie territoriali nel Regno Unito tra devolution e Brexit. Jovene, Naples
Closa C, Margiotta C, Martinico G (eds) (2020) Between democracy and law. The amorality of secession. Routledge, London
Edwards D (2018) Political change and social transformation, 1603–1641. In: Ohlmeyer J (ed) The Cambridge history of Ireland. Volume II. 1550-1730. CUP, Cambridge, pp 48–71
Elazar DJ (1987) Exploring federalism. University of Alabama Press, Tuscaloosa
Frosina L (2024) Separatismi e referendum. Teoria e prassi in prospettiva comparata. Jovene, Napoli
Haljan D (2014) Constitutionalising Secession. Hart, Oxford-Portland
Hirschl R (2014) Comparative matters. The Renaissance of comparative constitutional law. OUP, Oxford
Hofmann M (2009) Czechoslovakia, Dissolution of. Max Planck Encyclopedia of Public International Law, OUP, Oxford
Jackson VC (2012) Comparative constitutional law: methodologies. In: Rosenfeld M, Sajó A (eds) The Oxford handbook of comparative constitutional law. OUP, Oxford, pp 54–74.
Lijphart A (1977) Democracy in plural societies. Yale University Press, New Haven
Lijphart A (1995) Self-determination versus pre-determination of ethnic minorities in power-sharing systems. In: Kymlicka W (ed) The rights of minority cultures. OUP, Oxford, pp 275–287.
McCulloch A (2018) The use and abuse of veto rights in power-sharing systems: Northern Ireland's petition of concern in comparative perspective. Gov Opposit 53(4):735–756
McEvoy J (2006) The institutional design of executive formation in Northern Ireland. Reg Federal Stud 16(4):447–464
McGarry J, O'Leary B (eds) (2004) The Northern Ireland conflict: consociational engagements. OUP, Oxford
McGarry J, O'Leary B (2008) Consociational theory and peace agreements in pluri-national places: Northern Ireland and other cases. In: Ben-Porat G (ed) The failure of the Middle East peace process? A comparative analysis of peace implementation in Israel/Palestine, Northern Ireland and South Africa. Palgrave Macmillan, London, pp 70–96
Norman W (2006) Negotiating nationalism. Nation-Building, federalism, and secession in the multinational state. OUP, Oxford
O'Leary B (2019a) A treatise on Northern Ireland, Volume 1. Colonialism. OUP, Oxford
O'Leary B (2019b) A treatise on Northern Ireland, Volume 2. Control. OUP, Oxford
O'Leary B (2019c) A treatise on Northern Ireland, Volume 3. Consociation and Confederation. OUP, Oxford.
Örücü E (2006) Methodology of comparative law. In: Smits JA (ed) Elgar Encyclopedia of comparative law. Edward Elgar, Cheltenham, Northampton, pp 442–454

Palermo F (2019) Towards a comparative constitutional law of secession?. In: Delledonne G, Martinico G (eds) The Canadian contribution to a comparative law of secession. Legacies of the Quebec secession reference. Palgrave Macmillan, Cham, pp 265–282

Salamey I (2013) The government and politics of Lebanon. Routledge, London

Şen IG (2015) Sovereignty referendums in international and constitutional law. Springer, Heidelberg

Veach C (2018) Conquest and conquerors. In: Smith B (ed) The cambridge history of Ireland. Volume I. 600–1550. CUP, Cambridge, pp 157–181

Ward AJ (1994) The Irish constitutional tradition. Responsible government and modern Ireland, 1782-1992. Catholic University of America Press, Washington

Weinstock D (2001) Constitutionalizing the right to secede. J Polit Philosophy 9(2):182–203

Whitten LC (2023) Constitutional change in Northern Ireland. Bennett Institute for Public Policy – Institute for Government. Available via http://www.instituteforgovernment.org.uk/. Accessed 5 July 2025

Whysall A (2019) A Northern Ireland Border Poll. The Constitution Unit, London.

Wilford R (2009) Consociational government: inside the devolved Northern Ireland Executive. In: Taylor R (ed) Consociational theory. McGarry and O'Leary and the Northern Ireland conflict. Routledge, London-New York, pp 180–195

Wolff S (2011) Post-conflict state building: the debate on institutional choice. Third World Quart 32(10):1777–1802

The Welsh Exception: Gradualism and the Consolidation of Constitutional Asymmetry

Giulia Aravantinou Leonidi

Abstract This chapter examines the evolution of the devolution process in Wales from its inception in 1998 through 2025, situating the analysis within established scholarship and landmark institutional reforms. It also undertakes a comparative perspective on Scotland, highlighting key divergences and discussing convergences in legislative authority, institutional development, and policy outcomes. In particular, the author maintains that distinct historical contexts and political dynamics have shaped the unique devolutionary paths of the two nations. Particular attention is given to the initial arrangements established by the Government of Wales Act 1998, which established a devolution model markedly different from Scotland's immediate assumption of legislative powers, tracing the expansion of Welsh legislative powers through subsequent Westminster legislation. What may be termed the "Welsh exception"—the incremental and iterative process through which Wales has consolidated devolved authority—will be considered in detail, with a focus on how this path marked by gradualism has contributed to the entrenchment of constitutional asymmetry within the United Kingdom.

1 Introduction

The United Kingdom's devolutionary framework has long been defined by asymmetry, both in its formal structures and in its practical operation. While Scotland, Wales, and Northern Ireland have all acquired devolved powers, the journey of Welsh devolution has been shaped by a distinctive gradualism that sets it apart from the more immediate and comprehensive legislative autonomy secured by Scotland. This article explores what may be termed "the Welsh exception": the incremental and iterative process through which Wales has consolidated devolved powers, and how this path has contributed to the institutionalization of constitutional asymmetry within the United Kingdom.

G. Aravantinou Leonidi (✉)
Zayed University, Abu Dhabi, United Arab Emirates
e-mail: ioulia.aravantinouleonidi@zu.ac.ae

F. Savastano et al. (eds.), *Between Asymmetry and Secession*,
https://doi.org/10.1007/978-3-032-29603-0_12

The academic literature on devolution is particularly rich and provides important theoretical and empirical foundations for understanding these dynamics. Scholars have conceptualized devolution variously over time as administrative decentralization, substantive self-governance, or a hybrid model, and have debated how these frameworks apply to the UK's asymmetrical constitutional settlement. Beyond these conceptual debates, attention has been directed to the political forces that have either driven or constrained the transfer of powers, including the role of major political parties, the shifting tides of public opinion, and the evolving practices of intergovernmental relations. Against this backdrop, Wales and Scotland exemplify two divergent models of territorial self-government within the same constitutional order. The historical and institutional roots of this divergence are particularly significant. Scotland, with its long-established legal system, was institutionally prepared for broad legislative autonomy from the outset. Wales, by contrast, lacked a distinct legal order, which limited the scope of its initial settlement and produced a conferred-powers model that vested only executive powers in the Welsh institutions. Wales' differing structural starting point necessitated a more incremental transfer of powers, with successive Acts of Parliament gradually expanding Wales' legislative authority. By contrast, Scotland assumed wide-ranging powers at the beginning of devolution, enabling a more immediate form of constitutional self-assertion.

This historical path dependency has had enduring consequences for the development of territorial politics in the UK. Whereas Scotland has often leveraged its devolved powers to pursue a nation-building project that frequently places it in direct tension with Westminster, Wales has pursued a more pragmatic strategy of incremental empowerment, emphasizing collaboration, consensus-building, and institutional adaptation (Rawlings 2022). This approach has fostered a distinct model of shared governance that reflects Wales's evolving political identity within the Union. It also highlights the different constitutional logics at work within the UK: Scotland's devolution has been more explicitly nationalist in orientation, while Welsh devolution has been more gradualist, seeking to carve out space for distinctiveness without necessarily framing it in terms of separatism.

The consolidation of constitutional asymmetry thus emerges as a defining feature of the UK's territorial constitution. The comprehensive powers of the Scottish Parliament contrast sharply with the iterative development of the Welsh Senedd, while Northern Ireland's trajectory has been shaped by its unique political and security context (Murphy, Evershed 2021; Knox 2025), which has curtailed its capacity for sustained policy innovation despite similar formal powers and has made it a start- and-stop devolution model. In this sense, the Welsh case demonstrates how asymmetry is not merely an institutional arrangement but also a political strategy—one that reflects the challenges of accommodating diverse national identities within a state that resists the symmetry associated with classical federalism.

This chapter makes three central contributions. First, it situates Welsh devolution within the broader theoretical debates on asymmetrical governance and multilevel constitutionalism, with particular attention to the role of gradualism in shaping Wales's distinct trajectory. Second, it examines how the incremental empowerment of Welsh institutions has consolidated a model of constitutional asymmetry that is qualitatively different from Scotland's path. Third, it considers the implications of the Welsh exception for the stability and resilience of the Union, especially in the context of contemporary constitutional disruptions such as Brexit, which have tested the capacity of asymmetrical arrangements to manage territorial diversity. In advancing these arguments, the essay maintains that Wales's incremental path to devolution should not be seen as a "lesser" or derivative version of Scottish autonomy within the devolution framework. Rather, the Welsh case exemplifies a distinctive model of constitutional development in multinational states: one that embeds autonomy gradually, through negotiation and adaptation, while consolidating asymmetry as a stable feature of the UK's evolving constitutional order.

2 Devolution: Origins and Impact

Devolution has been described as the most significant constitutional change the United Kingdom has experienced since the Great Reform Act of 1832.[1] During his electoral campaign in the Midlothian constituency, William Gladstone declared: *"If we can make arrangements under which Ireland, Scotland, Wales, portions of England can deal with questions of local and special interest to themselves more efficiently than Parliament now can, that, I say, will be the attainment of a great national good*" (Bogdanor 1999).

Gladstone's vision was realized much later under Tony Blair's Labour government, though not without encountering resistance from those who, even today, view devolution to Scotland, Wales, and Northern Ireland as the final stage in the definitive decline of Great Britain (Hitchens 1999; Redwood 1999; Marr 2000; Paterson 2002).

In attempting to reconstruct the factors that contributed to the reshaping of the British constitutional framework, it is clear that devolution plays a central role in this process. It marked the transformation of the United Kingdom from a unitary state into a quasi-federal one, bringing about what has been termed the "devolved state" (Torre 2007a, b; Volpe 2007). It also altered the very way the United Kingdom is conceived. In the past, the English tended to regard the United Kingdom as the home of a single nation—the British nation. Today, in light of the profound changes introduced by devolution, the United Kingdom is more accurately understood as a multinational and multilevel state in which several nations (English, Scottish, Welsh, and Northern Irish) coexist (Caravale 2017; McEwen 2022).

Although devolution is often regarded as a relatively recent phenomenon, largely associated with the reforms of a Labour government, its origins can be traced back to the nineteenth century, well before the Labour Party itself was established. In

[1] The Reform Act of 1832, promoted by Lord Grey, was a legislative intervention that inaugurated a period of significant transformations in the British parliamentary system. Its approval was greeted with enthusiasm, as it renewed the antiquated electoral system after a series of failed attempts.

many respects, it represents the direct legacy of nineteenth-century Home Rule. The demands of Irish Home Rulers, subsequently echoed by the autonomist movements in Scotland and Wales, laid the foundations for nationalist currents that matured over the early decades of the twentieth century. These eventually coalesced into two enduring political forces: the Scottish National Party (SNP) and Plaid Cymru. By the 1970s—most notably between 1970 and 1979—these parties had become central actors in what many contemporaries perceived as a fundamental challenge to the constitutional integrity of the United Kingdom. Devolution—conceived as the broad reform movement that redistributed territorial powers to the sub-state regions of Scotland, Wales, and Northern Ireland—raises two fundamental and interrelated constitutional questions that have been consistently emphasized in the scholarly literature. The first concerns whether it is possible, or indeed desirable, to reach a definitive resolution to the challenges posed by Scottish nationalism and the enduring instability of the Northern Irish question, thereby strengthening the Union through the formal recognition of the distinctive characteristics of its constituent nations. The second relates to the advisability of preserving the inherently asymmetric character of the devolution settlement.

2.1 Devolution as a Brake on Centrifugal Forces: The Inception of Asymmetry

With regard to the first question, it is important to recall that the principal objective of devolution was to forestall secession within the United Kingdom by containing the centrifugal pressures generated by nationalist movements in Scotland and Wales, while in Northern Ireland, it sought to secure the participation of the Catholic nationalist minority in government. In Scotland, nationalists welcomed the introduction of devolution during the sweeping reforms initiated by the Blair government in the late 1990s, interpreting it not as a brake but as a catalyst for separatist aspirations. Sinn Féin in Northern Ireland similarly endorsed devolution, regarding it as a preliminary step toward detachment from the United Kingdom. By 2008, nationalist parties had assumed positions of power in all three devolved assemblies—through coalition arrangements in Wales and Northern Ireland, and as a minority government in Scotland. Against this backdrop, the Scottish National Party advanced a proposal to hold a consultative referendum on independence, a process that culminated in the government's February 2010 White Paper, *Scotland's Future: Draft Referendum (Scotland) Bill Consultation Paper*. This initiative reinvigorated opponents of devolution, who reiterated the claim that devolved governance accelerates fragmentation within the United Kingdom and inexorably propels the state toward disintegration. Many journalists and political commentators at the time adopted a markedly alarmist tone, suggesting that, since the introduction of devolution, Britain had entered a trajectory of irreversible decline (Stockwell 2025). Those concerned about the potential disintegration of the United Kingdom have been particularly unsettled by the asymmetry of the devolution settlement: Scotland has frequently been depicted as seeking to transcend the limits of devolved autonomy, while England has appeared hesitant to articulate a distinct national identity for fear of amplifying centrifugal pressures. From the perspective of constitutional theory, such anxieties are not surprising, since asymmetric arrangements are often regarded as inherently unstable. Federal theorists from Where onwards have stressed the importance of symmetry and balance, warning that differentiated autonomy may encourage, rather than suppress, secessionist demands. Yet more recent contributions in comparative federalism, particularly those of Stepan and Elazar, suggest that asymmetry may be a functional necessity in plurinational states, serving as a pragmatic accommodation of diversity rather than a harbinger of dissolution. In this light, it is worth recalling Vernon Bogdanor's cautionary observation that, with respect to the long-term effects of devolution, "it is far too early to tell." His position echoes Walter Bagehot's 1872 reflection, in the second edition of *The English Constitution*, that the consequences of the 1867 Reform Act could not yet be reliably assessed. Both underscore a key principle of constitutional development: institutional change cannot be evaluated in the short term, since political actors and electorates require time to adjust their expectations and disengage from prior constitutional habits. As Bruce Ackerman and other constitutional theorists have argued, transformative reforms unfold in "constitutional moments" whose meaning and durability only become apparent across decades, not years. From a comparative perspective, this dynamic is evident in multinational federations such as Canada, Belgium, and Spain, where asymmetrical devolution has generated persistent tensions but has also created enduring frameworks for negotiation. Like these cases, the United Kingdom's settlement should not be judged solely against an idealized model of federal equilibrium, but rather as part of an ongoing process of constitutional experimentation in a multilevel polity.

What can already be asserted with confidence, however, is that devolution has moved the United Kingdom decisively beyond the traditional unitary paradigm. Its significance lies not merely in institutional adjustment but in the introduction of a framework that is, in historical terms, wholly alien to the British constitutional tradition. The only partial precedent, the Northern Irish Stormont Parliament (1921–1972), illustrates the limits of comparison: imposed unilaterally by Westminster rather than conceded in response to nationalist claims, Stormont represented an exercise in containment rather than accommodation. By contrast, devolution in Scotland and Wales emerged from negotiation with nationalist movements, aligning the United Kingdom more closely with the logic of "holding-together" federations than with its own historical tradition of centralized sovereignty. In this sense, the British case contributes to wider debates in comparative federalism by illustrating both the risks and the adaptive potential of asymmetrical constitutional design in multinational states. The Northern Irish experience of devolution was profoundly shaped by the province's enduring political-religious conflict and by the first-past-the-post electoral system, which ensured the sustained dominance of the Protestant unionist party. Scotland and Wales, by contrast, developed under political, social, and economic conditions fundamentally distinct from those of Northern Ireland. In these cases, the trajectory of devolution has been closely bound to the evolving role of political parties—not only within Edinburgh and Cardiff, but also in Westminster. The functioning of devolution has often depended less on formal constitutional provisions than on the capacity of political actors to manage relations across different levels of government. Divergences between the exercise of devolved and central competences have frequently been addressed through informal practices of negotiation and coordination, rather than by invoking the Joint Ministerial Committee. As much of the literature on British constitutional development has noted, tensions between center and periphery have tended to sharpen when shifts in majority control at either the devolved or central level created partisan incongruence. In this respect, the politics of devolution has underscored the extent to which the United Kingdom's constitutional order relies on political conventions and flexible arrangements, rather than rigid institutional mechanisms, to manage intergovernmental relations.

2.2 Asymmetry and the Constitutional Paradox of Devolution

The second major issue raised by devolution concerns its asymmetry and the extent to which such an arrangement can generate a stable constitutional framework.

From the standpoint of constitutional theory, asymmetry poses a challenge to the principle of equal citizenship: while Scotland, Wales, and Northern Ireland all benefit from devolved powers, England—the largest and most populous component of the Union—remains excluded. The most striking expression of this imbalance lies in parliamentary representation. MPs from the devolved nations sitting at Westminster retain the right to vote on matters affecting England, whereas English MPs cannot vote on issues reserved to Scotland, Wales, or Northern Ireland. This anomaly, famously termed the *West Lothian Question* after Tam Dalyell's campaign in the late 1970s, illustrates what constitutional theorists describe as the "representation paradox" of asymmetrical governance: the very mechanisms designed to accommodate national diversity risk generating new inequalities at the center.

England's disadvantaged position is particularly paradoxical. Despite being the most populous, geographically extensive, and economically dominant part of the Union, it lacks its own parliament or assembly. Theoretically, the creation of an English Parliament might resolve this imbalance. Yet the absence of political demand for such an institution, combined with the near certainty that it would rival Westminster itself, has rendered this option politically unviable.

This difficulty was underscored by the Kilbrandon Commission in 1973, which rejected outright the idea of an English Parliament. The Commission reasoned that a federation composed of England, Scotland, Wales, and Northern Ireland would be so asymmetrical as to prove unworkable, since England's demographic and economic weight would inevitably dominate the system. Comparative federal theory lends weight to this conclusion: federations in which a single unit vastly outweighs the others—such as Canada with Ontario, or Spain with Castile—tend to struggle with balancing equality and effectiveness, often relying on informal accommodations rather than rigid federal symmetry.

A more pragmatic response within the British context has been captured by the slogan "English Votes for English Laws" (EVEL). This measure, endorsed by both the Conservative Party and the SNP, reflects what constitutional scholars term a functional rather than structural response: rather than redesigning the state along federal lines, EVEL seeks to mitigate representational inequality within the existing Westminster framework. Since 2006, successive proposals have advanced this approach, culminating in the Cameron government's announcement in the Queen's Speech of May 27, 2015, and its inclusion in the Conservative Party's manifesto.

Nonetheless, several commentators have highlighted the risks of embedding EVEL within the constitutional order. One potential consequence is that, in cases where a government depends on Scottish MPs for its majority, the House of Commons could effectively become bifurcated, producing two distinct majorities depending on the subject of legislation. In such circumstances, the government might be unable to secure passage of its preferred measures—an outcome often described as a "two-tier Parliament." The West Lothian Question is, in short, the direct product of the asymmetry that has become the hallmark of devolution. Over time, a number of remedies have been proposed: the creation of an English Parliament, the introduction of EVEL, and the establishment of regional assemblies in England. The latter option, however, was effectively foreclosed following the decisive rejection of regional devolution in the North East referendum of November 2004. In line with the Conservative Party's 2015 General Election manifesto, a significant step toward addressing the issue was taken in October of that year, when the House of Commons approved amendments to its Standing Orders to implement EVEL.[2] Under the new procedure, the Speaker was empowered to determine whether a bill applied only to England, or to England and Wales. In this task, the Speaker was assisted by the Clerk of Legislation and the Speaker's Counsel, both members of the parliamentary administration charged with the crucial function of filtering and classifying legislation. These rules applied to government bills, motions, and statutory instruments, and although they partially redressed the asymmetry of the settlement, they did not fundamentally alter the constitutional balance. As for the specter of separatism, those who describe the United Kingdom as "artificial" often overlook the enduring ties that sustain it, embodied in the institutional presence of its major unionist parties—Labour, Conservative, and Liberal Democrat. Yet in an era marked by recession and economic crisis, these parties have suffered electoral setbacks and a decline in influence, most visibly in Scotland, where successive elections have confirmed the Scottish National Party as the dominant political force. The referendum on Scottish independence of September 18, 2014, nevertheless demonstrated that the Union continues to rest on strong common interests and resilient shared institutions, capable of withstanding even the shock of a

[2] Rawlings, Richard. 2022. "Wales and the United Kingdom: A Territorial Constitutional Policy Drive." Territory, Politics, Governance 10 (5): 714–32.

direct secessionist challenge. There is thus little justification for the conclusion that asymmetric devolution, despite its undeniable tensions, cannot provide a stable constitutional response to nationalist pressures. Indeed, asymmetry has long been a feature of the British constitutional order, in which the component nations of the Union have historically been governed through arrangements tailored to their specific circumstances. On this basis, it is reasonable to endorse the view that asymmetric devolution need not represent a threat to the continuity of the United Kingdom. Rather, it may function as a pragmatic mechanism for containing the centrifugal dynamics of Scottish nationalism—a thesis sharply at odds with predictions that depict devolution as the first step toward the dissolution of the Union. At the same time, one cannot ignore that devolution poses challenges to two of the fundamental principles of the British constitutional order: the equality of benefits conferred by the state regardless of geographical location, and the principle of parliamentary sovereignty. With respect to sovereignty, in theory, it remains preserved, since the devolution statutes do not prevent Westminster from legislating for Scotland, Wales, and Northern Ireland, even in devolved matters. In practice, however, critics are partly vindicated, since devolution does impose a de facto limitation on Parliament's sovereignty. In Northern Ireland, this limitation is entrenched in the Belfast Agreement, a treaty between two states—the United Kingdom and Ireland—under which the British government may exercise authority in Northern Ireland only in accordance with the treaty (Kelly 2017). Following the adoption of the *Scotland Act 2016*, an additional limitation was introduced[3] through recognition of the permanence of Scottish institutions and the formalization of the Sewel Convention (Winetrobe 2005). The United Kingdom's withdrawal from the European Union introduced a new layer of constitutional complexity with profound implications for the devolution settlement. The central difficulty concerns the distribution of powers repatriated from Brussels to the devolved nations, a process that has reopened longstanding questions about the balance between central authority and territorial autonomy (McEldowney 2013; Anthony and Morison 2005). In 2018, the House of Lords Constitution Committee underscored the need for constructive dialogue between the UK government and the devolved administrations to ensure that repatriated competences were managed in a manner consistent with the principles of devolution (HL 2018). Both the Scottish and Welsh governments submitted amendments to the draft EU Withdrawal Bill, arguing that, in its original form, the legislation threatened to undermine the very foundations of devolution by recentralizing powers that, in principle, should have been devolved. The dispute over repatriated competences revealed the fragility of the UK's territorial constitution in the post-Brexit context. In Scotland, the controversy fed into a broader narrative advanced by the SNP, which presented Brexit—opposed by a majority of Scottish voters—as evidence of the structural limits of devolution within a Union still governed by the principle of parliamentary sovereignty. In Wales, although nationalist

[3]The Legislative Consent Motion (commonly known as the Sewel motion) requires the Scottish Parliament to pass a resolution consenting to Westminster's enactment of legislation on matters within its devolved competence.

claims were less pronounced, concerns about the encroachment of Westminster powers nevertheless sharpened intergovernmental tensions (Tierney 2018). Nowhere, however, were the constitutional consequences of Brexit more acute than in Northern Ireland. The need to preserve the open border between Northern Ireland and the Republic of Ireland, a cornerstone of the 1998 Good Friday Agreement, led to the adoption of the Northern Ireland Protocol. This arrangement effectively kept Northern Ireland aligned with certain EU regulatory frameworks, creating a de facto regulatory border in the Irish Sea. While designed as a compromise, the Protocol was politically contentious, particularly among unionists who perceived it as weakening Northern Ireland's place within the Union. In 2023, the Windsor Framework sought to address these concerns by introducing new mechanisms to ease checks on goods moving from Great Britain to Northern Ireland and by creating the so-called "Stormont brake," granting the Northern Ireland Assembly the power to object to the application of new EU rules. While the Framework represented a pragmatic attempt at recalibration, it underscored once again how Brexit has destabilized the constitutional equilibrium of the United Kingdom by layering external commitments onto an already asymmetrical internal settlement. Taken together, these developments demonstrate how external shocks—most notably the UK's departure from the EU—can reverberate through domestic constitutional arrangements, intensifying territorial grievances and testing the resilience of asymmetrical governance. Brexit has thus functioned as a stress test for devolution: in Scotland and Wales, by reigniting debates about sovereignty and self-determination, and in Northern Ireland, by intertwining the future of devolution with the preservation of peace and cross-border cooperation (Keating 2022; Minto and Wyn Jones 2025).

3 The First Steps of the Devolution Process in Wales

In July 1998, the *Government of Wales Act* was enacted. Welsh devolution reflected the long history of Anglo-Welsh relations and the convergence of interests that had bound the destinies of the two nations together since the era of Edward I. The provisions adopted for Wales in this first devolution statute highlighted its historical, political, economic, and cultural distinctiveness, as well as its position of subordination vis-à-vis England. For the first time in the British constitutional order, the Act introduced a clear distinction between primary and secondary legislative authority, a feature more typical of continental legal systems (Forman 2002; Torre 2014). The Welsh devolution settlement[4] established the National Assembly for Wales, a unicameral body composed of 60 members, elected partly in single-member constituencies by simple plurality and partly in regional constituencies through proportional

[4] The political and legal assimilation of Wales began in 1284 under Edward I (Longshanks) with the Statute of Rhuddlan, later completed by the Act for the Government of Wales 1535.

representation by list.[5] The Assembly was granted only limited autonomy, confined to administrative functions transferred through delegated legislation. The transfer of normative powers from the central government took place through two distinct procedures: the first relied on *Orders in Council*, while the second depended on *primary legislation*. Delegated legislation concerned specifically enumerated subject areas that traditionally fell within the competence of the Secretary of State.[6] This arrangement amounted to executive devolution rather than legislative devolution, since no primary legislative powers were conferred—unlike in Scotland, where such powers were granted. Thus, a wholly unprecedented model of devolution and decentralization emerged, unfamiliar to the British political system. It inevitably raised questions about the effectiveness of an assembly without primary legislative powers, particularly in a context where—unlike in systems such as Germany's—no clear principles had been developed to regulate the relationship between primary legislation and subordinate legislation enacted by subnational entities.

3.1 Legislative Devolution at Last?

Following the enactment of the *Government of Wales Act* (1998), criticism arose over the fact that an Assembly deriving its legitimacy from popular election was unable to exercise the quintessential functions of a representative body—namely, primary legislative authority (Hazell and Sinclair 1999). This was considered an absurdity, a genuine paradox, such that some even came to regard the pre-devolution arrangement—where the Welsh Office enjoyed broad functional capacity but lacked

[5] The National Assembly for Wales, with its sixty members, is the smallest of the devolved legislatures. Research conducted by the UK Changing Union project (2012–2015) found that lower chambers in EU states have, on average, 267 members, and suggested increasing the size of the Welsh Assembly to 100 members for a sub-state parliament representing about three million citizens. By comparison, the Northern Ireland Assembly has 108 members for a population of two million; the Stormont House Agreement (December 23, 2014)—incorporated into the *Northern Ireland (Stormont House Agreement) Bill* 2015—proposed reducing this to 90. The question of enlarging the Welsh Assembly is not new: the Richard Commission on the Powers and Electoral Arrangements of the National Assembly (2006) recommended an increase, though its suggestions on composition were not implemented in the *Government of Wales Act 2006*. The issue was revisited in the Assembly Commission's The Future of the Assembly: ensuring its capacity to deliver for Wales (January 2015) and, most recently, in A Parliament that works for Wales. The report of the Expert Panel on Assembly Electoral Reform (November 2017) also proposed adopting the Single Transferable Vote and extending the franchise to sixteen-year-olds.

[6] In particular, according to Schedule 2 of the Government of Wales Act 1998, these areas included: agriculture, forestry, fisheries and food; culture (including museums, galleries, and libraries) and sites of historical and artistic interest; economic development; education; the environment and water protection; health and social services; road infrastructure; housing policy; industry; local government; town and country planning; transport; sport; leisure and tourism; and the Welsh language.

the legitimacy typical of representative institutions—as preferable. Devolution was meant to fill this gap by creating an Assembly whose powers matched the status of an elective body. Yet paradoxically, the Assembly—whose members were regularly elected by the Welsh electorate—was excluded from the legislative process, its role reduced to that of a mere "executor" of policies determined in London (Burrows 2000). This paradox, which had marked Welsh institutional life since the Assembly's inception, was not resolved by the *Government of Wales Act* (2006). That Act failed to deliver the radical reform envisaged in the *Richard Report* and the subsequent *White Paper*, both of which had promised to mitigate the asymmetry (Torre 2000). This would have transformed the UK's devolution settlement by conferring legislative powers on Welsh institutions equivalent to those exercised by the Scottish Parliament. The Welsh model aspired to emulate the Scottish Parliament's significant legislative powers, yet Scotland and Wales remained, and remain, institutionally distinct realities within the framework of British devolution. From the outset, it was clear that further adjustments would be necessary to make the Welsh autonomy regime effective. Many commentators noted both the limited scope of the Assembly's influence over the legal framework applicable to Wales and the often-poor quality of the legislation it produced. In July 2002, the Welsh Assembly Government appointed a commission chaired by Lord Richard of Ammanford, former Leader of the House of Lords, with the task of reviewing the functioning of the devolution settlement. The commission began its work in September 2002, undertaking the difficult task of redefining the terms of Welsh devolution. Its final report—known as the *Richard Report*—was published in March 2004 (Commission on the Powers and Electoral Arrangements of the National Assembly for Wales 2004). The report made clear the commission's vision for the Assembly's future, offering a dual proposal for its realization. As the report stated: "The Assembly is the democratically elected representative body for the whole of Wales. The Welsh Assembly Government should be able to formulate policies within clearly defined fields and should have the power to implement all the stages for effective delivery, in partnership with the UK Government and other stakeholders. The Assembly Government should be able to set its own priorities and timetables for action. It should be accountable to the people of Wales through the elected Assembly for its policies and their implementation." Having considered the consequences of expanding the limited powers conferred upon the Assembly by the 1998 Act, the commission recommended dividing the institution into two separate bodies—one executive, the other legislative—thus accelerating the revision of the 1998 settlement, which it described as an "interim constitution." The tone and scope of these recommendations suggested the prospect of a radical constitutional reform, one that would transform the Assembly into a body with significantly enhanced legislative powers (Rawlings 2004; Trench 2005; McAllister 2004). However, the political implications of the *Richard Report* were not fully anticipated, even within the Labour Party. Numerous initiatives were promoted by both Welsh political figures and scholars to supplement the commission's proposals and assess their feasibility for adoption by Welsh and UK institutions. Shortly after the publication of the report, on October 6, 2004, the Assembly passed a motion urging legislative amendment of the 1998 Act. In June 2005, the

Secretary of State for Wales issued the White Paper *Better Governance for Wales*. Echoing the dissatisfaction with the devolution settlement, the White Paper noted: "Experience has shown that the Assembly's current legislative powers are too fragmented to enable the Assembly Government to implement its policies as effectively as it should. The Assembly's powers do not amount to a coherent whole; they arise under many different Acts and vary both in their scope and in their significance to the discharge of the Assembly's functions." This was Labour's response to the Richard Commission, pledging that if re-elected, the party would expand the Assembly's secondary legislative powers, revise the GWA's provisions on legislative competence, formally separate the Assembly's executive and legislative branches, and reform the electoral system. Within a few months, the proposals of the *Richard Report* and the White Paper were combined into the *Government of Wales Bill* (2005). After a complex legislative process, the bill received royal assent, becoming the *Government of Wales Act* (2006). The 2006 Act provided for the expansion of the Assembly's legislative powers through a three-stage process.[7] It also created the Welsh Assembly Government as a body distinct from the National Assembly, effectively abolishing the *corporate body* established by the 1998 Act. Another innovation was the establishment of the Welsh Consolidated Fund and the introduction of new financial provisions. From the perspective of legislative technique, it is noteworthy that the method of defining competences adopted in both the 1998 and 2006 Welsh statutes differed from that of the *Scotland Act*, instead resembling the approach taken in the devolution acts of the 1970s.[8] Finally, the

[7] The first phase was characterised by Westminster's reliance on "framework powers," designed to expand the Welsh Assembly's discretion in the legislative field while formally preserving the ultimate supervisory authority of Parliament. The second phase provided for a substantial transfer of competences in areas where the Assembly was already exercising powers originally conferred under the Government of Wales Act 1998. Such transfers were effected through Orders in Council, adopted with the joint consent of the National Assembly for Wales and the UK Parliament, thereby embedding a mechanism of shared constitutional control. The third phase, expressly contemplated by statute, was marked by the referendum on conferring upon the Assembly primary legislative competence in subject areas where it had previously exercised only subordinate legislative authority.

[8] The statute provides for an explicit enumeration of the competences devolved to Wales, while applying a residual clause with respect to those matters reserved to Westminster. The Richard Report, after considering and rejecting the tripartite model of legislative competences adopted in Northern Ireland—distinguishing between excepted, transferred, and reserved powers—recommended instead a scheme modelled on Scotland. Under this proposal, only the matters reserved to the exclusive competence of Westminster would be enumerated, while the residual clause would operate in favour of the Welsh Assembly. By contrast, in Scotland, the devolution of primary legislative competences was achieved through a clear specification of matters reserved exclusively to Westminster ("reserved matters"), with all other fields assigned to the Scottish Parliament ("devolved matters"). The model adopted for the distribution of legislative competences of the Scottish Parliament is therefore residual in nature. This model, which is also found in several federal systems, represented an innovative departure from the earlier Scotland Act 1978, as it inverted the logic of enumerating devolved powers. As Hazell and Sinclair observe: "The major difference from the devolution legislation of the 1970s is that the Scotland Act 1998 does not specify the powers devolved to the Scottish Parliament. The 1978 Act had a schedule defining the powers of the

Government of Wales Act (2006) set the stage for the referendum of March 3, 2011, in which voters were asked whether the Assembly should be granted primary legislative powers, thereby moving the Welsh model closer to the Scottish parliamentary framework.

3.2 Toward a New Model of Devolution for Wales: The Wales Act 2014 and the Wales Act 2017

Further confirmation that Wales has consistently lagged behind Scotland in the devolution process came with the passage of the *Wales Act 2014* in December 2014. Following the recommendations of the Silk Commission, the Act granted Wales greater autonomy in fiscal matters, adopting a framework modeled on the *Scotland Act 2012*. However, the provisions required approval by referendum—a referendum which, to date, has not been held. After the publication of the second part of the Silk Commission's report, which contained recommendations on the limitations of the current Welsh devolution regime, the Secretary of State for Wales, Stephen Crabb, presented to the Westminster Parliament in February 2015 a document prepared with the contributions of all major Welsh political forces and in collaboration with members of the academic community. At the time of presenting the bill, the Secretary of State for Wales declared that it "sets out in detail how the Government plans [...] to create a stronger, clearer, and fairer devolution settlement for Wales that will stand the test of time." The UK Government's Command Paper, *Powers for a Purpose: Towards a Lasting Devolution Settlement for Wales* (February 2015), outlined the mechanisms by which the executive intended to introduce a new model of devolution for Wales. Unlike the earlier settlement, which was based on specific transfers of powers to the Welsh National Assembly, this new framework—consistent with the Silk Commission's recommendations—conferred primary legislative authority in all areas not explicitly reserved to the UK Parliament at Westminster. This was achieved through the adoption of a *reserved powers model*, a technique generally used in federal systems and already applied in Scotland and Northern Ireland. In the Queen's Speech of May 27, 2015, the Government announced the introduction of another *Wales Bill*, which would devolve competences in areas such as energy, transportation, and the regulation of local elections. On October 20, 2015, the Draft Wales Bill was presented to Parliament. This bill aimed to implement the commitments made in the St. David's Day Agreement and the recommendations of the second report of the Silk Commission. The bill was received without great enthusiasm either in political circles or in academic debate.

new parliament in the smallest detail; and gave extensive powers to the Secretary of State to intervene. The 1998 Act is a far more confident and generous measure. Following the model of the Government of Ireland Act 1920 it simply lists the powers reserved to Westminster, with all the remainder devolved to Edinburgh."

Nevertheless, deepening the Welsh devolution process remained high on the Government's political agenda, as demonstrated by the Queen's Speech of May 28, 2016. Only a few days later, the *Wales Bill 2016–2017* (Bill 5) was introduced. The new proposal initially found favor with the new Secretary of State for Wales, Alun Cairns, who expressed hope for the swift conclusion of an agreement between UK and Welsh ministers on the revised text.

On January 31, 2017, the *Wales Act 2017* was enacted. The new devolution statute for Wales consists of five parts and seven schedules. Like the *Scotland Act 2016*, it grants permanent status to Welsh institutions. It also formally recognizes the existence of a distinct body of Welsh law, composed of legislation enacted both by Westminster and by the Cardiff Assembly. The *Wales Act 2017* adopts the reserved-powers model of competence distribution, following the Scottish precedent, and introduces an analogous provision concerning the formalization of the legislative consent motion (Moon 2017; Evans 2020; Wales Governance Centre 2020). In April 2018, Wales fully entered the fifth stage of devolution—legislative devolution—under which the National Assembly for Wales may legislate on any matter not expressly reserved to the Westminster Parliament, such as defense or foreign policy (House of Commons Library 2018).[9]

3.3 Deepening Autonomy: Recent Constitutional and Political Developments in Welsh Devolution

Recent years have witnessed profound developments in Welsh devolution, consolidating its institutional maturity while exposing new tensions in the relationship between Cardiff and Westminster. The most significant reform is the Senedd Cymru (Members and Elections) Act 2024, which received Royal Assent in June 2024 and will reshape Welsh democracy at the 2026 election. The legislation expands the Senedd from 60 to 96 members, introduces a new system of proportional representation across 16 larger constituencies, and replaces the previous Additional Member System with a closed-list model designed to improve proportionality and support gender parity. As Adam Evans has observed, the Senedd Cymru (Members and Elections) Act 2024 represents the culmination of two decades of debate over the adequacy of the Senedd's institutional capacity. By expanding membership from 60 to 96, the reform addresses long-standing concerns, first articulated by the Richard Commission, regarding the Assembly's ability to discharge its legislative and scrutiny functions effectively. Yet Evans underscores that this achievement comes at a

[9] The so-called "fifth stage" of Welsh devolution came into effect on April 1, 2018, marking a fundamental constitutional shift. This stage moved Wales from the earlier conferred powers model—under which the Assembly could legislate only in areas explicitly devolved—to a reserved powers model, whereby the Assembly is empowered to legislate on any matter not expressly reserved to Westminster. This brought Wales closer in line with the Scottish settlement and was widely regarded as consolidating the incremental trajectory of Welsh constitutional development.

significant cost: the adoption of a closed-list proportional representation system, which he interprets as a decisive shift away from the aspirational, deliberative ethos that once characterized reform debates. In this respect, the 2024 settlement embodies what he terms a movement from "aspiration to cold-headed reality," privileging pragmatic institutional enlargement over more ambitious democratic innovation (Evans 2025; Griffiths 2024). The 2026 boundary review has already produced a new electoral map, notable not only for its structural innovation but also for the symbolic decision to adopt Welsh-only constituency names, underscoring the growing centrality of the Welsh language to political identity. This cultural emphasis was further consolidated by the passage of the Welsh Language and Education (Wales) Act 2025, which commits the government to creating one million Welsh speakers by 2050, introduces local Welsh-language learning plans, and establishes a new National Institute for Learning Welsh (Lloyd Williams et al. 2024). In parallel, constitutional reform has extended into the economic domain. A landmark proposal, the Crown Estate (Devolution to Wales) Bill (Democracy and Boundary Commission Cymru 2024; Welsh Language and Education (Wales) Act 2025; United Kingdom Parliament 2025), passed its House of Lords report stage in July 2025 without opposition and is widely expected to transfer control of Wales's Crown Estate assets—including lucrative offshore wind and marine rights—to the Welsh Government. Support for the measure has been unanimous among Welsh local authorities, with Gwent becoming the last of 22 councils to endorse it in June 2025. Alongside this, ongoing debates about the devolution of justice have gained momentum, with the Welsh Government pressing for the phased transfer of judicial and policing powers in line with the recommendations of the Commission on Justice in Wales and the Independent Commission on the Constitutional Future of Wales. This push highlights both the gradualist character of Welsh constitutional development and its aspiration toward a more distinct legal identity, even as practical negotiations with London remain unresolved. Fiscal developments have further shaped the devolutionary landscape (Welsh Government 2025). The First Supplementary Budget 2025–26 increased Welsh Government resources by nearly £600 million, raising total spending to £29.5 billion, while the UK Government's 2025–29 Spending Review projected average annual funding for Wales of £22.4 billion, representing a 0.9% real-terms revenue increase and placing Wales ahead of England, Scotland, and Northern Ireland in per capita allocations. These financial adjustments reflect both the opportunities and the limitations of devolved fiscal autonomy, with Cardiff still heavily dependent on Treasury allocations while seeking greater control over resources such as the Crown Estate. The political context has been equally dynamic. Traditional unionist parties—Labour, Conservative, and Liberal Democrat—have seen declining influence, particularly in Scotland but increasingly in Wales as well, where Plaid Cymru has risen in prominence, and Reform UK has emerged as a disruptive force. Polling in early 2025 placed Plaid at 30%, Reform at 25%, and Labour at only 18%, signaling an unprecedentedly competitive Senedd election in 2026 (Senedd Research Service 2025a, b). Within Labour itself, tensions between Cardiff and Westminster have sharpened: First Minister Eluned Morgan has articulated a distinctively Welsh strategy—termed the "red Welsh way" (Morris

2025)—which emphasizes devolution of welfare powers, infrastructure investment, and economic sovereignty, and explicitly criticizes the centralizing tendencies of Keir Starmer's leadership in London. Commentators have warned that Starmer's failure to deliver on promises of a "partnership in power" with Welsh Labour risks further destabilizing the relationship between Cardiff and Westminster at a crucial juncture. Taken together, these developments illustrate both the deepening of Welsh devolution and its exposure to new strains. Institutional reforms such as the Senedd expansion and electoral redesign signal a maturing devolved polity; legislative initiatives such as the Crown Estate Bill and justice devolution debates underscore Wales's pursuit of greater constitutional and economic autonomy, while fiscal adjustments demonstrate the continued reliance on central transfers even amidst modest gains in funding. Finally, the intensifying political competition and divergence between Welsh and UK Labour exemplify the contested nature of devolution's future trajectory (Payne 2025). In this sense, Wales offers a striking example of how gradualism, asymmetry, and political contestation interact to consolidate devolved governance while simultaneously testing the resilience of the UK's territorial constitution.

4 Conclusions

The journey of Welsh devolution reveals the emergence of what might now be termed the "Welsh exception." In contrast to the more advanced Scottish model of autonomy, the Welsh settlement has been characterized by caution, negotiation, and gradual accretion of powers. This has been grounded in the different historical and political roots of the quests for autonomy of the two British nations. Thus, from the limited framework of the Government of Wales Act 1998 to the more ambitious provisions of the Wales Acts of 2014 and 2017, the Senedd has slowly consolidated its authority and its powers. This incrementalism, or gradualism, often regarded as a weakness in the past, has in practice enabled Welsh institutions to evolve, taking into account at the same time public opinion and political realities, promoting and embedding a culture of consensus and shared governance.

Comparison with Scotland has proven crucial in providing evidence of how different constitutional and political contexts have generated divergent paths. In fact, while Scotland has used its devolved powers to pursue an explicit project of national self-assertion, culminating in the unfortunate independence referendum of 2014, Wales has prioritized institutional consolidation and the steady development of a distinct political identity within the UK.

Recent developments have both tested and reinforced this pattern. Brexit, one of the most significant events in the UK's contemporary institutional life, has reopened long-standing questions about the distribution of competences and the resilience of intergovernmental arrangements, exposing the limits of trust between Cardiff and Westminster. Yet the experience also underscored the ability of Welsh institutions to assert themselves within the evolving territorial constitution. The recent adoption of landmark legislation shows how Wales has progressively moved from the tentative executive model of the late 1990s to a more confident and constitutionally salient legislature, thus confirming the ever-evolving nature of the devolution process in the United Kingdom.

Furthermore, the Welsh experience is of extreme importance for its contributions to the discussion on decentralization processes, as it illustrates both the potential and the controversial features of asymmetrical devolution. In fact, if on one hand, incremental reform in Wales has provided a sustainable path toward greater autonomy and a unique pattern, on the other, the persistence of asymmetry raises questions about equality, representation, and sovereignty—questions that still resonate across the board of the Union.

The study has tried to demonstrate how Wales represents, within the devolution framework, a unique and outstanding example of gradualism in the acquisition of relevant legislative powers. This characteristic has shaped a unique model of asymmetric autonomy and has, in time, promoted the institutionalization of national distinctiveness. The analysis provided in this essay is not meant to be definitive in any way, as the topic deserves future and more in-depth investigation.

References

Anthony G, Morison J (2005) Here, there, and (maybe) here again: the story of law-making for Post-1998 Northern Ireland. In: Hazell R, Rawlings R (eds) Devolution, law making and the constitution. Imprint Academic, Exeter, p 178

Burrows N (2000) Devolution. Sweet & Maxwell, London

Caravale G (2017) A family of nations. Asimmetrie territoriali nel Regno Unito tra Devolution e Brexit. Jovene, Napoli

Commission on the Powers and Electoral Arrangements of the National Assembly for Wales (2004) Report of the Richard Commission. The Stationery Office, London

Democracy and Boundary Commission Cymru (2024) Review of Senedd Constituencies 2026. Democracy and Boundary Commission for Wales

Evans G (2020) Devolution in Wales: From Assembly to Parliament. UK Constitutional Law Blog, 15 April 2020

Evans G (2024/2025). Senedd Reform: from aspiration to cold-headed reality? The Political Quarterly, online first. https://onlinelibrary.wiley.com/journal/1467923x

Forman FN (2002) Constitutional change in the United Kingdom. Routledge, London

Government of Wales Act 1998 (c. 33)

Griffiths JD (2024) Making the case for more politicians: a survey experiment to assess public support for expanding the Senedd. Parliam Aff 77(2):285–309

Hazell R, Sinclair D (1999) The British constitution in 1997–98: Labour's constitutional revolution. Parliam Aff 52(1):161 ff

Hitchens P (1999) The abolition of Britain. Quarter Books, London

House of Commons Library (2018) Twenty Years of Devolution in Wales, 1998–2018. Wales: Current Constitutional Position, 31 July 2018

House of Lords, Select Committee on the Constitution (2018) 9th Report of Session 2017–19, European Union (Withdrawal) Bill, HL Paper 69, 29 January 2018. https://publications.parliament.uk/pa/ld201719/ldselect/ldconst/69/69.pdf

Keating M (2022) Between two unions: UK devolution, European integration and Brexit. Territ, Politics, Gov 10(5):629–645. https://doi.org/10.1080/21622671.2022.2050939
Kelly R (2017) English Votes for English Laws. House of Commons Library Briefing Paper, no. 7339, 20 June 2017
Knox C (2025) Polarisation and inequality: 'Peace' in Northern Ireland. J Soc Policy:1–23
Law Wales (2024) Senedd Cymru (Members and Elections) Act 2024. 8 July 2024
Lloyd Williams S, Siôn ap Gruffudd G, Haf Gruffydd Jones E (2024) The development of welsh language education since devolution. Wales J Edu 26(2):72–90
Marr A (2000) The day Britain died. Profile Books, London
McAllister L (2004) The Richard Commission—Wales's alternative constitutional convention? Contemp Wales 17:128–139
McEldowney J (2013) The impact of devolution on the UK parliament. In: Horne A, Drewry G, Oliver D (eds) Parliament and the law. Hart Publishing, Oxford, p 215
McEwen N (2022) Irreconcilable sovereignties? Brexit and Scottish self-government. Territ, Polit Gov 10(5):733–749
Minto R, Wyn Jones R (2025). UK intergovernmental relations: on state-form, sovereignty and Brexit. Territory, Politics, Governance, 1–20
Moon D (2017) Welsh devolution and the problem of legislative competence. J Legal Policy:5–6
Morris S (2025) Eluned Morgan to Set Out 'Red Welsh Way' in Speech Criticising Starmer. The Guardian, 6 May 2025
Murphy MC, Evershed J (2021) Contesting sovereignty and Borders: Northern Ireland, devolution and the union. Territ, Polit, Gov 10(5):661–677
O'Brien M, Stapenhurst R, Johnston N. Parliaments as Peacebuilders in Conflict-affected Countries
Paterson L (2002) Is Britain disintegrating? Changing views of 'Britain' after devolution. Reg Fed Stud 12(1):21–42
Payne S (2025) Reform UK and Plaid Cymru Vie for Gains in Labour Stronghold of Wales. Financial Times, May 2025
Rawlings R (2004). Say Not the Struggle Naught Availeth: The Richard Commission and After. Aberystwyth. Centre for Welsh Legal Affairs
Rawlings R (2022) Wales and the United Kingdom: a territorial constitutional policy drive. Territ Polit Gov 10(5):714–732
Senedd Cymru (2024) Senedd Cymru (Members and Elections) Act 2024, c. 8
Senedd Research Service (2025a) What Does the UK Government's 2025 Spending Review Mean for Wales? Senedd Research Articles, August 2025
Senedd Research Service (2025b) What's in the Welsh Government's First Supplementary Budget 2025–26? Senedd Research Articles, July 2025
Stockwell L (2025) Contesting Regional Sovereignty from Below: The Unsettling Effect of Unilateral Independence and Autonomy Referendums. Territory, Politics, Governance, June, 1–24. https://doi.org/10.1080/21622671.2025.2510653
Tierney S (2018) Devolution and the repatriation of competences: the house of lords constitution committee reports on the EU withdrawal bill. The Constitution Unit Blog, 29 January 2018
Torre A (2007a) Devolution (dir. comp.). Enciclopedia giuridica Treccani, supplément XV:6–7
Torre A (2007b) Le metamorfosi del governo territoriale: lo Stato devoluto è una nuova forma di Stato? In: Torre A (ed) Processi di devolution e transizioni costituzionali negli Stati unitari (dal Regno Unito all'Europa), 309–338
Torre A (2014) Regno Unito. In: Carrozza P, Di Giovine A, Ferrari GF (eds) Diritto costituzionale comparato. Roma–Bari, Laterza
Trench A (2005) The Assembly's future as a legislative body. In: Osmond J (ed) Welsh politics come of age: responses to the Richard Commission. Institute of Welsh Affairs, Cardiff
United Kingdom Parliament (2025) Crown Estate (Devolution to Wales) Bill, HL Bill 21
Volpe L (2007) Summary Ending: verso la 'forma devoluta' dello Stato costituzionale?, 1151–1176
Wales Act 2014, c. 29 (UK)
Wales Act 2017, c. 4 (UK)

Wales Governance Centre (2020) Securing a fairer framework for devolved powers in Wales. Cardiff University, Cardiff
Welsh Language and Education (Wales) Act 2025 (2025)
Winetrobe B (2005) A partnership of parliaments? Scottish law making under the Sewel Convention at Westminster and Holyrood. In: Hazell R, Rawlings R (eds) Devolution, law making and the constitution. Exeter, Imprint Academic, pp 39–67

Federalism and Asymmetry as Viable Alternatives to Secession? Crisis, Changes, and Perspectives of the "Spanish Autonomic State"

Laura Frosina

Abstract The study analyzes the most recent political and constitutional debate concerning the crisis and reform prospects of the decentralization system of the Spanish State. Adopting a historical-constitutional approach, it first reconstructs the territorial question of the Basque and Catalan nationalities within the "autonomic" State, which has undergone significant transformations over time, yet remains incomplete and undefined at the constitutional level. In particular, the study focuses on recent developments regarding Catalonia's new financial model and the reform of the Basque Country's Statute, currently under debate. Finally, the article examines the potential transformation of the autonomous State into a federal and asymmetric model as a possible solution capable of curbing centrifugal dynamics and separatist movements, which, especially in recent years, have highlighted the critical issues and weaknesses of the "autonomic" model.

1 The *Territorial Question* between Federalism, Asymmetry, and Secession

The *territorial question* in Spain constitutes first and foremost a historical problem, intrinsically linked to key stages in the country's processes of democratization and modernization, which has not found a complete and satisfactory resolution throughout its historical and constitutional evolution.[1] However, this does not imply denying that the constituent compromise of 1978 regarding the autonomous model represented an undisputed achievement of Spanish democracy. It enabled a country emerging from a

[1] The need to avoid disruptions in Spain's transition to democracy explains why the historic regional problem, labeled by some more specifically as the "Catalan problem," was not resolved, causing frustration among those who aspired to a profound restructuring of the territorial model. See Ortega y Gasset (2014), pp. 56–57.

L. Frosina (✉)
Department of Political Sciences, Sapienza University of Rome, Rome, Italy
e-mail: laura.frosina@uniroma1.it

F. Savastano et al. (eds.), *Between Asymmetry and Secession*,
https://doi.org/10.1007/978-3-032-29603-0_13

long-standing dictatorship to create a constitutional framework for social coexistence, grounded in the integration of pluralism, the recognition of territorial diversity, and the affirmation of national unity. The experience of the autonomous State has led to the development of a quasi-federal system that has proven to operate effectively, guaranteeing a high degree of territorial decentralization and a full integration of society.

Nonetheless, nearly 48 years after the entry into force of the Constitution, the autonomous model's main features—its open, undefined nature and limited constitutional grounding—which initially facilitated its adaptation to the diverse territorial needs, are increasingly revealing their limitations, contributing to dysfunctions, inequalities, and different distortions within the system. The most evident shortcomings that have afflicted the Spanish autonomous State over the past decades include: the chaotic distribution of competences between the State and the Autonomous Communities, which has resulted in a flood of appeals before the Constitutional Court; the lack of effective territorial coordination by the central government, largely due to the absence of a Senate—or any other institutional body—capable of representing territorial interests; a deficit of institutional loyalty and the weakness of interterritorial cooperation mechanisms; and finally a flawed and uncertain system of regional financing, incapable of ensuring equality and interterritorial solidarity.[2]

These critical issues within the autonomous system, both structural in nature and developed throughout its evolution, have generated significant territorial inequalities. This has created fertile ground for the emergence of renewed secessionist demands, confederal impulses, or calls for extreme bilateralism, all of which have, in turn, fueled a sharp polarization of the political debate, oscillating between secessionist options and proposals for recentralization.[3]

In contrast, within the doctrinal debate, there is a broad consensus on the need to overcome the main problems of Title VIII of the Constitution through a constitutional reform oriented towards federalism (Aja 2014; Aragón Reyes 2016; Camara Villar 2018; Rubio Llorente 2014).

The transformation of the autonomous State into a fully federal model is an objective pursued not only by a large part of the academic doctrine but also by several political forces, foremost among them the *Partido Socialista Obrero Español* (Spanish Socialist Workers' Party—PSOE).

This transition to federalism is viewed as a means of institutional rationalization and a "salvific" political-constitutional solution capable of averting scenarios of fragmentation or disintegration posed by secessionist political agendas.

The renewal of the constitutional compromise through a federal pact, constitutional amendments introducing federal techniques and mechanisms aimed at improving the distribution of powers, territorial representation at the institutional level, interterritorial cooperation, and the system of autonomous financing, are

---

[2] For these and other issues concerning the autonomic State, see Muñoz Machado (2017), pp. 10–12. More recently, see the various contributions published in the book edited by Galera Victoria (2024), *passim*.

[3] On these issues, see, most recently, De Miguel Barcena (2025).

widely shared constructive objectives. However, they are not sufficient to fully resolve the territorial question. One of the fundamental critical issues—of which the Catalan independence crisis represents only the tip of the iceberg—is the role of constitutional, legal, and cultural asymmetry, which is and continues to be a defining feature of the Spanish territorial model. If not adequately addressed, this asymmetry risks remaining a structural and unresolved problem for the autonomous State (Arrieta Alberdi 2025).[4] This paper will examine the most constitutionally relevant factors of asymmetry, both static and dynamic, in order to reflect—in the concluding section—on the role that asymmetry might play within a renewed federal framework capable of countering secessionist and disintegrative trends that threaten territorial integrity and national unity.

2 The Asymmetric Constitutional Dimension of the Autonomous State and Its Weakening in Practice

The application of asymmetry in the context of plurinational federalism and regionalism is a relatively recent tool for managing differences and resolving conflicts in contemporary constitutionalism (Tarlton 1965; Mastromarino 2010). Asymmetry can be characterized as *de jure* or *de facto* (Watts 2005), depending on whether it is recognized and institutionalized at the constitutional or legislative level, or remains merely a cultural, economic, and social phenomenon.

Spanish regionalism is commonly considered an asymmetrical system, similar to the Italian one, as it displays territorial differences of varying nature and extent, mainly stemming from historical factors. In particular, the Spanish Constitution of 1978 introduces elements of differentiation, which result in distinctions of identity and asymmetries—or micro-asymmetries—either permanent or temporary, depending on whether they are intended to address structural or merely transitory territorial issues or problems (López Aguilar 1997; Aja 1999). The main differentiation, which holds more symbolic identity value than legal significance, is found in Article 2 of the Constitution. This article recognizes and guarantees the right to autonomy of the nationalities and regions within the framework of the indissoluble unity of the Spanish nation, thereby making a distinction between these two territorial entities. This constitutional provision—essentially aimed at recognizing the historical and identity-based specificities of Galicia, the Basque Country, and Catalonia (Monti 2021)—has not led to a significant differentiation between the two territorial categories in the evolution of the autonomous State. Nevertheless, it holds strong symbolic value for the historical nationalities, which have historically demanded—and continue to demand—differentiated legal treatment by virtue of

[4] Reference is made to the reflections of Herrero y Rodriguez de Miñón (2010), p. 38, who observes that asymmetric plurinationality is a distinctive feature of the autonomous State, a fundamental part of its structure, whose failure to recognize it can cause problems and generate tensions that, if not resolved, threaten the integrity of Spain.

this constitutional recognition. In reality, this distinction—which, in the initial phase of the establishment of the autonomous State, marked a division between the so-called fast-track and slow-track Autonomous Communities—has become increasingly blurred over time. This assimilation between the two types of autonomy was due both to the process of constitutional homogenization imposed on the model of territorial decentralization by the main political parties (*Partido Socialista Obrero Español*—PSOE and the *Partido Popular*—Popular Party—PP), and to the decision of some Autonomous Communities of Andalusia, Valencia, Aragon, the Canary Islands, and the Balearic Islands to define themselves as historical nationalities—or simply as nationalities—within the framework of the second-generation statutory reforms (García Roca 2005).[5]

A permanent constitutional differentiation of the territorial system is represented, however, by the additional provision that recognizes the *derechos históricos*, which have been implemented through the economic and financial regimes of the Basque Country and Navarre—systems known as *Concierto* and *Convenio económico* (Garcia de Pablos 2020). In addition to this constitutional asymmetry, there are also some forms of permanent micro-asymmetry, known as *hechos diferenciales,*[6] provided for in several articles of the Constitution, which recognize and protect, for example: linguistic diversity and the co-official status of regional languages (Art. 3), regional symbols and flags (Art. 4), insular specificity (Third Additional Provision), and local, foral, or special civil rights existing in certain Autonomous Communities (Art. 149.1.8).[7]

The aim of the Spanish Constituent was, therefore, to address the territorial question by recognizing the historical and legal specificities of certain territories within the unitary framework of the autonomous State, without introducing elements of permanent differentiation between the various Autonomous Communities. The aim was to lay solid foundations to advance, in the long term, towards an increasingly cohesive, homogeneous, and stable model capable of preserving internal pluralism (Castellà Andreu 2018). In essence, the decision was not to crystallize a two-tier system of autonomy, as established, for example, by the Italian Constitution, but rather to design an open and dynamic model aimed at overcoming—after five years—the structural differences between the two types of autonomies, while

[5]In a critical sense, on the risks of generalizing asymmetry in the second-generation statutory reforms, see García Roca (2005), pp. 73 et seq.

[6]According to the Pan-Hispanic Dictionary of Legal Spanish, hechos diferenciales means "Certain cultural, historical, geographical, economic, or social characteristics of some Autonomous Communities to which constitutional or legal recognition of particular powers is linked."

[7]Based on the constitutional text, it is therefore possible to make a distinction among the historical nationalities of 1978: Euskadi, Catalonia, and Galicia; to which, since 2007, Andalusia, Aragon, Valencia, the Balearic Islands, and the Canary Islands have been added, having self-defined as nationalities; singular autonomies fully included under the First Additional Provision: Euskadi and Navarre; territories with their own civil law (foral law): Euskadi, Navarre, Catalonia, Galicia, Aragon, and the Balearic Islands.

maintaining only the Basque and Navarrese economic and financial regimes and the *hechos diferenciales*.[8]

In the initial decades of the development of Spain's autonomous system, there was a clear political will to harmonize and standardize the territorial framework through a series of political and legislative measures. Notable among these were the Pactos Autonómicos of 1981 and 1992, agreed upon by the PSOE and the PP, as well as the 1982 Organic Law for the Harmonization of the Autonomous Process (LOAPA), which was subsequently declared largely unconstitutional by the Constitutional Court (Hernández Lafuente, González García 1992–1993). Another key instrument was the reform of the Statutes of Autonomy, through which the Autonomous Communities gradually expanded their scope of powers, pursuant to Article 148(3) of the Spanish Constitution, thus aligning with the other regions (Alvarez Conde 2007; Balaguer Callejón 2010). Added to these elements was a legislative expansion of the State through a broad, and at times abusive, interpretation of the so-called bases, which in some cases limited the legislative autonomy of the Autonomous Communities and their corresponding implementing laws (so-called *legislación de desarollo*).

This process of homogenization and levelling out of differences provoked a reaction from Basque, Catalan, and Galician nationalist parties, who felt they had lost their constitutionally recognized uniqueness and began to demand renewed differentiation and asymmetry. These demands were formally articulated in the 1998 *Barcelona Declaration*, signed by Convergence and Union (*Convergència i Unió*—CiU), the Basque National Party (*Partido Nacionalista Vasco*—PNV), and the Galician Nationalist Bloc (*Bloque Nacionalista Galego*—BNG). The declaration proposed the transformation of the autonomous model into a federal, plurinational, and asymmetrical State, featuring, among other elements, a Senate representing nationalities and regions, a special financial regime for Galicia and Catalonia, and enhanced representation and participation of territorial autonomies within the framework of the European Union. During the 1990s, the political debate surrounding the reform of the territorial model centered on the contrast between a persistent trend towards homogenization—supported by some Autonomous Communities and encapsulated in the well-known formula *café para todos*—and a renewed proposal for an asymmetrical federal model advocated mainly by the historical nationalities, summarized as *champán para las nacionalidades*. This context created fertile ground for the emergence of various pressures and impulses that converged in reform proposals and second-generation statutory reforms approved in the early years of the new century. While some Autonomous Communities, such as the Basque Country and Catalonia, sought to further differentiate themselves by demanding greater autonomy, recognition of their national identity, and even self-determination, others aimed to narrow the gap with the historical nationalities by proclaiming themselves as such and strengthening their competences and

[8] For historical rights and differential facts, see in particular García Roca (2000) and Herrero y Rodriguez de Miñón (1998).

self-government. The metaphor of the hare and the tortoise, used by some scholars to describe Spanish regionalism (Blanco Valdés 2008; Pradera 1993), also accompanied this latest wave of statutory reforms, which introduced further elements of complexity, differentiation, and heterogeneity within the autonomous State.

The overall evolution of the first 20 years of the decentralization model, here summarized in its key stages, has intensified certain structural weaknesses and underlying tensions, giving rise to new demands and, to use a term frequently employed by the Catalan independence movement, attempts at outright disconnection from Spain, which have seriously challenged the indissoluble unity of the nation.

3 Claims of the Historical Nationalities: The Cases of the Basque Country and Catalonia

The frustration experienced by the Basque and Catalan Communities due to the homogenization of autonomy and competences—and the resulting dilution of their territorial distinctiveness during the 1990s—led moderate Basque and Catalan nationalists to shift from autonomism to independentism. This is not surprising, given that both Communities have a strong national identity with deep historical roots and a long tradition of self-government, on which their uniqueness within the autonomous State depends.

The demands for external self-determination—also expressed as derecho a decidir—put forward by peripheral nationalist movements have become intertwined, in the new century, with calls for statutory reform. These demands have established themselves on the country's political scene, altering its political and constitutional stability. The correlation between the denial of asymmetry and the rise in secessionist claims has been evident in the evolution of both the Basque and Catalan autonomous experiences (Monti 2021).

3.1 The Singularity of the Basque Country and the Lack of a Statutory Reform

In the Basque Country, this process towards greater autonomy until independence, promoted by the Basque Nationalist Party jointly with the parties of the Basque Nationalist Front (*Abertzale Left*), materialized in the 2003 proposal for a statutory reform, known as the *Ibarretxe Plan* (Solozábal Echavarría 2005). The latter, as is well known, was approved by the Basque Parliament but subsequently rejected as a draft organic law by the *Cortes Generales*. The *Plan* presented several elements of deliberate ambiguity: while its preamble invoked the right to decide (*derecho a decidir*) over the Basque Country's future, it simultaneously called for a pact of free association compatible with the development of a composite, plurinational, and asymmetrical State—sketching an undefined model of confederalism and shared sovereignty between the State and the Basque Country (López Basaguren 2008, 2009). This statutory reform was deemed incompatible with the Constitution because it sought to change the type of State through an organic law—a result that, if anything, could only have been achieved through a constitutional amendment, which—as is well known—does not face material limits in the Spanish constitutional order, as it does not adhere to a model of militant democracy. The Plan was a document of extraordinary political significance as it marked a radical shift in the trajectory of Basque nationalism. The latter moved toward the goal of independence, moving away from the previous moderate approach, which was essentially based on the full implementation of the Statute of Guernica through the transfer of residual competences from the central government.

The Basque independence movement reached its peak in 2007 with the approval of the so-called *hoja de ruta*, which outlined a series of milestones leading up to a referendum on the Basque territorial issue. This was followed, in 2008, by the approval of *Law 9/2008,* on *popular consultation of the Basque electorate on the issue of peace and political normalization*, which provided for the holding of a referendum on the cessation of ETA violence as a precondition for initiating dialogue and negotiations with the terrorist organization, as well as the adoption of an agreement on the right to decide (*derecho a decidir*), to be submitted to a referendum of the Basque electorate.[9] This law, known as the second *Ibarretxe Plan*, gave rise to one of the first and most significant rulings by the Constitutional Court on secession and referendums—namely, Judgment No. 103/2008—which declared it unconstitutional because it infringed upon the exclusive competence of the State to call referendums (Art. 149.1.32 of the Constitution) and violated the unity of the Spanish nation, enshrined in Article 2 of the Constitution.[10] In its ruling, the Court clarified that granting the Basque people the ownership of the right to decide is equivalent to assigning sovereignty to a fraction of the Spanish people, thereby violating the fundamental principle that the Spanish people as a whole are—and remain—the sole holders of national sovereignty, which is the foundation of the Constitution and the source of all political power.

This phase of radicalization of the more moderate Basque nationalism, focused on secessionist claims, represented more of a temporary episode in the long political and institutional evolution of the Autonomous Community. Soon after, its demands shifted toward a deepening of regional self-government and greater asymmetry and bilateralism within the constitutional framework of the autonomous State. The issue of the right to decide, strongly supported in a secessionist key by EH Bildu and the parties of the *Frente Abertzale*, has always remained part of the political debate on autonomy. However, in the more moderate reinterpretations put forward by the Basque nationalism of the PNV, it has lost the unilateral

[9] Tajadura Tejada (2009).

[10] On this ruling, see López Basaguren (2009).

and distinctly pro-independence character that marked the phase of the *Ibarretxe Plan*.

The PNV's return to a moderate position can be explained, at least in part, by the institutional reforms that followed, which entailed the transfer of competencies and the further development of the regional tax system. These measures contributed, albeit only partially, to fulfilling key political and social aspirations of the Basque Autonomous Community.

Especially during the last three legislatures (XI, XII, and XIII), the establishment of coalition governments between the PNV and the Socialist Party of Euskadi (*Partido Socialista de Euskadi*—PSE)—along with the Basque nationalists' parliamentary support to the two most recent coalition governments at national level led by Pedro Sánchez—created new political conditions conducive to a shift in the approach to the territorial question, with a definitive renunciation of unilateralism. The governing parties have centered their political agenda on strengthening self-government, particularly through the transfer of outstanding powers and the approval of a fully lawful statutory reform supported by broad political consensus within the Basque Parliament. The main challenge, however, lies in forging an agreement between nationalist and non-nationalist forces on the content of the reform, which all parliamentary factions now consider essential to replace the outdated and unrevised 1979 statute. The recognition of the Basque nation as a political entity, holder of the *derecho a decidir*, and the provision for a referendum allowing the Basque people to democratically and legally determine their own political and constitutional future represent the most contentious and divisive issues at the heart of the political debate, in direct conflict with the positions held by the main national political parties.[11]

In light of these political divisions, the Basque statutory reform risks becoming stalled, preventing the historic nationality from adopting a new statute. This would result in not only forgoing new forms of constitutional asymmetry compatible with the principles of equality and solidarity upon which the autonomous state is founded, but also missing out on a statutory evolution similar to that undertaken by other Autonomous Communities that have adopted new statutes over the past two decades.

This paradox—manifesting as a form of statutory stagnation for the Basque Autonomous Community—confirms the close relationship between asymmetry and secession, and supports the validity of using the former as an alternative to the latter.

---

[11] For an analysis of the positions held by various constitutional scholars on the issue of the right to self-determination, see Ruipérez Alamillo (2002). On the contents of the right to decide, see, especially, Tudela Aranda (2016). On the limits of the right to decide, see Corcuera Atienza (2009).

3.2 Catalonia between Asymmetry, Secession, and the Long-Awaited Reform of Fiscal Autonomy

In Catalonia, the situation is even more complex, as the nationalist issue—similarly influenced by the process of progressive homogenization and the elimination of asymmetries within the autonomous State—has deteriorated into a more radical attempt at unilateral and unconstitutional secession (Castellà Andreu 2016).

It is important to recall that the roots of the Catalan question date back to the constituent phase, during which a shared territorial model was peacefully accepted, one that did not entail any specific legal status for Catalonia, but was instead limited—predominantly—to the recognition of an identity-based asymmetry, as reflected in Article 2 of the Spanish Constitution.[12]

Until the early 2000s, moderate Catalan nationalism—closely tied to the institutional figure of Pujol—had a distinctly autonomist character, disconnected from any form of independence claim.[13] The prevailing political approach was always to negotiate with central governments—through governance agreements—for new powers or financial arrangements, to strengthen self-government, even beyond the limits of the Statute, without a clear idea of how to translate the distinctiveness of Catalonia as a historical nationality within the autonomous State (De Carreras Serra 2010).

Political dissatisfaction with the absence of a specific model of autonomy for Catalonia—comparable, for instance, to the Basque model—soon resurfaced among various Catalan parties, both nationalist and non-nationalist. This discontent led to the political maturation and drafting of the new Statute of Autonomy of 2006. The Catalan Statute, which represented a fundamental milestone in the redefinition of Catalonia's autonomy within the autonomous State, was strongly supported by both nationalist and autonomist parties as a means to recover the special status lost following the generalization of autonomy brought about by the implementation of the "café para todos" model. The new Statute, in its original formulation, introduced a specific and highly developed regime of differentiation for Catalonia, based on the full recognition of its historical, cultural, and linguistic distinctiveness (Carrillo 2008). It significantly expanded the range of powers attributed to the Autonomous Community and reinforced the regional self-government of the Generalitat, while explicitly refraining from any reference to secession or self-determination (Tornos Mas 2007; Viver Pi-Sunyer 2008). The strongly asymmetrical and autonomist character of the new Statute appeared, in the years following its approval, to have satisfied the main demands of Catalanism, addressing some of the unresolved issues related to the territorial question. The intervention of the Constitutional Court, through Ruling No. 31/2010 on the Catalan Statute, instead represented a step back

[12] On the origins of Catalan nationalism and its evolution, see, among others, F. De Carreras Serra (2010).

[13] On Pujolism as an autonomist form of nationalism that rejects the separatist option, see Caminal i Badia (2001).

from that achievement, as it declared several statutory provisions unconstitutional and provided a constitutionally compliant reinterpretation of many others. In doing so, it significantly curtailed the autonomist and innovative scope of the Statute, dashing the hopes of Catalan nationalist and autonomist parties to advance toward asymmetric federalism through the instrument of statutory reform.[14] The intervention of the Constitutional Court marked the beginning of a deep crisis in relations between Madrid and Barcelona, which intensified in 2012 with Prime Minister Rajoy's rejection of the so-called *Pacto Fiscal* proposed by the Catalan Government. This initiative aimed to introduce an economic and financial model similar to the Basque *concierto económico*.

As noted by some scholars (Poggeschi 2018), the controversial ruling on the Statute and the refusal of the *Pacto Fiscal* laid the groundwork for the emergence of the independence movement and the advancement of the secessionist agenda, which developed in several stages and came to be known as the *procés*. The harsh response of the State institutions to Catalonia's demands for statutory and financial asymmetry influenced the definitive shift of Catalan nationalism from autonomism to independentism, and its evolution toward a unilateral path that led to the holding of two entirely illegitimate popular consultations on independence, in 2014 and 2017.[15] The radicalization of Catalan pro-independence parties, the adoption of unilateral strategies, the intransigence of the central government, and the judicial repression exercised by the State have constituted the defining features of the *procés* (Ferraiuolo 2017; Di Martino 2018). It has gone down in history for the complete unwillingness of both sides to negotiate a politically and legally shared solution, and for the democratic and constitutional rupture that occurred over the course of its development. In particular, the 2017 Catalan independence referendum, followed by the declaration of independence by the regional Parliament—declared unconstitutional by Rulings No. 114 and 124/2017, respectively—marked the definitive breaking point with the central government, leading, for the first time in Spanish constitutional history, to the application of the coercive clause provided for in Article 155 of the Constitution (Albertí Rovira 2018).

The Catalan independence issue, which thus escalated into a serious political and constitutional crisis, found a path toward resolution only following the political and governmental changes that have taken place at both the national and regional levels over the past five years, leading to the abandonment of unilateralism and judicial avenues in favor of dialogue and negotiation. The resumption of dialogue and negotiations—which are, moreover, fundamental components of Spain's political and governmental stability—has formed the foundation of the process to resolve the Catalan crisis (Mastromarino 2014).

The openings and agreements reached by the last two Sánchez-led coalition governments and the Catalan independence parties, together with the historic victory of

---

[14] Among the numerous commentaries, see AA.VV. (2010), pp. 9–68; Castellà Andreu (2010). For a critical perspective, as outlined above, see in particular Pérez Royo (2011), and compare with Requejo Rodríguez (2011).

[15] A reference on these consultations may be made to Frosina (2024), pp. 247–264.

the Catalan Socialist Party (PSC) in the most recent regional elections in May 2024—which saw the loss of the independence majority after 12 consecutive years—have created favorable political conditions to initiate a phase of pacification and political-institutional normalization in the Autonomous Community. This development was formally confirmed by the approval of Organic Law No. 1/2024 on amnesty, which was recently largely upheld as constitutional by the Constitutional Court.

Although at this stage the goal of secession appears, at least temporarily, to have been set aside, achieving a more pronounced asymmetry—primarily based on a new model of financial autonomy for Catalonia—remains one of the main priorities for both *Esquerra Republicana de Catalunya* (Republican Left of Catalonia—ERC) and Junts per Catalunya (Together for Catalonia, Junts).

The agreement for the appointment of Salvador Illa, signed between the *Socialists and the Catalan Republicans* at the start of the XV legislature, includes provisions for the approval of a *Fiscal Pact,* the key elements of which have already begun to be implemented in the understanding reached within the State-Generalitat Bilateral Commission convened in mid-July 2025.

In this latest agreement—considered a partial success by the *Republicans* and a complete failure by the *Junts independents*—the central tenets of the Fiscal Pact were confirmed. These include the transfer to the Catalan Tax Agency of the management and collection of 100% of the taxes paid in Catalonia, alongside the payment to the State of a fixed quota (still undefined) for public services provided in the region, and, finally, a solidarity contribution to the other Autonomous Communities "to help ensure equity among the territories."[16]

The proposed financial model has so far been outlined only in broad terms and still requires a detailed definition of both the financial amounts and the implementation timelines, as well as significant legislative reforms to enable its enactment and full application.

However, its potential implementation is viewed by some Autonomous Communities as creating an unjustified asymmetry in favor of Catalonia. Consequently, these Communities are calling for a reform of the common financing system through a revision of the *Organic Law on the Financing of the Autonomous Communities* (LOFCA), while also demanding stronger financial autonomy arrangements for themselves, without further widening the existing gap with Catalonia as a historical nationality.

These recent developments highlight the persistent challenges in resolving the Catalan issue and illustrate how a model of targeted asymmetry continues to face difficulties in gaining firm establishment within the Spanish autonomous State.

[16] Above the contents of the new *Fiscal Pact,* see Lago Peñas (2024).

4 Prospects for Reform of the Autonomous State and the Difficulties of Reconciling Asymmetry and Cooperation

The failure to implement the demands for differentiation persistently advanced by the Basque Country and Catalonia, together with the widespread dissatisfaction among the other Autonomous Communities regarding the disorganized and uneven functioning of the regional model, has brought the issue of constitutional reform of the State's structure back to the forefront of political, social, and academic debate (Galera Victoria 2024; Durbán Martín, Palao Gil 2025).

As highlighted in this paper, the intensification in recent decades of certain unresolved historical and constitutional issues—particularly those related to the identity of the historical nationalities and to the role of asymmetry and bilateralism in the evolution of the decentralization model, which came to a head with the unconstitutional drifts of the attempted Basque statutory reform and the Catalan crisis—has exposed the limits of the statutory reform process, the finite expandability of the regional model, and the centrality of constitutional revision in addressing the territorial question.[17] In both political and academic discourse, the prospect of a federal reform is widely supported and appears to have evolved into a fundamental cultural option—even before being a constitutional one—and into an institutional solution deemed essential to ensure the survival of the autonomous State.[18] The most broadly shared "theoretical-general" proposal is that of a comprehensive constitutional restyling aimed at consolidating a common space of coexistence—cohesive and based on solidarity—that guarantees the unity of the State, the integration of pluralism, and respect for diversity, moving in the direction of "una España cohesionada en la diversidad." If the intended outcome is clear, the mechanisms and tools to make it practically operational remain less so. There is a broad consensus on the federal option as an almost salvific solution for the autonomous State, as well as full awareness of its missing components. However, what seems to be lacking is a shared—if only embryonic—vision of this new model to be defined at the constitutional level and implemented through political and legislative means. The challenge remains of how to reshape and rationalize the distribution of powers between the State and the Autonomous Communities, how to reform the second chamber and the system of interterritorial conferences, and how to implement the reform of fiscal federalism—reconciling the needs for cohesion and cooperation with those of differentiation and asymmetry, which must find a stable balance within the constitutional framework. Above all, the demands for diversification, as extensively highlighted in the paper, if not adequately addressed at a systemic level, risk escalating and causing short-circuits—sometimes paralyzing—in the functioning of the State. In the current political phase, particularly in the Basque Country, the central

---

[17] On the connections between constitutional revision and statutory reforms, see Ortega Álvarez (2015) and Montilla Martos (2015).

[18] On the Democratic Revitalization of Autonomous Spain through Federalism, see Caamaño (2014).

issue remains the statutory reform, which has failed to take off mainly due to political divisions over the question of self-determination, while in Catalonia, the core issue seems to have shifted in recent months from secession to the reform of fiscal autonomy. These are not issues confined to these individual territorial realities but rather deeper dilemmas that impact the political and constitutional life of the State. The issue of Basque statutory reform affects the broader and delicate question of secession referendum and its controversial constitutional admissibility, while the matter of Catalonia's new financial regime also involves the other Autonomous Communities, which mostly consider this differentiation constitutionally unfounded, unjustified, and discriminatory, and claim the right to receive equal treatment. These brief reflections highlight the difficulty of resolving some problems of the historical nationalities through asymmetric and bilateral solutions that are not based on full acceptance by the other territorial autonomies and on a prior revision of the "territorial constitution."

The federalization of the autonomous model, through the introduction of institutions, procedures, and institutional bodies typically associated with federal systems, cannot disregard an underlying framework that identifies a solution to the vexed question of the historical nationalities. This could involve, for example, an asymmetric federalism based on the definitive constitutional recognition of asymmetry, or a model of cooperative federalism tempered by micro-asymmetries, *derechos históricos*, and bilateral channels. Opening the constitutional "*melón*" (can of worms) is highly daunting due to the plurality of political and territorial aspirations—sometimes conflicting—that would need to be reconciled within the scope of a broad constitutional reform. For this reason, at the academic level, it is suggested to aim for a reform proposal in which consensus is not a prerequisite to start the process, but rather a goal to be progressively and painstakingly achieved at the parliamentary level. The problem with constitutional reform lies in its excessive procedural complexity, which makes the constitutionally prescribed procedures in Articles 167 and 168 difficult to implement in practice, relegating Spain for about 48 years to a sort of constitutional stalemate, evidenced by the overall approval of only four constitutional reforms. The excessive rigidity of the Constitution, which clashes with a theoretical and jurisprudential view supporting the absence of substantive limits to constitutional revision, makes achieving the goal of reforming the "territorial constitution" particularly difficult—especially in the current context marked by greater political polarization and a more intense territorial conflict than in the past.

The future of the autonomous State thus hinges on this delicate and slippery terrain of constitutional revision and on the challenge of outlining a federal model capable of satisfying the differing political and territorial demands, including those of the historical nationalities, that make up Spain's complex and diverse territorial reality. From the very moment that the constitutional reform project is approved, Spain will have to demonstrate its ability to transform into a State capable of preserving and strengthening national unity through the integration of pluralism and the recognition of territorial differences.

References

AA.VV (2010) Valoración general de la sentencia 31/2010 del Tribunal Constitucional. Revista Catalana de Dret Públic no 1, 9–68

Aja E (1999) El Estado Autonómico. Federalismo y hechos diferenciales. Madrid, Alianza

Aja E (2014) Estado autonómico y reforma federal. Madrid, Alianza

Albertí Rovira E (2018) Cuestiones constitucionales en torno a la aplicación del artículo 155 CE en el conflicto de Cataluña. Revista d'estudis autonòmics i federals no 27, 1–23

Álvarez Conde E (2007) Reforma constitucional y reformas estatutarias. Madrid, Iustel

Aragón Reyes M (2016) Sustituir o reformar el Estado autonómico? Revista Española de Derecho Constitucional no 108, 359–373

Arrieta Alberdi J (2025) Problema territorial o de convivencia? Una historia y dos propuestas. In: Durbán Martín I, Palao Gil J (coord.) Constitución y Estado Autonómico. Cartografía del debate sobre la reforma territoriale. Valencia, Tirant Lo Blanch, 529–582

Balaguer Callejón F (2010) Reformas estatutarias y organización institucional. In: Ortega Alvarez LI, Camara Villar G, Montilla Martos JA, Balaguer Callejón F (dirs) Reformas estatutarias y organización institucional. Sevilla, Instituto Andaluz de Administración Publica, 33–45

Blanco Valdés R (2008) La seconda decentralizzazione spagnola: fra riforma confederale e stato possibile. In: Gambino S (a cura di), Regionalismi e statuti. Le riforme in Spagna e in Italia. Milano, Giuffrè, 103–136

Caamaño F (2014) Democracia federal. Apuntes sobre España. Madrid, Turpial

Camara Villar G (2018) La organización territorial de España. Una reflexión sobre el estado de la cuestión y claves para la reforma constitucional. Revista de Derecho Político no 101, 395–430

Caminal i Badia M (2001) El pujolisme i la ideologia nacionalista de Convergència Democràtica de Catalunya. In: Culla i Clarà JB (coord.), El pal de paller. Convergència Democràtica de Catalunya (1974–2009). Barcelona, Editorial Pòrtic

Carrillo M (2008) El nuevo estatuto de autonomia de Cataluña, en el marco de las reformas estatutarias en España. Revista de Derecho no 15(1), 61–90

Castellà Andreu JM (2010) La sentencia del Tribunal Constitucional 31/2010 sobre el Estatuto de Autonomía de Cataluña y su significado para el futuro del Estado autonómico. Federalismi.it no. 18

Castellà Andreu JM (2016) Tribunal Constitucional y proceso secesionista catalán: respuesta jurídico-constitucionales a un conflicto político-constitucional. Teoría y Realidad Constitucional no 37, 561–592

Castellà Andreu JM (2018) Estado autonómico: pluralismo y integración constitucional. Madrid, Marcial Pons

De Carreras Serra F (2010) La tradición histórica y el catalanismo actual. Cuadernos de Alzate no 42, 20–34

Corcuera Atienza F J (2009) Los límites del "derecho a decidir" (comentario de la STC 103/2008). Revista Española de Derecho Constitucional no 86, 303–41

De Miguel Barcena J (2025) Autodeterminación, secesión y derecho a decidir en el Estado autonómico. In: Durbán Martín I, Palao Gil J (coord.), Constitución y Estado Autonómico. Cartografía del debate sobre la reforma territorial, Valencia, Tirant Lo Blanch, 493–528

Di Martino A (2018) Il conflitto costituzionale in Catalogna: origini, svolgimento, prospettive. Costituzionalismo.it no 1, 49–107

Durbán Martín I, Palao Gil J coord. (2025) Constitución y Estado Autonómico. Cartografía del debate sobre la reforma territoriale. Valencia, Tirant Lo Blanch

Ferraiuolo G (2017) Sovranità e territorio alla prova della crisi catalana. Federalismi.it no. 17

Frosina L (2024) Separatismi e referendum. Teoria e prassi in prospettiva comparata. Napoli, Jovene

Galera Victoria A coord. (2024) La cuestión territorial en España. Un debate histórico, político y constitucional necesario. Granada, Comares

García Roca J (2000) A que llamamos, en Derecho, hechos diferenciales. Revista Vasca de Administración Pública no 11, 73–110

García Roca J (2005) El riesgo de la generalización de asimetrías en las reformas estatutarias y los límites del principio dispositivo. In: Martín Delgado I, Ortega Álvarez LI (coord.) La reforma del Estado Autonómico. Madrid, Centro de Estudios Políticos y Constitucionales, 85–110
Garcia de Pablos J F (2020) El concierto economico vasco y el convenio con Navarra. Los regimes tributarios y financierios forales. Madrid, Entrelineas Editores
Hernández Lafuente A, González García MA (1992–1993) Los Acuerdos Autonómicos de 28 de febrero de 1992: negociación, contenido y desarrollo. Documentación Administrativa no 232–233, 135–183
Herrero y Rodriguez de Miñon M (1998) Los derechos forales como derechos históricos. Revista Española de Derecho Constitucional, no 52, 53–80
Herrero y Rodriguez de Miñon M (2010) El derecho constitucional de la plurinacionalidad. Iura Vasconiae, no. 7, 35–51
Lago Peñas S (2024) La reforma de la financiación autonómica y el pacto catalán. Cuadernos de la Información Económica no 303, 20–27
López Aguilar J (1997) Constitución, autonomía y hecho diferencial. Cuadernos de derecho público no 2, 26–74
López Basaguren A (2008) Trasformazioni dello Stato autonomistico e riforma dello Statuto del Paese Basco: tra rottura ed "accomodamento" a convenienza. Federalismi.it no. 18
López Basaguren A (2009) Sobre referendum y comunidades autónomas: la ley vasca de la "consulta" ante el Tribunal constitucional (consideraciones con motivo de la STC 103/2008) Revista d'estudis autonomics i federals no 9, 202–240
Mastromarino A. (2010) Il federalismo disaggregativo. Un percorso costituzionale negli Stati multinazionali. Milano, Giuffrè
Mastromarino A (2014) Addomesticare la secessione: Indipendentismo e integrazione europea in dialogo. Percorsi costituzionali no. 3, 639–664
Monti M (2021) Federalismo disintegrativo? Secessione e asimmetria in Italia e Spagna. Torino, Giappichelli
Montilla Martos JA (2015) Reforma federal y Estatutos de segunda generación. Cizur Menor, Thomson-Aranzadi
Muñoz Machado M (2017) Ideas para una reforma de la Constitución. idpbarcelona.net/docs/actual/ideas_reforma_constitucion.pdf, 10–12
Ortega Álvarez L (2015) Reforma constitucional y reforma estatutaria. Madrid, Civitas
Ortega y Gasset J (2014) España invertebrada y otros ensayos. Madrid, Alianza Editorial
Pérez Royo J (2011) La STC 31/2010 y la contribución de la jurisprudencia constitucional a la configuración de un Estado compuesto en España: elementos de continuidad y ruptura, e incidencia en las perspectivas de evolución del Estado autonómico. Revista Catalana de Dret Públic no 43,121–149
Poggeschi G (2018) La Catalogna: dalla nazione storica alla repubblica immaginaria. Napoli, Editoriale Scientifica
Pradera J (1993) La liebre y la tortuga: Política y administración en el Estado de las Autonomias. Claves de razón práctica 38:24–33
Requejo Rodríguez P (2011) La posició del Tribunal Constitucional espanyol després de la STC 31/2010. Revista Catalana de Dret Públic 43:317–341
Rubio Llorente F (2014) Una propuesta de federalización. Madrid, Fundación Coloquio jurídico europeo, 13–29
Ruipérez Alamillo J (2002) Encuesta del derecho de autodeterminación. Teoría y Realidad Constitucional, no. 10–11
Solozábal Echavarría JJ (2005) Reflexiones contitucionales sobre la propuesta de modifica estatutaria de Ibarretxe. Revista Española de Derecho Constitucional no 73, 255–279
Tajadura Tejada J (2009) Referéndum en el País Vasco (Comentario a la STC 103/2008). Teoría y Realidad Constitucional no 23, 363–385
Tarlton C (1965) Symmetry and asymmetry as elements of federalism: a theoretical speculation. J Polit 27

Tornos Mas J (2007) Los estatutos de Cataluña. Madrid, Iustel
Tudela Aranda J (2016) El derecho a decidir y el principio democrático. Teoría y Realidad Constitucional no 37, 477–497
Viver Pi-Sunyer C (2008) La riforma dello Statuto della Comunità Autonoma di Catalogna: principali novità e problemi di costituzionalità. Diritto e Società no 3, 315–349
Watts RL (2005) Comparative Perspectives on Asymmetry in Federalism. *Asymmetry series* no. 4, Institute of Intergovernmental Relations, Queen's University

Federalism from the Bottom: The Role of Basque Country and Catalonia in Shaping Federalism in Spain

Adriano Dirri

Abstract The purpose of this chapter is to demonstrate that Spain represents a unique federal model shaped from the bottom, especially by the Basque Country and Catalonia. It examines how peculiar constitutional asymmetries—historical rights (*derechos forales*) and *hechos diferenciales*—have shaped the Spanish territorial Constitution since 1978, contributing to its federalising process. By discussing the latest academic scholarship on federal theory, this chapter examines the interplay between sovereignty, legal pluralism and sub-national autonomy. To this end, the federal jurisprudence of the Constitutional Tribunal will be recalled, as well as the recent developments under Sánchez, whose concessions—especially the 2024 Amnesty Act—have temporarily mitigated the Catalan crisis. Lastly, this chapter argues that Spain requires the constitutional recognition of its multinational reality as well as the entrenchment of asymmetry, preventing regression into homogenisation while preserving unity within diversity.

1 The *Territorial Question* between Federalism, Asymmetry and Secession

The purpose of this chapter is to strengthen the following argument: despite the territorial conflict, Spain fully represents a federal model, albeit far from the classical federal experiences. This paper will consider the rationale of the Spanish Constitution, with specific regard to its peculiar territorial organisation, especially focusing on the impact of historical rights (*derechos históricos* in Spanish) and the *hechos diferenciales* over secession claims. By analysing the latest academic debate about the "definition" of federalism (par. 1.1), this chapter will reappraise the "location" of Spain in federal studies; to this end, it will also consider those features connected to the entrenched autonomy of the sub-national entities. The odyssey of

A. Dirri (✉)
LUISS Guido Carli University, Rome, Italy
e-mail: adirri@luiss.it

F. Savastano et al. (eds.), *Between Asymmetry and Secession*,
https://doi.org/10.1007/978-3-032-29603-0_14

the Spanish federalising process will be taken into account. More specifically, the struggle for differentiation, which has been largely overlooked by the central government (par. 1.2), eventually led to two different waves of secessionist attempts from the Basque Country and Catalonia, and the latter provoked a serious constitutional conflict. In this regard, sovereignty claims and the (ambiguous) constitutional dispositions over territorial organisation will be recalled, as well as the role of historical rights (*fueros*) and the *hechos diferenciales*. The latter have been relevant for nationalities because they are considered the main constitutional tool for strengthening their autonomy and asymmetry, far from the "ordinary" autonomous communities. Besides the crucial role of the Constitutional Tribunal and, above all, its judgments in the past decade, the latest developments will be taken into consideration, such as the Amnesty Law (par. 1.3). Currently, the Sanchez government coalition is based on the external support of several nationalist movements, with whom the Prime Minister bargained several concessions over autonomy and self-determination. In the concluding remarks (par. 1.4), it is argued that even though the conflict has been temporarily halted through measures taken by ordinary legislation, nothing in the future may impede a setback in building constitutional asymmetry without a constitutional reform. Therefore, the call is to expressively acknowledge the multinational character of Spain as well as entrench constitutional asymmetry.

2 Federal Theory and Spain, *Aka* Federalism and *Estado Autonomico*

One of the most contentious and controversial issues in federal studies is the interplay between territory and law. In federal systems, the relationship between different sources of authority within the same constitutional polity and framework has its roots in the sovereignty debate as well as in legal pluralism. These features are at the epicentre of academic scholarships, and the manifestation of this tension becomes the thorny issue in federal constitutions. Firstly, to what extent may the category "federalism" be extended to all experiences marked by internal legal pluralism? Secondly, how far may the category "federalism" be expanded and broadened to include constitutional experiences beyond the classic federal models? Thirdly, to what extent may bottom-up (territorial) claims contribute to federalising processes in a context of constitutional rigidity?

These are only a few of the questions that may arise from a constitutional standpoint. It does not mean that other disciplines, such as political science and the history of political institutions, are not helpful. But their analysis goes beyond the purpose of this chapter, whose scope is limited to underscoring how Spain contributes to federal theory through the examination of the "special" relationship that Catalonia, on the one hand, and the Basque Country, on the other, have with the central state after two decades of secessionist claims—claims that appear to be temporarily halted.

The question of "territory" in federal constitutional studies is central when it comes to understanding bottom-up claims in relation to their territorial and non-territorial accommodation (Malloy and Palermo 2015). Similarly, it sheds light on the connection between law and identity at the sub-national level, which is to some extent generally constrained by the (Federal) Constitution. The latter allows for the presence of or is directly "composed of" different cultural identities. Therefore, the relationship between territory and law becomes crucial in understanding federal dynamics. Territory is not (only) where the law should be applied but where it is applied. Consequently, as has been rightly stated, "territory is not simply a geographical area in which laws happen to be applied but an aspect of the laws themselves" (Doyle 2018, p. 891).

Law with a special geographic referent may play a clarificatory role in fixing and ascertaining legal pluralism and identities. This is the case of Spain and the special regime for the Basque Country, Navarra and Catalonia, as envisaged by the first additional provision and the first and fourth transitional provisions. Moreover, specific constitutional provisions may reconcile plural identities through their recognition within a broader constitutional "container" to make sure that these identities do not implicitly have the chance (legally speaking) to undertake the path towards secession. This, again, is the case with the ambiguous formulation of Article 2 of the 1978 Spanish Constitution (Solozabal Echavarria 2018; San Anton Moracho 2018) (see par. 1.2).

Hence, regarding secession, it may be argued that constitutional silence (Jackson 2016) has proven to be the best option within the constitutional framework, paving the way for both constitutional agreement (where possible) and constitutional interpretation. However, in the shadow, the core issue is still sovereignty. In fact, beyond the debate about secession as taboo (Mancini 2012) and the "comparative constitutional law of secession" (Palermo 2019), the issue lies in the contestation of the constitutional order by sub-national identities. This is the limit—when sub-national groups question the Constitution's own authority to regulate secession (Doyle 2018, p. 901). It would also mean that secessionist claims do not consider other avenues for accommodating diversity, including constitutional federal processes, within the context of a rigid Constitution. The Constitution is contested as the supreme source of law according to Kelsen and the *Stufenbau* theory (Carrozza 2019, pp. 73–75). It is as if, in the case of Spain, the Constitution foresees the possibility of pursuing specific legal status and competences for special communities within a system that may be included among federal countries.

The starting point remains the debate around federalism, its manifestations and the constitutional devices for accommodating groups (*i.e.* federal arrangements). Spain is often positioned somewhere in the middle; this is the reason why the country has been called *Estado autonómico*. This definition has been made on the basis of the classic models of federations; for that purpose, it is useful to consider the latest scholarship debate on the issue.

Nevertheless, it should be kept in mind that the Spanish experience has been distinguished from classic models of federalism, especially the United States and Germany, in light of diverse federalising processes. This bias may hide the fact that

Spain is characterised by "multiple sources of authority within a single geographical territory", which mirrors legal pluralism (Ryan, 2020, p. 493). Still, the struggle is strictly connected to the concept of dual sovereignty, or distinct sources of sovereign powers. This standpoint does not address legal pluralism as legal identities, with territorial autonomy not deriving from original sovereign power. This is the theoretical gap that needs to be addressed, also because federal scholars know that "every system of federalism is developed in response to unique circumstances" (Ryan, 2020, p. 499). Thus, the federal model based on dual sovereignty should not serve as the groundwork for understanding federal dynamics in diverse constitutional environments and processes such as Spain.

The relevance of the Spanish territorial organisation from 1978 onwards is strictly connected to the meaning of the word "federalism". To this end, it is useful to underline the recent scholarly debate. A "working definition" presupposes the identification of key elements of the subject. In this case, it means identifying the most important features of federal constitutions, which necessarily include both dual and cooperative federations and their archetypes, the United States and Germany. It is not the scope of this paper to analyse traditional scholarships, which may be found elsewhere (Hueglin and Fenna 2015; Palermo and Kössler 2017; Popelier 2021). Broadly speaking, the most useful description still lies in Elazar, who identified federalism as a particular constitutional framework grounded in the "self-rule and shared-rule" formula (Elazar 1987).

Recently, Fenna and Schnabel have pointed out the relevance of autonomy vis-à-vis the co-determination constitutional dynamic in federal systems. They argue that the gist of federalism lies in the following idea of autonomy: the Federal Constitution provides for a central government and a set of governments for the "constituent" units into which the state is territorially divided; there is a direct relationship with the people, inasmuch as each layer of government has its own representative system and exclusive powers; and the status of the levels of government are constitutionally protected (Fenna and Schnabel 2024, p. 14). Conversely, problems emerge as far as "co-determination" (shared rule) is concerned. The main issues at stake are the role of intergovernmental relations (IGRs) and the process of decision-making at the central level through the second chamber. According to them, for Elazar, shared rule meant the existence of a shared central government and not, only and mainly, the procedures of lawmaking. In fact, if IGRs and second chambers are considered the heart of federalism, many would find that while the former is ineffective in either shaping lawmaking or representing sub-national units, the latter lacks a normative dimension and is part, instead, of the politics of federalism (Ferran and Sanjaume-Calvert 2022, p. 2; Fenna and Schnabel 2024, pp. 9, 10, 15).

Criticisms have been raised against the downgrading of the co-determination principle on the basis of, for example, the jurisprudence of the Canadian Supreme Court (Supreme Court of Canada, 2011), which has also stressed that IGRs cannot override constitutional provisions (Supreme Court of Canada, 1998 and 2023). Without any doubt, the IGR dimension is crucial to the functioning of federalism, but, as everyday politics, it is not related to the "constitutional essence" of federalism. That essence means harmonising the plural allocation of powers among the layers of government (including by-laws at the municipal level) and *politically* preventing the unilateral transfer of powers towards the centre as well as the unilateral processes advanced by strong sub-national entities (Hueglin and Mueller 2025, pp. 401–405). Still, Fenna and Schnabel focused their attention on constitutional amendment processes related to the normative powers of sub-national units rather than ordinary lawmaking procedures. They stressed that IGRs are a form of joint governance and not "rules" since they presuppose a "hard veto power, which constituent units rarely enjoy in their relations with central government" (Fenna and Schnabel 2025, pp. 408–413).

The inner problem of comparative law and federalism lies in understanding the relationship between the central government and sub-national entities. In fact, Fenna and Schnabel often recall the role of "constituent units" and, therefore, sovereignty as the groundwork for territorial accommodation between centre and periphery. That debate echoes Tierney's works, where federalism is considered a particular constitutional idea and practice. He stated that a federal constitution "creates one central government, but it also creates territorial government for each of its constituent territories", in addition to the fact that territorial polities, within a single polity (the federal state), retain "their constitutional personality and carries its particular constitutional subjecthood from constituent moment into constitutional form and hence into lived constitutional practice" (Tierney 2018, p. 57; Tierney 2022). The shortcoming of this view resides in sovereignty and in the historical formation of federal states. Therefore, other notable examples, including Spain, are left to different qualifications, such as "disaggregative federations" (Mastromarino 2013).

In a similar vein, plural constituent power theory leaves in the background the differences between devolution unitary states—the United Kingdom and Italy—and Spain, which shares fewer constitutional features with the former than with federal countries (Aroney et al. 2024, p. 602). The main reason is that Spain represents an additional example of a process from unity to plurality, without distinguishing the procedures of constitutional amendment or power conferral to sub-units in devolutionary unitary states. That is the difference with Italy, where sovereignty belongs to the people and remains in the national Parliament. In fact, while the central government and special regions are on equal footing in the approval of statutes of autonomy through a constitutional law, the powers and functions of ordinary regions are listed in Article 117 of the Constitution and are, therefore, amendable by a constitutional revision. In addition, with regard to "differentiated" autonomy (Article 116.3), the national Parliament plays the key role, since it may unilaterally revoke the functions allocated according to Article 116.3 (Palermo 2021, pp. 139–145; see also Savastano; Severa in this volume).

Differently, the territorial Constitution of Spain not only allows for the presence of regions and nationalities but also distinguishes two different procedures for accessing autonomy as well as recognising historical rights (*fueros*) and *hechos diferenciales*. These features are "enough" to make Spain a federal country because of the constitutional entrenchment and the necessary convergence between centre and periphery in the federalising process.

3 The Spanish (Federal) Distinctiveness between Homogenisation, Asymmetries and "Federal" Jurisprudence

In analysing the territorial Constitution of Spain, the starting point is the 1978 constitution-making process (Arato 2017, pp. 187–194). During the transition (Rubio Llorente 1991), the two leading parties—the Union of the Democratic Centre (Unión de Centro Democrático (UCD)) and the Spanish Socialist Workers' Party (Partido Socialista Obrero Español (PSOE))—sponsored decentralisation to various degrees, also as a tool for strengthening democracy (Balaguer Callejón 2019, pp. 423–431), especially the latter, which promoted pluri-nationality and even self-determination (Moreno 2010, pp. 160–177). The centre-left and left-wing parties adopted a pragmatic strategy and opted for a territorial model that could bridge the gap with other political forces (Jaria 1999). The result was that decentralised and/or federal demands were registered both from the centre (top down) and from historical communities (bottom up) with their parties (especially the Basque Country and Catalonia), supported by the PSOE and its allies (Moreno et al. 2019, pp. 246–249).

Therefore, the main agreement among the political parties during the constitution-drafting process was the rejection of centralism, alongside a delaying formula over autonomy that would satisfy all territorial claims and the recognition of historic nationalities as special. This balance was contained in the two principles under Article 2, which stand as the basis for Title VIII and its implementation: the indissoluble unity of the Spanish nation, the common and indivisible homeland of all Spaniards and the right to autonomy of the nationalities and regions of which it is composed, together with solidarity among them all. These core principles followed the 1931 constitutional framework, but the purpose was to overcome the principle of homogenisation among the autonomous communities, which was embodied in the draft Constitution of January 5, 1978. Afterwards, plural autonomous communities with their peculiarities were identified through the inclusion of two avenues for recognising territorial pluralism and highlighting specific legal traditions in communities with "stronger" legal identity. The principle of plurality in the territorial Constitution was encapsulated in different access routes, different autonomous initiatives and procedures for drafting statutes, different distributions of powers and the institutional organisation of the communities: in short, multiple (potentially) constitutional asymmetries. The Constitution implicitly envisages the presence of three autonomous communities (Catalonia, Galicia and the Basque Country) with extensive powers and others with weaker autonomy (Blanco Valdés 2014; Blanco Valdés 2012, p. 122; Cagiao y Conde 2022).

This open-ended solution recognised the legal and historical specificities of certain communities without acknowledging their territorial autonomy (a constitutional asymmetry). Thus, federalism has become the bone of contention between the historical communities (*nacionalidades*) and the central government, which has led to secessionist claims (Frosina in this volume; Monti 2021). Despite this, the federal nature of the Spanish constitutional architecture cannot be denied. Firstly, the features of the multilayered system must be traced in the bottom-up initiatives of the territories and not, for example, in bicameralism; secondly, the Constitution envisages several differentiations among the autonomous communities; and thirdly, fiscal autonomy was granted to the historical communities of the Basque Country and Navarra, according to their medieval *fueros*.

Hence, the comparative perspective shows how innovative the Spanish constitutional solutions regarding procedures and institutions are. In addition, even though some scholars argue that Spain is not a federal state because the principle of "shared sovereignty" cannot be detected, it is nonetheless evident that regional basic laws are above ordinary legislation and possess a "constitutional nature".[1] Lastly, the utility of the Senate lies in its veto power in the constitutional amending process, since it is in part (one-quarter) composed of members appointed by regional legislative councils (Hueglin and Fenna 2015, pp. 129–131, 234). This is an additional feature that continues to be relevant, since the de facto or "substantial federalisation of the system has occurred upon the initiative of the Autonomous Communities with the consent of the central government" (Aroney 2017, p. 21).

Other scholars considered Spain as a state in transformation from unitary to federal, highlighting the rationale that IGRs are the engine of the federalising process (Agranoff and Ramos Gallarin 1997). By contrast, others focused their attention on the multiple ethnoterritorial concurrences in the country, which produced a non-linear process with "chiefly elements of heterogeneity and plurality". This was mainly based on two premises: the differential fact and the centralist inertia in the plural accommodations of differentiated claims. Despite the differing views, IGRs were still deemed relevant in the process, though without considering the contribution coming from the bottom, especially from Catalonia and the Basque Country (Moreno 1997, pp. 73, 75–76).

The unique configuration of Spain is justified by the rigidity of the Constitution as well as by the role of the autonomous communities in the constitutional amending process, while their autonomy is expressed through their statutes. Therefore, federalism in the Spanish Constitution might be considered—at the beginning—almost an "empty box", except for the historical rights in specific territories, until the Constitution is "filled" by territorial autonomy through their statutes as "sub-constitutional regulations" and by the judgments of the Constitutional Tribunal (Colino 2009, pp. 263–264).

Despite some ambiguities, the richness of the territorial organisation of the Spanish constitutional framework should be highlighted. Firstly, the only "permanent" territorial asymmetry is represented by the first additional provision to the Constitution that protects and respects the historic rights of the territories with traditional charters (*derecho foral*). Secondly, non-territorial asymmetries or "micro-asymmetries", relate to, for example, the recognition of languages (Article 3 Constitution) and local rights (Art. 149.1.8). Thirdly, the standard and

[1] Despite the Constitutional Tribunal having more recently lowered its rank (*infra*).

fast-track procedures: the former, according to Article 143 grants the right to initiate the process to Provincial Councils concerned with a qualified majority and, afterwards according to Article 146 by the Spanish Parliament, the proposed statute must be approved. Through this procedure, the autonomous communities may assume their "own" competences (Article 148.1), while they must wait 5 years for the enlargement of their powers (Article 148.2). By contrast, the fast-track procedure envisages the possibility of circumventing the 5-year term and was basically reserved for those *territories* that already had their statutes at the time of the promulgation of the Constitution or provisional regimes (Second Transitional Provision)[2] (Monti 2021, pp. 32–33). In that way, the Spanish Constitution granted the special status to Catalonia, the Basque Country and Galicia. Despite that, the Constitution left the door open to multiple asymmetries, depending on which subject matter communities are able to pick and choose. In sum, "different tracks, speeds, historical legacies, and voluntary thresholds of autonomy make the existence of very different regional profile possible" (Sala 2014, pp. 114–115).

The multiple prospects of constitutional asymmetry were "sacked" by the major political parties, whose direction was more in favour of homogenisation rather than differentiation. Pushing towards uniformity was not the expectation of the historical communities. At the beginning of the 1980s, during the first stage of "federalisation", the 17 autonomous communities were created and their statutes adopted. Afterwards, the path to homogenisation was fuelled by the new statutes at the end of the 1980s, when an additional agreement over the autonomous communities took place in 1992 (second stage) (Munoz Machado 1992; Montaner 1996). They were considered a turning point in the evolution of the autonomous model (Blanco Valdés 2014; Blanco Valdés 2012, pp. 234–238), which was steadily opposed by Catalonia and the Basque Country during the 1990s and labelled *café para todos*. Despite different claims (Monti 2021, p. 38), the two nationalities started to advocate for a pluri-national federal state, with constitutional asymmetries and differentiation between "ordinary autonomous communities" and special nationalities. These positions found their way into the asymmetry of the Spanish Constitution: *hechos diferenciales* and historical rights. Within the third stage (Martinico 2010; Ruiz and Rico Ruiz 2006), both gave substance to their claims through the adoption of radical (secessionist) autonomous statutes (the Ibarretxe Plan and the 2006 Catalan Statute), whose consequence was a constitutional conflict with the central government and the involvement of the Constitutional Tribunal (Sala 2014, pp. 116–117).

Therefore, it is useful to recall the role of the Spanish Constitutional Tribunal. Since the beginning, it has referred to autonomy as a limited and distinct power

[2] "The territories which in the past have, by plebiscite, approved draft Statutes of Autonomy and which at the time of the promulgation of this Constitution, have provisional autonomous regimes, may proceed immediately in the manner contemplated in section 148, subsection 2, if agreement to do so is reached by the overall majority of their pre self-government higher corporate bodies, and the Government shall be duly informed. The draft Statutes shall be drawn up in accordance with the provisions of section 151, subsection 2, where so requested by the pre Autonomous assembly" (Senate Standing Orders, section 143).

from sovereignty because an autonomous territorial organisation is part of the whole and can in no case be opposed to the principle of unity. Rather, autonomy has its constitutional meaning within the realm of Article 2 of the Constitution (STC 4/1981). Shortly after, the Court highlighted the difference between the political nature of the autonomous communities and that of municipalities (STC 25/1981). A few years later, in declaring unconstitutional part of the *Ley Orgánica de Armonización del Proceso Autonómico* (LOAPA), the Court stated that the alleged equality of rights of the autonomous communities lacked a constitutional basis, on the one hand, and did not specify the uniqueness of the nationalities, on the other (STC 76/1983). In addition, for the Court, the Constitution is not a pact among historical territories that maintained "*unos derechos anteriores a la Constitución y superiores a ellas*". With these judgments, the Court highlighted the "constitutional distance" between classic federal models and Spanish federalism.

This was the constitutional interpretation of Spain's territorial organisation before the secessionist claims of the nationalities. The first test was the constitutionality of the Basque Parliament Law No. 9/2008, which called for a popular consultation to ascertain support for the beginning of negotiations with the central government in matters of peace and political normalisation. This judgment (STC 103/2008) was extremely important since it stated that referendums on sovereignty issues (regardless of their binding nature) must be conducted within the procedure set out in Article 168 for constitutional amendments (López Basaguren 2009). It was followed by the Constitutional Court's judgment on Catalonia's sovereignty claims: it started when the Court struck down the most important features of the 2006 autonomy statute, which affirmed the subordinate role of the latter in respect of the Constitution (Russo 2021, pp. 150–153), as well as declared that the sole sovereign people is the Spanish People (STC 31/2010). The Catalan secessionist "uprising" reached its peak between 2015 and 2017, which saw an open constitutional conflict. The Court, in judging the Catalan Declaration of Sovereignty in 2014, stressed once again that territorial alteration (secession) was possible only through constitutional amendments (STC 42/2014). Subsequently, the Court declared Catalan Law No. 10/2014 on referendums unconstitutional on grounds similar to those of 2008 (STC 31 and 32/2015). Lastly, among other judgments (STC 259/2015), the Court was called to rule over the law on the secessionist referendum held on October 1, 2017. The Court declared such type of legislation unconstitutional, both on procedural and on substantial grounds (STC 114 and 124/2017) (Castellà Andreu 2019, pp. 408–409; Bilbao Ubillos 2024, pp. 16–22).

These judicial precedents have highlighted the federal possibilities of the Spanish constitutional framework through its most critical issues: sovereignty and secession. This has been largely discussed by constitutional scholars (Adam 2017), but here it is argued that the potentialities of Spanish constitutional asymmetries are still not fully empowered, since they rest mainly on the historical rights of the nationalities.

4 Legal Pluralism and Territorial Claims: *Derecho Foral*, *Hechos Diferenciales* and Latest Developments during the Sanchez Era

Legal pluralism in Spain is often debated, especially concerning its impact on the different branches of law, without disregarding its consequences for the constitutional framework and federalism. Historical rights (*derecho foral*) are that part of local law that survived legislative and political unification, i.e. the construction of Spain as a constitutional democracy through various stages, beginning with the fall of Barcelona in 1714 and the Nueva Planta decrees of 1716, which made the Kingdom of Spain a French-style centralised state. These norms were collected especially in the Basque Country (1959), Catalonia (1960), Galicia (1963) and Navarra (1973). The Constitution acknowledged them in the first additional provision, and this must be connected to the *hechos diferenciales* for nationalities (Alpa 2023, p. 124).

Historically, it is worth recalling that among the obstacles at the time of the drafting and adoption of the Spanish Civil Code in the nineteenth century—based on the French model—there were the legal systems operating in the "foral" regions. Thus, from a legal standpoint, building a centralised and unitary state was not an easy task. Catalonia fiercely opposed homogenisation in civil law; among the reasons was the "import" of French rules, which were even closer to the Catalan civil framework (Dyson 2019, p. 134).

According to Article 149.1.8 of the 1978 Spanish Constitution, the autonomous communities have powers over the development of civil, *foral* and special rights, where they exist. In this matter, all autonomous communities have modified their code as well as adopted legislation broadening rules and institutions within the realm of *foral* rights. It is worth noting that in Catalonia, legislative activity has been very extensive, to the point that "*que la Compilacion se ha convertito en un element secundario del ordenamiento juridico privado*". Far more different and unique is the special fiscal regime of the Basque Country and Navarra, because they have kept the system of *Concierto economico*, through which both regulate and collect relevant taxes such as value-added tax (VAT) and personal income tax (IRPF) (Aja 2003, p. 185).

In addition to this kind of territorial asymmetry, *hechos diferenciales* represent a non-territorial differentiation. These include the recognition of special languages (Carbonneau and Jiménez-Salcedo 2024, pp. 269–288), fiscal regimes, unique institutions at the communal level and local police forces. Beyond the debate over broader or narrower interpretations of the constitutional provisions related to the *hechos diferenciales*, their role is strongly connected to Article 2 of the Spanish Constitution, which empowers territorial claims of the nationalities (Di Martino 2018, pp. 68–69). This presupposes the existence of people(s) with specific legal personality within the Spanish constitutional framework. This political reality has also acquired a legal dimension because the Constitution and the statutes recognise the existence of characteristics only for some autonomous communities and endow them with normative consequences in the form of rights, powers, institutions and special procedures (Aja 2003, p. 173). This represents a clear recognition of different legal, political and social traditions, which were kept intact at the time of the adoption of the Constitution (Tomás Y Valiente 1995, p. 28). In other words, *hechos diferenciales* cannot be extended to other autonomous communities since they are by definition "*elementos de una personalidad historico-politica diferenciada en algunas CCAA*" (Aja 2003, pp. 174–175).

These were the grounds of secessionist claims, which meant, for the nationalities, the existence of Spain as a multinational state. Two directions were undertaken: first, the road to unilateral secession was constitutionally unsuccessful (McRoberts 2022, pp. 217–256), and the only result was the broadening of the territorial cleavage between the central government and Catalonia; the second path has been the building of a stronger fiscal autonomy. Besides reconciliation with Catalan institutions, fiscal autonomy currently represents the main issue at stake. In fact, while the *concierto economico* is not contested in the Basque Country and Navarra, in Catalonia, it is slightly different. While for the former, fiscal autonomy as a *foral* right has been maintained without discontinuity over time, for Catalonia, it was suppressed, considering the fierce opposition to the 1936 military coup. The result has been that, from 2010 onwards, Catalan government authorities have been claiming this kind of "privilege", which initially started with more modest claims concerning levels of inter-territorial solidarity (Bossacoma Busquets and Sanjuame-Calvet 2019, pp. 454–455).

Therefore, secessionist claims differ between the Basque Country and Catalonia for a "constitutional reason". On the one hand, Basque nationalism in the past decade has been more focused on financial autonomy, with positive results; on the other hand, Catalonia "experimented" with radical claims aimed at unilateral secession while also considering the behaviour of the central government. The constitutional issue at stake is Catalonia's desire to link its claims to the first additional provision, since the Constitutional Tribunal has stated that historical rights are the constitutional basis for territorial asymmetry, but only for the Basque Country and Navarra (STC 214/1989). Consequently, the claimed existence of Catalan historical rights, recognised, for example, in Article 5 of the Catalan Statute, is more or less a dead letter (STC 31/2010) (Monti 2021, pp. 236–237).

The Catalan question remained at the centre of Spanish politics; with the advent of the Sánchez era (beginning in early 2020), a different political path was undertaken, that of the "normalisation" of political relations between the central government and Catalonia. The future of the autonomous community was set to be discussed in the "Table for Dialogue"—the centrepiece of the PSOE-*Esquerra Republicana de Catalunya* (ERC) pact. The initiative was modelled on the 1977 Moncloa Pact, but the main issue was the differences between ERC and *Junts per Catalunya* (JxCat): the former pursued dialogue with the Sanchez government, while the latter favoured unilateralism. This project required pardons for Catalan leaders who had remained in Spain, which represented only the first step towards normalisation (McRoberts 2022, pp. 275–292). Subsequently, the role of Catalonia and its nationalist forces became even more important for the formation of Sanchez's third government in October

2023. In exchange for the support of nationalist movements, especially JxCat, Sanchez agreed to several compromises, among them the Amnesty Law, to normalise the relationship with Catalonia and open a cross-cutting dialogue (Moreno Martínez 2025). This was proof of pragmatism since the Amnesty Act (*Ley Orgánica 1/2024, de 10 de junio, de amnistía para la normalización institucional, política y social en Cataluña*) represents an instrument to normalise the relationship between Catalonia and the central government rather than a measure to redress rights violations arising from criminal convictions (Bassocoma Busquets 2024). The Amnesty Act was challenged before the Constitutional Tribunal, which upheld the validity of the legislation with only minor declarations of unconstitutionality. In fact, the Court (137/2025) acknowledged the pragmatic view of the Act and considered this "move" as a suitable means of lowering constitutional and political conflict, given that it has been one of the most important conflicts within the Spanish constitutional framework (Tirapu-Sanuy 2025).

The secessionist claim has also been halted, thanks to the agreement over a new Fiscal Pact, a subject matter that was often advocated by nationalists in Catalonia (see Frosina in this volume). As said above, the Constitutional Tribunal (STC 31/2010) made Article 5 of the Catalan Statute inoperative, which impeded the activation of historical rights. Despite that, the "normalisation" of relations with Catalonia also passed through the new Additional Provision 17 of the *Ley Reguladora de las Bases del Régimen Local* (LBRL), introduced by Decree-Law No. 6/2023. This legislative innovation has given effect to Article 5 of the Statute since according to this new provision, the LBRL must be applied in light of Catalonia's historical rights, "*respetando en todo caso la posición singular en materia de sistema institucional recogida en el artículo 5* [...] *así como las competencias exclusivas y compartidas en materia de régimen local y organización territorial* [...]". It is the first time that an ordinary law has recognised Catalonia's specific position. Therefore, it makes possible the broadening of asymmetry in other matters, such as civil law, culture and language in education (Ridao Martín 2025, pp. 163–169).

To sum up, this evolution confirms that the only way forward is to strengthen Catalonia's constitutional asymmetry by recognising its historical rights alongside the reinforcement of its fiscal autonomy. Nevertheless, the main issue remains "alive" since the adoption of an ordinary law does not set aside the sovereignty claims of the nationalists in Catalonia. This is because, in the history of the Spanish federalising process, homogenisation trends have often prevailed through legislative measures of the central government. The solution—perhaps the only viable option—remains a constitutional reform that recognises the distinctiveness of the nationalities without prejudice to the other autonomous communities.

5 Conclusions: The Way Forward

The 1978 constitutional dispensation was considered by the Basque Country and Catalonia the starting point for the recognition of their special status among the autonomous communities. However, these expectations were often thwarted by homogenisation trends which fuelled secessionist attempts. Nevertheless, the Spanish Constitution allows for a wide range of constitutional asymmetries or, to recall Kierkegaard, several dimensions of the possibility, which has caused anxiety in the two nationalities regarding their autonomy.

In fact, a combined reading of the constitutional provisions related to autonomous communities—Part VIII, historical rights, and hechos diferenciales—makes Spain a federal state, although different from the classical model. There are strong arguments in support of this view, such as the constitutional revision procedure and the autonomous statutes, which have "a constitutional dimension [...] that ranks them above the legislation of either level of government" (Sala 2014, pp. 125–127). In addition, the Spanish Constitution acknowledges different kinds of asymmetries that had been overlooked until secessionist movements emerged in the Basque Country and Catalonia. Therefore, recognising the multinational character of Spain might represent the first step towards constitutional asymmetries (Anderson 2020). In addition, it would provide an opportunity to clarify the relationship between plurinationalism and the indissoluble unity of Spain (Tornos Mas 2019, pp. 401–402). This solution would overcome the ambiguities of the current constitutional framework, which was invoked by both Catalonia in favour of the unilateral secession and the legitimacy of the right to decide (the democratic principle), and by the central government in favour of the rule of law (the principle of legality) (López-Basaguren 2019, pp. 365–388). Furthermore, although Sanchez was able to defuse the issue with pragmatism, this settlement remains anchored in ordinary legislation. For these reasons a reconciliation through a constitutional revision seems the most viable option, given the fragility of the Sanchez government, whose survival depends on the support of Catalan nationalist parties, especially JxCat.

References

Adam EC (2017) The constitutional court of Spain: from system balancer to polarizing centralist. In: Aroney N, Kincaid J (eds) Courts in Federal Countries: federalists or Unitarists? University of Toronto Press, Toronto, pp 367–403

Agranoff R, Ramos Gallarín, JA (1997) Toward Federal Democracy in Spain: an examination of intergovernmental relations. Publius: J Fed 27(4):1–38

Aja E (2003) El estado autonómico: federalismo y hechos diferenciales. Alianza, Madrid

Alpa G (2023) I principi generali. Giuffrè, Milano

Anderson P (2020) Decentralisation at a crossroads: Spain, Catalonia and the territorial crisis. Ethnopolitics 19(4):342–355

Arato A (2017) The adventures of the constituent power: beyond revolutions? Cambridge University Press, Cambridge

Aroney N (2017) Constituent power and the constituent states: towards a theory of the Amendment of Federal Constitutions. Jus Politicum: Revue de droit politique 17:5–31

Aroney N, Duke G, Tierney S (2024) A theory of plural constituent power for federal systems. Glob Const 13(3):591–611

Balaguer Callejón F (2019) Federalism and democratic quality: the contribution of territorial pluralism to constitutional democracy. In: López-Basaguren A, Escajedo San-Epifanio L (eds) Claims for secession and federalism. Springer, Cham pp 423-431

Blanco Valdés RL (2012) Los rostros del federalismo. Alianza Editorial, Madrid
Blanco Valdés RL (2014) El laberinto territorial español: del cantón de Cartagena al secesionismo catalán. Alianza, Madrid
Bossacoma Busquets P (2024) The Catalan process of Independence and the Spanish Amnesty Act. Int J Const Law Blog, 20 June 2024, available at: https://www.iconnectblog.com/the-catalan-process-of-independence-and-the-spanish-amnesty-act/
Bossacoma Busquets P, Sanjaume-Calvet M (2019) Asymmetry as a device for equal recognition and reasonable accommodation of majority and minority nations. A country study on constitutional asymmetry in Spain. In: Popelier P, Sahadžić M (eds), Constitutional asymmetry in multinational federalism. Federalism and internal conflicts. Palgrave Macmillan, Cham, pp 429-460
Cagiao y Conde J (2022) Democracia y nación. España en el laberinto plurinacional. Catarata, Madrid
Carbonneau JR, Jiménez-Salcedo J (2024) The limits of linguistic diversity in a federal context: a comparative view of Canada, Spain and Germany. In: Mathieu F, Guénette D, Gagnon AG (eds) Comparative federalism. Federalism and internal conflicts. Palgrave Macmillan, Cham, pp 269–288
Carrozza P (2019) Kelsen y constitucionalismo contemporáneo: la continua presencia de los temas kelnesianos. Estudios de Deusto 67(1):55–82
Castellà Andreu JM (2019) Constitution and Referendum on Secession in Catalonia. In: López-Basaguren A, Escajedo San-Epifanio L (eds) Claims for Secession and Federalism. Springer, Cham, pp 405-422
Colino C (2009) Constitutional change without constitutional reform: Spanish federalism and the revision of Catalonia's statute of autonomy. Publius: J Federal 39(2):262–288
Di Martino A (2018) Il conflitto costituzionale sulla Catalogna: origini, svolgimento, prospettive. Costituzionalismo.it 1:49–107
Doyle O (2018) The silent constitution of territory. Int J Const Law 16(3):887–903
Dyson M (2019) Comparative legal history: methodology for morphology. In: Moréteau O, Masferrer A, Modéer KA (eds) Comparative legal history. Edward Elgar Publishing, Cheltenham, pp 110–138
Elazar DJ (1987) Exploring federalism. University of Alabama Press, Alabama
Fenna A, Schnabel J (2024) What is federalism? Some definitional clarification. Publius: J Fed 54(2):179–200
Fenna A, Schnabel J (2025) Defining federalism: a rejoinder to Hueglin and Mueller. Publius: J Fed 55(2):408–413
Ferran R, Sanjaume-Calvet M (2022) Defensive federalism: tackling the two faces of the territorial tyranny of the majority — a revised federal institutional design. In: Raquejo F, Sanjaume-Calvet M (eds) Defensive federalism: protecting territorial minorities from the "tyranny of the majority". Routledge, Abingdon, pp 1–21
Hueglin T, Mueller S (2025) A reply to Fenna and Schnabel's (2024) "what is federalism?". Publius: J Fed 55(2):399–407
Hueglin TO, Fenna A (2015) Comparative federalism. A systematic inquiry, 2nd edn. University of Toronto Press, Toronto
Jackson VC (2016) Secession, transnational precedents, and constitutional silences. In: Levinson S (ed) Nullification and secession in modern constitutional thought. University Press of Kansas, Lawrence, pp 314–342
Jaria J (1999) La forma del Estado en los debates constituyentes. In: Aparicio MA (ed) La Descentralización y el Federalismo: Nuevos Modelos de Autonomía Política (España, Bélgica, Canadá, Italia y Reino Unido). Cedecs, Barcelona, pp 13-28
López Basaguren A (2009) Sobre referendum y comunidades autónomas: la ley vasca de la "consulta" ante el Tribunal Constitucional (consideraciones con motivo de la STC 103/2008). Revista d'estudis autonomics i federals 9:202–240

López-Basaguren A (2019) Claims for secession in Catalonia. Rule of law, democratic principle and federal alternative. In: López-Basaguren A, Escajedo San-Epifanio L (eds) Claims for secession and federalism. Springer, Cham, pp 365–388

Malloy TH, Palermo F (2015) Minority accommodation through territorial and non-territorial autonomy. Oxford University Press, Oxford

Mancini S (2012) Secession and self-determination. In: Rosenfeld M, Sajó A (eds) The Oxford handbook of comparative constitutional law. Oxford University Press, Oxford, pp 481–501

Martinico G (2010) The new "Estatutos de autonomìa" in Spain: a brief overview of the literature. Persp Fed 1:1–15

Mastromarino A (2013) The adhesion of the Spanish autonomic state to the Disaggregative model of federalism: a possible way. In: López-Basaguren A, Escajedo San-Epifanio L (eds) The ways of federalism in Western countries and the horizons of territorial autonomy in Spain. Springer, Berlin–Heidelberg, pp 711-730

McRoberts K (2022) Catalonia: the struggle over independence. Oxford University Press, Oxford

Montaner LC (1996) Los estatutos de autonomía y los pactos autonómicos. Revista de estudios regionales 44:47–68

Monti M (2021) Federalismo disintegrativo? Secessione e asimmetria in Italia e Spagna. Giappichelli, Torino

Moreno L (1997) Federalization and ethnoterritorial concurrence in Spain. Publius: J Fed 27(4):65–84

Moreno L (2010) Federal democracy in plural Spain. In: Burgess M, Gagnon AG (eds) Federal democracies. Routledge, Abingdon, pp 160–177

Moreno L, Colino C, Hombrado A (2019) Spain: constitutional transition through the gradual accommodation of territories. In: Anderson G, Choudhry S (eds) Territory and power in constitutional transitions. Oxford University Press, Oxford, pp 237–254

Moreno Martínez V (2025) Entre la independencia y la reconciliación: el proceso soberanista catalán y la amnistía. In: Parlamento y Constitución. Anuario, Cortes de Castilla-La Mancha—UCLM, Toledo, pp 135–177.

Munoz Machado S (1992) Los pactos autonómicos de 1992: la ampliación de competencias y la reforma de los estatutos. Revista de administración pública 128:85–106

Palermo F (2019) Towards a comparative constitutional law of secession? In: Delledonne G, Martinico G (eds) The Canadian contribution to a comparative law of secession. Palgrave Macmillan, Cham, pp 265–282

Palermo F (2021) Asymmetries in the Italian regional system and their role model. In: Arban E, Martinico G, Palermo F (eds) Federalism and constitutional law. The Italian contribution to comparative regionalism. Routledge, London, pp 136-151

Palermo F, Kössler K (2017) Comparative federalism. Constitutional arrangements and case law. Hart Publishing, Oxford

Popelier P (2021) Dynamic federalism. A new theory for cohesion and regional autonomy. Routledge

Ridao Martín J (2025) Reconstruir l'asimetria: els drets històrics com a via de modulació o excepció de les competències i normes de l'Estat a Catalunya (CA-ES). Revista Catalana de Dret Públic 70:153–171

Rubio Llorente F (1991) Minorias y mayorias en el poder constituyente. Anuario de Derecho Constitucional y Parlamentario, 3.

Ruiz-Rico Ruiz GJ (2006) La reforma de los Estatutos de Autonomía: actas del IV Congreso de la Asociación de Constitucionalistas de España. Tirant lo Blanch, Valencia

Russo AM (2021) Sistema delle fonti e pluralismo territoriale tra (in) crisi ed (in) emergenza negli Stati composti. DPCE Online, 50(Sp.): 132–206.

Ryan A (2020) Federalism as legal pluralism. In: Berman PS (ed) The Oxford handbook of global legal pluralism. Oxford University Press, Oxford, pp 491–527

Sala G (2014) Federalism without adjectives in Spain. Publius: J Fed 44(1):109–134

San Anton Moracho L (2018) (Re)definiendo España: una aproximación a la génesis del articulo 2 de la Constitución Española. Huarte de San Juan, 25: 193–220.
Solozabal Echavarria JJ (2018) Art. 2. In: Rodríguez-Piñero Y Bravo Ferrer M, Casas Baamonde ME (eds) Comentarios a la Constitución Española, vol I. Wolters Kluwer, Madrid, pp 61-73
Tierney S (2022) The federal contract. A constitutional theory of federalism. Oxford University Press, Oxford
Tierney S (2018) Federalism and constitutional theory. In: Jacobsohn G, Schor M (eds) Comparative constitutional theory. Edward Elgar Publishing, Cheltenham, pp 45–65
Tirapu-Sanuy JM (2025) The Catalan Amnesty in the Spanish constitutional court: a triumph of pragmatism over principle. VerfBlog, 7/12, https://verfassungsblog.de/the-catalan-amnesty-in-the-spanish-constitutional-court/. https://doi.org/10.59704/d16f7effe3ceb6e6
Tomás y Valiente F (1995) Uniformidad y diversidad en las Comunidades Autonomas en la legislacion Estatal y en la doctrina del Tribunal Constitucional. In: Uniformidad o diversidad de las comunidades autónomas. IEA, Barcelona, pp 513–524.
Tornos Mas J (2019) Secession and federalism. The Spanish case. In: López-Basaguren A, Escajedo San-Epifanio L (eds) Claims for secession and federalism. Springer, Cham, pp 389-404
Ubillos JMB (2024) Spain as a Democratic State Governed by the Rule of Law and the Catalan Secessionist Process. Hague J Rule Law 16:3–30

Autonomy and Differentiation: The Evolution of Italian Regionalism Between Unitary Vocation and Pluralist Impulse

Federico Savastano

Abstract The essay addresses the attempt to formalize and expand asymmetrical arrangements within the Italian regional system through the implementation of so-called differentiated regionalism, introduced by the 2001 constitutional reform and now provided for in Article 116, paragraph 3, of the Constitution. It argues that these forms of asymmetry represent not a structural principle of the legal system but rather exceptional and circumscribed instruments, which must remain functional to the preservation of the principle of unity of the Republic and the safeguarding of substantive equality. The potentially improper expansion of this mechanism risks generating systemic inequalities if not accompanied by effective guarantees in terms of essential levels of services (LEPs), parliamentary oversight, financial sustainability, and procedural transparency. While Italian regionalism is open to flexible forms of autonomy, it cannot structurally tolerate fragmentation inconsistent with the supreme principles of the constitutional order.

1 Autonomy as a Structuring Principle of the Italian Regional State

The 1948 Italian Constitution marked a decisive turning point in the configuration of the State, formally enshrining the overcoming of administrative centralism and recognizing the regions as autonomous entities endowed with their own powers. Article 5 unequivocally affirms the principle of autonomy, to be understood not merely in administrative terms but as the acknowledgment of the normative and political capacity of territorial communities. This represented a clear break from the unitary model of the nineteenth-century State, delineating a pluralistic framework that, in its original intent, sought to reconcile the unity of the Republic with the enhancement of local autonomies.

F. Savastano (✉)
Department of Political Sciences, Sapienza University of Rome, Rome, Italy
e-mail: federico.savastano@uniroma1.it

F. Savastano et al. (eds.), *Between Asymmetry and Secession*,
https://doi.org/10.1007/978-3-032-29603-0_15

The compromise reached within the Constituent Assembly reflected the dialectical tension between two opposing constitutional visions: on the one hand, the unitary impulse of the national State and, on the other, the drive toward a territorial articulation of public power capable of reflecting the diversity of identities and local needs, hence the dual decision to establish the regions and to distinguish between ordinary statute regions and special statute regions. The latter, introduced ab initio through transitional provisions, responded to specific historical, cultural, and political circumstances that demanded more advanced forms of autonomy. The grounds for such differentiation were manifold: the need to safeguard linguistic minorities (as in Trentino-Alto Adige and Valle d'Aosta), insular contexts with particular administrative and infrastructural characteristics (Sardinia and Sicily), or deeply rooted political claims (as in the case of Friuli Venezia Giulia) (Patroni Griffi 2021).

This asymmetric arrangement did not imply a denial of the principle of equality but, rather, represented its substantive implementation, in the sense of adapting the institutional organization of the State to the country's structural diversities (Staiano 2017). Autonomy was thus conceived as a unifying factor, rather than as a source of disaggregation. Italian regionalism was therefore characterized from its inception by a persistent tension between institutional uniformity and the recognition of territorial pluralism (Bin 2017). This tension remained latent for decades due to the prolonged inertia in the actual implementation of regionalism, until the critical juncture represented by the 2001 reform of Title V.

Within the constitutional architecture of the postwar period, regional autonomy assumes a foundational role—not only with regard to the distribution of public power but also in shaping the very identity of the Republic. This approach anticipated many of the conceptual and institutional challenges that would emerge more clearly in subsequent decades as constitutional reflection increasingly focused on the meaning, scope, and implications of differentiation. The underlying idea remained that of a State which considers territorial autonomies as constitutive elements of its own structure and not as contingent or revocable concessions.

On this foundation, a model of regionalism developed that was structurally oriented toward symmetry, wherein differentiations were historically conceived as functional responses to specific linguistic, geographical, or social needs—as evidenced by the general commitment to the Mezzogiorno enshrined in the constitutional text in force until 2001.[1]

---

[1] The "Southern Question" received explicit constitutional recognition in the 1948 Italian Constitution, particularly through the XIII Transitional and Final Provision, which directly referred to the Mezzogiorno by envisaging "measures in favour of the populations of the islands and of mountainous or otherwise disadvantaged areas." This provision confirmed the urgency—already perceived during the Constituent Assembly's deliberations—of addressing the historical territorial imbalances affecting the national fabric. Beyond this transitional norm, Article 3, paragraph 2, entrusted the Republic with the duty to remove economic and social obstacles that constrain substantive equality, while Article 119, in its original formulation, authorized the State to implement special interventions in favor of the South ("in order to achieve specific objectives, and in particular to promote the development of the Mezzogiorno and the Islands, the State may allocate special grants to individual Regions"). With the reform of Title V in 2001, the explicit reference to the

It is precisely in light of this symmetrical and cooperative constitutional architecture that one must assess the significance and scope of the principle of differentiation introduced by the 2001 reform and its effective role within the broader framework of the Italian regional model.

Italian constitutional history reveals a persistent dialectic between the imperative of maintaining state cohesion and the progressive acknowledgment—first administrative, then political—of territorial diversity, in line with the spirit of Article 5 of the Constitution. From the postunification centralist paradigm, based on a concentrated conception of sovereignty, the evolution of regionalism has consistently unfolded within parameters favoring symmetry—even when temporarily interrupted by asymmetrical provisions such as the special statutes.

In this perspective, the territorial organization of the Republic has consolidated itself as a unitary system that tolerates functional exceptions but does not evolve into a radically pluralistic configuration. Even the 2021 constitutional amendments did not inaugurate a genuine transition toward differentiated federalism but rather accentuated the potential of a regulated and cooperative regionalism, within which the central State continues to perform a role of guarantee and rebalancing (Durst 2024).

Against this backdrop, Constitutional Law No. 2 of 7 November 2022 was enacted, amending Article 119 of the Constitution and introducing, in its final paragraph, the principle of insularity, thereby affirming that "the Republic recognizes the peculiarities of the islands and promotes the necessary measures to overcome the disadvantages deriving from insularity." This provision reinstated within the constitutional text a focus on the island territories that had been removed by the 2001 reform (Frosini 2020; Carboni 2022).

This historical and institutional background supports the conclusion that Italian regionalism has never been structurally anchored to the principle of differentiation—neither in axiological terms nor in organizational ones. The provision set forth in Article 116, paragraph 3, is inscribed within a normative continuum oriented toward symmetry and interinstitutional cooperation and does not constitute the natural culmination of a disaggregative or competitive trend in regional governance.

This essay seeks to demonstrate that regional differentiation, although expressly provided for by Article 116 of the Constitution, represents not a foundational principle of Italian regionalism but rather an exceptional and conditional mechanism operating within a system that remains, in its essence, symmetrical and collaborative.

Mezzogiorno was removed, replaced by general principles of equalization and solidarity. Nonetheless, the implementation of differentiated regionalism in the absence of effective guarantees concerning the essential levels of services (LEPs) risks producing a constitutional fracture. Such a dynamic could undermine the very territorial balance that the Constitution, since its inception, has sought to pursue and safeguard.

2 The Historical and Political Reasons for Statutory Differentiation

The adoption of special statutes for certain regions has, since the constituent phase, represented a solution aimed at accommodating and composing heterogeneous—often divergent—demands emerging within the national territory. The positioning of these regions outside the ordinary framework ought to be interpreted not as a concession to centrifugal forces but rather as the expression of a selectively adaptive form of regionalism, capable of absorbing elements of discontinuity without undermining the unitary principles of the constitutional order.

Such asymmetry finds its roots in a plurality of historical circumstances linked to specific events: the presence of internationally protected linguistic minorities, as in Trentino-Alto Adige and Valle d'Aosta; the condition of insularity and the severe infrastructural deficits affecting Sicily and Sardinia; and the geopolitical hinge role played by Friuli Venezia Giulia in the Cold War frontier context. These objective conditions, already noted by constitutional scholars in the earliest commentaries, justified recourse to more intense forms of autonomy, articulated through statutes vested with a para-constitutional status (Patroni Griffi 2021).

Beyond contingent motivations, special-regime regionalism has assumed paradigmatic significance, standing as an alternative model to the ordinary one and, prospectively, inspiring a differentiated evolution of the system. Italian regionalism has historically developed along a dual track of autonomies, driven by a twofold rationale: derogatory, in the case of the special regions, and translational, in the case of the ordinary ones. This dual structure reflects two distinct cultural matrices—namely, Iberian regionalism and Central European federalism—synthesized within the Constituent Assembly's deliberations (D'Atena 2014).

What was initially conceived as an exceptional response has progressively become a benchmark for subsequent claims to autonomy, generating a gradual destabilization of constitutional symmetry. The dualism between special and ordinary regions has fostered a dynamic interpretation of autonomy, opening space for legal and institutional solutions grounded in territorial specificity. Unsurprisingly, the Constitutional Court has consistently interpreted special autonomy as a clause of maximal expansion, justifying it through the historical singularity and sociocultural distinctiveness of the relevant territories.

An essential, albeit often overlooked, aspect concerns the prejuridical foundation of the special autonomies, rooted in preexisting collective identities recognized by the State as expressions of constitutional pluralism. These entities originated not from abstract administrative constructs—as in the case of the ordinary regions, shaped around statistical demarcations—but from a process of historical and cultural sedimentation, conferring upon their special status an anthropological depth (Silvestri, cited in D'Atena 2014). This distinction has deeply influenced the constitutional treatment of the special regions, which—already in the early republican period—were characterized by a full form of autonomy, with their respective statutes enjoying direct constitutional relevance (Mobilio 2021, p. 302).

According to the paradigm that emerged in the aftermath of the Second World War, the function of the special statute regions was not merely to respond to local demands but also to act as a pillar of cohesion and stabilization for national unity. The political-legal compromise reached in the Constituent Assembly tended to recognize the special regimes as a constitutional safeguard for deeply rooted historical and territorial identities (Mobilio 2021, p. 305).

In a comparative analysis, the Italian model of statutory differentiation aligns with analogous European experiences, where state unity coexists with differentiated regional orders. Italian special autonomies—despite their originality—anticipate elements that now characterize the evolutionary and flexible regionalism adopted in systems such as those of Spain, Belgium, and the United Kingdom (D'Orlando 2025). What emerges is a framework in which differentiation is not merely tolerated but also valorized as a tool for systemic inclusion and adaptability.

From this perspective, special autonomy constitutes a constitutional laboratory that has paved the way for a critical reconsideration of the very notion of uniformity. It has revealed the insufficiency of a regionalism based solely on the egalitarian distribution of competences, laying the foundations for a more sophisticated model—capable of accounting for territorial disparities and the functional differentiation among regional entities. Such a development now requires a critical reassessment of the principle of equality, which can no longer be confined to formal homogenization but must instead be articulated in a differential and territorial key, with a view to achieving genuine national cohesion (Lagrotta 2025; Bifulco 2023; Mobilio 2021, pp. 310–312).

3 Title V of 2001: An Opening to "Bottom-Up" Differentiation?

The 2001 constitutional reform—the most extensive amendment ever introduced into the Italian constitutional text (Mangiameli 2012)—marked a pivotal juncture in the development of Italian regionalism, profoundly reshaping the relationship between the State and the regions. While preserving the overarching structure of the form of State, the new Title V introduced elements of radical innovation, most notably the explicit recognition, under Article 116, paragraph 3, of the possibility for regions with ordinary statutes to obtain additional forms and particular conditions of autonomy (Mangiameli 2017). Far from constituting a marginal exception, this provision has gradually acquired systemic significance, functioning as an entry point to a differentiated model of regionalism no longer grounded in the original dichotomy between special and ordinary regions but rather in the capacity of individual regions to formulate and substantiate coherent proposals for the extension of their competences.

Article 116, paragraph 3, has often been interpreted as an enabling clause for a model of negotiated autonomy, capable of accommodating autonomist aspirations within an institutionally regulated framework. The procedural nature of the provision—which requires a formal agreement between the State and the region, to be ratified by a national statute—means that access to enhanced autonomy is not automatic but contingent upon a thorough assessment of constitutional compatibility and systemic sustainability (Tarli Barbieri 2024). In this respect, differentiation under Article 116 is grounded in a dynamic form of legitimation, in contrast to the static entrenchment that characterizes special statutes.

The reform, thus, made the principle of differentiation available to all regions, not by virtue of a predetermined status but as the outcome of a political and institutional initiative that necessitates bilateral agreement with the State. In so doing, Italian regionalism breaks away from the rigidity of preordained statutory arrangements, opening itself to a logic of negotiation structured through a formal legislative process involving Parliament and, potentially, subnational entities as well. The reform thereby dismantled the dogma of institutional symmetry, enabling differentiation not only in the content of devolved powers but also in the procedures by which those powers are conferred.

However, this process should have been accompanied by a comprehensive reformulation of the very concept of autonomy and of the prerequisites necessary for its concrete implementation—taking into account not only the institutional framework but also the actual administrative capacities and the ability to guarantee rights uniformly across the national territory (Mobilio 2021, p. 214). The introduction of concurrent legislation under Article 117 has further increased the complexity of the division of competences, promoting a regulatory interdependence between the State and the regions. This framework, however, has generated numerous jurisdictional conflicts and an abundant body of constitutional case law, which has progressively redefined the scope of regional autonomy within more stringent limits. The Constitutional Court, in its role of interinstitutional balancing, has attempted to ensure coordination between the various levels of government, though without fully resolving the tensions inherent in the coexistence of shared legislative competences (D'Atena 2014).

It is within this context that the process of differentiation for the ordinary regions has taken shape, with requests advanced through draft agreements prompting a lively debate on the balance between national unity and territorial pluralism. Differentiated regionalism thus emerges as a symptom of the crisis of the symmetrical model, exposing the inadequacy of a uniform conception of public power distribution (Bin 2019). Article 116, in its intrinsic ambiguity, has served as a catalyst for the redefinition of the principle of autonomy—not as a rigid framework but as an open field for institutional innovation (Mangiameli 2017).

The scholarly debate—which, in the case of differentiated autonomy, has at times been marked by politically or ideologically influenced approaches (Caravita 2019)—has also highlighted the risk that a disjointed application of the provision may give rise to systemic inequalities among regions. Mobilio has emphasized that the absence of a clearly defined set of essential levels of services (LEPs) constitutes a structural constraint on the implementation of differentiation, as it precludes any meaningful assessment of whether the newly configured institutional arrangements effectively guarantee the uniform protection of fundamental rights (Mobilio 2021, pp. 220–222). It has been observed that the successful realization of differentiation presupposes not only coherent political will but also adequate administrative capacity and a clear definition of LEPs as a safeguard for constitutional rights (D'Atena 2014). In the absence of these conditions, differentiation risks exacerbating territorial disparities rather than remedying them.

The valorization of the principle of differentiation also requires a systematic reinterpretation of Title V, which cannot be approached as a collection of isolated provisions but must be understood as an integrated framework to be harmonized with the fundamental principles of the constitutional order—including the legal and economic unity of the Republic, the principle of solidarity, and substantive equality. In its Judgment No. 192 of 2024, the Constitutional Court reaffirmed that the allocation of competences must be consistent with the guarantee of essential levels of services and the protection of fundamental rights so as to prevent differentiation from degenerating into structural inequality (Saitta 2025). From this perspective, the 2001 Title V may be interpreted not merely as a compendium of norms on regional autonomy but also as a genuine constitutional project aimed at institutional polycentrism (Mangiameli 2017).

Differentiated regionalism, initially conceived as a mechanism for adapting the legal order to territorial specificities, has thus become a litmus test for the resilience of the principle of autonomy in its dynamic dimension. It demands a robust procedural framework grounded in transparency, participation, and strict adherence to constitutional constraints—without which the risk of territorial fragmentation becomes not merely theoretical but also tangible. The current debate demonstrates that the success of differentiation depends on the capacity of the political-institutional system to secure a balance between autonomy and cohesion and between diversity and substantive equality (D'Atena 2014; Mangiameli 2017; Mobilio 2021).

4 The Improper Use of Differentiation: A Principle Expanding Where It Shouldn't

The extension of the principle of differentiation to regions with ordinary statutes has raised profound questions regarding the systemic coherence of the Italian regional framework. Although Article 116, paragraph 3, of the Constitution formally confines such differentiation to regions that explicitly request it, the interpretative and procedural developments surrounding its application have gradually deviated from the provision's original rationale. Rather than producing a normatively coherent and procedurally disciplined framework, what has emerged is a proliferation of informal practices and unilaterally formulated draft agreements—frequently devoid of adequate public scrutiny or a rigorous evaluation of the general interest (Patroni Griffi 2021).

This drift has been exacerbated by the absence of a sufficiently structured normative framework capable of regulating the differentiated process. The bilateral negotiation, inspired by a quasi-contractual model, has acquired opaque features, circumventing the ordinary circuits of democratic legality. The result has been a landscape in which differentiation has ceased to function as an exceptional and targeted instrument of institutional adaptation and has instead been recast as a generalized lever for political demands for expanded competences—decoupled from any genuine assessment of the requesting region's administrative and financial capacity (Bin 2022). Such an approach has undermined the credibility of the broader autonomy system, transforming differentiation into a mechanism more akin to a political claim for redistribution of power than a constitutionally grounded mode of governance.

This dynamic has exposed a fundamental distortion of the institution: instead of serving the constitutional aim of calibrated and functional adaptation, it has increasingly become a vector for systemic disarticulation. On multiple occasions, the negotiation process has overlooked essential ex ante evaluations concerning fiscal costs, interinstitutional implications, and distributive effects. Differentiation has thereby become a form of institutional pressure exerted outside the canonical structures of accountability, often driven by subnational political actors seeking internal legitimacy. The absence of transparent and effective oversight mechanisms has amplified the risks of a competitive (and disintegrative) trajectory for Italian regionalism (Poggi 2024).

In its landmark Judgment No. 192 of 2024, the Constitutional Court drew a clear line against this trajectory, affirming that differentiation cannot serve as a source of structural inequality, nor may it impair the guarantee of fundamental rights or compromise the legal and economic unity of the Republic. Article 120, when read in conjunction with Article 117, paragraph 2, letter m), imposes that any differentiated attribution of functions be conditional upon the prior determination of essential levels of services (LEPs), as well as upon the financial sustainability of the resulting arrangements (Mone 2024; Saitta 2025; Sterpa 2025). This interpretative stance reinforces the view that legitimate differentiation must be embedded within a nationally coordinated and sustainable constitutional project, capable of harmonizing local demands with the overarching imperative of solidarity.

From this vantage point, the lack of an organic procedural discipline and the inadequacy of the implementing legislative framework must be regarded as critical weaknesses (Poggi 2024). Law No. 86 of 2024, in its original formulation, was partially struck down for its anticipation of an undifferentiated transfer of entire subject matters—contrary to the constitutional requirement of identifying specific functions, in accordance with the principles of subsidiarity, differentiation, and adequacy (Tucciarelli 2025). The Court further ruled out the applicability of the mechanism to regions with special statutes, reaffirming the distinctiveness of the constitutional channels of autonomy. This clarification confirms that Article 116 cannot serve as a generalized shortcut to enhanced autonomy but must be strictly constrained by the structural limits of the constitutional system.

The concrete experience of preliminary agreements—such as those entered into by Lombardy, Veneto, and Emilia-Romagna[2]—has revealed the fragility of the current framework. Confidential negotiation has been preferred over public deliberation, and proposals for decentralization have often exceeded the effective administrative capacity of the requesting regions. No meaningful impact assessments have been conducted, nor have mechanisms for inclusive participation by territorial communities been activated. This procedural and functional asymmetry threatens to weaken the entire architecture of regional autonomy, generating unmitigated territorial gaps and distributive inequities. Differences in the quality and scope of public services risk becoming more pronounced, institutionalizing a geography of inequality among the regions.

The very nature of differentiation is thereby compromised: what was conceived as an exceptional mechanism has been transformed into an ordinary instrument of institutional pressure, deployed more for political competition than for rationalizing the allocation of powers. In this context, differentiation no longer responds to logics of administrative efficiency or subsidiarity but functions as a revendicatory tool, often driven by identity-based strategies and status-related claims. This deviation from the original function of the principle calls for a systematic reconsideration of the entire mechanism, beginning with the establishment of a procedural discipline capable of ensuring transparency, parliamentary oversight, and ex ante evaluation of its effects on the constitutional guarantees of rights and on national financial equilibrium (Ferrara 2025). Only a genuinely multilevel governance system, rooted in the principles of solidarity, subsidiarity, and institutional responsibility, can ensure that differentiation remains a tool of cohesion rather than a pretext for deepening the structural inequalities of the Republic.

5 Differentiation Tested by Constitutional Jurisprudence: From Conditional Legitimacy to Systemic Reconstruction

The constitutional litigation that has accompanied the implementation of differentiated regionalism has constituted a moment of both clarification and redefinition of the boundaries within which differentiation may operate without undermining the fundamental principles of the constitutional order. In this regard, the Constitutional Court's Judgment No. 192 of 2024 stands as a genuine turning point, not only for

[2] In 2017, the regions of Lombardy, Veneto, and Emilia-Romagna initiated negotiations with the central government to obtain expanded forms of autonomy pursuant to Article 116, paragraph 3, of the Constitution. These negotiations led to the drafting of preliminary agreements in 2018; however, the process subsequently stalled due to the absence of a clear legislative framework and shifts in the political landscape. The requests—broad in scope and formulated in a highly heterogeneous manner—raised serious concerns regarding the cohesion of the State and the fairness of differentiated regionalism, particularly in the absence of a prior definition of the essential levels of services (on this point, see Pallante 2019).

the breadth of the issues addressed but also for the depth and rigor of the theoretical framework underpinning it.

The Court reaffirmed that the principle of differentiation must be interpreted and applied within a systematic reading of the form of the State. Article 116, paragraph 3, constitutes not a rupture clause but rather a mechanism functionally integrated into the constitutional architecture, aimed at enhancing regional autonomy in harmony with the entirety of Title V and with the supreme principles of the Constitution. From this perspective, differentiation cannot result in a regression of rights guarantees, nor may it produce an unreasonable distribution of public resources in violation of the principle of substantive equality enshrined in Article 3 of the Constitution (Saitta 2025).

From a procedural standpoint, the Court underscored the imperative of strengthening the role of Parliament, which cannot merely act as a ratifying body for the agreement between the State and the region. Rather, it must exercise a substantive control over both the legitimacy and the policy soundness of requests for differentiated autonomy. The power of amendment, although compatible with the quasi-contractual nature of the process, must be exercised in a manner that ensures procedural transparency and inclusiveness, with institutional deliberation and representation of the general interest fully safeguarded (Casanova 2025).

The Court's jurisprudence has further emphasized the necessity of determining the essential levels of services (LEPs) prior to any conferment of differentiated competences. In the absence of fully defined LEPs, any hypothesis of devolution risks generating unsustainable asymmetries across the national territory, thereby compromising the uniform protection of civil and social rights and the foundational principle of territorial solidarity. This requirement is reflected in the Court's interpretive construction of Article 117, paragraph 2, letter m), which it identifies as an unwaivable clause safeguarding social rights throughout the Republic (D'Orlando 2025).

The judgment also highlighted the irreducible nature of the principle of the legal and economic unity of the Republic, recognizing the legitimacy of differentiated regionalism only insofar as it serves the objective of social cohesion and the full inclusion of all regional communities in the collective life of the nation. It is within this normative key that the Court's assertion is to be understood: differentiation must not result in fragmentation but must instead be oriented toward the enhancement of the common good and the most effective protection of the rights of individuals and social formations (Sterpa 2025).

Accordingly, the Court outlined a model of differentiated regionalism conceived as variable in geometry yet internally coherent with constitutional principles: a framework that precludes any form of institutional privilege and demands a rigorous justification of autonomist claims. What emerges is a conception of differentiation that is conditional, functional, and reversible—admissible only where the constitutional prerequisites of equality, solidarity, and sustainability are duly and demonstrably fulfilled.

6 Structural or Exceptional Asymmetry? Reflections on the Preconditions for Differentiated Autonomy

The principle of differentiation, as delineated in Article 116, paragraph 3, of the Italian Constitution, compels a profound reflection on the nature and ultimate purpose of the Italian model of regionalism. At the core of this inquiry lies the fundamental question of whether the constitutional system should be anchored in a symmetrical framework for the distribution of public powers or, rather, in a variable-geometry model of regionalism, in which asymmetry ceases to be an exceptional concession and becomes a structural and physiological component of the system. Over the past two decades, both scholarly and jurisprudential debates have increasingly revealed the existence of a theoretical dualism that directly implicates the form of the State itself, raising pressing questions concerning the relationship between unity, pluralism, and territorial cohesion.

On the one hand, the notion has taken root that differentiation constitutes a structural element, fully consonant with the principle of subsidiarity and with the valorization of territorial autonomies as expressions of a mature institutional pluralism. Within this framework, differentiated regionalism is the natural outgrowth of a polycentric, adaptive, and multilevel State architecture—aligned with the constitutional evolutions observable in several European jurisdictions. The experiences of Spain, Belgium, and the United Kingdom, among others, attest to a broader tendency in composite constitutional democracies toward flexible models of power allocation, inspired by considerations of efficiency, proximity, and functional adequacy (D'Orlando 2025). Article 116, paragraph 3, is thus construed as a dynamic provision, capable of accompanying gradual transformations in the relationship between the State and its regions, without undermining the constitutional balance.

On the other hand, however, there is growing awareness of the dangers posed by an expansive and unstructured conception of differentiation—one that risks hollowing out the unitary nature of the system. Under this view, enhanced autonomy cannot be claimed as a subjective right of the regions but must rather be regarded as a faculty subject to the fulfilment of stringent and objectively verifiable conditions. These include demonstrable administrative efficiency, financial sustainability of the proposed competences, consistency with the national interest, and strict compliance with a formalized procedural pathway. Differentiation, therefore, is admissible only where supported by a thorough and transparent evidentiary process, capable of demonstrating that its exercise does not compromise the principle of equality among citizens and territories (Ferrara 2025; Tucciarelli 2025).

These constitutional imperatives were unambiguously articulated by the Constitutional Court in Judgment No. 192 of 2024, which reaffirmed the indispensability of three fundamental preconditions: the prior determination of the essential levels of services (LEPs), the preservation of the legal and economic unity of the Republic, and the guarantee of substantive equality throughout the national territory (Saitta 2025). The Court warned of the systemic risks inherent in a disorganized implementation of differentiation, which could result in structural inequalities, undermine the principle of solidarity, and jeopardize the overarching constitutional project of social and territorial cohesion.

In light of these premises, it becomes evident that asymmetry cannot assume a constitutive value within the regional framework unless it is strictly delimited and duly justified. Rather, it must be conceived as a residual and selective instrument, applicable only in the presence of peculiar territorial needs that warrant departure from the symmetrical model. Absent such conditions, the expansion of regional competences would risk generating fragmentation within the system, exacerbating disparities in treatment and fostering tensions among public entities, with potentially grave repercussions for the unity of the Republic.

Nevertheless, from a medium- to long-term perspective, it is not to be excluded that the legal order may evolve toward a model of regulated differentiated regionalism—grounded in objective, public, and verifiable criteria. Such a model would require a solid, unified, and coherent normative framework, capable of reconciling openness to differentiation with unwavering adherence to the Constitution's fundamental principles, prominently including solidarity, unity, and equality. Within this vision, differentiation could serve a legitimate function in enhancing institutional efficiency and modernizing governance, but only insofar as it is embedded in a systemic and carefully monitored architecture, designed to forestall any drift toward particularism or institutional competition. The contemporary challenge lies precisely in defining this balance: to transform differentiation from a source of constitutional instability into a responsible mechanism of institutional adaptation.

7 Differentiation and Autonomy Between Aspiration and Limitation

The trajectory reconstructed in this essay reveals the profoundly ambivalent nature of the principle of differentiation within the Italian model of regionalism. Conceived as a means of enhancing territorial particularities within the framework of republican unity, differentiation has progressively assumed problematic features, especially when activated in the absence of a coherent normative and procedural architecture. The enduring tension between uniformity and diversity cannot be evaded—nor resolved—through interpretive shortcuts or opaque political arrangements. Rather, it demands a fundamental reconsideration of the very meaning of autonomy within the form of State as delineated by the Constitution.

In the Italian constitutional order, regional autonomy is to be understood as a structuring principle, not as a contingent concession. Within this framework, differentiation represents a legally permissible yet constitutionally constrained possibility, operative only where it remains consistent with the principles of solidarity, territorial cohesion, and substantive equality. Its implementation is contingent upon the fulfilment of stringent prerequisites: an adequate technical inquiry, the prior determination of essential levels of services (LEPs), the full implementation of fiscal federalism, financial sustainability guarantees, and—crucially—a transparent and effective parliamentary oversight mechanism (Tucciarelli 2025).

In this light, differentiation appears not as a constitutive element of the system of autonomies but rather as an exceptional and purposive derogation, whose admissibility is conditional upon its compatibility with the substantive unity of the Republic. Asymmetry may indeed be regarded as a sign of institutional maturity only when oriented toward the common good—not when driven by territorial opportunism. The risk of fragmentation is far from theoretical: it materializes wherever the principle of autonomy is instrumentalized for self-referential or revendicatory ends.

The evident opacity that has characterized certain negotiations between regions and the central government, the lack of a sufficiently articulated legislative framework, and the unresolved definition of LEPs have contributed to fostering a context in which differentiated claims have, at times, taken on unilateral characteristics. As noted by numerous scholars, the structure of Law No. 86 of 2024 is vulnerable precisely because of its lack of systemic coherence and institutional safeguards (Poggi 2025; Staiano 2023a, b). The resulting systemic tension is one that the Constitutional Court has sought to recalibrate through Judgment No. 192, reaffirming the primacy of the general interest and the necessity of subordinating differentiation to a demanding and publicly verifiable procedural framework.

The recent turn toward instruments of direct democracy—such as the proposed abrogative referendum concerning Law No. 86—further demonstrates how differentiated regionalism has become a focal point of intense conflict between political legitimacy and constitutional sustainability. A prospective ruling by the Constitutional Court on the admissibility of the referendum lies at the heart of this conflict and may represent a further testing ground for the principle of popular sovereignty—one that must be balanced against the protection of fundamental rights and the internal coherence of the constitutional system (Poggi 2025).

It falls to constitutional scholarship to contribute to the reconstruction of an interpretive framework that restores differentiation to its proper normative function, shielding it from instrumentalization. In this regard, Italian regionalism must be reimagined not as a mere aggregation of discrete autonomies but as the coherent articulation of a system that recognizes diversity as a constitutional value while tempering its effects through institutions and procedures capable of guaranteeing the equality of rights and the unity of the Republic. This approach finds confirmation in a significant strand of legal scholarship, which maintains that differentiated autonomy can only be sustainable if accompanied by mechanisms of redistributive solidarity and by a shared national discipline (Di Majo 2020; Vernata 2019).

Only within such boundaries can differentiated autonomy be conceived as an integral component of a pluralist and solidaristic constitutional order—one capable of meeting the challenges posed by territorial complexity without sacrificing the foundational principles of equality, solidarity, and republican unity.

References

Bifulco R (2023) Lo stato delle regioni a vent'anni dalla legge costituzionale n. 3 del 2001. Il diritto della Regione 2:36–54
Bin R (2017) L'attuazione dell'autonomia differenziata. Forum di Quaderni costituzionali, 20 April
Bin R (2019) Le materie nel dettato dell'articolo 116 Cost. Forum di Quaderni costituzionali, 26 June, 1–14
Bin R (2022) L'autonomia differenziata: politica o burocrazia? Le Regioni, Bimestrale di analisi giuridica e istituzionale 6:1153–1158
Caravita B (2019) Un doppio binario per l'approvazione del regionalismo differenziato. federalismi.it 13:1–5
Carboni GG (2022) La stagione dell'insularità. federalismi.it 22:20–30
Casanova D (2025) Regionalismo differenziato e riforma dei regolamenti parlamentari. Spunti a partire dalla sentenza della Corte costituzionale n. 192 del 2024. federalismi.it – paper, 30 April
D'Atena A (2014) Passato, presente... e futuro delle autonomie regionali speciali. Rivista AIC 4:1–15
D'Orlando E (2025) Uguaglianza nel godimento dei diritti e buon governo delle risorse pubbliche: LEP, costi e fabbisogni standard, federalismo fiscale, nella cornice dello Stato regionale cooperativo. federalismi.it – paper, 30 April
Di Majo L (2020) Regionalismo differenziato: una questione di metodo, prima ancora del merito. Rivista AIC 1:232–265
Durst L (2024) L'organizzazione territoriale in Italia tra regionalismo e autonomia differenziata: un percorso degli ultimi venti anni. Nomos – Le attualità del diritto 3:1–32
Ferrara A (2025) Tra favorevoli e contrari all'autonomia differenziata: è possibile trovare una comune convergenza per la realizzazione di un regionalismo d'esecuzione da avviarsi in via asimmetrica?. federalismi.it – paper, 30 April
Frosini TE (2020) «Insularità» e Costituzione. Rivista giuridica del Mezzogiorno 1:247–254
Lagrotta I (2025) La pars costruens della sentenza della corte costituzionale n. 192/2024 in materia di autonomia differenziata. Judicium, 1 April
Mangiameli S (2012) Regionalism and reforms: resolved issues and open problems. In: Mangiameli S (ed) Italian Regionalism Between Unitary Traditions and Federalist Processes: a contribution to the study of the crisis of the form of state in Italy, Giuffrè, Milan
Mangiameli S (2017) Il regionalismo italiano dopo la crisi e il referendum costituzionale. Appunti per concludere una lunga transizione. Italian Papers on Federalism 1:1–27
Mobilio G (2021) Differenziazione e specialità nella incerta evoluzione del regionalismo italiano. In: Cosulich M (ed) Il regionalismo italiano alla prova delle differenziazioni. Atti del Convegno Annuale dell'Associazione "Gruppo di Pisa" Trento, 18–19 September 2020. Editoriale Scientifica, Naples
Mone D (2024) Il modello di autonomia differenziata del ddl Calderoli tra finalità dichiarate e finalità perseguite: il nodo delle risorse finanziarie. Nuove Autonomie 1:95–110
Pallante F (2019) Ancora nel merito del regionalismo differenziato: le nuove bozze di intesa tra Stato e Veneto, Lombardia ed Emilia-Romagna. federalismiit 6:1–35
Patroni Griffi A (2021) Entry "Regionalismo differenziato". In: Bifulco R, Celotto A, Olivetti M (eds) Digesto delle discipline pubblicistiche. UTET, Turin, pp 317–338
Poggi A (2024) Il regionalismo differenziato nella "forma" del d.d.l Calderoli: alcune chiare opzioni politiche, ancora nodi che sarebbe bene sciogliere. federalismiit 3:iv–xiv
Poggi A (2025) Il referendum sul regionalismo differenziato: i principi, l'attuazione, le Corti e la sovranità popolare. federalismi.it 1:iv–ix
Saitta A (2025). Quale futuro per l'autonomia differenziata? La risposta è nella sentenza n. 192 del 2024. federalismi.it – paper, 30 April
Staiano S (2017) Articolo 5. Carocci, Rome
Staiano S (2023a) Salvare il regionalismo dalla differenziazione dissolutiva. federalismi.it 7:iv–xv

Staiano S (2023b) Salvare il regionalismo differenziato dai suoi epigoni attardati. Rivista giuridica del Mezzogiorno 4:987–994
Sterpa A (2025) Le due "sentenze sorelle" sul regionalismo differenziato: legge Calderoli e referendum sotto la lente della nazione. federalismi.it – paper, 30 April
Tarli Barbieri G (2024) «Il passaggio dall'idea al fatto è sempre penoso». L'autonomia differenziata tra mito e realtà. Diritti regionali 1:81–112
Tucciarelli C (2025) Note introduttive. federalismi.it – paper, 30 April
Vernata A (2019) Il regionalismo differenziato alla prova della Costituzione. Costituzionalismoit 2:1–26

The Material Dimensions of Italian Regionalism

Francesco Severa

Abstract This essay examines the substantive dynamics of Italian regionalism within the broader framework of constitutional pluralism. It argues that Italy's regional system, while formally decentralized, is characterized by an intrinsic *artificiality*: a model not rooted in identity-based federalism but in the political reconstruction of pluralism after the centralized, authoritarian experience of the twentieth century. The analysis traces the evolution of center–periphery relations from the 1948 Constitution to the 2001 reform, highlighting the dominant role of the Constitutional Court in shaping the principles of subsidiarity and *loyal cooperation*. Over time, judicial mechanisms have been complemented by increasingly political forms of integration, privileging negotiation and coordination over adjudication. The result is a flexible, dialectical model of governance, where national unity and regional autonomy coexist within a continuous process of institutional recomposition—an expression of Italy's enduring attempt to transform conflict into cooperation within a plural constitutional order.

1 The Italian Regional Path and Its Rationale

To begin with a clarifying consideration: the regional dimension of the Italian constitutional system—already present as a substantive element in the original 1948 Constitution and later further emphasized by the 2001 reform—can hardly be regarded as the ultimate expression of a federalization process. Nor can it be convincingly interpreted as an ex post attempt to revive certain autonomist dynamics in a federal key (Rolla 2022; Caravita 2006a; Reposo 1993; Bognetti 1991; De Vergottini 1990).

From the first perspective, the historical process of constructing Italian statehood (the Risorgimento and the ensuing unification process, as traditionally defined by "institutional" historiography) had nothing specifically *federal* in nature. It was not

F. Severa (✉)
Sapienza University of Rome, Rome, Italy
e-mail: francesco.severa@uniroma1.it

F. Savastano et al. (eds.), *Between Asymmetry and Secession*,
https://doi.org/10.1007/978-3-032-29603-0_16

established through a dialectical or "contractual" relationship among pre-existing state entities willing to transfer part of their sovereignty to a higher, supranational authority (La Pergola 1969). On the contrary, the territorial and political fragmentation that had characterized the Italian peninsula since the fall of the Roman Empire was resolved in the nineteenth century through annexation to the Savoy State and the creation of a typically centralized constitutional order—both politically and administratively—modeled on post-revolutionary France (Stanco 2012; Antonacci 1996; Ciuffoletti 1994; De Francesco 1994).

Turning to the second perspective, claims for self-government within the unified Italian State have rarely—if ever—been primarily identity-based; rather, they have been political in nature (Carboni 2020; Bartole 1999; with regard to Sardinia, Demuro et al. 2013; with regard to Sicily, Armao 2024; Ruggeri 2022; Giarrizzo 1975). With the exception of a few linguistic minorities located along the northern borders (Poggeschi 2010; Palermo and Woelk 2008; Pizzorusso 1993), other "independence-oriented" expressions have generally been linked to territorial factors (such as insularity—see Constitutional Amendment No. 2 of 2022 - Tucciarelli 2025; Carboni 2022) or to the protection of specific territorial models of economic development (for instance, the "Mitteleuropean" integration pattern of northern Italian regions, recently implemented through the differentiated autonomy mechanism under Article 116(3) of the Constitution - see Bertolissi 2025; Morrone 2025).

Nevertheless, most of these centrifugal tendencies have been reabsorbed within a framework of extraordinary autonomy, by recognizing to five regions—those either hosting significant linguistic minorities or located on islands—the possibility of enjoying special forms and conditions of autonomy through constitutional statutes (Article 116 of the Constitution; see Cortese and Woelk 2023). This exceptional regime coexists with an ordinary framework of regional autonomy, which applies to the remaining regions and operates according to a fundamentally *translational* logic (D'Atena 2022 - see also Grazzini et al. 2020), that is based on a transfer of competences from the center to the periphery. The very existence of such an exceptional regime confirms, *a contrario*, the broader cultural and ethnic homogeneity of Italy, which has allowed the autonomist model to be structured around a single, uniform formula applicable nationwide—without the need to accommodate each disaggregating claim individually. Many geopolitical scholars view this feature as a strength of the Italian system (Fabbri 2018).

This leads to the conclusion that Italian regionalism—in both its ordinary and special variants—should be conceptually situated within the powerful pluralist impetus that characterized the country's post-war constituent process (Sturzo 1962). This impetus manifested not only in political terms—through party and trade-union pluralism, freedom of expression, the personalist principle, and substantive equality—but also institutionally, through a non-hierarchical structure of the Republic founded on the integration of multiple decision-making centers, each endowed with its own (often elective) legitimacy and, consequently, its own constitutional weight. The "regional path" thus imposes upon the Italian legal order a distinct notion of unity, "constructed on the basis of a re-composable regional pluralism, rather than presumed where an inexorable bureaucratic pluralism operates, nourished by uncontrolled sectoral interests" (Amato 1972).

2 An "Artificial" Regionalism Within the Dynamics of Institutional Pluralism

Pluralism in the Italian constitutional order operates as a form of logical bifurcation. Parliament was conceived as a bicameral institution, with no substantial differences in the electoral systems of its two chambers but with the intent of imposing a certain *deliberative slowness* upon parliamentary debate and of ensuring the highest degree of consensus in legislative decision-making (Palermo and Nicolini 2013). The executive, in turn, was designed with a dual nature—hierarchical in shaping political direction yet collegial in decision-making (Ruggeri 1981). The continuum between Parliament and Government, anchored in the confidence relationship, is balanced by two guarantor bodies—the President of the Republic and the Constitutional Court—both capable of expressing countermajoritarian instances (Morrone 2019, 2021; Ruggeri 2024). The judiciary, for its part, possesses an organizational apex—the High Council of the Judiciary (Consiglio Superiore della Magistratura)—yet exercises no collective power, as each judge is bound only by the law (Article 101(2) of the Constitution; see Biondi 2024; Luciani 2020).

How, then, does regionalism participate in this "game"? It functions as a counterweight to the centralizing tendencies of the executive. It complements the central executive power by creating other loci for the exercise of governmental authority—not fully concurrent but *ratione materiae* competent—within a system of functional distribution that originally favored the State but was rebalanced in favor of the periphery through the 2001 constitutional reform (Constitutional Law No. 3 of 2001).

The "autonomist pluralism" is enshrined among the fundamental principles of the 1948 Constitution, particularly in Article 5, which postulates the necessary coexistence of the State and local autonomies within a multiplicity of overlapping territorial layers—coinciding with, but also distinct from, the State itself—each capable of identifying a political community endowed with self-government and its own legislative or administrative competences (Ronchetti 2018; Luciani 1997). This principle is reaffirmed in the solemn declaration of Article 114, as amended in 2001, which establishes that the Republic is "constituted by the State, the Regions, the Metropolitan Cities, the Provinces, and the Municipalities." These are all loci of sovereignty, mutually coequal, self-legitimating, and endowed with full political, normative, and administrative autonomy, albeit with a specific division of functions and competences, further supported by the general principle of subsidiarity (Demuro 2006; Mangiameli 2002).

What must be emphasized is that each of these autonomist components was not built upon a preexisting political, ethnic or cultural claim but rather grounded in territorial division—one that roughly respects geographically and socially homogeneous areas, defined not only by physical contiguity but also by anthropic connections deriving from patterns of urban, industrial, and service development. In this perspective, territory becomes the sole true instrument delimiting peripheral autonomy. It constitutes the space of the community itself—the citizens who inhabit it and share a sense of political belonging within it. It is as if, from the delimitation of space, a political will and a set of interests emerge, which the corresponding territorial entity must protect or represent—not the other way around.

The theoretical consequences of this conception are essentially threefold: (1) the shared territorial element is sufficient to confer political character upon the resident community, irrespective of further differentiations of a cultural or identitarian nature; (2) the protection that the representative territorial entity must ensure to its residents assumes a general dimension, extending broadly to the collective interests of all; (3) each of the entities through which national sovereignty is articulated must be linked to its citizens through forms of representation inspired by democratic principles.

In this sense, within the Italian constitutional framework, autonomy is inherently *artificial*: it is not designed to accommodate specific centrifugal impulses but is rather rooted in a deliberate historical-political rationale—namely, the overcoming of the centralized State, viewed as a facilitator of totalitarian drift, which historically had always opposed autonomist aspirations (Caravita 1994).

This idea permeates the entire republican institutional structure. At the peripheral level as well, it manifests through systems of government based on a binary model: an elective assembly and an executive. Unlike the State level, however, autonomies do not possess their own political guarantor institutions but only administrative oversight mechanisms, in part traceable to the national executive (such as municipal secretaries), or other forms of scrutiny over regional and local activity—both normative (the possibility for the central government to challenge regional laws before the Constitutional Court) and administrative or accounting (the supervisory role of the "Corte dei Conti" - Court of Auditors). Furthermore, the binary structure of autonomous institutions is not modeled on a confidence relationship between assembly and executive, as occurs at the national level, but rather on verticalized arrangements, whereby the head of the regional or municipal executive (the President of the regional government or the Mayor) is directly elected, with mechanisms designed to ensure a politically aligned assembly majority. This last aspect is of particular relevance.

The verticalization of the regional form of government in Italy has represented—and continues to represent—a historical trend, solidified by the 1999 constitutional reform (Constitutional Law No. 1 of 1999, introducing the direct election of the Regional President). In most regions, the assembly majority is directly or indirectly linked to the election of the President, thereby ensuring stable support for regional policies. Given the President's power to appoint members of the regional executive, this development has politically curtailed the role of regional councils, to the point of overexposing the position of the regional President—not only in internal governance but also, and above all, in relations with other components of the pluralistic State, particularly the central government.

Here lies the crucial point: the coexistence of multiple loci of sovereignty within the republican framework raises the problem of their organic and functional integration. Above all, it poses for constitutional scholars the question of identifying the *legal instruments* of such integration. In traditional systems where autonomist pluralism stems from a genuinely federalist matrix, the task of integration is entrusted to political dialogue between center and periphery—two politically characterized entities, often even through the existence of regional political parties (as in Spain or, differently, in Germany), called to confront each other within shared representative institutions. The most typical institutional expression of this dynamic in federal States is a bicameral parliament, where one chamber is either regionally elected (as in the US Senate) or composed through designation by regional executives (as in the German Bundesrat).

This was not provided for in Italy's 1948 Constitution, and despite numerous constitutional reform proposals aimed at establishing a "Chamber of the Regions" (most notably the 2016 "Renzi–Boschi" reform, approved by Parliament but rejected in the confirmatory referendum), such an institution still does not exist today. This absence is a direct consequence of the *artificial* nature of Italian regionalism, which lacks genuinely differentiated or alternative peripheral political forces.

How, then, has the integration of autonomous entities within the pluralistic State been pursued?

In what constitutional historians call the "First Republic" (from 1948 to the early 1990s), the vehicle of integration was essentially political and material rather than institutional. It operated not through specific bodies—such as a chamber of the regions—but through the political consonance between central and peripheral levels of government, mediated primarily by political parties. During that period, Italy lacked regionally based parties of significance; national parties fully controlled peripheral institutions, serving as the effective vehicles of mediation between autonomist pluralism and state unity. Legally, Article 127 of the Constitution, in its original formulation, entrusted Parliament and the State with the identification of the "national interest," guiding both central and peripheral institutions. With regard to regional functions, regional legislation remained confined within the competences established by the State, under forms of coordination always determined by central authorities. Autonomist pluralism thus found expression essentially in administrative differentiation—that is, through multiple centers of attribution of the same sovereignty: nothing more than plural administrative articulations of a single State sovereignty.

With the transition, in the 1990s, to a different phase of the Republic's history—marked by the dissolution of traditional mass parties (the Christian Democracy and the Communist Party) and the emergence of a major autonomist force, *Lega Nord* (Northern League)—this essential mediating element disappeared. The constitutional strengthening of regional roles culminated in the 2001 reform, which reversed the previous scheme by granting regional autonomies broad independence in determining their own political direction, exercised through a legislative function on par with that of the State. This development made it even more urgent to identify instruments for integrating the various centers of sovereignty—yet such instruments have never been systematically codified nor institutionally embedded.

The early 2000s reform did not provide for specific venues of political coordination between the center and periphery. The establishment of a permanent Conference between the State and regions—experimentally in place since 1983—was not constitutionalized but rather left to ordinary legislation (first through Law No. 400 of 1988, then through Legislative Decree No. 281 of 1997). This, unsurprisingly, entails significant limitations. Moreover, the judicial resolution of conflicts between powers before the Constitutional Court remains the only effectively conclusive means of addressing disputes between center and periphery, though incapable of preventing them. Particularly in the sphere of legislative powers, *direct action* before the Constitutional Court (Article 127) has become the primary instrument for resolving conflicts between State and regional legislation.

This predominantly judicial approach to the systemic integration of autonomist pluralism has not always yielded positive results; it has often instead deepened the ambiguity surrounding the boundaries of competence (Caruso 2021). More generally, the interpretive work of the Constitutional Court has reinforced the systemic tendency to regulate integration through adherence by the interacting institutions to a set of general principles—an implicit *code of conduct* developed through constitutional interpretation and practice. The following pages aim to bring some conceptual order to this complex model.

3 Why Is There No "Chamber of the Regions" in Italy?

As previously noted, Italy has never had a national parliamentary body conceived to represent regional interests. Even where the Constitution prescribes that the Senate shall be "elected on a regional basis" (*Article 57*, *Constitution*), this textual formulation has been interpreted merely as a binding indication for the delineation of electoral constituencies. Under the electoral law enacted in 2005 (the so-called *Calderoli Law*), that constitutional provision was even construed as precluding the introduction of a nationwide majority premium in the Senate—hence, the bonus was applied on a regional basis, with all the ensuing difficulties in achieving homogeneous majorities between the two chambers.

In truth, the establishment of a permanent institutional forum for territorial interests within the legislative process would provide a tangible expression of interdependence, ensuring an ineliminable dimension of dialogue and interorganic coordination (Gianfrancesco 2017). The dynamic process of integration among republican institutions, together with the frequent instances of overlap and blurring of competences and powers, would thereby find an ideal venue for realization and resolution.

Now, should one argue that in an interdependent system the task of synthesizing and reconciling competence-related conflicts ought to be entrusted to a *Chamber of the Autonomies*, designed to give voice to territorial interests, one would, in effect, be choosing to relocate the entire construction of pluralism onto the political plane. This, in itself, cannot be deemed a negative solution, yet it reasonably presupposes a genuine political *alterity* between the center and periphery—or, more precisely, the existence of a truly alternative and decentralized party system, emancipated from the logic of nationally channeled consensus. Absent such differentiation, the risk is that a "parliamentarized" interdependence—guaranteed and constructed within a politically homogeneous landscape centered exclusively at the national level—would suffocate the ascending and descending dialectic essential to an authentically pluralist system of territorial autonomies.

In Italy, this danger appears particularly concrete. A reconfigured parliamentary structure—one remodeled according to an asymmetric bicameralism and oriented toward granting greater weight to territorial instances—would not necessarily suffice, in itself, to strengthen the process of integration that the Constitution envisions as grounded in the ongoing exchange among the multiple institutions composing the Republic. More generally, such an institutional design does not even appear to be a necessary or sufficient condition for establishing a truly decentralized model. As Caravita (2006b) aptly observed, "No one disputes the typically federal character of countries such as Canada, Belgium, or Spain, where the Senate, for various reasons, does not represent the federated entities and in any case does not perform such a representational function; and, conversely, in Germany, Austria, Switzerland, Australia, or even the United States, the proper functioning of the federal system certainly does not depend solely on the existence of a chamber representing the federated entities."

In this perspective, the strengthening and constitutionalization of the *Conference system* (*sistema delle Conferenze*) might prove more coherent with the Italian model of constitutional integration. The idea of establishing, within the Presidency of the Council of Ministers, a permanent forum for dialogue between the central and regional governments dates back to the 1980s, primarily as a means of providing a consultative arena to assist in shaping the national political direction—embodied and coordinated by the head of the executive—while respecting autonomist claims. Substantively, legislative developments progressively reinterpreted the collegial nature of the national government in a plural sense: no longer merely *structural* (rooted in ministerial plurality and the functional equality of all ministers) but also *substantive*, necessarily open to the cooperation of regional autonomies.

This understanding also explains what most scholars identify as the chief structural defect of the Conference system—namely, that it fosters dialogue among *executives* while almost entirely excluding the *assembly* component, which nevertheless exists at the regional level. Yet this is, in truth, an expression of the very *artificiality* of Italian regionalism discussed above and, in a certain sense, appears coherent with it.

The integration of regional pluralism within the national unitary dimension occurs not through political-party mechanisms but rather through the necessary *plurality* of political direction, which must find synthesis in the Prime Minister. Such synthesis cannot disregard the regional component, which must be granted participation—however consultative—in the national formulation of the Republic's political aims. In Italy, what is needed is not, except in limited and exceptional cases, a *political integration* of the autonomies but rather a *constant integration of autonomous wills*—of the proportional sovereignties they express—which must find a place within the national political direction. Once this purpose is clarified, it becomes easier to understand why the answer lies not in establishing a "Chamber of the Autonomies" but in creating a *permanent system of consultation* among the ultimate holders of autonomous powers (Fabrizzi 2024).

4 The Principle of Loyal Cooperation and Legislative Integration

The pronounced jurisdictional character of Italy's integration mechanism between the center and periphery has meant that the Constitutional Court—through its case law in *direct actions*—has developed the essential principles meant to guide the model, especially in relation to boundary issues between state and regional legislative competence as structured by Article 117 of the Constitution in its 2001 amended form. As is well known, the new text assigns to the State the *exclusive* exercise of legislative power in certain subject matters specifically listed in paragraph 1; it then establishes *concurrent* competence—state framework legislation and regional implementing legislation—in a further list set out in paragraph 2; finally, it entrusts regional legislatures with *general residual* competence for all subject matters not included in the preceding two paragraphs.

Through its decisions, the Court has progressively shaped the exchange between State and regional legislation, effectively adhering to the view that it is ultimately the central level that concretely structures the room for maneuver of peripheral lawmaking, by leveraging the *expansive force* of certain subjects of exclusive state competence. This is the idea the Court conveys when it speaks of the *crosscutting nature* (*trasversalità*) of certain matters—such as environmental protection, the regulation of economic competition, or the determination of the *essential levels of benefits relating to civil and social rights*—which, when regulated by state statute, inevitably affect a plurality of competences and may impinge indiscriminately upon both state and regional spheres, thereby setting *minimum* standards that compress regional legislative power (see Judgments No. 282 of 2002, No. 407 of 2002, No. 14 of 2004; D'Atena 2002). In the well-known Judgment No. 303 of 2003, the Court wrote: "To limit the unifying activity of the State to those matters expressly attributed to it in exclusive legislative power or to the determination of principles in matters of concurrent competence, as the applicants maintain, would indeed surround regional legislative competences with ironclad guarantees, but it would also unduly devalue unitary instances which—even in constitutional arrangements strongly pervaded by institutional pluralism—justify, under certain conditions, a derogation from the normal distribution of competences [one need only consider, in this respect, the concurrent legislation (konkurrierende Gesetzgebung) in the German constitutional order, or the Supremacy Clause in the United States federal system]".

Starting from this premise, in addition to *transversality*, the Constitutional Court has identified further "flexibility devices" capable of drawing back toward the center (both) legislative regulation (and administrative management) in areas requiring unitary exercise. In this sense, the Court has read Article 118(1) in an extensive manner: that provision sets out a *subsidiary* allocation of administrative functions between the State and substate entities, favoring the attribution of functions to less peripheral levels of government whenever a more or less pronounced need for "unitary exercise" emerges. In the aforementioned 2003 judgment, the Court extends this principle to the division of legislative competences, clarifying that "the upward dynamic introduced by Article 118(1) cannot remain without consequences for the exercise of the legislative function; the principle of legality—which requires that even functions assumed by subsidiarity be organized and regulated by statute—logically excludes that individual Regions, through differentiated rules, may organize and regulate administrative functions attracted to the national level and affirms that only state law may attend to such a task." This implies that the State must be allowed to legislate even beyond the limits drawn by Article 117 whenever the need arises to regulate administrative activity that, for reasons of unitary exercise, must be attracted to the state level.

Transversality and the *upward (centralizing) tendency* inherent in the principle of subsidiarity are thus two clear manifestations of how both doctrine and the Constitutional Court immediately sought to contain the disintegrating tendencies of the new autonomist pluralism introduced by the 2001 reform. The division of legislative power between the center and periphery was promptly bound to a flexible regime that, in some cases, appears to derogate from the rigid—and seemingly simple—scheme of Article 117 by introducing mechanisms that retrieve the national unitary instance and, in a sense, leave to the State the decision whether to compress or allow the expansion of regional competence. The *ratione materiae* distribution is therefore conceived not so much by the field of impact as by the *purpose* pursued: where the latter implicates national interest, the expansion of central competence is permitted.

Reasoning in terms of purposes—that is, the political interpretation of legislative objectives—shifts the issue one level further. The scheme for dividing the legislative function is made flexible by evaluative mechanisms that necessarily relate to the political direction pursued by the State. Reasons of political direction justify the prevalence of state legislation and qualify its competence. It is therefore no accident that the Constitutional Court has increasingly emphasized in its case law that where state law must prevail for reasons of *transversality* or unitary exercise of functions, such prevalence must be exercised through procedures for *sharing* the State's political direction with that of the regions. The justices speak here of the *principle of loyal cooperation*: the legitimacy of the State's prevailing action—aimed at pursuing unitary administrative needs—must be assessed *in concreto* with regard to the forms of involvement of peripheral levels, the degree of such involvement, and the actors involved. Numerous decisions have struck down legislative provisions that, depending on the case, failed to require *agreement* (*intesa*) or the *opinion* of the State-Regions Conference—or that required only an opinion rather than a more structured *intesa* (see Judgments No. 222 of 2005, No. 383 of 2005, No. 76 of 2009, No. 31 of 2024). In essence, the Court has invalidated legislation that disregards the necessary confrontation among the plurality of political directions composing the nation or that fails to attempt their integration.

This has concerned not only the administrative plane but also the legislative one—for example, in cases of delegated legislation. A paradigmatic decision is No. 251 of 2016, which declared unconstitutional Law No. 124 of 2015, an ambitious attempt to reform the public administration. Because the reviewed legislation affected a plurality of subject matters—some within state and others within regional competence—the Court held that the adoption of the delegated decrees required prior *intesa* within the Conference system, and not mere consultation, as the statute provided. In that case, the justices appeared to identify in the forms of legislative delegation—combined with a prior *intesa* for the issuance of the delegated decrees—"the solution that best embodies cooperation" between the State and the regions (Severa 2020a). In the absence of a constitutionally enshrined instrument enabling regional representatives to influence the formation of "complex" normative acts directly, it is, in effect, the national legislature itself that may prefer legislative delegation as the means to secure the necessary dialogue with the regions, particularly when far-reaching, pervasive reforms are contemplated.

In practice, a model of regional participation in national legislation based on consultation also emerged during the Covid emergency. Decree-Law No. 6 of 23 February 2020—the first in a long series of measures introducing containment policies impinging even upon constitutionally protected liberties reserved to statutes—provided that such measures would be enacted through one or more Prime-Ministerial Decrees, adopted "upon the proposal of the Minister of Health, [after hearing the ministers competent by subject-matter], as well as the Presidents of the competent Regions, where the measures concern exclusively one or certain specific Regions, or the President of the Conference of Regional Presidents, where they concern the national territory" (Article 3). Substantively, the Decree-Law supplied a broad umbrella for the strengthened statutory reserve regarding restrictions on personal freedoms in response to the pandemic, while the ensuing Prime-Ministerial Decrees operationalized the progressively stricter measures—*agreed with the regions* through the legally mandated, albeit nonbinding, consultation.

In this procedural sequence, the concertation formula between the center and periphery relied on a very *weak* linkage. No binding *intesa* was required between the State and regions, nor even a mandatory opinion. What was required was the political sharing of choices—certainly in the form of joint responsibility but without insurmountable constraints imposed by territorial entities upon governmental decisions (Severa 2020b). Here, loyal cooperation is projected entirely onto the political plane, in such a way that any disagreement cannot freeze the issuance of governmental measures.

It can therefore be said that loyal cooperation is not so much a principle of *sources of law*—a method for resolving boundary disputes between state and regional legislation—as it is a genuine *criterion of institutional action*, indeed a *method of government* (Caruso 2021). It requires the State to justify instances of prevalence or to embed them within procedures that impose forms of concertation—even *weak* ones, yet still meaningful—aimed at compelling convergence among divergent political directions, where such divergence truly exists. The problem, in Italy, is that scrutiny of these guarantees—the review of the legitimacy of such encroachments—is not fundamentally political (it is not entrusted to a "Chamber of the Regions") but, as noted, jurisdictional: ultimate synthesis occurs only before the Constitutional Court. The forms and procedures that give concrete shape to loyal cooperation are thus not left to the autonomous determination of the institutions involved; they reach full completion only through the Court's judicial review. Or do they?

5 Substantive Forms of Litigation between the State and the Regions

This final observation compels us to address a concluding element of interest. It is evident that, from this perspective, the procedural rules governing proceedings before the Constitutional Court become a key factor shaping the dialogue between the center and periphery. The interpretation of these rules, as well as the practices that emerge through their use, plays an essential role in configuring the structure of Italian regionalism.

Access to the Court for disputes concerning the division of legislative competences between the State and the regions is essentially provided through a single channel. Under Article 127 of the Constitution, the State may bring a direct action before the Constitutional Court within 60 days when it believes that a regional statute exceeds the region's competence in relation to any constitutional parameter. Conversely, a region may challenge a state statute only when it considers that its own legislative competences have been infringed—thus, solely with reference to the division of powers under Article 117.

This asymmetry is significant: it effectively entrusts the State with a general function of *constitutional oversight* over regional legislation, as though the State were the guarantor of the legislation's conformity with the Constitution. From the regional perspective, by contrast, recourse to the Court remains a defensive guarantee—an instrument to protect against the compression of its legislative sphere, rather than an assertion of parity.

In practice, however, this differentiation has been mitigated through the Constitutional Court's expansive interpretation. In Judgment No. 198 of 2018, the Court clarified: "Regions may invoke parameters of constitutional legitimacy other than those governing the division of competences between the State and the Regions only under two conditions: when the alleged violation is potentially capable of reverberating upon constitutionally guaranteed regional powers, and when the applicant Regions have adequately reasoned the redundancy of the alleged constitutional infringement upon the division of competences, identifying the specific competence affected and providing sufficient argumentation to that effect."

This enlargement of the scope of regional actions—based on the concept of *redundancy*—has effectively strengthened the subjective protection of regional institutions against encroachments upon their constitutionally guaranteed powers. The result has been a genuine rebalancing of the positions of the central and regional levels, allowing for the easier correction of certain state tendencies toward restricting regional prerogatives. Moreover, such a review operates immediately upon the enactment of the state law, within 60 days, thus amounting to an *abstract review of legislation*.

Despite this attempt at balancing the two institutional entities, recent years have witnessed the consolidation of practices aimed at reducing judicial litigation between the State and the regions. This has resulted both from a marked restraint in state-initiated challenges and from the strengthening of *extrajudicial negotiation* between the two levels of government based on the idea that conflicts between the center and periphery may be resolved during a *prelitigation* phase. The trend first emerged in 2019, when the then-President of the Constitutional Court, Marta Cartabia, noted in her annual report the considerable number of principal constitutionality proceedings terminated with a declaration of *cessation of the matter in dispute* or dismissal due to the modification of the contested legislation following an agreement between the parties. In substance, judicial review of regional laws has been increasingly used by the State as a *pressure instrument*, inducing regions to amend their legislation, upon which the government, in turn, withdraws its challenge.

This tendency was further consolidated in October 2023, when the Presidency of the Council of Ministers issued a directive to its administrative departments ordering the *rationalization of litigation* between the State and the regions (Directive published in the *Official Gazette*, 25 October 2023). Under this act, ministerial departments are required not only to identify potential constitutional defects in regional laws but also to explore the margins for possible negotiation in view of prospective amendments by the regions concerned. The Department for Regional Affairs is then tasked with deciding whether to proceed with a constitutional challenge, taking into account, as a politically relevant factor, any formal *commitment to repeal* undertaken by the President of the affected region.

What deserves emphasis here is the emergence—also in normative terms (Politi 2023)—of a clear *material trend* aimed at transferring competence disputes between the center and periphery into an essentially *political dynamic*: a direct exchange between executives culminating in a reciprocal, quasi-contractual commitment to manage the division of competences and the exercise of powers. The principal action before the Constitutional Court thereby becomes an *ancillary instrument* to political negotiation—if not an outright *lever* to promote, or even compel, dialogue between divergent institutional instances.

There also exists, in fact, a second avenue for access to the Constitutional Court in matters of competence between the center and periphery: the *conflict of powers between entities* (*conflitto tra enti*), conceived as a remedy against acts—typically nonlegislative—of either the State or a region that may infringe the constitutionally protected prerogatives of the other. Yet such proceedings remain marginal today, accounting for only 0.5% of the Court's total decisions in 2024 (down from 3.3% in 2010). This statistical marginality reinforces the conclusion that the dialogue between central and regional institutions continues to revolve primarily around the *legislative function* and the perennial need to define its boundaries of competence.

6 Conclusions

What emerges from the foregoing analysis is, in essence, a *disharmony* between a constitutional model centered on the *jurisdictional transposition* of the conflict between center and periphery—particularly regarding the distribution of legislative competences and sources of law—and an evolving *interorganic dialogue* increasingly grounded in the regional level's willingness to participate in the formation of the national political direction. In other words, there has been a genuine *flight from litigation*, driven by the idea that the integration of autonomies is best achieved through *factual processes of policy-sharing* between the two levels of government.

This development entails, first and foremost, a reduction in the role of regional assemblies, which are increasingly overshadowed—within the regional form of government—by the *President of the Regional Executive*, directly elected and the undisputed protagonist of dialogue with the central government, all the more so because the *prejudicial* resolution of competence disputes between the State and the regions relies directly on the expression of will of the regional executive, now the privileged counterpart in this dialogue—an imbalance already denounced in scholarly analyses of the *Conference system*.

Moreover, *loyal cooperation* transcends its function as a mere interpretive mechanism for resolving conflicts of legislative competence and evolves into a *governing model*—a principle for organizing integration within the Italian plural constitutional system. The transfer of competences, alongside a reasserted tendency toward centralization, increasingly rests upon a continuous *dialectical exchange* between the two poles, between the two institutional levels. In short, Italy has consolidated a *flexible model of concurrence* among the plural levels of autonomy—one attentive to political negotiation rather than to a rigid recomposition of the distributional scheme.

If the boundaries among sources of law blur amid the uncertainties of power recomposition, interinstitutional dialogue, and the shifting balance between the center and periphery, what truly matters is to grasp the *informal dynamics* shaping the definition and interpretation of constitutional principles. At the core lies the original vocation for *pluralism* that characterizes the Italian model of regionalism—not the exaltation of regional identities but the *autonomist deconstruction* of central power. The goal is to *disintegrate sovereignty* in order to *reconstitute it* upon a framework of *permanent integration*, on a principle of continual recomposition of the center-periphery dynamic. The underlying idea is that the *national political direction* must be the product of integrating all the political directions of these plural components—*unity and autonomy* as the dual expressions of a *dynamic institutional system*, enriched by its diversity and strengthened by its capacity for *shared synthesis*.

References

Amato G (1972) La via italiana alle Regioni. In: Serrani D (ed) La via italiana alle Regioni. Milano

Antonacci N (1996) Centralismo e federalismo nell'Italia del XIX secolo. Una riflessione. Scienza & Politica. Per una storia delle dottrine, 15

Armao G (2024) Ubi insula, ibi jus speciale. Il principio di coesione insulare alla prova del regionalismo differenziato. Nuove Autonomie, 1

Bartole S (ed) (1999) Le Regioni alla ricerca della loro identità culturale storica. Giuffrè, Milano

Bertolissi M (2025) Autonomia differenziata. Materiali controcorrente. Giappichelli, Torino

Biondi F (2024) Il Consiglio Superiore della Magistratura. Organo dell'autonomia o luogo di potere? Il Mulino, Bologna

Bognetti G (1991) Federalismo. Digesto delle discipline pubblicistiche. UTET Università, Torino

Caravita B (1994) Territorio degli enti territoriali minori. In: Enciclopedia giuridica. Istituto dell'Enciclopedia Italiana, Roma

Caravita B (2006a) Stato federale. In: Cassese S (ed) Dizionario di Diritto pubblico. Giuffrè, Milano

Caravita B (2006b) Le sedi della concertazione. federalismi.it, 23

Carboni GG (2020) Il regionalismo identitario. Cedam, Torino

Carboni GG (2022) La stagione dell'insularità. federalismi.it, 22

Caruso C (2021) Cooperare per unire. I raccordi tra Stato e Regioni come metafora del regionalismo incompiuto. In: Cosulich M (ed) Il regionalismo italiano alla prova delle differenziazioni, Napoli

Ciuffoletti Z (1994) Federalismo e regionalismo. Da Cattaneo alla Lega, Bari-Roma

Cortese F, Woelk J (eds) (2023) Autonomie speciali e regionalismo italiano. Un bilancio. FrancoAngeli, Milano

D'Atena A (2002) Materie legislative e tipologia delle competenze. Forum di Quaderni costituzionali

D'Atena A (2022) Dove vanno le Regioni? Rivista AIC, 4

De Francesco A (1994) Ideologie e movimenti politici. In: Sabbatucci G, Vidotto V (eds) Storia d'Italia I: Le premesse dell'Unità, Bari-Roma

De Vergottini G (1990) Stato federale. In: Enciclopedia del diritto, vol XLIII, Milano

Demuro G (2006) Commento all'articolo 114 della Costituzione. In: Bifulco R, Celotto A, Olivetti M (eds) Commentario alla Costituzione. UTET, Torino

Demuro G, Mola F, Ruggiu I (eds) (2013) Identità e autonomia in Sardegna e Scozia. Maggioli Editore, Rimini

Fabbri D (2018) L'insospettabile omogeneità degli italiani. Limes, 5

Fabrizzi F (2024) Il Parlamento nella "Democrazia decidente". Il ruolo delle Camere oggi. Il Mulino, Bologna

Gianfrancesco E (2017) Parlamento e Regioni: una storia ancora in attesa di un lieto fine. Il Filangeri

Giarrizzo G (1975) Sicilia politica 1943-1945. La genesi dello Statuto regionale. Consulta Regionale Siciliana (1944–1945) Saggi introduttivi, Palermo

Grazzini L, Lattarulo P, Macchi M, Petretto A (2020) Asymmetric decentralization: some insights for the Italian case. Politica Economica 1

La Pergola A (1969) Residui contrattualistici e struttura federale nell'ordinamento degli Stati Uniti. Giuffrè, Torino

Luciani M (1997) Unità nazionale e principio autonomistico alle origini della Costituzione. In: Franceschini C, Guerrieri S, Monina G (eds) Le idee costituzionali della Resistenza. Atti del convegno di studi, Roma

Luciani M (2020) Il Consiglio superiore della magistratura nel sistema costituzionale. Osservatorio AIC 1

Mangiameli S (2002) La riforma del regionalismo italiano. Giappichelli, Torino

Morrone A (2019) Suprematismo giudiziario. Su sconfinamenti e legittimazione politica della Corte costituzionale. Quaderni costituzionali

Morrone A (2021) Suprematismo giudiziario II. Sul pangiuridicismo costituzionale e sul lato politico della Costituzione. federalismi.it 12

Morrone A (2025) Lo Stato regionale dopo la sent. n. 192 del 2024. Giustizia Insieme

Palermo F, Nicolini M (2013) Il bicameralismo. Pluralismo e limiti della rappresentanza in prospettiva comparata. Napoli

Palermo F, Woelk J (2008) Diritto costituzionale comparato dei gruppi e delle minoranze. Cedam, Padova

Pizzorusso A (1993) Minoranze e maggioranze. Einaudi, Torino

Poggeschi G (2010) I diritti linguistici. Un'analisi comparata. Carocci Editore, Roma

Politi F (2023) La direttiva sulla "razionalizzazione" della procedura governativa di esame delle leggi regionali. Prime considerazioni. Rivista AIC 11

Reposo A (1993) Stato federale. In: Enciclopedia giuridica, vol XXX, Roma

Rolla G (2022) Il pensiero federale e lo Stato unitario autonomistico. Note introduttive. DPCE Online, numero speciale

Ronchetti L (2018) Unità e indivisibilità della Repubblica: la sovranità popolare e l'interdipendenza nel nome della Costituzione. costituzionalismo.it, 1

Ruggeri A (1981) Il Consiglio dei ministri nella Costituzione italiana. Giuffrè, Milano

Ruggeri A (2022) Il senso della specialità e la vicenda dell'autonomia siciliana (dalle esperienze del passato una lezione per l'avvenire). Nuove Autonomie, 1

Ruggeri A (2024) Fino a che punto possono tenersi distinte le vicende della forma di governo da quelle della forma di Stato? federalismi.it 24

Severa F (2020a) Sui raccordi tra livelli di governo in tempo di emergenza. Biolaw Journal—Rivista di Biodiritto 1

Severa F (2020b) Centro e periferia: la partecipazione alla funzione legislativa come elemento di unificazione. Rivista Gruppo di Pisa, 2

Stanco G (2012) Le prospettive del policentrismo in Italia. Radici e costruzioni identitarie tra storiografia e dottrina giuridica. A&C Revista de Direito Administrativo e Constitucional 49

Sturzo L (1962) La Regione (1921). In: Sturzo L (ed) Regioni e Mezzogiorno. Roma

Tucciarelli C (2025) Nuove forme della specialità? Le isole come questione di diritto costituzionale. federalismi.it 20

Dynamics of the Belgian Asymmetric Federalism and Reform Perspectives

Paola Piciacchia

Abstract This chapter examines the dynamics of Belgium's asymmetric federalism, focusing on the interplay between its complex institutional structures and the evolving political landscape. It analyzes how historical compromises have led to a unique federal arrangement characterized by varying degrees of autonomy among regions and communities. Numerous factors and centrifugal forces have shaped the development of Belgium's federalization process, leading to the requirement for further reforms.

1 Introduction: The Federalization Process of Belgium

The Belgian model of the federal State deserves particular reflection. This experience, unique in the world, provides, in fact, a valid example of how the dynamics of federalism have followed multilevel trajectories, responding to a continuous process of federalization (Friedrich 1968) in which unity and diversity as well as integration and differentiation have attempted to recompose themselves in an "ultra" complex system of governance strongly conditioned by historical roots and political, cultural, and social factors. In particular, linguistic tensions have been one of the preponderant factors in the path pursued by the Belgian State, proof of which is that language and culture were among the first competences of the central State transferred to the communities since 1970.

Belgian federalism was built not on the basis of a preestablished theoretical model but through an essentially evolutionary logic and empirical adaptation to the needs of a complex reality. It is, in fact, part of the national collective conscience of a country historically marked by linguistic, social, and economic conflicts, which have strongly influenced its institutional transformation, and whose nature is such that it has imposed itself as a "variable geometry" system (Uyttendaele 1997).

P. Piciacchia (✉)
Sapienza University of Rome, Rome, Italy
e-mail: paola.piciacchia@uniroma1.it

F. Savastano et al. (eds.), *Between Asymmetry and Secession*,
https://doi.org/10.1007/978-3-032-29603-0_17

The complexity of the federal system reflects, in this sense, the "subtles" (Born 2013) of the historical, political, and socioeconomic balances underlying its development and is the result of an evolutionary path that, since the 1970s, has led Belgium, initially a unitary State and governed by the Constitution of 1831, to a process of federalization culminating in the 1993 reform of the Constitution, which, for the first time in Article 1, explicitly consecrated it as a federal State composed of communities—French, Flemish, and German (Article 2 of the Constitution)—and regions—Walloon, Flemish, and Brussels (alongside which Article 4 of the Constitution also recognizes four linguistic regions: the French speaking, the Dutch speaking, the German speaking, and the bilingual Brussels-Capital).[1]

Therefore, although it was only in 1993 that the federal structure was consecrated at the constitutional level, federalism in Belgium was not born suddenly. It was the culmination of a long transformation of the State, carried out over decades—especially starting from the 1970s—to meet the needs of a society divided by numerous fractures. We are referring here to the six waves of reforms—those of the years 1970–1973, 1980–1983, 1988–1990, 1992–1993, 2001, and 2012–2014—which were the result of subtle understandings and negotiations between the political forces and the components of the Belgian State.

At first, the existence of two important communities, each striving for autonomy—Flanders (Dutch speaking), which claimed cultural autonomy, and Wallonia (French speaking), which claimed economic autonomy—had already brought forth, starting from the 1960s, a series of requests that resulted in the constitutional reforms of 1970, 1980, and 1988. The 1970 revision recognized the existence of the two great cultural communities (the Dutch Community and the French Community) and the three regions (Flemish, Walloon, and Brussels), while the 1980 revision created the German-speaking Community and attributed to the communities and regions (except Brussels) a legislative competence exercised through their own representative assemblies and their own governments. Then, in 1988, the Brussels-Capital Region was also endowed with its own competences, own Parliament, and own government, and the competences of the communities and regions were extended.

After the constitutional reform of 1993, a further step was taken in 2001 with the fifth reform of the State—also the result of a delicate compromise between the opposing needs of the French-speaking and Flemish parties—which was achieved not through a constitutional reform but through the approval of two special laws of 13 July, which attributed new competences to the regions and communities, taking them away from the State.

The persistence of conflicts between the Flemish and Francophones over linguistic and institutional issues—due in particular to the Flemish request for a split in the Brussels-Hal-Vilvorde constituency and the controversy over the appointment of burgomasters in the six Flemish municipalities with special status on the outskirts

---

[1] Linguistic regions are territorial circumscriptions that serve to delimit the scope of particular legislation, the linguistic legislation that regulates the use of languages in different fields by virtue of the Constitution.

of Brussels—led to the agreement of 11 October 2011 on the sixth State reform following the very long government crisis that began in 2010 and lasted 588 days. The sixth reform of the State was accomplished between 2012 and 2014 through the approval of numerous special and ordinary laws on the division of competences and through a constitutional revision that restructured bicameralism, which significantly weakened the Senate.

Further demands on the Flemish side and, this time, also on the French-speaking side soon led to the idea of a seventh state reform, whose purpose is to improve not only the constitutional architecture—specifically in the Brussels-Capital Region—but also the rationalization of competences to avoid unnecessary overlaps between levels of government, for example in the healthcare sector, as the resulting difficulty in managing the Covid-19 pandemic had sadly taught.

In the government agreement that gave birth to the De Croo Government on 1 October 2020—following the longest crisis, which lasted 662 days without a majority government—the preparation of the seventh state reform was among the objectives of the new executive, which envisaged "une nouvelle structure de l'État à partir de 2024 avec une répartition plus homogène et plus effective des compétences dans le respect des princes de subsidiarité et de solidarité interpersonnelle," with the aim of strengthening both the autonomy of the federated entities and the power of the federal State.[2]

In 2024, the changes had not yet been adopted, but the need to reform federalism continued to be the basis of the Government Agreement of 31 January 2025 of the Arizona[3] coalition, formed after the legislative elections of 9 June 2024 and which led to the birth, on 3 February 2025, of the current De Wever Government. In the Government Agreement, explicit reference was made to reforms—without constitutional change—in the sphere of federalism, with the aim of increasing the responsibility of each entity, strengthening mutual solidarity between the federal government and the federated entities, and promoting interfederal cooperation.

For decades now, Belgian federalism has been characterized by pressures that make it a system not yet fully accomplished, requiring continuous adjustments. But in order to understand the need for such adjustments, it appears appropriate to analyze their nature and main characteristics.

[2] Government Agreement, 30 September 2020, p. 79.

[3] Formed by the New Flemish Alliance (N-VA), the center-right and right-wing party with the most votes in the final elections (24 seats), whose leader is the current Prime Minister Bart de Wever; the Reformist Movement (MR), a liberal and conservative-inspired party representing Wallonia and the French-speaking Community, which came second in the 2024 elections with 20 seats; the Christian Democrats (Christen-Democratisch en Vlaams (CD&V), a center-right party of Catholic-Christian inspiration that obtained 12 seats in the election; Avanti (Vooruit), a social democratic political party active in Flanders and the Brussels-Capital Region which won 13 seats in the 2024 federal elections; and, finally, Les Engagés, a centrist and social-liberal French-speaking party that obtained 5 seats in 2024.

2 The Characteristics of Belgian Federalism

An analysis of the competences and organizational features of the federated entities confirms the complexity of the Belgian federal system, whose true scope must be assessed in light of what each of them represents within the system itself.

The first feature to be highlighted is the structure, characterized by profoundly different constituent parts: the communities, "composed with a purely personalistic criterion, by well-defined and differentiated ethnic groups", and the regions, "formed on an essentially territorial basis" (Biscaretti di Ruffia 1994).

Although in Belgium, according to part of the doctrine (c. Mertes 1999), cannot fully speak of constitutive autonomy by not having, the federated entities, the power to adopt its own constitutions[4] but we can only speak of a limited power of self-organization[5] granted in 1993 with the fourth reform of the State to only six of the federated entities and then extended in 2012–2014 with the sixth reform of the State also to the Brussels Region- Capital and the German-speaking Community (Peiffer 2017), the autonomy of the federated entities in the federalization process began to materialize with the affirmation of an extended regulatory power, i.e. through the attribution of the power to legislate on the matters transferred to them and also with the recognition of a certain fiscal autonomy. As early as 1980, the French and Flemish Communities were able to legislate on cultural matters, while the Walloon and Flemish Regions had been given powers in various fundamental sectors, such as the environment. Furthermore, as will be seen later, autonomy came to be recognized, pursuant to Article 167, paragraph 3c, of the Constitution, allowing the communities and the regions to sign international treaties and conventions on matters within their respective competence.

The characteristics of Belgian federalism have long been described in the Belgian constitutional doctrine (Delpérée 1996, 1998, 2000), which defined it, firstly, as a federalism of "superposition" due to the presence, on the same territory, of two categories of federated entities competing for a dual claim to autonomy: the communities (French, Flemish, and German speaking) and the regions (Walloon, Flemish, and Bruxelles), which do not coincide territorially with each other, generating great complexity in the distribution of competences. Secondly, it is a federalism of "dissociation," as it derives from the decomposition of a unitary State (Verdussen 2011). Thirdly, it is a federalism of "confrontation," marked by several distinct and "dualist" parts due to the presence of two large linguistic communities (French and Flemish) facing each other—one in the North and the other in the South and partly in the Center. This framework makes Belgian federalism "asymmetric," both from a territorial point of view (an asymmetry of origin, given the territorial noncoincidence between the communities and the regions) and from a

[4] Despite Flanders' claims to have its own constitution.

[5] Which takes the form of power to issue *ordonnances spéciales* and *décrets speciaux*, adopted by a two-thirds majority of votes cast, provided that a majority of the members of the competent parliaments are present (Articles 118, § 2, c. 1, and 3 and 123, § 2, c. 1 and 3).

point of view of competences (an asymmetry in their attribution) (Verdussen 2015).

The Belgian constitutional framework meets the requirements of the federal State since it ensures the principle of "equality" between the entities composing it; "equivalence between the rules"—i.e., the equal normative value of acts issued by their respective representative bodies (laws, decrees, and ordinances); the "exclusivity of attributions"—noninterference by others in regulating matters entrusted to each entity using its own financial means, an exclusivity that the Constitutional Court supervises[6]; and the "identity of responsibilities," meaning that the same immunities granted to national parliamentarians apply to those of the federated entities, just as the particular criminal proceedings envisaged for ministers apply to members of the governments of the communities and regions (Delpérée-Verdussen 1997).

At the same time, the principle of "participation" is guaranteed, which takes shape through both cooperation between the various federated entities, consistent with federal loyalty (Article 143 of the Constitution), and the collaboration of the communities and regions in the exercise of powers organized at the federal level, more precisely in constitutional provisions aimed at guaranteeing the role of linguistic groups within federal institutions (as in the case of the Council of Ministers, which requires equal composition between the Dutch and French or in the articulation of Parliament into linguistic and political groups).

For their part, federated entities are held (Born 2013, pp. 206–207) to respect, on the one hand, the principle of federal loyalty enshrined in the aforementioned Article 143, which also requires, in fact, upholding the principle of proportionality, which prohibits an authority from exercising its competences in a way that makes it difficult for another to perform its own. On the other hand, pursuant to Article 6, paragraph 1, VI, c. 3, of the special law of 8 August 1980, they are required to respect the principle of the free movement of people, goods, services, and capital; commercial and industrial freedom; as well as the general regulatory framework of the economic union and the monetary unit within the country.

Having said this, it is through the analysis of competences and organizational features that we fully understand the complexity of the Belgian federal system, whose true soul must be evaluated in light of what each federated entity represents within the system itself.

[6] In Belgium, there are no competing competences; however, the Constitutional Court sometimes admits a field of hierarchical competences between the federal authority and the federated collectivities in cases where the federal authority lays down minimal rules applicable throughout the territory of the State, while the federated authorities may, within the scope of their competences, supplement them.

3 The Division of Competences between Functional Asymmetries and Distributive and Devolutive Transfers

In Belgium, eight federated entities hold legislative (or quasi-legislative) power: the Flemish Community and the Flemish Region, which share the same bodies (Flemish Parliament and government) and whose territorial base corresponds to the Dutch linguistic region; the French Community, which has the French linguistic region as its territorial base; the German-speaking Community, which coincides with the German-speaking region; the Walloon Region, whose territory corresponds to the French and German linguistic regions; and the Brussels-Capital Region, which has the bilingual Brussels-Capital Region as its territory.

Alongside them, mention should also be made of the Brussels-Capital Joint Community Commission (CoCoM)—whose bodies consist of an assembly composed of all the members of the Brussels regional Parliament and a college that includes the members of the Brussels government, and which exercises legislative power similar to the regional one—and of the French Community Commission (CoCoF) of Brussels-Capital, whose legislature is formed by all the French-speaking members of the regional Parliament and whose executive is composed of all the French-speaking members of the regional government and which has no legislative power but can only issue administrative decrees.

Both, although they are not public communities but moral public persons, are endowed with powers similar to those of communities and regions and, therefore, also legislative power.

The Belgian federal State is characterized by a division of areas of competence, which intersect extensively but do not overlap entirely.

The distribution of powers among the components of the federal State is based on the principles of attribution and exclusive competence.[7] It means the federated bodies exercise only the competences specifically conferred on them by the Constitution and institutional reform laws and that each federated body is exclusively competent in matters attributed to it within the limits of its territory or area of competence. Federal law does not prevail over the law of federated entities (except in tax matters[8]), and the federal authority does not exercise protection over them, with the exception of Brussels, where a form of protection is conferred on the King (i.e., the executive) and the House of Representatives in certain areas established by

[7] That principle is attenuated by Article 10 of the special law of 8 August 1980, which provides for the possibility of activating a kind of implicit powers of the communities and regions and which authorizes marginal invasions into federal competence when the matter lends itself to differential treatment.

[8] Tax matters are concurrent competences governed by Article 170 of the Constitution, which recognizes only the federal legislator as having the power to adopt fiscal measures, without taking into account the competences of the communities and regions, and recognizes the prevalence of tax law over tax decrees and ordinances. This prevalence has been confirmed several times by the Constitutional Court. (See CC, arrêts No. 119/2007, 19 September 2007, B.4.1.; No. 68/2008, 17 April 2008, B.6.4; and No 5/2019, 23 January 2019, B.8.). See Verdussen et al. 2019.

the Law of 12 January 1989 relating to Brussels institutions, in order to preserve the international role and capital function of the Kingdom.

However, numerous factors make the distribution of competences in Belgium particularly complex. Although, in fact, the Constitution laid down in the 1993's reform at Article 35 the general criterion for the attribution of specific powers to the federal State and residual powers to federated entities, this constitutional provision was never implemented in the absence of approval of the special law which under paragraph 2° of Article35 of the Constitution should have fixed the terms and conditions for the division of residual powers between the community and the regions and also determined the date of the entry into force of the same Article 35. The latter, in any case, could not have preceded the inclusion in Title III of the Constitution of an article determining the list of exclusive matters of the federal State, as specified by the transitional provision of the same Article 35 Constitution. As a consequence, the criterion applied continued to be the relative criterion for the attribution of competences to federated entities and the residual criterion for state competences.

Precisely, the failure of the entry into force of Article 35 explains one of the complexities of the division of powers between the various components of the Belgian federal State which was built up over time in a pragmatic manner, resulting the transfers in favor of the federated entities from negotiations and agreements "plus soucieux de reposer sur des équilibres politiques que de constructing un système cohérent et fonctionnel" (Faniel et al. 2021, p. 129).

It is worth underlining how special laws play a fundamental role in the distribution of competences. The special laws are provided for by various constitutional provisions (e.g. Articles. 4, 35, 39, 115, 118 of the Constitution), placed below the Constitution and subordinate to it and although they differ from the ordinary ones in terms of approval methods—require in both Chambers the majority of votes in each linguistic group, the presence of the majority of the members of each Group and the favorable vote of 2/3 of the voters (Article 4 uc) -, they remain formally laws enacted under the bicameral procedure (for which the House of Representatives and Senate have the same powers under Article 77 of the Constitution), and therefore are not superordinate to ordinary ones. However, a supremacy of the *loi spéciale* over ordinary law is recognized (Lejeune 1996) when it contains provisions that can be construed as an extension and completion of the Constitution regarding the definition of the division of competences between the State, the communities, and the regions. In any case, due to the majority requirements for their adoption, they are imposed on all ordinary legislators and public authorities. In this sense, they are considered "materially constitutional," serving as reference rules for the Constitutional Court in reviewing the conformity of laws and decrees (the primary sources of federated entities) with rules governing the distribution of competences (Lejeune 2021, pp. 100–101).

In this case, the federal, regional, and community legislators are required to respect the *loi spéciale*, and any law, decree, or ordinance contrary to it may be annulled by the Constitutional Court. Since there is, in principle, no subordination between the different categories of federal, community, or regional legislative acts, in this case, we speak of a hierarchy on a material level, by virtue of which "the content of a legislative provision is considered pre-eminent and becomes therefore limit for another legislative provision" (F. Leurquin-De Visscher, 1996). Controversial in doctrine is the nature of these special laws, which require a particular majority for approval. They have often led scholars to draw an analogy with italian constitutional laws: from which, however, they remain decidedly distinct given the profound diversity of the procedure for revising the Constitution (Leurquin and DeVisscher 1996).

In light of the above, the division of competences between the central State, the communities, and the regions is fundamentally established according to the "attribution criterion": the competences that belong to the federated entities are enumerated by the Constitution (albeit limited), by the special laws of 8 August 1980 and 12 January 1989, and by the ordinary law of 31 December 1983, while competences not expressly attributed to the federated entities are the prerogative of the central State.

In truth, no constitutional provision explicitly lays down the criteria for the attribution of residual competences to the central State. However, legal doctrine believes (Lejeune 2021, p. 504) that it can be deduced from the original general competence of the unitary State, which was later transformed into a federal State.

Generally speaking, the central state is responsible for legislating on international relations; defense; police power; maintenance of public order; civil security; civil protection; civil, commercial, and corporate law; the Constitutional Court; the organization of the judiciary; federal administrative justice; the Council of State; criminal law and criminal procedure; money and financial policy; and labor and social security law.

Alongside the competences that may be regarded as residual in the sense outlined above, the Constitution or special laws expressly confer certain competences upon the central State. Within the Constitution, however, a distinction must be drawn between, on the one hand, those provisions that refer to legislation and were adopted after the first federal reform of 1970, which attributed legislative powers to the federated entities and in relation to which the federal authority retains exclusive competence; and, on the other hand, those constitutional provisions that also refer to legislation but predate 1970. In the latter case, the mere reservation of a specific matter to legislation does not automatically establish a division of competences between the federal authority and the federated entities. Rather, the competences of the respective legislators are determined by the general rules governing the allocation of powers laid down in the Constitution and special laws, albeit implicitly (Lejeune 2021). It is then necessary to evaluate on a case-by-case basis. In fact, in some cases it is accepted that matters also provided for by provisions prior to 1970 are "due to the nature of the things" to be attributed to the federal legislator: thus for example for the matter relating to Belgian nationality, that relating to political rights, the administrative police, to the competences of the courts, etc. Similarly, the attribution of powers to the federal authority may also result from various reservations formulated by the special law concerning the attribution of powers to the communities and regions.

However, the framework governing the allocation of competences has become even more complex due to the introduction of an additional criterion alongside the attribution criterion. Indeed, the allocation of competences was initially carried out through a "distributive" transfer (from the central State to the federated entities). It was subsequently complicated by a "devolutionary" transfer (i.e. a transfer between the federated entities themselves), which was institutionalized at the constitutional level through Articles 137, 138, and 139. This latter mechanism disrupted the symmetry of the distributive transfer by creating an overlapping allocation of competences: institutions established to exercise community competences were also granted the exercise of regional competences, and, conversely, regional institutions were entrusted with competences originally belonging to the community level.

Horizontal transfers of competences between federated entities represent the truly distinctive feature of Belgian federalism. They stem from the overlapping territorial areas within which federated entities exercise their powers and allow an entity to acquire new competences without requiring a constitutional amendment, but merely through an agreement between the entities concerned. These dynamics have further complicated the institutional landscape and the distribution of competences among federated entities (Faniel et al. 2021, p. 140).

As regards community competences, these are defined by Articles 127–129 of the Constitution and essentially include: cultural matters (listed in detail in Article 4 of the Special Law of 8 August 1980, such as language, fine arts, radio, television, sport, tourism, etc.); education; personalized matters (i.e. those concerning the relationships that may arise between individuals and services with a social purpose, and therefore relating to healthcare and assistance to persons); the use of languages in administrative matters in relation to the aforementioned subjects; cooperation between Communities; international cooperation, including the conclusion of treaties; and scientific research.

In addition to this general breakdown, under Article 130, §1, of the Constitution, the German-speaking Community has jurisdiction in the same matters as other communities, except in the field of language use, where its competence is limited to teaching in establishments set up, subsidized, or recognized by the public authorities.

On the other hand, as regards the powers of the regions, they are those laid down in Articles 6, 6a, and 7 of the special law of 8 August 1980, which essentially concern the economy in the broad sense, territorial development, economic policy, agricultural policy, energy policy, public works and transport, the environment, nature conservation, rural renewal, and housing.

The regions, like the communities, are also competent in scientific research relating to the subjects within their jurisdiction. It is worth remembering that in all the matters listed above, the regions have exclusive competence, except in certain cases, such as economic competences, where they are required to respect principles established by the federal authority, which moreover remains competent for monetary policy, financial and savings policy, pricing and revenue policy, etc. Finally, the regions are also competent in the organization and exercise of ordinary supervision of the provinces and municipalities, the general financing of local authorities, and intermunicipal cooperation.

Communities and regions also have "accessory" competences that allow them to fully exercise their main competences. This means that the Communities and Regions' full range of powers entails the obligation to interpret the provisions conferring material competences upon them broadly, so as to encompass, as inherent powers, all aspects that may reasonably be connected to those competences, even where they might initially appear to fall within the residual competence of the federal authority or of another territorially competent entity.

Thus, they can adopt measures relating to the infrastructure necessary to exercise their skills and can create decentralized services, plants, and businesses and/or take equity participations; in the same way, community and regional governments can carry out expropriations for reasons of public utility. The implied powers of the communities and regions may be assimilated to the abovementioned accessory powers, which allow them to regulate competences belonging to the central State when this is necessary for the exercise of community and regional competences (even if the Court of Arbitration has in the past specified that the impact on the federal matter must be marginal and that the matter must be able to lend itself to differentiated treatment) (Uyttendaele 1997).

Finally, the Constitution, in Article 167(1), assigns an important role to the Communities and Regions in the field of international relations: they may conclude international treaties in matters within their competence subject with the activation of mechanisms for information and concertation with the central State, which retains a power of control by being able to come to a halt even in the procedure for concluding the treaty.

Still with regard to international relations, it is worth specifying how the Constitution, in Article 169, Ic, has provided—with the aim of guaranteeing compliance with international or supranational obligations—a temporary power to replace the federal State with community and regional bodies in the event that they fail to take the necessary measures to comply with these international obligations.

Finally, it is worth remembering that the legislator (Article 92bis et ter, L. spéc., 8 August 1980) also provided for the possibility for the federated entities to conclude "cooperation agreements" among themselves in relation to the creation and joint management of services and institutions, the joint exercise of their own competences, or the development of common initiatives.

4 Organizational Features of Communities and Regions and Equivalence of Rules

Directly proportional to the cultural and territorial complexity of the Belgian federal structure is the complexity of the organization of community and regional institutions, which are strongly influenced by the asymmetry of origin and the asymmetry in the attribution of competences envisaged by the Constitution.

Since 1993, the Communities and Regions have enjoyed constitutive autonomy, as outlined above, allowing them to regulate certain aspects concerning the election, organization, and functioning of their institutions (Article 118 of the Constitution). They are also provided with Councils directly elected by the people (Article 116 of the Constitution) and possess their own legislative and executive bodies.

Given that, by virtue of this asymmetry, on the Dutch side the Council of the Flemish Community also exercises the competences of the Council of the Flemish Region—a faculty recognized by Article 137 of the Constitution for the French Community as well, which, however, has not used it to date—it should be noted that there are currently five elective Assemblies (Article 115 of the Constitution): the Flemish Council, the Council of the French Community, the Council of the German-speaking Community, the Walloon Regional Council, and the Council of the Brussels-Capital Region. The 1993 reform extended the direct election of the members of the Councils to all the communities and regions, which was previously limited only to the Councils of the German-speaking Community and the Brussels-Capital Region. The Councils are elected for 5 years without the possibility of dissolution, and their parliamentarians—whose causes of ineligibility and incompatibility are established by special law of 8 August 1980, integrating Article 119 of the Constitution, which places incompatibility with the office of minister or national parliamentarian—enjoy the same prerogatives as members of the national Parliament.

The composition varies from Council to Council. The functions of the Councils are the same as those of the national Parliament, and they exercise full competence in the areas assigned to them. In carrying out their legislative function, they issue (see paragraph 1) acts having the force of law, called "decrees" (except for the Brussels-Capital Region, which issues "ordinances," which "formally" do not possess the force of law but can equally repeal, supplement, and modify laws within the region itself). As for the procedure, the rules are, in principle, similar to those of the national Parliament.

As for the governments, they are elected by majority vote of the relevant Councils, to which they are accountable and by which they may be overthrown through a constructive vote of no confidence adopted by an absolute majority—applicable both to the entire government and (unusually) to individual ministers. Governments participate, together with the Councils, in carrying out the legislative function through the rights of initiative and sanction and perform the executive function through the promulgation of decrees and ordinances, the issuance of necessary regulations and decrees of execution, and the day-to-day management and direction of administrative services.

From the above, it follows that the primary or secondary acts issued by these entities are placed on the same level as the acts, primary or secondary, issued by the central State. Accordingly, the decrees adopted by the Flemish, Walloon, and Brussels-Capital Regions, as well as by the Flemish, French, and German-speaking Communities, through which the regional or community legislature regulates matters falling within its competence, have the same legal force as ordinary federal legislation. Consequently, they may repeal, amend, or replace existing federal laws (Articles 127–130 and 134 of the Constitution; Article 19(2) of the Special Law of 8 August 1980).[9]

5 The Brussels Peculiarity

Finally, the territory of Brussels-Capital, which is characterized by a "rare complexity," occupies a particular place (Nihoul 1996, p. 230) because of its bilingual character. As a consequence, it is, in fact, possible to distinguish four types of local institutions on the same territory: one of a regional nature—the Brussels Capital Region—and the other three of a community nature—the French Community commission, the Flemish Community commission, and the common community commission, which overlap and are characterized by different bodies, each with a legal personality but composed of the same representatives, who thus find themselves exercising distinct skills depending on the body in which they sit. As for the Brussels-Capital Region, it is worth underlining how, unlike the other regions, its autonomy is subject to particular restrictions, which are resolved—but only in the case of preserving the international role and functions of Brussels-Capital—through the activation of mechanisms aimed at suspending the acts of the Brussels Region or creating powers to replace the central State.

6 The Mechanisms for the Prevention and Resolution of Conflicts between the Components of the Federal State

The complex relationship between the central State and the federated entities inevitably gives rise to mechanisms aimed at regulating and/or preventing conflicts and encouraging collaboration between the federal State and its components through mutual information, participation in the development of rules, concertation, and common agreement. Therefore, in order for respect for federal loyalty, referred to in Article 143, Ic, to be guaranteed, the constituent and special legislators have decided to attribute to particular institutions—such as the Constitutional Court, the Council of State, the Senate, and the Committee of Concertation—the task of preventing and/or regulating conflicts.

The Constitutional Court, pursuant to Article 142 of the Constitution, adjudicates conflicts of competence between the federal State and the federated entities and reviews the constitutionality of laws, decrees, and ordinances primarily related to

[9] Similarly, regulations or *arrêtés* of general application, therefore legislation that the community or regional government can issue for the execution of the aforementioned decrees, have the same value as the *arrêté* royal, while the *arrêté ministériel*—which the community or regional government can authorize to be issued by one of its members—is placed on the same level as the federal *arrêté ministériel*.

compliance with Articles 10, 11, and 24 of the Constitution, as specified in Article 142, 2°, of the Civil Code and any other provision determined by special law (Article 142, 3°, of the Civil Code).

In addition to its other functions, the Senate also performs an advisory role in the resolution of conflicts: in fact, pursuant to Article 143, it rules—after an attempt at concertation between the interested parties which however rarely reaches a solution, with a reasoned opinion to the Concertation Committee—on conflicts of interest that may arise between the Assemblies of the federal State, the communities, and the regions (but CoCom and CoCoF must also be included, the latter introduced by the special law) due to a draft law, proposal or amendment. However, this opinion does not bind the authorities responsible for deciding on the conflict of interest.

Then there is the "Concertation Committee," which is a purely political body, provided for by Article 31 of the Law of 9 August 1980. This body is made up of 12 members in equal proportion (six of French expression and six of Dutch expression)—half of whom represent the federal government (the Prime Minister and five ministers), while the other half represent the federated entities (the Minister President of the Walloon Government, the Minister President of the Government of the French Community, the Minister President of the Government of the Brussels Capital Region, one minister of the Brussels Government from a group other than that of the Minister President, and finally two ministers of the Flemish Government). Its main purpose is to promote concertation and cooperation between the State, the communities, and the regions, and to this end, it forms special committees called "interministerial conferences," which serve as the privileged place for meeting and dialogue. It also intervenes (pursuant to Article 56 RCR) in the event that the Council of State considers that the provisions of a draft law exceed the competence of the State: in this case, the draft is sent to the Committee for the expression of a reasoned opinion, and the examination of the draft law is suspended.

The Council of State, on the other hand, also plays an important role in the prevention and resolution of conflicts: through its "Legislation Section," it is competent to intervene in the development of all regulations, both at the federal level and at the community and regional levels, by issuing mandatory opinions verifying compliance with the division of competences. In addition, through its "Administration Section," it has the power to annul any law, decree, or ordinance lacking "external" or "internal" legality.

7 Conclusion: Toward the Seventh Reform of Federalism

A synthesis of the characteristics of Belgian federalism highlights, first of all, its evolutionary nature, deriving from progressive adjustments resulting from compromises between opposing political forces divided between autonomist and secessionist forces.

Second, it highlights the extent to which centrifugal and dissociative dynamics contributed to the construction of that asymmetry—although intentional and not accidental (Delpérée 2022) and rooted in the desire to overcome disputes and conflicts—which makes the Belgian model still unfinished to this day.

Fruit of a bipolarity (Verdussen 2011) between French-speaking and Flemish entities—the architects of all negotiations that have led to the reforms till date—the model is increasingly at the center of criticism for the excessive stratification of competences, aggravated by devolutive attribution between entities, for its excessive complexity, especially regarding Brussels-Capital, and for the difficulty of coordination on fundamental public policies such as climate and the environment.

This asymmetry results in transfers of competences realized in some way *à la carte* and capable of giving birth to subtle legal mechanisms, which, through derogatory or exceptional rules, allow the law to be adapted to regional specificities (Behrendt and Vandenbosch 2017). Add to this the extensive use of implicit competences by federated entities, in particular by the Flemish Community. This practice was at the origin of incremental changes in the distribution of competences, especially since it was validated on several occasions by the Constitutional Court; this allows us to speak today about a "reform of the latent State" (Nève De Mévergnies and Romainville 2025a).

The seventh reform of the State (Delvaux 2022) today imposes itself as urgent, even though the first months of the De Wever Government—which on 17 June 2025 resolved the suppression of the Senate, an institution that remains essential in a federal State and whose elimination in Belgium risks weakening the fragile balance of the federal system (Nève De Mévergnies and Romainville 2025b)—do not argue in favor of a rational approach to reforms.

References

Behrendt C, Vandenbosch S (2017) Le réaménagement de la répartition des compétences dans le fédéralisme asymétrique belge. Civitas Europa 38(1):241–254

Biscaretti di Ruffia P (1994) Costituzioni straniere contemporanee. Le Costituzioni di sette Stati di recente ristrutturazione. Giuffré, Milano

Born CH (2013) Quelques réflexions sur le système de répartition des compétences en matière d'environnement et d'urbanisme en droit belge. Revue juridique de l'environnement, 5, special issue

Delpérée F - Verdussen M (1997) La responsabilité penale des ministres fédéraux, communautaire et régionaux. Bruylant, Bruxelles

Delpérée F (1998) Le système constitutionnel de la Bélgique. Larcier, Bruxelles

Delpérée F (2000) Le droit constitutionnele de la Bélgique. Bruylant, Bruxelles

Delpérée F (1996) L'ordinamento federale belga, (con scritti di Delpérée, Guiglia, Leurquin-De Visscher, Orru, Verdussen). Giappichelli, Torino

Delpérée F (2022) Éloge de la complexité, AA.VV., Dossier: Belgique 2030. Revue générale, 1

Delvaux G (2022) La Belgique à quatre, vers une simplification du fédéralisme belge ? Analyse des perspectives institutionnelles à l'aube d'une Septième réforme de l'État. Faculté de droit et de criminologie, Université catholique de Louvain, thèse

Faniel J, Istasse C, Lefebve V, Sägesser C (2021) La Belgique, un État fédéral singulier. Courrier hebdomadaire du CRISP 15(2500):7–266

Friedrich CJ (1968) Trends of federalism in theory and practice. Frederick A. Praeger

Lejeune MA (1996) Introduction aux droit et aux institution de la Belgique fédérale. La Charte, Bruxelles
Lejeune Y (2021) Droit costitutionnel belge. Larcier
Leurquin F, De Visscher (1996) Fonti del diritto. L'ordinamento federale belga, (con scritti di Delpérée, Guiglia, Leurquin-De Visscher, Orru, Verdussen), Giappichelli, Torino
Mertes C (1999) L'autonomie constitutive des Communautés et des Régions. Corrieur Hebdomadaire, 1650-1651,1-58
Nève De Mévergnies M, Romainville C (2025a) L'exercice Asymétrique De Compétences Fédérales En Belgique : Une Modification De La Répartition Des Compétences Qui Ne Dit Pas Son Nom? Blog Juspoliticum
Nève De Mévergnies M, Romainville C (2025b) Requiem pour le Sénat de Belgique : ces voix que l'on se prive d'entendre
Nihoul P (1996) Le autorità brussellesi. In: Delpérée F (ed) L'ordinamento federale belga. (con scritti di Delpérée, Guiglia, Leurquin- De Visscher, Orru, Verdussen), Giappichelli, Torino
Peiffer Q (2017) L'autonomie constitutive des Communautés des entités fédérées. Corrieur Hebdomadaire, 2350-2351,1-64
Uyttendaele M (1997) Institutions fondamentales de la Bélgique. Bruylant, Bruxelles
Verdussen M (2011) La Belgique. Un fédéralisme bipolaire mû par une dynamique de dissociation. In: Seymour M, Laforest G (eds) Le fédéralisme multinational: Un modèle viable? Peter Lang, Bruxelles, pp 211–225
Verdussen M (2015) Asymétrie. In: Uyttendaele M, Verdussen M (eds) Dictionnaire de la Sixième Réforme de l'État. Larcier, Bruxelles, pp 69–72
Verdussen M, Romainville C, Bonbled N (eds) (2019) Les grands arrêts sur le partage des compétences dans l'État federal. Éditions Larcier, Bruxelles

The Case of Flanders: Flemish Nationalism as a Driver of the Federalising Process—and a Belgian Split? Insights from the Post-2024 Elections

Andrea Fiorentino

Abstract This chapter examines Flemish nationalism as both the primary driver of Belgium's federalisation and a potential catalyst for state dissolution. It begins by tracing the historical and constitutional roots of the ethno-linguistic divide between Flemish and Francophone communities, showing how this divide has shaped Belgium's asymmetric and increasingly disaggregated federal model. It then turns to the 2024 elections, highlighting the electoral gains of Flemish pro-independence parties—*Nieuw-Vlaamse Alliantie* (N-VA) and *Vlaams Belang* (VB)—and assessing their capacity to challenge the unity of the Belgian state. Despite mounting centrifugal pressures, the chapter argues that the Belgian split pursued by Flemish secessionists remains unlikely, owing to a combination of constitutional constraints, political strategies and conventions, limited popular support, controversies over Brussels, and external deterrents.

1 Introduction

It has rightly been observed that the Belgian case can be regarded as "a pilot case in the study of secessionism, at least in the context of consolidated democracies", particularly from the perspective of comparative public law (Mastromarino 2014, pp. 911–912).

Indeed, since at least the early 2000s, there has been a radicalisation of Flemish nationalist parties advocating for the independence of Flanders, accompanied by their consistent success in both federal and regional elections. The results of the triple elections held on 9 June 2024—European, federal, and regional/community—confirm and reinforce this trend (Di Domenico 2024). Despite a highly fragmented party landscape, the vote rewarded, above all, the right-wing nationalists of the *Nieuw-Vlaamse Alliantie* (N-VA), which became the leading federal party for the third consecutive time, securing 16.7% of the vote (following 17.6% in 2010,

A. Fiorentino (✉)
UnitelmaSapienza University of Rome, Rome, Italy
e-mail: andrea.fiorentino@unitelmasapienza.it

F. Savastano et al. (eds.), *Between Asymmetry and Secession*,
https://doi.org/10.1007/978-3-032-29603-0_18

20.26% in 2014, and 16.03% in 2019). N-VA also maintained its position as the most voted party in the Flemish Parliament, with 23.88%, continuing a dominance that has remained uninterrupted since 2004. The party's statute may raise concern among those who care about the future of the Belgian state: at the heart of its institutional agenda is the goal of establishing an independent and republican Flanders, as the result—consistent with the political course set out by its leadership—of a gradual "evaporation" of the Belgian state, progressively hollowed out through the devolution of its powers to the federated entities and the European Union.

However, even more alarming was the anticipated success of a Flemish far-right party with an even more vehemently secessionist stance: *Vlaams Belang* (VB). The party emerged as the largest in the European elections, narrowly surpassing N-VA (14.50% vs. 13.96%), though it fell short—contrary to polling predictions—at both the federal and regional elections, where it came in a close second (with 13.77% and 22.66%, respectively). VB's performance in the regional vote brought the party close to its peak in 2004, when its predecessor, Vlaams Blok, secured 24% of the vote before being dissolved shortly thereafter, following a conviction for violating anti-racism and anti-xenophobia legislation. In its platform, VB advocates for a "Czechoslovak-style" solution: should it obtain a parliamentary majority, either alone or in coalition, the Flemish Parliament would first declare sovereignty and subsequently initiate negotiations with Wallonia to arrange an orderly separation of Belgium to be completed within 5 years. Should no agreement be reached within that period, the party proposes that Flanders proceed with a unilateral declaration of independence.

In light of recent developments, it is worth reflecting on the institutional implications of Flemish nationalism for Belgian statehood from a historical-constitutional perspective. Such an inquiry must begin by revisiting the historical centrality of the ethno-linguistic divide between the Flemish and French communities within the Belgian legal system (Colella 2016)—an enduring reality that has long driven and continues to drive a semi-permanent process of institutional and constitutional transformation. Understanding how this multinational dimension underpins Belgium's unique federal architecture is essential to assessing the possible trajectories of a federalising process that has been unfolding for over half a century, with particular attention to the prospect of a dissolution of state unity as a result of the secession of Flanders.

2 Flemish Ethno-Linguistic Identity as the Driving Force of the Belgian Federalising Process

The features of the Belgian federal state—and, consequently, any meaningful reflection on its future—cannot be properly understood without first considering the highly complex political and social foundations that have shaped its evolution.

The population of the Kingdom of Belgium is approximately 11.76 million (2024), divided into two principal national communities united by a centuries-long political history yet separated by a linguistic boundary that has remained largely unchanged since the twelfth century. In the North, the Dutch-speaking population of Flanders numbers approximately 6.82 million, accounting for about 58% of Belgium's total population. In the South, the Walloon Region is home to roughly 3.69 million Francophones (31.4%), alongside a distinct German-speaking minority of approximately 79,500 individuals (0.7%) residing near the eastern border with Germany. Brussels, with just under 1.25 million inhabitants (10.6% of the national population), is officially bilingual but features a clear Francophone majority—Flemish speakers constitute less than 15% of the city's residents. This imbalance largely results from a long-standing process of so-called Frenchification, driven by Brussels' attractiveness as the administrative and financial capital of the Belgian state and, more recently, the *de facto* capital of the European Union (EU).

Originally, the two groups coexisted peacefully, resisting the French occupation (1792–1815) and later fighting for independence from the United Kingdom of the Netherlands (1830), subsequently adopting a constitution (1831—still in force today) that was progressive for its time. This fundamental law established a parliamentary monarchy within a unitary state and recognised the linguistic freedom of every Belgian.

From the outset, however, Walloon minority's hegemony became apparent. This dominance was based on the economic wealth of a region rich in mining and textile industries and on the political pre-eminence of social, bureaucratic, and military elites educated in French—the language of the upper classes at that time and the vehicle of Enlightenment ideals. The *de facto* imposition of French by the ruling social classes as the sole official language in acts of public authority and judicial proceedings —despite the Dutch dialects spoken by the predominantly rural and deeply Catholic population of Flanders—was intended to promote the formation of a homogeneous Belgian nation. However, this objective ultimately proved unsuccessful. Indeed, Frenchification efforts promptly sparked the emergence of a Flemish nationalist movement: a political movement grounded in an ethno-cultural conception of nationhood that initially demanded the recognition and protection of its language and culture and subsequently sought the creation and development of a social, political, and institutional space for the free and autonomous expression of a distinct Flemish identity.

It is primarily within the Flemish Community that the "active" element of the ethno-linguistic conflict lies—a confrontation that persistently animates Belgium's political and institutional life. Nationalist and identity-based claims, both autonomist and secessionist, are predominantly rooted in the Flemish population. Conversely, the national consciousness of the Francophone Community is considerably weaker, being anchored instead in a civic and voluntarist conception of nationhood rooted in the French revolutionary tradition, as well as in the socio-economic emancipation demands of Wallonia. Walloon independence movements, divided between separatists and advocates of union with France, are largely "reactive" to Flemish nationalism and occupy an irrelevant position within the political landscape.

Flemish nationalism, leveraging the strength of its majority social base through the process of democratisation—which commenced with the introduction of plural male suffrage in 1892, advanced with the establishment of universal male suffrage in 1919, and culminated in universal suffrage in 1948—gradually eroded the political monopoly previously held by the Francophone elites. The introduction of the linguistic issue into the country's political agenda subsequently led, as early as 1898, to the recognition of Dutch as the second national language through the so-called law of equality (Dutch: *Gelijkheidswet*) (Jahn 2015, pp. 82–83) and, in 1921, to the establishment of the territoriality principle governing the use of each language. The latter followed the failure, due to Francophone resistance, of an attempt to impose bilingualism throughout the entire state.

A qualitative leap towards parity between the two dominant ethno-linguistic groups occurred only after the Second World War, as a result of profound social and economic transformations (Carrozza 2011, p. 994), amounting to a genuine Copernican revolution. The decline of Wallonia, marked by an irreversible industrial crisis, alongside the economic rise of Flanders, driven by the expansion of the service sector and the emergence of the Port of Antwerp as Central Europe's gateway to global trade, further strengthened Flemish national consciousness.

The sharp linguistic divide, deepened by the reversal of the previous socioeconomic cleavage, soon transformed the party system. Between 1968 and 1978—against the backdrop of escalating ethno-linguistic tensions, with student protests centred at the University of Leuven—the main Belgian political parties (Christian Democrats, Liberals, and Socialists) split along linguistic lines. The establishment of a federal party system composed of parties accountable solely to their respective linguistic communities was consolidated through the emergence and rise of regional parties without counterparts. These included, above all, Flemish parties, notably the *Volksunie*, founded in 1954, which was a predecessor of the N-VA and a driving force behind federalisation, but also Walloon parties such as the *Rassemblement wallon*. This development was reinforced in the early 1980s by the creation of two distinct green parties, which were linguistically divided from their inception (De Winter et al. 2006, p. 938).

Belgian society progressively split into two distinct compartments, resulting in the formation of two completely separate and non-communicating public spheres, each nurtured and shaped by media (press, radio, and television) in its own language (Billiet et al. 2006, p. 914). This division has also acquired a political-ideological dimension, with left-wing parties predominating in Wallonia (primarily the *Parti Socialiste* (PS)) and centre to centre-right parties dominant in Flanders—namely, *Christen-Democratisch en Vlaams* (CD&V), *Open Vlaamse Liberalen en Democraten* (Open VLD), and the previously mentioned N-VA and VB (Popelier 2019, pp. 21–22). Complicating coexistence is the fact that the latter are generally reluctant to support, through Flanders' higher fiscal contributions, the generous welfare standards in the declining Wallonia, fostering mutual distrust that further erodes solidarity within the federal state (Carrozza 2011, p. 1003). It is worth noting that the divide and political polarisation between the Flemish and Walloon party systems is entrenched by the demarcation of electoral districts along linguistic lines.

The politicisation of the ethno-linguistic divide, propelled by Flemish nationalism, laid the groundwork for the deconstruction of the former unitary state through the launch of a dissociative (Delpérée 2000, pp. 388–393) or disaggregative (Mastromarino 2010) federalising process—still ongoing—which has unfolded through six state reforms (1970, 1980, 1988–1989, 1993, 2001, and 2011–2014) (Popelier and Lemmens 2015, pp. 15–33), each representing a chapter in what has been described as a "never-ending roman-fleuve" (Rimanque 1994, p. 446). Preceded by two decades of regionalisation, the Belgian federal state, formally established by the 1993 constitutional revision, embodies a *sui generis* model of federalism Its distinctive features lie in the multiple institutional expressions of the division of Belgian society into two ethno-linguistic groups whose relationship is asymmetric due to the greater demographic and economic strength of the Flemish component compared with its Walloon counterpart.

This is not the place for an in-depth discussion of the characteristics of the Belgian federal state. Nevertheless, it is worth briefly mentioning the complex institutional mechanisms introduced in an attempt to accommodate diversity, particularly the Flemish demands for recognition of their self-perception as a "community of destiny". These mechanisms are the result of an ongoing search, through the negotiation of institutional and constitutional reforms, for a balance aimed at ensuring coexistence between the two linguistic groups—an inherently unstable balance, marked by a "persistent tension, oriented towards guaranteeing economic, social, and political continuity, but also towards overcoming the recurrence of social conflicts" (Mastromarino 2014, p. 912).

First, it is essential to highlight the primary element of asymmetry within the Belgian federal system, established by the constitutional law of 24 December 1970. Namely, the provision—following the 1963 division of the territory into four linguistic regions (Flemish, French, bilingual, and German-speaking)—of two distinct but largely overlapping federated entities: three Communities (Flemish, French, and German-speaking) and three Regions (Flanders, Wallonia, and Brussels-Capital), the latter established with about a decade's delay. While the regions, designed to exercise the so-called *territorialisable* competences, responded to Walloon demands for territorial governance and decentralisation in socio-economic matters as a means of counteracting the industrial decline of Wallonia, the communities emerged from Flemish nationalist claims for a form of political unity grounded in identity, culture, and language (Mabille 1997, pp. 350–351). Accordingly, the latter were assigned key competences related to language, education, and culture, along with other so-called *personalisable* competences concerning the individual's interaction with public administration services (healthcare, social assistance, etc.).

The Flemish, true to their prevailing ethno-cultural conception of nationhood, aimed at further developing their community to the extent that it ultimately absorbed the Flanders Region: this was achieved through the fusion of the parliamentary assemblies and executive bodies of the Flemish Community and Region, utilising the provision offered by Art. 137 of the Constitution. Conversely, the French Community did not avail itself of this possibility but instead, under Art. 139 of the Constitution, transferred many competences to the Walloon Region, as well as to the French Community Commission of Brussels.

This complexity is further compounded by additional arrangements aimed at ensuring, through institutional asymmetry, substantive parity of political power between the Flemish and French groups in federal decision-making within a multinational federal state characterised by a bipolar or dyadic structure (Popelier 2019, p. 40). Above all, consider the legal requirement of linguistic parity in the composition of the Council of Ministers (Art. 99 Constitution), which guarantees the over-representation of the French-speaking minority in the federal government but makes its formation significantly complex. After federal elections, parties must engage in typically protracted negotiations to strike a delicate balance between two poles: the need for political homogeneity within coalitions and their democratic legitimacy, understood as the ability to reflect the preferences of the majority of voters within each linguistic community (Popelier 2019, pp. 21–22). The necessity to achieve a compromise-based balance that is not only political but also linguistic has conferred distinctive features on the Belgian parliamentary system, making it a prototype of "consociational" or "consensus" democracy (Lijphart 1999).

Additional constitutional safeguards based on linguistic affiliation are also provided. In both chambers of Parliament—where the two communities are represented proportionally to their respective demographic weight—members must be registered with either the Flemish or the French linguistic group (Art. 53 Constitution). This division is particularly relevant, for instance, in the adoption of so-called special majority laws concerning institutional reforms (such as those defining the competences of the communities or transferring powers to the regions), which require not only a two-thirds majority of all votes cast but also a majority within each linguistic group (Art. 4 Constitution). Each linguistic group is further entitled to trigger the "alarm bell" (Art. 54 Constitution): if at least three-quarters of the members of a linguistic group consider that a bill (excluding money bills and special majority law bills) would seriously harm intercommunity relations, they may submit a motion to that effect; in such cases, the legislative process is suspended, and the motion is referred to the Council of Ministers, which must, within 30 days, issue a reasoned opinion and invite the chamber to decide on both the opinion and the potentially amended bill. This mechanism has been invoked only twice (in 1985 and 2010), effectively functioning as a *de facto* veto, primarily through its deterrent effect (Dupont 2015, pp. 389–390). The legislative process for a bill may also be suspended, and a consultation phase initiated—if any federal or federated parliamentary assembly considers that the bill would seriously harm its interests or disrupt the federal balance (Art. 143 Constitution).

With regard to the division of powers, the linguistic, socio-economic, and ideological-political divide, marked by mutual distrust and limited willingness or capacity to cooperate, has resulted in a predominantly dual federalism based on the exclusive distribution of legislative competences between the federal state and the federated entities. However, the Sixth State Reform (2011–2014) resulted in a strengthening of mechanisms for intergovernmental cooperation (Angelini and Benvenuti 2016; Rossi 2016; El Berhoumi et al. 2016), which were further enhanced during the COVID-19 pandemic emergency (Delledonne 2022).

3 Flemish Nationalism After the 2024 Elections: Belgium on the Brink of Dissolution?

The strong representation and veto powers of the two linguistic communities, which imbue the federal decision-making process with "confederal features aimed at consensus seeking", characterise the Belgian federal state as dyadic or bipolar. In a dyadic system, it is the interaction and conflict between the two main linguistic groups, rather than the formal structuring of the state into multiple federated entities, that constitutes the central element shaping the overall federal architecture (Popelier and Lemmens 2015, pp. 76–77, 88). Its dynamics can therefore be described not so much in the classical terms of an institutional relationship between centre and periphery, but rather as a distinctive form of confrontation between the peripheries. This situation engenders instability and fragility within the federal arrangement, particularly where, as in the case of Belgium, one national group predominates demographically, politically, and economically (Watts 2007, p. 234; Popelier and Lemmens 2015, p. 77). This entails a risk of paralysis in the federal decision-making process, which has frequently materialised in Belgium. One only need consider the often protracted negotiations following federal elections to form coalitions capable of supporting a linguistically balanced government that is also as politically homogeneous as possible. The record remains the 541 days of negotiations required after the 2010 elections to form a governing majority. More recently, following the 2024 elections, 236 days of negotiations were required to establish a government.

The federal system, designed to accommodate diversity through institutional mechanisms aimed at reconciling the demands of unity with those of autonomy, ultimately tends to fuel centrifugal and destructive tendencies (Reuchamps and Caluwaerts 2014; Popelier and Lemmens 2015, p. 86). Difficulties in the federal decision-making process arising from the institutionalised conflict between the ethno-linguistic communities often lead to further devolution of powers to substate entities, progressively eroding the authority of the central government and laying the groundwork for its gradual hollowing out. The political crisis following the 2010 elections provides a clear illustration: it was resolved only after an agreement was reached on the Sixth State Reform, which devolved significant competences to the regions and communities.

Given the increasingly prominent role of Flemish nationalism in recent years—driven by N-VA and VB, which together secured 46.54% of the vote at the community level and 30.47% at the federal level in 2024 (resulting in 44 of the 88 seats in the Flemish linguistic group)—it is worth considering the future of the Belgian federal state. In light of the extensive veto powers held by linguistic groups in both government formation and decision-making, what future lies ahead for Belgian statehood? At a theoretical level, at least three scenarios seem possible, beyond the tangled *status quo*. The first, involving a radical break, is the unilateral secession of Flanders from the rest of Belgium, which could either claim to be the legal successor of the federation or constitute a new state. The second is that continued devolution to overcome federal paralysis could lead to a transformation of the federal state into a looser "confederation"—or even to its negotiated partition. The third, in line with the trajectory of the Sixth State Reform and further developed during the pandemic emergency, envisions the survival of the federation through a balanced combination of greater autonomy for the federated entities and enhanced cohesion and intergovernmental cooperation. The central question for the present analysis is therefore how likely it is that Flemish nationalism ultimately lead to a split of the Belgium state.

For now, Flemish independence—whether through unilateral secession or as the culmination of a negotiated dismantling of the federation between the two national communities—appears to be an unlikely scenario. To date, no parliamentary initiative has ever been formally launched in that direction.

Firstly, regarding the pre-legal ground of the legitimacy of the Belgian system, it should not be underestimated that, despite undeniable tensions, a Belgian national consciousness is rooted among public opinion. This consciousness prevails over separatist demands and is expressed and renewed during national holidays (such as Belgian National Day, celebrated on 21 July) and at pro-Belgium political events across the country. It reflects a civic sense of belonging that does not conflict with substate identities or the broader European supranational identity, but rather coexists with and complements them. In 2014, a survey by the Institute for Social and Political Opinion Research (ISPO) revealed that only 6.4% of Flemings supported separatism—a percentage that rose during periods of institutional crisis, such as in 2007 and 2010, but never exceeded 12%. Instead, a large majority of Flemings consistently expressed support for the transfer of additional powers to Flanders (Swyngedouw et al. 2015). When compared with the electoral success of the separatist parties, these data give rise to what has been called "the Flemish paradox": an apparently paradoxical phenomenon explained by the willingness of segments of the non-separatist electorate to vote for separatist parties because of their positions on issues other than the institutional question, such as the N-VA's socio-economic policies or VB's anti-immigration stance. Such voting behaviour has become increasingly acceptable as a result of the success of the strategy pursued by Flemish nationalists over recent decades to hollow out and delegitimise the Belgian state (Huysseune 2016; Maddens 2017).

Secondly, on the political front, the only party currently advocating for a unilateral secession in the short term is the radical right-wing and xenophobic *Vlaams Belang*. As previously noted, this party envisages that, once it has either obtained a majority on its own or entered a coalition with the N-VA, the Flemish Parliament would declare sovereingty and subsequently open negotiations with Wallonia for an orderly separation of Belgium to be concluded within a maximum of 5 years. Should no agreement be reached by then, Flanders would secede unilaterally. Although support for the party is growing, its rise to institutional power currently appears very unlikely. Since the late 1980s, VB has been subject to a strict *conventio ad excludendum*—the so-called *cordon sanitaire*—which entails the refusal of major political parties to form any electoral alliance with it and their commitment to exclude it from coalition negotiations at all government levels. This political veto is justified either by VB's incompatibility with democratic values or by other parties' fear of being associated with it and punished by the electorate (Biard 2021). While N-VA officially pursues Flemish independence under its statute and, unlike other mainstream parties, has never formally adhered to the *cordon sanitaire*, it has so far resisted any temptation to ally with VB to achieve its objectives. Still, the issue remains controversial within the nationalist-conservative party. During the campaign for the elections of 9 June 2024, polling data suggesting that N-VA and VB might secure a majority of seats in the Flemish Parliament led some N-VA figures, notably including the then Flemish Minister-President Jan Jambon, to leave open the possibility of a post-election coalition with VB. However, the party leader, Bart De Wever, closed off any debate on the matter in May 2024, publicly stating for the first time that he felt no affinity with VB and firmly ruled out forming a government with that party. Ultimately, the *cordon sanitaire* held once again. Following the elections, on 30 September 2024, a new government took office at the regional level, led by N-VA's Matthias Diependaele, supported by a three-party coalition of N-VA, CD&V, and the Flemish socialist party *Vooruit*. At the federal level, after protracted negotiations from which VB was excluded, the De Wever government was sworn in on 3 February. This government is the first led by an N-VA figure and is supported by a coalition that includes, on the Flemish side, N-VA, CD&V, and *Vooruit* and, on the Francophone side, the liberal *Mouvement réformateur* (MR) and the centrist *Les Engagés* (LE). That said, it does not seem impossible that the *cordon sanitaire* may eventually be broken. Signs in this direction are indeed already visible at the local level, where, following the municipal elections of 13 October 2024, some independent lists have formed coalition agreements with VB—for example, in Ranst (Antwerp province) and Izegem (East Flanders).

It is noteworthy that the coalition agreements underpinning the federal and regional governments led by the N-VA contain no explicit reference to the party's long-term plans for Flemish independence. This reflects a strategy that envisages an intermediate stage consisting of a "confederation" of states united under the same monarchy, but sharing only economic and monetary union and common foreign and defence policies. The term "confederation" is used here in a non-technical sense: the proposed arrangement would not constitute an international union of independent sovereign states establishing a joint, parity-based organisation to exercise certain functions, but rather a new constitutional framework aimed at minimising federal competences in favour of quasi-state entities (Dumont and Van Drooghenbroeck 2007, p. 2). The Flemish government agreement for the 2024–2029 term (*Vlaams Regeerakkoord 2024–2029*), while calling for a more autonomous international role for Flanders, a stronger voice in EU decision-making, and "full autonomy […] in defining its democracy and organising its administration", also emphasises the importance of "efficient and constructive collaboration with other levels of government", including the federal level, in order to achieve "more coherent and effective decisions in the interest of the Flemish". Similarly, the 2025–2029 federal coalition agreement vaguely calls for a state reform aimed at "a more homogeneous and effective distribution of competences", while specifying that it should be pursued "without the support of extremist voices". At the same time, it commits the federal government to major economic and social reforms through strengthened cooperation and coordination across levels of government, within a framework that enhances both individual responsibility and mutual solidarity. This cooperative emphasis is undoubtedly favoured by the current political landscape, in which the Flemish and Francophone coalition parties simultaneously govern their respective federated entities.

The N-VA nationalists remain far from being able to unilaterally meet the high constitutional thresholds required to advance their gradualist plans for independence—a path firmly opposed not only by Walloon parties but also by mainstream Flemish ones. In this context, just as it did following its entry into the Michel government in 2014, the N-VA has shown a readiness to moderate and temporarily shelve its maximalist positions in order to seize the opportunity to govern and translate electoral support into policy influence. As the last federal coalition agreement illustrates, the party has even demonstrated openness to the idea—at odds with its former slogan "Belgium does not work"—that effective federal policies can be pursued within a framework of cooperative federalism. This is exactly where the ultimate stabiliser of Belgium's inherently unstable federal equilibrium comes into play: a political culture that resists extra-constitutional ruptures, such as a parliamentary declaration of sovereignty or a secession referendum, and remains deeply committed instead to the art of compromise. This inclination towards negotiation is necessitated by the dyadic architecture of the federal system, which serves as a mechanism for the mediated reconciliation of the political-identity divide within society. As scholars have long observed, "the vehemence of the secessionist discourse is, if not neutralised, at least strongly mitigated precisely by the institutionalised political formula of the country, characterised by procedures that ensure broad participation of linguistic communities in public decision-making, as well as by the continual recourse to compromise" (Mastromarino 2014, p. 914).

Finally, it is important to remember an issue that cannot be resolved even through negotiation, making the separation of Flanders unlikely: the fate of Brussels. Brussels is currently a bilingual territory in which multiple jurisdictions overlap in a particularly complex manner—the federal government, the Brussels regional government, the Flemish and French communities, and the Joint Community Commission. The Brussels-Capital Region, which has a strong French-speaking majority but is entirely surrounded by Flemish territory, holds strategic importance as the capital of both Belgium and Flanders, the seat of the principal institutions of the European Union and the headquarters of the North Atlantic Treaty Organization (NATO), and a major economic and financial centre. Therefore, Brussels is the subject of opposing and potentially irreconcilable claims. On the one hand, Flemish nationalists oppose the increasing Frenchification of the Flemish municipalities surrounding the Brussels Region, with a view to strengthening Flanders's claim to Brussels as its capital in the event of independence. On the other hand, many Walloons aspire to retain Brussels as their capital in the event of Flemish secession by establishing territorial continuity between Wallonia and the Brussels Region through the transfer of Flemish municipalities with significant French-speaking minorities (the "facility municipalities", which already benefit from special linguistic policies compared to those of the communities). Given the difficulty of assigning Brussels to either side and the impossibility of dividing it along ethno-linguistic lines, one proposed solution is to make Brussels a separate third state, potentially granting it the status of a capital district within either a Belgian confederation or the European Union, modelled on Washington, D.C., or the Australian Capital Territory. The Brussels factor is also a powerful deterrent to secessionist ambitions due to its European significance. A secessionist Flemish state would find itself outside the EU and would need to apply for membership, requiring approval from all member states—a process far from certain. A pre-emptive rejection, also motivated by concerns about the solvency of Belgium's high public debt, could be used to discourage secessionist moves. Moreover, in the event of an escalation of ethno-national conflict, the threat of the EU institutions relocating from Brussels could serve as an additional stabilising factor (Jahn 2015, p. 87).

4 Conclusion: The Belgian Split as a Fiction

On 13 December 2006, Belgian viewers were stunned as the French-speaking public broadcaster RTBF interrupted regular programming with a breaking news report: Flanders had just declared independence. The king had fled, politicians were in shock, and crowds had gathered at Brussels Airport. For several long minutes, many believed it was real. Only later did a caption reveal the truth: it was a fiction.

Bye Bye Belgium, the faux news special aired by the French-speaking public broadcaster, was a provocative media experiment. Its goal was to spark reflection on the future of the Belgian state amid mounting tensions between Flemings and Francophones. But the reaction was swift and indignant. Politicians denounced it as dangerous manipulation, a "media coup" that undermined public trust. Yet, with remarkable foresight, the broadcast anticipated what would follow: two of the most acute political crises in Belgium's history. Between 2007 and 2011, the country teetered on the edge of paralysis, at one point going 541 days without a federal government.

Yet, almost 30 years later, the imagined secession remains just that—a fiction. As this chapter has shown, Flemish nationalism has undoubtedly shaped Belgium's federal architecture. Through persistent demands for autonomy and identity recognition, it has driven a disaggregation of state powers and institutions. However, the path to independence remains blocked—not only by legal and institutional constraints but also by political pragmatism and limited public support. The *cordon sanitaire* still isolates the far-right VB. N-VA, despite its nationalist rhetoric, governs through compromise and has set aside its secessionist goals when in office. Most importantly, the Flemish electorate continues to favour greater autonomy rather than outright statehood. Moreover, the dispute over the future status of Brussels is one of the major obstacles to Belgium's division. Additionally, the risk of EU exclusion for an independent Flanders and losing Brussels as a European capital strongly deter secession.

Despite persistent divisions and conflicts, Belgium appears destined to endure, resisting the siren call of a split by managing its differences through evolving institutions and continued compromise.

References

Angelini F, Benvenuti M (2016) Il federalismo belga alla luce della sesta riforma dello Stato. Istituzioni del Federalismo 1:181–227

Biard B (2021) Challenging the cordon sanitaire in Belgium: a diachronic analysis. In: Caluwaerts D, Reuchamps M (eds) Belgian exceptionalism. Belgian politics between realism and surrealism. Routledge, New York, pp 79–92

Billiet J, Maddens B, Frognier AP (2006) Does Belgium (still) exist? Differences in political culture between Flemings and Walloons. West Eur Polit 29(5):912–932

Carrozza P (2011) Lo Stato belga e la sua crisi. Diritto pubblico comparato ed europeo 3:994–1004

Colella L (2016) La diversità linguistica come «elemento strutturale» della forma di Stato multiculturale belga. Diritto pubblico comparato ed europeo 4:1121–1144

De Winter L, Swyngedouw M, Dumont P (2006) The politics of Belgium: institutions and policy under bipolar and centrifugal federalism. West Eur Polit 29(5):933–956

Delledonne G (2022) Il federalismo asimmetrico del Belgio di fronte alla crisi pandemica. DPCE Online 54(Spec):353–368

Delpérée F (2000) Le droit constitutionnel de la Belgique. LGDJ, Paris

Di Domenico L (2024) The Belgian triple vote: the recurrent search for a compromise. In: Cerruti T, Savastano F (eds) The European Parliament Elections in 2024. Giappichelli, Torino, pp 163–175

Dumont H, Van Drooghenbroeck S (2007) Le statut de Bruxelles dans l'hypothèse du confédéralisme. Brussels Studies, Document 10

Dupont N (2015) Il federalismo belga al bivio. Diritto pubblico comparato ed europeo 2:381–402

El Berhoumi M, Dumont H, Hachez I (2016) La sixième réforme de l'État: l'art de ne pas choisir ou l'art du compromis? Larcier, Bruxelles

Huysseune M (2016) The Flemish Paradox: the hegemony of pro-independence parties in a region largely indifferent towards independence. Ethnopolitics 16(4):352–368

Jahn E (2015) International politics. Springer, Heidelberg

Lijphart A (1999) Patterns of democracy: government forms and performance in thirty-six countries. Yale University Press, New Haven

Mabille X (1997) Histoire politique de la Belgique. Facteurs et acteurs de changement. CRISP, Bruxelles

Maddens B (2017) Secessionist strategies: the case of Flanders. Secession and counter-secession. An international relations perspective. CIDOB, Barcelona, pp 55–62

Mastromarino A (2010) Il federalismo disaggregativo. Un percorso costituzionale negli Stati multinazionali. Giuffrè, Milano

Mastromarino A (2014) Evaporazione vs solidificazione: la sfida belga. Istituzioni del Federalismo 4:909–937

Popelier P (2019) Asymmetry and complexity as a device for multinational conflict management: a country study of constitutional asymmetry in Belgium. In: Popelier P, Sahadžic M (eds) Constitutional asymmetry in multinational federalism. managing multinationalism in multitiered system. Palgrave, Cham, pp 17–45

Popelier P, Lemmens K (2015) The constitution of Belgium: a contextual analysis. Hart Publishing, Oxford

Reuchamps M, Caluwaerts D (2014) Le fédéralisme belge, creuse-t-il sa propre tombe? Outre-Terre. Revue Européenne de Géopolitique 3(40):45–58
Rimanque K (1994) Quelques remarques sur le "perpetuum mobile" de la réforme de l'État en Belgique. Les réformes institutionnelles de 1993: vers un fédéralisme achevé? Bruylant, Bruxelles
Rossi S (2016) Belgio, uno Stato «a incastro». Le Regioni 4:649–667
Swyngedouw M, Abts K, Baute S, Galle J, Meuleman B (2015) Het communautaire in de verkiezingen van 25 mei 2014. Analyse op basis van de postelectorale verkiezingsonderzoeken 1991–2014. Centrum voor Sociologisch Onderzoek, Leuven
Watts RL (2007) Multinational federations in comparative perspective. In: Burgess M, Pinder J (eds) Multinational federalism. Routledge, Abingdon–New York, pp 225–247

Towards a Geopolitical Theory of Separatism: Spatial Reason and Dimensions of Relation, the Hybrid Order, and the Function of Government

Francesco Barbaro

Abstract This essay proposes a geopolitical theory of separatisms, built through the systematisation of a body of conceptual tools already formulated by the author in previous research. It begins with a critique of legal thought on the matter, caught in what is defined as the labyrinth of sovereignty. In turn, it critically scrutinises those elements of geographical thought that, if properly adapted, can be repurposed for the study of the subject. The theoretical proposal is then presented, bringing together in an integrated framework the spatial reason of separatisms; the dimensions of relation—vertical, horizontal, and diagonal; the paradigm of contemporary hybrid order, arising from the crisis of the foundational categories of modern political order; and the different forms in which power relates to this, from which emerges the centrality of a function of government capable of rising to the complexity of contexts and situations. Finally, the theory is succinctly applied to the case of the Western Balkans.

1 Introduction: A Critique of Legal Thought

Geopolitical thought conceives phenomena of power through the lens of space. In this, it differs from legal thought, which examines them through the filter of norms. Accordingly, rather than *secession*, we shall prefer to speak of *separatism*: first, because the former is only one of the possible forms of the latter and, second, because the term secession reflects a preferential interest in the constitutional mechanics of that case, whereas the term separatism reveals a sensitivity more closely oriented to the dynamics whereby one political space detaches from another.

In this essay, then, we propose to present our geopolitical theory of separatisms, systematising in organic form a set of theoretical-conceptual tools we have already formulated—in relation to this specific theme and not only—in recent years. Such a

F. Barbaro (✉)
Sapienza University of Rome, Rome, Italy
e-mail: francesco.barbaro@uniroma1.it

F. Savastano et al. (eds.), *Between Asymmetry and Secession*,
https://doi.org/10.1007/978-3-032-29603-0_19

task, however, cannot fail to engage critically with geographical thought and, even earlier, with legal thought.

Indeed, the academic debate on separatist phenomena has thus far been dominated by legal approaches, mostly aimed at establishing their soundness from a moral or procedural standpoint. From a review of the literature, we can identify the following main positions.

A first strand privileges the defence of a right to national self-determination (Moore 1998). In our view, it raises the problem of defining and recognising the status of nationhood itself. In fact, it is neither self-evident nor unambiguous what renders an ethnopolitical community worthy—or not—of being defined as a nation. It would be scarcely credible to claim that this is exhausted in the aspiration to, or the attainment of, sovereign power over a territory. In the case of aspiration, the floodgates of disorder would be opened, since any group could self-define as a nation and thus claim self-determination, with possible recursive effects. In the case of attainment, by contrast, recognition of that principle would be reduced to a post hoc ratification of power relations as the outcome of the separatist conflict—thereby disavowing the very idea of law as a transcendence of the state of nature. Nor is it at all clear who, from the outside, can or should have the authority to recognise and legitimise some groups as national and others not. All the more so, given the lack of an effective international authority—i.e. one superordinate to nations—any such third party would itself suffer from a deficit of recognition and legitimacy.

A similar weakness in legal authority afflicts just-cause theories of secession, which envisage such an option as a remedy for serious rights violations suffered by a community (Buchanan 2004). Here, too, from our point of view, international organisations display their full fragility. This is due not only to a problem of investiture but above all of political operability: namely, the fact that such organisations reproduce within themselves the very imbalances and conflicts that characterise international politics. This cannot but invalidate the impartiality required of anyone called upon to render such a judgment. Put differently, precisely because states conceive of themselves as *summa potestas superiorem non recognoscens*, international organisations will remain hostage to their interests and competition. In addition, other no less thorny problems arise. It is by no means clear, indeed, which criteria should be used to establish a cause as just—or more just than another—and a violation as grave—or graver than another. Nor is it at all obvious that the most appropriate solution to such violations is the assignment of sovereign power over a territory or that such an assignment constitutes a guarantee against further violations.[1]

Faced with the difficulty of judging separatisms on the basis of their moral legitimacy, an alternative is to ground judgment on method rather than on merit. This position starts from the idea that territorial collectivities have the right to manage their membership in, or separation from, a state on consensual bases. Interest thus shifts to the procedures by which the separation process takes place so as to assess

[1] The experience of the present shows, rather, that the recognition of new sovereignties has facilitated the perpetuation of new violence against new minorities.

their congruence with standards of constitutionality and democratic legitimacy (Norman 2003). This approach is almost entirely agnostic about the substantive reasons sustaining a separatist claim. Inevitably, this fosters degraded political conduct. On the same footing as national self-determination or remedying serious violations, one thus places separatist projects motivated by predatory ends—as in the case of peripheral areas that seek to appropriate local resources—and withdraws them from national redistribution. Or else, the threat of secession can be used as a bargaining lever to obtain advantages in terms of greater autonomy, resource drainage, or other political pay-offs. Yet the procedural theories have another weakness, perhaps even more serious: the removal of conflict. To assume that a separation process must follow predefined and linear institutional procedures is to ignore not only the reasons for the process but also the concrete context in which it unfolds and the relations it implies among multiple actors—relations that place it in a liminal zone where the legal progressively loses its grip in favour of the political.

The various legal approaches, despite their diversity, share a common underlying bias. More or less implicitly, they assume—without adequate problematisation—the cornerstone of the modern political paradigm: the claim of a univocal correspondence between geo-historically determined forms of community, space, and power—namely, between nation, territory, and sovereignty. Yet this axiom is weakened by the fact that the political order to which it refers has long exhibited the signs of a severe crisis. In this sense, separatist phenomena are all the more interesting in that, with their load of conflict and instability, they help to lay that crisis bare.

This argument readily brings to mind John Agnew's (1994) concept of *territorial trap*. It presupposes that the disciplines studying international politics are caged by three assumptions: sovereignty as a territorial fact, i.e. that sovereignty is exercised exclusively over a defined territory; a clear distinction between domestic and foreign politics, such that each develops separately from the other; and the complete correspondence between the state and the society living on its territory, that is, that the former is an expression of the latter. On closer inspection, however—in the case of separatisms but more generally in today's global political context—two of these assumptions are explicitly denied from the outset, while another is, so to speak, inverted. First, it is evident that political space is not homogeneous and, in particular, that a separatist community does not identify with the state of which it is part. The lack of correspondence between the two, therefore, is anything but "trapped". Second, the distinction between inside and outside is called into question by the separatist claim itself, which aims precisely to reconfigure them, not to mention that, as we shall see, conflict brings to bear interactions between inside and outside that further destabilise this distinction. Finally, that sovereignty is a territorial fact—i.e. that it seeks to realise itself as exclusive power over a defined territory—is rather tautological. Reversing the terms, and instead focusing on territory as a sovereign fact, helps illuminate a critical aspect: the surreptitious character of the claim that a political space must necessarily be the object of exclusive, i.e. sovereign, power.

This brings us full circle in our critique of legal thought. Within a separatist conflict, one typically witnesses a clash between a state's intent on defending its territorial integrity and a community seeking to separate in order to realise its self-determination. Or, upon the collapse of central power, one sees various peripheral powers pitted against each other over portions of territory. In any case, however, each of these actors juridically appeals to the same principle, grounded precisely in that conception of exclusive power over political space. But if what is at stake is exclusive power, the parties deny each other's reasons: one and the same principle cannot justify them both. Hence, any attempt at a solution will run into a dead end, and each party will continue to wander through the meanders of what we have already called the *labyrinth of sovereignty* (Barbaro 2023).

2 A Critique of Geographical Thought

If reasoning grounded in the legal principle of sovereignty imprisons us in a labyrinth, it is worth asking whether something akin to Ariadne's thread might be extended to us by geographical thought.

Within the conceptual repertoire of geographical and geopolitical studies, there is no shortage of tools that can be repurposed for the study of separatisms. It is nonetheless a fact that no fully developed theorisation on the subject has yet been produced within this disciplinary field,[2] which has mostly touched it only tangentially. We must therefore engage critically with the literature, extract from it those indirectly useful tools, and rework them so as to adapt them properly to an original theoretical synthesis.

Friedrich Ratzel (1903) introduced into nascent political geography the idea of the state as an organism installed upon a soil and predisposed to grow vertically through rooting and horizontally through expansion. In this sense, territory is conceived as nourishment. That a state may lose rather than acquire it is thus understood as a pathological condition, linked to its decline and the concomitant development of other state organisms. It should be clarified that for Ratzel, the term *state* does not identify exclusively the institutional form consecrated by the modern age but designates any political community capable of rooting itself and expanding territorially. This explains how, later, scholars aligned with classical geopolitics could apply the same concepts to the scenario of the Pan-Regionen (Haushofer 1931) or the Großräume (Schmitt 1941)—strategic macro-regions in which individual states, if anything, may function as hegemonic centres. Since these are political spaces less homogeneous than a nation state and in competition with one another to define a global order, territorial loss is all the more likely to be understood as a symptom of crisis.[3] Yet among various scholars—polygenetically, owing to its extreme intuitive appeal—the same idea takes hold: if phenomena of separation can weaken the adversary's political space, then it may be strategic to support them or,

[2] As confirmed by the absence of dedicated entries in leading geographical dictionaries (Gregory et al. 2009; Kobayashi 2020).

[3] Kjellén (1916), however, had already warned that the overextension of a political space could lead to its disintegration.

at least, logical to sympathise with them.[4] It is hard to deny, however, that the reflections of classical geopoliticians are more or less marred by adherence to a point of view internal to the political subjectivity of their respective countries. This constitutes a genuine paradox for an approach that starts from strongly objectivist epistemological premises. It is therefore unsurprising that separatist phenomena are treated mainly as a symptom of decline to be resisted or as potential strategic tools to be wielded. In any case, such readings do not offer reflections on the ontology or aetiology of separatisms, nor on their distinctive spatial phenomenologies—in other words, they do not help explain what they are, why they take place, and in what forms they manifest themselves.

In the post-war period, political geography was deeply influenced by Richard Hartshorne's work. He was openly hostile to geopolitics, which he helped to banish, going so far as to describe it as "steeped in error, exaggeration, and intellectual poison" (Hartshorne 1954, p. 176). Yet his research interests continued to revolve around the foundational theme of the discipline: the relationship between space and power. He certainly pursued them on the basis of different epistemological assumptions: to nomothetic aspirations—i.e. the search for general laws—he opposed an idiographic approach, grounded in the study of particular cases. According to Hartshorne (1939), geography is characterised by the peculiarity of its method, consisting in the analysis of *areal differentiation*, that is, the heterogeneous distribution of phenomena in space. This enables its ultimate aim: identifying and studying particular spaces—regions—and the combinations of factors that define them. Such combinations can be interpreted as structures that fulfil functions (Hartshorne 1950), one of the primary ones being territorial cohesion. It is here that so-called *centripetal* and *centrifugal* forces—terminology drawn from the urban geographer Charles Colby (1933)—come into play as decisive factors, favouring, respectively, the integrity and fragmentation of a territory. Focusing on the centrifugal forces, congenial to separatist processes, we can say that for the American geographer, they are fundamentally an irregular or fragmented territorial morphology, unstable or contested borders, pronounced socio-economic disparities, and, above all, the absence of what he called the *idea of the state*—that is, the raison d'être of a political space as shared by its members. This approach undoubtedly has the merit of highlighting the opposition between contrary forces acting upon a territory and which may have, among their outcomes, the separation of one of its parts. As conceived, however, this opposition is reduced to an inert balance among factors that are, in reality, little more than attributes ascribed to political space. Consequently, it does not translate into a dialectic, a dynamic between two or more political

[4] Mahan (1890), in relation to naval conflicts, addressed American independence from the European imperial powers. Kjellén (1916) sided with the Poles against the Austro-Hungarian Empire and with the Ukrainians against the Russian Empire. Mackinder (1919) and Bowman (1921) supported the creation of small states as a *cordon sanitaire* between Germany and Russia. Spykman (1942) applied logics of fragmentation to the Rimland and to Latin America. Haushofer (1931) and Schmitt (1941) endorsed the independence of African and Asian colonies against the thalassocratic empires.

subjectivities. Nor could it, for the simple reason that the latter are not recognised in their role as living forces animating the process. This schema, therefore, does not allow us to get to the core of separatism as conflict by analysing its reasons, stakes, and modes of development.

There are, moreover, numerous studies—not only geographical but also economic, sociological, anthropological, and the like—that are focused on single aspects that can rightfully be read as centrifugal factors. Elongated or indented morphologies, as well as fragmented and archipelagic configurations, had already been highlighted by Derwent Whittlesey (1939). Decades later, unstable and contested borders were analysed in Michel Foucher's authoritative work (1991) as both a material and discursive device. It is clear, however, that such elements of material geography cannot by themselves offer an exhaustive explanation of separatist phenomena. Nor are they sufficient to determine them—thinking so would amount, well past its time, to a form of geographical determinism—whereas they may at most provide favourable conditions for their development.

From the analysis of economic factors, two possible and opposite tendencies emerge. The first is what we may call the *separatism of the poor*. Ted Robert Gurr (1970) grounds his study of political protest and revolt in the concept of *relative deprivation*—the perceived gap between what a group believes it is entitled to and what it actually receives—acknowledging its applicability also in territorial terms. Michael Hechter (1975) interprets the Celtic nationalisms of the British Isles (Irish, Scottish, and Welsh) as a reaction to a centuries-long dynamic of *internal colonialism* exercised by England. From this perspective, separatisms would be the outcome of a minorities' frustration in the face of an inequitable spatial distribution of values. The second tendency we may term the separatism *of the rich*, paraphrasing Dalle Mulle (2017). According to this reading, when resource drainage rises, internal economies of scale decline, and the costs of exchange with the outside fall, a wealthy region is incentivised to separate (Bolton and Roland 1997; Alesina and Spolaore 2003). More generally, even when attentive to associated socio-psychological implications, interpretations centred on economic factors tend to surreptitiously attribute to them a monocausal determinist value they evidently cannot bear. It would be logically problematic, after all, to claim that two opposite elements such as poverty and wealth could constitute the linear cause of the same political phenomenon, namely separatism. Ironically, having escaped the labyrinth of sovereignty, we would find ourselves cast into that of economism.

Moreover, economic readings tend to neglect almost entirely, despite its centrality, the identity dimension. By contrast, among studies devoted to the latter—almost all centred on the concept of nation—a strand highlights how the economic, social, and political factors of an international order can exert from the outside a decisive influence on the internal dynamics of an ethno-political community. We can thus define this approach as *exogenous* and *structural*, since it considers the nation the product of exogenous conditioning exerted by the constitutive structures of the superordinate political order. The two most representative contributions in this regard, published in the same year, explain the genesis of the purported correspondence between state, nation, and territory in different ways. Ernest Gellner (1983) traces it to the rise of nineteenth-century industrial society, whose needs for standardised skills and cultural homogeneity were met through the creation of a national school and the reorganisation of administrative apparatuses. Benedict Anderson (1983), on the other hand, traces it to the disintegration of universalist Christian society and the advent of modernity: the perceptual revolution of secular time[5] and the linguistic-cultural revolution of printing books and newspapers in the vernacular fostered feelings of national belonging. These analyses have the merit of identifying factors that, in different periods and for different reasons, facilitated the emergence of national communities through separation—from pre-modern universal empires in Anderson's account and from plurinational states of industrial modernity in Gellner's. Their explanatory capacity, however, is limited to the geo-historical contexts they reconstruct and on which they are calibrated, verging on deterministic hermeneutic circles. Thus, also because of their dissonance,[6] they do not provide a basis for a general theorisation of separatist phenomena.

Furthermore, they tend to neglect that national identity may have an autonomous consistency, even independent of, for example, socio-economic conditioning, as the outcome of a cultural and territorial sedimentation. In reaction to this orientation, an alternative approach has emerged, focused on the role of endogenous identity traits in the construction of ethno-national communities, which is why we define it as *endogenous* and *ethno-symbolic*. Anthony D. Smith (1986), in particular, shows how the political-cultural elites of ethno-national communities select and politicise pre-existing identity elements—among which is the idea of a homeland—to construct mythic-symbolic complexes in support of strategies aimed at asserting territorial sovereignty. Walker Connor (1994), in turn, starts from the distinction between patriotism as loyalty to the state and, on the other hand, nationalism as loyalty to the ethno-national community founded on a sense of common descent. Of the latter, he highlights a non-rational component, capable of transcending—and at times counteracting—socio-economic conditioning and its cost-benefit logic. This approach finally places at the centre the substance of the identity of communities aspiring to become nations and, through separation, to acquire territorial sovereignty. Nonetheless, such theories essentially offer no satisfactory explanations of the reasons and modes of separatist conflicts. Moreover, even while recognising the intermediation of political-cultural elites and their intervention on those very contents, they do not provide specific tools for analysing these elites' discursive practices of power. This, by contrast, is precisely the aim of a third approach, which we define as *constructivist*, in that it conceives political spaces essentially as products of the construction of representations, and as *critical*, precisely because it seeks to deconstruct the latter. This methodological perspective—embodied in critical geopolitics (Ó Tuathail 1996)—on the one hand, obscures the concrete dimension of

[5] Anderson here draws on Walter Benjamin's (1974) notion of *homogeneous, empty time*, enabled by secularised calendars and clocks.

[6] Notably, Gellner conceives the nation as a functional instrument of industrial society, in a top-down homogenising dynamic, whereas for Anderson, it constitutes instead the goal of a bottom-up particularist process.

geopolitical facts, namely that which exists beyond representations and, in fact, constrains them as a tangible, inescapable limit. On the other hand, it imputes to actors a rationality that is often patently contradicted by their actions and by their own discourses.

3 A Theory for Separatisms

The partiality and insufficiency of the various readings thus call for a theoretical synthesis that systematises these elements in an organic, coherent framework. Separatisms arise as a centrifugal and revisionist movement, opposed to a centripetal and conservative power. The centripetal and centrifugal characters ought to be referred not solely to factors abstractly concerning a state's subjective viewpoint in relation to its territory—as Hartshorne maintained—but also to distinct, opposing political subjectivities vying for control of that space. It is these subjectivities that actively embody the role of centripetal and centrifugal forces—not the spatial factors, which, at most, condition the context and the situation in which the conflict takes shape. The spatial reason of separatism must therefore be sought in the existential condition of a community situated on a territory and which perceives, conceives, and lives in particular ways not only the territory itself—as theorised by Lefebvre (1974)—but also the relationship between its own identity and that territory, as well as that between itself and the central power holding ultimate control over that territory, and other powers that, from within or without, may harbour designs upon it. The nation, therefore, is defined not by the claim to or the acquisition of a juridical prerogative but precisely by those ways of perceiving, conceiving, and living its relations with territory and with others' power, as bound up with its own existence.

A clarification is in order regarding these—as we define them—*modes of geopolitical being*.[7] They must undoubtedly be investigated in their essence, but not only and not so much by deconstructing them with the aim of unmasking representations of power as by appreciating their concrete effects on the subject's relations with territory and with other powers.

The separatist conflict, moreover, is not the product of a determinism generated by this complex of relations; rather, it matures when these relations lead to a breaking point influenced by the *context*—i.e. the structure given by the relations among the stable elements of a political space—and by the *situation*—i.e. the combination of dynamic elements that disturb the stability of that political space. The community thus finds itself in a context and a situation to which it ascribes existential value, whether in terms of opportunity or of threat. Otherwise, it would be difficult to explain why in so many cases—perhaps most—the identity and territorial

[7] We employ this expression to highlight the epistemological premises of our research, which can be traced to a form of phenomenological ontology (Barbaro 2025a, 2026).

preconditions are not, in themselves, sufficient to trigger a dynamic of separation. Like many other political facts, then, separatism is a phenomenon strongly characterised in relational, contextual, and situational terms.

Within this framework, the various factors analysed in the literature come into play. Morphological factors may constitute obstacles to be overcome (e.g. Biafra "enclosed" by the Niger Delta, 1967–1970) or favourable elements to be used as levers or strengths (e.g. colonies distant from the colonising states). Economic factors may constitute both a motive for separation and a means to support it (e.g. Catalonia). Ethno-symbolic factors are undoubtedly fundamental in that, on the one hand, they provide the discursive arguments for mobilising the community in a separatist direction (e.g. the invention of a "Padanian" identity; cf. Giordano 2001), but, on the other hand, they refer to those identity preconditions whose existential value is activated by context and situation (e.g. ethnic and religious cleavages in the Balkans).

Context and situation are thus fundamental to understanding geopolitical conflicts in general and separatist conflicts in particular—in both spatial and temporal senses. It is the context of Western political modernity that has structured geopolitical devices such as nation and sovereignty, and it is the situation of its crisis that renders recourse to those devices contradictory—turning sovereignty, precisely, into a labyrinth. In a diachronic sense, the paradigm shift from the modern to what we shall later define as the *hybrid* is thus relevant. The transition towards a possible new spatial order or *Nomos*—to use a lexicon dear to Carl Schmitt (1950)—also highlights what is interesting in a diatopic sense: namely, the trans-scalar dynamic whereby the scale at which separatist conflict occurs and the scale at which the global political space is being reorganised condition and reinforce each other—the latter currently seeming to move towards the definition of new macro-regional spaces, or Großräume (Barbaro 2026).

The relational, contextual, and situational traits of separatisms can be traced back to the nature of geopolitical facts as phenomena of a systemic ontology that is complex and chaotic in the specialist sense, that is, marked by a pronounced sensitivity to initial conditions and to perturbing factors and, above all, by the presence of an innumerable quantity of variables interacting in non-linear ways (Barbaro 2025b; 2026). Among these, human variables—often of a voluntaristic nature and therefore anything but rational—play a major role. This heightens the self-organising character of social phenomena, ipso facto revealing that the ambition to exercise sovereign, homogenising control over political space is little more than an illusion. The drive towards homogenisation—typical of the modern state and so evident as to have been widely grasped polygenetically (Gottmann 1973; Paasi 1986; Sack 1986; Taylor 1994; Elden 2013)—should arguably be understood as a projection of the desire to realise the ideological assumption of correspondence among nation, sovereignty, and territory and to secure the integrity of the latter.

Such an effort is destined to be frustrated by another constitutive feature of political spaces, which we have elsewhere defined as *transitionality* (Barbaro 2024; 2026). By this term we mean, first, that political and cultural phenomena tend, in themselves, to be distributed unevenly across territory. Second, we refer to the existence of particular spaces whose very identity is deeply connected to their representing a transition area between other spaces that are, by contrast, strongly defined. Such areas constitute privileged sites of transitions that are both spatial and temporal: that is to say, they are the places where changes in the global political order most readily find triggers and outlets. In this sense, it is easy to understand how transitional regions—consider Eastern Europe, the South China Sea, or the Middle East—constitute, in a certain way, *the hinge joints of the world.*

By virtue of their peculiarities, transitional regions are more prone to the action of centrifugal phenomena, such as, precisely, separatisms. Conversely, the latter may often be the object of interest to external powers that intend to use them—perhaps indirectly and covertly—to further their projects of reorganising macro-regional or global spaces (e.g. the North Atlantic Treaty Organization (NATO) and Russia in Ukraine), and this brings trans-scalar dynamics back into play. Such complexity requires a conceptual tool capable of reducing it and bringing to the surface the main lines of force acting upon the field of separatist conflicts. As we have seen, Ratzel refers to the verticality whereby the political organism roots itself in the soil and to the horizontality by which it expands across it. This schema, however, does not include such an essential element as the interaction among different political organisms, thus remaining severely limited in its explanatory power. Precisely for this reason, just as we did with centripetal and centrifugal forces, we deem it more useful to push to the utmost the heuristic potential of this tool by expanding its application to the relation among political subjectivities. We thus recover what, in other contexts, we have introduced as *the dimensions of relation*—where to the two traditional ones, as will shortly be clear, we had added a third (Barbaro 2025b, 2026).

With respect to separatisms, the first and most obvious dimension is the vertical one, which pits the centripetal force of the state against the centrifugal force of the separatist component. Within the labyrinth of sovereignty, the stakes will thus be territorial integrity for the conservative subject and self-determination for the revisionist one (e.g. here, too, Catalonia). This is, clearly, the most classical form of separatist conflict. But in the event of the collapse of central power, a horizontal dimension will ensue, in which the components previously subordinate to it contend among themselves for parts of the defunct state's territory (e.g. the dissolution of Yugoslavia). Yet all the more when the separatist conflict invests a transitional region—as we have already noted—it is reasonable to expect external actors to intervene in order to steer the process in favour of their strategic aims (e.g. Bosnia and Kosovo; Crimea and Donbas). A situation of this kind will see the emergence of a third dimension that, refracting between the first two, will inevitably disturb them and which, precisely for this reason, we have elsewhere defined as *the diagonal dimension* (Barbaro 2025b, 2026). An external power may, for example, strike at the vertical dimension—i.e. the balance of power between central and centrifugal forces—in order to reap advantages in its own horizontal dimension, namely in terms of projecting influence. Or it may act upon the horizontal dimension—for instance, on competition among different centrifugal powers—in order to shape the vertical grip of one or another over the territory. The diagonal is thus a dimension that intersects the other two, and this transversality makes even more evident a feature that concerns the dimensions of relation as a whole: they are not mutually exclusive traits but may alternate or coexist, developing and interacting in non-linear ways.

The diagonal dimension, at any rate, inevitably calls into question the concept of the *hybrid*, for it is there that the latter evidently finds the most congenial space to manifest. However, a critical reflection upon the very essence of the hybrid is necessary. According to the most traditional and widespread meaning, this would lie in the introduction of non-conventional instruments, alongside conventional ones, within conflict (Hoffman 2007). For our part, we contest such a view that, by focusing on a symptom rather than on the phenomenon's reasons, obscures both its temporal and, above all, its spatial implications. It merely registers the proliferation of such instruments, allegedly employed by everyone, everywhere, at any time, and in the same ways.[8] This reading thus prevents us from grasping the peculiarities that constitute the hybrid as a geopolitical order. Any instrument conceived for peaceful uses can be repurposed offensively: a knife, for instance, may be used to prepare a meal for a friend or to slit an enemy's throat. But if everything is hybrid, then nothing truly is, and the very category loses its explanatory value so that—as we have often argued elsewhere—*in the night of the hybrid all cows stand in a grey zone*. In our view, then, the hybrid must be distinguished from the non-conventional, and the peculiarities of its paradigm must be sought rather in the placing under tension of the fundamental categories upon which a political order rests—in our case, the modern one: namely, in the crisis of the oppositional pairs inside/outside, friend/enemy, peace/war, or military/civil (Barbaro 2025a; 2026).

This crisis has significant consequences for conflicts, beginning precisely with separatist ones. It is no coincidence, after all, that they re-emerged forcefully after the Cold War and then again at the end of the unipolar moment—that is, at junctures when the international order, amidst fissures and creaks, underwent profound changes. Separatisms, as we have already seen, represent in themselves an instance of reconfiguring the inside/outside boundary. At the same time, however, this spatial differentiation is violated by third-party actors who, indirectly or covertly, act to influence the conflict in line with their strategic interests. In parallel, then, the friend/enemy distinction is likewise strained: the state discovers that it faces as enemies components internal to its own political space, while it becomes increasingly difficult to detect and frame the hostile activities of external actors. This, in turn, renders it more difficult to distinguish between a state of peace and a state of war: the latter is no longer the object of formal declarations and is no longer limited to strictly military action but—immersed in a cone of shadow that grants attackers plausible deniability—sublimates into an unbounded competition in both modes of action and choice of targets. It follows that even the civil/military distinction is neutralised: first, because, by their very pervasiveness, digital technologies lend themselves to offensive repurposing—which recalls the instrumental meaning of the hybrid in the

[8] This represents a constant from the myth of the Trojan horse to today's drones and in the strategies of Western powers, as well as of revisionist ones such as China or Russia, and also in those of Israel.

strategic tradition—and, second, because attacking the civil sphere of adversary communities makes it possible to strike indirectly, together with their vertical resilience, their room for manoeuvre in the horizontal dimension of external relations—and this, instead, brings us back to the peculiarity of the diagonal dimension.

The crisis of these foundational categories of political order does not necessarily mean their demise but certainly signifies their reconfiguration—whose outcome is, however, hard to foresee, though it seems oriented towards a reorganisation of the international order into *large spaces* or spheres of influence. What is certain is that the absence of stable categories renders it challenging to act incisively upon the dynamics of order-change and, prior even to that, to understand them. If such understanding can no longer rest upon the plane of knowledge—i.e. already-given, general, and structured epistemes—then it must rest on a different plane: that of *the minimum sense-bearing epistemic units*, as we have defined information (Barbaro 2025a, 2026). In fact, information is the instrument by which the complexity of chaotic, self-organising systems such as the political can be reduced in order to produce new syntheses—that is, to construct new knowledge and new representations, including those that may be malevolently administered to the adversary so as to induce him to make choices to his detriment and to one's own advantage.

It remains to be clarified what type of power can operate effectively—both on the informational plane and on the more strictly geopolitical plane—within such a hybrid and complex context. It will not be what we have called *the Juridical*: the most classical form of modern power, of a strongly telluric nature inasmuch as it is tied to the definition of a spatial and, precisely, juridical order of the Earth—respectively *Ortung* and *Ordnung* in Schmitt's (1950) lexicon; symbolised by the archetype of the *polis* (Gottmann 1973), it is bent towards the realisation of Plato's ideal of security (Plato 1907). The Juridical, indeed, conceives of its power in space as exclusive and thus sovereign and, when confronted with phenomena such as separatisms, can only lose itself in the labyrinth of sovereignty. Nor will it be the type of power we have defined as *the Economic*[9], evidently thalassic in character, insofar as it is tied to the freedom of commercial flows, and corresponding to Gottmann's image of the *Alexandrian system*, which—not by chance—aptly expresses Aristotle's ideal of openness to opportunity (Aristotle 1831). The Economic, after all, tends by nature towards globalisation and its deterritorialising logics: but this renders it simply inadequate for grappling with phenomena such as separatisms, where what truly matters are elements like territory, identity, and security. It will therefore be another type of power, not a mere alternative to the first two but a transcendence of their antinomy: what we more properly identify as *the Political*. This concretely corresponds to *the function of government* that, while not harbouring the Juridical's pretension to determine space, neither surrenders to entropy as the Economic does; rather, it is bent towards realising the ends of the community, starting from an understanding of context and situation and through an adaptive interaction with

[9]The Economic may be regarded as kindred to what, in other works, we have identified as *Technique* (Barbaro 2026), by virtue of their shared totalising and self-referential tendency.

them. The function of government, as indicated by its Latin etymology, is therefore intended to steer the community between security and opportunity, as between land and sea—hence its strongly *amphibious* nature (Barbaro 2023). If Gottmann does not conceptualise it and thus provides no archetype for it, we propose here that of the κοινόν (koinón), namely the leagues of poleis that self-organise for a—precisely, as the Greek etymology this time indicates—common end. The ideal will therefore be that of φρόνησις (phrónēsis), that is, knowledge translatable into action and, ultimately, wisdom. Albeit not theorised and in an intuitive—that is, unselfconscious—form, an approach of this kind has enabled the parties involved to find alternatives to separation and repression in cases such as Nunavut in Canada (1999), Greenland within Denmark (2009), the federalisation of Belgium (1993), and European regionalism, which has provided various sub-state communities with channels of representation and margins for trans-scalar action within the European Union.

4 The Case of the Western Balkans: Conclusions

Having proposed a systematic theorisation of separatisms, the most effective way to test its validity is through application to a concrete case. Within the limits of this essay, we intend succinctly to do so in relation to the Western Balkans, which, by virtue of their geopolitical peculiarities, constitute a privileged laboratory for the study of separatisms and their conflict dynamics.

The spatial reason for separatist phenomena in this region lies in its marked transitionality, to be understood both in terms of internal differentiation—ethnic, cultural, religious, and socio-economic—and of its intermediate position between the European and Russian spheres. This explains the historical alternation of phases of cohesion under external powers and of fragmentation once those powers receded. In the Cold War context, the Yugoslav state achieved unity and independence, thanks to a combination of factors: the charismatic leadership of Tito; a system of self-managed socialism selectively open to Western markets; an international positioning of non-alignment, which made it a reference point for the entire Third World; and a federal framework capable of absorbing centrifugal pressures. These pressures were by no means absent, but the central power addressed them in the vertical dimension by alternating repression and concessions.

The end of bipolarism and the crisis following Tito's death led to the collapse of the federal centre and to the separation of ethno-national communities. The conflict thus shifted to the horizontal dimension, where these communities fiercely contested portions of the defunct Yugoslav state. The instability of the area and its strategic value in the reorganisation of international political spaces favoured the intervention of external actors. NATO, interpreting US strategic interests and framing its action within the UN doctrine of responsibility to protect, intervened militarily, decisively conditioning the outcome of the conflicts. The EU, in addition to the accession of Slovenia and Croatia, promoted partnership initiatives, limited however by their high degree of conditionality. Russia exerted influence through ties with the Orthodox world, a privileged relationship with Serbia, and energy and infrastructure projects. Turkey sought to maintain its presence among Muslim communities, while China consolidated a strategic penetration through massive investments under the Belt and Road Initiative, which—unlike those of the EU—were largely devoid of formal conditionality.

All these interventions—expressions of the Juridical when grounded in schemes of sovereignty or of the Economic when centred on the logic of flows—operated in the diagonal dimension, acting upon the verticality of Balkan states to enhance their own horizontal projection of influence. Such dynamics reflect the emergence of a hybrid paradigm of power, in which the modern distinctions between inside/outside, friend/enemy, peace/war, and civil/military are destabilised. The Western Balkans thus continue to constitute a theatre of information warfare, fuelled both by Russian representations and by Euro-Atlantic ones. Yet, so far, the hybrid competition has not been matched by the emergence of what we have called the Political: that is, a power capable of exercising the function of government in order to move beyond the labyrinth of sovereignty—as it might be, for instance, through the recognition of a special status for Serbian sacred sites in the area currently under Kosovar administration.

In conclusion, separatist phenomena are not mere accidents in the life of political spaces but rather indicators of the stability and of the evolution of the order upon which they rest. They arise from spatial reasons intimately bound to the transitionality of politico-cultural identities and of power relations across multiple scales. The conflicts they engender therefore unfold along several dimensions: the vertical one, between central power and the separatist community; the horizontal one, between separatist communities contending over portions of territory; and the diagonal one, refracting between the former two and enabling external actors to shape their outcome. This calls into question the hybrid paradigm of power, rooted in the crisis of the modern order and of its categories. To adapt to such a context, it is necessary to understand its dynamics and to draw from that understanding the guidance needed to prevent territory—pulled forcefully in opposing directions—from being torn apart like the body of Pentheus by the fury of the Bacchantes.

References

Agnew J (1994) The territorial trap: the geographical assumptions of international relations theory. Rev Int Polit Econ 1(1):53–80

Alesina A, Spolaore E (2003) The size of nations. MIT Press, Cambridge MA

Anderson B (1983) Imagined communities: reflections on the origin and spread of nationalism. Verso, London

Aristotle (1831) Politica. In: Bekker I, Brandis CA, Bonitz H (eds) Aristotelis Opera. Reimer, Berlin, pp 1252–1342

Barbaro F (2023) La problematica geopolitica dei separatismi nel labirinto della sovranità. Studi Politici 2(1):111–125

Barbaro F (2024) The Balkans as a transitional region between internal circles and global squarings in the paradigm of hybrid power. In: Prokorović D, Sellari P, Mifsud E (eds) Global security and international relations after the escalation of the Ukrainian crisis. Institute of International Politics and Economics, Belgrade, pp 413–428

Barbaro F (2025a) Spazio, potere, informazione. Una nuova teorizzazione geopolitica. Università di Roma "La Sapienza", Roma

Barbaro F (2025b) Geopolitica e spazi digitali. Edizioni Nuova Cultura, Roma

Barbaro F (2026) Information and Technique between Hybrid Order and the Regional Reorganisation of Global Political Space. A System of Geopolitical Theory. In: Dolan CJ (ed) International Relations – Power, Politics, and Perceptions. IntechOpen, London, 10.5772/intechopen.1013971

Benjamin W (1974) Über den Begriff der Geschichte. In: Tiedemann R, Schweppenhäuser H (eds) Gesammelte Schriften. Suhrkamp, Frankfurt am Main, pp 690–708

Bolton P, Roland G (1997) The breakup of nations: a political economy analysis. Q J Econ 112(4):1057–1090

Bowman I (1921) The new world: problems in political geography. World Book Company, Yonkers-on-Hudson, NY

Buchanan A (2004) Justice, legitimacy, and self-determination: moral foundations for international law. Oxford University Press, Oxford

Colby CC (1933) Centrifugal and centripetal forces in urban geography. Ann Assoc Am Geogr 23(1):1–20

Connor W (1994) Ethnonationalism: the quest for understanding. Princeton University Press, Princeton

Dalle Mulle FM (2017) The nationalism of the rich: discourses and strategies of separatist parties in Catalonia, Flanders, Northern Italy and Scotland. Routledge, London

Elden S (2013) The birth of territory. University of Chicago Press, Chicago

Foucher M (1991) Fronts et frontières. Un tour du monde géopolitique. Fayard, Paris

Gellner E (1983) Nations and nationalism. Blackwell, Oxford

Giordano B (2001) The contrasting geographies of "Padania": the case of the Lega Nord in Northern Italy. Area 33(1):27–37

Gottmann J (1973) The significance of territory. University of Virginia Press, Charlottesville

Gregory D, Johnston R, Pratt G, Watts MJ, Whatmore S (eds) (2009) The dictionary of human geography. Wiley-Blackwell, Chichester

Gurr TR (1970) Why men rebel. Princeton University Press, Princeton

Hartshorne R (1939) The nature of geography: a critical survey of current thought in the light of the past. Annals of the Association of American Geographers, Lancaster

Hartshorne R (1950) The functional approach in political geography. Ann Assoc Am Geogr 40(2):95–130

Hartshorne R (1954) Political geography. In: James PE, Jones CF (eds) American geography: inventory and prospect. Syracuse University Press, Syracuse, pp 167–225

Haushofer K (1931) Geopolitik der Pan-Ideen. Weltpolitische Bücherei, Bd 21. Zentral-Verlag, Berlin

Hechter M (1975) Internal colonialism: the Celtic fringe in British national development, 1536-1966. Routledge & Kegan Paul, London

Hoffman FG (2007) Conflict in the 21st century: the rise of hybrid wars. Potomac Institute for Policy Studies, Arlington, VA

Kjellén R (1916) Staten som lifsform. Hugo Gebers Förlag, Stockholm

Kobayashi A (ed) (2020) International encyclopedia of human geography, 2nd edn. Elsevier, Amsterdam

Lefebvre H (1974) La production de l'espace. Anthropos, Paris

Mackinder HJ (1919) Democratic ideals and reality: a study in the politics of reconstruction. Constable, London

Mahan AT (1890) The influence of sea-power upon history, 1660–1783. Little, Brown, Boston

Moore M (ed) (1998) National self-determination and secession. Oxford University Press, Oxford
Norman W (2003) Domesticating secession. In: Macedo S, Buchanan A (eds) Secession and self-determination: NOMOS XLV. New York University Press, New York, pp 191–237
Ó Tuathail G (1996) Critical geopolitics. Routledge, London
Paasi A (1986) The institutionalization of regions: a theoretical framework for understanding the emergence of regions and the constitution of regional identity. Fennia 164:105–146
Plato (1907) Leges. In: Burnet J (ed) Platonis Opera, vol V. Oxford University Press, Oxford, pp 624–947
Ratzel F (1903) Politische Geographie oder die Geographie der Staaten, des Verkehres und des Krieges, 2. Umgearb, Aufl. R. Oldenbourg, München
Sack RD (1986) Human territoriality: its theory and history. Cambridge University Press, Cambridge
Schmitt C (1941) Völkerrechtliche Großraumordnung mit Interventionsverbot für raumfremde Mächte. Ein Beitrag zum Reichsbegriff im Völkerrecht. 2., erw. Aufl. Deutscher Rechtsverlag, Berlin
Smith AD (1986) The ethnic origins of nations. Blackwell, Oxford
Spykman NJ (1942) America's strategy in world politics. The United States and the balance of power. Harcourt Brace, New York
Taylor PJ (1994) The state as container: territoriality in the modern world-system. Prog Hum Geogr 18(2):151–162
Whittlesey D (1939) The Earth and the State: a study in political geography. Henry Holt, New York

Navigating Separatism in Bosnia and Herzegovina: A Constitutional Perspective

Edin Skrebo

Abstract The purpose of this chapter is to address the issue of secessionist tendencies in Bosnia and Herzegovina within the broader context of the country's constitutional solutions. Starting from some basic historical and political coordinates, the question of secession in Bosnia and Herzegovina will be addressed by illustrating the particular ethnic federalism that the state adopted for the first time in its history with the signing of the Dayton Peace Agreement and the simultaneous adoption of the new Constitution (1995). In this way, it will be possible to illustrate how the constituents adopted the federal system in order to simultaneously give space and autonomy to the ethnic specificities that characterise the country and safeguard the state integrity of Bosnia and Herzegovina. With these aims, the constituent members adopted a consociational political-institutional system alongside the federal system to safeguard the role of the different ethnic components as much as possible. In this context, after outlining its main characteristics, we will try to understand how the current federal and power-sharing system has influenced, positively or negatively, the secessionist movements that have been present in the country since the 1990s.

1 Autonomy as a Structuring Principle of the Italian Regional State

Scholars estimate that there are currently about 200 (latent or active) secessionist territorial claims in the world (Margiotta 2009, p. 214). Not even the European continent is an exception to this general observation. Suffice it to mention, by way of example, the cases of the United Kingdom (Scotland, Northern Ireland), Spain (Catalonia and the Basque Country), Belgium (Flanders) and Italy (South Tyrol and

E. Skrebo (✉)
University of Milan-Bicocca, Milan, Italy
e-mail: edin.skrebo@unimib.it

F. Savastano et al. (eds.), *Between Asymmetry and Secession*,
https://doi.org/10.1007/978-3-032-29603-0_20

Veneto). Moreover, even a supranational organisation like the European Union is not immune to internal secessionist pressures: Brexit is a prominent example.[1]

However, the geographical area of Europe that has become synonymous with the division and fragmentation of state territory into small, hostile and unstable units is the Balkans (Góra 2020, p. 38), so much so that the term "Balkanisation"[2] has been coined to describe this phenomenon. Indeed, since the Paris Peace Conference (1919), the Balkan region has been the subject of a progressive and multiple division of the territory of the states established there. This continued until the 1990s, when the last act of this "Balkanisation" was completed with the dissolution of the former Yugoslavia (Glenny 2017, p. 112 ff). However, almost three decades after the end of this tragic conflict, there are still significant centrifugal forces of a secessionist and territorial nature and territorial claims in the Balkans. Specifically, to mention only the most important cases, there is the political (and not so political) conflict between Serbia and Kosovo following the latter's declaration of independence in 2008, the secessionist claims of the ethnic Albanian population of the Republic of North Macedonia, the tensions between Slovenia and Croatia over the maritime borders in the Istria region, and, last but not least, the interference and political pressure of the Serbian and Croatian political classes on Bosnia and Herzegovina (BiH) and on the Serbian and Croatian populations living there, which have on several occasions manifested themselves as incentives for secessionist policies (Malcolm 2002, p. 253).

This chapter is dedicated to the case of Bosnia and Herzegovina. In particular, the purpose of this study is to address the issue of secessionist tendencies in Bosnia and Herzegovina in the broader context of the constitutional solutions adopted in the country. Starting from some basic historical and political coordinates, the question of secession in Bosnia and Herzegovina is addressed in the broader perspective of ethnic federalism, which the state adopted for the first time in its history with the signing of the Dayton Peace Agreement (DPA) and the simultaneous adoption of the new Constitution (1995) (Trnka 2009, pp. 45–71). In this way, it will be possible to illustrate how the framers of constitutional text adopted the federal system in order to give space and autonomy to the specific ethnic groups that characterise the country and safeguard the state integrity of Bosnia-Herzegovina. In this sense, the Constitutional Assembly also adopted a consociational political-institutional system of power-sharing in order to safeguard the role of the different ethnic groups as much as possible. In this context, and taking into account the main features of the constitutional system, we will try to understand how the current federal system and power-sharing have influenced, positively or negatively, the secessionist movements that have been present in the country since the 1990s. In particular, we will try to understand the extent to which the federal solution and power-sharing system have influenced the management of secessionist pressures or, on the contrary, have exacerbated such politics.

---

[1] See Anderson (2018), pp. 4–44; Kostov (2020), pp. 11–196; Duerr (2015), p. 44; Kochenov and Van Den Brink (2016), pp. 67–92; Closa (2016), pp. 240–264.

[2] See Oxford English Dictionary (2013).

This study is structured as follows. Specifically, Sect. 2 will provide the reader with a brief overview of the secessionist movements that have been present in Bosnia and Herzegovina since the dissolution of Yugoslavia, of which the country was a federal Republic until 1992, and the political-territorial solutions that have been proposed during the conflict. Section 3 examines the form of ethno-territorial federalism that Bosnia and Herzegovina adopted with the Dayton Peace Agreement. In particular, this section will relate the asymmetrical federal solution to secessionist pressures. Section 4 will try to provide the coordinates of the democratic power-sharing system as a tool to reduce tensions between different ethnic groups. Finally, Sect. 5 will be devoted to the conclusions, in which an attempt will be made to answer the question of how the federal system based on ethnicity and territory, together with the power-sharing system, have influenced the secessionist movements in Bosnia and Herzegovina.

2 Bosnia and Herzegovina: Between Independence, Secession and War

The disintegration of the Socialist Federative Republic of Yugoslavia began slowly but surely in the decade following the death of Josip Broz Tito (1980) and ended tragically with the conflicts that engulfed this geographical area (1991–1999) (Pirjevec 2014). The mutual tensions between the Republics that constituted Yugoslavia, together with the severe economic crisis and the political project—especially of the Serbian political elite—of re-centralising the state, with less autonomy for the Republics and provinces, contributed to the dissolution of Yugoslavia, followed by armed conflict (Silber and Little 1997, p. 37 ff).

Following the example of Slovenia and Croatia, Bosnia and Herzegovina—one of the six Republics that constituted the Yugoslav Federation—called a referendum on independence, which was held between 29 February and 1 March 1992 (Pejanović 2023, pp. 115–132). Sixty-four per cent of the population voted for independence. However, the subsequent international recognition of Bosnia and Herzegovina also coincided with the outbreak of war between three main ethnic groups: Bosniaks, Bosnian Serbs and Bosnian Croats. Indeed, Bosnia and Herzegovina is historically characterised by the coexistence of three different religious faiths (Muslims, Orthodox and Catholic Christians, and a small Jewish community), which also coincide with the three main ethnic groups residing in the country: Bosniaks, Serbs and Croats. This ethnic and religious mix had important implications during the break-up of Yugoslavia and the formation of the new state of Bosnia-Herzegovina. Indeed, the majority of Bosniaks and Bosnian Croats voted in favour of declaring independence from Yugoslavia. On the other hand, the Bosnian Serbs, who had close links with neighbouring Serbia, boycotted the referendum, fearing that they would lose their links with Serbia and become a minority in the new state (Silber and Little 1997, pp. 222–230). In this context, and also as a result of political pressure from Milošević, the Bosnian Serbs began as early as 1990–1991 to organise autonomous territorial units where this ethnic group was in the majority and where the municipalities were administered by the largest Serb party (SDS) (Burg and Shoup 2000, p. 32 ff). Even before the referendum on independence was held in Bosnia and Herzegovina (February–March 1992), the Bosnian Serbs had unilaterally proclaimed the establishment of the Republic of the Serbs People of Bosnia and Herzegovina (January–February 1992), after holding a consultative referendum only in regions with a Bosnian Serb majority, which was subsequently declared unconstitutional by the Constitutional Court of the Socialist Republic of Bosnia and Herzegovina (Silber and Little 1997, p. 258). In this climate, the international recognition of the state of Bosnia and Herzegovina and the separatist tendencies of the Bosnian Serbs led to an armed conflict between the army of Bosnia and Herzegovina and the army of the Bosnian Serbs (VRS), who fought over the territories where the Bosniak and Bosnian Serb populations were in the majority. At the same time, the ethnic Croat population, under considerable pressure from neighbouring Croatia, had begun to form Croat communities in Bosnia and Herzegovina in November 1991 under the leadership of the largest Croat party (HDZ). However, this did not stop the Bosnian Croat political class and the Bosnian Croat population from supporting the independence referendum. Moreover, until 1993, the army of Bosnia and Herzegovina and the Croatian Defence Council (HVO) had formed a military and political alliance against the army of the Serb Republic of Bosnia and Herzegovina. However, under strong pressure from Croatia, this pact was broken in 1993, and the three main ethnic groups clashed with their respective armies (Shrader 2003, p. 65). Only in 1994, with the Washington Agreement, did the Bosniaks and Croats, under pressure from the USA, sign an alliance and form the Federation of Bosnia and Herzegovina as a territorial unit with a majority of Bosnian Croats and Bosniaks, which today constitutes a federal entity of Bosnia and Herzegovina. This was followed in November–December 1995 by the Peace Agreement for Bosnia and Herzegovina, also known as the Dayton Peace Agreement (Holbrooke 1999, pp. 231–287; Slye 1996, pp. 459–473).

Within this complex ethnic, religious, political, and historical framework that characterises Bosnia and Herzegovina, and which we have only briefly touched on here, some useful considerations begin to emerge for the argument of this contribution. Indeed, the first thing to note is that the population of Bosnia and Herzegovina is divided into three main ethnic and religious groups—Bosniaks (50% of the total population), Bosnian Serbs (30%) and Bosnian Croats (15%)—and other minority groups.[3] Another aspect that should be emphasised is the formation of territorial units, in the context of the independence of Bosnia and Herzegovina from Yugoslavia, characterised by the search for ethnic homogeneity. In fact, the policy of the Bosnian Serbs, and later of the Bosnian Croats, was to create self-proclaimed territorial entities capable of gathering the majority population of their own ethnic group in order to break the territorial unity of Bosnia and Herzegovina. Another useful aspect to highlight is that the three ethnic groups present in Bosnia and Herzegovina have not shared a common vision of the state since the first attempts to achieve independence

[3] Agency for Statistics of Bosnia and Herzegovina.

from Yugoslavia. On the one hand, the majority Bosniaks were in favour of an independent Bosnia and Herzegovina, but there was a lack of decentralised structures and models to mitigate the country's territorial and ethnic diversity. Similarly, the ethnic Croat population had supported the country's independence but at the same time called for the creation of political and territorial structures that would guarantee their own political and institutional role, as well as a degree of territorial autonomy (Yee 1996, pp. 180–181). From these initial positions, however, the Bosnian Croat political class—also under pressure from Croatia—moved towards a secessionist policy, which led to a real armed conflict. On the contrary, from the very beginning of the disintegration of Yugoslavia, the Bosnian Serbs were highly critical of the possible independence of Bosnia and Herzegovina (Bieber 2006, pp. 18–20). Moreover, the Bosnian Serb political class did not want to lose its privileged relations with the Serbian political class if the country left Yugoslavia. The international recognition of Bosnia and Herzegovina thus coincided with the unilateral proclamation of an autonomous Serbs region and an extremely aggressive military policy towards Bosnia and Herzegovina, which then led to the creation of Republika Srpska, one of the two federal entities that make up Bosnia and Herzegovina today. Finally, it can be added that since the creation of the state of Bosnia and Herzegovina in 1992, the three main ethnic groups have not reached a point of agreement, not only on the form of the state to be created but also on a common sense of belonging. On the contrary, territorial and ethnic secessionist movements have characterised Bosnia and Herzegovina since its inception as a state (Gaeta 1996, p. 148).

There are two other aspects of the formation of the state of Bosnia and Herzegovina that are directly related to the war that took place there between 1992 and 1995. Even before the outbreak of the conflict, the international community and the European Community had proposed a federal or semi-federal solution to guarantee a large degree of autonomy for the different ethnic groups and the integrity of the state (Weller 1996, pp. 89–94). The "Carrington-Cutileiro Plan" of February 1992, named after mediators Lord Carrington and José Cutileiro, was the final outcome of the peace conference organised by the European Community in Lisbon. At the heart of the proposed peace plan were two aspects to which the European mediators had paid particular attention. The first was the sharing of political power between the country's three main ethnic groups. The second was for the state to devolve many of its responsibilities to the local communities into which the peoples of Bosnia and Herzegovina were divided. Despite initial opposition from the Bosnian Serbs, the plan was signed by the three main political leaders of the ethnic groups involved but was soon rejected by the Bosniaks, who could not accept an ethnic division of the territory that could have led to discrimination against minority groups (Vranić 2013, pp. 51–52). After this first attempt, and following the start of armed clashes between the different factions, in January 1993, United Nations Special Envoy Cyrus Vance and European Community Representative Lord Owen began negotiating a peace proposal with the leaders of the three main ethnic groups. The proposal, which later became known as the "Vance-Owen peace plan", envisaged the division of Bosnia and Herzegovina into ten semi-autonomous regions (defined as cantons) with a clear ethnic division. In practice, what was defined as the "cantonalisation" of the territory of Bosnia and Herzegovina consisted of a kind of confederation of micro-territories based on ethnicity, with a very weak role for the central state. The failure of this second plan was followed by another round of negotiations in July 1993, during which UN mediators Thorvald Stoltenberg and David Owen presented a new peace plan that would have divided Bosnia and Herzegovina into a union of three ethnic republics. Specifically, the plan would have given 53% of the territory to the Bosnian Serbs, 30% to the Bosniaks and 17% to the Bosnian Croats. However, as mentioned in the previous pages, the peace agreement was not reached until 1995, under heavy pressure from the US administration (Greenberg and McGuinness 2000, pp. 45–53). The first point to emphasise here is the fact that the international community, in each of the peace plans presented, including the Dayton peace plan, has consistently proposed a federal solution, not only in order to reconcile and defuse the secessionist tendencies of the various groups present in the territory but also to achieve the dual objective of preserving the integrity of the state in the broader context of the autonomy of the individual groups. However, the federalism proposed in Bosnia and Herzegovina and then actually adopted with the 1995 Constitution, which is also Annex IV of the Dayton Peace Agreement, is an ethnic federalism in which the territorial aspect merges with that of ethnic affiliation (Šarčević 2009, p. 68).

The further aspect that emerges from the peace plans summarised above—and which constitutes the second point of interest for this article—is that the federal system proposed for Bosnia and Herzegovina is also accompanied by a model of consociational democracy based on power-sharing elements (Keil 2013, p. 125 ff). In fact, the recognition of the ethnic factor is evident not only in the proposal to adopt an ethnic-based federal system but also in the fact that the ethnic factor is institutionalised with the adoption of a political system shared by the three main ethnic groups. In this way, it is possible to guarantee equal representation of the ethnic groups within the legislative and executive powers (O'Brien 2010, pp. 338–340). In addition, the ethnic groups have a high degree of autonomy in managing their own interests. Also, they have institutional tools in the legislative and executive branches, such as the power of veto, to guarantee the interests of their own ethnic group and equal participation in the composition of the executive.

3 Ethnic Federalism in Bosnia and Herzegovina

The constitutional order of Bosnia and Herzegovina, as established by the General Framework Agreement for Peace in Bosnia and Herzegovina, manifests a unique and complex form of ethno-territorial federalism. Enshrined in Annex 4 of the Agreement, which serves as the Constitution of Bosnia and Herzegovina, this model of governance was conceived not solely as a means of political organisation but primarily as a mechanism for conflict resolution and ethnic accommodation following the devastating war of 1992–1995. It represents a *sui generis* federal model that combines elements of consociational democracy, territorial division and ethnic parity (Woelk 2008, pp. 91–96).

The Constitution of Bosnia and Herzegovina establishes a decentralised state composed of two entities: the Federation of Bosnia and Herzegovina and Republika Srpska. In addition, the District of Brčko was subsequently constituted as a self-governing administrative unit under the direct sovereignty of the State of Bosnia and Herzegovina, following the Final Award of the Arbitral Tribunal in 1999 (Ademović et al. 2012, pp. 81, 315–326).

Pursuant to Article I (3) of the Constitution, Bosnia and Herzegovina consists of the aforementioned entities, which are recognised as constituent units with their own constitutions and legislative, executive and judicial authorities, provided they do not conflict with the Constitution of the State (Steiner and Ademović 2010, pp. 108–112). This establishes a federal structure that is highly asymmetric and ethnically delineated, given the predominance of particular ethnic groups within each entity: Bosniaks and Croats in the Federation of Bosnia and Herzegovina, and Serbs in Republika Srpska (Ademović et al. 2012, pp. 385–441). The Federation of Bosnia and Herzegovina is further divided into ten cantons, each possessing its own government and legislature, which also reflects ethnic balances. In contrast, Republika Srpska functions as a centralised entity without internal federal divisions but remains constitutionally bound to ensure the rights of all constituent peoples throughout its territory (Ademović et al. 2012, pp. 329–375).

Central to the constitutional order is the doctrine of "constituent peoples", namely Bosniaks, Croats and Serbs, along with "Others" and citizens. This concept, affirmed in the Preamble and further elaborated in the jurisprudence of the Constitutional Court of Bosnia and Herzegovina (notably the U-5/98 decision),[4] underscores the parity of these three ethnic groups throughout the territory of Bosnia and Herzegovina, irrespective of their numerical majority in either entity (Begić and Delić 2013, pp. 450–453).

This ethno-national parity is reflected in both territorial governance and the structure of public institutions. At the state level, the tripartite Presidency comprises one Bosniak and one Croat elected from the Federation of Bosnia and Herzegovina, and one Serb elected from Republika Srpska (Article V). The Parliamentary Assembly, the state-level legislative authority, consists of the House of Peoples and the House of Representatives. The House of Peoples, in particular, institutionalises ethnic parity by comprising 15 delegates: five Bosniaks, five Croats and five Serbs, indirectly elected by the respective entities' legislatures (Article IV).

Although it does not explicitly refer to ethnicity, two-thirds of the 42 members of the House of Representatives must be elected in the electoral districts of the Federation of Bosnia and Herzegovina, while the remaining third must be elected in the districts of Republika Srpska. Once again, therefore, there is a clear intention to

[4] Constitutional Court of Bosnia and Herzegovina, Decision U-5/98 III Partial Decision, 29 January 2000.

equalise the roles of the two federal entities and their respective populations, albeit proportionally.

The same principles of ethnic equality apply to the formation of the government. In fact, no more than two-thirds of ministers can be appointed from the Federation of Bosnia and Herzegovina, thereby ensuring that a minimum number of ministers are appointed from the other entity. Furthermore, a precise ethnic balance is required when allocating ministries. Each minister must appoint a deputy who does not belong to the same "constituent people" as themselves (Constitution, Article V(4)).

This model of ethno-territorial federalism leads to a multi-layered institutional architecture, characterised by both horizontal and vertical division of powers. At the vertical level, competencies are allocated among the state, the entities and, within the Federation, the cantons. Article III of the Constitution delineates the exclusive competences of the state, which include foreign policy, foreign trade, customs policy, monetary policy and immigration, while all other functions are retained by the entities unless expressly transferred by mutual agreement (Meškić and Pivić 2011, pp. 602–608).

At the horizontal level, institutional functioning is contingent upon mechanisms that ensure ethnic representation and safeguard collective rights. These include the "vital national interest" vetoes in legislative bodies. The decision-making procedure set out in the Constitution for the House of Peoples allows for a veto to be raised if a deputy believes that a bill, or part of it, violates the "vital interest" of the constituent people to which they belong. In this case, only the club to which the deputy who raised the veto belongs shall meet. If the club also votes in favour of the veto, the President of the Chamber must establish a committee comprising one representative from each constituent people. This committee's task is to find a shared solution, with a view to a subsequent vote. However, if the committee is unable to resolve the crisis within 5 days, the matter is referred to the Constitutional Court. Through an *ad hoc* "emergency" procedure, the Court must provide a reasoned opinion on whether there has been a violation of "vital interests". If the Court recognises that the act, or part of it, is harmful, it is referred back to its proponent, who must then reformulate the bill so that it does not violate those interests. Conversely, if the Court does not recognise the harmful nature of the bill, it is returned to the House for a second vote, after which it cannot be vetoed in this way (Karić 2016, p. 67 ff).

However, the veto that may be exercised by members of the Presidency is different, as they protect not the vital interests of the constituent peoples but rather those of the entities in which they were elected. According to the Constitution (Article V), the Presidency must take certain decisions concerning specific matters unanimously. If such consensus is not reached, however, the decision may be taken by a simple majority in a second vote, namely with the favourable vote of two out of three members of the Presidency. If the dissenting member considers that the majority's decision is contrary to the vital interests of their entity may raise a suspensive veto. Once a member of the Presidency has raised a veto on a matter, the National Assembly of Republika Srpska is obliged to express its opinion on the veto, provided that the veto was raised by a member elected in the territory of this entity. Similarly, if the suspensive veto has been invoked by a Bosniak or a Croat, the relevant club within the House of Peoples of the Federation of Bosnia and Herzegovina will express its opinion on the veto. If, within 10 days of the veto being invoked the parliamentary assemblies of the entities recognise, by a two-thirds qualified majority, that the entity's vital interests have been harmed, the Presidency's decision shall automatically be disapplied.[5]

It should also be noted here that the veto is not primarily intended to protect the interests of the entities, as stated in the constitutional provision, but rather to safeguard the interests of the constituent peoples. This is demonstrated by the fact that decisions subject to veto are sent to Entity Assemblies for their opinion on the merits to be sought. However, in the case of the Federation of Bosnia and Herzegovina, only delegates from the House of Peoples who belong to the same constituent people as the member of the Presidency who raised the issue are entitled to express their opinion (Balić et al. 2023, pp. 409–414; Montanari 2019, pp. 11–13).

The judiciary similarly reflects this ethno-federal model. The Constitutional Court of Bosnia and Herzegovina comprises nine judges: four selected by the House of Representatives of the Federation, two by the National Assembly of Republika Srpska and three appointed by the President of the European Court of Human Rights. This composition ensures both internal legitimacy and international oversight, reinforcing the hybrid and transitional nature of the post-conflict federal arrangement (Išerić et al. 2023, pp. 75–81; Montanari 2020, pp. 713–718).

The ethno-territorial model, though initially successful in securing peace and a modicum of stability, has faced sustained criticism for perpetuating ethnic divisions, impeding democratic development and obstructing the emergence of a civic political culture. The European Court of Human Rights, in the landmark *Sejdić and Finci v. Bosnia and Herzegovina* judgment (2009),[6] found the Constitution to be in violation of the European Convention on Human Rights due to the exclusion of non-constituent peoples from eligibility for election to the Presidency and the House of Peoples. Despite international and domestic calls for constitutional reform, the deeply entrenched ethnic veto powers and entity-based interests have hindered substantive change (Bonifati 2020, pp. 1–6; Milanović 2010, p. 1).

Additionally, the requirement for entity representation and the ethno-national key in public administration have contributed to bureaucratic fragmentation and inefficiency. The overlapping authorities between the state, the entities and, in the Federation, the cantons have led to legal uncertainty and administrative redundancy (Mujanović 2020, pp. 6–9).

The ethno-territorial federalism of Bosnia and Herzegovina, as institutionalised by the Dayton Constitution, represents a paradigmatic case of a conflict-resolving federal arrangement grounded in ethnic accommodation and power-sharing (Anderson 2013, p. 164 ff). While it has succeeded in halting open conflict and preserving territorial integrity, its long-term viability as a constitutional order conducive to integration, democratic governance and European integration remains contested. Any reform of this complex structure must carefully balance the need for

[5] Constitution, Article V, para. 2, lett. d.

[6] *Sejdić and Finci v. Bosnia and Herzegovina*, Nos. 27996/06, 34836/06, ECtHR (Grand Chamber), 22 December 2009.

institutional functionality with the imperative of ensuring the collective rights of Bosnia and Herzegovina's constituent peoples, thereby maintaining the delicate peace achieved in Dayton.

4 Power-Sharing System and the Role of International Actors in Bosnia and Herzegovina's Stability

In post-conflict societies characterised by deep ethno-political cleavages, the establishment of a democratic power-sharing system is often deemed an essential mechanism for fostering peace, ensuring political stability and preventing the resurgence of violence (Grewe and Riegner 2011, p. 29 ff). In this way, Bosnia and Herzegovina represents one of the most complex cases of ethnic conflict resolution in Europe, having emerged from the devastating war of 1992–1995 through the Dayton Peace Agreement. The Constitution of Bosnia and Herzegovina introduces a deeply consociational model of governance designed to reduce tensions and ensure equitable representation among the country's three constituent peoples: Bosniaks, Croats and Serbs. This first part of the section explores the role of democratic power-sharing, as constitutionally defined, in reducing ethnic tensions in Bosnia and Herzegovina and examines its benefits and limitations in light of contemporary challenges.

The Constitution of Bosnia and Herzegovina establishes a power-sharing framework rooted in consociational democracy, a theory most prominently associated with political scientist Arend Lijphart. According to Lijphart, power-sharing in divided societies entails the inclusion of major ethnic groups in the decision-making process through grand coalitions, proportionality, mutual vetoes and segmental autonomy (Lijphart 1977, p. 23 ff). These principles are embedded within Bosnia and Herzegovina's constitutional architecture in several key ways.

Firstly, the tripartite Presidency, composed of one Bosniak and one Croat (elected from the Federation of Bosnia and Herzegovina) and one Serb (elected from Republika Srpska), ensures that each constituent people is directly represented at the highest level of executive authority. Secondly, the bicameral Parliamentary Assembly, particularly the House of Peoples, reflects ethnic parity by including equal representation of Bosniaks, Croats and Serbs, thereby institutionalising mutual oversight and consent.

Thirdly, the Council of Ministers—Bosnia and Herzegovina's executive government—is structured to reflect ethnic balance, with each constituent people guaranteed representation in key ministerial posts. Furthermore, the decision-making procedures in legislative bodies are designed to protect vital national interests through the mechanism of the "vital national interest" veto, which allows representatives of each ethnic group to block legislation perceived as threatening their collective rights, as described in the previous section (Balić and Izmirlija 2013, p. 121).

The introduction of these power-sharing mechanisms has played a significant role in preventing a relapse into conflict and maintaining a fragile peace in Bosnia and Herzegovina. By formally recognising the political equality of the three constituent peoples and guaranteeing them participation in all branches of government, the Constitution creates a framework where no single group can dominate the political system unilaterally (Cooley 2020, pp. 1–10).

This inclusive approach has been instrumental in reducing ethnic tensions by offering security and political voice to all groups, thereby deterring unilateralism and fostering interethnic cooperation in state institutions. In this sense, democratic power-sharing has acted as a conflict management tool, facilitating post-war reconciliation and reducing the incentives for secessionist or irredentist politics (Kasapović 2005, p. 7 ff).

Moreover, the Constitutional Court of Bosnia and Herzegovina has played an essential role in interpreting and upholding the principle of equality among constituent peoples. In the landmark decision U-5/98, the Court affirmed that all three groups are constituent peoples throughout the entire territory of Bosnia and Herzegovina, regardless of numerical majority, reinforcing the notion of collective equality and thereby defusing regional and ethnic tensions.

Despite its stabilising function, the democratic power-sharing model in Bosnia and Herzegovina is not without serious limitations. The primary criticism of the existing arrangement is that it institutionalises ethnic divisions, often at the expense of democratic functionality and civic representation. The rigid emphasis on ethnic identity has led to the exclusion of citizens who do not identify as one of the three constituent peoples—referred to as "Others"—from running for key state offices, including the Presidency and the House of Peoples.

Furthermore, the system of ethnic vetoes and entity-based voting in the House of Representatives often leads to political deadlock and policy paralysis, impeding the effective functioning of state institutions. This has had negative repercussions for governance, economic development and European integration efforts. In practice, democratic power-sharing has sometimes served to entrench ethnic elites and obstruct much-needed structural reforms (Zdebo 2023, p. 172 ff).

While the power-sharing model has been vital in maintaining peace, a growing consensus exists—among domestic actors, international organisations and civil society—that constitutional reform is necessary to transition towards a more functional, civic-oriented democracy. Such reform should aim to preserve the collective rights of constituent peoples while simultaneously expanding individual rights and political participation for all citizens (Bieber 2006, p. 20).

This could be achieved through the introduction of non-ethnic quotas, the enhancement of the role of civil society in public affairs and the reform of electoral laws to allow for cross-ethnic political representation. Additionally, the full implementation of rulings by the European Court of Human Rights would be a step towards harmonising Bosnia and Herzegovina's constitutional system with European standards and values (Romaniello 2016, pp. 81–94).

The democratic power-sharing system embedded in the Constitution of Bosnia and Herzegovina has played an indispensable role in reducing ethnic tensions and maintaining post-war stability. It has succeeded in ensuring representation and safeguarding the rights of the country's three constituent peoples (Keil 2012, p. 206 ff). However, its long-term effectiveness is undermined by its rigid ethnic structures, discriminatory provisions and institutional inefficiencies (Perry 2002, p. 3). Moving forward, constitutional reform that balances group rights with individual freedoms is essential to building a more inclusive, democratic and unified Bosnia and Herzegovina. Such reform must not abandon the principles of power-sharing but must modernise them to align with the broader democratic aspirations of all citizens of the country (Marko 2006, p. 209).

Since the signing of the Dayton Peace Agreement in 1995, Bosnia and Herzegovina has been under the continuous and structured oversight of international actors, whose primary objective has been to safeguard the country's territorial integrity, preserve peace and guide the transition towards democratic governance and Euro-Atlantic integration. Among these actors, the Office of the High Representative (OHR) has occupied a central and unique position, functioning as the principal authority for civilian implementation of the DPA. Alongside the OHR, the European Union (EU), the Organization for Security and Co-operation in Europe (OSCE), the North Atlantic Treaty Organization (NATO) and the United Nations have played vital roles in supporting state building, monitoring compliance and countering secessionist tendencies that threaten the fragile post-conflict order.

This second part of the present section analyses the evolving role of international actors, with particular emphasis on the OHR, in responding to separatist pressures and fostering long-term stability in BiH. It assesses the legal foundations, practical interventions, challenges and critiques associated with the international presence in BiH's domestic affairs.

The Office of the High Representative was established under Annex 10 of the Dayton Peace Agreement, with a mandate to oversee the implementation of the civilian aspects of the peace settlement. The OHR derives its legitimacy from both the Peace Agreement and the endorsement of the international community, notably the United Nations Security Council and the Peace Implementation Council (PIC) (Beglerović 2022, pp. 403–406).

The 1997 Bonn PIC Conference significantly expanded the powers of the OHR, granting it "Bonn powers": a suite of extraordinary competencies that include the authority to impose laws, amend constitutional provisions and dismiss elected or appointed officials who obstruct the peace process. These powers, though never codified in a single legal instrument, have enabled the High Representative to act decisively in circumstances where domestic consensus is absent or threatened by ethnic nationalism (Banning 2014, p. 289 ff). In particular, the OHR may adopt legislative acts valid for the legal system of Bosnia and Herzegovina by its own decision, in areas where internal legislative power is unable to make decisions due to internal conflicts or a lack of will regarding issues that are sensitive yet necessary for the country.

The OHR has played a critical role in reinforcing the sovereignty of the State of Bosnia and Herzegovina, counteracting centrifugal forces emanating from entity-level political structures, especially those advocating secession or undermining central institutions. The High Representative has also functioned as a guardian of the Dayton constitutional order and a mediator in resolving inter-ethnic disputes. In fact, the OHR has the power to dismiss any public official, including those who have been elected, if their behaviour contravenes the principles of the peace agreement (Dijkstra and Raadschelders 2022, pp. 297–304).

Since its inception, the OHR has been at the forefront of addressing separatist rhetoric and actions, particularly from political actors in the Republika Srpska (RS), where calls for independence or referenda challenging the authority of the state have periodically escalated. The High Representative has employed a range of instruments to counter these challenges (Ker-Lindsay 2016, p. 13 ff).

The OHR has used its Bonn powers to remove individuals from office for activities deemed contrary to the peace agreement or threatening to the constitutional order. For instance, numerous officials—at both entity and municipal levels—have been dismissed for obstructing the return of refugees, promoting ethnic intolerance or questioning Bosnia and Herzegovina's sovereignty.

To strengthen the functionality of state institutions and dilute the impact of separatist strategies, the OHR has imposed key state-level legislation. These include laws on state border service, public broadcasting, a unified army and a single judiciary, among others. These measures have been instrumental in consolidating Bosnia and Herzegovina's institutions and curbing the autonomy of entity-level actors to operate unilaterally.

The OHR has worked in conjunction with the Constitutional Court of Bosnia and Herzegovina and international legal experts to ensure the supremacy of the state Constitution and the rule of law. In cases where entity-level legislation conflicts with the Dayton framework, the OHR has often acted to prevent the erosion of the state's authority.

While the OHR has been the most visible and interventionist international actor, it has operated within a broader framework of multilateral engagement.

The EU has supported institutional reform and integration efforts through the Stabilization and Association Process (SAP). It has used conditionality as a tool to encourage political cooperation and discourage ethno-nationalist obstruction (Venneri 2007). However, its influence has been constrained by the limited political consensus within BiH and by its reluctance to assume the assertive role previously played by the OHR.

NATO's initial military stabilisation mission, followed by the EU's Operation Althea under the European Union Force (EUFOR), has ensured a secure environment conducive to civil reconstruction. EUFOR continues to maintain deterrence against the use of force by nationalist elements and supports law enforcement when required (Boštjančič Pulko et al. 2016, p. 1 ff).

The OSCE has played a critical role in promoting democratic governance, human rights and electoral reform. The United Nations, while less directly engaged in daily political oversight, has supported institutional capacity building and provided political legitimacy to international actions through Security Council resolutions.

The international administration in Bosnia and Herzegovina has not been without criticism. Several key concerns have emerged.

The democratic legitimacy of international actors within Bosnia and Herzegovina's constitutional order is a widely debated topic. The use of the Bonn powers, particularly the imposition of laws and the dismissal of officials without judicial recourse, has raised concerns about the democratic deficit in the country's governance model (Kulanić 2011, pp. 172–175).

Also, the prolonged international tutelage has arguably fostered political dependency among domestic actors and discouraged the development of local accountability mechanisms.

As international attention has shifted elsewhere and calls for the closure of the OHR have grown, its capacity to intervene decisively has diminished, even as nationalist rhetoric has resurged.

Despite these challenges, many scholars and policymakers argue that the OHR remains a necessary safeguard, particularly given the persistent threats of entity-level secession, the fragility of state institutions and the unfinished nature of constitutional reform.

International actors, and particularly the Office of the High Representative, have been indispensable in managing Bosnia and Herzegovina's transition from war to peace. By upholding the Dayton constitutional framework, countering separatist movements and fostering institutional development, they have preserved the integrity of the state against considerable odds (Gilbert 2022, p. 39 ff).

Nevertheless, the current moment demands a recalibration of this role: moving from externally enforced stability to internally generated legitimacy and resilience. While the long-term goal must be full sovereignty and functional democracy for BiH, the cautious and conditional withdrawal of international oversight should be predicated on genuine and irreversible reforms, especially in the areas of rule of law, minority protection and constitutional equality (Babuna 2014, p. 3 ff).

The continued involvement of the OHR and international partners remains essential until Bosnia and Herzegovina is sufficiently stable, unified and democratic to assume full responsibility for its governance and future trajectory within the European family of nations.

5 Conclusions: Ethno-Federalism, Power-Sharing and Secession in Bosnia and Herzegovina

The post-conflict political architecture of Bosnia and Herzegovina represents a paradigmatic case of institutional engineering in a deeply divided society. Rooted in the 1995 Dayton Peace Agreement and codified in the Constitution of Bosnia and Herzegovina, the country's governance framework is built upon three interdependent pillars: ethno-federalism, consociational power-sharing and a persistent threat of secessionist rhetoric and manoeuvring, particularly emanating from Republika Srpska. While each of these elements individually reflects international efforts to balance peace, representation and autonomy, their intersection has generated a fragile equilibrium that has proven difficult to reform and is highly susceptible to political deadlock and centrifugal pressures (Keil 2012, pp. 214–217).

The federal structure of Bosnia and Herzegovina is, by design, an ethno-territorial arrangement. The two entities—the Federation of Bosnia and Herzegovina and Republika Srpska—reflect not merely administrative divisions but also the legacy of wartime territorial consolidation along ethnic lines. The Federation itself is subdivided into ten cantons, often delineated by ethnic majorities, while the Brčko District represents a neutral, jointly administered area to prevent further entrenchment of territorial claims.

This ethno-federalism was intended to appease nationalist demands and provide a degree of autonomy to major ethnic groups. However, in practice, it has institutionalised ethnic exclusivity and produced a fragmented polity in which ethnicity is the principal axis of political identity, legal representation and public administration. The result is an uneven federation with significant asymmetry between the relatively centralised Republika Srpska and the internally fragmented Federation (Trnka 2009, p. 55).

The consociational elements of Bosnia and Herzegovina's constitutional order—tripartite Presidency, parity in the House of Peoples, ethnic quotas in public institutions and the "vital national interest" veto—are manifestations of a power-sharing ethos designed to secure peace and inclusivity in the aftermath of genocide and ethnic cleansing. These mechanisms have been instrumental in stabilising the country and preventing the reoccurrence of violence. They ensure that no single ethnic group can unilaterally dominate state institutions and that major decisions necessitate interethnic cooperation, if not consensus.

Yet the success of power-sharing in maintaining peace must be weighed against its cost to democratic functionality and societal integration. The rigid ethnic structuring of the state has excluded "Others" (citizens not identifying as Bosniak, Croat or Serb) from key political offices, as highlighted in judgments by the European Court of Human Rights. Moreover, ethnic veto powers have enabled minority obstructionism, creating chronic legislative paralysis and eroding citizens' trust in state institutions (Begić and Delić 2013, p. 463).

Perhaps the most enduring and destabilising aspect of Bosnia and Herzegovina's political system is the persistent threat of secession. While the Dayton Agreement affirmed the sovereignty and territorial integrity of BiH, it simultaneously empowered sub-state units with significant autonomy. The ambiguity of this arrangement, especially in the absence of a shared national identity and amidst ongoing nationalist agitation, has allowed secessionist narratives to flourish.

Leaders in Republika Srpska have periodically issued calls for referenda on independence, threatened withdrawal from state-level institutions and passed legislation aimed at restoring entity competencies or undermining state sovereignty. These moves, although not legally sanctioned, exploit the decentralised nature of the state and the ethnic legitimacy conferred by the Dayton framework. Such actions not only threaten the cohesion of the state but also place BiH at odds with its constitutional commitments, international obligations and long-term aspirations for European integration (Savanović et al. 2020, p. 99 ff).

In particular, the current political crisis in Bosnia and Herzegovina, marked by the secessionist ambitions of Republika Srpska, represents the most significant challenge to the country's constitutional order and territorial integrity since the 1995 Dayton Peace Agreement. At the centre of this turmoil is Milorad Dodik, the President of the Republika Srpska entity, whose actions have escalated tensions and raised concerns both domestically and internationally. In early 2025, Dodik was convicted by the Court of Bosnia and Herzegovina for defying the authority of the High Representative, resulting in a 1-year prison sentence and a 6-year ban from holding public office. Rather than complying with the Court's decision, Dodik and the Republika Srpska leadership intensified their separatist agenda. This included enacting laws that reject the jurisdiction of Bosnia and Herzegovina's central judiciary and police within Republika Srpska, effectively establishing a parallel legal and institutional framework. Furthermore, the National Assembly of this entity adopted a new constitutional project that lays the groundwork for secession, granting the entity the authority to form its own army and judiciary (Sahadžić 2025; Fella 2024, pp. 12–18).

These unilateral actions directly contravene the Dayton Accords, which prohibit the independence of any entity within Bosnia and Herzegovina. The High Representative, Christian Schmidt, has warned that such secessionist attempts threaten the country's territorial integrity and will not be tolerated. In response to the escalating crisis, NATO and EUFOR have expressed readiness to prevent any destabilisation of Bosnia and Herzegovina, emphasising their commitment to maintaining peace and security in the region.

The secessionist drive of Republika Srpska poses a significant threat not only to the stability of Bosnia and Herzegovina but also to the broader Balkan region. It undermines the country's aspirations for European integration and risks reigniting ethnic tensions that could lead to renewed conflict. To safeguard the peace and unity achieved over the past three decades, it is imperative for the international community to take decisive action. This includes enforcing the Dayton Accords, supporting Bosnia and Herzegovina's central institutions and countering external influences that seek to destabilise the region (Davidović and Sahadžić 2025).

Taken together, the triad of ethno-federalism, power-sharing and secessionist threats constitutes a deeply interdependent and self-reinforcing system. Ethno-federalism provides the territorial and institutional infrastructure for ethnic autonomy, power-sharing ensures ethnic representation but often blocks reform, and secessionist rhetoric leverages both structures to assert nationalist agendas. This feedback loop has contributed to a systemic stalemate that inhibits not only constitutional reform but also economic development, social cohesion and progress towards Euro-Atlantic integration.

Moreover, international actors, while instrumental in maintaining peace, have not yet succeeded in facilitating a transition from this conflict-management model to a functional, inclusive and civic-oriented democracy. The Office of the High Representative, though empowered to intervene decisively, has faced growing resistance and declining legitimacy, while the European Union's policy of conditionality has been weakened by internal divisions and enlargement fatigue (Woelk 2016, p. 33).

Resolving this stalemate requires a nuanced and gradual rethinking of Bosnia and Herzegovina's constitutional order. Any reform must recognise the need to balance collective rights with individual freedoms, preserve ethnic representation while expanding civic participation and reinforce state sovereignty without denying cultural and political pluralism. Ethno-federalism cannot be dismantled overnight, but it can be transformed to allow for more integrative policies, cross-ethnic political platforms and functional governance. Power-sharing should evolve from ethnic quotas to mechanisms based on inclusive deliberation and democratic merit. Secessionist agendas must be disincentivised not only through legal prohibitions but also through incentives for cooperation, economic interdependence and shared governance (Kingsbury 2021, pp. 9–21).

Ultimately, the experience of Bosnia and Herzegovina offers a cautionary tale about the long-term consequences of institutionalising ethnicity in post-conflict governance. While such arrangements may be necessary to end hostilities and guarantee representation, they must not become permanent barriers to unity, democracy and progress. The challenge facing Bosnia and Herzegovina today is not merely to preserve peace but also to transcend the logic of war that continues to shape its institutions.

References

Ademović N, Marko J, Marković G (2012) Ustavno Pravo Bosne i Hercegovine. Konrad Adenauer Stiftung, Sarajevo

Anderson LD (2013) Federal solution to ethnic problems. Accommodating Diversity. Routledge, London

Anderson AB (2018) Overview: the diversity and complexity of separatist movements in Europe. J Ethnopolit Minor Issues Europe 17(3):4–44

Babuna A (2014) European Integration, Bosnia-Herzegovina and Stability, in the Western Balkans: a new strategy. Perceptions XIX(2):1–32

Balić L, Izmirlija M (2013) Consociation in Bosnia and Herzegovina: practical implementation of the theoretical principles. South-East Eur J Polit Sci I(3):121–134

Balić L, Woelk J, Vlaški B (2023) Veto rights. In: Sahadžić M, Banović D, Barbarić D, Marković G (eds) Citizens, Constitution, Europe: glossary of essential constitutional concepts in BiH. Univerzitet u Sarajevu, Sarajevo, pp 409–414

Banning T (2014) The 'Bonn Powers' of the high representative in Bosnia Herzegovina: tracing a legal figment. Goettingen J Int Law 6(2):259–302

Begić Z, Delić Z (2013) Constituency of peoples in the constitutional system of Bosnia and Herzegovina: chasing fair solutions. ICON-S 11(2):447–465

Beglerović N (2022) The role, expectations and challenges of high representative in Bosnia and Herzegovina. Polit Central Europe 18(3):397–432

Bieber F (2006) After Dayton, Dayton? The evolution of an unpopular peace. Ethnopolitics 5(1):15–31

Bonifati L (2020) Molto rumore per nulla? Dieci anni dalla sentenza Sejdić-Finci. Forum di Quaderni costituzionali 1:59–70

Boštjančič Pulko I, Muherina M, Pejič N (2016) Analysing the effectiveness of EUFOR Althea operation in Bosnia and Herzegovina. Eur Perspect J Eur Perspect Western Balkans 8(1):14–39

Burg SL, Shoup PS (2000) The war in Bosnia-Herzegovina: ethnic conflict and international intervention. Routledge, London

Closa C (2016) Secession from a Member State and EU Membership: the view from the Union. Eur Const Law Rev 12:240–264

Constitutional Court of Bosnia and Herzegovina, decision U-5/98 III Partial Decision, 29 January 2000

Cooley L (2020) Consociationalism and the politics of the census in Bosnia and Herzegovina and Northern Ireland. Political Geography

Davidović M, Sahadžić M (2025) The tipping point in BiH's constitutional struggle: prohibition from Holding Office for the President of the Republika Srpska. VerfBlog

Dijkstra GSA, Raadschelders JCN (2022) The high representative in Bosnia and Herzegovina: the unusual institutional arrangement of a non-authoritarian, yet controlled, democracy. World Aff 185(2):285–311

Duerr GME (2015) Secessionism and the European Union The Future of Flanders, Scotland, and Catalonia. Rowman & Littlefield, Lanham

Fella S (2024) Bosnia and Herzegovina: secessionism in the Republika Srpska. House of Commons. Library, London

Gaeta P (1996) Symposium: The Dayton Agreements: a breakthrough for peace and justice? The Dayton Agreements and International Law. Eur J Int Law 7:147–163

Gilbert AC (2022) International intervention and the problem of legitimacy encounters in postwar Bosnia-Herzegovina. Cornell University Press, Ithaca

Glenny M (2017) The Balkans, 1804-2012: Nationalism, War and the Great Powers di Misha. Granata Books, London

Góra S (2020) Separatism in the Balkans. Annales Universitis Mariae Curie-Sklodowska, Lublin-Polonia XXVII(2):29–46

Greenberg MC, McGuinness ME (2000) From Lisbon to Dayton: International Mediation and the Bosnia Crisis. Words over War: Mediation and Arbitration to Prevent Deadly Conflict, pp 35–75

Grewe C, Riegner M (2011) Internationalized constitutionalism in ethnically divided societies: Bosnia-Herzegovina and Kosovo Compared. In: von Bogdandy A, Wolfrum R (eds) Max Planck Yearbook of United Nations Law, vol 15, pp 1–64

Holbrooke R (1999) To end a war. The Modern Library, New York

Išerić H, Sahadžić M, Banović D (2023) The Judiciary of Bosnia and Herzegovina. In: Sahadžić M, Banović D, Barbarić D, Marković G (eds) Citizens, Constitution, Europe: glossary of essential constitutional concepts in BiH. Univerzitet u Sarajevu, Sarajevo, pp 313–320

Karić M (2016) Consociational democracy in theory and practice: the case of Post-war Bosnia and Herzegovina. International University of Sarajevo, Sarajevo

Kasapović M (2005) Bosnia and Herzegovina: consociational or liberal democracy? Politička misao XLII(5):3–30

Keil S (2012) Federalism as a tool of conflict-resolution: the case of Bosnia and Herzegovina. L'Europe en formation 363:205–218

Keil S (2013) Multinational Federalism in Bosnia and Herzegovina. Routledge, London

Ker-Lindsay J (2016) The hollow threat of secession in Bosnia and Herzegovina: legal and political impediments to a unilateral declaration of independence by Republika Srpska. Research on South Eastern Europe, London

Kingsbury D (2021) Separatism and the State. Routledge, London

Kochenov D, Van Den Brink M (2016) Secessions from EU Member States: the imperative of Union's neutrality. Eur Pap 1(1):67–92

Kostov C (ed) (2020) Separatism and regionalism in Modern Europe. Logos Verlag, Berlin

Kulanić A (2011) International political actors and state-building process in Bosnia-Herzegovina. Epiphany-J Transdiscip Stud 4(1):167–184

Lijphart A (1977) Democracy in plural societies. Yale University Press, New Haven

Malcolm N (2002) Bosnia: a short history. Pan Books, London

Margiotta C (2009) L'ultimo diritto. Profili storici e teorici della secessione. Il Mulino, Bologna

Marko J (2006) Constitutional Reform in Bosnia and Herzegovina 2005-06. Eur Yearb Minor Issues Online 5(1):207–218

Meškić Z, Pivić N (2011) Federalism in Bosnia and Herzegovina. ICI-J 5(4):597–617

Milanović M (2010) Sejdic and Finci v. Bosnia and Herzegovina. Int Leg Mater 49(2):281–320

Montanari L (2019) La complessa soluzione istituzionale adottata in Bosnia ed Erzegovina: finalità ed effetti nel passare del tempo. Eur Divers Autonomy Pap 2:1–27
Montanari L (2020) The use of comparative and international law by the Constitutional Court of Bosnia and Herzegovina. In: Ferrari GF (ed) Judicial cosmopolitism. the use of foreign law in contemporary constitutional systems. Brill, Leiden, pp 708–744
Mujanović J (2020) Bosnia and Herzegovina's eroding Dayton constitutional order. J Labour Soc Aff Eastern Europe 2:1–19
O'Brien J (2010) The Dayton Constitution of Bosnia and Herzegovina. In: Miller L, Aucoin L (eds) Framing the state in times of transition. United States Institute of Peace Press, Wasghington DC, pp 332–449
Oxford English Dictionary, 2013
Pejanović M (2023) The Statehood of Bosnia and Herzegovina in the 20th and 21st Centuries. University Press, Sarajevo
Perry V (2002) Constitutional reform and the 'Sprit' of Bosnia and Herzegovina. Eur Centre Minor Issues 7:1–14
Pirjevec J (2014) Le guerre jugoslave 1991-1999. Einaudi, Torino
Romaniello M (2016) Ethnic federalism in question: the case of Bosnia and Herzegovina. In: Benedizione L, Scotti VR (eds) Proceedings of the Conference, Twenty years after Dayton. The Constitutional Transition of Bosnia and Herzegovina. LUIS Academy, Rome, pp 81–94
Sahadžić M (2025) Constitutional Standoff in Bosnia and Herzegovina: drama in four acts (so far). Centre for Constitutional Change
Šarčević E (2009) Dejtonski Ustav: Karakteristike i karakteristični problem. Konrad Adenauer Stiftung, Sarajevo
Savanović A, Vranješ A, Vranješ N, Budimir Z (2020) Izvori, geneza i priroda secesionističke retorike u Republici Srposkoj. Politička misao 57(1):93–126
Sejdić and Finci v. Bosnia and Herzegovina, Nos. 27996/06, 34836/06, ECtHR (Grand Chamber), 22 December 2009
Shrader CR (2003) The Muslim-Croat Civil War in Central Bosnia A Military History, 1992–1994
Silber L, Little A (1997) The Death of Yugoslavia. Penguin, London
Slye R (1996) The Dayton Peace Agreement: constitutionalism and ethnicity. Yale J Int Law 21:459–473
Steiner C, Ademović N (2010) Constitution of Bosnia and Herzegovina. Commentary. Konrad Adenauer Shtiftung, Sarajevo
Texas A&M University Press, College Station
Trnka K (2009) Specificities of the constitutional arrangement of Bosnia and Herzegovina. Revus-J Const Theory Philos Law 11:45–47
Venneri G (2007) Modelling States from Brussels? A critical assessment of the EU-driven state-building of Bosnia and Herzegovina. Cyprus Center Eur Int Aff 7:1–42
Vranić I (2013) The International Community's Peace Plans in Croatia and Bosnia and Herzegovina 1991-1995. Croat Stud Rev 9:17–72
Weller M (1996) Peace-keeping and peace-enforcement in the Republic of Bosnia and Herzegovina. Max-Planck-Institut für ausländisches öffentliches Recht und Völkerrecht, pp 70–177
Woelk J (2008) La Transizione costituzionale della Bosna ed Erzegovina. Dall'ordinamento imposto allo Stato multinazionale sostenibile? CEDAM, Padova
Woelk J (2016) The constitutional transition of Bosnia and Herzegovina between nationalism and European conditionality. In: Benedizione L, Scotti VR (eds) Twenty years after Dayton. The constitutional transition of Bosnia and Herzegovina. LUISS Academy, Rome, pp 21–48
Yee S (1996) The new constitution of Bosnia and Herzegovina. Eur J Int Law 7:176–1992
Zdebo A (2023) Doomed to fail? Rebound effect and conflict management problems in Bosnia and Herzegovina. Polska Akademia Umiętności XXXII(1):169–184

The Right of Withdrawal from the European Union

Federico Savastano

Abstract This chapter examines how the once-unthinkable idea of a Member State leaving the European Union evolved into a concrete legal option through Article 50 of the Treaty on European Union (TEU). It first links the politicisation of withdrawal to the eurozone crisis, Grexit debates and the loss of the Union's attractiveness, before reconstructing the pre-Lisbon framework based on general international law and the Vienna Convention, particularly the *rebus sic stantibus* clause. The chapter then traces the political and doctrinal path from early federalist projects to the unilateral withdrawal clause and analyses in detail the Lisbon procedure, highlighting its legal uncertainties and potential strategic uses. Drawing on federal experiences and the Canadian Supreme Court's opinion on Québec, withdrawal is read as a "proceduralised secession" requiring negotiation and agreement. The conclusion argues that, although exit is legally possible today, the Union's deep constitutional embeddedness makes a complete disentangling from its legal and political order virtually impossible.

1 Leaving Europe: From a Theoretical Case to a Plausible Hypothesis

For decades, the hypothesis that a State might wish to leave the common European home was considered so unrealistic that it was never taken into account, either theoretically or legally.

The *in progress* construction of the European Union and its gradual transformation from an international to a supranational organisation meant that, for many years, the issue of withdrawal from the Union was not included in the founding Treaties—a gap that was filled only with the Treaty of Lisbon, after having first been proposed a few years earlier in the never-ratified Constitutional Treaty of 2004.

F. Savastano (✉)
Department of Political Sciences, Sapienza University of Rome, Rome, Italy
e-mail: federico.savastano@uniroma1.it

F. Savastano et al. (eds.), *Between Asymmetry and Secession*,
https://doi.org/10.1007/978-3-032-29603-0_21

The fact that this normative vacuum was addressed only after nearly 50 years from the signing of the Treaty of Rome was due not to a belated awareness of the problem but rather to two substantive reasons.

First was the legal nature of the Community, which until the signing of the Single European Act was markedly different from its current form.

Second, during the Union's expansion phase—which led to the inclusion of 28 Member States—Europe represented an immense vehicle for the dissemination of rights and economic opportunities, making the very idea of a State's withdrawal hardly conceivable.

Indeed, which government would have renounced the "four freedoms" and the opportunity to access a vast new market?

More than the normative intervention introduced by the Lisbon Treaty, it was the economic and financial crisis that rendered the hypothesis of withdrawal by certain Member States not merely a surreal academic exercise but also a concrete eventuality—albeit one with largely unpredictable consequences.

This became apparent when the term *Grexit* began to circulate in journalistic discourse, referring to the crisis in relations between Greece and the European Union.

The impact of the crisis on the stability of the European Union manifested itself in three main ways.

First, it fuelled *Euroscepticism* and, thus, strengthened those political movements that identified Europe as the scapegoat for national economic difficulties. All national governments of the Member States faced the electoral rise of Eurosceptic parties and reacted by changing their own stance towards Brussels in an attempt to stem the internal loss of votes that threatened their political stability. Eurosceptic movements thus brought to the forefront of public debate in all Member States the question of the possibility of leaving the European Union—a topic that had previously been entirely marginal and confined to a few nationalist circles.

Second, it is well known that Europe's response to the crisis was based on austerity policies, highly unpopular and deeply felt in many Member States. One reaction to these measures was the revival of the theory of *competitive devaluation*, according to which a State that decided to leave the Union could reap significant economic benefits by devaluing its own currency, thereby gaining a competitive advantage over the slow and cumbersome European bloc.

The third and undoubtedly most significant consequence of the crisis was that it represented the first true test of the Union's effectiveness. Never before in its history had the Community—and later the Union—been confronted with such a complex situation. The severe economic difficulties faced by Member States put the credibility of European institutions to a harsh test, precisely at a time when they were expected to demonstrate maximum efficiency (Caravita 2012). The European project, after all, was born to provide common solutions to problems too great for individual States to tackle alone; if it proves incapable of doing so, it risks losing its very raison d'être.

The loss of the Union's attractiveness is partly illustrated by the recent case of Iceland—a candidate country for accession that, after applying in 2009, obtaining official candidate status in 2010, and having already closed 11 of the 35 negotiation chapters of the *acquis communautaire*, decided to suspend negotiations and withdraw its application for membership, thereby definitively renouncing accession to the Union.

This case closely resembles that of Norway: the Scandinavian State submitted an application for membership three times and, on two occasions—in 1972 and 1994—even signed the Treaty of Accession, only to withdraw following the negative outcome of the respective confirmatory referendums.

As mentioned earlier, the first *borderline* situation that seriously drew attention to the issue of withdrawal was that of Greece—a country on the brink of economic and financial collapse and default. Athens faced dramatic moments, caught between its debts to the International Monetary Fund, negotiations with European institutions and other Member States, and the looming risk of being unable to pay public employees' salaries. The harsh austerity period that ensued led to the spread—initially among right-wing Greek parties such as *Golden Dawn*—of the belief that Greece could perform better outside the Union by returning to the old drachma and freely devaluing it. This possibility was even contemplated at the time by the Tsipras government, though it was ultimately abandoned thanks to the agreement reached with Brussels and Frankfurt (Triulzi 2015; Grasso 2015).

As for precedents, prior to Brexit, there had been no genuine cases of withdrawal from the Union. However, three episodes may be mentioned in which certain territories originally subject to the Treaty of Rome altered their status and ceased to be covered by the Treaties.

The first concerns Algeria, which at the time of the establishment of the European Economic Community (EEC) was an integral part of French territory. In 1962, Algeria declared its independence from France and thereby automatically exited the Community system.

A completely unique case is that of Greenland, which became part of the Community following Denmark's accession in 1973. Pursuant to a referendum held in 1979 and greater autonomy granted by the Copenhagen government, Greenland left the EEC in 1985 without declaring independence from Denmark, which remains a Member State. To formalise the withdrawal, the *Treaty on Greenland* was adopted, amending the founding Treaties to exclude the application of Community law to Greenland's territory and establishing a special relationship akin to that applied to French overseas territories.

Finally, as of 1 January 2012, the Council of the Union modified the status of Saint Barthélemy, a French overseas collectivity, which had requested exemption from European rules due to its geographical remoteness and its small, tourism-based economy.

While these episodes must be duly reported and considered, they cannot be regarded as precedents of genuine withdrawals, since in none of them did a signatory State of the founding (or accession) Treaties formally request or declare its intention to leave the Union.

2 The Unlimited Duration of the Treaties and Withdrawal Under International Law

Before the Treaty of Lisbon introduced Article 50 of the Treaty on European Union (TEU), academic doctrine was divided between two opposing views: the first maintained that withdrawal from the Treaties was legally impossible; the second traced the issue back to the norms of general international law.

Both the Treaty on European Union (Article 53) and the Treaty on the Functioning of the European Union (Article 356) expressly provide that the Treaties are concluded for an *unlimited duration*. These provisions, taken together with the "definitive" limitation of State sovereignty in favour of the European legal order, were interpreted as evidence of the irreversible nature of the process of integration, thereby rendering any withdrawal by a Member State legally impossible (Weiler 1985).

The fact that even the preparatory works of the 1957 Treaty of Rome contained no reference to the possibility of withdrawal further reinforced this interpretation (Di Rienzo 2012).

This view, however, was challenged by several constitutional courts of the Member States,[1] which repeatedly emphasised the notion of a *transfer of competences* rather than a *renunciation of sovereignty*.[2] Consequently, they affirmed the principle that, by virtue of its inherent sovereignty, a State must retain the right to withdraw (Nicotra 2003).

Another line of scholarly thought held that in the absence of explicit provisions, the rules applicable to a potential withdrawal by a Member State were to be found, in general, in international law and, in particular, in the 1969 Vienna Convention on the Law of Treaties, whose Part V deals specifically with the *invalidity, termination and suspension* of treaties (Tesauro 2012).

Customary international norms such as *desuetude* or *contrary custom* have never been considered applicable to the European case, nor do the Treaties contain final terms or express or implied *resolutive conditions*.

With regard to withdrawal, the Vienna Convention distinguishes between two situations: (a) cases in which treaties include explicit clauses of denunciation or withdrawal and (b) cases in which the treaties are silent on the matter.

Two provisions are particularly relevant in this context (Rieder 2013). First, Article 54 of the Convention provides that the termination of a treaty or the withdrawal of a party may take place either (a) in conformity with the provisions of the

[1] Particularly relevant in this context are the decisions of the German Federal Constitutional Court (Bundesverfassungsgericht)—notably *Solange I* (*BVerfGE* 37, 271, 29 May 1974), *Solange II* (*BVerfGE* 73, 339, 22 October 1986), the *Maastricht* judgment (*BVerfGE* 89, 155, 12 October 1993), the *Bananenmarkt* case (*BVerfGE* 102, 147, 7 June 2000), and, of course, the *Lisbon* judgment (*BVerfGE* 123, 267, 30 June 2009).

[2] Of particular interest on this subject is the distinction between "shared sovereignty" and "pooled sovereignty" (Fabbrini 2015).

treaty itself or (b) at any time, by consent of all the parties after consultation with the other contracting States. Sub-paragraph a, concerning explicit clauses, is the one that applies to the European Union following the entry into force of the Lisbon Treaty; sub-paragraph b refers instead to a consensual mechanism of termination.

Article 56, by contrast, governs cases in which a treaty contains no provisions regarding termination, denunciation, or withdrawal. Paragraph 1 establishes a general rule against the unilateral denunciation of treaties, stating that such a treaty cannot be subject to denunciation or withdrawal except in two situations: (a) where it is established that the parties intended to admit the possibility of denunciation or withdrawal or (b) where a right of denunciation or withdrawal may be implied from the nature of the treaty (Christakis 2011).

Paragraph 2 further provides that a withdrawing State must notify the other parties of its intention at least 12 months in advance.

As to the causes of termination, international law recognises six: abrogation (Article 59)—the conclusion of a subsequent agreement between the same parties containing provisions incompatible with those of the earlier treaty; extinction of the subject—where one of the contracting parties ceases to exist; impossibility of performance (Article 61)—arising from the disappearance or destruction of the object of the treaty; material breach (Article 60)—where one party fails to fulfil its obligations; fundamental change of circumstances (Article 62); and renunciation—where a party waives a right under a treaty that confers only advantages and no obligations.

A further cause of termination is contained in Article 64, which provides that if a new *peremptory norm of general international law (jus cogens)* emerges and conflicts with an existing treaty, the latter becomes void and terminates *ex nunc*.

Among these causes, the one most relevant to the European context is the fundamental change of circumstances, traditionally known under international law as the *clausula rebus sic stantibus*.

Under Article 62 of the Convention, the parties may invoke a fundamental change of circumstances as a ground for terminating, withdrawing from, or suspending the operation of a treaty.

The Convention, however, does not leave the notion of "circumstances" undefined. Article 62(1) precisely sets out the conditions under which the clause may be invoked: only those circumstances that constituted an essential basis of the parties' consent to be bound by the treaty, and whose alteration has the effect of radically transforming the extent of the obligations still to be performed, may be taken into account.

A European State could therefore, in principle, have withdrawn from the Union by invoking a fundamental change of circumstances that had motivated its signature or accession to the founding Treaties—an economic crisis, for instance, could certainly fall within the scope of this clause.

The applicability of the *rebus sic stantibus* principle—undeniable, in any case, as it forms part of *jus cogens*—has been confirmed by the Court of Justice of the European Union, which has held that the *jus cogens* norms relating to the termination and suspension of treaties on the ground of *rebus sic stantibus* are binding upon the Union's institutions and form part of the Community legal order.[3]

In summary, prior to the entry into force of the Lisbon Treaty, a Member State of the European Union could have declared its unilateral withdrawal only either with the consent of all the other Member States or by invoking an unforeseen and fundamental change of circumstances that had radically affected its ability to comply with its obligations of membership.

A useful parallel can be drawn with the United Nations: the UN Charter does not explicitly provide for a right of withdrawal, and no precedent of withdrawal has ever occurred.[4] International law scholarship generally holds that any withdrawal from the United Nations would be governed by the principles of general international law—in particular, by the *rebus sic stantibus* clause—applicable where a State no longer considers itself able to fulfil the obligations imposed by the UN Charter and participate in the international organisation.

3 The Path Towards the Introduction of a Unilateral Withdrawal Clause

The already mentioned absence—even in the preparatory works of the 1957 Treaty of Rome—of any reference to the possibility of withdrawal from the Community clearly reveals the deliberate intention of the founding fathers not to allow Member States to leave the new organisation or, at least, not to make such a possibility explicit.

The idea of introducing a clause on unilateral withdrawal was first raised during the preparatory works of the Spinelli Draft Treaty. The proposal, presented by the Danish member Jens-Peter Bonde, was immediately opposed by members of Spinelli's *Crocodile Club* and ultimately rejected as being inconsistent with the federalist spirit underpinning their draft Treaty.

A second attempt to formalise the possibility of denunciation of the Treaties occurred with the Herman Report of 1994, the second major project for a federalist reform of the Community. Unlike the Spinelli proposal, the Herman project (Schiffauer 1999) aimed at a comprehensive reorganisation of the Treaties into a single code consolidating the *acquis communautaire* and defining the objectives of the Union. Article 44 of that project concerned the Union's capacity to conclude treaties, and paragraph 7 provided that "the Treaties shall be denounced in accordance with the procedures laid down for their conclusion".

[3] *Case C-162/96 A Racke GmbH & Co v Hauptzollamt Mainz* [1998] ECR I-3655, para 46 (ECJ).

[4] The only case that may be regarded as analogous to a withdrawal is that of Indonesia, which in 1965 unilaterally announced its departure from the United Nations as a form of protest against the election of Malaysia as a non-permanent member of the Security Council. However, Indonesia's "withdrawal" was interpreted merely as a temporary absence since the country resumed participation in the activities of the organisation in September 1966.

A more decisive proposal emerged from the "Penelope Project" of 2002 (Mattera 2003). Article 103 of that draft Treaty—coordinated by François Lamoureux under the direction of President Romano Prodi—explicitly contemplated the possibility of withdrawal from the Union. However, such a right was reserved solely for those Member States unable to adopt subsequent revisions of the Constitutional Treaty. The purpose was, therefore, to allow a State to withdraw in the event of constitutional amendments it could not endorse while remaining closely associated with the Union (Di Rienzo 2012).

A more concrete step towards the introduction of a withdrawal clause came with the Draft Treaty establishing a Constitution for Europe, subsequently taken up by the Treaty establishing a Constitution for Europe. The principal motivation behind the introduction of the withdrawal clause was of a political nature: the work of the Convention coincided with preparations for the major 2004 enlargement to Central and Eastern Europe, and it was the new candidate States, many of them emerging from the experience of the Warsaw Pact—which had admitted neither *de jure* nor *de facto* the possibility of exit—that most strongly advocated the inclusion of such a provision.

The proposal, advanced by Vice President Giuliano Amato, provoked intense debate within the Convention. There was no unanimity regarding the advisability of granting Member States the possibility of leaving the Union nor consensus on the procedural modalities that such a withdrawal should follow.

The text of what was to become Article I-60 of the Constitutional Treaty drew explicitly on the 1969 Vienna Convention on the Law of Treaties, and several alternative options were discussed during the preparatory phase: eliminating the article altogether, thereby abandoning the introduction of any voluntary withdrawal clause; avoiding the establishment of a unilateral right of withdrawal, instead recognising merely a right to *request* withdrawal—thus making departure conditional upon the conclusion of a binding agreement between the Union and the withdrawing State; limiting the right of withdrawal to cases of non-ratification of constitutional amendments (as envisaged in the Herman Report); introducing a period, to be defined between 5 and 20 years after withdrawal, during which the departing State would be precluded from reapplying for membership; creating fixed and limited periods of *self-suspension* for Member States; and establishing the status of "associated member" for States wishing to renounce full membership.

The issue generated considerable division within the Convention, reflecting the broader tension between those favouring a federalist vision of the Union and those adhering to a more intergovernmental approach.

Ultimately, the Convention opted for the inclusion of the withdrawal clause in Article I-60 of the Constitutional Treaty. Under this provision, a Member State could withdraw by notifying the European Council of its intention and by concluding an agreement with the Union, to be approved by the European Parliament and adopted by the Council acting by a qualified majority (72% of the Council members, excluding the withdrawing State, representing at least 65% of the Union's population).

The introduction of the clause was delayed by the failure of the Constitutional Treaty to enter into force, following its rejection during the national ratification process. Nevertheless, the proposal was revived and successfully incorporated into the Treaty of Lisbon, which finally enshrined the right of unilateral withdrawal in European primary law.

4 The Withdrawal Procedure Under the Provisions of the Lisbon Treaty

Article 50 of the Treaty on European Union, as consolidated by the Treaty of Lisbon, formalised and proceduralised the so-called *Eurexit*, establishing, first of all, that the right of withdrawal belongs to every Member State wishing to exercise it in accordance with its own constitutional requirements.

The procedure to be followed by the withdrawing State consists in notifying its decision to the European Council, with which it must define the terms of its separation through an agreement negotiated in accordance with Article 218(3) of the Treaty on the Functioning of the European Union (TFEU).

The Council is the institution entrusted both with receiving the notification from the withdrawing State and with approving the withdrawal agreement. It also decides who shall conduct negotiations with the departing State on behalf of the entire Union. The withdrawal becomes effective either upon the entry into force of the withdrawal agreement or, failing such agreement, 2 years after the notification has been submitted to the European Council by the withdrawing State.

Naturally, the members of the Council and the European Council representing the withdrawing State do not take part in the deliberations or decisions concerning that State. The Council, without the participation of the representatives of the withdrawing State, acts by qualified majority, defined in Article 50(4) TEU as 72% of the members of the Council representing the participating Member States, accounting for at least 65% of the population of the Union.

Article 50 concludes, in paragraph 5, by providing that should a State which has withdrawn from the Union wish to rejoin, it must apply under the ordinary accession procedure set out in Article 49 TEU. There is, therefore, no automatic right of re-entry, and a former Member State seeking readmission would lose any exception, benefit, or *opt-out* previously negotiated during its former membership.

In light of Article 50 TEU and Article 218 TFEU, the process for a consensual separation between the Union and a Member State may be summarised as follows:

The Member State formally notifies the European Council of its intention to withdraw from the Union.

The European Council appoints the Union's negotiator and establishes guidelines on the basis of a recommendation from the Commission, which that negotiator must follow in order to agree on the terms of withdrawal and the framework for future relations between the Union and the withdrawing State.

Once an agreement is reached, it must be approved by the European Parliament and by the Council acting by qualified majority under Article 238(3)(b) TFEU.

The procedure set out in the Treaties undoubtedly simplifies the legal framework for withdrawal compared to the past when the absence of specific provisions required recourse to general international law. However, it still presents several noteworthy issues.

Paragraph 1 of Article 50, as noted, refers to the right of *any* Member State to withdraw "in accordance with its own constitutional requirements". This raises two significant questions.

First, as a provision of the Treaties, the competence to interpret Article 50—and, where necessary, to resolve disputes arising from it—lies with the Court of Justice of the European Union (CJEU). Some scholars have suggested that this could theoretically place the CJEU in the position of assessing whether a Member State has complied with its own constitutional requirements—effectively acting as the ultimate arbiter of domestic constitutional law (Friel 2004). Such a hypothesis, however, is widely regarded as improbable (Wyrozumialy 2012).

Second, particular attention must be paid to those States whose constitutional provisions make explicit reference to membership of the European Union. For instance, the Preamble to the German Basic Law (Grundgesetz) explicitly speaks of "the German people, united in a united Europe". It is thus difficult to conceive how Germany could withdraw from the Union "in accordance with its constitutional requirements" without amending the text of the Basic Law itself.

Of great importance is also the clause providing that—unless otherwise agreed—withdrawal takes effect automatically after 2 years from notification, even in the absence of a concluded agreement. The withdrawing State could, therefore, use this rule strategically during negotiations or as leverage to undermine the process.

Another noteworthy aspect concerns paragraph 4 of Article 50, which excludes representatives of the withdrawing State from the deliberations of the European Council and the Council on matters concerning that State. While politically understandable, the provision makes no mention of Members of the European Parliament (MEPs), who may thus continue to perform their functions even when called to decide on matters relating to the withdrawal process of their own State—including giving consent to the negotiated withdrawal agreement (Hofmeister 2010). Some scholars have viewed the exclusion of the State's representatives from the Council as a violation of the democratic principle of representation while considering the continued participation of the State's MEPs as an unintended compensatory mechanism. However, it seems more accurate to affirm that Members of the European Parliament represent the citizens of the Union as a whole, not their individual Member States, unlike members of national governments represented in the Council.

Further differences can be observed between the withdrawal procedure under Article 50 and the accession procedure under Article 49 TEU. The most significant concerns the role of the Commission: while central to the accession process, it plays a relatively marginal role in withdrawal, being limited to issuing recommendations for the opening of negotiations. During accession, the Commission accompanies and supervises candidate States throughout the negotiation process. In the case of withdrawal, by contrast, Article 218(3) TFEU provides that the Council shall designate the Union's negotiator or head of the negotiating team, without mentioning the Commission.[5]

Other distinctions concern the duration and voting requirements: accession negotiations are open-ended and potentially indefinite, whereas withdrawal negotiations are limited to 2 years. Accession requires unanimity in the Council, while withdrawal, only a qualified majority (Nicolaides 2013).

The withdrawal procedure described in the Treaties applies, in any event, only where the separation between the Union and a Member State occurs consensually or, at least, through responsible use of the legal instruments provided by the TEU. Should negotiations fail or should the withdrawing State refuse to engage in them, the situation would become considerably more complex.

As repeatedly noted, after 2 years from the notification of withdrawal, the separation becomes effective even without an agreement. The question remains whether such withdrawal occurs automatically upon expiry of the 2-year period—as the Brexit experience suggests—and what forms of responsibility may arise for a State disregarding the procedural requirements set forth in the Treaties.

The German Constitutional Court, in one of its landmark decisions on national sovereignty and relations with the European Union—the *Maastricht Urteil*—stated that Germany remains a "Master of the Treaties": it voluntarily limited its sovereignty to further European integration yet retains the power to reclaim it through a contrary act of domestic law. This reasoning has been interpreted by some as support for the possibility of unilateral withdrawal based on the State's ultimate sovereignty vis-à-vis treaty obligations.

However, the principle of *actus contrarius* affirmed by the German Court does not appear compatible either with the norms of Union law or with those of international law. In any case, it must be observed that the withdrawal procedure can apply only where the withdrawing State itself consents to initiate it. If a State were to withdraw unilaterally and in disregard of the established procedure, the available legal instruments would encounter the same limits of enforceability typical of international law. In such circumstances, political and economic relations would, in practice, prevail over legal mechanisms.

[5] In fact, as will be seen, the European Commission plays a key role, particularly because the Council—as in the case of *Brexit*—may decide to appoint it as the Union's negotiator. Although the Council is not legally bound to do so, the Commission's institutional structure makes it the most suitable body to perform this function, thereby confirming its position as a central institution even within the withdrawal procedure (Curti Gialdino 2017).

5 The Right of Secession in Federal Legal Systems

The *sui generis* nature of the European Union invites consideration of experiences other than those arising under traditional international law. Viewing the European project as a form of *federal experience*[6]—and taking into account the type of withdrawal envisaged by Article 50 TEU—the hypothesis of *Eurexit* may also be analysed as a form of secession. In this respect, it is worth revisiting the concept of a *right to secession* in federal systems.

It must be stated at the outset that no unilateral right to secession exists within federal legal orders.

Nevertheless, the advisory opinion of the Supreme Court of Canada on the proposed secession of Québec offers an instructive precedent. Following the 1995 referendum, in which the federalist side narrowly prevailed with 50.6% of the votes against 49.4% in favour of secession, the Canadian government sought the Court's opinion on whether the francophone province possessed an actual legal right to secede.

The Supreme Court delivered a negative opinion, reaffirming the non-existence of any unilateral right of secession. Even if the people of Québec had voted in favour of independence, no legal obligation would thereby have arisen for the federal government, nor would any automatic separation have taken effect.

The decision rested primarily on the inapplicability of the principle of self-determination to peoples who are neither colonial subjects nor under foreign domination. Since the Québécois enjoy the full exercise of fundamental democratic rights within Canada, the principle of self-determination could not be invoked in their case.

Nonetheless, the Court recognised the legitimacy of a referendum as an instrument of political expression. It emphasised, however, that even a positive outcome in favour of secession would merely trigger negotiations between the seceding province and the federal government. The right to secession, in other words, must be balanced against other constitutional principles, such as constitutional rigidity and the rule of law. Secession is therefore possible, but only in agreement with the federal State and the other provinces.

The significance of this landmark decision lies above all in its transformation of secession from a substantive right into a procedural framework.

The analogies between the Canadian Court's reasoning and the procedure established by Article 50 TEU are evident. In both cases, the declaration of intent constitutes merely the beginning of negotiations, not an act of immediate separation. Moreover, secession—whether of a province or of a Member State—must occur in agreement with the other constituent units, not unilaterally. This logic is reflected in

[6] Particular support is given to the view that "the name (federal State) does not necessarily correspond to the thing (federalism), and, above all, the thing (federalism) may exist even without the name (federal State); or, put differently, federal models of government may be adopted even in countries that do not formally define themselves as federal" (Caravita 2006).

the European context, where the Council, composed of representatives of the Member States' governments, serves as the Union's negotiator, rather than the Commission, which acts as an independent central body.

Most importantly, what unites the Canadian and European experiences is the attempt to proceduralise withdrawal—to bring within the framework of law situations that have traditionally been managed and resolved *de facto*.

6 Withdrawal or Secession?

The introduction of Article 50 TEU by the Treaty of Lisbon represents an attempt to *proceduralise* withdrawal from the European Union, shifting the centre of gravity of the issue from the domain of international law to that of Union constitutional law.

Both international law and federal constitutional jurisprudence, however, tend to address the problem of separation between legal orders by promoting consensual solutions. The Vienna Convention and the Canadian Supreme Court's opinion on Québec alike emphasise the importance of *agreement* and *negotiation* between the parties involved.

In this sense, the European Union—as is often the case—stands as a unique entity: one that both transcends and incorporates elements of international and federal experiences. There is little doubt that the content of Article 50 TEU is deeply inspired by the Canadian judgment on Québec. The reference to a Member State's own *constitutional requirements* as the basis for expressing its intention to withdraw and thereby initiating a process of negotiation with the Union mirrors the very sequence articulated by the Canadian Court: referendum → negotiation → agreement → secession.

The Québec ruling further reinforces the constitutionalisation of withdrawal from the Union by excluding the applicability of the principle of self-determination of peoples to entities that are neither colonial nor subject to foreign domination. That principle—a creature of international law—is, according to the Canadian Court's reasoning, clearly inapplicable to the European Union, which is founded on the free and voluntary adhesion of its Member States.

A traditional argument in favour of the *internationalist* view holds that the Member States of the Union remain sovereign States—far more so than a province such as Québec or any subnational entity seeking secession. Yet this reasoning is flawed at its foundation: European States have voluntarily transferred part of their sovereign powers to the Union. Moreover, in an age of globalisation and erosion of the nation State, can sovereignty still meaningfully be understood as *superiorem non recognoscens*—a power subject to no higher authority?

The interwar period was characterised by widespread unilateral denunciations of treaties, whose consequences are tragically well known. In the aftermath of the Second World War, international and regional organisations were established to secure peace among nations. Their primary method was to require States, as a condition of membership, to accept limitations upon their sovereignty in the name of peaceful coexistence. The goal was precisely to temper the notion of *superiorem non recognoscens*, subjecting States to the law of the international organisations they joined, governed by treaty-based international law. Sovereignty thus became a relative legal concept—voluntarily limited by States and variable according to the relationship between a State and an international organisation or between a federated State and its federal authority.

The real difference lies, rather, in historical and cultural factors. It is far more difficult to persuade a European State—endowed with centuries of history, political culture, and strong national identity—to accept a limited or transferred sovereignty than it is for a young State or a former colony to do so.

Ultimately, the precise terminology—whether *Eurexit* should be classified as withdrawal or secession—is of limited importance. What truly matters is the interaction between international norms and Union law in governing the separation between two legal orders.

The legal nature of the Union and the consolidated version of its founding Treaties suggest reliance on constitutional mechanisms: tools that enable conflicts to be managed consensually, in advance, and in compliance with the principle of legality.

To leave the European Union in an orderly, peaceful, and consensual manner is therefore possible, provided the procedures set out in the Treaties are respected—but the legal and structural impact of such a departure is profound.

The Union shapes the very States that compose it; it draws upon shared traditions and values and has itself become a vehicle for their diffusion and development. To withdraw is a difficult choice—but to disentangle oneself completely from the Union, to erase its past imprint and resist its ongoing influence, is virtually impossible.

References

Caravita B (2006) Lineamenti di diritto costituzionale federale e regionale. Giappichelli, Turin

Caravita B (2012) La grande sfida dell'Unione europea tra prospettive di rilancio e ombre di declino. federalismi.it 1:1–6

Christakis T (2011) Article 56, 1969 Vienna Convention. In: Corten O, Klein P (eds) The Vienna Convention on the Law of the Treaties: a commentary. Oxford University Press, Oxford

Curti Gialdino C (2017) Le trattative tra il Regno Unito e l'Unione europea per la Brexit alla luce dei primi due cicli negoziali. federalismi.it 16:2–37

Di Rienzo A (2012) Art. 50 TUE. In: Curti Gialdino C (ed) Codice dell'Unione europea operativo. Simone, Napoli

Fabbrini S (2015) Which European Union? Europe after the euro crisis. Cambridge University Press, Cambridge

Friel RJ (2004) Providing a constitutional framework for withdrawal from the EU: Article 59 of the Draft European Constitution. Int Comp Law Q 53(2):407–428

Grasso G (2015) Il referendum greco e la questione democratica nella (ri)costruzione del soggetto politico europeo. Osservatorio AIC 2:1–11

Hofmeister H (2010) Should I Stay or Should I Go? A critical analysis of the right to withdraw from the EU. Eur Law J 16(5):589–603

Mattera A (ed) (2003) Pénélope. Projet de Constitution de l'Union Européenne. Clémen Juglar, Paris

Nicolaides P (2013) Withdrawal from the European Union: a typology of effects. Maastricht J Eur Comp Law 20(2):209–219

Nicotra IA (2003) Il diritto di recesso e il Trattato che istituisce la Costituzione europea. In: Lucarelli A, Patroni Griffi A (eds) Studi sulla Costituzione europea. ESI, Naples

Rieder CM (2013) The withdrawal clause of the Lisbon Treaty in the light of EU citizenship: between disintegration and integration. Fordham Int Law J 37(1):147–174

Schiffauer P (ed) (1999) Quale carta costituzionale per l'Unione europea? European Parliament, Luxembourg

Tesauro G (2012) Diritto dell'Unione europea. Cedam, Padua

Triulzi U (2015) La crisi della Grecia è la crisi dell'Europa? federalismi.it 15:2–7

Weiler JHH (1985) Alternative to withdrawal from an international organization: the case of the European Economic Community. Israel Law Rev 20(2–3):282–298

Wyrozumialy A (2012) Withdrawal from the Union. In: Blankets HJ, Mangiameli S (eds) The European Union after Lisbon: constitutional basis, economic order and external action. Springer, Berlin–Heidelberg

Brexit as a Type of Secession: Withdrawal from European Treaties, National Identity and Human Rights

Eleonora Iannario

Abstract *Brexit* is certainly one of the most significant events in the integration process, which has clarified the functioning of Article 50 of the Treaty on European Union (TEU), as introduced by the entry into force of the Lisbon Treaty, regulating the right to withdraw from the European Union. After presenting the exit from the EU as a form of legal separation that takes place within an almost federal framework, it will be emphasised how *Brexit* bears important conceptual similarities with secession. The aim is to highlight how the process of a state withdrawing from a supranational organisation is a testimony to the intertwined nature of the European constitutional landscape.

1 Taking Back Control: *Britain's Exit* and the Reclamation of National Sovereignty

1.1 "Fog in the Channel, Continent Cut off": The Role of Populism and Sovereigntism

The United Kingdom and the European Union have always had a complex, uneasy, full of *opt-out* and never linear relationship (Caravita 2017, 2020). The UK's position has shifted repeatedly. Initially, it was sceptical of the European project due to a range of complex international entanglements: its management of the Commonwealth; a general reluctance to cede sovereignty, as later exemplified by *Brexit*; and a pronounced concern over sectors, such as coal and steel, where early European cooperation was particularly prominent. These factors led the UK to remain outside the initial dynamics of European integration, opting instead to strengthen its ties with its historical ally, the United States (Savastano 2023, pp. 40–41). Churchill himself recognised that British identities have historically taken shape among a persistent tension between two competing conceptions: a

E. Iannario (✉)
LUISS Guido Carli University, Rome, Italy

F. Savastano et al. (eds.), *Between Asymmetry and Secession*,
https://doi.org/10.1007/978-3-032-29603-0_22

vision of Britain as exceptional and isolated, on the one hand, and as an integral part of Europe, on the other (Douglas-Scott 2023, p. 257[1]).

However, following the withdrawal from its colonial Empire, together with the gradual decline of its international role and the unfavourable economic context, the United Kingdom submitted its application to join the then European Economic Community on 10 May 1967. It therefore became a European member relatively late, officially on 1 January 1973 (during the second enlargement), only to withdraw nearly 50 years later.

Therefore, the UK's relations with the continental institutions have always been marked by an invisible but at the same time well-perceived mistrust that has functioned as a curtain of separation between the island and the continent (Kerry 2016; Martinelli 2025, pp. 8–10[2]). Consequently, all stages of the dialogue between London and Brussels were characterised by uncertainty and clashes: from the moment the Community was born to the moment the United Kingdom joined it and when the Union achieved the goal of the single currency until the UK decided to leave this supranational organisation (Savastano 2019, p. 7). Owing to the persistent ambiguities surrounding the United Kingdom's affiliation with European institutions, the *Brexit* issue emerged (Tanca 2018, pp. 341–360). Hence, the general orientation has always been one of semi-distancing, even though the UK's influence and contribution to European integration in both political and legal terms is indisputable (Biondi 2017, pp. 2–7). Eventually, it soon became clear that the UK and the EU were two different things, and the divergence proved fatal (Savastano 2019, p. 45).

It is essential to take into account the distinguishing elements between British and continental European cultures, reflecting, from a historical perspective, an alterity symbolised geographically by the two shores of the English Channel. Nevertheless, it cannot be denied that common law has represented an original order alternative to the Romanist tradition not only due to its *sui generis* institutions and organisational methods but also because it is rooted in a culture of the relationship between subject and authority that is profoundly different from its continental counterpart (Martinelli 2025, pp. 10–11). Therefore, British exceptionalism has

---

[1] Churchill captured some of this in his famous "three great circles" speech in Llandudno in 1948, in which he stated: "The first circle for us is naturally the British Commonwealth and empire. Then there is the English-speaking world in which we, Canada, and the other British Dominions and the United States play so important a part. And finally there is United Europe. These three majestic circles are coexistent and if they are linked together there is no force or combination which could overthrow them or even challenge them...[In doing so] we hold the key to opening a safe and happy future to humanity, and will gain for ourselves gratitude and fame."

[2] A particularly significant perspective for reconstructing the relationship between the United Kingdom and the European Union over the past decades is offered by Kerry in European Union: Prime Ministers' Speeches and Party Manifestos since 1970. House of Lords Library Note, No. 2016/015, 15 March 2016. See also Martinelli, who expresses the conviction that all the reasons underlying this unresolved relationship, which constitutes the basis of many particular issues, can be traced back to a cultural motivation: the British have never truly perceived themselves as European citizens, as they are unable to accept the attribution and homogenisation of their own national characteristics within the framework of continental reality.

emerged over time as a powerful narrative (Douglas-Scott 2023, p. 255), emphasising how Britain's geographic insularity enabled the creation of singular institutions of liberty, such as the common law, parliamentary sovereignty and *habeas corpus*.

Of course, the transformations of the British Constitution have deeply influenced both the way the legal system has evolved over time and the very concept of sovereignty: from devolution to the protection of fundamental rights and from the affirmation of referendums to participation in major international assemblies. In this context, characterised by an absence of revolutionary or dramatic rupture, the United Kingdom's accession, first to the European Communities and later to the European Union, marked a turning point in the redefinition of sovereignty within the British legal order (Martinelli 2025, pp. 218–219).

It is evident that one of the founding elements behind the United Kingdom's decision to leave the EU lies in the *Brexiters*' desire to reclaim political and legal sovereignty, even at the expense of all the competences shared with other Member States since 1972. It is thus worth reflecting on the notion of sovereignty, which is claimed to be re-established on two levels: the exclusive sovereignty of constitutional organs over decisions affecting the lives of the British people and the full reaffirmation of parliamentary sovereignty, interpreted according to the norms and dynamics of contemporary democracy (Martinelli 2025, p. 217).

From that point onwards, there was a marked reduction in sovereignty conceived as the absolute prerogative of British institutions, previously perceived as virtually immune to external interference in decision-making. Simultaneously, the classical principle of "parliamentary sovereignty" was relativised (Douglas-Scott 2023, p. 285[3]), as regulatory frameworks in several areas began to be directly shaped by European Union law. Consequently, the necessity of withdrawing from the supranational entity of the European Union came to be perceived as essential to restore internal boundaries of decision-making power, free from the constraints of a shared authority (Marquand 2006, p. 175[4]).

In other words, the principal mantra of *Brexiteers*—"taking back sovereignty" (Douglas-Scott 2023, pp. 307–314[5])—was largely fuelled by a nostalgic, Victorian

[3] Douglas-Scott speaks about the "Death of Parliamentary Sovereignty".

[4] Marquand describes the UK's antipathy to European federation as a "neurosis" since it entails the abolition of the ancient doctrine of parliamentary sovereignty, which has been the cornerstone of the English Constitution for centuries.

[5] The author contends that sovereignty comprises both external and internal dimensions. Externally, it refers to a state's capacity to be recognised by the international community as an independent and equal entity among other states. Internally, sovereignty can be understood primarily in terms of parliamentary and popular sovereignty. The former holds particular resonance in the United Kingdom, where the Westminster Parliament has traditionally been seen as possessing unlimited legislative authority exercised through representative democracy. However, this conception may come into tension with popular sovereignty, especially when the people express their will directly through referendums. Such tension became particularly evident in the context of *Brexit*, where appeals to "taking back sovereignty" were often marked by conceptual confusion and contradiction. In this process, several actors were notably excluded or marginalised—these included international organisations, courts, constituent nations and territories of the UK (such as Scotland, Northern Ireland, Wales and Gibraltar), as well as certain individuals, namely EU citizens residing in the UK who were denied a vote in the referendum and UK nationals living in the EU.

and imperialist vision of the United Kingdom as a global reference point. In fact, some scholars (Douglas-Scott 2023, pp. 250–251[6]) have interpreted *Brexit* as an expression of "post-colonial melancholia", a sense of loss and yearning for a bygone imperial era imagined as glorious and redemptive. Therefore, the proponents of *Brexit* believed that the UK, in the medium to long term, would be able to pursue its interests more effectively by disengaging from a common European identity (Martinelli 2025, p. 220).

This conviction went hand in hand with the emergence of an increasingly pronounced English nationalism, often associated with hostility towards immigration and Euroscepticism (Kenny 2021, pp. 678–695). Nationalism, indeed, was closely tied to a sense of *Britishness* (Ryan 2018, pp. 154–160[7]). Economic, cultural and political elements have been mobilised in the discursive construction of *Britishness* and its separation from the older Anglo-British imaginary. These cultural factors, reinforced by economic resentment, have been further consolidated by opposition to the EU (Keating 2022, p. 641).

"Fog in the Channel, Continent cut off",[8] well-known aphorism that once seemed a distant expression of English arrogance, thus took on renewed significance during the referendum on EU membership, illustrating the enduring desire among much of the British population to distinguish itself from the continent. This inherent predisposition towards separation significantly shaped the decision to pursue *Brexit*. In fact, at the core of the choice to leave the European Union stood a major element of the British historical and cultural identity: an insularity often experienced as a form of otherness in relation to continental Europe (Martinelli 2025, pp. 7–9). Further dividing points, such as political choices, economic challenges and opposition to large-scale immigration, were undoubtedly important but ultimately contingent.

Globalisation, along with the process of increasing European integration and the consolidation of the four foundational pillars of the EU, has often had the effect of fuelling both populism and sovereigntism. More precisely, these broad openings contributed to the financial crisis at the turn of the millennium, which had a significant impact on socio-economic inequalities. In the case of populism, the European Union served as an ideal scapegoat for channelling popular discontent against the "external" cause of society's ills; in the case of sovereigntism, it constituted the "other" political order from which to defend oneself and against which to reassert

---

[6] The author explores the theme of *post-imperial nostalgia*. This perspective is also echoed in popular and patriotic cultural narratives that present Britain's history as an epic and morally uplifting tale, depicting the nation as small but heroic and as a civilising force in the world.

[7] Ryan provides an analysis that connects the notion of *Britishness* to the values of the British Empire, where it was projected abroad as a desirable attribute, alongside Christianity and other symbols of civilisation. By contrast, the current post-imperial context presents a very different task: that of constructing Britishness for those considered "outsiders" within the borders of the United Kingdom, rather than exporting it overseas.

[8] The popular maxim comes from a headline that appeared in *The Times* in the 1930s, which demonstrated a fine work, a refined piece of writing, steeped in irony and intellectual smugness. It is relevant to take this sense of superiority into account when researching the reasons for the choices of the Britons.

national identity (Savastano 2019b, pp. 252–253). Both movements capitalised on values such as "post-materialism" and invoked themes such as "post-colonial nostalgia" and the aspiration for the United Kingdom to reclaim its former greatness, thereby further stimulating pro-*Brexit* discourse (Horder 2025, pp. 167–168).

The ties of EU membership were in fact an easy target, all in order to attract support. The UKIP Party has based its political orientation on sovereigntist and strongly anti-European positions. To counter its electoral rise, the Conservative Party has adopted a markedly Euro-critical approach, promoting the referendum on the UK's stay in the European Union. It instrumentalised issues such as immigration, economic governance and national sovereignty, rejecting the idea of an "ever closer union". This approach contributed to legitimising latent Eurosceptic sentiments (Savastano 2019b, p. 255). In an attempt to stem UKIP's growing popularity, then Prime Minister David Cameron pledged to renegotiate a more favourable relationship with the EU and to hold a referendum on the UK's stay by 2017. On 10 November 2015, he sent a letter to the President of the European Council, Donald Tusk, putting forward proposals for reform that his government considered essential, requesting reform in four key sectors: economic governance, sovereignty, competitiveness and immigration (Douglas-Scott 2023, p. 286). Furthermore, Cameron strongly defended the deal as a pragmatic step in the national interest and declared that, in the event of agreement on these points, he would support the *Remain* campaign. Subsequent to this event, the reactions in the UK to the renegotiation deal were divided: eurosceptics dismissed it as meaningless, while *pro*-EU groups and businesses viewed it more positively (Savastano 2019b, p. 259). Nonetheless, the agreement was conditional on a *Remain* outcome in the 23 June 2016 referendum and would not take effect otherwise.

1.2 The Referendum on EU Membership

The renegotiation was overtaken by the referendum on continued EU membership, a referendum that many accused David Cameron of calling primarily to resolve internal divisions within the Conservative Party, rather than to serve the national interest (Douglas-Scott 2023, pp. 287–288). The referendum was conducted under the *European Union Referendum Act*, passed on 17 December 2015, stipulating that a referendum would be held in the United Kingdom on the country's continued membership in the European Union by 31 December 2017 (Savastano 2019, p. 47). Notably, the Act did not require the government to implement the outcome; it was advisory rather than legally binding. Nevertheless, in a policy paper issued in February 2016, the government stated that it felt under a "democratic duty"[9] to give effect to the will of the people.

[9] The Process for Withdrawing from the European Union, HM Government, 29 February 2016, 7, par. 2.1.

British citizens, Commonwealth citizens residing in the United Kingdom, Gibraltar residents eligible to vote in European Parliament elections and British citizens living abroad who had been registered on the electoral roll within the previous 15 years were thus called upon to answer the following question: "Should the United Kingdom remain a member of the European Union or leave the European Union?" with voters offered the choice between "Remain a member of the European Union" and "Leave the European Union".

The vote on the UK's exit from the European Union, driven by emotions and a deep sense of British national identity, counted 72.2% of eligible voters. Of these, 51.9% voted in favour of *Leave* (17,410,742 votes), while 48.1% supported *Remain* (16,141,241 votes) (Curti Gialdino 2017). Hence, the decision to exit the European Union prevailed. Then 26,033 spoiled or blank ballots represented 0.08% of the total. It is interesting to point out how only Scotland, Northern Ireland and London voted in favour of remaining in the EU; conversely, in all other areas, *Leave* triumphed (Savastano 2019, pp. 48–51). In response, the British government declared, "the British people have voted for *Brexit*" (May, 2019[10]), framing the withdrawal as a unified, patriotic act: a "red, white and blue *Brexit*" (May, 2019[11]) for the entire United Kingdom. The UK's expressed intention to depart from the European Union, following the outcome of the referendum held on 23 June 2016, has given rise—and will continue to give rise—to complex and multifaceted challenges within the European space, many of which involve considerable and complex repercussions. In the near future, the referendum on EU membership will likely be widely perceived and interpreted as one of the final remnants of the imperial legacy gradually fading from the British collective consciousness. For some scholars, *Brexit* constituted a manifestation of post-imperial angst (Dorling and Tomlinson 2019).

However, the referendum resulted in a profound political and social divide, with cross-cutting splits between *Leave* and *Remain* supporters within both the Conservative and Labour parties, thereby fuelling uncertainty and instability.

Even among the *Brexiteers* themselves, there existed a fundamental division between liberals and nationalists, particularly on the central and critical issue of immigration (Ryan 2018b, pp. 35–56). On one hand, Labour supporters advocating for a soft *Brexit* sought to retain the economic benefits of European integration without being subject to EU legislation and wished to preserve the free movement of goods, services, capital and people. On the other hand, the Nationalist wing led by Nigel Farage aimed to put an end to uncontrolled immigration: Farage's billboard, portraying supposed waves of migration at Europe's borders, became a striking symbol within a fragile debate overshadowed by the persistent spectre of borders (Rowlands 2018, pp. 68–69).

[10] Full text of Theresa May's speech introducing her "new Brexit deal", Brexit Central. https://brexitcentral.com/full-text-of-theresa-mays-speech-introducing-her-new-brexit-deal/.

[11] PM Speech on the Union, Stirling, 4 July 2019, https://www.gov.uk/government/speeches/pmspeech-on-the-union-4-july-2019.

Above all, *Brexit* constituted a resounding rejection of migration policy, fuelled—among other factors—by the sharp rise in migration flows from new EU Member States after 2004 (Savastano 2015[12]).

The *Leave* campaign targeted a transformation of the UK's existing political and economic order, while the *Remain* side attempted to instil sufficient doubt about the risks associated with such a change. Moreover, leaving the EU was depicted as a means for Britons to reclaim greater autonomy and freedom from arbitrary political interference, as well as to increase control over national economic resources.

The influence of the *Leavers*' arguments lay in framing the European Union as a threat to the UK's sovereignty, identity and territorial integrity. In fact, Michael Gove notably used the analogy of a kidnapping, suggesting that the innocent United Kingdom was being held hostage and mistreated by the EU. This rhetoric was echoed in UKIP's slogans such as "We want our country back"[13] and "We must break free of the EU and take back control of our borders", which framed immigration as the root cause of numerous social problems.

Conversely, the *Remainers*, who viewed continued EU membership as a source of economic benefit, civil rights, freedoms and international standing, found themselves defending a *status quo* that failed to generate the level of enthusiasm required to present a compelling and ambitious vision for the future development of the Union.

In other words, there existed a "hope deficit" that arguably enabled the *Leavers* to mobilise national hostility towards immigrants, who were perceived as the most tangible and visible symbol of what needed to change. Indeed, large segments of the public had long dreamt of *Brexit* as the path to an independent nation capable of determining its own destiny. Pessimism and widespread insecurity—symptoms of a deeper dissatisfaction afflicting a significant portion of the English population—combined with a strong sense of national belonging, led to outbursts directed against migrants. This antagonistic attitude drew upon a variety of cross-cutting concerns. Firstly, there was a widespread perception that large numbers of immigrants were coming to Britain to find work and to benefit from the UK's rich welfare system. Secondly, the British people were concerned about national security and the rising crime rate associated with border management. Finally, there was a cultural dimension, marked by anxiety about the integration of individuals from different cultural backgrounds and the potential vulnerability of the British social fabric to fast changes. Central to these collective narratives was the belief that a cohesive Britain could "stand alone" (Horder 2025, pp. 66–67) reinforced by the imperial memory of having ruled the world by the early nineteenth century as a "Great Power" and leading state, thus requiring no oversight from a threatening continental power

[12] See also the letter sent by UK Prime Minister David Cameron to the President of the European Council, Donald Tusk, dated 10 November 2015.

[13] See the slogan "We want our money back" in the Press Conference following the Dublin European Council, MargaretThatcher.org, Document No. 104180.

(Douglas-Scott 2023, pp. 210[14]). These discourses were further sustained by apprehensions about the prospect of a European army, concerns over a globalist *pro*-EU agenda promoting a presumed uncontrolled migration and the persistent claim that Britain's sovereignty was being ceded to Brussels or that the legacy of victory in the Second World War fundamentally clashed with the idea of a shared European identity.

It had become evident that the great solution to these issues was encapsulated in the idea of sovereignty, portrayed as the tool by which the British people could reclaim control over their nation.

1.3 Understanding the Referendum

The 2016 referendum, with the *Leave* victory, constituted a fundamental *constitutional moment*—as emphasised by authoritative scholars (Martinelli 2022[15])—which was neither an oversight by a Prime Minister nor an unforeseeable event and even less the result of a colossal misunderstanding. All these interpretations were widely present in the debates on both sides of the Channel, tending to trivialise, especially on the part of commentators most critical of this decision, an affair that as a whole is far from being ascribable to a single cause and reducible to mere contingent dynamics.

As highlighted above, the roots of *Brexit* run deep, reflecting a historically unresolved relationship between the United Kingdom and continental Europe, made distinct by enduring tensions across historical, geographical, cultural, political, and legal dimensions (Martinelli 2022, p. 10).

While the 1975 referendum temporarily settled the question of EEC membership in favour of the *pro*-European side, it did not eliminate long-standing British reservations towards deeper integration, particularly regarding sovereignty and alignment with continental models. The referendum outcome was less an expression of genuine European enthusiasm than a pragmatic endorsement of the economic benefits of Common Market membership. Over the ensuing decades, British governments, especially under the Conservatives, sought to maximise these advantages while carefully limiting political integration, securing numerous *opt-outs* (notably from the single currency) without renouncing EU membership altogether. The

---

[14] In the second half of the nineteenth century, the concept of a "Greater Britain" gained currency. The project was supported by prominent Victorian intellectuals; for example, the radical politician Charles Dilke, in his travel account *Greater Britain* (1868), used the term to refer specifically to English-speaking territories, inhabited by White populations and governed autonomously, as a potential union between the mother country and the colonies.

[15] This expression must be understood in a double sense: as an event situated within the broader context of the relationship with European institutions that has contributed to a redefinition of the British Constitution and as an intense sequence of problems, circumstances and conflicts that have led to legislative changes and judicial interventions and have redefined the Constitution as it ought to be understood in the current historical moment.

Labour government pursued modest constitutional reforms inspired by continental principles, including devolution, the incorporation of the European Convention on Human Rights (ECHR) through the *Human Rights Act 1998* and the establishment of the UK Supreme Court via the *Constitutional Reform Act 2005*. Nonetheless, this act failed to hold a referendum on joining the euro, a missed *constitutional moment* that could have consolidated the UK's European orientation and prevented the resurgence of nationalist sentiment. This defeat contributed to a broader reversal of integrationist momentum.

The 2016 Brexit referendum marked the culmination of this shift. Although the *Leave* vote prevailed by a narrow margin, it signified a deep and deliberate decision with constitutional implications that cannot be dismissed as either transient or marginal.

From a constitutional point of view, the referendum demonstrated its force to the extent of initiating the procedure laid down in Article 50 of the Treaty on European Union (TEU), in accordance with the modalities provided by British constitutional law. It was a decision taken by the electorate, delegated to it by the representative democratic circuit, which in practice was never challenged in Parliament, despite the fact that the majority of Members of Parliament (MPs) had supported the *Remain* position (Martinelli 2025, pp. 106–107). In this context, the triggering of Article 50 TEU assumed the significance of a genuine dividing line. On the one hand, it was necessitated by the legal value attributed to the *Brexit* referendum, itself a consequence of the incorporation of this instrument within the framework of the contemporary British Constitution. On the other hand, however, it also represented the limit of the referendum's binding force in favour of *Leave*. In other words, while the electorate expressed the will to exit the European Union, it could not, evidently, determine the terms and conditions of that withdrawal. Consequently, once Article 50 TEU was invoked, the focus of the process shifted away from the referendum result and onto the negotiations: an arena removed from the expression of popular will, within which everything could potentially be reconsidered (Martinelli 2025, p. 109).

Therefore, the analysis has shown that this context has profoundly influenced the interpretation of the relationship between parliamentary sovereignty and the expression of popular will, as well as the assessment of the constitutional role assumed by the referendum: an increasingly central role in matters that reach the very foundations of the state's structure and which is now beginning to be absorbed into a sort of constitutional domain not entirely subject to the political will of Westminster (Martinelli 2025, p. 260).

1.4 2019 Elections

In 2016, the public discourse surrounding the referendum prominently featured ideals like "sovereignty" and "freedom". By 2019, however, these narratives had been eclipsed by a prevailing sense that failure to deliver *Brexit* legally would have represented a broader betrayal of "democratic principles" by the political elite (Horder 2025, pp. 78–79). In fact, the 2019 December General Elections constituted a kind of "ritual of renewal" (Horder 2025, p. 32) aimed at honouring the 2016 referendum. The new political initiative of Nigel Farage, leader and founder of the Brexit Party, was likely perceived as particularly compelling, precisely because it appeared to offer a means of preserving a form of "true democracy" that many feared was slipping away. For many *Brexiters*, those elections represented a fundamental transformation of the social order: the destruction of a declining old regime and the birth of a new, unified and restored one. *Brexit* was driven not just by the desire of its supporters to assert their position but rather by a transformation intimately bound to the "paradox of sacrifice" (Horder 2025, p. 64) repeatedly invoked by *Leave* advocates. More specifically, the exit from the EU was perceived as an opportunity to regenerate trust and restore the sanctity of democracy, thereby reconstituting a social body seen as fragmented. In this sense, *Brexit* supporters quite literally placed the European project upon a sacrificial altar, in the hope that the pain of economic loss might be redeemed by the gain of social renewal. At that point, the European Union was widely regarded as a technocratic and largely remote organisation: it functioned as a symbolic target embodying the perceived causes of national decline, economic inequality and rapid demographic change (Dorling and Tomlinson 2019; Sobolewska and Ford 2020).

The period between 2016 and 2020, and especially between May's 2017 election win and Johnson's 2019 triumph, was dominated by the issue of *Brexit*. Therefore, in March 2017, May triggered Article 50 of the Lisbon Treaty, thereby initiating a 2-year countdown within which the United Kingdom was expected to sever all sovereign ties with the European Union.

Public opinion continued to be sharply divided not only between proponents of maintaining the closest possible relationship with the European Union but also among advocates of *Brexit* themselves. The latter disagreed as to whether withdrawal should have involved a total rupture of political and economic arrangements or whether it would have been better to adopt a "Norwegian" or "Swiss" model, marked by substantial cooperation without full membership (Horder 2025, p. 38). Regardless of the position taken, the national debate was intensely heated and all-encompassing. It is no coincidence that Boris Johnson's *Get Brexit Done* slogan[16] resonated so strongly during the 2019 election campaign, so much so that, although the Brexit Party failed to win a single parliamentary seat, it played a pivotal role in enabling both the re-election of Johnson and the Conservative Party and the eventual implementation of a "Hard *Brexit*" for the United Kingdom. Securing 365 Members of Parliament, Conservative candidates removed any possibility of forming a "progressive alliance" (Horder 2025, p. 41) capable of obstructing the United

[16] Conservative and Unionist Party Manifesto 2019, *Get Brexit Done*. Unleash Britain's Potential, 47–48: "Once we get Brexit done, Britain will take back control of its laws. As we end the supremacy of European law, we will be free to craft legislation and regulations that maintain high standards but which work best for the UK. We want a balance of rights, rules and entitlements that benefits all the people and all the parts of our United Kingdom."

Kingdom's withdrawal. With their commanding majority, the Conservatives acquired the parliamentary advantage necessary to overcome the legislative stalemate and ratify the revised Withdrawal Agreement, thus cementing the United Kingdom's exit from the European Union formally on 31 January 2020.

This result was also facilitated by the strategic interventions (Horder 2025, p. 53[17]) of Farage, who consistently evoked the memory of the noble dead, framing their sacrifice as a conduit to the sacred ideal of democracy. In his rhetoric, *Brexit* transcended pragmatic considerations of trade and economics; it was envisioned as a pivotal moment of collective renewal, capable of fostering social solidarity in the context of ongoing structural deterioration.

2 The United Kingdom's Withdrawal from European Union Treaties

The EU was established to offer collective solutions to challenges too vast for individual Member States. In view of this broad objective, candidate countries must adopt the 35 chapters of the *acquis communautaire* and align themselves with the Union's common principles and values in order to obtain official candidate status.

For decades, the possibility that a Member State of the Union might want to leave the common European house was considered so unrealistic that it was not even considered on a theoretical, as well as legal, level (Rieder 2013, p. 156). On the contrary, the *federalising process* and its gradual transformation from an international to a supranational organisation (Caravita 2020) meant that the subject of withdrawal from the Union was not included in the founding Treaties. Only the entry into force of the Lisbon Treaty in 2009, after having been proposed a few years earlier in the never-ratified 2004 Constitutional Treaty, introduced this possibility (Savastano 2019, p. 121; Caravita 2020, pp. 216–217).

2.1 *Article 50 TEU*

A Member State wishing to exercise its right of withdrawal is required to act in accordance with its own constitutional requirements. The procedure to be followed entails notifying the European Council of the decision to exit, after which the modalities of

[17] "This is now actually about more than just delivering Brexit. This is in fact about democracy itself. This is about our nation. This is about those who for hundreds of years, built this nation, defended this nation, sacrificed so much so that we could be a nation. This is about who we are as a people and as a country […] it is also about our place in the world. And our standing in the world. […] I want us to re-establish where we should be in the world. Being represented, being represented in the higher councils across the globe by somebody from the European Commission is—I would suggest—not worthy of who we are as a people."

withdrawal are to be determined in an agreement negotiated pursuant to Article 218.3 of the Treaty on the Functioning of the European Union (Article 50.2 TEU).

The Council is the institution responsible for receiving notification from the withdrawing state, for authorising the Withdrawal Agreement and for designating the EU's negotiator, who will conduct the talks on behalf of the entire Union. The actual exit becomes effective either upon the entry into force of the Withdrawal Agreement or, failing that, 2 years after the submission of the notification to the European Council by the withdrawing state (Article 50.3 TEU).

Naturally, the members of the Council and of the European Council representing the withdrawing state shall not participate in the deliberations concerning that state (Curti Gialdino 2017, p. 6). The Council, excluding the representatives of the withdrawing state, shall act by a qualified majority, which, as specified in Article 50, second sub-paragraph, means 72% of the participating Member States representing at least 65% of the EU population (Article 238 TFEU, par. 3, b).

Article 50 concludes in paragraph 5 by stipulating that should a former Member State seek to rejoin the Union, it must follow the ordinary accession procedure provided for in Article 49 TEU. Accordingly, a state that has withdrawn from the Union cannot automatically regain membership; it must apply for accession as any new candidate would (Rieder 2013, pp. 155–160; Savastano 2019, p. 134). Therefore, Article 50 TEU provides that the Treaties shall cease to apply to the withdrawing state from the date of entry into force of the Withdrawal Agreement or, failing that, 2 years after the notification of its intention to withdraw, unless the European Council, in agreement with the Member State concerned, unanimously decides to extend this period.

2.2 Negotiating the Exit: From May's Letter to Withdrawal Activation

The official act that marked the beginning of the process leading to the United Kingdom's withdrawal from the European Union was the letter sent by Prime Minister Theresa May to the President of the European Council, Donald Tusk, on 29 March 2017.[18] The government then started the official process to exit the EU. This followed the procedure set out under Article 50 TEU, which was inserted into the TEU by the Lisbon Treaty in 2009 and required the UK to formally notify the EU of its intention to leave and to negotiate with the EU a Withdrawal Agreement (Douglas-Scott 2023, p. 370). In this respect, Article 50 TEU[19] does not prescribe a

---

[18] *Article 50 notification letter from the United Kingdom*, 29 March 2017, after which President Tusk has convened the European Council on 29 April 2017.

[19] See, with regard to the United Kingdom, Department for Exiting the European Union (DExEU), which was a ministerial department from 14 July 2016 to 31 January 2020 responsible for overseeing negotiations to leave the EU; with regard to the European Union, European Commission, *Negotiating documents on Article 50 negotiations with the United Kingdom. Documents published as part of the European Commission's approach to transparency on Article 50 negotiations with the United Kingdom.*

specific form for the withdrawal notification. In this case, the United Kingdom employed the usual diplomatic channels, delivering the notification in the form of a six-page letter. The notification letter articulated a fundamental principle that underpinned all six of its pages: the United Kingdom expressed its intention to leave the Union but not Europe (Savastano 2019, p. 73). For this reason, its objective was to preserve a *special relationship* (Martinelli 2025, p. 18[20]) with what would continue to be its primary geographical and strategic context.

The declaration of the intent to withdraw was contained on the first page of the letter, which also referred to the internal constitutional steps leading to the decision: the referendum result, parliamentary approval and Royal Assent to the *European Union (Notification of Withdrawal) Act 2017*. The remaining five pages can be read as a preamble to the negotiation process, laying out a set of principles intended to guide the steps that would follow (Savastano 2019, p. 74).

Moreover, Prime Minister May repeatedly emphasised that the pursuit of a deep and special partnership would serve not only British interests but also those of the European Union. The letter was thus designed to demonstrate the mutual desirability of reaching a Withdrawal Agreement in the interest of both parties. It argued that the achievement of the goals outlined in the letter would be beneficial to the wider international community, provided negotiations had been conducted in a constructive spirit.

Among the priorities articulated were placing citizens' rights at the core of the negotiations, fostering mutual respect and sincere cooperation to affirm and uphold shared European values while negotiating the Withdrawal Agreement, pursuing a comprehensive and ambitious framework for future relations, addressing the issue of the Irish border and establishing a UK-EU free trade area, alongside the ability for the UK to negotiate independent trade agreements with third countries.

Indeed, in order to safeguard human rights in the *post-Brexit* era, it was chosen to primarily protect the status of EU citizens residing in the UK and British citizens living in other EU Member States who, following the withdrawal, ceased to hold EU citizenship. Under EU law, these individuals were entitled to equal treatment with the nationals of the host state in many respects, a feature of EU citizenship, but this no longer applies after *Brexit*. Prior to the 2016 referendum, some proponents of *Brexit* maintained that such rights would be preserved as "acquired rights" (i.e. rights not automatically extinguished when a treaty ceases to apply) under the 1969 Vienna Convention on the Law of Treaties (Douglas-Scott 2023, p. 489). However, despite certain assurances made during the referendum campaign and repeated pleas by those affected not to be treated as "bargaining chips" (Douglas-Scott 2023, p. 490), their rights were frequently neglected throughout the *Brexit* process. It was the EU that insisted that EU citizens' status be protected and guaranteed under the EU Withdrawal

[20] The terminology once again evokes a notion closely akin to the *special relationship* that Churchill famously articulated in his Fulton (Missouri) speech of 5 March 1946, referring to the bond between the United Kingdom and the United States. As noted by Martinelli, Churchill's position regarding the relationship between the United Kingdom and Europe was so deeply embedded in broad sectors of the political system and public opinion as to justify the conclusion that "we are with Europe, but not of it. We are linked but not compromised".

Agreement. Under that Agreement, it was established that EU nationals residing in the UK, as well as UK nationals living in other Member States, would be allowed to continue exercising the rights conferred under EU law as of 31 January 2020, in accordance with the principles of equal treatment and non-discrimination. EU citizens who had already established residence in the UK and wished to preserve their legal status were required to apply for a residence permit and demonstrate a minimum of 5 years of continuous presence in the country. Although the relevant reference date for calculating residence was set at 31 December 2020, the end of the transition period, applications could be submitted until 30 June 2021 (Caravita 2020, p. 221).

Regarding migration from the European Union, EU law provides for the expulsion of EU citizens who fail to find employment within 3 months of entry or who commit criminal offences (Douglas-Scott 2023, p. 491[21]).

UK legislation introduced a distinction between individuals with “settled status”, referring to those who had been lawfully residing in the UK for over 5 years and were thus eligible for permanent residence and those with “pre-settled status”, referring to those with less than 5 years of residence, who could acquire settled status upon reaching the required duration, even beyond 31 December 2020.

With regard to the rights enjoyed by EU citizens under EU law while residing in the UK, it can be deduced that these remained subject to enforcement by UK courts. Additionally, for a period of 8 years from the date of entry into force of the agreement, UK courts retain the ability to submit preliminary references to the Court of Justice of the European Union in cases of interpretative uncertainty. For its part, the European Commission continues to oversee the proper application of the EU legal framework concerning Union citizens residing in the United Kingdom.

3 The Relationship Between *Demos*, *Telos* and *Ethos*

Over the past few decades, the United Kingdom has undergone, in an especially intense manner, many of the challenges and transformations currently facing modern European states.

These challenges provide the backdrop for a profound reconfiguration of the United Kingdom as a territorial political entity. It represents a significant example of “spatial rescaling” (Keating 2022, p. 629), a process through which functional systems, citizen demands, collective identities, political communities and governance institutions shift to new levels: above, below and across the territorial state.

In this context, the devolution reforms, initially unsuccessful in the 1970s but implemented at the end of the century, constitute a major attempt to stabilise territorial governance, politics and public policy. Nonetheless, these reforms have been partial and were not accompanied by a broader constitutional renewal, leaving

[21] Douglas-Scott asserts that “this vilification of migrants has, however, been a feature of *Brexit*, dating back to the Referendum campaign”.

unresolved crucial questions concerning the nature of the state, sovereignty and territorial cohesion. Devolution occurred during the UK's membership in the European Union, which provided an important external support framework for the new territorial configuration, as well as opening the way to new forms of multilevel governance (Keating 2022, p. 630). Conversely, the United Kingdom's withdrawal from the European Union represented an attempt to reinvent the unitary, sovereign nation state, a construct the UK has never fully embodied, and certainly not since the late twentieth century (Ryan 2018b, p. 36). This process has therefore destabilised the system of devolution and territorial politics within the island.

The concepts of the nation state and the union are theoretical models, and the United Kingdom can be seen as fitting one or the other at different times (Douglas-Scott 2023, pp. 339, 409[22]). They may also be viewed as positions along a spectrum, indicating varying degrees of unity. This means that they offer distinct perspectives on three constitutive elements of any political entity: *demos*, *telos* and *ethos* (Keating 2021). The *demos* refers to the people in whom sovereignty is ultimately vested, thus forming the basis of legitimate authority traditionally attributed to the sovereignty of the Parliament, thereby avoiding the contentious issue of defining the people itself. Then *telos* links integration to the idea of a union grounded in accommodation, compromise and entrenched rights, serving as the instrument through which the union may contribute to the achievement of desirable substantive goals. Finally, the *ethos* concerns shared values that may constitute the foundation of citizenship and belonging.

Whereas nation state constitutions often claim a common normative foundation, in unions, these values tend to be more contested. Some constitutional provisions rest on shared foundational principles, including a common understanding of *demos*, *telos* and *ethos*. Other constitutional systems, by contrast, provide institutional mechanisms for cooperation within a union in the absence of an agreement on those foundations (Keating 2022, p. 631). The territorial constitution of the United Kingdom must be understood as an instance of the latter.

After the 2016 referendum, *Brexit* highlighted the extent to which external (EU membership) and internal (devolution) dimensions of sovereignty were deeply interconnected (Nicolini 2013, p. 21), revealing the need for renewed reflection on both fronts. Despite resistance to cutting devolved powers, *Brexit* was pursued as if the UK were a unitary state, and the UK *Internal Market Act* ended up centralising power in practice. It imposed a system of mutual recognition for goods and services, which allows less regulatory divergence in the devolved territories than had been

[22] The author prefers the expression "union State" over "unitary State" to describe the United Kingdom, as it does not constitute a wholly homogeneous entity. In his view, the notion of a "union State" denotes a state in which the centre does not exercise direct control over every part of the territory. The UK, indeed, is not unitary by nature but is marked by a plurality of institutional arrangements across its various constituent parts. So the United Kingdom may be described as a "union State" composed of four nations, as it does not possess a uniform legal system across its entire territory, and it can be argued that it lacks a single, unequivocal sovereignty.

permitted under the EU's internal market regime. Remarkably, the British government even revived the use of the term "unitary state" (Keating 2022, p. 635).

For proponents of *Brexit*, EU membership was seen as fundamentally at odds with a unitary vision of the state grounded in parliamentary sovereignty. Nevertheless, if the United Kingdom is understood as a union rather than a unitary state, striking parallels emerge between the two entities. Both the United Kingdom and the European Union can be characterised as asymmetric, quasi-federal unions in which *demos*, *telos* and *ethos* are continually contested and renegotiated and in which the locus of sovereignty remains disputed. In this sense, they may be understood as post-sovereign political entities that challenge traditional constitutional categories.

EU membership provided a discursive space in which post-sovereign conceptions of sovereignty could be developed, and it enabled a broader framework for devolution than would likely have been achievable otherwise. In fact, the Union supplied the regulatory framework for the internal market within the United Kingdom itself, ensuring regulatory harmonisation at the sub-state level. An additional notable European influence was provided by the *European Convention on Human Rights* (ECHR), which was incorporated into UK domestic law through the *Human Rights Act 1998*. Under this Act, courts may assess the compatibility of legislation and government actions with the Convention. This ECHR played an even more binding role in the devolution statutes: any court may invalidate devolved legislation that conflicts with the ECHR. This has had a profound effect, decoupling the protection of human rights from both nationality and the notion of a unified *demos*. A British Charter of Rights long championed by the Conservative Party as a Eurosceptic and nationalist alternative to the *Human Rights Act* would, by contrast, tie rights more closely to the concept of *Britishness*. Although the ECHR is formally unaffected by *Brexit*, it remains within the scope of the UK's Eurosceptic agenda and is likely to re-emerge as a subject of political contestation.

Europeanism was at odds with the British nationalism embraced by the *Leave* campaign, which relied on the notion of a unified *demos*. This kind of unionism in the United Kingdom undoubtedly contains an "assimilationist" component, aimed at building a unified nation and state. At the same time, a "patriotic" element highlights the value of national traditions, which affirms and values the traditions of the constituent nations, as well as a more "contractual" interpretation, in which loyalty is conditional and contingent (Keating 2021). Despite these different expressions, all forms of unionism share a fundamental attachment to the principle of sovereignty and to the supremacy of Westminster.

Following the United Kingdom's accession to the European Union in the twentieth century, this vision came to be rooted in the doctrine of the absolute sovereignty of Westminster. In that context, unionism sought to ground itself in a higher *ethos* of shared values and norms, often invoked as "British values" such as democracy, liberty, the rule of law and respect for diversity (Dicey 1959; Keating 2022, p. 641[23]).

[23] Here, the author refers to the view based on the principle of absolute parliamentary sovereignty, whose most renowned exponent was Dicey AV.

The *European Union Withdrawal Bill 2017* originally proposed that all competences repatriated from the EU would return to Westminster, regardless of whether they had been classified as reserved or devolved under the devolution settlements. Any powers deemed unnecessary at the central level could later be returned to the devolved administrations. Devolution, in this light, was conceived as a "third way" (Keating 2022, p. 639) between secessionist nationalism and traditional unionism, and it broadly reflected what most people in the peripheral nations of the UK appeared to want. The constitutional choice thus seemed to lie between a renewed, devolution-based unionism and separation. *Brexit*, however, posed a serious challenge to advocates of this "third way" between unitary statehood and secession. The UK was faced with a binary outcome: either remain within the EU or leave it entirely with no viable alternatives. As a result, the *momentum* has shifted towards demands for secession.

4 The Right to Secession

Early European federalists, such as Spinelli, recognised the benefits of adopting a federal model. In fact, the European Union demonstrates several features typically associated with federalism, most notably the division of competences between the central authority and sub-state levels (Douglas-Scott 2023, p. 402). The Treaty of Lisbon, which entered into force in 2009, contributed to the formal clarification of such a distribution by setting out the categories of competences in the Treaty on the Functioning of the European Union (TFEU) and assigning exclusive competences to the Union under Article 3 TFEU.

The European Union today represents an evolving federal model, developed in accordance with Article 1, paragraph 2, of the TEU (Caravita 2020, pp. 87–89[24]). The 24 titles of Part III of the TFEU govern areas in which decision-making processes, varying between the European method and the intergovernmental one, involve both the representation of citizens and that of the Member States. Therefore, considering the European Union as a federal experience and taking into account the type of withdrawal outlined in Article 50 TEU, the hypothesis of *Eurexit* may also be studied as a form of secession (Caravita 2020, p. 224; Closa 2017, pp. 1–11; Frantziou 2022, p. 75[25]). In this sense, it is worth revisiting the concept of the right to secession within federal systems. According to Schmitt (Schmitt 1984, p. 478), the agreement between states forming a confederation or a federation is a free treaty insofar as the decision to join the federation depends on the will of the member. While the act of joining is voluntary, the agreement is not a contract that can be unilaterally terminated at will, as it governs more than discrete and measurable legal

[24] Caravita adopts the perspective of the *European federalising process*.

[25] Frantziou states that Brexit is not a form of secession within the traditional vocabulary of international law or the framework of decisional secession from federal states.

relations. Rather, through accession to a federation, a state becomes part of a broader political system, which can take more or less complex forms. Thus, the formal possibility of withdrawal must reckon with the material consequences of exclusion from the legal order to which it belonged.

This perspective stems from the conviction that integration policy regards the European Union as an entity that has transcended its status as a special-purpose association (Nettesheim 2021[26]) and has evolved into a political body that, in cooperation with the Member States, pursues a general political agenda oriented towards the common values enshrined in Article 2 TEU. Consequently, the EU is not solely based on supranational governance; certain domains are structured contractually, requiring intergovernmental consensus among the participating Member States, in light of the obligations arising from the Treaties. Therefore, mechanisms for the termination of this contractual relationship are indeed embedded within the framework of European integration. As early as 2004, the Treaty establishing a Constitution for Europe explicitly provided for the right of withdrawal.[27]

As a further confirmation of the inherently difficult nature of decisions concerning secession—understood as the detachment of a territory from a political entity to which it had originally adhered—one may refer to the approach tentatively adopted within the framework of the European legal order, where the sovereign authority of the Member States remains significantly present (Caravita 2020, p. 58). In the view of the Court of Justice, the EU withdrawal clause reflects the sovereign prerogative of Member States to secede, an act that eludes legal limitation by the supranational order (Simoncini 2023, pp. 171–194). Thus, a "sovereign" right of withdrawal has always been implicit within the legal order of the European Union. Today, the Lisbon Treaty has made this implicit right explicit through Article 50 TEU, which offers a procedural mechanism aimed at facilitating a structured and non-confrontational disengagement (Schütze 2023, pp. 119–130).

It must be noted that there is no unilateral right to secession in federal legal systems. As the most authoritative recent scholarship suggests (Caravita 2020, pp. 53–54), the issue of secession today should be addressed by moving away from the traditional, static conception tied to the nineteenth- and twentieth-century idea of state sovereignty. Instead, it should be studied through a dynamic lens that defines secession not as the separation of one group from another pre-existing group but as a process aimed at territorial detachment, regardless of whether its ultimate goal is achieved. In this sense, secession is an option within political-constitutional and thus federal dynamics.

[26] According to Nettesheim, the traditional "principal-agent" dynamic between the Member States and the EU is inverted, with European institutions instructing the constitutional organs of Member States not only on the actions they are required to undertake but also on those from which they are expected to abstain. This reflects a conception of integration policy that no longer regards the EU as a mere agent of the Member States, considered as principals.

[27] The Constitutional Treaty of the European Union, approved by the Intergovernmental Conference on 18 June 2004, Article I-60: *Voluntary withdrawal from the Union*.

The link between federalism and secession is unequivocal (Savastano 2019; Caravita 2020). Secession tends to be more actively pursued in multinational federations, which often represent constitutional contexts seeking innovative constitutional and institutional solutions. Secession is clearly intertwined with federal processes, particularly in the diverse relationships between central and sub-national institutions, especially when a specific minority is territorially concentrated. This issue characterises a wide range of federal models, including the European Union and within its Member States, most notably, the Scottish and Catalan questions. The role of constitutional law is to channel such conflict, to rationalise it and govern it through legal norms. For this reason, any potential political-constitutional right to secession forms an integral part of the study (Doyle 2023, pp. 91–114[28]) of federalism and of political systems based on autonomy, whether or not it leads to actual separation.

The foregoing reflections invite a closer examination of the similarities between *Brexit*, secession and state succession (Vidmar 2018, p. 447) since the constitutional dynamics of the UK's withdrawal bear resemblance to various secessionist movements worldwide (Skoutaris 2019, p. 210). These analogies are visible both in the domestic legal architecture established in the aftermath of the referendum—particularly the *European Union (Withdrawal) Act 2018*, which aimed to preserve legal continuity in a manner typical of secession scenarios—and in elements of the political rhetoric that helped drive *Brexit* forward. As highlighted in the preceding paragraphs, indeed, *Brexit* drew upon a shared underlying narrative that elevates national identity as a central, unifying force within political and social life, as commonly seen in secessionist movements (Weiler 2017, pp. 12–13).

First, rather than invoking the subjugation of a specific group, *Brexit* articulated a broader discontent with European supranationalism and the perceived absence of genuine popular authorship within the EU framework. This reveals an important dimension of the withdrawal—namely, the emphasis on nationhood or national sovereignty—as closely aligned with key features of secession, even in the absence of any substantiated claims of inequality or subordination. Moreover, a nationwide referendum does not necessarily constitute a credible assertion of a homogeneous national *demos* capable of unambiguously justifying a right to secede (Frantziou 2022, p. 74). Rather than offering a pluralistic conception of the popular will, *Brexit* appealed to the outcome of the referendum as the voice of a unified, monolithic people. Much like secessionist claims, it portrayed only a part of the people as the people (Martinico 2019, pp. 87–104), thereby raising concerns about the democratic legitimacy of such a reductionist narrative. Then *Brexit* reflected a simplified vision of direct democracy, one grounded in contested appeals to national identity. In this respect, it shares with other secessionist movements a troubling pattern of equating democracy solely with the "sovereign will"[29] of the people or with

[28] The author investigates whether the four constituent entities of the United Kingdom can be said to hold a secession right and whether a political constitution can legitimately accommodate such a right.

[29] See Supreme Court Judgments, *Reference re Secession of Quebec* [1998] 2 SCR 217, par. 67.

unqualified majority rule while sidelining other constitutional principles. In adopting such an approach, much like secession itself, *Brexit* has put the assumed interdependence between the rule of law and democratic legitimacy (Frantziou 2022, p. 74).

With regard to these complex legal systems, it is appropriate to recall the case of the Canadian Supreme Court judgment[30] regarding the proposed secession of Quebec (Caravita 2020, p. 225; Frantziou 2022, pp. 70–71; Savastano 2019, pp. 139–141). After the 1995 referendum in which federalists narrowly defeated separatists, the Canadian government asked the Court about the francophone province's right to secede, but the Court firmly denied the existence of any unilateral secession right. Although the Québécois had voted to separate, no legal obligation would arise for the federal government, nor would any automatic secession occur. Nevertheless, the Court sustained the legitimacy of using a referendum and emphasised that even a favourable outcome would simply have triggered negotiations between the seceding province and the federal government. It thus emerged how the right to secession must be balanced with other constitutional principles, such as constitutional rigidity and the rule of law. Secession is therefore possible, but only in agreement with the central government and the other provinces.

The importance of this well-known Canadian opinion lies especially in shifting secession from a substantive to a procedural dimension, precisely what occurred through the proceduralisation of a Member State's withdrawal from the EU by activating Article 50 TEU for the first time in the case of the United Kingdom. In both cases, the intention to withdraw does not automatically result in the termination of the legal relationship; rather, it triggers a legally regulated process based on negotiation and respect for constitutional principles.

There are several analogies between the Canadian Court's ruling and the procedure established under Article 50 TEU. Notable among these are that the declaration of intent merely triggers negotiations, as stipulated by the Treaties, and that secession must occur in agreement with the other provinces; just as at the European level, it must occur through the Council composed of Member State government representatives rather than through the Commission as a central and independent body. However, what most strongly links the Canadian and European cases is the attempt to proceduralise the exit from a federation, an effort to bring under the rule of law situations that are typically conducted and resolved *de facto*.

This brief overview of secession highlights how a phenomenon traditionally regarded as *extra ordinem* has gradually been reframed as a legal option, largely due to the jurisprudential contribution of the Canadian Supreme Court.

Ongoing scholarly debates on this matter, as well as its constitutional implications, have rightly led the academic literature to acknowledge the emergence of a "comparative constitutional law of secession" (Palermo 2019, pp. 265–282) owing to the functional and procedural approach that has been developed. *Brexit*, then, serves both as an internal precedent within the EU framework regarding the legal

[30] See Supreme Court Judgments, *Reference re Secession of Quebec* [1998] 2 SCR 217.

and political feasibility of withdrawal and as a valuable comparative model for federalisation trajectories shaped by secessionist aspirations.

Brexit could perhaps be regarded as a potential example of "consensual secession" (Frantziou 2022, p. 72), rather than a form of internationally protected secession, insofar as it gives effect to the democratically expressed will of the British people to leave the European Union, a will recognised in Article 50 TEU. This provision grants a Member State an almost unqualified right to withdraw, exercised under its sole sovereign responsibility. Therefore, Article 50 TEU operates as a *lex specialis* in relation to Article 54 of the Vienna Convention on the Law of Treaties and may be understood as more than a mere intergovernmental mechanism (Frantziou 2022, p. 73). Article 50 TEU outlines a step-by-step procedure for withdrawal, to be carried out within the institutional framework of the EU, and establishes the legal foundation upon which future relations may be negotiated. Nevertheless, the only substantive requirement imposed by Article 50 TEU—the obligation to act in accordance with the withdrawing state's own constitutional requirements—implies that it is for the Member State concerned to determine a withdrawal process that remains "Union-conform" (Tatham 2012, p. 149). This does not mean, however, that withdrawal is entirely devoid of procedural safeguards. The Court of Justice of the European Union[31] has clarified that Article 50 TEU must be interpreted in light of the broader constitutional values and fundamental rights of the Union, not solely according to its textual content. Even so, the specific content of a Member State's constitutional requirements is not something the EU may define or enforce. Therefore, the ultimate decision to withdraw remains a matter of "sovereign choice".[32] Article 50 TEU thus articulates a single substantive constitutional condition, which the withdrawing state is best placed to evaluate. Beyond this, the provision accommodates a broad spectrum of withdrawal modalities.

Concluding, Brexit is expected to have a lasting impact on the traditional understanding of central issues in constitutional law, as it has challenged the boundaries between state sovereignty and supranational integration, as well as the relationship between federalism, secession, and membership in a political order. It therefore calls for a reconsideration of the concept of the State in light of increasingly dynamic processes of integration and disintegration. Indeed, although the negotiations and subsequent approval of both the Withdrawal Agreement and the Trade and Cooperation Agreement proved particularly difficult in the UK, *Brexit* marked a turning point in both the theory and practice of secession. It reflects, to a certain extent, the approach adopted by the Canadian Supreme Court in its landmark case *Reference re Secession of Quebec*, which has come to be seen as a model of regulated and consensual secession (Caravita 2022). The provisions of Article 50 TEU, the mechanisms for resolving membership, the management of interdependencies between legal systems and the inclusion of a transitional period to facilitate the

[31] CJEU, *Andy Wightman and Others v Secretary of State for Exiting the European Union*, C-621/18, 10 December 2018.

[32] Ivi par. 50.

detachment all exemplify a coordinated, albeit *sui generis*, approach to secession (Fasone and Martinelli 2023).

5 Concluding Remarks

The end of the withdrawal and future partnership agreements between the EU and the United Kingdom proved to be exceedingly complex, notwithstanding the fact that the UK had long benefited from numerous *opt-outs* from the Treaties (Fasone and Martinelli 2023), most notably those concerning the Charter of Fundamental Rights and convergence towards the Economic and Monetary Union. While the UK often held back European integration because of its strong national identity and legal system, it also played a major role in advancing the EU through important economic and legal contributions. In this context, *Brexit* has provided important insights into the functioning of Article 50 TEU, establishing itself as a new milestone in the study of the right to secede from federal systems. Moreover, the case of the United Kingdom has offered important responses regarding both the resilience of the European legal order and the increasingly indispensable role it plays within the legal systems of EU Member States.

Therefore, *Brexit* has intensified pressures on supranational political entities like the European Union and reawakened the discourse surrounding the nation state, particularly by positioning migration as both material and symbolic concerns. The fear of losing cultural identity and control over national borders was pivotal in shaping the 2016 referendum. The treatment of the "stranger" within British society, moreover, highlights deep socio-cultural divisions, both across national boundaries and within domestic communities (Rowlands 2018, pp. 68–69). In this light, *Brexit means Brexit*[33] became not just a political slogan but also a legal and historical affirmation, removing any realistic prospect of reversal in what stands as one of the most consequential events in the history of European integration. It must be clearly stated that, despite the heavy blow inflicted by the exit of a prestigious Member State, *Brexit* ultimately represented a victory for the European Union. It was a success because *Britain's exit* discouraged the diffusion of Eurosceptic sentiment in other EU Member States, instead shedding light on the complexity involved in withdrawing from such a deeply embedded form of membership, particularly in relation to financial, socio-economic and organisational costs.

Most importantly, *Brexit* demonstrated the operability of Article 50 TEU and, more broadly, the legal framework regulating the separation between two legal orders. The withdrawal from the European Union, comparable in many respects to the secession of a federated state, or at least situated midway between secession within federal systems and a simple withdrawal from an international treaty, nonetheless had the crucial function of formalising a political event. This carried with it

[33] The battle slogan coined by Theresa May and frequently repeated in her public speeches.

a significant consequence: the process of separation could unfold without infringing upon the rights of both British and EU citizens, which were safeguarded at each stage (Savastano 2019, pp. 199–203). Nevertheless, the *post-Brexit* exclusion of the EU Charter from UK law, and the often fragile status of EU citizens' rights, means that rights protected under the *Human Rights Act* become even more important after *Brexit* (Douglas-Scott 2023, p. 494). However, this very law remains at risk of repeal in the future. Will the rights once protected by the EU continue to be safeguarded with the same robustness as before?

Furthermore, it could be argued that the conceptual symmetry between entry into the EU and withdrawal from it reflects a sovereign logic that is consistent in principle with the voluntary foundation of EU membership and the spirit of loyal cooperation expressed in Article 4 TEU. Nevertheless, the absence of explicit provisions in Article 50 TEU to safeguard shared constitutional values and the rights involved in EU citizenship raises serious concerns, since it enables the Union to abdicate its obligations towards individuals it has previously regarded as integral members of its legal and political order.

Moreover, it is crucial to take into account the legal consequences of a Member State's withdrawal from the European Union. It is important to consider, in this respect, that Article 50 TEU not only addresses the withdrawal negotiations but also specifies that these should take into account the framework for the future relationship between the withdrawing state and the Union. The legal systems of the Member States have become so deeply intertwined with that of the European Union that disentanglement cannot be achieved through the mere denunciation of the Treaties. The complexity of the relationship between legal orders requires a thorough impact assessment for each individual area of regulation. The response of the UK government was relatively prompt and took the form of the *European Union (Withdrawal) Bill*. This was the most significant of a series of legislative acts adopted to manage the withdrawal process. Through this Bill, the *European Communities Act 1972* was repealed with effect from the date of entry into force of the Withdrawal Agreement, and a process of "domestication" of all applicable EU norms into UK law was initiated.

Another noteworthy aspect concerns the fact that, even if the challenges posed by technical and regulatory complexity have been overcome, the legal orders nonetheless remain significantly interconnected. In particular, practical experience has demonstrated that the withdrawing state cannot reasonably expect to continue its legal existence unaffected by the future development of EU law, which had shaped its legal framework throughout the years of its membership. In fact, with the enlargement of the European Union, the acceding states have been under constant obligation to align themselves with the *acquis communautaire*.[34] From a legal per-

[34] The European Commission has outlined a range of constitutive elements of European identity, which incorporate geographical, historical and cultural dimensions. The sharing of ideas and values, along with a common history, cannot be defined by a fixed formula and should be reconsidered by each new generation (Communication from the Commission to the European Parliament and the Council, Enlargement Strategy and Main Challenges 2006–2007, annexed special report on the EU's capacity to integrate new members, Brussels, 8.11.2006, COM(2006) 649 final). Accordingly,

spective, the harmonisation of national laws across multiple policy areas in the European Union creates a unified regulatory space. The ongoing processes of legal approximation in the various areas of EU competence have contributed to the establishment of a shared legal *acquis*. Such processes have resulted in providing individuals with a more expansive and reliable set of opportunities than would be available within the confines of national legal orders. For this reason, leaving the European Union entails a comprehensive reorganisation of a country's legal and institutional system across all substantive sectors shaped over decades by EU legislation and jurisprudence. *Brexit* tested how membership of the European Union entails the creation of very strong relationships and interconnections such that their orderly and systematised disentanglement is practically impossible (Savastano 2019b, p. 260).

It is clear that the United Kingdom faced significant challenges in carrying out *Brexit* due to the deep interconnection between domestic and EU legal systems, which rendered their separation highly complex (Martinelli 2025, p. 219). In fact, *Brexit* has resulted in a "constitutional dismemberment" (De Vergottini 2023, p. XIV) on a scale far exceeding early expectations.

Despite lacking a formal Constitution, the European Union is nonetheless governed by three foundational texts that collectively fulfil the functions and reflect the structure of a modern constitutional order: the Treaty on European Union, the Treaty on the Functioning of the European Union and the Charter of Fundamental Rights. Together, these texts play a role akin to that of national constitutions. These norms are embedded in a legal and political synergy that cannot simply be replicated within a purely national framework. Accordingly, just as entry into the EU requires compliance with the 35 Copenhagen chapters, continued membership implies full integration of the *acquis*. Withdrawal, in turn, necessitates a process of deconstructing those 35 chapters (Caravita 2017, p. 3[35]). The operation in question has succeeded in the context of *Brexit*. It demonstrates that the most constitutionally complex challenge for any federated structure—namely the act of secession—can indeed be carried out in a structured and lawful manner. Furthermore, the UK's decision to leave the EU conveyed precisely those narratives of self-determination characteristic of secessionist movements and was perceived as a form of schism or apostasy, much in the same way as secessions typically are (Frantziou 2022, p. 69). Such an interpretation of *Brexit* would indeed reflect the constitutional functioning of the EU, insofar as "the formalisation of the exit procedure in the EU Treaties reinforces, in itself, a more federal view" of the Union (Pohjankoski 2018, p. 850).

It is easy to view the United Kingdom as an exceptional case. Indeed, it remains the only country to have voted to leave the EU. Yet it may be more fruitful to interpret it as a case study in how the relocation of power is challenging traditional modes of governance, which have proven inadequate in addressing internal political tensions, economic pressures and the relationship with the supranational order. The European Union has emerged strengthened, if not in the short term, then at least

any country has the right to submit an application for membership, provided it is willing to adopt the *acquis communautaire*.

[35] The author refers to Brexit as a "constitutional gamble".

over the medium to long term (Milani 2019). Far from weakening the Union, *Brexit* revealed the EU's ability to withstand a major rupture, confirming its institutional robustness in navigating such a critical juncture akin to a secession.

References

Biondi A (2017) Conclusioni del convegno 'Brexit: ad un anno dal referendum, a che punto è la notte?'. Federalismi.it 18:2–7

Caravita B (2017) Brexit: ad un anno dal referendum, a che punto è la notte? Federalismi.it 16:2–4

Caravita B (2020) Quanta Europa c'è in Europa? Percorsi e prospettive del *federalizing process* europeo. Giappichelli, Turin

Caravita B (2022) Secession, withdrawal, and the experience of the European Union. Federalismi.it 4:1–10

Closa C (2017) Troubled membership: secession and withdrawal. In: Closa C (ed) Secession from a Member State and withdrawal from the European Union. Cambridge University Press, Cambridge, pp 1–11

Curti Gialdino C (2017) Le trattative tra il Regno Unito e l'Unione europea per la Brexit alla luce dei primi due cicli negoziali. Federalismi.it 16:2–37

De Vergottini G (2023) Prefazione. In: Fasone C, Martinelli C (eds) L'impatto della Brexit sul modello Westminster. Giappichelli, Turin, pp XI–XVII

Dicey AV (1959) Introduction to the study of the law of the constitution, 10th edn. Macmillan, London

Dorling D, Tomlinson S (2019) Rule Britannia: Brexit and the End of Empire. Biteback Publishing, London

Douglas-Scott S (2023) Brexit, Union, and Disunion: The Evolution of British Constitutional Unsettlement. Cambridge University Press, Cambridge

Doyle O (2023) Leaving the Union: constitutionalising secession rights in the United Kingdom. In: Fasone C, Martinelli C (eds) A multilevel constitutional perspective on Brexit: from local to global. Giappichelli, Turin, pp 91–114

Fasone C, Martinelli C (2023) Introduction – Brexit as a multilevel constitutional challenge. In: Fasone C, Martinelli C (eds) A multilevel constitutional perspective on Brexit: from local to global. Giappichelli, Turin, pp 1–15

Frantziou E (2022) Was Brexit a form of secession? Global Policy 13:69–78

Horder M (2025) What brexit means. An anthropology of polarization and cultural change in Britain. Routledge, New York

Keating M (2021) State and nation in the United Kingdom: the fractured union. Oxford University Press, Oxford

Keating M (2022) Between two unions: UK devolution, European integration and Brexit. Territ Polit Gov 10(5):629–645

Kenny M (2021) Governance, politics and political economy – England's questions after Brexit. Territ Polit Gov 10(5):678–695

Kerry E (2016) European Union: Prime Ministers' Speeches and Party Manifestos since 1970. House of Lords Library Note, No. 2016/015, 15 March

Marquand D (2006) Federalism and the British: anatomy of a neurosis. Polit Q 77(2):175–183

Martinelli C (2022) La Brexit come «constitutional moment». Federalismi.it 10:2–33

Martinelli C (2025) Brexit and the British Constitution. Giappichelli, Turin

Martinico G (2019) Constitutionalists' guide to the populist challenge: lessons from Canada. In: Closa C, Margiotta C, Martinico G (eds) Between democracy and law: the amorality of secession. Routledge, London, pp 87–104

Milani G (2019) Chi di secessione ferisce…: la brexit e il Regno (dis)Unito. Federalismi.it – Osservatorio Brexit, 83–87
Nettesheim M (2021) Exclusion from the EU is possible as a last resort. VerfBlog
Nicolini M (2013) La costruzione territoriale dell'identità costituzionale tra finzioni giuridiche e "trauma" della secessione. Studi parlamentari e di politica costituzionale, 7–32
Palermo P (2019) Towards a comparative constitutional law of secession? In: Delledonne G, Martinico G (eds) The Canadian contribution to a comparative law of secession. Legacies of the Quebec Secession. Palgrave, London, pp 265–282
Pohjankoski P (2018) 'Secession' and 'Withdrawal' from the European Union as constitutional expressions. Eur Const Law Rev 14(4):845–854
Rieder CM (2013) The withdrawal clause of the Lisbon Treaty in the light of EU citizenship (between disintegration and integration). Fordham Int Law J 37(1):146–174
Rowlands A (2018) On the promise and the limits of politics: faith-based responses to asylum seeking. In: Ryan B (ed) Fortress Britain? Ethical approaches to immigration policy for a post-Brexit Britain. Jessica Kingsley Publishers, London and Philadelphia, pp 68–93
Ryan B (2018) Conclusions. In: Ryan B (ed) Fortress Britain? Ethical approaches to immigration policy for a post-Brexit Britain. Jessica Kingsley Publishers, London and Philadelphia, pp 154–160
Ryan B (2018b) Migration, morality and States. In: Ryan B (ed) Fortress Britain? Ethical approaches to immigration policy for a post-Brexit Britain. Jessica Kingsley Publishers, London and Philadelphia, pp 35–56
Savastano F (2015) Sulle conseguenze di un eventuale Brexit. Federalismi.it 23:2–9
Savastano F (2019) Uscire dall'Unione europea. Brexit e il diritto di recedere dai Trattati. Giappichelli, Turin
Savastano F (2019b) L'Unione europea e il mondo globale: una scelta costituzionale irreversibile? In: Allegri G, Sterpa A, Viceconte N (eds) Questioni costituzionali al tempo del populismo e del sovranismo. Editoriale Scientifica, Naples, pp 247–264
Savastano F (2023) Trasformazioni costituzionali nell'allargamento dell'Unione europea. Giappichelli, Turin
Schmitt C (1984) Dottrina della Costituzione (1928). Giuffrè, Milan
Schütze R (2023) Future(s) of and for the Union: some thoughts after Brexit. In: Fasone C, Martinelli C (eds) A multilevel constitutional perspective on Brexit: from local to global. Giappichelli, Turin, pp 119–130
Simoncini M (2023) Profili costituzionali della giurisprudenza europea sulla Brexit. In: Fasone C, Martinelli C (eds) L'impatto della Brexit sul modello Westminster. Giappichelli, Turin, pp 171–193
Skoutaris N (2019) On Brexit and secession(s). In: Closa C, Margiotta C, Martinico G (eds) Between democracy and law: the amorality of secession. Routledge, London, pp 195–212
Sobolewska M, Ford R (2020) Brexitland: identity, diversity, and the reshaping of British politics. Cambridge University Press, Cambridge
Tanca A (2018) Brexit: l'esito di una relazione problematica. Quaderni Costituzionali 2:341–360
Tatham A (2012) "Don't mention divorce at the wedding, darling!": EU accession and withdrawal after Lisbon. In: Eeckhout P, Biondi A, Ripley S (eds) EU law after Lisbon. Oxford University Press, Oxford, pp 128–154
Vidmar J (2018) Brexit, democracy and human rights: the law between secession and treaty withdrawal. Wis Int Law J 35(2):426–457
Weiler JHH (2017) Secessionism and its discontents. In: Closa C (ed) Secession from a member state and withdrawal from the European Union: troubled membership. Cambridge University Press, Cambridge, pp 12–31

The Future of Cohesion Policy in the Wake of the RRF: Towards Inexorable Centralisation?

Antonia Maria Acierno

Abstract This contribution examines the evolution of the European Union's cohesion policy and the growing tension between its original mission—reducing territorial disparities—and the new strategic priorities that emerged following the pandemic and the creation of the Recovery and Resilience Facility (RRF). After reconstructing the historical and institutional development of cohesion, the article highlights how the rise of a highly centralised governance model, built on the "cash for reforms" logic, is progressively weakening the partnership principle, the territorial embeddedness of cohesion policy and the role of regional authorities. The analysis shows that the ongoing debate on the post-2027 framework, particularly the proposal for Single National Plans, risks exacerbating this centripetal shift. The conclusions stress the need to reinforce multi-level governance and to strengthen national institutional mechanisms—especially the conference system—to prevent further marginalisation of regions and to preserve cohesion policy's founding mission of addressing territorial inequalities.

1 The Origins of Cohesion Policy and Its Institutional Implications

Cohesion policies, through redistributive measures, aim to "remedy the imbalances that Community action for the internal market causes to the detriment of the weaker regions" (Predieri 1996). Indeed, the European trajectory (Manganaro 2022; Manzella 2009) of cohesion policies has ancient origins that first emerged, in embryonic form, in the preamble to the 1957 Treaty of Rome, which explicitly urges European peoples "to strengthen the unity of their economies and to ensure their harmonious development by reducing the differences existing between the various regions and the backwardness of the less favoured regions".

A. M. Acierno (✉)
Luiss Guido Carli University, Rome, Italy
e-mail: aacierno@luiss.it

F. Savastano et al. (eds.), *Between Asymmetry and Secession*,
https://doi.org/10.1007/978-3-032-29603-0_23

However, it was not until 1986 that a more explicit formalisation of cohesion policies was established, with Article 23 of the Single European Act providing for the inclusion in Part 3 of the European Economic Community (EEC) Treaty of a Title V entitled "Economic and social cohesion".

In the aftermath of the 1988 structural funds reform, which was initiated by five regulations and came into force in 1989, the Maastricht Treaty of 1993 formally institutionalised economic and social cohesion, elevating it from its status as an "economic instrument for overcoming regional inequalities" to that of an "objective of the Union" (Manganaro 2022), alongside the single market and economic and monetary union (Commission Communication 2004; Chessa 2020). Nevertheless, the principle of cohesion was not established solely through the Maastricht Treaty. Indeed, Article 7D of the Amsterdam Treaty—which was signed on 2 October 1997 and came into force on 1 May 1999—expressly states: "Without prejudice to Articles 77, 90 and 92, and given the place occupied by services of general economic interest in the shared values of the Union as well as their role in promoting social and territorial cohesion, the Community and the Member States, each within their respective powers and within the scope of application of this Treaty, shall take care that such services operate on the basis of principles and conditions which enable them to fulfil their missions."

References to the principle of cohesion can also be found in the 2000 Charter of Fundamental Rights of the European Union (Azzena 2011), where the promotion of social and territorial cohesion is reaffirmed with regard to access to services of general economic interest (Article 36).

Similarly, in the Draft Treaty establishing a Constitution for Europe (not ratified)[1] (Lucarelli and Patroni Griffi 2003), it is expressly reiterated that the Union must "promote economic, social and territorial cohesion and solidarity among Member States".

The Treaty of Lisbon, which came into effect in 2007, formally expressed the need to balance the internal market with sustainable and inclusive growth. This was enshrined in Title XVIII of the Treaty (Articles 174–178), which replaced the original name relating to "economic and social cohesion" with "economic, social and territorial cohesion".

Due to the constraints of brevity, the present study does not address the various communications, manuals, guidelines and tools produced by the European Commission and the Interact Programme concerning cohesion policy.

There is no doubt (Azzena 2011), however, that the fact that the affirmation of the principle of cohesion has undergone constant evolution in various and heterogeneous sources has, on the one hand, inevitably contributed to the difficulty of defining an elusive concept (Cinnirella 2024) but, on the other hand, has favoured and guided the often bumpy path of social Europe (Patroni Griffi 2018a).

---

[1] As is well known, the Treaty was approved by the European Council on 18 June 2004 and by the European Parliament but was subsequently rejected by France (29 May 2005) and the Netherlands (1 June 2005) in their respective national referendums.

The principle of cohesion, which is ontologically related to the principles of subsidiarity (Di Stefano 2003), solidarity (Azzena 2011) and equality (Balboni 2001), thus becomes the means by which to realise and strengthen the statehood of the European order (Azzena 2011).

The aforementioned cohesion has been identified as a functional tool for advancing the process of European integration. However, it is important to note that this cohesion has also had a notable impact on the political and administrative structures of the Member States. This impact has been seen in the emergence of multi-level governance (Hooge 1996), which has resulted in "a transformation in the sense of a heterarchical relationship between administrations, both at the national level—where we have seen the break-up of the state and the reorganisation of powers assigned to regions and local authorities—and at the supranational level, where—as a result of the Europeanisation of regional development policy—relationships, including direct ones, have been established between the European Commission and regional administrations".

It is no coincidence, moreover, that, starting in the 1970s, specifically with the establishment of the European Regional Development Fund (ERDF) in 1975, it became possible to gradually break through the "federal blindness"– the so-called Landesblindheit (Ipsen 1966) concept coined by Ipsen—which, since the 1950s, had almost monopolised the European legal system.

Until then, in fact, in line with the traditional internationalist approach that characterised the European Economic Community, the prevailing view was that only the national governments of the Member States could participate in decision-making processes (Chessa 2020).

This thesis essentially endorsed a considerable marginalisation of sub-state territorial entities in the Community legal system (Chessa 2020) and was partly supported by the eminently centralised structure of the Member States, with the exception of what could be defined as the *exception and a half* of federal Germany and Italy, where, as is well known, the long process of implementing the Italian regions (Mangiameli 2012; Berti 1976; Staiano 2017), with the exception of the special regions, only began in the 1970s, thus inaugurating what has been aptly described as the "perennial, confused transition of Italian regionalism" (Patroni Griffi 2021).

The first formal recognition of sub-national levels of government at the European level occurred in 1985, with the regulation of Integrated Mediterranean Programmes (Council Regulation (EEC) No. 2088/85 of 23 July 1985) (Caretti 1996), which stipulated that the plans should be drawn up "at the appropriate geographical level by the authorities designated by each Member State concerned".

However, it was the 1988 reform of the Structural Funds that further delineated the gradual emergence of local government levels in both the planning and implementation of European interventions (Caretti 1996), thereby rendering local authorities recipients of shared responsibilities in these processes.

Exemplary in this regard is Article 4 of Council Regulation (EEC) No. 2052/88 of 24 June 1988 on the tasks of the Structural Funds and their effectiveness and on coordination of their activities among themselves and with the operations of the

European Investment Bank and other existing financial instruments, according to which "Community operations shall be such as to complement or contribute to corresponding national operations. They shall be established through close consultations between the Commission, the Member State concerned and the competent authorities designated by the latter at national, regional, local or other level, with each party acting as a partner in pursuit of a common goal. These consultations are hereinafter referred to as the 'partnership'. The partnership shall cover the preparation, financing, monitoring and assessment of operations."

This marked the commencement of a transition, later sealed by the Maastricht Treaty, from the so-called *functionalist regionalism* of the European Community—in which the involvement of regional and local authorities was restricted to the pursuit of certain objectives of economic and social cohesion policy, which the local governments themselves did not participate in defining—to so-called *institutionalist regionalism* (Caretti and Tarli Barbieri 2024), which echoed the "Europe of the Regions" already advocated in 1970 by Denis de Rougemont in his *Lettre ouverte aux Européens*.

In this work, the Swiss philosopher conceptualised regions as emerging entities, envisaging them as centres of cultural influence and, most significantly, as spaces for civic participation (Saint-Ouen 2014).

As previously stated, the Maastricht Treaty was instrumental in elevating the regions to a more prominent role within the European arena. This transition was facilitated by three significant innovations (D'Atena 2022). Firstly, the codification of the principle of subsidiarity introduced greater flexibility into the division of powers between different bodies, enabling regions to establish forms of partnership within the fund programming process. Secondly, the introduction of the possibility for Member States to be represented at Council of Ministers meetings by members of regional governments, initiated upon the request of the German Länder, contributed to the regional representation. Thirdly, the establishment of the Committee of the Regions played a crucial role in promoting regional involvement.

1.1 The Committee of the Regions and Cohesion Policy

The Committee of the Regions, in accordance with Article 300 of the Treaty on the Functioning of the European Union (TFEU), provides assistance to the European Parliament, the Council and the Commission in legislative and decision-making processes.

The composition of the body in question is such that it consists of representatives of local and regional authorities from the Member States (D'Atena 2022).[2] Initially,

[2] Individual representation guaranteed to regions is found in the three federal states of the Union and in two states with regions endowed with legislative powers, namely Spain and Portugal. In addition to these two states, before Brexit, the United Kingdom was also considered. The Italian case is rather peculiar in this regard, as Italy is the only state with regions with legislative powers in which individual representation of the regions is not guaranteed: in fact, out of 20 regions, only 14 have guaranteed full membership at the regional level.

the Committee possessed extremely limited prerogatives, to the extent that even the other Community institutions refused to recognise it. However, between 1995 and 2004, there was a change of pace, strengthening its position within the European institutional framework, although it should be reiterated that it has never been formally recognised as an institution (Decoster et al. 2019). Indeed, the origins of this body, which was formally established in 1994, are quite old. Notably, as early as 9 May 1960, the European Parliamentary Assembly, the precursor to the European Parliament, had proposed the establishment of a consultative committee on regional economies (European Committee of the Regions et al. 2020). This decision was implemented following the enactment of the Single European Act in 1988, which led to the establishment of the Consultative Council of Regional and Local Authorities as an advisory body to the Commission (Aliberti 2018).

However, the establishment of the European Committee of the Regions must be considered within the historical and geopolitical context that followed the fall of the Berlin Wall on 9 November 1989 (European Committee of the Regions et al. 2020).

However, the establishment of the European Committee of the Regions must be considered within the historical and geopolitical context that followed the fall of the Berlin Wall on 9 November 1989.

It was during this period that, at the instigation of the then French President François Mitterrand, a project was promoted for a political union for the European Community in which to place the new Federal Republic of Germany (German reunification had taken place on 3 October 1990) (European Committee of the Regions et al. 2020). The primary objective of the initiative was to enhance the involvement of the German Länder and the Belgian regions in the European legislative process (European Committee of the Regions et al. 2020). However, following the Maastricht Treaty, the proposal was reduced in scope, with the intention of establishing an advisory body being deemed sufficient for regions with strong legislative powers to take part in European governance through their participation in the EU Council of Ministers (European Committee of the Regions et al. 2020; McCarthy 1997).

Although, as mentioned above, Article 13 of the Treaty on European Union (TEU) does not include the Committee of the Regions in the list of European Union institutions[3] (Decoster et al. 2019), the reforms of the Treaties between 1997 and 2004, initiated with the aim of preparing for the enlargement of the EU to 27 Member States (achieved in 2007 with the accession of Romania and Bulgaria), have contributed significantly to the strengthening of its role (Decoster et al. 2019).

The Treaty of Amsterdam is particularly significant in this regard, as it guaranteed the Committee of the Regions administrative and budgetary autonomy (Decoster et al. 2019). The Treaty of Lisbon further expanded the scope of the Committee's advisory role, extending the range of matters subject to mandatory consultation and authorising it to bring cases before the Court of Justice of the European Union as a semi-privileged claimant in cases where it is excluded from the legislative process or

[3]Article 13 lists only the European Parliament, the European Council, the Council, the European Commission, the Court of Justice of the European Union, the European Central Bank and the Court of Auditors among the institutions of the European Union.

in cases of violation of the principle of subsidiarity (Decoster et al. 2019). It is evident that this possibility is not recognised, for example, in the case of the European Economic and Social Committee (EESC) (Decoster et al. 2019).

With regard to cohesion policy, the Committee of the Regions plays a pivotal role. By means of its advisory function, the Committee seeks to influence European policies, particularly those relating to regional development and territorial cohesion, in a manner that aligns with the specific needs of the territories.

In this regard, it is noteworthy that the Committee of the Regions has established a special commission responsible for territorial cohesion policy and the EU budget (COTER). As will subsequently be evidenced, this commission is firmly opposed in today's public debate to any form of centralisation of cohesion policy after 2027.

The role of the Committee of the Regions with regard to cohesion policy is, among other things, detailed in various provisions of the Treaty on the Functioning of the EU.

In particular, Article 175 TFEU stipulates that every 3 years, the European Commission shall submit to the European Parliament, the Council, the Economic and Social Committee and the Committee of the Regions a report on the progress made towards achieving economic, social and territorial cohesion. Concurrently, the Committee of the Regions and the Economic and Social Committee will fulfil an advisory function within the ordinary legislative procedure, whereby the European Parliament and the Council will adopt specific measures deemed necessary outside the Funds, without prejudice to measures decided upon in the context of other Union policies.

Article 177 TFEU also provides for consultation of the Committee of the Regions and the Economic and Social Committee as part of the ordinary legislative procedure by which the European Parliament and the Council define the tasks, priority objectives and organisation of the Structural Funds. In accordance with Article 177 TFEU, the same procedure is employed to define the general rules applicable to the funds, as well as the provisions necessary to ensure the effectiveness and coordination of the funds among themselves and with other existing financial instruments. Furthermore, a Cohesion Fund is established to provide financial contributions to projects in the field of the environment and trans-European networks in the area of transport infrastructure. In accordance with Article 178 TFEU, the implementing regulations relating to the European Regional Development Fund are to be adopted by the European Parliament and the Council. This process is to be undertaken in accordance with the ordinary legislative procedure and must be preceded by consultation with the Economic and Social Committee and the Committee of the Regions. Despite the existence of a regulatory framework, the effectiveness of the advisory work carried out by the Committee of the Regions has often been considered somewhat disappointing, particularly with regard to the failure to take on board the recommendations that the Committee addresses to the Council on draft regulations concerning the Structural Funds, which frequently take the form of actual amendments (Marchetti 2011). This absence of responsiveness on the part of European institutions in considering the opinions of the Committee of the Regions is accompanied by the fragmentation of the institutional structures of individual Member States, which often exhibit highly diverse forms of decentralisation. This has resulted in regions and local authorities favouring dialogue with national governments rather than with European institutions (Marchetti 2011). This demonstrates that the process of enhancing the role of the regions in Europe remains firmly anchored to the constitutional models of the individual Member States, meaning that decisions taken at the European level can only exert a marginal influence (Chessa 2020).

With regard to the Committee of the Regions, the prevailing scholarly consensus (Hönnige et al. 2015) that its influence on the European decision-making process is negligible due to its purely advisory role is partly contradicted by empirical studies. These studies have demonstrated that a significant percentage of the European Commission's legislative proposals on regional matters have taken the Committee of the Regions' position into account (Neshkova 2010).

A recent evolutionary study on the relationship between the European Parliament and the Committee of the Regions is also of interest. This study (Decoster et al. 2019) highlights how the relationship between these two institutions, initially characterised by a high degree of mistrust, has improved greatly over time, resulting in fruitful cooperation. The initial endorsement of the Committee of the Regions by the Treaty of Amsterdam, which empowered the European Parliament to consult the Committee directly, and the Treaty of Lisbon, which introduced an obligation for the European Parliament to consult the Committee on legislative proposals within its remit, was followed by the signing of a mutual cooperation agreement between the two bodies (Decoster et al. 2019).

Confirming the greater—albeit still imperfect—involvement of the Committee of the Regions in the European decision-making process, there are various examples of opinions issued by the Committee of the Regions that have been effectively taken on board by the Council of the EU (or during negotiations with the Parliament and the Commission).

For instance, consider the Drinking Water Directive (recast 2018). In this case, the Committee proposed amendments that were subsequently adopted by both the Parliament and the Council. These amendments included the inclusion of a flexible derogation for small water suppliers and greater transparency towards citizens.[4]

A more recent case study, which involved the European Parliament and the Council reaching a compromise agreement on the regulation of a European Health Data Space (EHDS) on 14 March 2024, also demonstrates the incorporation of various amendments proposed by the Committee of the Regions. These amendments call for greater involvement of regions and local authorities, as well as the need to support new additional infrastructure through innovative funding programmes.[5]

As will be demonstrated in conclusion, the Committee of the Regions is playing an active role in emphasising the necessity to uphold the role of regions and local authorities in the ongoing debate concerning the EU's long-term budget for the post-2027 era.

---

[4] Quality of water intended for human consumption | European Committee of the Regions.

[5] Lo spazio europeo dei dati sanitari | Comitato europeo delle regioni.

2 The "Identity Crisis" of Cohesion Policy

Despite constituting one-third of the European Union's budget, the European Union's cohesion policy has long been characterised by a certain "identity crisis" (Hunter 2023), as its objectives have changed so much that its clear definition has been lost (Petit 2004). In this sense, cohesion policy has evolved to become increasingly "protean" (Opinion of Mr Advocate General Bot delivered on 2 April 2009) in nature. In fact, as rightly pointed out in a review (European Court of Auditors 2025a) published in June 2025 by the European Court of Auditors, cohesion policy—despite Article 174 of the TFEU, which defines its objective or, rather, its founding mission as reducing territorial disparities—has included an increasing number of priorities, including the green and digital transition, research and innovation, employment, education, cross-border cooperation, sustainable transport and social inclusion.

In particular, cohesion policy has returned to the forefront of public debate, monopolising the current public discourse, alongside the emergence of new public priorities that, in the wake of the recent implementation of Next Generation EU (NGEU), are unfolding in the context of negotiations on the future of the EU budget and the new EU legislative cycle (Schwab 2024).

In March 2025, following President Von der Leyen's proposal for the so-called Rearm Europe Plan, the Joint White Paper for European Defence Readiness 2030 was published. This document, while ostensibly seeking to enhance the flexibility of the European Union's instruments, unambiguously reaffirmed the objective of orienting cohesion policy towards investments in defence and security. In particular, it was expressly stated: "The development of a strong and resilient European defence industry will support European competitiveness and promote regional development and economic growth" (European Commission 2025a). Shortly thereafter, the conclusions of the white paper were explicitly reflected in the communication entitled "A modernised Cohesion policy: The mid-term review", presented on 1 April 2025 by the European Commission.

In particular, in this communication, "the Commission proposes to create two new specific objectives within the existing scope of the European Regional Development Fund (ERDF) and Cohesion Fund support". Specifically, the first new objective authorises Member States to voluntarily reprogramme funds allocated to strengthening the productive capacities of defence companies, circumventing restrictions relating to geographical location or company size but complying with state aid rules. Conversely, the second new specific objective pertaining to defence encourages the construction of "resilient defence or dual-use infrastructure to foster military mobility in the Union". Moreover, Raffaele Fitto, the Executive Vice President of the Commission responsible for Cohesion and Reforms, has identified five priorities for the mid-term review of EU cohesion policy: competitiveness, defence (especially for regions along the eastern border), housing, water resilience and energy transition. This development confirms the increasingly versatile and multifaceted nature of cohesion policy. This expansion carries with it the risk of weakening the territory-based approach that is characteristic of cohesion policy, thus leading to an increase in the territorial disparities that cohesion policy is designed to address and equalise (European Court of Auditors 2025b). Furthermore, it is inevitable that tensions will emerge between the historical objectives, which could be more accurately described as identity related, of cohesion policy and the new objectives of the Union, particularly in the context of a community budget that will be incapable of financing such disparate priorities concurrently. This will serve to exacerbate the risk that the expenditure allocated to reducing territorial disparities will be reduced in order to favour policies considered more strategic.

However, even prior to the mid-term review in April 2025, the Recovery and Resilience Facility contributed significantly to this identity crisis in cohesion policy. As is well known, the Facility pursues the goal of strengthening the twin transition and the cohesion and resilience of the European Union, as does the cohesion policy. However, the two policies differ from each other in other respects, as will be seen.

In this sense, it is noteworthy that the extensive reflection on the future of cohesion policy—which has involved, in various capacities, the advisory bodies of the European Union, Member States, regional and local authorities and stakeholders (Margaras and Alvarez 2025)—has been triggered precisely by the influence exerted by the Recovery and Resilience Facility on cohesion policy.

It is of particular interest to note the work carried out by the European Commission, which established a group of high-level specialists to examine the future challenges of cohesion policy. The work of this team of experts was concluded in February 2024 with the presentation of a report, which was subsequently incorporated into the ninth Cohesion Report. The report "Forging a sustainable future together: cohesion for a competitive and inclusive Europe" emphasised the necessity of adopting the performance-based approach of the Recovery and Resilience Facility in an innovative and non-pedantic manner.

3 A Comparison Between the Recovery and Resilience Facility and Cohesion Policy: Challenges and Lessons Learned

As previously stated, the Recovery and Resilience Facility—the primary expenditure programme of *Next Generation EU* (Dermine 2023; Buti and Fabbrini 2023; De Witte 2021; Leino-Sandberg and Ruffert 2022)—and cohesion policy are associated with a number of congruent objectives, primarily encompassing the twin transition and the cohesion and resilience of the European Union. The financial allocations for these two programmes are comparable, with €530 billion designated for cohesion and €723.8 billion for the RRF, and both programmes support similar investment types (European Commission 2024).

This phenomenon is exemplified by the legal foundations upon which the Next Generation EU initiative is established: Articles 122 and 175 of the TFEU.

In particular, Article 175(3) TFEU, the flexibility clause (De Witte 2021)[6] that allows for the adoption of "specific actions outside the Funds" in the field of cohesion, forms the legal basis for the so-called RRF Regulation (EU Regulation 2020/241).

As articulated by the European Commission in the annexes to the proposal for a regulation of the European Parliament and of the Council establishing the Recovery and Resilience Facility (COM(2020) 408 final ANNEXES 1 to 3), the overarching objective of this Facility is to "effectively contribute to the strengthening of the growth potential, job creation and the economic and social resilience of the Member State, to mitigate the economic and social impact of the crisis and to contribute to the strengthening of economic, social and territorial cohesion".

In this preamble, there is therefore clear justification for the use of Article 175(3) TFEU as the legal basis for the so-called RRF Regulation.

This justification is articulated in Article 4(1) of the RRF Regulation, which explicitly identifies the promotion of economic, social and territorial cohesion as the general objective of the Facility, although it is accompanied by a dozen other objectives of a highly diverse nature (Dermine 2023).

From an operational point of view, however, the two instruments differ significantly. It is no coincidence that numerous analyses have been carried out comparing cohesion policy and the RRF (European Court of Auditors 2023; Adalid 2024; Zeitlin et al. 2023; Darvas and Weslau 2023; Centurelli 2022; Corti et al. 2024; Bachtler et al. 2024; Molica et al. 2024a), which will be summarised below.

With regard to the financial aspects, the RRF is funded by the EU budget, which is financed by own resources and contributions from the Member States. By contrast, the RRF, as part of the NGEU, is entirely financed by loans from the capital markets.[7]

Furthermore, there are some discrepancies in the similarity of the policy objectives pursued by the two instruments. While cohesion policy is ontologically suited to long-term objectives aimed at bridging the gaps between regions, the RRF is a temporary instrument whose main purpose is to stem the economic and social consequences of the COVID-19 pandemic.

However, as far as our analysis is concerned, the main difference between the two instruments is in terms of governance.

As reiterated by the Commission itself, the RRF "is an innovative, performance-based instrument, where payments are made to Member States, as beneficiaries, upon delivering reforms and investments preagreed in national recovery and resilience plans […] Focused on the timely and efficient implementation of Member States' plans, the performance logic of the RRF makes payments conditional on concrete outcomes. Disbursements thus depend on the delivery of the preagreed

[6] Since 2002, many measures have been adopted on the basis of Article 175 paragraph 3 TFEU (European Solidarity Fund, 2002; European Globalisation Adjustment Fund, 2006; European Fund for Aid to the Most Deprived, 2014; Structural Reform Support Programme, 2017; Reform Support Programme, 2020; Just Transition Fund, 2020).

[7] Article 5(1) of Council Decision (EU, Euratom) 2020/20253.

investments and reforms rather than the final costs incurred" (European Commission 2023).

In particular, the NGEU has sealed a truly new "method of government". This "method of government" (Fasone and Lupo 2023) takes the form of a conditional mechanism known as "cash for reforms" (Leino-Sandberg 2023), which stipulates that the disbursement of European resources is conditional upon the submission of strictly performance-based National Recovery and Resilience Plans (PNRRs) by individual Member States wishing to benefit from them. As a result, the receipt of NGEU funds is no longer an automatic consequence of reporting the costs incurred, as is traditionally the case with cohesion funds, but follows the satisfactory achievement of the objectives and targets set by Member States in their national plans, which are assessed through constant bilateral dialogue, and often informal, between the European Commission and the governments of the individual Member States during both the definition and implementation phases of the individual plans.

Moreover, while the RRF is implemented under direct management, cohesion policy funds are implemented under shared management (European Commission 2024). It is evident that, on a European level, the European Commission—through its internal organisational structure (the Secretariat-General for Recovery and Resilience—RECOVER and DG ECFIN)—directly manages the RRF, whereas in cohesion policy, it shares responsibility with the Member States. At the national level, in the case of the RRF, each Member State has designated a state administration to act as coordinator of the Plan, integrating the single point of contact with the Commission. In cohesion policy, however, there are countless national and regional authorities in the Member States involved in the programming and implementation of individual programmes (European Commission 2024).

Furthermore, the cohesion policy is not only in accordance with the principle of territoriality but also fosters a bottom-up decision-making process, thereby proactively engaging local actors and civil society (Schwab 2024).

Conversely, the RRF, being exempt from the partnership principle, does not allocate a driving role for regional actors in the formulation of national plans. This is formally reflected in Article 18(4)(q) of the RRF Regulation, which stipulates that national plans must include, but not necessarily only, "a summary of the consultation process" with regional and local authorities and civil society (such as the social partners) (Adalid 2024). This has resulted in the almost total and generalised marginalisation of regional authorities in the preparation of the plans.

This has been emphasised since the implementation of the plans by the Committee of the Regions (Committee of Regions 2021, 2022), which, in 2024, following a further investigation (CoR-CEMR 2024), confirmed the ongoing exclusion of the regions, even during the revision of the plans through the preparation of the RepowerEU chapters.

Similar findings were also reached in the interesting survey conducted as part of the "Regions for EU Recovery" (R4EUR) initiative, created in 2020, which includes more than 30 European regions from nine Member States (Austria, Belgium, Finland, France, Germany, Italy, Poland, Slovakia and Spain).

The present study's findings are consistent with those of a survey conducted as part of the "Regions for EU Recovery" (R4EUR) initiative, which was established in 2020 and encompasses over 30 European regions from nine Member States (Austria, Belgium, Finland, France, Germany, Italy, Poland, Slovakia and Spain). While the report (Regions for EU Recovery 2022) corroborates the pervasive marginalisation of regional entities in the execution of the RRF, it concomitantly underscores a partial realignment of this tendency, manifesting solely in Åland, Flanders and Lower Austria. In these regions, the implementation of the RRF has facilitated an augmentation in the involvement of the regions, thereby counterbalancing their initial exclusion from the formulation of the plans.

According to the majority of respondents, the primary risks identified by local and regional governments in the implementation of the RRF are potential overlaps and a lack of coordination with the European Structural and Investment Funds.

Conversely, the European Court of Auditors has identified that the concurrent existence of the RRF and cohesion funding introduces heightened absorption risks, primarily attributable to the inherent deficiencies within public administrations tasked with implementing two distinct policies concurrently (Mendez and Bachtler 2024; Barbero et al. 2023).

In this sense, although many parties advocate for the adoption of a performance-based approach in cohesion policy, akin to that employed by the RRF, the potential risks of implementing the RRF model within the Structural Funds cannot be understated.

Indeed, the European Court of Auditors has raised concerns regarding the subordination of RRF payments to Member States on the condition of the satisfactory achievement of previously agreed targets and objectives. This has led to the question of whether the RRF can be regarded as a performance-based instrument. This issue is further compounded by the marginalisation of regional authorities and the presence of numerous critical issues within the RRF model. These include a lack of attention to actual results (European Court of Auditors 2024) and a low level of transparency in the use of funds.

For this reason, it is imperative to enhance the instruments utilising the financing-not-linked-to-costs model, which is both generalised and enshrined in the NGEU. This enhancement should be informed by the lessons learned from the RRF (European Court of Auditors 2024).

4 Concluding Remarks Looking to the Near Future

Nevertheless, the primary legacy of the RRF model as incorporated within the European Commission's communication on the mid-term review of cohesion policy appears to overlook the lessons learned thus far from the RRF. Instead of orienting cohesion policy towards a more results-oriented approach, it appears to be influenced solely by the centripetal drift of its governance from the RRF model (Acierno 2023).

Indeed, the mid-term review unambiguously directs post-2027 cohesion policy towards centralisation. In this sense, the Commission's proposal (European

Commission, Communication 2025b) to establish 27 Single National Plans (SNPs) for reforms and investments is emblematic. These SNPs, for each Member State, encompass a range of areas of intervention, including fisheries, the Cohesion Fund, the European Social Fund, the Common Agricultural Policy Funds, the European Regional Development Fund, the Internal Affairs Fund, and others (e.g. the Social Climate Fund) (Mehlbye et al. 2025).

While the centralisation of European funds may, in principle, accelerate and streamline the process of their disbursement, it is important to note that this may result in the marginalisation of regional actors and the distortion of the territorial anchoring of cohesion policy (Hunter 2025).

In this sense, the mid-term review, in the wake of the RRF's lack of attention to the territory (Carrosio et al. 2022; Ferraiuolo 2022; Patroni Griffi 2022),[8] supports the paradigm of so-called hyper-Lisbonisation and re-nationalisation. This is characterised by an increasingly centralised governance of cohesion policy, with the objectives of the policy being subordinate to the short-term and rapidly evolving sectoral priorities of the EU agenda (Molica et al. 2024b). This is detrimental to the reduction of territorial disparities, which should be the core mission of the cohesion funds.

The risks of marginalisation of the regions that emerge from the mid-term review were immediately apparent to the Committee of the Regions. The Committee has, as previously mentioned, been openly and firmly opposing any form of possible centralisation. It has called for the active and full involvement of local and regional authorities in the management of decisions on the definition of investment priorities, including in new instruments such as the Competitiveness Fund (Cor Press release 2025a). The Committee of the Regions has reiterated the necessity to preserve the fundamental principles of cohesion policy, including the place-based approach, the partnership principle, the subsidiarity (Leino-Sandberg 2024) principle and multi-level governance, within the renewed post-2027 cohesion policy framework (CoR Press release 2025b).

How, then, can the regions be enhanced?

Clearly, institutional remedies to stem the marginalisation of regional authorities and revitalise autonomy must be sought in the constitutional models of individual Member States, which provide for forms of decentralisation that are sometimes profoundly heterogeneous.

In conclusion, it may be useful to mention the Italian case, given that Italy[9] is the state with the lowest level of involvement of local authorities in the planning phase

[8] Although the Italian NRRP allocates 40% of distributable investments to the South, a study by ANCE (*PNRR: revisione e stato di attuazione delle misure di interesse per le costruzioni, 8 maggio 2024*) shows that only 29% of PNRR projects have been launched in the South, compared to 40% in the North and 36% in the Centre.

[9] Italy, among other things, is also experiencing a series of difficulties with regard to expenditure under the Structural Funds programmes. In March 2025, Italy declared payments amounting to approximately 3.7 billion (4.95% of the total 74 billion planned). On this point, see Servizio Studi della Camera dei deputati (2025), *La politica di coesione in Italia*, June 2025, p. 20 ff.

of the PNRR (National Recovery and Resilience Plan),[10] having implemented what has been defined as a "federalism of mere execution [...]in this paradigm, local authorities are entrusted exclusively with the implementation of political and administrative decisions taken at national and European level within their respective local areas. They only sporadically engage in forms of 'upstream' sharing or participation (even if only for information purposes) with the political bodies representing those areas" (Cecchetti 2022).

In order to attempt to "reverse the trend" and thus collaterally streamline the pursuit of the objectives of the National Recovery and Resilience Plans and the cohesion policy aimed at reducing territorial disparities, it appears to be a priority to enhance the principle of loyal cooperation (Agosta 2008) between the different levels of government (Dirri 2024) through what the Italian Constitutional Court itself has defined as "the main instrument that allows the regions to play a role in determining the content of certain state legislative acts that affect matters of regional competence", namely the "conference system".[11]

In this perspective, the desired *constitutionalisation* (Dirri 2024) of the conference system—understood, in accordance with the established position of the Constitutional Court,[12] as the typical forum for the implementation of the principle of loyal cooperation—could be the most suitable solution, responding to a form of cooperative regionalism expressed in a European dimension. The promotion of political mediation in institutional liaison forums is therefore the challenge to be overcome in order to enable more widespread participation by the regions in European decision-making processes (Caridà 2018). This is especially true in a system such as Italy's, which suffers from the absence of a chamber representing the regions in a bicameral system that has retained its equal structure (Patroni Griffi 2018b).

Furthermore, as has been rightly emphasised, the necessity for collaboration between different levels of government is common to almost all composite states (Dirri 2024; Palermo 2018).

References

Acierno AM (2023) La governance del Piano nazionale di ripresa e resilienza nel prisma dei rapporti endogovernativi. Diritto Pubblico Europeo - Rassegna Online 19(1)

Adalid S (2024) Interactions between cohesion policy and next generation EU. "Planned financing" and the transformation of European economy. Legal perspectives of the EU Cohesion Policy (ed. Ottaviano), Giappichelli, Turin

[10] On this point, Italy ranks behind Romania, Spain, France and Croatia: "Italy is the worst performer as its NRRP does not include a section on any consultation process" (see European Committee of the Regions, 2021, EU Regional and Local Barometer, Brussels, pp. 34–35).

[11] Ruling No. 33/2011 (Point 5.5. of the Considerato in diritto).

[12] Constitutional Court, Judgments Nos. 192/2024; 106/2020; 195/2019; 36/2018; 308/2011; 33/2011; 31/2006; 62/2005; 116/1994.

Agosta S (2008) Leale collaborazione tra Stato e Regioni. Giuffrè, Milan

Aliberti C (2018) Il ruolo del Comitato delle Regioni nell'assetto istituzionale dell'Unione europea. Diritti regionali

Azzena L (2011) Il principio di coesione come indicatore del quantum di statualità, Politiche di coesione e integrazione europea. Una riforma difficile ma possibile (ed. Colombini), Jovene, Naples, p 110 ff

Bachtler J, Mendez C, Downes R (2024) Charting a new course for cohesion policy after 2027, EoRPA Report 24/3, European Regional Policy Research Consortium

Balboni E (2001) Il principio della coesione economica e sociale nell'ordinamento comunitario e nella recente esperienza dell'Unione. La difficile Costituzione europea (ed. De Siervo), Il Mulino, Bologna, p 26 ff

Barbero J, Christensen M, Conte A, Lecca P, Rodríguez-Pose A, Salotti S (2023) Improving government quality in the regions of the EU and its system-wide benefits for cohesion policy. J Common Mark Stud 61

Berti G (1976) Art. 5. Comm. della Cost. Branca, Rome-Bologna

Buti M, Fabbrini S (2023) Next generation EU and the future of economic governance: towards a paradigm change or just a big one-off? J Eur Public Policy 30:4

Caretti P (1996) Le regioni tra programmazione statale e comunitaria: il caso dei Fondi strutturali. Fondi strutturali e coesione economica e sociale nell'Unione europea (ed. Predieri), Giuffrè, Milan, p 257

Caretti P, Tarli Barbieri G (2024) Diritto regionale. Giappichelli, Turin

Caridà R (2018) Leale collaborazione e sistema delle conferenze. Cedam, Padua

Carrosio G, Cicerone G, Faggian A, Urso G (2022) How place-sensitive are the national recovery and resilience plans? Recovery Watch series

Cecchetti M (2022) L'incidenza del PNRR sui livelli territoriali di governo e le conseguenze nei sistemi amministrativ. Rivista AIC 3

Centurelli G (2022) Next Generation Eu e fondi strutturali. L'evoluzione dei sistemi di gestione e controllo ed elementi di semplificazione nel periodo 2021-2027. Rivista giuridica del Mezzogiorno 1

Chessa O (2020) L' «Europa delle Regioni»: illusioni e disillusioni. Federalismi.it 7

Cinnirella C (2024) Solidarity and cohesion in EU law. Legal perspectives of the EU Cohesion Policy (ed. Ottaviano), Giappichelli, Turin, p 71

Commission Communication (2004) Third Report on economic and social cohesion [COM(2004) 107 final]

Committee of Regions (2021) Regional and local authorities and the National Recovery and Resilience Plans, Bruxelles

CoR Press release (2025a) Il futuro bilancio dell'UE deve essere ambizioso e stabilire regole chiare per consentire alle regioni di affrontare le sfide strutturali ed emergenti, affermano i leader locali a Brest, Il futuro bilancio dell'UE deve essere ambizioso e stabilire regole chiare per consentire alle regioni di affrontare le sfide strutturali ed emergenti, affermano i leader locali a Brest | Comitato europeo delle regioni

CoR Press release (2025b) Cohesion Policy post 2027: linking investments and reforms must not lead to a more centralised governance, Cohesion Policy post 2027: linking investments and reforms must not lead to a more centralised governance | European Committee of the Regions

CoR-CEMR (2022) Implementation of the Recovery and Resilience Facility: The perspective of Local and Regional Authorities. Results of the CoR-CEMR targeted consultation

CoR-CEMR (2024) Implementation of the Recovery and Resilience Facility: The perspective of Local and Regional Authorities. Results of the CoR-CEMR targeted consultation

Corti F, Pedralli M, Pancotti C (2024). The recovery and resilience facility: key innovations and the interplay with cohesion policy, ZEW Discussion Papers, No. 24-040, ZEW - Leibniz-Zentrum für Europäische Wirtschaftsforschung, Mannheim

D'Atena A (2022) Diritto regionale. Quinta edizione, Giappichelli, Turin, p 413

Darvas Z, Weslau L (2023) First lessons from the Recovery and Resilience Facility for the EU economic governance framework, study for the European Parliament, Economic Governance and EMU Scrutiny Unit, IPOL IDA(2023)741748

De Witte B (2021) The European Union's Covid-19 Recovery Plan: the legal engineering of an economic policy shift. Common Mark Law Rev

Decoster F, Delhomme V, Rousselle J (2019) The Committee of the Regions and the European Parliament: an evolving relationship. The European Parliament in times of EU crisis. Dynamics and Transformations (ed. Costa), Palgrave Macmillan, London

Dermine P (2023) Le plan de relance "Next Generation EU" de l'Union européenne. Analyse constitutionnelle d'une initiative historique, Bruylant, Bruxelles

Di Stefano A (2003) Le politiche strutturali dell'Unione europea e il principio di sussidiarietà. Politica comunitaria di coesione economica e sociale e programmazione economica regionale (ed. Sapienza), Milan

Dirri A (2024) La leale cooperazione nell'assestamento del PNRR: un regionalismo «esecutivo» per il superamento dei divari territoriali. Osservatorio costituzionale, 1

European Commission (2023) Recovery and Resilience Facility: Two years on. A unique instrument at the heart of the EU's green and digital transformation, COM (2023) 99 final

European Commission (2024) External supporting study – Case study on the functioning of the RRF and other EU funds

European Commission (2025a) Joint white paper for European Defence Readiness 2030, Brussels, 19.3.2025 JOIN(2025) 120 final, 17–18

European Commission (2025b) Communication from the Commission to the European Parliament, the European Council, the Council, the European Economic and Social Committee and the Committee of the Regions. The road to the next multiannual financial framework, Strasbourg, 11.2.2025 COM(2025) 46 final

European Committee of the Regions, B. Wassenberg (2020) The History of the Committee of the Regions (1994-2019) – 25 years of cities and regions furthering European integration. 2020, https://data.europa.eu/doi/10.2860/501, p 195 ff

European Committee of the Regions (2021) EU Regional and Local Barometer, Brussels

European Court of Auditors (2023) EU financing through cohesion policy and the Recovery and Resilience Facility: A comparative analysis (Review, 1/2023)

European Court of Auditors (2024) Performance-orientation, accountability and transparency – lessons to be learned from the weaknesses of the RRF (Review 2/2024)

European Court of Auditors (2025a) The Future of EU Cohesion Policy: Drawing lessons from the past" (Review 04/2025)

European Court of Auditors (2025b). Opinion, 2

Fasone C, Lupo N (2023) Learning from the Euro-crisis. A new method of government for the EU's economic policy coordination after the pandemic. Sant'Anna Legal Studies (STALS) Research Paper, 4

Ferraiuolo G (2022) Correzione delle asimmetrie territoriali. Rivista AIC 3

Hönnige C et al (2015) Consultative Committees in the European Union. No Vote – No Influence? ECPR Press, Colchester

Hooge L (1996) Cohesion Policy and European Integration: building multi-level governance. Oxford University Press

Hunter A (2023) Addressing Cohesion Policy's identity crisis in a changing European Union. Discussion paper Europe's political economy programme

Hunter A (2025) Cohesion policy's mid-term review: stress-testing regional development in a new EU era. European policy centre

Ipsen HP (1966) Als Bundesstaat in der Gemeinschaft. Problemedes europäischen Rechts, Frankfurt, p 256

Leino-Sandberg P (2023) Recovery and resilience facility two years after- quo vadis EU money? Verfassungsblog

Leino-Sandberg P (2024) Cohesion policy and the principle of subsidiarity: a legal analysis, ZEW Discussion Papers, No. 24-042, ZEW - Leibniz-Zentrum für Europäische Wirtschaftsforschung, Mannheim

Leino-Sandberg P, Ruffert M (2022) Next generation Eu and its constitutional ramifications: a critical assessment. Common Mark Law Rev:433 ff

Lucarelli A, Patroni Griffi A (2003) Studi sulla Costituzione europea. Percorsi e ipotesi, Edizioni scientifiche italiane, Naples

Manganaro F (2022) Politiche di coesione. Enciclopedia del diritto. I tematici, Giuffrè, Milan, p 842 ff

Mangiameli S (2012) Il regionalismo italiano dall'unità alla Costituzione e alla sua riforma, Milan

Manzella GP (2009) The turning points of EU Cohesion policy, Report Working Paper, Investment Bank, Luxembourg

Marchetti A (2011) Il comitato delle regioni nella definizione delle politiche comunitarie di coesione, Politiche di coesione e integrazione europea. Una riforma difficile ma possibile (ed. Colombini), Jovene, Naples, p 165 ff

Margaras V, Alvarez E (2025) The future of cohesion policy. Current state of the debate, EPRS | European Parliamentary Research Service, PE 767.217

McCarthy RE (1997) The Committee of the Regions: an advisory body's tortuous path to influence. J Eur Public Policy 4(3)

Mehlbye P, Böhme K, Schön P, Martin D (2025) 27 national plans: include the territorial reality! Spatial Foresight

Mendez C, Bachtler J (2024) The quality of government and administrative performance: explaining Cohesion Policy compliance, absorption and achievements across EU regions. Reg Stud 58

Molica F, Santos AM, Conte A (2024a) Measuring achievements: can cohesion policy programmes effectively monitor their performance? Investigaciones Regionales – J Reg Res 62

Molica F, de Renzis A, Bourdin S (2024b) Between re-renationalisation and hyper-Lisbonisation: the long goodbye to the EU Cohesion Policy original goals. GSSI Discussion Paper Series in Regional Science & Economic Geography, Discussion paper, 10

Neshkova MI (2010) The impact of subnational interests on supranational regulation. J Eur Public Policy 17(8)

Opinion of Mr Advocate General Bot delivered on 2 April 2009

Palermo F (2018) Beyond second chambers: alternative representation of territorial interests and their reasons. In: Perspectives on Federalism, vol 10, issue 2

Patroni Griffi A (2018a) Ragioni e radici dell'Europa sociale: frammenti di un discorso sui rischi del futuro dell'Unione. Federalismi.it

Patroni Griffi A (2018b) Per il superamento del bicameralismo paritario e il Senato delle autonomie: lineamenti di una proposta. Federalismi.it

Patroni Griffi A (2021) Regionalismo differenziato. Digesto delle discipline pubblicistiche. Aggiornamento (ed. Bifulco, Celotto, Olivetti), UTET, Milan, 319

Patroni Griffi A (2022) Il Piano Nazionale di Ripresa e Resilienza e il regionalismo differenziato nella dimensione della coesione territoriale. Rassegna di diritto pubblico europeo 1

Petit Y (2004) La cohésion économique et sociale: objectif ou politique de la Communauté et de l'Union européenne. L'Europe et les régions: quinze ans de cohésion économique et sociale (ed. Leclerc), Bruylant, Bruxelles

Predieri A (1996) Europeità dei fondi strutturali: compendio e metafora. Fondi strutturali e coesione economica e sociale nell'Unione europea (ed. Predieri), Giuffrè, Milan, 28-259

Regions for EU Recovery (2022) REGIONS FOR EU RECOVERY Benchmark study on the implementation of the Recovery and Resilience Facility at the regional level

Saint-Ouen F (2014) «Denis de Rougemont, penseur original de la Fédération européenne». L'Europe de Denis de Rougemont, Academia-L'Harmattan, Louvain-la-Neuve

Schwab T (2024) Quo Vadis, cohesion policy? European regional development at a crossroads. Intereconomics 59(5):284–292

Staiano S (2017) Costituzione italiana. Art. 5, Rome
Zeitlin J, Bokhorst D, Eihmanis E (2023) Final report October 2023. Rethinking the Governance and Delivery of the Cohesion Policy Funds: Is the Recovery and Resilience Facility (RRF) a Model? European Commission

Kolibri 360 GmbH
Ferdinand-Jühlke-Straße 7
99095 Erfurt, Deutschland
produktsicherheit@kolibri360.de